ARTHUR VENO is widely regarded as one of the most controversial experts on bikers, as he works with both police and bikers. He is the author of *The Brotherhoods: Inside the Outlaw Motorcycle Clubs*, a registered psychologist and former Director of the Center for Police and Justice Studies at Monash University, Australia. He counts amongst his friends members of several major outlaw motorcycle clubs, including the Hell's Angels, Bandidos and Gypsy Jokers. At the same time he has students, friends and colleagues who are serving police members in Canada, USA and Australia. Once dubbed by bikers 'The Mad Professor', he is now known simply as 'The Professor'.

KAREN SIMS has had a long-standing educational interest in understanding the outlaw motorcycle subculture dating back to 1985. Veno has dubbed her 'the data hound' because of her unique abilities to track down even the most obscure publications.

The Mammoth Book of

Bikers

EDITED BY ARTHUR VENO

ROBINSON

RUNNING PRESS
PHILADELPHIA · LONDON

Constable & Robinson Ltd
3 The Lanchesters
162 Fulham Palace Road
London W6 9ER
www.constablerobinson.com

First published in the UK by Robinson,
an imprint of Constable & Robinson, 2007

A copy of the British Library Cataloguing in
Publication Data is available from the British Library

UK ISBN 978-1-84529-538-7

7 9 10 8 6

First published in the United States in 2007
by Carroll & Graf Publishers
This edition published in 2007 by Running Press Book Publishers

9 8
Digit on the right indicates the number of this printing

Library of Congress Cataloging-in-Publication Data is available on file

US ISBN 978-0-7867-2046-0

Running Press Book Publishers
2300 Chestnut Street
Philadelphia, PA 19103-4371

Visit us on the web!
www.runningpress.com

CONTENTS

PREFACE

I have been called "a biker apologist" by one government and banned from an international conference on one-percenter outlaw motorcycle clubs by the police (they call the clubs "gangs") for being too "pro biker". On the other hand, I have been accused of "rehashing the same pro cop crap" and being "a police informant" by some bikers. The old adage, "You can please *some* of the people *some* of the time . . . but you can't please *all* of the people *all* of the time" accurately reflects responses to my twenty-odd years of working in biker and police circles. I don't mind this hassle – I believe it demonstrates that I "tell it like it is".

The selections presented in this Anthology have been collected with the help of colleague Karen Sims. Together, we have included writings that we believe to best define the history of one-percenter motorcycle clubs and the debates surrounding them. Although we had opposing views and consequently differences of opinion on some aspects of the outlaw biker subculture, such as whether they are deemed to be criminal organizations, we worked out a compromise between the two of us. The editorial comments can be viewed as a collaborative effort by both editors and no distinctions are made between their impressions.

Much has been written about outlaw bikers – books, articles, features and so on – but the material is usually polarized between two extremes, being either pro or (as is more often the case) anti-biker. The present collection is unique. It includes offerings by bikers, popular authors, academics, and policemen – providing readers with enough raw material to make up their own minds.

EDITOR'S NOTE

Some authors in this volume (for example William Dulaney) use an accurate "within club" term when speaking of "Charters" of the Hells Angels Motorcycle Club – the general term being "Chapters".

And regarding the missing apostrophe in "Hells Angels", this is the currently accepted form, adopted by the club itself. Nevertheless, some writers opt for the technically correct "Hell's Angels". Readers should therefore note that both versions are accurate for the purposes of this book.

PART 1

Birth of
the Outlaw Biker

"There is over 120 years of history here. Someone has to tell it."

William Dulaney

Two years after the first reliable motorcycle was produced, motorcycle clubs were formed. And they have been thriving ever since. In 1924 the American Motorcycle Association (AMA) was founded, quickly dubbing any non-affiliated clubs "outlaws". Thus a black-and-chrome counter-culture was born, destined to become an international phenomenon.

In fact, most "outlaw" motorcycle clubs (as defined by the American Motorcycle Association) formed between the 1920s and 1940s were harmless groups of guys and girls with a desire to escape the humdrum by riding collectively on "club runs" or by testing their skills at organized motorcycle races. But from the beginning, motorcyclists have been bound by a love of bikes, the treatment they receive as riders, and an overall lifestyle associated with motorbiking. This near-mythical bond between biker and bike still exists.

From its very birth the motorcycle has attracted those who love the freedom of the open road. The sheer power of the machine, the high speeds it is capable of achieving, and exposure to the elements produces an adrenaline rush that cannot be fathomed by car drivers. The concentration required to operate a motorcycle blocks all bullshit from your mind, focusing attention on the near-addictive high of riding. If motorcycles influence your life, then you are part of the motorcycling community.

If the 1920s saw the "birth" of outlaw bikers, the 1940s saw them come of age. The end of the Second World War in 1945 heralded the return of thousands of young servicemen, many of whom – thanks to military training – possessed the necessary skills to ride. Furthermore, many of these survivors were eager to recapture the comradeship and excitement of active service. As motorcycling went some way to satisfying these needs, motorcycle clubs enjoyed a post-war boom. But the event that spawned the modern image of the outlaw biker occurred in 1947 at the tiny Californian town of Hollister. By all accounts some motorcyclists behaved badly. By today's standards the incident was tame: a few broken windows, one arrest, some riders doing burn-outs in bars and cheap restaurants. Nevertheless, the mayhem at Hollister was seized upon by *Life* magazine and blown out of proportion. Meanwhile, a young film-maker named Stanley Kramer picked up on the story and in 1953 released a movie entitled *The Wild One*.

The impact of this movie – starring Marlon Brando and Lee Marvin – cannot be overstated. The clothing, modified bikes, biker badges, and many other features of current outlaw clubs can be traced directly to this motion picture. In fact, the movie made such a strong statement of rebellion in its portrayal of alienated bikers that it was banned in several countries, including Britain and Australia. Nevertheless, *The Wild One* was the medium by which the culture was spread around the globe when, several years after its release, it was finally screened overseas (the British Board of Film Censors lifted its ban in 1968). Thus, by the 1960s, the scene was set for an expansion of outlaw biker subculture across the English-speaking world.

Meanwhile, the American Motorcycle Association was keen to distance itself from events like Hollister, reputedly declaring that: "Ninety-nine per cent of motorcyclists are law-abiding citizens and the actions at Hollister are a result of outlaw motorcyclists and non-motorcyclists." Of course, the AMA was referring to non-members when it spoke of "outlaw" motorcyclists and clubs, but those who embraced the biker image as depicted in *The Wild One* immediately declared themselves "one percenters". The terms "outlaw" and "one percenter" soon became blurred: but as far as the media and police were concerned, both "outlaw" and "one-percenter" clubs were simply "gangs".

And so, between the late 1940s and late 1960s most present-day one-percenter clubs officially began, including – among many others – the Hells Angels, the Bandidos, and the Pagans.

But the one-percenter clubs were not considered a serious problem for law enforcement agencies until another watershed event: the alleged rape of two teenage girls at Monterey, California, in 1964 by two members of the Hells Angels Motorcycle Club. This incident led to the Lynch Report (named after Thomas Lynch, California Attorney-General at the time), which identified outlaw motorcycle clubs as criminal entities. Despite put-downs by the likes of journalist Hunter S. Thompson ("As a historical document, it read like a plot synopsis of Mickey Spillane's worst dreams"), the Lynch Report was the first time that politicians defined outlaw motorcycle clubs as organizations worthy of law enforcement attention.

The years of the Vietnam War which ended in 1975 was the next big event to produce a large influx of outlaw motorcyclists. Largely for the same reasons that attracted Second World War survivors to motorcycling, Vietnam Vets swelled the ranks of one-percenter clubs. Meanwhile, the hippy counter-culture of the 1960s and early 1970s introduced two other factors into the biker fraternity: drugs and internationalization. But while the hippies eventually disappeared into "the system", giving up their alternative lifestyle and dress code, outlaw bikers retained their distinctive style. And outlaw bikers still live by their own rules, expressing their rejection of mainstream culture and society.

FIRST CONTACT

Brock Yates

Brock Yates is a freelance writer and Harley-Davidson rider. While Brock wasn't part of the early years of motorcycling history, his ability to capture the essence of early subculture – and in particular, the machines outlaw bikers ride – makes for a fascinating read. The following piece is short, but it powerfully describes youthful impressions, providing readers with a glimpse into the early years of outlaw motorcycle clubs.

The noise. The god-awful death rattle issuing from the bowels of his infernal machine. He had been a quiet kid, one of those bashful back-markers in elementary school, a pasty-faced runt lost in the playground stampedes and the adolescent classroom chatter. Now, suddenly, as a junior in high school, he had reinvented himself, a transmogrification of quasi-lethal intensity.

Among the brush-cut and bobby-soxed hierarchy of 1950s teenage life, he cut a wide swath, swooping among the Goody Two-shoes aboard his black-and-chrome monster. Wrapped in a wide-collared leather jacket studded with chrome, he was someone to be reckoned with, a stern-faced stud on a bad-ass motorcycle.

His classmates watched him in a confused state of part scorn, part envy, from the vantage point of establishment tools: teenagers operating in the mainstream of conventional lusts over fast cars and faster women. But the notion of a motorcycle – no, make that a Harley-Davidson motorcycle – was beyond the pale, drifting into the lurid red-light districts occupied by the devil drug, marijuana, and the white-slave trade. Other guys tried the zooter gig, fashioning themselves in duck's-ass haircuts and peg pants in open defiance of the conventions of khaki and gray flannel – the Fonzi-like prototypes later to be immortalized in *Grease* and other fifties flashbacks. But the over-the-top gesture, the ultimate fuck-you to the straight arrows and suck-ups of the day was that mother-humper Harley from hell.

"Wheels" of any kind beyond a Schwinn was the ultimate guy fantasy. Decades would pass before the booming middle class could afford to outfit its high-schoolers with automobiles, much less anything as exotic as motorcycles. The periodicals of the early 1950s swooned over the alleged menace of "hot-rodders," a California manifestation involving youths aboard chopped and channeled flathead Fords who engaged in such sociopathic madness as "drag racing" and death-defying games of "chicken." These exotic little home-built machines, hacksawed out of prewar Fords, were viewed as a motorized expression of the newly discovered teenage species known as "juvenile delinquents." This alleged rabble, sporting T-shirts with Camel packs rolled into the sleeves, represented a new surge of Visigoths marauding through the nation's streets. The dreaded hot rods (a contraction of "hot roadster") would be chronicled in countless hysterical magazine and newspaper stories of the day, culminating in the 1955 cult film *Rebel Without a Cause*, starring that paradigm of 1950s punkdom, James Dean. Drag racing, as portrayed in the film's deadly duel, shook moms and pops out of their Barcaloungers from coast to coast. Images of every kid in America behind the wheel of a hopped-up Ford or, God forbid, a thundering Harley slashing through the suburbs at suicidal speeds, seared their suburbanite brains. Hot rods. Motorcycles. Leather jackets, and in the distance the fearsome tribal drumbeats of rock 'n' roll. The fall of Rome was upon them.

Among the foot-sloggers, the kid on the Harley-Davidson enjoyed an automatic status reserved for those with "wheels" of all types, but in his case they belonged to a mysterious, exotic and faintly ominous, flame-belching motorcycle. A scrubbed classmate from the suburbs was also among the anointed, but purely as a midget leaguer. Somehow he had talked his father into letting him buy a used, clapped-out motor scooter, a lumpy Cushman powered by a one-lung lawnmower engine. On days when he rode it to school, he parked it near the Harley, a dinghy moored in the shadow of that battleship, unworthy of notice by the ship's owner.

The Harley guy would leave class, cloaked in his leather armor on even the warmest days, and stride past the Cushman in total disdain. Legging over the Harley, he fiddled briefly with the fuel value and the choke before commencing his ritual attack on the kick starter, leaping and cursing as his booted foot rocked up and down on the chromium lever. The monster would fart and grumble, fitfully barking in protest against the intrusion by its master. Finally, after minutes of refusal, the mighty engine would awaken, spewing clouds of raw gas and fire from its twin pipes, rattling windows and sending decent folk scurrying, their ears covered against the din. Once satisfied that the beast was awake, he would settle into its saddle and, rolling his gloved right hand on the handlebar throttle, rev the engine until the plugs cleared and the last living creature within earshot had been intimidated. Then, with his left hand he would reach for the shifter, jam the thing into gear, and roar away, weaving and yawing in a shower of gravel. To the witless squares who knew no such power, it was like witnessing a moon shot almost twenty years hence.

Properly costumed, he had become a member of a tiny, exclusive clique headquartered in a grease-stained warren on the edge of town. There a strange, lanky man ran a dealership for Harley-Davidson motorcycles. It was off-limits to decent folk, a corral for outriders and bandits, bikers and weirdos who rode motorcycles, more a collection of shacks than a real building. The floors were soaked black with motor oil and littered with shards of piston rings, broken chains, shattered cylinder heads, and bent forks – the effluvia of a thousand haphazard repairs. Outside leaned a rabble of old motorcycles, bare-boned frames, piles of shredded tires, and broken engines, a graveyard of outlaw machinery tended by the gaunt man who knew all and was all regarding motorcycles – the high priest in the smoky Harley temple.

One day the suburbanite ventured into the forbidden place, naively searching for a part for his Cushman. This was akin to asking the gunnery officer on the USS *Missouri* for a box of BBs. A Cushman motor scooter in a Harley-Davidson store? Send in the clowns! What's that pie-faced twit doing intruding with that puny, gutless slug among real men's machines? The dealer slouched inside, appearing nearly as filthy as the soot-stained walls. He grunted a response to the kid's question, barely deigning to deal with a noncultist. Other men lurked against the workbenches. They wore grimy denims and sported heavy engineer's boots gleaming with caked motor oil. They smoked heavily, filling the morbid room with gray clouds that mingled with the belching and backfiring of the Harley they were attempting to tune with large screwdrivers. The outlander had clearly stifled conversation, and it would remain so until he departed, leaving them to stand in silent witness to the rattle-bone thud of the big machine under the dealer's crude ministrations. The kid never returned. Nor did anyone he knew who was considered a member of decent society ever enter those dreaded precincts.

Who were those men? The term "biker" would not become part of the national slang for another decade, and they were therefore nameless outriders – supplicants to a small but true faith centered around a brutish machine that fit between their legs. Most rode Harley-Davidsons, but others traveled on giant Indians – a similar large American-made motorcycle that remained a steadfast rival, albeit with sagging sales and loyalties. While hard-edged motorcycle gangs were at the time forming in California, the notion of outlaw organizations coalescing around Harleys and Indians in dinky cities was unthinkable. Motorcycle gangs might exist in sybaritic California, where debauched movie stars and other bohemians played their evil games, but not in the great heartland, where motorcycles sputtered on the dark and mysterious perimeter. For most Americans banditry as defined by such strange and frightful cults as the Hells Angels was still beyond their ken in the early 1950s.

The men who hung around the little motorcycle shop were for the most part lost souls: disoriented and disillusioned WWII veterans, functioning alcoholics, unemployed factory workers, and a few rebellious teenagers, all of whom found solace in the radiated strength of the big bikes. Power was available at the kick of the leg and the flick of the wrist. Equality came at the end of an exhaust pipe, and every Buick-driving Babbitt better know it. Still, the riders were marginalized, meaningless and essentially ignored, crackpots who dressed strangely and hung out in sleazy bars and rode noisy motorcycles. Fringe players in the grand American scheme whose sullen expressions of independence seemed harmless and irrelevant. Beyond the noise and bluster of their blowsy motorcycles, who cared about them, save for a few addled teenagers who retained a fearful fascination for their monster machines?

The suburbanite fitfully tried to keep up with his Harley-rider classmate, wrestling as he could against middle-class conventions but lacking the money, much less the social chutzpah, to make the leap aboard a Harley – which, truth be known, he and his peers viewed with a combination of fear and lurid fascination. He managed to marshal sufficient funds by selling the Cushman to obtain a tiny Czechoslovakian CZ-125, with a cylinder barely as large as a Harley carburetor but still a legitimate motorcycle. It would be a source of considerable pride for him to later learn that in fact James Dean himself had entered the world of bikes on a sister unit, rising then into fast British twins before killing himself behind the wheel of a Porsche 550 Spyder sports-racing car. Still, it was not enough. The Harley-Davidsons – with their seventy-four-cubic-inch "Knucklehead" engines – larger than the sixty-seven-cubic-inch power plants of the Volkswagen Beetles that were beginning to arrive on these shores – remained alone; the baddest, grumpiest, surliest motorcycles on earth.

So what if any number of Brit bikes, BSAs, Triumphs, Nortons, et al., could wax a Harley in a head-to-head race? So what if Harleys leaked oil like sieves and burned valves and warped their cylinder heads? So what if their tub-thumping exhausts infuriated proper folk? So what if only the lower orders rode and coveted them? So what if Harley-Davidson was not a nice machine? So what if the people who rode them scared the wee-wee out of the good burghers? Wasn't that the point?

His CZ-125 was eventually traded for a collection of used sports cars and the rigors of family raising and career chasing. So too for his classmate on the Harley, who gave up his leathers for white perma-press shirts – complete with plastic mechanical pencil holders – and an engineering career in that paradigm of establishmentarianism, General Motors.

His short-lived rebellion was over, and his old Harley had no doubt ended up on the rubble pile behind the shop, now long since demolished and replaced by a miniature golf course and driving range. But his statement had been made, and it would play a minuscule role in the expanding legend of Harley-Davidson, which was about to become one of those precious few machines elevated beyond mere function to the apotheosis of a globe-spanning lifestyle. Its role is a curious one, a duality of good and evil, of raffish innocence and snarling pugnacity. No other icon of the machine age, be it a Ferrari or a Porsche automobile, a rare WWII fighter plane, or a megapriced, English-built Vincent Black Shadow motorcycle, possesses this ambiguity of purpose.

Harley-Davidson prospers worldwide, thanks to its lofty status. It has a patina of history and tradition that cannot be created even by the canniest and most creative of advertising wizards. It is hardly the most technologically advanced or best performing of its breed. Quite to the contrary. The current Harley-Davidson is in essence an antique. Its basic design dates back to 1936 and, in a broad engineering sense, to a French twin-cylinder concept developed at the end of the nineteenth century. It is the perfect flintlock rifle. The world's most refined sundial. But with that antiquity comes tradition and a storied continuity that defies imitation. The Japanese – long masters of the art of creating high-performance engines and capable of making vastly superior motorcycles of all kinds – are frantically dumbing down their product lines in slavish attempts to build faux Harley-Davidsons. The results are perfect replications of the venerable Milwaukee original, but hopeless and hollow gestures. They bring nothing to the table to counter Harley's near century-old aura.

Within that essentially hundred-year saga lies a series of stops and starts and the elements of both success and failure. Contradictions abound, and in a broad sense this grand old machine's persona broadly represents that of the nation that created it – and that radiates its personality around the globe. Rooted in Milwaukee, Harley-Davidson symbolizes the best and the worst of a nation whose growth has been fitful, rebellious, disjointed, and cursed by raging crosscurrents and blurred imagery. If perception equals reality, the source of the Harley mystique begins not with the founding of the company in 1903 by the brothers Davidson, Arthur, William, and Walter, and their friend William Harley, but rather in a steamy farming town in Northern California on Independence Day, 1947.

800 POUNDS OF STEEL

Ross Fuglsang

Ross Fuglsang accurately describes the development of the Harley-Davidson motorcycle as a symbol of American culture, and the significance of Harley customization as a means of self-expression for outlaw bikers.

What is it about a motorcycle which so endears it to the male psyche? Attempts to analyze the bond between man and machine are similar: placed in opposition to the comfort and security of the all-too-confining automobile, it becomes the "very icon of wildness." In a ritual paean to the motorcycle, Robert Hughes preaches that a bike extends its rider "into the environment, all senses alert. . . . The bike flows into it in a state of heightened consciousness that no driver, with his windows and heater and radio, will ever know. It is the total experience." Of the Harley-Davidson "look" he helped create, Willie G. Davidson said, "The bike conveys a mechanical forcefulness – it's not totally tamed. We don't cover up the nuts and bolts because they're part of the mechanical beauty of the bike."

A Harley is more than just nuts and bolts and transportation to fanatical owners. It is a lifestyle "embroidered into the fabric of Americana," Carl Ciati writes in *Popular Mechanics*. "It's a look, a sound, a riding position, a certain style." It is devotion to mechanical beauty which inspires such loyalty that men tattoo the Harley-Davidson bar and shield logo on their bodies. And, because it was for years the last vestige of the American motorcycle industry, the Harley myth incorporates a sense of pride and patriotism. When Honda reigned as sales leader, hardcore Harley loyalists stood firm, seeing in the "You meet the nicest people on a Honda" campaign a "veiled and underhanded swipe at the Harley rider, who was by implication somehow mad, bad and dangerous to know."

All of this excitement surrounds a machine that was, in truth, an accident, the happy result of early attempts to refine the internal combustion engine. And, as is often the case with technological innovations, no one person can take sole credit for the invention of the motorcycle. In the process of developing an air-cooled, four-stroke engine for automotive use, Gottlieb Daimler constructed a petrol-powered bicycle in 1885. Within a matter of a few years the *motorrad* appeared in large numbers in France and Germany and by 1896 these contraptions, flitting about at a top speed of about 24 mph, had taken on the familiar shape of the modern motorcycle. Motorcycle historians Richard Hough and L. J. K. Setright note that the motorcycle has "suffered ever since from its self-imposed engineering limitations as well as from its despised social standing." That it survived at all in a world satisfied with the horse and wagon (and one in the process of developing a horseless carriage) they call a "pleasing paradox." Those early machines were, after all, noisy and uncomfortable, and the engines were especially sensitive to every bounce and jiggle. Every trip was an adventure.

But its fickle temperament may have been the machine's saving grace. Early motorcycles demanded great dedication and mechanical skill of their riders. Those first-generation bikers were up to the task, though, since they were often the machine's designers and builders, well aware of the machine's moods and limitations. Motorcycles were also not for the fainthearted. Early riders earned their reputations as "iron men." In return, motorcycles provided "a very special delight, a unique amalgam of rigour and exuberance, the paradox of detachment from the world and yet intimate engagement with it." Who cared that the over-powered bicycles were temperamental, noisy, dirty, painful and completely anti-social – they were fun.

The first two decades of this century were a period of technical innovation that redeemed some of the least appealing aspects of cycling. Up to that point, riders pedaled or ran alongside their bikes to get them started. Because of the cycle's low power, riders often had to jump off and push them up hills. Even more damaging to the industry was the fact that there were too many manufacturers, too few mechanics and too many designs. When it became standard practice to incorporate a small four-stroke engine into a standard safety bicycle frame, replacing the bottom bracket, the motorcycle's future brightened. This design improved the motorcycle's balance by lowering the center of gravity and better distributing the weight of engine and rider.

Both rider and machine changed in the early years of this century. Hough and Setright identify a new type of man taking up motorcycling. The iron men became the minority, replaced by those looking for utility. "The new owner," they note, "would entertain no romantic notions about his machine, and usually had no mechanical knowledge whatever." To that end, between 1905 and 1915, practically every modern motorcycle design feature appeared: spring forks for comfort; handlebar controls for mixing oil, fuel and air; improved dynamos for starting and lighting; V-belts and an occasional chain drive; and fat tires that could be repaired and changed in a matter of minutes rather than hours. "Here at last was a motorcycle which really looked like a motorcycle," write Hough and Setright. "Here was the machine which was to spark off a wave of new manufacturers, a new sport, a new contribution to – or in some ways a new threat to – society."

With this semblance of standardization and organization came the necessity of racing, the tests of speed and endurance and of the rider's skills. Prior to 1903 a handful of men would occasionally gather at horse tracks and bicycle velodromes to race their machines at speeds in excess of 30 mph. In this country, 1903 saw the formation of the Federation of American Motorcyclists, which in 1908 put together its first organized event, a two-day endurance run around New York City and Long Island. The president of the Harley-Davidson Motor

Company, Walter Davidson, mounted an early Harley to face off against and defeat 84 other riders representing 22 different makes of motorcycle.

The first Harley-Davidson had rolled out of the one-room Milwaukee machine shop operated by Bill and Walter Davidson and William Harley in 1903. A year earlier the first Indian motorcycle sprang out of Springfield, Massachusetts. These two manufacturers, along with Henderson and Excelsior, would come to define motorcycling in the United States and pretty much reign over racing and endurance contests early in the century. Harley-Davidson's famed Wrecking Crew dominated the sport between 1916 and 1921. But 1921 also saw sales of Harley-Davidsons slump, prompting the company to pull out of racing. The FMA itself had collapsed in 1919, replaced in 1923 by the American Motorcyclists Association (AMA).

The United States motorcycle industry had run up against a new obstacle, the automobile, and it did not fare well. By 1919 sales figures had faltered and "motorcycling in America had almost died." The composition of motorcycle ridership changed with the times as well. Cycling became "proletarian" as those who could afford them took to automobiles. More importantly for the industry, however, motorcycling essentially became a *man*'s hobby:

> There remained a sizable number of gentlemen, young and not so young, who regarded poodle-faking and the weather protection of the motor car with scorn. Believing "he that travels fastest travels alone," they managed to satisfy themselves – if nobody else – of their sturdy masculinity by bestriding a good lusty motorcycle.

Ridership, because of increased competition from other modes of transportation, was being whittled down to a hard core of riders who truly enjoyed the sensation and rigour that only the motorcycle could provide. Technical skill and mechanical knowledge were still important, but not essential; potential buyers needed transportation that was reliable and versatile. The best bikes survived, barely, and after World War I they provided cheap and utilitarian transportation. Despite technical advances that improved speed, handling and comfort, the domestic market for motorcycles became increasingly narrow.

Motorcycles fared better in Europe, possibly because of the industry's infrastructure and less intense competition from automobile companies. From the beginning, in America, the Harley-Davidson Motorcycle Company stressed service. Its efforts to establish a national network of dealers and parts suppliers, along with its intrinsic conservatism, may have been what kept the company afloat during the lean years between the wars. European firms also had the advantage of years of experience, and could take advantage of geographical and climatic differences. To survive, Harley-Davidson pitched its line of reliable, heavy-duty bikes to its two prime markets: police departments and the military. The Department of the Interior used Harleys to patrol Yellowstone Park, and delivery drivers and rural lettercarriers went about their jobs on servicars and sidecar-equipped motor bikes.

European manufacturers, especially those in Great Britain and Germany, dominated the youthful motorcycle market. Industry histories concentrate on European designs and innovations; Harley-Davidson, Indian and other American makes rate only brief asides. The explanation for this focus is fairly simple: the look of a motorcycle is of equal importance to manufacturing and sales. Even slight changes in design, like the placement of the gear shift or the location of the speedometer, become major issues. Hough and Setright concentrate almost exclusively on European bikes, and Vic Willoughby's *Classic Motorcycles* offers an in-depth look at 40 European machines he considers "yardsticks" of motorcycle engineering.

Styling was not an immediate concern in this country, however. Size and power were what mattered most. After introducing a V-twin (two-cylinders mounted in a V shape) in 1909, Harley-Davidson came to dominate the American market. As T. A. Hodgdon points out in *Motorcycling's Golden Age of the Fours*, big bikes, twins and fours (four cylinders), came to define this country's motorcycles. And despite flirtation with smaller bikes and fours, Harley-Davidson's conservative focus on large-displacement twins (750–1,400 cc's) earned it a reputation for intractability and stagnation. German and British firms concentrated on speed and handling and perfecting their small-bore single and twin-cylinder engines. To Europeans, stodgy Harleys and Indians were huge and unwieldy; Willoughby goes so far as to call them "agricultural." Only in America did the styling of hogs and Super Chiefs come to be considered "classic." There was an obvious reason for this focus, however. In competing against automobiles, American motorcycle manufacturers had to offer some semblance of comfort on roads that by and large would not be paved until the 1950s. Also, motorcycles had to travel farther than smaller European models between fuel stops. If American manufacturers needed a rationale for big bikes, that was it.

A cross-country endurance run by Wells Bennett in 1922 pointed up many of the hazards faced by this country's early bikers. Riding a Henderson four, Bennett left Los Angeles and within 50 miles ran out of paved road. From there on, one-third of his route was composed of sand and gravel cut with deep ruts: "Plugging along in second gear mile after mile, Bennett had trouble keeping his balance. It was necessary to cross from one side of the road to the other many times, in order to keep in the furrows. This was very strenuous work and just a sample of what was to come." With Flagstaff behind him he was in the mountains bouncing "over 68 miles of assorted rocks, chuck holes and sand," only occasionally getting out of low gear. Outside of Winslow, Arizona, he fell into a dry wash and his 450-pound bike sank into the sand. The trip continued in a similar vein, with the occasional sand dune thrown in for variety, until he hit Emporia, Kansas, after 100 hours in the saddle. From St. Louis to New York City he had the advantage of paved roads, but cold October nights wearied him and a brush with street car rails left him bruised and battered on the side of a New Jersey highway. He managed to set a transcontinental record – six days, 15 hours and 13 minutes – an improvement of some seven hours over the previous mark, but only because the weather had been dry and his bike suffered no damage more serious than a series of flat tires.

Before World War I, to attempt a lengthy trip on a small bike with a limited range was folly. When Hough and Setright acknowledge that American manufacturers went in for bulk rather than mechanical innovation, it is because that is what worked. In the 1920s and 1930s a cyclist could hope for, at best,

5,000 miles before having to discard an off-brand bike that was either out of production or just unfixable. The dependability offered by Harley-Davidson and Indian was an increasingly important issue, as was the dealer's mechanical support. Added to the mix in the United States was that the automobile quickly became a symbol of middle-class striving. A car in the garage, or more likely on the curb, was a sure sign of success. The motorcycle's working-class image is one it has never completely overcome.

Inherent design limitations also hurt the motorcycle's American marketability. It could not comfortably transport a family (unless the rider had a sidecar). As Hough and Setright mention, cycling was a solo adventure for men. Motorcycles were at the mercy of weather. Early on cars had similar problems and "automobilists" stored their vehicles in the winter, but by 1914 some cars had roll-up windows and heaters, and the Fisher Closed Body Corporation turned out 150 enclosed chassis in 1910. Henry Ford's Dearborn. Michigan, assembly line hit its stride in the 1920s, churning out cars that for $245 compared favourably to the cost of a two-wheeler. In the end, affluent Americans turned their backs on bikes. Harley-Davidson's production of motorcycles dropped by almost two-thirds – 28,189 to 10,202 – from 1920 to 1921, and it would not top that 1920 sales figure again until 1942.

Motorcycling's image and the nation's waning interest in racing was further damaged by the deaths of a number of high profile racers in the 1920s. Motordromes, which were often just steeply banked wooden tracks, were regularly referred to as "murderdromes." By the 1930s flat track and dirt track racing had lost their luster, and road construction and the automobile made cross country runs less than riveting. Outside of delivery drivers and police officers, motorcycling became the province of the eccentric and the anti-social. Harley-Davidson, always a wizard at advertising and public relations, began to stress respectability and recreational themes in pitching its product. The company used its in-house publication. *The Enthusiast*, to promote safe riding. It was, and still is, "a publication that cultivates and celebrates much of what is good about riding in the company of like-minded people."

The AMA, propped up financially by Harley-Davidson since

1928, sanctioned nearly 300 motorcycle clubs in the 1930s, but they were on the decline amid Depression hardship. Harley-Davidson historian David Wright observes that "those who were in clubs became more and more a subculture, wearing clothes available only from a motorcycle dealer." As Martin Norris argues, these clubs represented the "responsible" riders. They "had their own strict dress codes, and members wore uniforms that were almost military in appearance." Yet they were the ones who were, and still are to some extent, overlooked when people think of bikers. Organized clubs sponsored mixers, charity events, races and hill-climbing contests. And, like *The Enthusiast*, AMA clubs promoted responsible motorcycling as a family activity.

Before the end of World War II, J. Edgar Hoover's FBI and various other government agencies were preparing the country for an inevitable spate of juvenile delinquency and crime. Deciding who would lead the fight against the approaching menace and resolve the techniques to be used in the coming battle were hotly contested by sociologists and criminologists. In *A Cycle of Outrage*, James Gilbert documents both the growing public awareness of delinquency, beginning in 1943, and a series of Senate hearings which focused national attention on the battle between the Justice Department and the Children's Bureau, setting the tone for the next decade. The result of the war years, he concludes with some irony, was that the country was prepared for the worst – and got it.

According to Gilbert, the 1940s and 1950s were characterized by a variety of threats to the middle-class family. Changes in youth culture inspired confusion and fear in older Americans unprepared and unwilling to accept such rapid social change. The end result was hostility and suspicion between generations, and the belief that teenagers had somehow lost their moral bearings: "In the postwar world, the changing behavior of youth, in terms of speech, fashions, music and mores, appeared to erase the boundaries between hijinks and premature adulthood and even delinquency." Taken together, events of the era validated increased concern, as well as increased expenditures for adolescent counseling, education and law enforcement.

In *The Fifties* David Halberstam paints a friendlier, if no less disconcerting, portrait of America. Conformity and materialism were the rule and deviance came at a pretty price. His snapshot descriptions of McDonalds, Holiday Inns, suburban Levittowns and television sitcoms reveal a society inconducive to and increasingly intolerant of nonconformists, free spirits and rebels. The Beats, exemplified by Jack Kerouac and Allen Ginsberg, looked outside "the system" for freedom. The growing youth culture that idolized Marlon Brando, Elvis Presley and James Dean identified with being misunderstood, especially by parents. There was, Halberstam concludes, a "blandness, conformity, and lack of serious social and cultural purpose in middle-class life in America," and those with the temerity to turn their backs on it were "the pioneers of what would eventually become the counterculture."

Perceptions of increased delinquency, the growing popularity of rock and roll music and hot-rodding, the new social mobility and economic independence of adolescents, and changing definitions of right and wrong dovetailed with the older generation's Cold War hysteria and fear of anarchy and conspiracy. What Gilbert calls a premature adult culture, "thrust upon the American public by communications media that emphasized everything new and threatening," could easily have been mistaken for radical change. The situation was no less confusing for adolescents who had to adapt to new technology, which was "changing their lives every day in ways obvious and not so obvious; that's why they were afraid."

In 1954 *Newsweek* offered a special report on violence in America. Crimes of violence – manslaughter, assault, murder – were up 33 percent from the years 1937 to 1939. Rapes were up 80 percent. Juvenile delinquency and youth gangs were singularly menacing: "More and more they are going in for big-time crime. They carry guns, and they're even quicker than adult criminals to kill." Criminologists blamed the moral breakdown on global tensions; the only cure was "a stiffening of the moral fabric of the nation and a spiritual renaissance." Los Angeles and its overburdened police force become the focus of the story, but capsule summaries of crime in nine cities revealed the issue to be of nationwide concern.

But violence and street gangs have always been a part of American culture, we just choose to ignore them whenever possible. In the 1950s Harrison Salisbury coined the term the "shook-up generation" to describe the growing incidence of gangs and youth violence. His concern is summarized in one sentence: "What are we going to do about our young people?" Though focused on New York City street gangs, Salisbury sheds light on the changing nature of gangs and what concerned Americans at the dawn of a new decade. Most disturbing to him is the potential violence presented by future generations of suburban teens. With fathers spending too much time at work, Salisbury describes isolated homes and emotionally starved children: "In too many homes the mother is too busy with an eternal round of social activities to have any real relationship with her children. The end result is unhappiness in the midst of plenty." Where mothers took charge of the home, Salisbury suggests boys rebelled and displayed "extreme masculine attitudes, violence and even sadism."

Rootlessness, mobility and a burgeoning population also figured into Salisbury's equation. "People are pouring into California from all parts of the United States. They represent a mixture of ethnic groups and cultural backgrounds. The result of this heavy population movement is identical with the New York picture – friction between the newcomers and old-timers. . . ." James Q. Wilson addresses the mixture of disparate peoples and changes in community standards in an article in *The Public Interest*. His survey of 1,000 Boston homeowners in 1968 found that the "urban problem" ultimately consisted of a failure of accepted community standards.

Cars and motorcycles provided one outlet for alienated young men and motorheads who might have felt unfairly constrained, isolated, or just out of place in post-war America. Richard Reeves, describing his own experience in the fifties, allows the '55 Chevy "historical significance by pointing out that putting a big engine in a small car meant that for the first time the poor (or at least the middle class) could drive as fast as the rich.' In hot-rod culture, with its roots running as far back as the Model T, kids bought stock automobiles and tinkered until they had the most unique machine possible, one that would reflect who they were or who they wanted to be. If they could shut down someone else's rod, all the better.

Harley-Davidsons similarly attracted men and boys who wanted to express themselves mechanically but could not afford an automobile. The bikes were familiar to World War II vets, and by design Harleys were rugged and fairly cheap. With a bit of work they could also be quite fast. But even more important for later generations of cyclists, Harley 74s (74 cubic inches), the bike of choice for the early outlaw clubs, were easy to repair and easy to personalize. Harley enthusiast Alf Walle writes that Harleys were revered by motorcycle clubs because they could be stripped down to their essentials with a minimum of tools and experience, and could easily reflect the rider's personality through customized paint jobs and an array of bolt-on parts.

It was within this motorcycle subculture that a more focused outlaw subculture took shape in the 1940s and 50s. Randal Montgomery contends that a "delinquent subculture is organized so as to render certain skills [fighting, avoiding authority] as focal points of status achievement." Those skills that early outlaw motorcycle clubs valued emphasized mechanical skill and the ability to ride. Clubs and club members also put a priority on toughness, excitement and autonomy, and the objective of intentionally seeking out trouble was to demonstrate hyper-masculine toughness. Since most members of early outlaw clubs were unskilled or semi-skilled laborers, J. Mark Watson, a former member of a club himself, believes they escaped otherwise dull lives through the excitement generated by the club. The motorcycle provided mechanically inclined, working-class youths a level playing field on which to compete in those skills which were important to them. They suspended competition in a game they could not win – middle-class striving – by creating and emphasizing an artificial culture in which they made their own rules.

ENTER THE OUTLAW MOTORCYCLE CLUB

William L. Dulaney

William Dulaney is a former member of an outlaw motorcycle club and continues to ride his 1953 Harley-Davidson FLE on a daily basis. Here he focuses on the early development of motorcycle club culture.

Perhaps the first emergence of an enduring motorcycle club, one that still exists as of this writing, appeared in 1936. This group was called the McCook Outlaws, hailing from Cook County, Illinois, which encompasses the city of Chicago. The McCook Outlaws were later to become the Chicago Outlaws, now known as the Outlaws Motorcycle Club. According to a 26-year member of the Outlaws Motorcycle Club, older members of his organization related to him that they congregated for the purposes of long distance touring – which was quite an adventure aboard a foot-operated clutch and hand-shifted motorcycle traveling largely on unpaved dirt roads – and racing, which included hill-climbing, flat quarter-mile dirt tracks, and oval wooden board tracks. A secondary but enduring biker pastime was the massive consumption of alcohol and general good-natured debauchery. Organizational symbols of the McCook Outlaws were stenciled on the back of mechanics' overalls, which consisted simply of the club's name; leather vests and jackets, as well as club-specific logos and symbols were yet to make their debut. It is interesting to note that according to the Outlaws Motorcycle Club History website the club's organizational logo (i.e., "Charlie," a skull centered over two crossed pistons and connecting rods, similar to a Jolly Roger pirate's flag) was heavily influenced by the attire worn by Marlon Brando's character "Johnny" in the 1954 film *The Wild One*.

An all-female motorcycle club called The Motormaids has maintained an American Motorcyclist Association club charter for more than 60 years (the AMA granted their charter in 1940). While the Outlaws Motorcycle Club may arguably lay claim to a slightly longer lineage, they have experienced at least two organizational identity permutations during their tenure. The Motormaids, however, has maintained a singular identity and overall governing structure since their inception and thus may well be the oldest established motorcycle club in the world, older even than the world famous Hells Angels Motorcycle Club, which formed in 1947, who also maintain their original organizational identity.

The Japanese attack on Pearl Harbor, which kick-started American involvement in World War II and the resultant compulsory military service of young American men, clamped the brakes down hard on the acceleration of motorcycle club diffusion across the country. However, the sound of Japanese bombs exploding in Pearl Harbor were to be anything but the death knell of motorcycle clubs.

At the end of World War II young men returned from combat in droves. Many found the transition back to a peaceful civilian life a more monotonous chore than they could handle. Some combat vets were trained in riding motorcycles, specifically Harleys and Indians, while serving overseas. Other servicemen who weren't officially trained in the operation of military motorcycles would simply commandeer motorcycles and ride them about for much needed relief from the stress of armed conflict. Some who didn't have experience with motorcycles during the war did manage to work their way up to master-level partiers. Be they Army Air Corps flight crews, Seamen, Infantrymen, Airborne or Marines, the one constant thread that was sewn throughout their uniforms was the ubiquitous post-mission celebration. Many WWII veterans formed strong bonds with one another, relationships that transcended wartime, which likely began during basic training where men were forced into seemingly impossible and highly stressful situations in order to expedite the formation of an exceptionally high degree of interdependence. During actual combat, men became brothers-in-arms through the horrific experiences of war. They witnessed members of their unit being killed and wounded, they themselves being wounded or killing enemy soldiers, as well as other atrocities of war.

Upon their successful return from combat missions, marines, airmen, soldiers and sailors retired to the nearest drinking establishment in an attempt to drown the memories of battle with booze, to heal the scars of armed conflict with laughter, and to try and feel human again, if only for a short while. These men became brothers born of warfare, atrocity, and death, a kinship that runs deeper than blood relations. It is also important to consider the ages of these men: the average age of WWII servicemen was only 26. Many returning combat vets reported feelings of restlessness and a general malaise; their pre-war personalities had been forever changed. These men were likely experiencing varying degrees of Post Traumatic Stress Disorder (PTSD), a psychological diagnosis that wasn't officially recognized until 1980. The National Center for Post Traumatic Stress Disorder defines the disorder as:

A psychiatric disorder that can occur following the experience or witnessing of life-threatening events such as military combat, natural disasters, terrorist incidents, serious accidents, or violent personal assaults like rape. People who suffer from PTSD often relive the experience through nightmares and flashbacks, have difficulty sleeping, and feel detached or estranged, and these symptoms can be severe enough and last long enough to significantly impair the person's daily life.

Researchers have found that for some combat veterans, relief from the effects of PTSD can be found by engaging in interpersonal and leisure activities such as those involved with motorcycling. Thus, it seems logical that the horrors of war and the hell of combat may have melted down the pre-war personalities of these men only to recast them forever in a new form, a form that didn't fit well with the post-World War II American culture.

It should come as no surprise that when these men returned stateside and resumed their jobs punching time clocks, dressing in suits, reporting to managers, swinging hammers, or repairing automobiles, that very soon they started searching for "leisure" activities that could get their blood pumping once again. Veterans, searching for relief from the residual effects of their wartime experiences, started seeking out one another just to be around kindred spirits and perhaps relive some of the better, wilder social aspects of their times during the war. Soon enough American motorcycles became part of the equation, largely due to the high level of performance and excitement the cycles offered a rider, as well as for the relatively antisocial characteristic of loud exhaust pipes and the large, imposing size of the bikes. Add to this a post-war economic boom and a July 4th, 1947 Hollister, California incident as reported by *Life* magazine, and it seems that all the necessary ingredients, which were missing during the previous era, were now present and sufficient for a specific type of motorcycling organization to emerge.

"MOTORCYCLISTS TAKE OVER TOWN, MANY INJURED"

C.I. Dourghty

C.I. Dourghty Jr was a reporter with the San Francisco Chronicle.
The following story, which he filed on 6 July 1947, was soon taken up by newspapers around America.

Hollister. July, 5

State Highway patrolmen tonight imposed informal martial law in downtown Hollister to curb the riotous activities of an estimated 4000. Almost 60 persons were injured, three of them seriously. Several more arrests were made and a special night court session was convened to punish those charged with reckless driving and drunkenness. The outburst of terrorism – wrecking of bars, bottle barrages into the streets from upper story windows and roofs and high speed racing of motorcycles though the streets – came as participants in the annual "Gypsy Tour" sponsored by the American Motorcycle Association converged on Hollister for a three-day meeting.

Evening Lull

Shortly after dusk tonight, the force of 40 highway patrol officers, commanded by Captain L.T. Torres of San Benito County, forced a lull in the terrorism. Armed with tear gas guns, the officers herded the cyclists into a block on San Benito street, between Fifth and Sixth streets, parked a dance band on a truck and ordered the musicians to play. Hundreds of individuals who invaded the town yesterday for the motorcycle show, about 10 per cent of them women halted their riotous "play" to dance. Their formal ball at the American Legion Hall was canceled by police orders. The dancers scuffed their way through inches of broken glass, debris of bottle barrages thrown during the day. The officers stood almost shoulder to shoulder along the curb.

Request for Help

Captain Torres and his men were sent to the scene by Charles E. Raymond Cato of the highway patrol who received a formal request of assistance from Lieutenant Roy L. McPhail of the seven-men Hollister police department. The request for aid was made at 3:30 P.M. today. As the state officers moved in, hundreds of cyclists roared through the streets of Hollister, defying traffic regulations. Many of them were injured in spills and crashes. One man's left foot was virtually severed. Lieutenant McPhail was emphatic in his announcement to *The Chronicle* that he was asked for assistance by the State Highway Patrol. Police Chief Fred A. Earin of Hollister said: "It's just one hell of a mess."

Thursday

The motorcyclists gathering for a three-day program of social activities, races and hill climbing events scheduled to end tomorrow began "taking over the town" the evening of July 3. The momentum of their activities gained strength during the 4th of July. By evening, they were virtually out of control, the police reported. Riders, both men and women, steered their machines into bars, crashing fixtures and bottles and mirrors.

They defied all traffic regulations racing full speed through the streets and intersections. Hundreds loosed bottle barrages. Bartenders halted the sale of beer, believing the group could not afford whiskey. Riotous activities continued. The bars closed two hours earlier than permitted by law. The same curfew was to go into effect tonight. The groups defied the officers to curb their activities. As many arrests as possible were made by police. Judge Frank Butcher convened a special session of his court tonight to dispose of the cases as he did last night. The sentences ranged from $25 to $250 and up to 75 days in jail. One of the participants identified by the police as Jim Morrison, 19, of Los Angeles, was given 90 days in the county jail for indecent exposure. The emergency room at Hazel Hawkins Hospital was jammed to overflowing. The first case arrived early yesterday. Late tonight, more than 40 persons had been treated. The San Benito Hospital handled the overflow cases.

List of Injured

The most seriously injured were: Merton Kranzman, 20, Rural Rout NO. 4, Tular. Compound fracture of the right leg. Frank McGovern, 45, Rural Rout NO. 2, Chico. Left leg almost severed. Ted Boyde Jr., 20, 542 Williams street, Oakland. Possible skull fracture. With the riot under control for the moment, officers said there is no apparent organized leader of the activity. The "Gypsy Tour" attracted motorcyclists from California, Arizona and Oregon. The first day's meeting was attended by as many as 12,000 persons, according to official estimates. Races were to conclude the tour today. Officers late tonight had not decided whether they would be permitted. "You just can't run everybody out of town", said Captain Torres. The "tour" brought the largest amount of transients in recent history to Hollister. Hundreds slept in "haystacks" according to police and in the city park and squares.

FORTY HOURS IN HOLLISTER

John Dorrance

John was a freelance writer who, in this selection, succinctly describes the moral panic about bikers with some excellent in-depth journalistic research commencing with the "old timers" who were present for the Hollister "riots" in 1947.

"The movie picture didn't do it justice," says the elderly owner of the lumber and hardware store. He remembers watching the line of black motorcycles that rumbled into the tiny, dusty community of Hollister, California, on the Fourth of July, 1947.

"There were girls stripped to the waist throwing beer bottles. The town was closed off at both ends – they used the main street as a drag strip. The gutters were loaded with beer bottles."

Now three seasoned customers, old farmers and ranchers from the surrounding Diablo foothills, gather around the counter to listen to the familiar tale. Next to the 1961 earthquake that destroyed a few buildings downtown, the "motorcyclists' invasion" was the most exciting event ever to hit Hollister.

"It was like a festival for drunks," says one sun-burnt farmer. "Drunks laying in the gutter. Bottles all over. People throwing bottles from up above. What they did out on the track was a different story. But the bunch I seen in town, they were drunks." Another man recalls that he left town for three days to escape the roar from thousands of unmuffled Harleys and Indians.

"I've seen *The Wild One* twice," says the shop assistant, dumping finishing nails into a metal bin. "From what I've heard, the movie is really blown out of proportion. But mom tells stories of locals that got involved in the trouble-making."

The others smile at the middle-aged assistant's comment. In those years after World War II, he was only a small baby, and couldn't possibly have known what it was like. But the old people remember that weekend as "the time when the Hell's Angels came." And they probably wouldn't change their stories one iota — not even if someone interrupted long enough to explain that the Hell's Angels didn't even exist that Independence Day 10 years ago, when the "riot" came to town.

That weekend was destined to catapult the sleepy central California community of 4800 residents — Hollister's only claim to fame then was that the area produced 74 percent of all the garlic grown in the United States — into the maw of the national newspapers, *Life* magazine, and finally, the Hollywood film industry.

Late Saturday night, an industrious reporter from the *San Francisco Chronicle* had flown down for the weekend to cover what was supposed to be a calm gathering of motorcyclists. From Hollister, he filed a sensational story which was quickly picked up by the *New York* and *Los Angeles Times*.

The national press, nurtured on the grist of a world war, saw the story in a common light. Editors called the events of that holiday weekend the "battle for Hollister," and almost every article about the rally used the words "invasion," "havoc," or "wreckage." Two weeks afterward, a full-page photograph published in *Life* magazine forever branded the image of the motorcycling rioteer on the nation's conscience. Sprawled across the saddle of a straight-pipe Harley parked in a pile of beer bottles, a filthy, glassy-eyed biker grins at the photographer while casually swilling another brew. "Cyclist's Holiday," read the caption beneath the now-infamous photograph. "He and his friends terrorize a town."

The effects were immediate and damning. With a readership of nearly five million, *Life* was the largest weekly in America, and the image of the drunken biker fit with the already dark impressions many suburbanites held of those strange individuals who put two wheels under their rumps and rode – often in militaristic formation like the Nazis the nation had so recently defeated – around the countryside on loud, sinister machines. Several years before, a motorcycle gathering in Daytona Beach, Florida, had erupted in brawls and drunken riding, but it was small stuff compared with the battles then raging in Europe, and the story never made front-page news.

After the Hollister story broke, one town quickly cancelled its invitation to host a rally. Cities where future rallies were scheduled were phoning the American Motorcycle Association to ask if the gypsy tours would stay – *could* stay – safely under control.

"Make no mistake about it," exclaimed one AMA spokesman investigating the aftermath of the Hollister rally, "that publicity was bad. The sport was set back on its heels. No doubt the instigators of the havoc, if they have one spark of a sense of decency, are filled with regret." Hollister also marked the birth of the "outlaw" biker, with the AMA branding the gang element as the "one-percenters" who were ruining motorcycling for what Paul Brokaw, then editor of *Motorcyclist* magazine termed ". . . the tens of thousands of innocent, clean cut, respectable, law-abiding young men and women who are the true representatives of an admirable sport."

During the late 1940s, several rowdy clubs had indeed latched onto motorcycling, among them the Galloping Gooses, Satan's Sinners, and the Booze Fighters – all harbingers of the Hell's Angels who would form later in 1950. It was a small group of about 20 Booze Fighters parked in a trailer on main street, according to many of the rally participants, who instigated much of the trouble downtown. Rumor had it the Booze Fighters also caused a scene at the Veteran's Park when they refused to remove their gang jackets before competing in the straight racing. Another report claimed "the local 'toughies' figured they could further stir things up as the motorcycle riders would be blamed for everything."

Most organizers agreed that a minority of the riders caused the uproar, but the story varied depending on who was telling the tale. AMA officials had registered 1500 riders at Hollister, for example, and estimated the true count of the weekend's motorcyclists at 3000. The newspapers had apparently exaggerated the numbers. Carnage was slight at the Hollister "riot": the facts were less colourful in some instances than the papers that printed the stories of wildness.

Thursday afternoon the motorcyclists – including many reputable clubs from out of state, even two hundred leather-clad Motor Maids – began arriving in town to watch the races and participate in the planned events.

By Friday evening, downtown Hollister was packed. The town's daily four-page newspaper, the *Free Lance*, reported "moderately wild activities" – a few riders were drag racing and spinning donuts on the asphalt of the main street. In an effort to slow the number of hard-drinking riders, the bars closed down two hours early on Thursday night. A special session of night court convened to process a crowd of drunks and traffic violators – the small county jail was overflowing.

The next day, everything was peaceable at the Veteran's Park as the plank races and hillclimbs proceeded uneventfully. Downtown, the situation was deteriorating. For some, the Fourth of July binge had spilled over into the weekend. Bikes were ridden inside bars, beer bottles flew from the roof-tops – a fair number of riders were wiping out while drag-racing on the main street. The situation was beyond the capabilities of Hollister's seven-man police force. A radio call for reinforcements went out to the Highway Patrol late Saturday afternoon. The CHP quickly herded everyone into a two-block area of downtown – the crowd danced off the excess energy and alcohol to the strains of a makeshift band.

"Luckily, there appears to be no serious damage to the town," one city councilman told a reporter after things cooled down the next day. "These trick riders did more harm to themselves." Three motorcyclists had been seriously injured; one man suffered compound fractures of his right leg when struck by a cyclist swerving to avoid another rider spinning circles in the middle of the street. By early Sunday morning, the nearby hospital had treated 50 bikers for abrasions and broken bones.

After the Independence Day celebrations, Hollister quickly

returned to normal. Capacity crowds watched 50 of the nation's top racers perform at the half-mile flat track, and the park director invited everyone back next year. Downtown saw a half-ton of smashed beer bottles swept from the gutters of Hollister and a cracked window in the town's bank replaced. Some time later, the *Free Lance* noted that "county coffers were richer by some $2000 in fines and forfeited bails" – local stores reported doing $50,000 worth of business from the visiting cyclists. Two weeks later, the local markets had sold out of *Life* magazines, and Hollister residents were lending their soughtafter copies to friends and neighbors.

One of the millions who bought a copy of that issue was Frank Rooney, a New York writer. The image of the drunken rider fascinated Rooney. It played on his imagination for two years, until he wrote a short story called "Cyclists' Raid." It was one of his best. The plot centers around a vicious paramilitary motorcycle gang that ransacks a small town located, curiously enough, somewhere in California. Members of the "Angeleno Motorcycle Club" wore flat green goggles which gave them "the appearance of some tropical tribe with enormous semi-precious eyes, lidless and immovable." The gang drag races through the streets before fatally running down a young woman in the lobby of a hotel.

A Hollywood producer named Stanley Kramer read the story in *Harper's* magazine after its publication in 1951. Kramer traveled to Hollister to interview anyone he could about this rally that had begun to develop mythical qualities – some locals were already swearing the Hell's Angels had ridden in that weekend. Then the producer gathered together a band of hell-raising bikers much like the original Booze Fighters, and got them together with a relatively unknown young actor named Marlon Brando.

Kramer did not want to make a documentary, he said, but rather he wanted to capture ". . . the first big divorcement of youth from society" – the outlaw biker gang. His movie *The Wild One* hit mid–1950s audiences like the early warning of a malignant tumor. Despite its claimed fictional treatment, *The Wild One* harked back to Hollister.

"This is a shocking story. It could never take place in most American towns – but it did in this one. This," read big block letters across the screen at the start of the picture "is a public challenge not to let it happen again."

Recalls retired local racer Johnny Lamanto, who was 20 years old and motorcycle-crazy in the summer of 1947: "That movie really downed the motorcycle image. The way they made the picture, 90 percent wasn't the way it happened here. In them days there was mostly respectable clubs. There was no big gangs like this Marlon Brando bunch, where guys come in and park and harass the bars and all that."

The Hollister gathering was the first rally Lamanto had seen since before the war when the "Pacific Coast Racing Championships and Gypsy Tour" had been held at Bolado Park, 10 miles south of town. "When the gypsy tour came to town that year I didn't have a bike, so I went the 50 miles to San Jose and bought a 61-cubic-inch Harley. They had fantastic racing in those days."

The championships began in 1935 and grew steadily from a one-day motorcycle race into a three-day event with parades, dances, hillclimbs, controlled stunts, and national-caliber action on the tracks. In fact, the AMA used the Hollister event as a pattern during the 1930s for other gypsy tours throughout the country. And in 1940 (the last year before World War II interrupted the Hollister races), Captain Torres of the Highway Patrol expressed the overwhelming sentiments of Hollister's city government and the merchants' committee when he said: "I believe the cyclists should be invited here again next year, and the community should make every effort to that end."

At the next rally only seven years later, Captain Torres, and 35 other Highway patrolmen, would reinforce Hollister's handful of nervous police to help quiet the hundreds of rowdy, drunken bikers who had taken over a two-block section of the main street. One officer called the 1947 rally "the worst 40 hours in Hollister's history."

"Saturday afternoon it got a little out of hand," admits Johnny. He remembers some people tossing bottles onto the pavement, and riders spinning circles in the street with their machines. "The guys weren't vicious, but they were drag racing up and down. Yeah, I drag raced just like the rest of them. It actually didn't get that much out of hand. And it

simmered down right after they brought in the Highway
Patrol Saturday night."

"It depends on which perspective you have," adds Johnny's
wife, his girlfriend at the time of the rally. "A lot of the
merchants enjoyed having the rally come because the riders
brought a lot of money into town. But a lot of these townspeople
are 'horsey people' – ranchers and horsey people do not like
motorcycles."

Johnny nods his head in agreement. "Christ, I remember the
rodeo they used to have in Salinas years ago," he says. "You
couldn't walk down the street after the parade, there were so
many beer bottles."

The nearby rodeos, however, never stirred up the national
press like Hollister had. No citizens had been molested by the
cyclists, and the physical damage to the town was negligible.
Yet, the rally had the dubious distinction of being the first of
what the newspapers would call a "motorcycle riot." The
following year, the town of Riverside, 280 miles south of
Hollister, was subjected to drunken violence when another
gypsy tour stepped over the edge of common decency. This
time several police officers were attacked, and an unruly mob of
bikers bashed in a pickup truck. Riverside city councilmen
asked for a statewide ban on motorcycle events.

Meanwhile, state and local legislatures across the country
were taking steps to curtail or dampen motorcycle events as a
result of the news stories tumbling out of California. Alabama
unearthed an ancient law forbidding motorcycle activities on
Sundays, while in Kuskogee, Oklahoma, officials banned double riding in specified sections of their city.

"Hollister just had a one-day half-bike race at the Veteran's
Park after that '47," says Johnny. "But the merchants wanted
the gypsy tour back because – man, they made nothing but
money. Oh Christ, they got rich over it, you know. The bars
profited most, and the restaurants."

The city fathers of Hollister debated long and hard on
whether to allow another three-day rally to roar into their
community. Could they keep the rowdies under control next
time? The local paper reported that threats of bodily injury had
drifted indirectly to police officers during the rally; one such
vow "to bust open your jail if our pals aren't turned loose" was

realized shortly after 10 p.m. on Saturday night when companions of three locked up riders applied a crowbar to the door of
the jail behind city hall and freed their friends. Fred A. Earle,
the town's chief of police, had resigned 48 hours after the
weekend debacle. Having served the community for more than
three decades, the harried cop diplomatically told the city
council he was finally throwing in the towel "due to an increase
in my duties."

The subsequent decision to slice the festivities to one day
effectively killed the event. No hordes of Independence Day
bikers drag raced through Hollister or at the racetracks after
1947.

Larry Ketzel – founder of the Salinas Ramblers Motorcycle
Club, the local club of well-disciplined riders that had helped
sponsor and organize the 1947 rally – lives 30 miles west of
Hollister in the town of Salinas. He acts like a man badly burned
by the media. Ketzel claims that during the uproar, frantic
newsmen were collecting beer bottles to stack around the
motorcycle for grimmer-looking photographs.

"If you just used your head, you would realize it would be
impossible for a man to drink that much beer and still be sitting
up," Larry says about the photograph in *Life*. (Indeed, the
photographer who snapped the famous picture later admitted it
was posed.)

It has been almost 40 years since a Hollywood filmmaker also
stopped by Larry's former motorcycle dealership in Salinas to
gather information about the rally.

"We chewed the fat for half an hour," Larry recalls of his
discussion with Stanley Kramer. "He assured me there would
be nothing detrimental to motorcyclists in his picture." Larry
sadly shakes his head, trying to figure how over the years the
whole story had snowballed into hell. Maybe it's just the kind of
small town that can't keep a big secret. "Can't you just let that
thing die?" says Ketzel of Hollister's infamous legend.

Only a few days ago, a new reporter was hired on at the *Free
Lance*. An editor asked her if she had heard about the 1947 rally.

"Oh yeah," she replied. "Wasn't that the time when the
Hell's Angels came to town?"

CYCLISTS' RAID

Frank Rooney

The following story appeared in Harpers *Magazine.*
Little could be discovered about the author, but the tone
and perception of the work clearly identifies him as a
complete and total outsider to the world of motorcycles.
Along with Hollister, his story was the basis for Kra-
mer's Wild One.

Joel Bleeker, owner and operator of the Pendleton Hotel, was
adjusting the old redwood clock in the lobby when he heard the
sound of the motors. At first he thought it might be one of those
four-engine planes on the flights from Los Angeles to San
Francisco which occasionally got far enough off course to be
heard in the valley. And for a moment, braced against the
steadily approaching vibrations of the sound, he had the fantastic notion that the plane was going to strike the hotel. He
even glanced at his daughter, Cathy, standing a few feet to his
right and staring curiously at the street.

Then with his fingers still on the hour hand of the clock he
realized that the sound was not something coming down from
the air but the high, sputtering racket of many vehicles moving
along the ground. Cathy and Bret Timmons, who owned one of
the two drugstores in the town, went out onto the veranda but

Bleeker stayed by the clock, consulting the railroad watch he pulled from his vest pocket and moving the hour hand on the clock forward a minute and a half. He stepped back deliberately, shut the glass case and looked at the huge brass numbers and the two ornate brass pointers. It was eight minutes after seven, approximately twenty-two minutes until sundown. He put the railroad watch back in his pocket and walked slowly and incuriously through the open doors of the lobby. He was methodical and orderly and the small things he did every day – like setting the clock – were important to him. He was not to be hurried – especially by something as elusively irritating as a sound, however unusual.

There were only three people on the veranda when Bleeker came out of the lobby – his daughter Cathy, Timmons, and Francis LaSalle, co-owner of LaSalle and Fleet, Hardware. They stood together quietly, looking, without appearing to stare, at a long stern column of red motorcycles coming from the south, filling the single main street of the town with the noise of a multitude of pistons and the crackling of exhaust pipes. They could see now that the column was led by a single white motorcycle which when it came abreast of the hotel turned abruptly right and stopped. They saw too that the column without seeming to slow down or to execute any elaborate movement had divided itself into two single files. At the approximate second, having received a signal from their leader, they also turned right and stopped.

The whole flanking action, singularly neat and quite like the various vehicular formations he remembered in the Army, was distasteful to Bleeker. It recalled a little too readily his tenure as a lieutenant colonel overseas in England, France, and finally Germany.

"Mr. Bleeker?"

Bleeker realized the whole troop – no one in the town either then or after that night was ever agreed on the exact number of men in the troop – had dismounted and that the leader was addressing him.

"I'm Bleeker." Although he hadn't intended to, he stepped forward when he spoke, much as he had stepped forward in the years when he commanded a battalion.

"I'm Gar Simpson and this is Troop B of the Angeleno Motorcycle Club," the leader said. He was a tall, spare man and his voice was coldly courteous to the point of mockery. "We expect to bivouac outside your town tonight and we wondered if we might use the facilities of your hotel. Of course, sir, we'll pay."

"There's a washroom downstairs. If you can put up with that—"

"That will be fine, sir. Is the dining room still open?"

"It is."

"Could you take care of twenty men?"

"What about the others?"

"They can be accommodated elsewhere, sir."

Simpson saluted casually and, turning to the men assembled stiffly in front of the hotel, issued a few quiet orders. Quickly and efficiently, the men in the troop parked their motorcycles at the curb. About a third of the group detached itself and came deferentially but steadily up the hotel steps. They passed Bleeker who found himself maneuvered aside and went into the lobby. As they passed him, Bleeker could see the slight converted movement of their faces – though not their eyes, which were covered by large green goggles – toward his daughter Cathy. Bleeker frowned after them but before he could think of anything to say, Simpson, standing now at his left, touched his arm.

"I've divided the others into two groups," he said quietly. "One group will eat at the diner and the other at the Desert Hotel."

"Very good," Bleeker said. "You evidently know the town like a book. The people too. Have you ever been here before?"

"We have a map of all the towns in this part of California, sir. And of course we know the names of all the principal hotels and their proprietors. Personally, I could use a drink. Would you join me?"

"After you," Bleeker said.

He stood watching Simpson stride into the lobby and without any hesitation go directly to the bar. Then he turned to Cathy, seeing Timmons and LaSalle lounging on the railing behind her, their faces already indistinct in the plummeting California twilight.

"You go help in the kitchen, Cathy," Bleeker said. "I think it'd be better if you didn't wait on tables."

"I wonder what they look like behind those goggles," Cathy said.

"Like anybody else," Timmons said. He was about thirty, somewhat coarse and intolerant and a little embarrassed at being in love with a girl as young as Cathy. "Where did you think they came from? Mars?"

"What did they say the name of their club was?" Cathy said.

"Angeleno," LaSalle said.

"They must be from Los Angeles. Heighho. Shall I wear my very best gingham, citizen colonel?"

"Remember now – you stay in the kitchen," Bleeker said.

He watched her walk into the lobby, a tall slender girl of seventeen, pretty and enigmatic, with something of the brittle independence of her mother. Bleeker remembered suddenly, although he tried not to, the way her mother had walked away from him that frosty January morning two years ago saying, "I'm going for a ride." And then the two-day search in the mountains after the horse had come back alone and the finding of her body – the neck broken – in the stream at the foot of the cliff. During the war he had never really believed that he would live to get back to Cathy's mother and after the war he hadn't really believed he would be separated from her – not again – not twice in so short a time.

Shaking his head – as if by that motion he could shed his memories as easily as a dog sheds water – Bleeker went in to join Gar Simpson who was sitting at a table in the barroom. Simpson stood politely when Bleeker took the opposite chair.

"How long do you fellows plan to stay?" Bleeker asked. He took the first sip of his drink, looked up, and stared at Simpson.

"Tonight and tomorrow morning," Simpson said.

Like all the others he was dressed in a brown windbreaker, khaki shirt, khaki pants, and as Bleeker had previously observed wore dark calf-length boots. A cloth and leather helmet lay on the table beside Simpson's drink, but he hadn't removed his flat green goggles, an accouterment giving him and the men in his troop the appearance of some tropical tribe with enormous semi-precious eyes, lidless and immovable. That was Bleeker's first impression and, absurd as it was, it didn't seem an exaggeration of fancy but of truth.

"Where do you go after this?"

"North." Simpson took a rolled map from a binocular case slung over his shoulder and spread it on the table. "Roughly we're following the arc of an ellipse with its southern tip based on Los Angeles and its northern end touching Fresno."

"Pretty ambitious for a motorcycle club."

"We have a month," Simpson said. "This is our first week but we're in no hurry and we're out to see plenty of country."

"What are you interested in mainly?"

"Roads. Naturally, being a motorcycle club – you'd be surprised at the rate we're expanding – we'd like to have as much of California as possible opened up to us."

"I see."

"Keeps the boys fit too. The youth of America. Our hope for the future." Simpson pulled sternly at his drink and Bleeker had the impression that Simpson was repressing, openly, and with pride, a vast sparkling ecstasy.

Bleeker sat and watched the young men in the troop file upstairs from the public washroom and stroll casually but nevertheless with discipline into the dining room. They had removed their helmets and strapped them to their belts, each helmet in a prescribed position to the left of the belt-buckle but – like Simpson – they had retained their goggles. Bleeker wondered if they ever removed the goggles long enough to wash under them and, if they did, what the flesh under them looked like.

"I think I'd better help out at the tables." Bleeker said. He stood up and Simpson stood with him. "You say you're from Troop B? Is that right?"

"Correct. We're forming Troop G now. Someday –"

"You'll be up to Z," Bleeker said.

"And not only in California."

"Where else for instance?"

"Nevada – Arizona – Colorado – Wyoming."

Simpson smiled and Bleeker, turning away from him abruptly, went into the dining room where he began to help the two waitresses at the tables. He filled water glasses, set out extra forks, and brought steins of beer from the bar. As he served the troop, their polite thank yous, ornate and insincere, irritated him. It reminded him of tricks taught to animals, the animals only being allowed to perform under certain obvious conditions of security. And he didn't like the cool way they stared at the two waitresses, both older women and fixtures in the town and then leaned their heads together as if every individual thought had to be pooled and divided equally among them. He admitted, after some covert study, that the twenty men were really only variations of one, the variations, with few exceptions, being too subtle for him to recognize and differentiate. It was the goggles, he decided, covering that part of the face which is most noteworthy and most needful for identification – the eyes and the mask around the eyes.

Bleeker went into the kitchen, pretending to help but really to be near Cathy. The protective father, he thought ironically, watching his daughter cut pie and lay the various colored wedges on the white blue-bordered plates.

"Well, Daddy, what's the verdict?" Cathy looked extremely grave but he could see that she was amused.

"They're a fine body of men."

"Uh-huh. Have you called the police yet?"

He laughed. "It's a good thing you don't play poker."

"Child's play." She slid the last piece of blueberry pie on a plate. "I saw you through the door. You looked like you were ready to crack the Siegfried line – single-handed."

"That man Simpson."

"What about him?"

"Why don't you go upstairs and read a book or something?"

"Now, Daddy – you're the only professional here. They're just acting like little tin soldiers out on a spree."

"I wish to God they were made of tin."

"All right. I'll keep away from them. I promise." She made a gesture of crossing her throat with the thin edge of a knife. He leaned over and kissed her forehead, his hand feeling awkward and stern on her back.

After dinner the troop went into the bar, moving with a strange co-ordinated fluency that was both casual and military and sat jealously together in one corner of the room. Bleeker served them pitchers of beer and for the most part they talked quietly together, Simpson at their center, their voices guarded and urgent as if they possessed information which couldn't be disseminated safely among the public.

Bleeker left them after a while and went upstairs to his daughter's room. He wasn't used to being severe with Cathy and he was a little embarrassed by what he had said to her in the kitchen. She was turning the collars of some of his old shirts, using a portable sewing machine he had bought her as a present on her last birthday. As he came in she held one of the shirts comically to the floor lamp and he could see how thin and transparent the material was. Her mother's economy in small things, almost absurd when compared to her limitless generosity in matters of importance, had been one of the family jokes. It gave him an extraordinary sense of pleasure, so pure it was like a sudden inhalation of oxygen, to see that his daughter had not only inherited this tradition but had considered it meaningful enough to carry on. He went down the hall to his own room without saying anything further to her. Cathy was what he himself was in terms which could mean absolutely nothing to anyone else.

He had been in his room for perhaps an hour, working on the hotel accounts and thinking obliquely of the man Simpson, when he heard, faintly and apparently coming from no one direction, the sound of singing. He got up and walked to the windows overlooking the street. Standing there, he thought he could fix the sound farther up the block toward Cunningham's bar. Except for something harsh and mature in the voices it was the kind of singing that might be heard around a Boy Scout campfire, more rhythmic than melodic and more stirring than tuneful. And then he could hear it almost under his feet, coming out of the hotel lobby and making three or four people on the street turn and smile foolishly toward the doors of the veranda.

Oppressed by something sternly joyous in the voices, Bleeker went downstairs to the bar, hearing as he approached the singing become louder and fuller. Outside of Simpson and the twenty men in the troop there were only three townsmen – including LaSalle – in the bar. Simpson, seeing Bleeker in the door, got up and walked over to him, moving him out into the lobby where they could talk.

"I hope the boys aren't disturbing you," he said.

"It's early," Bleeker said.

"In an organization as large and selective as ours it's absolutely necessary to insist on a measure of discipline. And it's equally necessary to allow a certain amount of relaxation."

"The key word is selective, I suppose."

"We have our standards," Simpson said primly.

"May I ask just what the hell your standards are?"

Simpson smiled. "I don't quite understand your irritation, Mr. Bleeker."

"This is an all-year-round thing, isn't it? This club of yours?"

"Yes."

"And you have an all-year-round job with the club?"

"Of course."

"That's my objection, Simpson. Briefly and simply stated, what you're running is a private army." Bleeker tapped the case slung over Simpson's shoulder. "Complete with maps, all sorts of local information, and of course a lobby in Sacramento."

"For a man who has traveled as widely as you have, Mr. Bleeker, you display an uncommon talent for exaggeration."

"As long as you behave yourselves I don't care what you do. This is a small town and we don't have many means of entertainment. We go to bed at a decent hour and I suggest you take that into consideration. However, have your fun. Nobody here has any objections to that."

"And of course we spend our money."

"Yes," Bleeker said. "You spend your money."

He walked away from Simpson and went out onto the veranda. The singing was now both in front and in back of him. Bleeker stood for a moment on the top steps of the veranda looking at the moon, hung like a slightly soiled but luminous pennant in the sky. He was embarrassed by his outburst to Simpson and he couldn't think why he had said such things. Private army. Perhaps, as Simpson had said, he was exaggerating. He was a small-town man and he had always hated the way men surrendered their individuality to attain perfection as a unit. It had been necessary during the war but it wasn't necessary now. Kid stuff – with an element of growing pains.

He walked down the steps and went up the sidewalk toward Cunningham's bar. They were singing there too and he stood

outside the big plate-glass window peering in at them and
listening to the harsh, pounding voices colored here and there
with the sentimentalism of strong beer. Without thinking further
he went into the bar. It was dim and cool and alien to his eyes and
at first he didn't notice the boy sitting by himself in a booth near
the front. When he did, he was surprised – more than surprised,
shocked – to see that the boy wasn't wearing his goggles but had
placed them on the table by a bottle of Coca-Cola. Impulsively,
he walked over to the booth and sat across from the boy.

"This seat taken?"

He had to shout over the noise of the singing. The boy leaned
forward over the table and smiled.

"Hope we're not disturbing you."

Bleeker caught the word "disturbing" and shook his head
negatively. He pointed to his mouth, then to the boy and to the
rest of the group. The boy too shook his head. Bleeker could see
that he was young, possibly twenty-five, and that he had dark
straight hair cut short and parted neatly at the side. The face
was square but delicate, the nose short, the mouth wide. The
best thing about the boy, Bleeker decided, were his eyes, brown
perhaps or dark gray, set in two distorted ovals of white flesh
which contrasted sharply with the heavily tanned skin on the
cheeks, forehead and jaws. With his goggles on he would have
looked like the rest. Without them he was a pleasant young man,
altogether human and approachable.

Bleeker pointed to the Coca-Cola bottle. "You're not
drinking."

"Beer makes me sick."

Bleeker got the word "beer" and the humorous ulping motion
the boy made. They sat exchanging words and sometimes
phrases, illustrated always with a series of clumsy, groping
gestures until the singing became less coherent and spirited
and ended finally in a few isolated coughs. The men in the troop
were moving about individually now, some leaning over the bar
and talking in hoarse whispers to the bartender, others walking
unsteadily from group to group and detaching themselves immediately to go over to another group, the groups usually two or
three men constantly edging away from themselves and colliding
with and being held briefly by others. Some simply stood in the
center of the room and brayed dolorously at the ceiling.

Several of the troop walked out of the bar and Bleeker could see them standing on the wide sidewalk looking up and down the street – as contemptuous of one another's company as they had been glad of it earlier. Or not so much contemptuous as unwilling to be coerced too easily by any authority outside themselves. Bleeker smiled as he thought of Simpson and the man's talk of discipline.

"They're looking for women," the boy said.

Bleeker had forgotten the boy temporarily and the sudden words spoken in a normal voice startled and confused him. He thought quickly of Cathy – but then Cathy was safe in her room – probably in bed. He took the watch from his vest pocket and looked at it carefully.

"Five minutes after ten," he said.

"Why do they do that?" the boy demanded. "Why do they have to be so damned indecent about things like that? They haven't got the nerve to do anything but stare at waitresses. And then they get a few beers in them and go around pinching and slapping – they—"

Bleeker shivered with embarrassment. He was looking directly into the boy's eyes and seeing the color run under the tears and the jerky pinching movement of the lids as against something injurious and baleful. It was an emotion too rawly infantile to be seen without being hurt by it and he felt both pity and contempt for a man who would allow himself to display such a feeling – without any provocation – so nakedly to a stranger.

"Sorry," the boy said.

He picked up the green goggles and fitted them awkwardly over his eyes. Bleeker stood up and looked toward the center of the room. Several of the men turned their eyes and then moved their heads away without seeming to notice the boy in the booth. Bleeker understood them. This was the one who could be approached. The reason for that was clear too. He didn't belong. Why and wherefore he would probably never know.

He walked out of the bar and started down the street toward the hotel. The night was clear and cool and smelled faintly of the desert, of sand, of heated rock, of the sweetly-sour plants growing without water and even of the sun which burned itself into the earth and never completely withdrew. There were only a few townsmen on the sidewalk wandering up and down, lured by the presence of something unusual in the town and masking, Bleeker thought, a ruthless and menacing curiosity behind a tolerant grin. He shrugged his shoulders distastefully. He was like a cat staring into a shadow the shape of its fears.

He was no more than a hundred feet from the hotel when he heard – or thought he heard – the sound of automatic firing. It was a well-remembered sound but always new and frightening.

Then he saw the motorcycle moving down the middle of the street, the exhaust sputtering loudly against the human resonance of laughter, catcalls, and epithets. He exhaled gently, the pain in his lungs subsiding with his breath. Another motorcycle speeded after the first and he could see four or five machines being wheeled out and the figures of their riders leaping into the air and bringing their weight down on the starting pedals. He was aware too that the lead motorcycles, having traversed the length of the street had turned and were speeding back to the hotel. He had the sensation of moving – even when he stood still – in relation to the objects heading toward each other. He heard the high unendurable sound of metal squeezing metal and saw the front wheel of a motorcycle twist and wobble and its rider roll along the asphalt toward the gutter where he sat up finally and moved his goggled head feebly from side to side.

As Bleeker looked around him he saw the third group of men which had divided earlier from the other two coming out of a bar across the street from Cunningham's, waving their arms in recognizable motions of cheering. The boy who had been thrown from the motorcycle vomited quietly into the gutter. Bleeker walked very fast toward the hotel. When he reached the top step of the veranda, he was caught and jostled by some five or six cyclists running out of the lobby, one of whom fell and was kicked rudely down the steps. Bleeker staggered against one of the pillars and broke a fingernail catching it. He stood there for a moment, fighting his temper, and then went into the lobby.

A table had been overthrown and lay on its top, the wooden legs stiffly and foolishly exposed, its magazines scattered around it, some with their pages spread face down so that the bindings rose along the back. He stepped on glass and realized one of the panes in the lobby door had been smashed. One of the troop walked stupidly out of the bar, his body sagging against the impetus propelling him forward until without actually falling he lay stretched on the floor, beer gushing from his mouth and nose and making a green and yellow pool before it sank into the carpet.

As Bleeker walked toward the bar, thinking of Simpson and of what he could say to him, he saw two men going up the stairs toward the second floor. He ran over to intercept them. Recognizing the authority in his voice, they came obediently down the stairs and walked across the lobby to the veranda, one of them saying over his shoulder, "Okay, pop, okay – keep your lid on." The smile they exchanged enraged him. After they were out of sight he ran swiftly up the stairs, panting a little, and along the hall to his daughter's room.

It was quiet and there was no strip of light beneath the door. He stood listening for a moment with his ear to the panels and then turned back toward the stairs.

A man or boy, any of twenty or forty or sixty identical figures, goggled and in khaki, came around the corner of the second-floor corridor and put his hand on the knob of the door nearest the stairs. He squeezed the knob gently and then moved on to the next door, apparently unaware of Bleeker. Bleeker, remembering not to run or shout or knock the man down, walked over to him, took his arm and led him down the stairs, the arm unresisting, even flaccid, in his grip.

Bleeker stood indecisively at the foot of the stairs, watching the man walk automatically away from him. He thought he should go back upstairs and search the hall. And he thought too he had to reach Simpson. Over the noise of the motorcycles moving rapidly up and down the street he heard a crash in the bar, a series of drunken elongated curses, ending abruptly in a small sound like a man's hand laid flatly and sharply on a table.

His head was beginning to ache badly and his stomach to sour under the impact of a slow and steady anger. He walked into the bar and stood staring at Francis LaSalle – LaSalle and Fleet, Hardware – who lay sprawled on the floor, his shoulders touching the brass rail under the bar and his head turned so that his cheek rubbed the black polished wood above the rail. The bartender had his hands below the top of the bar and he was watching Simpson and a half a dozen men arranged in a loose semi-circle above and beyond LaSalle.

Bleeker lifted LaSalle, who was a little dazed but not really hurt, and set him on a chair. After he was sure LaSalle was all right he walked up to Simpson.

"Get your men together," he said. "And get them out of here."

Simpson took out a long yellow wallet folded like a book and laid some money on the bar.

"That should take care of the damages," he said. His tongue was a little thick and his mouth didn't quite shut after the words were spoken but Bleeker didn't think he was drunk. Bleeker saw too – or thought he saw – the little cold eyes behind the glasses as bright and as sterile as a painted floor. Bleeker raised his arm slightly and lifted his heels off the floor but Simpson turned abruptly and walked away from him, the men in the troop swaying at his heels like a pack of lolling hounds. Bleeker stood looking foolishly after them. He had expected a fight and his body was still poised for one. He grunted heavily.

"Who hit him?" Bleeker motioned toward LaSalle.

"Damned if I know," the bartender said. "They all look alike to me."

That was true of course. He went back into the lobby, hearing LaSalle say, weakly and tearfully, "Goddam them – the bastards." He met Campbell, the deputy sheriff, a tall man with the arms and shoulders of a child beneath a foggy, bloated face.

"Can you do anything?" Bleeker asked. The motorcycles were racing up and down the street, alternately whining and backfiring and one had jumped the curb and was cruising on the sidewalk.

"What do you want me to do?" Campbell demanded. "Put 'em all in jail?"

The motorcycle on the sidewalk speeded up and skidded obliquely into a plate-glass window, the front wheel bucking and climbing the brick base beneath the window. A single large section of glass slipped edge-down to the sidewalk and fell slowly toward the cyclist who, with his feet spread and kicking at the cement, backed clumsily away from it. Bleeker could feel the crash in his teeth.

*   *   *

Now there were other motorcycles on the sidewalk. One of them hit a parked car at the edge of the walk. The rider standing astride his machine beat the window out of the car with his gloved fists. Campbell started down the steps toward him but was driven back by a motorcycle coming from his left. Bleeker could hear the squeal of the tires against the wooden riser at the base of the steps. Campbell's hand was on his gun when Bleeker reached him.

"That's no good," he yelled. "Get the state police. Ask for a half dozen squad cars."

Campbell, angry but somewhat relieved, went up the steps and into the lobby. Bleeker couldn't know how long he stood on the veranda watching the mounting devastation on the street – the cyclist racing past store windows and hurling, presumably, beer bottles at the glass fronts; the two, working as a team, knocking down weighing machines and the signs in front of the motion picture theater; the innumerable mounted men running the angry townspeople, alerted and aroused by the awful sounds of damage to their property, back into their suddenly lighted homes again or up the steps of his hotel or into niches along the main street, into doorways, and occasionally into the ledges and bays of glassless windows.

He saw Simpson – or rather a figure on the white motor-cycle, helmeted and goggled – stationed calmly in the middle of the street under a hanging lamp. Presumably, he had been there for some time but Bleeker hadn't seen him, the many rapid movements on the street making any static object un-important and even, in a sense, invisible. Bleeker saw him now and he felt again that spasm of anger which was like another life inside his body. He could have strangled Simpson then, slowly and with infinite pride. He knew without any effort of reason that Simpson was making no attempt to control his men but waiting rather for that moment when their minds, subdued but never actually helpless, would again take posses-sion of their bodies.

Bleeker turned suddenly and went back into the lobby as if by that gesture of moving away he could pin his thoughts to Simpson, who, hereafter, would be responsible for them. He walked over the desk where Timmons and Campbell, the deputy, were talking.

"You've got the authority," Timmons was saying angrily. "Fire over their heads. And if that doesn't stop them—"

Campbell looked uneasily at Bleeker. "Maybe if we could get their leader—"

"Did you get the police?" Bleeker asked.

"They're on their way," Campbell said. He avoided looking at Timmons and continued to stare hopefully and miserably at Bleeker.

"You've had your say," Timmons said abruptly. "Now I'll have mine."

He started for the lobby doors but Campbell, suddenly incensed, grabbed his arm.

"You leave this to me," he said. "You start firing a gun—"

Campbell's mouth dropped and Bleeker, turning his head, saw the two motorcycles coming through the lobby doors. They circled leisurely around for a moment and then one of them shot suddenly toward them, the goggled rider looming enormously above the wide handlebars. They scattered, Bleeker diving behind a pillar and Campbell and Timmons jumping behind the desk. The noise of the two machines assaulted them with as much effect as the sight of the speeding metal itself.

Bleeker didn't know why in course of watching the two riders he looked into the hall toward the foot of the stairway. Nor did it seem at all unreasonable that when he looked he should see Cathy standing there. Deeply, underneath the outward preoccupation of his mind, he must have been thinking of her. Now there she was. She wore the familiar green robe, belted and pulled in at the waist and beneath its hem he could see the white slippers and the pink edge of her nightgown. Her hair was down and he had the impression her eyes were not quite open although, obviously, they were. She looked, he thought, as if she had waked, frowned at the clock, and come downstairs to scold him for staying up too late. He had no idea what time it was.

He saw – and of course Cathy saw – the motorcycle speeding toward her. He was aware that he screamed at her too. She did take a slight backward step and raise her arms in a pathetic warding gesture toward the inhuman figure on the motorcycle but neither could have changed – in that dwarfed period of time and in that short, unmaneuverable space – the course of their actions.

She lay finally across the lower steps, her body clinging to and equally arching away from the base of the newel post. And there was the sudden, shocking exposure of her flesh, the robe and the gown torn away from the leg as if pushed aside by the blood welling from her thigh. When he reached her there was blood in her hair too and someone – not Cathy – was screaming into his ears.

After a while the doctor came and Cathy, her head bandaged and her leg in splints, could be carried into his office and laid on the couch. Bleeker sat on the edge of the couch, his hand over Cathy's, watching the still white face whose eyes were closed and would not, he knew, open again. The doctor, after his first examination, had looked up quickly and since Bleeker too had been bent over Cathy, their heads had been very close together for a moment. The doctor had assumed, almost immediately, his expression of professional austerity but Bleeker had seen him in that moment when he had been thinking as a man, fortified of course by a doctor's knowledge, and Bleeker had known then that Cathy would die but that there would be also this interval of time.

Bleeker turned from watching Cathy and saw Timmons standing across the room. The man was – or had been – crying but his face wasn't set for it and the tears, points of colorless, sparkling water on his jaws, were unexpectedly delicate against the coarse texture of his skin. Timmons waved a bandaged hand awkwardly and Bleeker remembered, abruptly and jarringly, seeing Timmons diving for the motor-cycle which had reversed itself, along with the other, and raced out of the lobby.

There was no sound now either from the street or the lobby. It was incredible, thinking of the racket a moment ago, that there should be this utter quietude, not only the lack of noise but the lack of the vibration of movement. The doctor came and went, coming to bend over Cathy and then going away again. Timmons stayed. Beyond shifting his feet occasionally he didn't move at all but stood patiently across the room, his face toward Cathy and Bleeker but not, Bleeker thought once when he looked up, actually seeing them.

"The police," Bleeker said sometime later.

"They're gone," Timmons said in a hoarse whisper. And then after a while, "They'll get 'em – don't worry."

Bleeker saw that the man blushed helplessly and looked away from him. The police were no good. They would catch Simpson. Simpson would pay damages. And that would be the end of it. Who could identify Cathy's assailant? Not himself, certainly – nor Timmons nor Campbell. They were all alike. They were standardized figurines, seeking in each other a willful loss of identity, dividing themselves equally among one another until there was only a single mythical figure, unspeakably sterile and furnishing the norm for hundreds of others. He could not accuse something which didn't actually exist.

He wasn't sure of the exact moment when Cathy died. It might have been when he heard the motorcycle, unbelievably solitary in the quiet night, approaching the town. He knew only that the doctor came for the last time and that there was now a coarse, heavy blanket laid mercifully over Cathy. He stood looking down at the blanket for a moment, whatever he was feeling repressed and delayed inside him, and then went back to the lobby and out onto the veranda. There were a dozen men standing there looking up the street toward the sound of the motorcycle, steadily but slowly coming nearer. He saw that when they glanced at each other their faces were hard and angry but when they looked at him they were respectful and a little abashed.

Bleeker could see from the veranda a number of people moving among the smashed store-fronts, moving, stopping, bending over and then straightening up to move somewhere else, all dressed somewhat extemporaneously and therefore seeming without purpose. What they picked up they put down. What they put down they stared at grimly and then picked up again. They were like a dispossessed minority brutally but lawfully discriminated against. When the motorcycle appeared at the north end of the street they looked at it and then looked away again, dully and seemingly without resentment.

It was only after some moments that they looked up again, this time purposefully, and began to move slowly toward the hotel where the motorcycle had now stopped, the rider standing on the sidewalk, his face raised to the veranda.

No one on the veranda moved until Bleeker, after a visible effort, walked down the steps and stood facing the rider. It was the boy Bleeker had talked to in the bar. The goggles and helmet were hanging at his belt.

"I couldn't stand it any longer," the boy said. "I had to come back."

He looked at Bleeker as if he didn't dare look anywhere else. His face was adolescently shiny and damp, the marks, Bleeker thought, of a proud and articulate fear. He should have been heroic in his willingness to come back to the town after what had been done to it but to Bleeker he was only a dirty little boy returning to a back fence his friends had defaced with pornographic writing and calling attention to the fact that he was afraid to erase the writing but was determined nevertheless to do it. Bleeker was revolted. He hated the boy far more than he could have hated Simpson for bringing this to his attention when he did not want to think of anything or anyone but Cathy.

"I wasn't one of them," the boy said. "You remember, Mr. Bleeker. I wasn't drinking."

This declaration of innocence – this willingness to take blame for acts which he hadn't committed – enraged Bleeker.

"You were one of them," he said.

"Yes. But after tonight —"

"Why didn't you stop them?" Bleeker demanded loudly. He felt the murmur of the townspeople at his back and someone breathed harshly on his neck. "You were one of them. You could have done something. Why in God's name didn't you do it?"

"What could I do?" the boy said. He spread his hands and stepped back as if to appeal to the men beyond Bleeker.

Bleeker couldn't remember, either shortly after or much later, exactly what he did then. If the boy hadn't stepped back like that – if he hadn't raised his hand. . . . Bleeker was in the middle of a group of bodies and he was striking with his fists and being struck. And then he was kneeling on the sidewalk, holding the boy's head in his lap and trying to protect him from the heavy shoes of the men around him. He was crying out, protesting, exhorting, and after a time the men moved away from him and someone helped him carry the boy up the steps and lay him on the veranda. When he looked up finally only

Timmons and the doctor were there. Up and down the street
there were now only shadows and the diminishing sounds of
invisible bodies. The night was still again as abruptly as it had
been confounded with noise.

Some time later Timmons and the doctor carried the boy, alive
but terribly hurt, into the hotel. Bleeker sat on the top step of
the veranda, staring at the moon which had shifted in the sky
and was now nearer the mountains in the west. It was not in any
sense romantic or inflamed but coldly clear and sane. And the
light it sent was cold and sane and lit in himself what he would
have liked to hide.

He could have said that having lost Cathy he was not afraid
any longer of losing himself. No one would blame him. Cathy's
death was his excuse for striking the boy, hammering him to the
sidewalk, and stamping on him as he had never believed he
could have stamped on any living thing. No one would say he
should have lost Cathy lightly – without anger and without that
appalling desire to avenge her. It was utterly natural – as natural
as a man drinking a few beers and riding a motorcycle insanely
through a town like this. Bleeker shuddered. It might have been
all right for a man like Timmons who was and would always be
incapable of thinking what he – Joel Bleeker – was thinking. It
was not – and would never be – all right for him.

Bleeker got up and stood for a moment on the top step of the
veranda. He wanted, abruptly and madly, to scream his agony
into the night with no more restraint than that of an animal
seeing his guts beneath him on the ground. He wanted to smash
something – anything – glass, wood, stone – his own body. He
could feel his fists going into the boy's flesh. And there was that
bloody but living thing on the sidewalk and himself stooping
over to shield it.

After a while, aware that he was leaning against one of the
wooden pillars supporting the porch and aware too that his flesh
was numb from being pressed against it, he straightened up
slowly and turned to go back into the hotel.

There would always be time to make his peace with the dead.
There was little if any time to make his peace with the living.

BIRTH OF THE TERROR

Brock Yates

Concise and beautifully written, Brock Yates's "Birth of the Terror" gives a biker's account of the transformation of outlaw bikers into one percenters, and is widely regarded as one of the best works in the genre.

Americans gaped in shock at the photograph on page 31 of the July 21, 1947, issue of *Life* magazine. Peering at the citizenry in boozy defiance and waving a beer bottle at the camera was a pudgy man on a motorcycle. Dozens of empties were littered on the pavement around the drunken rider's jackbooted feet. The caption, written in knife-edge *Life* style, enhanced the outrage:

On the Fourth of July weekend 4,000 members of a motorcycle club roared into Hollister, California, for a three-day convention. They quickly tired of ordinary motorcycle thrills and turned to more exciting stunts. Racing their vehicles down Main Street and through traffic lights, they rammed into restaurants and bars, breaking furniture and mirrors. Some rested on the curb. Others hardly paused. Police arrested many for drunkenness and indecent exposure but could not restore order. Finally, after two days, the cyclists left with a brazen

explanation. "We like to show off. It's just a lot of fun."
But Hollister's police chief took a different view. Wailed
he, "It's just one hell of a mess."

Lock up your daughters! The Huns are on the roll! Your town
may be next. The fat man on the Harley became riveted in the
skulls of millions of decent, law-abiding, God-fearing Americans as an alcohol-soaked harbinger of anarchy spreading
across the nation.

With that single black-and-white photograph in America's
most popular and respected newsmagazine, the images of motorcycling and of Harley-Davidson were altered forever. From
that moment on, motorcycles would be tinged with evil: pre-
datory machines ridden by raging barbarians. This legend
would be enhanced in years hence by magazine stories, songs,
and a spate of motion pictures. Despite the horror generated by
the photograph and its ensuing alteration of the image of
motorcycles – most specifically Harley-Davidsons – recent
research by cooler heads reveals that *Life* was involved –
perhaps unwittingly – in the age-old game of yellow journalism,
wherein a routine incident is cynically sensationalized.

The Gypsy Tour, a relaxed weekend jaunt, at Hollister had
been organized by the Salinas (California) Ramblers Motorcycle Club and the Hollister Veterans' Memorial Park Association as a weekend of motorcycle racing, touring, and recreation.
It was but one of dozens of such events, all part of the American
Motorcycle Association's schedule of competitions across the
nation. The races at the little city's $\frac{1}{3}$ -mile dirt track in Bolado
Park attracted expert riders from all over the West Coast, who
traveled to the garlic truck-farming center set in the gravelly
brown foothills of the Diablo and Gabilan mountains forty-five
miles south of San Jose. They began drifting into town on July
2. They rolled in, lone riders and clusters of three and four,
streaming across the dusty flats from tough working-class Bay
area towns like Oakland and San Jose. Other had trekked north
from Los Angeles and San Pedro, from San Bernardino and
Fontana, splay-legged on chuffing Knuckleheads and aged
Indians and a few English Nortons and BSAs. Most had
sleeping bags wrapped over their back fenders in preparation
for a weekend of camping in the clear, chilly desert nights. Some

oldsters came on hulking twins with their women huddled in sidecars, the ultimate luxury transportation. Into Hollister they powered, engines rumbling ahead of long brown swirls of desert grit, ready for action. By Friday evening, their numbers had swelled to perhaps two thousand. While no official count was ever made, best estimates place the peak crowd at about four thousand by the time the little city returned to normal.

Motorcycle clubs had existed in one form or another since the early 1920s. Most were benign, involved in touring and several forms of motor sports like track racing and hill climbing. But a tiny percentage had assumed a darker image. Embittered and disillusioned by the American dream during the Depression, gangs formed up, mainly in the grungy industrial districts of Southern California, to ride and drink together, subsisting on menial jobs and dealing in stolen motorcycle parts. Because Harley-Davidson was the most abundant and popular motorcycle, it was obvious that it would be the brand of choice, both as a possession and a source of stolen income.

Following World War II, thousands of veterans spilled out of the armed forces, disoriented and disenfranchised. Although the GI Bill of Rights offered the most liberal safety net for ex-soldiers in history, inevitably some drifted toward the fringes of society, unable to make the transition from the intensity of warfare to the comparatively pallid pace of civilian life. They, like the men who had returned from the Civil War and headed toward the great western frontier, or the World War I veterans who formed the so-called Lost Generation, were altered forever, inured to violence and incapable of coping with the strictures of organized society.

Worse yet, peace had not come easily to the late 1940s world. While the United States had not suffered greatly in the war compared to other nations (no physical damage to its cities, 323,000 deaths out of an estimated 50 million worldwide), its ascension to the position of most powerful nation on earth brought great burdens. The bellicose Soviet Union had seized all of Europe east of the Elbe River and, in the words of Winston Churchill, cut it off from the west with an "Iron Curtain." To strengthen the non-Communist European nations, the American government instituted the Marshall Plan and other aid programs to stimulate the recovery of their war-ravaged economies. This shift of funding away from the domestic infrastructure had caused violent strikes in the American coal and rail industries and created deep pockets of unemployment. Added to that was paranoia about the threat of Communist infiltration at the very highest levels of government and in the military. The nation remained strangely unsettled during a period when the tranquillity of peacetime should have pervaded the landscape.

Oozing around the edges were the rebels, for the most part veterans still in their early twenties who were not only restless but possessed of a new knowledge of and fascination with machinery. The war had exposed many of them to all manner of technical exotica – airplanes, tanks, trucks, weapons, power plants, electronic devices, etc., that had been unknown prior to the fighting. This newfound interest had led many into the hot rod and sports car movements and would prompt an explosion in automotive enthusiasm and a major market shift toward small high-performance cars in the decades to come. This was for the most part innocent fun – despite a short-lived media fascination with the perils of "hot-rodding" and "drag racing." But motorcycles produced a harder-edged group of devotees. These veterans, feeling cast out of normal society, embraced the motorcycle not only as a recreational diversion but as a weapon against the established order, a raucous, fire-breathing barbarian of a contraption, the exhaust rattle of which was not unlike that of a .50-caliber machine gun. As weapons for wreaking havoc among the citizenry, unmuffled Harley-Davidsons were adopted by hundreds of restless young men flung into the ennui of the postwar world. This phenomenon was most visible in the Los Angeles basin, which had become a locus of the displaced and the disconnected during the vast Dust Bowl migrations of the 1930s. From this ruck rose the first outlaw motorcycle clubs (never, to this day, do they refer to themselves as "gangs"). It was at Hollister that they made their national debut. Riding into the heat-ravaged town in company with multitudes of workaday motorcycle enthusiasts came hard-edged young riders from clubs with names like the Booze Fighters, the Pissed Off Bastards of Bloomington (POBOBs), the Winos, Satan's Sinners, the Galloping Ghosts, and the Market Street Commandos. There was a nihilistic element to their names, as opposed to those of the hot rod clubs that had formed up at the same time.

These carried simple, innocent names like the Road Runners, and the Glendale Stokers and Sidewinders, and while their members engaged in reckless street races on occasion, they operated with a boyish enthusiasm. This was harmless playtime compared to the violence-prone anarchy of the new-style motorcycle clubs.

They came to Hollister to raise hell. While a vast majority of the weekend's riders quietly encamped on the edge of Hollister and caused no trouble to the city's four thousand residents, a nucleus of perhaps five hundred bikers, led by the Booze Fighters and the POBOBs, congregated on Friday night in a few saloons lining San Benito Street in the center of town. The action spilled outside, and soon a two-block war zone was established between Fourth and Sixth Streets. Motorcycles were ridden on the sidewalks and thundered into the barrooms. Various riders attempted stunts for the drunken throng. Several failed miserably. A youth from Tulare broke his leg in two places; an Oakland biker fractured his skull; and one of the more senior rioters, a 45-year-old reveler from Chico, nearly severed his foot when his bike crashed. Brawls were unrelenting, and Hollister's five-man police force was quickly overwhelmed.

Motors roared, beer bottles shattered on the pavement, and drunken shouts pierced the still night. The party thundered on throughout Saturday as the cops attempted to restore order. Several of the worst offenders were tossed in the small jail behind city hall on nearby Fifth Street. Armed with crowbars, other bikers defiantly freed them, and the beer blast boiled onward.

Forty-nine arrests were made, for the most part on charges of public intoxication, disorderly conduct, indecent exposure, and assorted misdemeanors, to a point where a special session of night court ran until dawn on Sunday to process the offenders. Roughly fifty of the celebrants were treated at the local Hazel Hawkins Hospital, but aside from the aforementioned trio who damaged themselves in botched trick riding displays, there were no serious injuries. Considering the lurid tales generated by the incident, which implied death and destruction rivaling the St. Bartholomew's Day Massacre, the so-called Battle of Hollister was at best a skirmish and at the least a glorified drunken binge.

On Sunday, Hollister police sergeant Roy McPhail called the

California Highway Patrol for help. Thirty CHP officers, armed with riot gear and tear gas and joined by several Monterey County deputies, finally restored order. By Monday morning, most of the rioting bikers had blearily wobbled out of town. The great confrontation, a puny squabble when compared to the vast antiwar campus conflicts that would erupt twenty years later, dribbled to an end amid the reek of stale beer and the crunch of broken glass. Yet the seismic shift it caused for the world of motorcycling was the cultural equivalent of the immense, ominous Calaveras earthquake fault that bisected the little city two blocks to the west of the riot scene.

Surely the event would have been long forgotten had it not been for a veteran *San Francisco Chronicle* photographer named Barney Peterson and reporter C. J. Doughty. They had been assigned on Friday evening to fly via a small chartered airplane the ninety miles to Hollister to snap some photos of the brawl. But by the time they landed, the action was apparently at a low enough level that Peterson needed some theatrical license to produce a properly dramatic picture.

Peterson's shot, picked up by the Associated Press and *Life* and then seen around the world, was probably taken the following morning, in front of Johnny's Bar and Grille on San Benito Street. Despite the seminal impact it had on motorcycling in general and on Harley-Davidson in particular, there is considerable doubt about its veracity. Surely Peterson took the picture at the riot, and there is no question that the Harley-Davidson in the photo is an authentic precursor of the "choppers" that became favored among future bikers. It was a battered big twin, probably a prewar 74 with its front fender removed (this was to become a favored styling trick as more and more effluvia was removed from the basic motorcycle in the years to come). But there is more to the story, as has been revealed by motorcycle historian and columnist Jerry Smith of Coos Bay, Oregon. Long fascinated with the Hollister incident and the sea change it effected in worldwide motorcycling, Smith has done extensive research into the circumstances surrounding Peterson's photograph. In searching the archives of the *San Francisco Chronicle*, Smith discovered that the now-dead Peterson shot several pictures with his 4 × 5 Speed Graphic while in Hollister. Smith found three versions, notably different, of the famous photograph. What fascinated him was the litter of beer bottles at the rider's feet. In one photo the bottles were standing upright, although in the exposure used by *Life* they are strewn helter-skelter around the front tire and under the engine of the motorcycle. It appears that the bottles were carefully arranged for maximum impact. In another of Peterson's unpublished shots, the rider has repositioned his booted feet on the front forks and pretentiously draped a jacket over his left shoulder. On the back of the jacket is an emblem of a winged skull surrounded by the words "Tulare Raiders." The letters "DAVE" are clearly visible.

Smith and local historian Daniel Corral located eighty-three-year-old Gus DeSerpa, who was present at the scene as a curious local and confirmed that the pictures were in fact posed, with the bottles planted on the pavement and the motorcycle positioned for maximum impact. The rider has also been identified by Smith as one Eddie Davenport, although his current whereabouts, or even if he owned the motorcycle upon which he was sprawled, remain a mystery. While associates of the late Barney Peterson deny that he would stoop to faking a news photo, there is no debating that several poses were assumed by Davenport during the shoot. Whether Davenport did this on his own or at Peterson's instigation is a moot point. More central to the issue is the fact that a person or persons staged the infamous Hollister *Life* photograph simply to generate public outrage.

In an interview with Smith, DeSerpa recalled the incident in a way that calls into question the validity of the infamous photograph:

> My former wife and I said, "Let's go uptown and see all the excitement." And then we ran into these people. They were on the sidewalk, and there was a photographer, I think he was from the *Tribune* [sic]; anyhow, they started to scrape up the bottles with their feet, you know, from one side to the other, and then they took the motorcycle and picked it up and set it right in the glass. I told my wife, "Hey, that's not right, they shouldn't be doing that." Yeah, he [the guy on the bike] was pretty well loaded. He was just in the vicinity right there. I think they just got

him to sit down there. Because there was a bar right there,
Johnny's Bar. I think he came wandering out of that bar.
He comes staggering out, and "Hey, here's just the guy we
want; hey, how about you sitting on there so we can take a
picture?"

This was not the first time that the media made ad hoc
"adjustments" to a scene for maximum drama (the Marine
flag-raising on Iwo Jima's Mount Suribachi comes immediately
to mind). What is amazing is the durability of the picture and its
impact. *Life*'s caption writers also managed to amplify the
drama, implying that "4,000 members of a motorcycle club"
did the damage. In fact, it was a tiny cadre of perhaps 10 percent
of that number, representing perhaps a dozen small California
clubs. The distortion was unconscionable, but considering the
novelty embodied in the notion of a helpless rural town being
terrorized by a mob of Huns on motorcycles, who cared if the
facts were stretched a bit? Surely the people who actually saw
the picture in that issue of *Life* half a century ago represented
but a minuscule percentage of the population (although the
magazine reprinted it in its "25 Years Ago in *Life*" section in
1972). Yet its imagery is pervasive, as if it had been branded into
the brains of every citizen as a paradigm of motorcycling – as the
quintessential portrait of every man and woman who ever rode a
Harley-Davidson. Hollister was perfect for the *Life* cultural
spin. Like most of the elite media of today, the magazine was
New York based, urban and sophisticated to a fault, and endlessly disdainful of the tall-grass population. Motorcycles were
(until Malcolm Forbes end-ran the elitists in the 1970s) the
worst sort of a proletarian gadget – especially the hulking, noisy,
oil-spitting Harleys from that provincial brewery town called
Milwaukee. Riots among the great unwashed were to be expected. *Life* editors, perusing the national landscape from their
Olympian perch high above Manhattan, felt more than quali-
fied to pass judgment on a collection of grease-stained blue-
collar hooligans. That these images of outlawry and lawlessness
would be transferred to their own children at unlikely venues
like Yale and Columbia in another twenty years was incon-
ceivable. But in the summer of 1947, it was obligatory to sneer
at the slobs bullying a hick town in nowhere and not worry

about any broader implications the incident might have for society.

Today Hollister's downtown is part of a national historic district. San Benito Street's rows of Gothic and Greek revival buildings have been neatly restored. In the middle of the small business district still sits Johnny's Bar and Grille, the seedy metacenter of the infamous riot and the backdrop for the Peterson photograph. While Hollister celebrates its eighteenth-century Spanish mission and the growth of its agricultural empire, the notorious Battle of Hollister is unmarked by sign or symbol. Only in 1997 did bikers return in appreciable numbers for the fiftieth anniversary of the legendary event. The gathering was pure theater. As opposed to the original rioters like the Booze Fighters and the Tulare Raiders, who wore Levi's and T-shirts, the newcomers were decked out in expensive black leathers, looking infinitely more ominous than their predecessors. But this was faux menace. They were average citizens in search of a communal identity embodied in the swashbuckling raffishness of the Booze Fighters and their like. A noted Harley rider from the upper echelons of government, Colorado senator Ben Nighthorse Campbell, appeared briefly, properly costumed. He mingled with corporate executives, lawyers, doctors, and other professionals who came to Hollister to pose in front of Johnny's and to transport themselves, in spirit at least, to that wild moment when a cipher of a human in the grand scheme of things named Eddie Davenport drunkenly launched himself into immortality.

Hollister's original moment of fame appeared to pass quickly. Several major dailies, including the *New York Times* and the *Los Angeles Times*, gave the incident cursory coverage, but this being a time when television network news was in its infancy, videotape unknown, and satellite feeds unthinkable, coverage was limited to Peterson's staged photograph and a brief dispatch from the news wire services.

If there was any reaction to the Hollister riot among the Harley-Davidson management in faraway Milwaukee, there is none on the public record. With the prospect of strengthening sales in a pent-up postwar market, the company, led by second-generation president William H. Davidson, was surely more concerned with increasing production and adding new models than reacting to a ruckus in a dusty California farm town. The company's major rival remained much-hated Indian, America's only other serious motorcycle manufacturer, while the steadily increasing influx of lightweight, high-performance motorcycles from British manufacturers like Norton, BSA, Triumph, Royal Enfield, and Ariel posed a new threat. Imperiously, the Harley-Davidson management passed the word to its dealers that any servicing of the English bikes, even including the sale of lubricants, was forbidden. Meanwhile, plans moved ahead for the acquisition of a large former military propeller-manufacturing factory on the outskirts of Milwaukee and the introduction of a new cylinder head design for the big V-twin sixty-one- and seventy-four-cubic-inch models that formed the core of its business. These major advances were to be announced at a lavish dealer meeting set for Milwaukee's Shroeder Hotel in late November of 1947, where optimism about the company's seemingly robust future was sure to blot out any memories of the brief flurry of bad publicity surrounding Hollister and the *Life* magazine photograph.

But the brand on the American psyche was deep and permanent. As the St. Valentine's Day Massacre in Chicago had defined gangsterism and the Kent State shootings became a symbol of the Vietnam antiwar movement, Hollister's impact far exceeded the damage wrought by the actual incident. The little town would forever be linked with motorcycle hoodlums in general and specifically with Harley-Davidson riders. A few cuts and bruises, some arrests, and broken beer bottles were seemingly unimportant at the time, but thanks to Peterson's photograph, Hollister was elevated into the folklore of American violence along with the seven dead thugs of the "Bugs" Moran gang and the four students who would fall at Kent State in the spring of 1970. Four years later, *Harper's* magazine, a much-respected monthly celebrating its hundredth birthday, published a short story by a writer named Frank Rooney titled "Cyclists' Raid." It chronicled an assault on an unnamed town by a gang of motorcyclists that ended in the death of a central character, the daughter of a hotel owner named Joe Bleeker. Bleeker spotted the menace, in Rooney's words, as he stood "quietly looking, without appearing to stare, at a long, stern column of red motorcycles coming from the south, filling the single main street of the town with the noise of a multitude of piston [sic] and the crackling of exhaust pipes." Rooney's reference to a technically meaningless "multitude of piston" reveals a notable lack of knowledge about his subject, as do the accompanying drawings by a long-forgotten artist named David Berger. His motorcyclists are impeccably dressed like aviators, with leather flying helmets, khaki shirts and riding breeches, and high leather boots – as opposed to the scruffy denim of the drunks who rumbled in Hollister.

Rooney's raiders behave well enough at the beginning of the story, but soon go berserk, with "the motorcycles racing up and down the street, alternately whining and backfiring and one had jumped the curb and was cruising on the sidewalk." In the end the bikers ride off in quasi-military formation, leaving Bleeker's sweet-heart daughter dead and others injured. There is little point to the story other than to imply that out there in the hinterlands roved bands of motorized maniacs ready to blast into towns like modern day Quantrill's Raiders to rape and pillage and kill. *Harper's* was a widely read monthly, and Rooney's story prompted horrified comment in genteel suburban circles – circles removed by sociological light years from a small group of motorcyclists who had formed up in the sooty steel town of Fontana, California. There, at roughly the same time Rooney was composing his hyperbolic fantasy, the real thing – the motorcycle club that would rise into the realm of international legend – was coalescing in beat-up bars and rented shacks on the edge of town. The little band, organized in 1948, was composed of young men who traded the conventions of middle-class American life for a rigid cultism built around motorcycles, free-form sex, and endless boozing supported by small-time thievery, and bound together by a code of ethics based on fanatic collective loyalty. They would, for reasons lost to history, call themselves the Hells (sic) Angels.

Some believe this fearsome name was derived from a B-17 squadron – the 358th – of the 303rd USAF Bomber Group based in the English Midlands during World War II. The fact that Clark Gable, who was a known Harley-Davidson enthusiast, flew a few missions with the 358th may or may not relate to the story. Another theory sources the name from the 1930 Howard Hughes-produced extravaganza *Hell's Angels*, starring

Jean Harlow and Ben Lyon. Either way, the Hells Angels would establish themselves as the ultimate motorcycle club, the baddest, hardest riding, most rigidly disciplined, and ruthless of them all, at least in the minds of the general public. By 1950, a handful of similar clubs had been loosely organized up and down the West Coast, for the most part in hard-knuckle industrial towns like Fontana, Long Beach, San Pedro, Oakland, San Jose, and San Bernardino. The motorcycle of choice was the Harley-Davidson, which, in a sense, won by default, it being the most prolific brand in the nation. Indians were accepted by the clubs' membership, as were the few Triumphs and BSAs reaching the market. But slowly, with the demise of Indian in 1953 and the rise of jingoism among the clubs during the Vietnam conflict, the Harley would reach an exclusive, iconic status. During the formative years of the outlaw gangs, any number of motorcycle makes were acceptable – provided they bore the distinctive brands of their owners.

This involved cutting or "chopping" away effluvia like fenders, saddlebags, and chrome trim in order to reduce weight and thereby increase performance. But more important, chopping branded the motorcycle as beyond the fringe, openly contemptuous of mainstream riders and their mindless compliance with convention.

If the formation of the Angels and their ilk was a symptom of disillusionment with middle-class life, it was but a footnote to the widely chronicled beat movement blossoming during the early 1950s in the mildly addled brains of a twenty-one-year-old ex-merchant mariner and aspiring novelist named Jack Kerouac and his pal, twenty-four-year-old poet Allen Ginsberg. They, along with William S. Burroughs, the drug-fogged heir to the business-machine fortune, and twenty-year-old sometime poet Gregory Corso, were the pioneers of a post-transcendentalism that some critics claimed linked them, in a broad sense, with Thoreau and Whitman. It centered on a fascination with pacifism and a suspicion of the modern industrial age. But their open rebellion against middle-class mores, which involved flirtations with Zen, heavy drug use (Burroughs was a pioneer heroin addict), boozing, and wild sex (Ginsberg was openly homosexual), elevated them into a realm of outrageous behavior heretofore unknown to the good burghers of America. In 1950, even as the motorcycle gangs were forming on the cultural fringes, Kerouac was setting out on a disjointed, drug-and-alcohol-blurred journey aboard his beat-up Buick. His odyssey would lead to a marginally coherent semi-autobiographical novel featuring his alter ego Sal Paradise, and his pals Carlo Marx (Ginsberg) and Dean Moriarty – a pseudonym for long-time counterculture Olympian druggy Neal Cassady. *On the Road* was published seven years later. During this same time frame, Ginsberg produced his murky, controversial poem *Howl*, the subject of several showcase pornography trials, and Burroughs published a disjointed chronicle of a permanent state of heroin-crazed addiction called *Naked Lunch*. These three men, along with a few acolytes in Greenwich Village and San Francisco, were the founding fathers of the beat (shorthand for "beatitude") movement, which created the bedrock foundation of the counterculture that followed in the early 1960s. While Kerouac slowly drank himself to a hermit's death that would come in 1969, Ginsberg gained icon status among the hippies, leading demonstrations against the Vietnam war and becoming, with Bob Dylan, an informal poet laureate for the entire movement. While Burroughs and Corso drifted off center stage, Neal Cassady made an easy transition from beatnik to hippie and became a fixture in San Francisco's Haight-Ashbury scene before drugs and alcohol resulted in a lonely, drug-fogged demise before the decade had ended.

Operating on the perimeter of this vast, robust but ill-defined shift in the youth culture of the nation was a new breed of motorcyclists – also devoid of a defining political philosophy but surely better structured, more violent, and more scatological than the counterculturalists. The overall themes were similar: denial of the viability of normal middle-class life and the expression of that disdain with openly antisocial and shocking acts. But while the joint, acid, the hookah, love beads, and the guitar became the accoutrements of the beatniks and the hippies, the angrier, tougher men who formed the motorcycle clubs employed other, more culturally infuriating symbols, including German iron crosses, the hated Nazi swastika, and frightening club "colors" – the embroidered emblems worn on the back of leather or denim cutoff jackets. These quasi-military trappings often utilized SS-style death's heads, snakes, crossed bones, laughing skulls, etc. as symbols of supreme menace. The Hells Angels' colors were centered around the profile of a helmeted skull trailing a large feathered wing, displayed with fanatic reverence on an embroidered patch surrounded by the words "Hells Angels M.C. [motorcycle club]" with the name of the chapter ("Berdoo" for San Bernardino, Oakland, Vallejo, etc.). The exact origin of biker clubs' colors is unclear, although they probably date to pre-World War II and their use by more benign motorcycle organizations. By the late 1950s, colors were in universal use by the clubs (or "gangs," as they were known in the press and among the general public). Rivals to the Angels, like the Outlaws, which formed up at roughly the same time, also employed colors centered on a motorcycle theme. The Outlaws' colors, for example, presented a skull flanked by a pair of pistons – surely from a motorcycle. All the clubs, regardless of their location or size, formed their tightly knit organizations around a single talisman: a lusty, rackety brute of a motorcycle more often than not bearing the Harley-Davidson label.

It was sometime during this period that a particularly poetic motorcyclist (whether a gang member or not is lost to history) labeled his Harley a "hog." He was no doubt rhapsodizing about the machine's bulk and its sloppy, ill-mannered demeanor as compared to the smaller, more effete European bikes. The name stuck, much to the distress of the decent folk who rode Harleys, although in the future this colorful, if clearly pejorative, nickname would be heartily embraced by the most lily white of the marque's devotees.

The men in Milwaukee were aware of the rise of the new outlaw clubs but chose to ignore them. Their surrogates who ran the 50,000-member American Motorcycle Association denounced the Angels and their ilk as "one percenters," an outlandish minority of thugs and outsiders who bore no resemblance to the real world of motorcycling. This assault delighted the outlaws, who saw it as affirmation of their presence and began wearing patches denoting themselves as "One Percenters," the ultimate imprimatur of the hard-core biker.

The lifestyle of the clubs centered on unflagging group loyalty and mutual support, whether in bar fights or in paying debts. Revenues, used primarily to maintain low-rent clubhouses and for endless communal parties, came from petty thievery and trading in stolen motorcycle parts. Initiation rites – made frighteningly lurid by rumors that oozed through straight society – often involved group sex with the flinty women who rode with them but could not be members. Scruffy fashions featuring filthy, oil-soaked denims, long hair, tattoos, headbands, handcrafted jewelry, and beards were in many ways prototypical of the look adopted by the hippies a few years later, as were some of the more shocking, antisocial mores originated by the outlaws. But while conventional society reeled in stunned fury over the antics of the bikers, similar behavior was tolerated in the counterculturists in the sixties – mainly because Mr. and Mrs. America's sons and daughters were participating.

Assaults on the establishment by middle-class college students were generally viewed as acts of conscience by sympathetic media and academia, although they were often more violent and overtly antisocial. After all, the Hells Angels never spun off gruesomely homicidal mutations like the Weathermen, the Symbionese Liberation Army, or the Manson family. No Angel ever burned down an ROTC building or blew up a university laboratory or machine-gunned a bank guard in the name of a hazy people's revolution. Much like the Mafia, the motorcycle clubs were essentially isolated tightly knit cults whose battles were turf wars and who only ventured into the public domain when the media chose to spotlight them.

The Harley-Davidson company, operating in splendid isolation in the hinterlands of Milwaukee, continued to view the motorcycle market within a narrow perspective as old-line, traditional customers heaving their overweight bodies aboard belit and bechromed Harley cruisers known in the business as "dressers" – as in military "full dress." The notion that a collection of punks would actually saw up a perfectly good motorcycle in the name of an outlandish, antisocial fad was as confusing to them as the news from trend-setting California that more and more riders were turning to midsized, high-performance British and German bikes made by such well-known manufacturers as BMW, BSA, Triumph, and Norton.

While historians have described the fifties as pallid and feckless in comparison to the wild sixties, there were stirrings of discontent, as evidenced by the beat movement, the exploding popularity of rock 'n' roll, the California hot-rodders, and the rising tide of motorcycle gangs. The nation had changed radically since the end of the war. Paranoia about the Russian menace remained intense, and the nasty, undeclared war in Korea would kill and maim nearly as many Americans as the subsequent disaster in Vietnam, but the country appeared, superficially at least, to be heading in the words of Arthur Schlesinger Jr., into a "state of repose." The devastation of the Depression, followed by the manic effort during World War II, had enervated the nation, and despite Korea and the Cold War, much of the citizenry seemed to yearn for a return to the good life of the twenties. Save, of course, for a segment of young men who found the Babbitt-like normalcy insufferably boring. And at this point, the nation was able to afford such rebellions. Now the most powerful economy in the history of the world, America, offered unprecedented opportunity for diversion and recreation – including alternate lifestyles like those of the beats and the bikers. Thousands of dissidents were therefore provided the luxury of hating the establishment – based, ironically, on the largesse of that very entity.

They had, in theory, much to whine about. The liberal elite was in high dudgeon over the excesses of the McCarthy hearings and the endless assaults on civil liberties by the House Un-American Activities Committee. The blackballing of a group of Hollywood screenwriters with decided left-wing sympathies energized the film industry for the first time since the 1930s. In 1952, Stanley Kramer, a producer with openly liberal sensibilities, began producing a much-revised version of Frank Rooney's *Harper's* magazine story, starring a pair of hot young actors as motorcycle gang members. Marlon Brando and Lee Marvin were cast with gritty character actor Robert Keith in a picture titled *The Wild One*, which would once again reinforce the depredations of Hollister in the public psyche. As Johnny Stabler, the leader of a motorcycle gang called the Black Rebels, Brando rumbles into a little town called Wrightsville with his buddies and begins hanging out at Bleeker's Café. There the pouty, punk-faced Brando, decked out in a leather jacket and a jauntily angled military-style peaked cap (no doubt a studio costumer's interpretation of proper motorcycle gang garb), meets the female star, the long-forgotten Mary Murphy, and utters the only memorable line of the picture when, replying to her question, "What are you rebelling against?" he mumbles, "What have you got?" While Brando uses a 500 cc Triumph Speed Twin in the movie, the bad guy, Chino, a semicrazed former gang member played with his classic malevolence by Lee Marvin, enters the scene aboard a scruffy, flathead Harley-Davidson, thereby linking the brand to the rising legend of motorcycle hoodlumism.

Kramer's film was a middling commercial success and quickly forgotten by the public. Its longevity as a cult favorite is based purely on the fact that it was among the first to identify 1950s-style antiheroes in the Brando–James Dean mold (Dean's immortal but equally simpleminded *Rebel Without a Cause* would be released a year later), as well as to confirm that motorcycles were mechanical predators ridden by a new breed of outlaw. Dean employed an automobile – a hot-rodded Mercury – in his movie, but the role of the machine was the same: a device for angry youths rebelling against the smmary Ike and Mamie Good Life. Both pictures, *The Wild One* and *Rebel Without a Cause*, were fumbling attempts by Hollywood to describe a restlessness and isolation among the nation's youth that was being played out with infinitely more passion and intensity by Kerouac and his buddies and among the fledgling motorcycle clubs in grubby saloons and flophouses across the land.

THE WILD ONES

Michael Dregni

Michael Dregni offers fascinating insights into the making of the cult movie, The Wild One, *while painting an accurate picture of key events in early outlaw biker history.*

The Movie

In 1953, *The Wild One* starring Marlon Brando opened at a theater near you. Producer Stanley Kramer and director Laslo Benedek knew a good story when they saw one. They jumped on the Hollister incident, read the news accounts, shook their heads once more at the photograph, and fashioned a fictionalized account of the event. Their film began with a warning that bore echoes of the first lines of Dante's guided tour of Hell: "This is a shocking story. It could never take place in most American towns – but it did in this one. It is a public challenge not to let it happen again."

In the film, Marlon Brando played the leader of the Black Rebels Motorcycle Club, a cool cat named Johnny Strabler who wore a black leather jacket like a suit of armor against the world. Atop his Triumph Thunderbird, he led his gang on a Fourth of July ride up the California coast, stopping to wreak havoc at a motorcycle race before moving on to terrorize an innocent small town based on Hollister.

The opening scene of the movie provides a quick Hollywood-style sociological analysis of the roots of postwar disaffection that gave birth to motorcycle gangs. A highway patrolman who had just chased away Brando's gang warns another officer.

"Where'd that bunch come from?" an officer asks, playing the devil's advocate for a theater full of moviegoers asking themselves the same question.

"I don't know," responds the other patrolman, the voice of all-knowing wisdom. "Everywhere. I don't even think they know where they're going. Nutty. Ten guys like that gives people the idea everybody that drives a motorcycle is crazy. What are they trying to prove?"

"Beats me," answers the first officer, the voice of the common people. "Looking for somebody to push them around so they can get sore and show how tough they are."

When the gang arrives in town, it makes a beeline for Bleeker's Cafe and Bar. Members drop their change into the jukebox and order up rounds of beer. One townsgirl, taken by the excitement that follows the gang, says, "Black Rebels Motorcycle Club, that's cute! Hey Johnny, what are you rebelling against?"

With studied nonchalance, Johnny answered, "Whaddya got?"

He further explained his philosophy of life to the waitress named Cathy, played by Mary Murphy. She is curious about Johnny and his gang, and queries him: "Where are you going when you leave here? Don't you know?"

Johnny: "We're just gonna go."

Cathy: "Just trying to make conversation; it means nothing to me."

Johnny: "Look, on weekends, we go out and have a ball."

Cathy: "What do you do? I mean, do you just ride around, or do you go on some sort of picnic or something?"

Johnny: "A picnic? Man, you are too square; I have to straighten you out. Now listen, you don't go any one special place, that's cornball style. You just go!" he says to a snap of his fingers. "A bunch gets together after a week. It builds up. The idea is to have a ball. Now, if you gonna stay cool you gotta wail. You gotta put something down. You gotta make some jive, don't you know what I'm talking about?"

Obviously, she doesn't have a clue.

Soon, Johnny will take Cathy for a ride on his Triumph, giving society a taste of freedom on two wheels. "I've never ridden on a motorcycle before," Cathy exclaims with delight. "It's fast. It scared me. But I forgot everything. It felt good."

Then, the true bad guy shows his face. Lee Marvin and his gang of bad bad guys ride into town. As Cathy walks home from work, Marvin on his Harley-Davidson leads his gang to encircle the woman, spinning around in a kaleidoscope of revving bikes – the Indians circling the wagon train in the Wild West – moving in for the kill. Only Johnny can save her, whisking her away on his Triumph like a knight in shining armor.

The Anti-Hero

Brando's character was confusing to 1950s audiences. He was the bad guy and the good guy at the same time. This didn't make sense: Everyone knew full well that the bad guys wore black hats and the good guys wore white. It was repeated every Saturday matinee in the horse opera at the local theater.

Now, suddenly, here was Johnny wearing a black leather jacket and a black cap, terrorizing a town with his good-for-nothing bikers – and then midway through the movie another side of his character gradually comes to light. Johnny ain't all bad, just confused. Under the mask of that emotionless face and the armor of his jacket, he's introspective, questioning, maybe as confused about his direction in life as the audience is confused about his character. Johnny was the first anti-hero role in Hollywood.

Marlon Brando had the look down pat. "The part was actor-proof," he wrote forty years later in his autobiography, *Songs My Mother Taught Me*. That may have been a self-deprecating brag, or perhaps Brando didn't realize that in many ways he *was* Johnny.

Brando provided his own psychoanalysis of Johnny: "More than most parts I've played in the movies or onstage, I related to Johnny, and because of this, I believe I played him as more sensitive and sympathetic than the script envisioned. There's a line in the picture where he snarls, 'Nobody tells *me* what to do.' That's exactly how I've felt all my life. Like Johnny, I have always resented authority. I have been constantly discomfited by people telling me what to do, and have always thought that Johnny took refuge in his lifestyle because he was wounded – that he'd had little love as a kid and was trying to survive the emotional insecurity that his childhood had forced him to carry into adulthood. Because of the emotional pain of feeling like a nobody, he became arrogant and adopted a pose of indifference to criticism. He did everything to appear strong when inside he was soft and vulnerable and fought hard to conceal it. He had lost faith in the fabric of society and had made his own world. He was a rebel, but a strong part of him was sensitive and tender. At the time I told a reporter that 'I wanted to show that gentleness and tolerance is the only way to dissipate the forces of social destruction' because I view Johnny as a man torn by an inner struggle beyond his capacity to express it. He had been so disappointed in life that it was difficult for him to express love, but beneath his hostility lay a desperate yearning and desire to feel love because he'd had so little of it. I could have just as easily been describing myself. It seemed perfectly natural for me to play this role."

The movie was not a hit when it made its debut. Many theater-owners refused to screen such trash; others who dared to were read the riot act by do-gooders. "The public's reaction to *The Wild One* was, I believe, a product of its time and circumstances," Brando wrote. "It was only seventy-nine minutes long, short by modern standards, and it looks dated and corny now; I don't think it has aged well. But it became a kind of cult film."

The film struck a chord with a certain disaffected crowd that were tantalized by the rebellion – and by Brando's character. He was a romanticized Robin Hood on a cycle, offering would-be rebels an image to live up to. Sales of black leather jackets soared, Brando related in his autobiography, and suddenly became a symbol, although what the symbol stood for was not truly understood. It was the dawn of the juvenile delinquent craze, a horror mirrored in numerous paperback potboiler novels and Hollywood films. A new star was born riding on the wave of this craze, a young actor named James Dean, who in his film *Rebel Without a Cause* came to stand against everything society stood for.

Brando writes that he never expected *The Wild One* to have such an impact: "I was as surprised as anyone when T-shirts, jeans and leather jackets suddenly became symbols of rebellion. In the film there was a scene in which somebody asked my character, Johnny, what I was rebelling against, and I answered, '*Whaddya got?*' But none of us involved in the picture ever imagined it would instigate or encourage youthful rebellion. . . .

"After *The Wild One* was finished, I couldn't look at it for weeks; when I did, I didn't like it because I thought it was too violent."

Reading between the lines of Brando's autobiography, it seems obvious that *The Wild One* also played an important role in changing Brando's life, whether he realized it or not.

"I never knew that there were sleeping desires and feelings in our society whose buttons would be hit so uncannily in that film. In hindsight, I think people responded to the movie because of the budding social and cultural currents that a few years later exploded volcanically on college campuses and the streets of America. Right or wrong, we were at the beginning of a new era after several years of transition following World War II; young people were beginning to doubt and question their elders and to challenge their values, morals and the established institutions of authority. There was a wisp of steam just beneath the surface when we made that picture. Young people looking for a reason – any reason – to rebel. I simply happened to be at the right place at the right time in the right part – and I also had the appropriate state of mind for the role."

THE RIVERSIDE RIOTS

Bill Hayes

*William "Bill" Hayes lived through many of the early
years prior to the formation of today's better known
clubs. He was a founding member of the Boozefighters
Motorcycle Club, one of the principal clubs involved in
the Hollister mêlée. Here he describes a later incident,
known as the Riverside Riots.*

"*Our first club run as the East Bay Dragons MC pack was
Memorial Day 1959. We rode 40 miles to Alum Rock Park
near San Jose. We left Oakland at about nine that morning,
stretched out from Seventy-Ninth Avenue to Eighty-Second.
It took us five hours to go forty miles. On the way, we picked
up our riding buddy, Heavy Evans, who was living in Menlo
Park at the time.*

"*When we showed up at Alum Rock, we scared the holy hell
out of the families barbecuing in the park with their kids. The
minute they saw us ride up on our Harleys, they packed up their
picnic baskets, loaded up their station wagons, and made a
beeline for the exit gate. People were even more scared of us after
they saw the movie* The Wild One *with Marlon Brando.*"

          – Tobie Gene Levingston, President, East Bay
          Dragons MC, from the book, *Soul on Bikes*

Images are hard to shake, and once they've taken a media-driven stranglehold on your personality, all bets are off. "Hard" becomes "impossible," and basically – if the image is bad – you're sunk. You're stuck with it. You might as well be branded like one of Ben Cartwright's steers or have a neon-scarlet "A" that glows in the dark carved directly into your forehead. It's permanent and it just ain't gonna change.

Ever.

Don Knotts, for example, is the pure embodiment of an everlasting media *image*. He was destined to have a lifelong career as various incarnations of Barney Fife, Mr. Furley, and the Incredible Mr. Limpett. I'm pretty sure that his phone never rang with offers from tough-talking, raspy producers just begging him to get outfitted with tight, sleeveless camouflage muscle jerseys and start learning testosterone-laden lines for the character of *Big Doc the Ice Pick Maniac* in the next "Terminator" flick.

Don Knotts could've gained 150 pounds, chiseled himself into Mayberry's answer to Lennox Lewis, chugged steroids like Tic-Tacs, and he still would have been Barney Fife in everybody's mind. His ground-in image was set in stone. Period.

And *image* is, of course, the root of the word, *imagination*.

Another example: I'm sure that sports fans find it hard to look at Marv Albert in men's clothing now. The *imagination* immediately rockets us back to his *other wardrobe*, with or without the rug.

Another: It's difficult to see the lovely and talented Monica Lewinski standing straight up. The *imagination* tends to visualize her a little more . . . *relaxed*.

Images like these are locked in. There's nothing that can be done. No erasing. No "delete" button. No laser removal operations. No going back.

And some images continue to grow, to get even more and more intense. They not only transcend the "delete" button, but they shatter the whole machine as they leap through the monitor, rise from the pages, or drop down from the silver screen. Barney and his one-bullet "nipping things in the bud," Marv slipping out of his Armani in favor of something more *comfortable*, and Monica reaching quickly for the Kleenex are *not* the kind of images that *grow*. They simply *are*.

But the image of the American biker is different. Very different. It has never stopped expanding. It has never stopped growing.

The image of the three-piece-patch wearing biker – *especially in numbers*, in an unstoppable, invincible group – is as starkly rattling to most people as having a Vise-Grip locked around their Adam's Apple. The media learned this truth very early on and they learned how to cash in on it. The visual power of a long, seemingly endless line of steel and chrome V-twins, surrounded by a deafening roar, descended on a nervous, unsuspecting public many years ago like the crazed, fiery stallions from the Apocalypse, and this metal-edged snowball has never stopped rolling.

The classic *Life* magazine photo of the funeral of Sacramento Hells Angels president, James "Mother" Miles, the writings of Hunter Thompson, the low-budget exploitation biker flicks of the 1960s, and even scenes in the ultramodern, slick 2003 film *Leather & Iron*, all center on the mass movement of an urban army of *implied* bad men on bad machines.

A *pack*.

In any encounter there are always strategic aspects, but nothing – *nothing* – can take the place of the fear and cold-sweat awe that is generated by sheer and overpowering *numbers*. "Bikers Take Over a Town" was the kind of official headline hook that kicked the image into gear over a half-century ago. And it worked. It sold newspapers, magazines, and drive-in movie theater tickets. Vicarious thrills are always popular. But there are degrees. Most people who are comfortable with their given niche in methodic, *normal* society aren't connected to organizations that are even *capable* of "taking over a town."

American Dental Association Convention Erupts Into Brutal Rioting: Drunken Hygienists Seize Eight Floors of Chicago's Palmer House

Bourbon Street Reduced to Rubble by Knife-Wielding Rowdy Rotarians: Louisiana National Guard Called In to Take Back "The Big Easy" From Convention Partiers in Funny Hats

No, these headlines are never seen. And neither are the ones about bikers anymore. At least not very often. But they *could be*, and there's the difference. The media fear factor that began back in 1947 is still on a roll, precisely because the image has never changed. And it never will. Motorcycles are not for everybody. The lifestyle is not for everybody. And *everybody* knows this. But the air of mystery is profound. That is what makes the biker world so titillating. We all know how Monica stained her dress. On the other hand, most people don't have a clue as to how it feels to ride in the wind at 70 miles per hour, side-by-side in solid brotherhood with other bikers. They don't know what it's like to pull up in front of joints like Johnny's in Hollister, the All American in South Gate, The Crossroads or Cook's Corner, or any other bona fide biker bar, past or present. They've never casually parked their bike in line with all the others and comfortably strolled in for a cold one, just like in the movies.

There are 4,560,424 registered motorcycles in this country, according to the latest available stats (2001) published by the Motorcycle Safety Foundation in Irvine, California. The population of the U.S. (according to the national census conducted the year before, in 2000) was listed at 281,421,906. Simple math boils the percentage of the populace on two wheels down to around 1.6 percent. Eliminate the kids on the "crotch rockets," and the sedate "touring motorcycle enthusiasts" on their Gold Wings and the like, and you have a very, very elite group. Along with elitism go the seductive mysteries that accompany any such "secret society."

Although 1947 was a long time ago, to this day whenever Mr. and Mrs. Wholesome in the family Saturn sedan are even remotely close to a long, two-by-two procession of perceived motorcycle madness, they pray that the savages aren't hungry for even more human flesh.

The Boozefighters MC has fallen into one of the strangest, most oddly ironic social situations in the entire history of civilized, postindustrial human existence. They started a lifestyle that they were never really a part of. It's kind of like finding out that the Pilgrims didn't eat turkey on Thanksgiving.

Kind of . . .

Are the Boozefighters real "bikers?" Yep. They are genuine, pure, and authentic, no questions asked. But the *image* that shotgunned out of Hollister in 1947 redefined that word before it even had a chance to make Webster's, and the "biker" *definition* is the shaky social fulcrum that this whole image thing balances on. It is a definition that remains as subjective as the recipe for the perfect Bloody Mary. Following the Hollister "event," Frank Rooney's short story (*Cyclist's Raid*), and Stanley Kramer's production of *The Wild One*, however, the media's idea was forged in solid steel; the definition began to take on a life of its own.

Talking with the remaining Boozefighters "originals" is like fine-tuning an old analog tube radio. As you slowly and carefully move the dial in just the right way, suddenly all the static and fuzziness clears up. Gradually, everything becomes clear. A distorted *image* glides into straight-razor focus. Sitting face to face with surviving BFMC pioneers like Jack Lilly. Johnny and Jeannine Roccio, Gil Armas, Jim Cameron, Les Haserot, and Vern Autrey, one thing is undeniable – the Boozefighters definitely had a purpose in mind when they banded together, whether they formally voiced it or not.

Did they know that they were about to rip an enormous hole into the social fabric of America?

No.

Was their intention to flex some aggressive, post-wild-west, high-noon muscle, forcing meek and mild townspeople in small burgs everywhere to cry and beg for mercy? Did they intend to ride into town after town, swilling the mayor's finest whiskey (after kicking in his front door, of course), caging up all of the women under 25, so they could be used as cheap chattel by drunken "gang" members?

Please . . .

The originals all have one thing very much in common: They smile and they laugh. When you ask them about what "really happened" in Hollister – and the early days in general – they all get the same sheepish, kicking-the-stone grin that Opie had when Andy asked him why he put the frog in the school marm's desk drawer.

"Aw, Pa, I wuz just havin' some fun . . ."

Why did the originals climb on those bikes? Because it was fun. The *purpose* was pretty uncomplicated and basic. Did they think about seizing the shaking souls of an entire town? Did they think about the regal glory of commanding large sectors of concrete "turf?" Did they imagine their "club" as a conduit for drug peddling, violence, extortion, and gun running?

Let's revisit the first two requirements of an early Booze-fighter prospect for some answers:

1. *Get drunk at a race meet or cycle dance.*
2. *Throw lemon pie in each other's faces.*

Now, unless they were communicating in some secret club code, it appears that they pretty much wanted to drink, ride motorcycles, and, yeah Pa, just have some *fun*. And it seemed like a fairly simple goal at the time. But there are many definitions of "fun." Your basic sloppy drunken pie toss didn't provide particularly good fuel for a profitable media fire, so guys like Barney Peterson, Frank Rooney, and Stanley Kramer reached into *Cap'n Billy's Whiz Bag* and came up with "trouble with a capital T" to rope in the poor, timid citizenry of River Cities everywhere.

One of the most visible events of the Hollister episode was Jim Cameron riding his Indian into Johnny's Bar. It's a bit of a stretch to imagine that this was the first act in a series of vicious, calculated strikes designed to soften up the town before the actual "take over." According to the always-smiling Jim, "I rode it into the place and leaned it against the bar. I had to have *someplace* to put it. They were pretty nice about it . . . didn't think much of it . . . just asked me to lean it against the wall instead of the bar, so people could still have room to drink. OK, no problem."

Still grinning, Jim recently commented on a present-day Boozefighter's description of the legend of Hollister: "I think you've learned it better than any of us lived it . . ." And what most people have learned is a lot about something that never happened. It's been well over 50 years since Hollister, yet present-day websites like something called *Whole Pop Magazine* still carry accounts that state: "The Hell's Angels are the biggest gang, but they were not the first. 'The Booze Fighters' (sic) were the first of a new breed of motorcyclists, the outlaw gang. During a fourth (sic) of July revelry in 1947, they lived down to their name and terrorized an agricultural town, Hollister, California, getting themselves into the news and their story eventually into the movies (*The Wild One*)."

Even the venerable Hunter Thompson lapped up the hype. In his 1966 documentary epic, "*Hell's Angels*," Thompson talks about the predecessors of the HAMC: "Many of the Angels are graduates of other outlaw clubs . . . some of which, like the Booze Fighters (sic), were as numerous and fearsome in their time as the Angels are today. It was the Booze Fighters (sic), not the Hell's Angels, who kicked off the Hollister riot, which led to the filming of *The Wild One*."

Let's look at "numerous." In 1966, when Thompson's book was published, the Hells Angels had an estimated 463 members, based on statistics compiled by then California State Attorney General Thomas C. Lynch and other California law enforcement agencies. (This figure is also mentioned in Thompson's book.) In "their time" of 1947, the Boozefighters membership was approximately 60 members within three chapters, according to original wild one Vern Autrey. Then we come to "fearsome." The actual handwritten minutes of the Boozefighters' meeting of July 9, 1947, immediately following the "Hollister riot," were as follows: "July 9 Big meeting and a line of clatter about the rally (Hollister). Reading all about it in the papers. Big discussion on sprockets-handlebars etc. Red (Dahlgren) will be on a three months (probation). Not to miss no meetings for any reason or is to be automatically out."

The entire Hollister extravaganza was reduced to "a line of clatter" and "reading about it in the papers." Then it was on to a "big discussion" of "sprockets" and "handlebars." Oh, and by the way, Red better not miss "no meetings" again. This was sure enough an ominous powwow of "fearsome" desperados. The next month's minutes were equally terrifying: "Aug 27 (1947) Had a dandy beer bust Sat night & Sun. Plenty drunk – a good time was had by all . . ."

Frank Rooney's story had not yet been published when Riverside, California, hosted two post-Hollister motorcycle events; rallies on Labor Day of 1947, and the Fourth of July 1948. But Barney Peterson's photo had already been seen by most of America. Fertile seeds of dread instilled into "normal, God-fearing citizens" were already beginning to sprout and spread. The beast was alive!

The two Riverside events are often confused with one another, probably because they were held so close together and because they both occurred within a year of Hollister. Street racing, some fighting, and a lot of drinking in the local bars were certainly a part of both of these wingdings in Southern California's "Inland Empire," but the second event, Fourth of July 1948, really got the presses rolling.

RIVERSIDE AGAIN RAIDED BY GANG: ONE DEAD, 54 ARRESTED AS MOTORCYCLISTS STAGE RIOTS

This article featured what has become the second most famous photo ever connected with the Boozefighters: Vern Autrey and "Fat Boy" Nelson sitting on their parked bikes drinking bottles of beer. Teri Forkner was perched behind "Fat Boy." The caption read:

CYCLISTS TAKE OVER TOWN – As townspeople watch from the relative safety of the sidewalk, three motorcyclists whose sweaters read "Boozefighters Motorcycle Club," stop for a beer on one of Riverside's (Calif.) streets. More that 2,000 cyclists, in town for racing at a nearby track, took over the town and rode wildly about the streets. With one dead and 54 arrested in the second outbreak of rowdyism by motorcyclists in 11 months, Sheriff Carl F. Rayburn said he will sponsor no more motorcycle races in Riverside.

Okay, except that the picture wasn't taken in Riverside. Teri, the late wife of Wino Willie, was quick to identify the photo as having been taken in Hollister. "We were proud of that picture," she said, "but we were ticked off that it wasn't used in the *San Francisco Chronicle* story or in *Life* magazine, instead of that other picture that was staged with the drunk on the bike with the beer in each hand. This picture was actually taken in Hollister, July 4, 1947."

And the photo definitely made the rounds within the "biker as beast" press.

The December 1957 issue of the gossip tabloid *Top Secret* featured some pretty eminent literary landmarks, like *"SHOCKING NEWS FROM THE A-LABS: HUMAN*

SPERMS FOR SURVIVAL," and *"WHY NEGRO WO-MEN SAY . . . 'WHITE MEN ARE BETTER LOVERS.'"*

The magazine also included a "hot" exposé of high-profile, high-priced society call girl Pat Ward. Among her tawdry attributes was the fact that she was – gasp – a "biker!" Much of the text in the article, I believe, was ripe for a Pulitzer. This is serious literature. Pat Ward's former lover, Manny Trujillo – described as an "admitted spy, a former loyal student at a Communist Party school, and a black-leather-jacketed tough" – had a lot to say concerning his former "ol' lady":

> "She wouldn't bathe for days on end," he declares. "When she stayed in my place, the room smelled like something had died." Manny claims that Pat was a violent nymphomaniac, an insatiable lover who delighted in engaging in weird sexual acts. Whenever Trujillo refused – or was unable – to satisfy Pat's raging lust, the girl went into fits of screaming fury.

Naturally the only picture in the entire universe that could go along with the acrid spice of *Top Secret's* article was – yep – the recycled shot of Teri, "Fat Boy," and Vern. But this time the Boozefighters logo on the jackets had been surgically removed with whatever photographic technology an upper-echelon outfit like *Top Secret* had available to them at the time. And then there were those little, clandestine, taboo '50s "blackout" strips applied across the eyes of the villains, so as to not reveal the true identity of the devil himself. The caption above the picture dug deep into Hades: ". . . motorcycle gang of typical speed demons."

Sure! The very same "demons" that "took over" Riverside! Well, not exactly . . .

On July 17, 1948, Roger L. Abbott, undersheriff of Riverside County, released a notarized open letter to any and all news and press outlets concerning what *really* happened at the second "Riverside riot." I've not tampered with Undersheriff Abbott's document in any way – no grammatical corrections, nothing – this is his letter, pure, straight ahead:

> As beautiful and cultured Riverside, painfully emerges torn and bleeding from the wreckage and devastation of a

three day 4th of July celebration of several thousand motorcycle enthusiasts attending the Novice, Amateur, and National Championship 100 mile motorcycle races held under the auspices of the Riverside County Sheriff's Training Center, Incorporated, sponsored by the Bombers Motorcycle Club of Riverside and sanctioned by the American Motorcycle Association, one asks, "just what is the extent of damage caused by these hoodlums and tramps, these uncivilized demons, who ride exploding and fire-belching machines of destruction with abandon, hell-bent on destroying the property and persons of Riverside citizens, according to the newspapers?"

Well, an awning got torn on a down-town business house. A city park plunge office was entered and a flashlight stolen. Swimming suits were left lying on the bottom of the plunge. Motorcyclists? Maybe.

An automobile, driven by an impatient citizen was set upon by victims and their friends who resented being knocked down by this car and its driver when it was driven into their midst for failing to yield the right of way. The body of the car was dented and some of its glass was broken.

A bottle fell or was dropped out of a hotel window, a man's wallet was taken from his pocket, and three motorcycles were reported stolen, one of which has been recovered.

A city park official got a bloody nose during an altercation with a motorcyclist who wanted to sleep in the park, and who had imbibed too freely. This motorcyclist submitted peacefully to arrest by an officer and has plead not guilty to charges of assault and battery. The courts must decide on the issues involved.

That is the official total of damage to persons and property in what the newspapers have screamed nationally to be "a weekend of terror, resulting from an invasion of Riverside by hoodlums and their molls on motorcycles rioting in the streets and wrecking the city."

In order to clinch the matter, and to make sure that the wire services would carry the story to the entire nation, the news articles added the spicy bit that, "the invasion left forty-nine arrested and one killed." It was convenient to omit, for the sake of sensationalism, that this one person killed in all of Riverside County on that week-end was nearly a hundred miles from Riverside at the time he ran into a bridge abutment on the highway and was killed and at the time he ran into the abutment, according to authentic reports, was not going to or from the Rally in Riverside. As a matter of police record, there were no traffic accidents in the City of Riverside from Saturday afternoon July 3rd at 4:05 o'clock until Monday afternoon July 5th at 1:15 o'clock. There were no accidents at any time during the entire week-end in the city in which motorcycles were involved. It is doubtful if many cities of fifty thousand inhabitants in the nation can boast of such a record over that week-end.

Forty-nine persons arrested! Well, almost – 46 to be factual, and 8.7 percent of these were Riverside residents.

These people came to Riverside that weekend on a holiday. Some of them took on a too heavy cargo of beer and other drinks – and having become uninhibited, performed obediently for the hundreds of Riverside citizens who had come out of their homes to enjoy the fun. When the police decided it was time to put an end to the confusion and noise, they simply walked in and ordered the celebrants to disperse. If they could not, they were arrested and lodged in jail – if they did not, they were arrested for failure to disperse. Thirty minutes, and the job was accomplished. A number were arrested throughout the weekend for shooting fireworks, intoxication, drinking in public, and disturbing the peace. These were the methods used by the police to control the situation.

The following arrests have been used by news articles to point the finger of shame at Riverside's seduction, violation, and disgrace:

Drinking in public, 4 persons arrested
Drunk, 8 persons arrested
Drunk Driving, (motorcycle) 2 persons arrested
Drunk Driving, (automobile) 1 person arrested
Shooting Fireworks, 9 persons arrested
Disturbing the Peace, 12 persons arrested

Assault and Battery, 1 person arrested
Failure to Disperse, 8 persons arrested
Interfering with an Officer, 1 person arrested
Total, 46 persons arrested

This tabulation indicates that the Riverside Police Department had control of the situation at all times and acted with effective efficiency.

The State Forestry did not enter into the enforcement program but did drive a pickup truck through town on their way to an assignment.

Contrary to newspaper sensationalism on a national scale – Sheriff Rayburn did not invite the motorcycle fraternity to Riverside. It was the Riverside County Sheriff's Training Center Inc., the members of which are full time deputy sheriffs and who hold such a fund raising event each year to construct and maintain a training center with training facilities where officers of the Sheriff's Department and other law enforcement agencies of the County of Riverside can receive training for their jobs.

Sheriff Rayburn did not get his "trousers torn off in the riots of motorcycle raiders."

Sheriff Rayburn did not say he "would never invite the motorcycle fraternity back to Riverside again."

To say that the news services have been guilty of gross exaggeration and sensationalism in their presentation of this 4th of July week-end and last Labor Day week-end in Riverside is an understatement. However, they may be given consideration on the basis that such news balloons are often set adrift by young, inexperienced, overzealous and perhaps frightened newspaper reporters who are correspondents for large metropolitan newspapers and have wire service at their disposal. I am certain it was not, or is not, the intent of the vast majority of news editors throughout the nation to condone such reporting as they well know the practice of it would bring them into the same ill repute, good and bad alike, that the motorcycle sport now is burdened with.

In spite of all this, however, law enforcement cannot condone the unlawful acts of the few, which bring discredit to the many through unfavorable publicity, exaggerated or not.

Certainly the American Motorcycle Association recognized motorcycle clubs and the "outlaw" motorcycle clubs should reach an understanding to ensure the future of motorcycle sports without making the host city the victim of ill-will between those clubs.

Certainly stricter concentrated enforcement and education must be undertaken to eliminate the use of devices intended to increase rather than decrease exhaust noise. It was this irritating noise made by a liberal estimate of perhaps one hundred motorcycles, which sound caused the din, some of these no doubt, normally would have not done this had it been the American custom to celebrate Independence Day with all the noise possible.

The use of streets and highways for drag races and other motorcycle games must be abandoned.

Most of the arrests were made in the downtown area while three thousand of the motorcyclists were several miles out of twon [*sic*] enjoying clean healthy games and contests sanctioned by the American Motorcycle Association. It cannot be overlooked that not a single arrest was necessary at the track either day of the races or at the night field meet.

In view of the reports received through the mail our sympathy is extended to the thousands of dealers throughout the nation whose life savings are affected and to worthwhile clubs who are suffering and in some cases quite badly from the injustice of the reports.

Definitely, a change in attitude and acts of the one percent of irresponsible, intemperate and sometimes vulgar motorcyclist hiding behind the cloak of decency of the ninety-nine per cent of motorcyclists must be accomplished.

In reviewing the evidence developed in this report one is compelled to acknowledge that the nation-wide sensational publicity given the 4th of July week-end in Riverside, California was neither honest nor factual – but will in all likelihood hasten the day of a clean name for motorcycling and honest press reporting.

(This article may be used for news or publication
purposes)
(signed)
Roger L. Abbott
Undersheriff
Riverside County, California
(notarized)

Alrighty then . . . Seems like ol'Sheriff Roger wasn't particularly pleased about having his town (or as his old manual
typewriter put it, *twon* . . .), and the good citizens of Riverside,
being made into yet another field of poor, helpless grunion,
flopping aimlessly and unprotected as the evil, heavy-booted
bikers marched along the shore, stuffing them into buckets,
only to be devoured later at some depraved bacchanalian orgy
and drooling feast.

"*CYCLISTS TAKE OVER TOWN*"? Nope . . . just didn't
happen. . . .

But let's go back to that *image* thing. One image was good for
business, depending on the business you were in. And like a lot
of businesses, the nuts and bolts are screwed together behind
the scenes while the little people go on about their daily lives.
Wander into your local grocery and ask the first person you see
who's pushing a cart load of things like milk, bread, and a
twelver of Bud, just what the NASDAQ mark is up or down to
on the stock exchange today.

The same kind of thing was dead-on true in the early world of
the biker. As one faction (the media . . .) began to turn the
wheels of the commercial *image*, the people who actually made
the whole shebang work (the real bikers) were living the *truth*,
not acting out the more sensational *fiction*. The actual playing
out of the media creation unfortunately came later. After the
damage had been done. The original truth was all about *fun*.
Fun that can sometimes get a bit messy, like a pie in the face.
Fun that can even get somewhat out of hand, like when the
rodeo clown gets a pretty good whack from a bus-sized, aggravated bull. But a pie is still a pie, and a clown is still a clown –
we're not talkin' guns and SWAT teams here. Problem is that
splattered lemon meringue and red noses don't sell the way
mayhem and destruction do.

As I sat with some of the originals at Jack Lilly's home in the California desert – not far from where all the Riverside "activity" occurred – a strong, warm breeze was dropping down from the foothills, stirring things up along the flats. It was the perfect ambient atmosphere to begin to twist time into reverse, the ideal raw setting to explore the foul and sleazy truth about how over 50 years ago a "motorcycle gang of typical speed demons" took over yet another quiet, peace-loving town of meek, God-fearing, once-happy *Father Knows Best* families, shattering their innocence, burning their Christmas trees, carving vile graffiti into the fine paint on their new DeSotos, and laughing like Attila the Hun while the blood of murdered children ran ankle deep through the streets.

"I remember when we first got there," recalled Jack. "The first couple of guys that got drunk – I think it might have been Wino and John Davis – well, they had this douche bag they filled with wine. They were walkin' down the middle of the street – they just stopped traffic and were walkin' down the middle – one of them holdin' the bag, the other had the 'nozzle' in his mouth . . .

"And we had this big water drum with us, carried it in the old Model T pick-up with the trailer that used to go with us on all our runs. The drum had three Xs painted on it. At first I thought some of the guys brought some water for drinking, but they never drank water. Then I thought it might have been for washing, but they didn't wash either."

"It was filled with wine!" said Johnny Roccio.

Jack Lilly nodded and smiled at Johnny. As he continued to relive the Riverside run I thought of a line from Charlie Brechtel's tribute tune to Wino Willie – "*They rode them old motorsickles, didn't need no car . . .*" – the definition of a "real" biker.

"We got to Riverside," Jack remembered. "Havin' a good time, and I stayed too long. My wife was waiting for me up in Idyllwild. She'd given me a deadline to make it before dark 'cause I had a pretty weak battery on my VL. I could a bought a battery, too 'cause I was workin' at the time, but I always tried to nurse these damned old batteries. I'd buy Electro-lites at Western Auto, and I'd nurse them along, charging them for a couple of days, put them back in my motorcycle. First time I'd use them at night, you could see the light just shrinkin' back into it, so I'd have to follow a car with bright lights."

"Just like my old Knucklehead!" said Johnny.

"Same thing, huh? Why they'd build a motorcycle with a 2-amp generator and it took 10 amps to run the damn headlight, I'll never know. Anyway, I stayed way too late. I took off at dusk. I got halfway up the hill and the lights went out. I don't know if you've been up Idyllwild grade – if you have you know how twisty it is. Well, you don't want to go up there when there's no moon, no stars, and no headlight! I finally gave up and found a wide spot and pulled off. I thought, 'I'll sit here and wait for a car.' So here comes a car, and the son of a gun was a speed demon. I said, 'Hell, I can't catch *him*. I'll wait for the next one.' The next one came along and I followed him for a while, but all of a sudden he speeds up and leaves me. I wait for another one and the same thing happened. I finally figure that I was scaring the hell outta these people. They'd hear the sound of a motorcycle but couldn't see me following them! So they'd just speed off!"

"You shoulda waited for a truck!" said Johnny. "A loaded one!"

"I did! Finally! It was a pickup with a load of wood or something that he was taking up the hill . . . and *he* couldn't outrun me. Followed him all the way up the hill 'til the road splits at the end of town, where my wife was waiting for me in this nice cabin she had borrowed from a friend for the weekend. And she had fire in her eyes. Here it was about nine or ten o'clock, and I was supposed to be there before dark to take her out to dinner, but it took me forever to get up that hill in the dark!"

Evidently Jack left just before the remaining "*Cyclists Take Over Town*," but he vividly remembers the barbaric ride into Riverside: hordes of cruel Boozefighters storming the gates of this placid Southern California community, teeth undoubtedly filed to fine points to more easily tear into human flesh, coal-black souls and hearts bursting with depraved lust.

"We all dyed our hair bright red. Well, not all of us – me and 'Red Dog' already had red hair – but everybody else, all the other guys, the ones with brown hair, and blond hair, and so on, all suddenly had really bright red hair. Here's this whole group ridin' down the highway, a sea of red, following this Model T Ford pickup truck with our club trailer hooked to it. I don't understand how they got enough power outta that thing to pull that trailer – the Model T had like 20 horsepower brand new, I think – and that was about an 18- or 20-foot trailer with our bunks in it and that goofy water drum filled with wine up on the roof."

Johnny's wife, Jeannine, also remembered the 1947–1948 version of the evil Trojan Horse: "The trailer . . . *the* trailer . . . with the bunks . . . they had several bunks they built into it so the drunks could lay in there and dry out . . . and they had cases and cases of beer underneath . . ."

Their arrival must have looked like Hannibal crossing the Alps . . . you could just sense the pending carnage in the air.

"There was one little hamburger stand that caught our attention as we rode into town," said Jack, "because just past the hamburger joint there was a vacant lot where we could park the trailer. Well, on the way to the lot, the trailer got a flat. Just so happened that in the lot there was a piece of road equipment of some kind so, naturally, we just swapped the wheels from the trailer and the road equipment, and everything was fine. Another thing I don't understand, though, was why we had those little Model T wheels and tires on that trailer in the first place. How they held up that trailer, the bunks, and all that beer is still a mystery."

"The truck," added Johnny, "had a 2-by-12 for the seat, just a piece of wood, and they pounded 16-penny nails through that thing that would stick up just a little bit when you sat on it. And underneath it they had it hooked up to the coil. And if they didn't like you or something or wanted to be funny they'd pull a switch and you'd definitely jump off that SOB. It was a real jolt! They'd pull all kinds of stuff like that!"

Except, evidently, "stuff" like taking over a town. I guess things like bright red hair and electric seats were just a lot more *fun*.

The genesis of the biker lifestyle was born very innocently into a restless world that apparently needed some fear served up with its smiles. Or at least the media thought it did.

Jack, Johnny, Jeannine, Wino and all the rest of the originals seemed to have a little bit better grasp on the truth, a better grasp on just what constituted real fun, a better grasp on the definition – *and the image* – of a real "biker."

HELL'S ANGELS

William Murray

Illustrating the fascination with outlaw bikers at the time, this article was originally printed in the Saturday Evening Post *in 1965. It serves as a historical document, demonstrating the impact of Hollister and its aftermath. It is an excellent example of the attempts by Americans to understand the social change occurring during those tumultuous times.*

My first impression when I walked into the Blue Blaze was that I had blundered into some sort of obscene children's party. There were about 15 men in their early 20's, and five or six of their girls, standing at the bar, sitting around the small dance floor, huddled by the jukebox, shooting pool, perched out on a patio beside which a row of motorcycles gleamed silver and black in the light from an open doorway. The girls, with chalk-white faces and dark glasses, wore Levis and boots and sawed-off jackets. The men wore the same carefully ratty uniform, but with decorations: wings, swastikas, *Luftwaffe* insignia, cloth patches of a skull wearing a winged helmet, patches with the number "13." The decorations glinted oddly in the dim orange light, and the whole place had the ludicrous air of a costume party. Nonetheless, I was with two detectives, Inspector Larry

Wallace and another plainclothesman of the San Bernardino, Calif., sheriff's substation, and I was supposed to pass myself off as a detective. I was getting my first look at some members of the Hell's Angels, the most notorious and feared "outlaw" motorcycle club in California.

One Angel, fat and curly-headed and thick-lipped, with his back to the jukebox and an arm around the neck of a tiny girl with stringy blond hair, was swaying gently, but not in time to the music.

"Hey," he said, to no one in particular, "how's about we all get into the shower together?"

The girl laughed harshly, pushed him away, and joined the group around the pool table. The players were cursing and laughing with every shot. One young Angel with long, greasy locks and a pointed beard would run around the table every time he put a ball away and kiss everyone. "Mother, mother, mother," he'd exclaim and snap his fingers in the air. Around the dance floor, three couples swigged beer and joked with each other; one girl got up and began doing a slow jerk in time to the music, but she was quickly hauled back by her partner, a burly Angel with anchors tattooed on his biceps. She squealed with delight and flopped on his lap.

Otto, the Fontana club president, eyed us warily, but Wallace smiled. "No sweat, Otto," he said. "We're just having a look around. How's it going?"

"Lousy," Otto said. "The goddam heat is on everywhere."

Several Angels and girls gathered around him. It turned out that they blamed the press for some difficulties they had been running into. "We can't ride nowhere no more," one of them said. "We can't even wear our colors hardly, except around here." Otto was especially pessimistic about the way things were going. "We ain't even heard from that actor Sal Mineo since we let him know we wanted three grand, which don't seem like a lot for a whole damn movie, now does it?" he said bitterly.

At the bar the proprietress, a plump middle-aged woman, dispensed beer and whiskey. Angels were scattered along the length of the bar, but down at one end a small group of young Negroes drank silently together and warily surveyed the scene around them. I sat down next to a husky Angel of about 25, and a pretty blonde, whom I'll call Skip and Rosie.

"What do you guys keep coming around here for?" Skip asked me. "We ain't doing nothing. Why don't you leave us alone?"

"Yeah," Rosie said. "They want to make sure you take a bath, that's all."

"I took a bath, honey," he said.

"You didn't take one once for two months." Rosie said. "It's a good thing I got lousy sinuses."

"That was last year," Skip said, grinning. "Now we're as clean as all you good citizens, ain't we, Rosie?"

Rosie grinned.

"He don't care, anyway," Skip said. "To him. I stink. And to me, he stinks. The last cop that came in here got *his* bath, only it was in beer." Skip and Rosie walked off toward the dance floor. their arms around each other.

"Hey," the thick-lipped curly-head at the jukebox said to the room at large, "what do you say we all get under the shower together, huh?" Everybody ignored him.

A little later, as I headed back to the car with the two detectives, I told Wallace I thought maybe I should have told the Angels who I was. Then I could have hung around longer.

He took my arm and stopped me. "Listen," he said, "I don't know where you're going from here on, but don't ever make the mistake of underrating the Angels. They're tough and they're mean, and that's the truth. I don't think they'd be dumb enough to stomp on a journalist, but you can't count on it. And when they're all together, dressed up and partying, anything can happen.

"Now you take this bar here: We're going to have a real bad situation in there in a few weeks. You seen there was a few colored boys in there tonight? They've been staying away, but it looks like they're going to come on back. Now when we get a dozen or so of these colored boys in here with the Angels, well, you'll see what'll happen."

I asked Wallace if the Angels were racists. "No, not really." he said. "Maybe deep down they are. There ain't no Negro Angels. But the main thing is the Angels ain't *for* anybody, and that makes them anti-Negro and just about anything else."

The Hell's Angels have been around for 15 years, but they came to national prominence when they roared unexpectedly into

California's Monterey Peninsula on Labor Day weekend of 1964. According to newspaper reports, there were some 300 of them from all over the state, bearded and long-haired, bizarre-looking and foul-mouthed, noisy and menacing, all wearing their colors: swastikas, wings, Levis, the short denim jackets, the numeral "1," which means the wearer belongs to the "outlaw" one percent of clubs not affiliated with the American Motorcycle Association. They were making one of their celebrated "runs," a flocking together in some sparsely populated area in order to havé a party; the sort of party, authorities contend, that can degenerate into a drunken riot, such as the one that overwhelmed the small town of Hollister. Calif., back in 1947 or raged in the streets of Laconia, N.Il., last June.

In Monterey the Angels set up camp near the small town of Seaside, built a huge bonfire at the water's edge, and began to drink and roughhouse and paw the strange-looking women they liad brought along with them. They had come, they said, to solicit contributions from the membership to send the corpse of a dead buddy of theirs, who had recently been killed in a highway accident, back to his mother in North Carolina. And why Monterey? "Because we get treated good here," one of the Angels explained to a local reporter. "Most other places we get thrown out of town."

And so, under the watchful eyes of Monterey's police, the Angels proceeded to throw their fund-raising party. Here is California's Atty. Gen. Thomas C. Lynch's account of what happened next:

Early on the morning of September 6, complaint was made to Sheriff's officers by the erstwhile companions of two girls, aged 14 and 15, that they had been taken away from their boyfriends by some Hell's Angels at the site of the camp. Shortly, deputies found one completely nude and another with only a small amount of clothing on her. Both alleged that they had been raped by five to 10 men just prior to the arrival of the officers. They professed to be unable to identify any responsibles at that time. Some hours later, four men were arrested after being identifed by the girls. Two of the men identified themselves as presidents of the North Sacramento and Richmond Hell's Angels chapters. . . .

The next day the police escorted the Angels and their girl friends out of town, detaining the four suspects for questioning. The newspapers splashed stories all over the front pages, and a local politician named Fred S. Farr, a state senator, requested Attorney General Lynch to investigate not only this specific outrage but also the whole question of the Hell's Angels and outlaw motorcycle gangs in general. Alarm over such gangs was not new; the Hollister riot of 1947 had introduced outlaw motorcyclists to the nation and had inspired the movie *The Wild One*, starring Marlon Brando. What was new, however, was the almost panicky determination to do something about it.

Lost in all the hullabaloo was the fact, reported obscurely or not at all, that on September 25 all charges against the four Hell's Angels had, for some reason, been dropped. Still, the impression lingered on that foul deeds had been committed and the authorities had been aroused.

The attorney-general's report was made public at a press conference in the middle of March, about six months after the events in Monterey, and it caused an immediate sensation. For days it was almost impossible to buy a newspaper anywhere in California that didn't contain some terrifying account of what the Hell's Angels had been up to. "No act is too degrading for the pack." *Time* magazine wrote. ". . . But their favorite activity seems to be terrorizing whole towns." The article went on to describe how the Angels and some allies had all but wrecked the tiny town of Porterville, Calif., (population 7.991) in September, 1963. The attorney general's report itself cited 17 specific instances of "hoodlum activities." It declared that the offenses most commonly committed were forgery, assault, auto and motorcycle theft, rape, sex perversion and habitual use of dangerous drugs.

Nonetheless, on closer reading, the report turned out to be oddly temperate about what had actually been proven. It noted that the Monterey rape charges had been dropped because "further investigation raised questions as to whether forcible rape had been committed." It revealed that not one of the 17 instances of hoodlum activities had resulted in a major conviction, most not even in arrests. It turned out that 151 Angels or associates had actually been convicted of a felony and 85 had actually served time. The 1,023 misdemeanor convictions reported were mainly for traffic violations. Furthermore, these figures covered 15 years, a fact omitted from the report. This wouldn't qualify the Angels for Good Conduct Medals, but it did make for slightly less dramatic reading.

By the attorney general's own count, there were 463 Hell's Angels in the state, almost all of them either in the San Francisco Bay area or in and around Los Angeles. Two hundred and seventy-six ex-Angels were reportedly among the 438 other outlaw motorcyclists belonging to such groups as the Coffin Cheaters, Satan's Slaves, Devil's Henchmen, Outlaws, El Diablos, Gypsy Jokers and East Bay Dragons (a Negro outfit).

But lurid stories continued to appear regularly in the press. The Angels were suddenly everywhere, committing all sorts of atrocities. The climax came when the 18-year-old daughter of a police lieutenant was raped in Reseda. The girl had been lured into a house containing 12 to 20 men, including 3 to 11 (depending on which story one believed) of "the notorious Hell's Angels." The police rounded up 16 suspects and the girl's father subsequently shot down one of them, who had had nothing to do with the crime, in a corridor of the West Valley police station. Ultimately five suspects were indicted. None was a Hell's Angel.

About this time a newspaper called. The Porterville *Recorder* ran an editorial which indignantly took issue with the published stories that the Angels had gone berserk in Porterville. The truth was, said The *Recorder*, that at the first sign of trouble the Angels had been escorted peacefully out of town. The paper was annoyed that no credit had been given to the Porterville police department and allied enforcement agencies for having prevented exactly the sort of hell-raising the outside press claimed had taken place.

Shortly after the Porterville editorial, the Angels themselves showed up on, of all things, a half-hour television program on a local California station. It was called *Rebels on Wheels*, and showed the Angels in their hangouts around Fontana. Among their spokesmen were an almost inarticulate brute known as Blind Bob and a toughtalking brunette named Donna, who would have been pretty except for a scar that ran from the corner of her mouth practically to her earlobe. They were all puffing away on cigarette butts and their speech was oddly slurred either from drink or from whatever they were smoking.

The program was largely a protestation of innocence. Donna said the Angels were good guys, that charges against them were always dropped because the authorities never had anything to go on. Why did she hang around with the Angels? "Everybody believes in something. Some people believe in God. I believe in the Angels." A sociologist, Dr. Lewis Yablonsky, pointed out that society tended to aggrandize the Angels' behavior because "there is a touch of this in all of us." But the most vivid moment of the program came when Blind Bob, inarticulate during the interview, was shown planted on the back of his "hog," riding down the highway. He had handled that big, powerful machine with consummate ease, steering it casually with one hand, like Valenzuela bringing Kelso to the starting gate, the wind blowing hard into his face, and his mouth set in a tight grin of pure enjoyment.

As I thought about all these happenings – the Monterey accusations, the attorney general's report, the published accounts, the actual facts, my TV glimpse of the Angels themselves – I decided that whatever the Angels were, they were not simple, either by themselves or as a social phenomenon. I decided to try to get a clearer idea of them, and of those who dealt with them.

The five sergeants and lieutenants in the East Los Angeles sheriff's station all belonged to the Special Enforcement Detail. They were all agreeable but stern-looking men with short haircuts, and they were all in agreement. They thought the attorney general's report had not gone far enough. They felt they had matters under control in Los Angeles County ("You won't see an Angel wearing his colors on the sidewalk around here"), and they thought other areas ought to crack down harder. They told a number of atrocity stories about "Angel weddings," in which Angels earned "red wings," red-enameled USAF flight insignia, by committing indecent acts. It was all part of something the Angels called "showing class," acts defined as "real mind-snappers."

"Now," one of the sergeants said, "if you want to get in touch

with the Angels, we can give you a contact. Fellow named Ed
Roth. Call him up."

"He makes things for them," said another sergeant. "And he
likes them. Look, you might have to pay him something."

"Pay him something?"

"For the Angels," he said. "They're interested in money."

"What is Roth to you?" I asked.

"We have an agreement," a lieutenant said.

As I left, one of the sergeants handed me a card:

SHERIFF'S DEPARTMENT
COUNTY OF LOS ANGELES
PETER J. PITCHESS, SHERIFF

"Be sure you spell Peter J. Pitchess right," the sergeant said.
"He's the sheriff around here, and that's an elective office."

Ed Roth is called Big Daddy, and he has been praised by Tom
Wolfe in the title piece of a book, *The Kandy-Kolored Tanger-
ine-Flake Streamline Baby*, as one of the country's most brilliant
designers of custom-built automobiles. His designs were reproduced in plastic kits by the Revell Company and sold in the
hundreds of thousands. Big Daddy Roth Monster T-Shirts, in
200 different versions, went at the rate of 1,000 a day.

Roth had his own ideas about the Angels. "They're the Wild
Bill Hickoks, the Billy the Kids, the last American heroes we
have, man," he said over the phone. "They've got plenty of loot
now, and they're not *going* to talk to you. They're sick of all this
publicity." He said another reporter had gone to Bakersfield
with them last spring. "The cops had traps laid for them, and he
picked up all their traffic tickets. Man, he must have poured
twelve hundred bucks into the Berdoo [for San Bernardino]
treasury at least. But now they're mad as hell. The piece hasn't
come out yet, and they're sore about all this other crap that's
been done about them, and especially that TV program. You
saw Doug and Hambone, they were flying, man. Then they
promised to cut out all that stuff about marijuana, but they go
ahead and run it anyway. Just last night they had a meeting and
voted to turn the press off."

I told Roth I still wanted to talk to him.

"OK, come on down here," he said. "But don't wear a necktie."

Roth lives and works in Maywood, a desolate-looking, smog-filled community out toward Long Beach. He calls his small complex of boxlike buildings a studio, and there is a sign proclaiming: ROTH: MONSTERS THAT MEAN BUSINESS!

Big Daddy was out in back, working over his new car, a bright-yellow drag racer called Yellow Fang, which he said could hit 190 miles per hour in nine seconds from a standing start. Roth is in his early 30s, he is six feet three or four, and he must weigh close to 300 pounds. He sports a scraggly goatee and a moustache, and he was wearing a gaudy, flowered shirt with an "I Like Bikes" button on it. I found out later he's been happily married for years, has five children, and won't drive any of his own drag racers.

Big Daddy revealed that Sal Mineo was supposed to have coughed up $3,500 for the Berdoo treasury, and that the Angels were thinking of renting the corner of Sunset and Vine to put themselves on public display at 25 cents a look. He had advised them against it and urged them to hire a lawyer because their civil rights were being violated. I asked how all these projects jibed with the Angels' determination to avoid publicity. "They got to do something gigantic," Roth said. "Something that'll put them over, take the heat off." Later, he unveiled his newest creation, a Big Daddy T-Shirt with HELL'S ANGELS' FAN CLUB stenciled across the front.

Fontana is a sleepy-looking town in San Bernardino County, and the first thing that strikes you as you near it is the sheer flatness of the land, the wide country roads, criss-crossing each other endlessly, all but empty of traffic. There are no curves, and even on the back roads cars can go 70 miles an hour. It's a motorcycle paradise.

Seventeen thousand people live in Fontana itself, and they are almost all recent arrivals, drawn into the area by the great iron heart of Fontana, the Kaiser steel plant. You can see it for miles, its great, black chimneys and slag heaps soaring high above the palms and eucalyptus and citrus groves. The plant was built 20 years ago, during the war and, until it came, there were only a few thousand Okies and squatters, who grew oranges and lemons, raised chickens and rabbits. There are many Negroes and Mexicans in the area, and they live in desperate squalor, in rotting shacks and coops. The sun always shines, and it's always warm.

The first chapter of the Hell's Angels was founded here in 1950. Most of the Angels come from lower-income groups and have had little or no education. If and when they work, it is usually at menial tasks, on factory assembly lines or as garage mechanics. A few hold down white-collar jobs (Tiny, in Oakland, is the credit manager of a television-and-electrical-appliance store; Skip from Richmond was for seven years a clerk in a small food-chain outlet, until he was fired last July for refusing to quit the Angels). Most tend to move from job to job, taking work only when they absolutely have to. Their basic expenses are not high, since they often share houses and costs. Some refuse to work at all, but will live off the earnings of employed girl friends or from whatever they can steal. The police claim that the Angels are the country's ablest motorcycle thieves and geniuses at assembling a "hot" machine from the scattered parts they pick up here and there in their wanderings. In any case, whatever money they manage to acquire is only a means to an end, best symbolized by their clothes. The Nazi uniforms are worn only because they have become identified, through comic strips and men's adventure magazines, with the license to band together, to push people around, to be somebody. "When you walk into a place where people can see you, you want to look as repulsive as possible," said one Berdoo Angel. "We're bastards to the world and they're bastards to us."

The motorcycle is the chief instrument the Angels use in the achievement of freedom and power. The Harley-Davidson 74, the machine most of the Angels ride, is an awesome beast to start with – a roaring charger easily capable of 100 miles an hour, a concentration of power you can merge into, do tricks with, escaping at terrific speed from whatever is pursuing you, with your buddies front and back and all around, there to protect you, to smash through the sad square world that hems you in, leaving no past behind you, expecting nothing of the future, living strictly in the moment and the immediate thrill.

The Angels reduce a machine to its essence, jamming the seats down, stripping away the chrome and extras, replacing standard parts and fittings with improvisations of their own, turning what started out as a "garbage wagon" into a "chopper." Some Angels can dismantle a motorcycle in two hours. When they get through tinkering with it, the hog is a lean, dangerous beast.

A number of Angels have died on the highways, and most have had serious accidents. They refuse to wear crash helmets and shun leather, which affords some protection in a spill. They choose to live as close to death as possible, which is what attracts into their ranks the few members who come from prosperous backgrounds. "Yeah we're honest with each other, we can count on each other," one of the Oakland Angels told me. "I went through all that school and family jazz. It's all crap. Boy, am I glad the Angels took me in! I don't ever want to be anything *but* an Angel, and that's it!"

The Angels make a considerable show of being free from social restraint, but they also have a charter, elect a president, vice president, secretary, treasurer, and sergeant at arms, and collect dues. They must wear a uniform and drive a certain kind of motorcycle, must attend meetings regularly, must not join other clubs, and must do what the leader says. The conformity an Angel lives under would depress an executive trainee.

As for sex, the Angels believe in its cruder aspects, and in license. They are followed by coveys of sad little girls, mostly in their teens or early 20's. There is one girl to every four or five Angels, and the turnover is terrific. If a girl wants to be a mama and "pull a train," which means make herself available to everyone, then she'll be welcome at any Angel party. There are very few mamas around, and they don't last long. They sometimes get auctioned off to another Angel for a gallon of gas or a pack of cigarettes or as little as 12 cents.

The girls the Angels favor are their Old Ladies, and an Old Lady is a girl who belongs to one Angel, is often married to him and bears his children. Inspector Larry Wallace recalls bursting into an Angel pad to rescue a couple of children who had been living with their mothers and some Angels on beer and cornflakes in an apartment cluttered with cans of motor oil, sprockets, dirty dishes, garbage, empty beer cans and last month's sheets.

In Fontana, Friday is the night the Angels gather, and you will see them in the late afternoon, four or five of them, buzzing around an A & W Root Beer stand on Sierra Avenue, practically in the middle of town. They park their hogs there and sit down to munch hot dogs, while around them mothers with broods of children sip root-beer floats and sodas. In Fontana the Angels do not misbehave in public, and they are tolerated. "Four or five of them together, that's all right." Wallace says. "A whole bunch of 'em, ten or twelve or more, and we bust it up."

Larry Wallace has had to deal with the Angels ever since he arrived in Fontana seven years ago. He is 32, and he speaks with the kindly drawl of his native Oklahoma. When you first meet him he is likely to remind you of a plump, amiable little boy. Actually, Wallace hasn't much fat on him; he has been lifting weights since he was eight and he is a 235-pound chunk of muscle. He walks into bars, and tough customers make the mistake of concentrating on his kindly smile and innocent, light-gray eyes; they see easy pickings, and they come in swinging. What happens next, says Wallace mildly, "is just awful." He shuns all fancy footwork and modern refinements like the karate chop. "I just grabs 'em around the neck," he says dolefully, "and slam 'em up against something hard." Even the Angels respect Larry Wallace.

In his private office Wallace keeps a souvenir to remind himself of what the Angels mean to him. It's a two-by-four framed reproduction of a Modigliani woman he confiscated out of an Angel pad. The lady is sleepy-looking, long-necked, with a prim little mouth. An Iron Cross has been scrawled over her head and the word "help" is entwined in her hair. Around her neck hangs a Star of David with a swastika stamped into it, and there's a bullet hole in her throat, with a drawing of the bullet emerging from the back of her head. Scattered here and there are Angel maxims of the day:

As you were I was.
As I am, you will be,
　H. Himmler

Dope Forever
Forever Loaded

Honest officer, had I known my health stood in jeprody
(sic) I would never had lit one

And this rather plaintive one:

When we do right no one remembers.
When we do wrong, no one forgets.

Wallace watches the Angels as they shift around from place to
place, moving into apartments or small houses in shabby
neighborhoods, a dozen Angels and two or three girls sharing
the place, usually for a week or two or three, before moving on.
They are easy to keep track of because they always sport their
colors, run in packs, and make noise. "Between you and I,
they're just disgusting," says Wallace. "I mean, when you see
an Angel you don't forget him. They got to do this because they
couldn't do anything else."

During my visit to the Blue Blaze, the Angel who was most
eager to talk to me was a blond, pink-cheeked giant with a sweet
smile and soft handshake who introduced himself as Alvin Ray,
president of the Fresno chapter. The introduction alone made
Ray unusual, because Angels make a point of not saying who
they are or where they come from or what they do, and it's not
considered good form to ask. Alvin Ray was eager to show the
bike, but he wouldn't have it until the next day, and he was
going straight back to Fresno.

"You come to Fresno," he had said. "Find Ratcliff Sta-
dium, that's out on Blackstone Avenue. Ask for me at the
filling station across the street, they'll know where I am." He
smiled dreamily. "I'm sometimes hard to find." Later he said
he'd gone down to Selma, Ala., on his wonderful bike – not to
march with the civil-rights people or anything like that, but
just to see what was going on. "I thought maybe them niggers
was getting out of hand," he had said, with the same sweet
smile.

I decided to look up Alvin Ray, but nobody at the filling
station in Fresno admitted knowing anything about him or the
Angels. After some prodding, one of the attendants said he'd
heard rumors, that was all, to the effect that there had been
some motorcyclists in a house down the road a piece. "But they

ain't there now. They was thrown out of there about a week ago," he said.

The house was set back 100 or 200 yards from Blackstone Avenue, which is the main road north to Yosemite, and it was just one of many similar ones in the neighborhood – a one-story, white-frame, three-room bungalow with a tiny front yard and a general air of dilapidation. Nonetheless, it was hard to miss. Part of the fence had been flattened, all of the windows had been smashed, one of the fenceposts had been rammed through a door, and the branches of two small trees in the front yard had been torn away from the trunks and dragged grotesquely on the ground; between them, an armchair sprawled face down, gutted, its arms smashed. On the back of the chair, written in red ink, were the words:

> Hells Angels
> 13 M 69er
> Dee – Berdoo

I went into the house and stood in the center of what must have once been the living room. It was hard to tell, because I had never seen such utter chaos: Every piece of furniture had been smashed; debris littered the floors – broken glass, torn clothing, empty cans, wine and beer bottles, crockery, boxes. Every door had been ripped off its hinges, and a large hole gaped where an air conditioner had been torn away and carted off. The word "cops" had been scrawled in large red letters over a caved-in bed and used as a target for bottles and anything else that had come to hand. Under it was written "yea Fresno," over another swastika. All the walls had been defaced, and on one of them a partying Angel had carefully composed a poem:

> Day & Night –
> Whoever crashed; he painted & burnt
> But!!!!
> One day he crashed and –
> was burnt –
> and was also painted
> But!!!!!!
> Now he's off and running –

Strong –
He doesn't hold a grudge
But PLEASE don't get him wrong.
Because if you *CRASH*
It will certainly be your . . .!

The immediate neighbors were respectable people whose
houses were not more than a few yards away; they said that
the house had been rented to a single girl who had seemed all
right. The next morning the motorcyclists had started to arrive;
there must have been 20 or 25 of them, including their girls, and
their party had lasted nearly two weeks, until the police had
finally come without being summoned. No one had protested or
called for help. The man who lived directly in back of the house,
and who hadn't had a night's sleep in all that time, explained
why. "You're not going to buck an army," he said. "They
wouldn't have stood for it. They're like a bunch of animals."

I got a more direct idea of the sort of feeling the Angels can
inspire when I arrived in the San Francisco Bay area and began
to see something of the Oakland chapter and its leader, Ralph
(Sonny) Barger. Barger is 26 years old and has been an Angel
since he was 16. I had telephoned him directly and arranged to
meet him at his house. He lives with his Old Lady, a willowy
brunette named Elsie, and her two small children in a roomy old
house on a quiet rundown street in East Oakland. Barger has a
deep chest, and long, muscular arms, heavily tattooed, and his
full beard and lengthy, reddish hair make him look forbidding.
He stared at me out of cold, expressionless brown eyes, shook
my hand limply and turned to unlock the door. "The Old
Lady's out," he said. "I just got back from seeing my lawyer.
I'm going up on an assault rap in a couple of weeks, but I got
witnesses, and I'll beat it."

Barger's furniture was much used and battered, but it was
comfortable and had been recently dusted; there were a couple
of cheap framed landscapes on a mantel, and some photographs
of the kids. Everywhere I looked there were trophies – great
rococo clusters of wooden columns supporting cups, statuettes,
gilded toy motorcycles – all won by the Oakland. Angels in
various motorcycle shows and races. There was a Nazi flag on
the wall directly opposite a rack holding two semi-automatic

rifles, and on a side table a large photograph of Sonny staring into the camera and delivering himself of a rousing Bronx cheer.

We talked affably enough for half an hour or so, and at one point Barger grinned and said. "Well, nobody ever wrote nothing good about us, but then we ain't never done nothing good to write about." But the convivial atmosphere changed when five other Angels stopped by. At first they pointedly ignored me, talking over, around and through me directly at Sonny. The talk was mainly about what a bum deal they had been getting from everybody. Everytime a car slowed down in the vicinity, they would get up and glance quickly out the windows. One, a surly black-bearded youth named Buzzard, was sporting a porkpie hat and a cane he had picked up somewhere; he waved the cane about as he talked and jabbed it idly at me from time to time. I suddenly got the clear impression that he would have enjoyed using it on somebody. Buzzard was a Berdoo Angel, a refugee from the pressure being applied down south, and he was angrier at the press than most of the others. As soon as I could manage it, I said good-bye to Sonny and got out of the house.

A few days later a huge Negro made the mistake of dropping into the El Adobe, then the Angel bar in East Oakland, and getting into an altercation with one of them; he was taken out into the parking lot and jumped by the whole pack. After he had been carted away in an ambulance, and the police had begun asking questions, the Angels all agreed that the Negro had pulled a knife on their buddy; what could they have done but go to his assistance? No charges were preferred against them. The whole incident seemed to be regarded by the Angels involved as something of a lark. The Angels always claim, possibly with some justice, that they never start a fight but retaliate after provocation. Their retaliation is often massive, and out of all proportion, however: and there is always an atmosphere of potential violence about the Angels, even when they are in no danger. Singly or in groups of two or three, they are often easy to talk to. They can be sociable drinking companions, and a few of them are articulate. But in a body, especially when partying, they are unpredictable and dangerous.

Most of all, they are alone defiantly, aggressively alone. They have no friends, except other outlaw motorcyclists, and they haven't any natural allies. As self-proclaimed rebels, they'd be welcomed everywhere in beatnik circles and on some campuses today. But the Angels despise the new radicals. 'They're a bunch of Commie bastards," one of them said. Just last month six Angels charged into the student demonstration over Vietnam; one Angel got a split head and was arrested.

Isolated, highlighted and so few in number – there are probably fewer than 200 active members in the whole state – the Angels are playing a bizarre role, part menace and part fall guy. They are in a perfect position to be exploited by politicians anxious to impress the electorate, by policemen unable to put a stop to high-level crime, by hustlers looking for a new teen-age fad to launch, by reporters and commentators hungry for headlines, by entertainers who need new sensations to feed the hungry public. And in dealing with the Angels, who are genuinely antisocial and out of step and unattractive in the extreme, everybody looks good, no matter what his motives. Sonny Barger is almost right when he says, "All these mothers are using us and making a scene, and we ain't getting one damn cent out of it!"

What the Angels are getting out of it, in fact, is nothing but trouble. Even the Oakland Angels, who have suffered less from the publicity backlash of the attorney general's report than their sister chapters, have noticed that the police are keeping the heat on and it has become almost impossible for them to go off on their runs unmolested.

The last time they tried it, when they started out on what was supposed to be a statewide run to Bass Lake, a resort area north of Fresno, they were followed all the way by police and their progress was reported regularly in snappy, alarmist radio bulletins. Ultimately only about 150 riders, including girls and members of other outlaw clubs, got through, only to be met in Bass Lake by 100 heavily armed officers with dogs and all the latest electronic-tracking equipment. They were served with John Doe summonses, calling for them to appear in court to show why they shouldn't be restrained from ever coming back, and they found themselves confined to a small area of the resort and sealed off from the outside world by roadblocks and patrols. Furthermore, stores were reluctant to sell them anything. (Their beer supply was finally secured through the efforts of a blockade-running free-lance writer collecting material for a book.) When they pulled out, after an uneventful two days of mild carousing, they were escorted by the police and forced to leave a dozen of their members behind to clean up their campsite under the eye of forest rangers. The Boy Scouts couldn't have made less of a splash.

The Angels are puzzled and resentful at what has been happening to them, but this is because they have no clear conception of their position in society. The Angels are hipsters, but hipsters rarely see the world as clearly as the people they despise, the squares who, after all, manage to make society in their own image and run it to their own advantage. Hipsters, for the most part, don't know or ignore the fact that the odds are stacked against them, and the Angels are no exception. They are the sort of rebels who, in Germany in the 1920's, would have been recruited into the Brownshirts – chronic malcontents who enjoy smashing up beer halls, looting stores and breaking heads. When the party comes to power, they can never understand why.

"If they don't take this heat off us," Sonny Barger said one afternoon, "we're going to have to do something drastic. I sure would hate to see that happen." The implication was that the Angels would be forced into open warfare with the police, an occurrence I suspect the police would welcome.

At war or at peace, with the heat on or off, the Angels' barbarian image seems destined to last, and it makes it hard for some people to absolve them of anything. Even after it became clear they had had nothing to do with the Reseda rape, one police officer insisted that the suspects were really "just *like* the Angels." When rioting broke out in Laconia, N. H., during the 44th Annual New England Motorcycle Rally last June, the local police said it was all started by "a handful of Californians who call themselves Hell's Angels," and Mayor Peter Lessard declared he believed they'd been trained in riot techniques in Mexico. "Are the Communists behind it?" he asked darkly.

Well, there were no Angels in Laconia last June, and one of the offers the Angels actually did receive was from a television producer eager to find out when they were making their next run on a small town, so that the TV cameras could be on hand to record the carnage. The Angels are currently weighing that offer and dickering with another show that has offered them $2,000 for taped shots of Angels at work and at play.

The Angels believe more firmly than anyone else in their own press clippings, and it helps to sustain them when the cold winds blow. They are all – Sonny, Terry the Tramp, Tiny, Zorro, Fat Freddie, Ronnie, Skip, Jimmy, Magoo, Clean Cut, Mouldy Marvin, Buzzard, Gut, and everyone – convinced that far from being losers they are indestructible. "I wouldn't say we're losers," Sonny Barger said recently. "Whatever they do to us, we can take it because we want to be what we are, and there ain't nobody gonna change us."

LOSERS AND OUTSIDERS

Hunter S. Thompson

*This is a concise statement by one of America's most
creative and insightful writers of the 1960s. "Gonzo"
journalist Hunter S. Thompson rode and partied with
the Hells Angels, gathering research material for the
first full-length book on the club, simply entitled* Hell's
Angels. *Thompson's long-term association with the
Angels ended when he received a flogging at the hands
of a club member, due (according to Sonny Barger) to
his interference in a domestic dispute.*

Last Labor Day weekend newspapers all over California gave
front-page reports of a heinous gang rape in the moonlit sand
dunes near the town of Seaside on the Monterey Peninsula.
Two girls, aged 14 and 15, were allegedly taken from their dates
by a gang of filthy, frenzied, boozed-up motorcycle hoodlums
called "Hell's Angels," and dragged off to be "repeatedly
assaulted."

A deputy sheriff, summoned by one of the erstwhile dates,
said he "arrived at the beach and saw a huge bonfire surrounded
by cyclists of both sexes. Then the two sobbing, near-hysterical
girls staggered out of the darkness, begging for help. One was
completely nude and the other had on only a torn sweater."

Some 300 Hell's Angels were gathered in the Seaside-Monterey area at the time, having convened, they said, for the purpose of raising funds among themselves to send the body of a former member, killed in an accident, back to his mother in North Carolina. One of the Angels, hip enough to falsely identify himself as "Frenchy of San Bernardino," told a local reporter who came out to meet the cyclists: "We chose Monterey because we get treated good here; most other places we get thrown out of town."

But Frenchy spoke too soon. The Angels weren't on the peninsula twenty-four hours before four of them were in jail for rape, and the rest of the troop was being escorted to the county line by a large police contingent. Several were quoted, somewhat derisively, as saying: "That rape charge against our guys is phony and it won't stick."

It turned out to be true, but that was another story and certainly no headliner. The difference between the Hell's Angels in the papers and the Hell's Angels for real is enough to make a man wonder what newsprint is for. It also raises a question as to who are the real hell's angels.

Ever since World War II, California has been strangely plagued by wild men on motorcycles. They usually travel in groups of ten to thirty, booming along the highways and stopping here and there to get drunk and raise hell. In 1947, hundreds of them ran amok in the town of Hollister, an hour's fast drive south of San Francisco, and got enough press notices to inspire a film called *The Wild One*, starring Marlon Brando. The film had a massive effect on thousands of young California motorcycle buffs; in many ways; it was their version of *The Sun Also Rises*.

The California climate is perfect for motorcycles, as well as surfboards, swimming pools and convertibles. Most of the cyclists are harmless weekend types, members of the American Motorcycle Association, and no more dangerous than skiers or skin divers. But a few belong to what the others call "outlaw clubs," and these are the ones who – especially on weekends and holidays – are likely to turn up almost anywhere in the state, looking for action. Despite everything the psychiatrists and Freudian casuists have to say about them, they are tough, mean and potentially as dangerous as packs of wild boar. When push comes to shove, any leather fetishes or inadequacy feelings that may be involved are entirely beside the point, as anyone who has ever tangled with these boys will sadly testify. When you get in an argument with a group of outlaw motorcyclists, you can generally count your chances of emerging unmaimed by the number of heavy-handed allies you can muster in the time it takes to smash a beer bottle. In this league, sportsmanship is for old liberals and young fools. "I smashed his face," one of them said to me of a man he'd never seen until the swinging started. "He got wise. He called me a punk. He must have been stupid."

The most notorious of these outlaw groups is the Hell's Angels, supposedly headquartered in San Bernardino, just east of Los Angeles, and with branches all over the state. As a result of the infamous "Labor Day gang rape," the Attorney General of California has recently issued an official report on the Hell's Angels. According to the report, they are easily identified:

> The emblem of the Hell's Angels, termed "colors," consists of an embroidered patch of a winged skull wearing a motorcycle helmet. Just below the wing of the emblem are the Letters "MC." Over this is a band bearing the words "Hell's Angels." Below the emblem is another patch bearing the local chapter name, which is usually an abbreviation for the city or locality. These patches are sewn on the back of a usually sleeveless denim jacket. In addition, members have been observed wearing various types of Luftwaffe insignia and reproductions of German iron crosses. Many affect beards and their hair is usually long and unkempt. Some wear a single earring in a pierced ear lobe. Frequently they have been observed to wear metal belts made of a length of polished motorcycle drive chain which can be unhooked and used as a flexible bludgeon. . . . Probably the most universal common denominator in identification of Hell's Angels is their generally filthy condition. Investigating officers consistently report these people, both club members and their female associates, seem badly in need of a bath. Fingerprints are a very effective means of identification because a high percentage of Hell's Angels have criminal records.
>
> In addition to the patches on the back of Hell's Angels jackets, the "One Percenters" wear a patch reading "1 %-

*er." Another badge worn by some members bears the number
"13." It is reported to represent the 13th letter of the
alphabet, "M," which in turn stands for marijuana and
indicates the wearer thereof is a user of the drug.*

The Attorney General's report was colorful, interesting, heavily
biased and consistently alarming – just the sort of thing, in fact,
to make a clanging good article for a national news magazine.
Which it did; both barrels. *Newsweek* led with a left hook titled
"The Wild Ones," *Time* crossed with a right, inevitably titled
"The Wilder Ones." The Hell's Angels, cursing the implications of this new attack, retreated to the bar of the DePau Hotel
near the San Francisco waterfront and planned a weekend
beach party. I showed them the articles. Hell's Angels do
not normally read the news magazines. "I'd go nuts if I read
that stuff all the time," said one. "It's all bullshit."

Newsweek was relatively circumspect. It offered local color,
flashy quotes and "evidence" carefully attributed to the official
report but unaccountably said the report accused the Hell's
Angels of homosexuality, whereas the report said just the
opposite. *Time* leaped into the fray with a flurry of blood,
booze and semen-flecked wordage that amounted, in the end,
to a classic of supercharged hokum: "Drug-induced stupors . . .
no act is too degrading . . . swap girls, drugs and motorcycles
with equal abandon . . . stealing forays . . . then ride off again to
seek some new nadir in sordid behavior. . . ."

Where does all this leave the Hell's Angels and the thousands of
shuddering Californians (according to *Time*) who are worried
sick about them? Are these outlaws really going to be busted,
routed and cooled, as the news magazines implied? Are California highways any safer as a result of this published uproar?
Can honest merchants once again walk the streets in peace? The
answer is that nothing has changed except that a few people
calling themselves Hell's Angels have a new sense of identity
and importance.

After two weeks of intensive dealing with the Hell's Angels
phenomenon, both in print and in person, I'm convinced the
net result of the general howl and publicity has been to obscure
and avoid the real issues by invoking a savage conspiracy of

bogymen and conning the public into thinking all will be "business as usual" once this fearsome snake is scotched, as it surely will be by hard and ready minions of the Establishment.

Meanwhile, according to Attorney General Thomas C. Lynch's own figures. California's true crime picture makes the Hell's Angels look like a gang of petty jack rollers. The police count 463 Hell's Angels: 205 around Los Angeles and 233 in the San Francisco-Oakland area. I don't know about L.A. but the real figures for the Bay Area are thirty or so in Oakland and exactly eleven – with one facing expulsion – in San Francisco. This disparity makes it hard to accept other police statistics. The dubious package also shows convictions on 1,023 misdemeanor counts and 151 felonies – primarily vehicle theft, burglary and assault. This is for all years and all alleged members.

California's overall figures for 1963 list 1,116 homicides, 12,448 aggravated assaults, 6,257 sex offenses, and 24,532 burglaries. In 1962, the state listed 4,121 traffic deaths, up from 3,839 in 1961. Drug arrest figures for 1964 showed a 101 per cent increase in juvenile marijuana arrests over 1963, and a recent back-page story in the *San Francisco Examiner* said, "The venereal disease rate among [the city's] teen-agers from 15–19 has more than doubled in the past four years." Even allowing for the annual population jump, juvenile arrests in all categories are rising by 10 per cent or more each year.

Against this background, would it make any difference to the safety and peace of mind of the average Californian if every motorcycle outlaw in the state (all 901, according to the police) were garroted within twenty-four hours? This is not to say that a group like the Hell's Angels has no meaning. The generally bizarre flavor of their offenses and their insistence on identifying themselves make good copy, but usually overwhelm – in print, at least – the unnerving truth that they represent, in colorful microcosm, what is quietly and anonymously growing all around us every day of the week.

"We're bastards to the world and they're bastards to us," one of the Oakland Angels told a *Newsweek* reporter. "When you walk into a place where people can see you, you want to look as repulsive and repugnant as possible. We are complete social outcasts – outsiders against society."

A lot of this is a pose, but anyone who believes that's all it is has been on thin ice since the death of Jay Gatsby. The vast majority of motorcycle outlaws are uneducated, unskilled men between 20 and 30, and most have no credentials except a police record. So at the root of their sad stance is a lot more than a wistful yearning for acceptance in a world they never made; their real motivation is an instinctive certainty as to what the score really is. They are out of the ball game and they know it – and that is their meaning, for unlike most losers in today's society, the Hell's Angels not only know but spitefully proclaim exactly where they stand.

I went to one of their meetings recently, and halfway through the night I thought of Joe Hill on his way to face a Utah firing squad and saying his final words. "Don't mourn, organize." It is safe to say that no Hell's Angel has ever heard of Joe Hill or would know a Wobbly from a Bushmaster, but nevertheless they are somehow related. The I.W.W. had serious plans for running the world, while the Hell's Angels mean only to defy the world's machinery. But instead of losing quietly, one by one, they have banded together with a mindless kind of loyalty and moved outside the framework, for good or ill. There is nothing particularly romantic or admirable about it; that's just the way it is, strength in unity. They don't mind telling you that running fast and loud on their customized Harley 74s gives them a power and a purpose that nothing else seems to offer.

Beyond that, their position as self-proclaimed outlaws elicits a certain popular appeal, however reluctant. That is especially true in the West and even in California where the outlaw tradition is still honored. The unarticulated link between the Hell's Angels and the millions of losers and outsiders who don't wear any colors is the key to their notoriety and the ambivalent reactions they inspire. There are several other keys, having to do with politicians, policemen and journalists, but for this we have to go back to Monterey and the Labor Day "gang rape."

Politicians, like editors and cops, are very keen on outrage stories, and state Senator Fred S. Farr of Monterey County is no exception. He is a leading light of the Carmel-Pebble Beach set and no friend of hoodlums anywhere, especially gang rapists who invade his constituency. Senator Farr demanded an immediate investigation of the Hell's Angels and others of their Ilk – Commancheros, Stray Satans, Iron Horsemen, Rattlers (a Negro club), and Booze Fighters – whose lack of status caused them all to be lumped together as "other disreputables." In the cut-off world of big bikes, long runs and classy rumbles, this new, state-sanctioned stratification made the Hell's Angels very big. They were, after all, Number One. Like John Dillinger.

Attorney General Lynch, then new in his job, moved quickly to mount an investigation of sorts. He sent questionnaires to more than 100 sheriffs, district attorneys and police chiefs, asking for information on the Hell's Angels and those "other disreputables." He also asked for suggestions as to how the law might deal with them.

Six months went by before all the replies were condensed into the fifteen-page report that made new outrage headlines when it was released to the press. (The Hell's Angels also got a copy; one of them stole mine.) As a historical document, it read like a plot synopsis of Mickey Spillane's worst dreams. But in the matter of solutions it was vague, reminiscent in some ways of Madame Nhu's proposals for dealing with the Vietcong. The state was going to centralize information on these thugs, urge more vigorous prosecution, put them all under surveillance whenever possible, etc.

A careful reader got the impression that even if the Hell's Angels had acted out this script – eighteen crimes were specified and dozens of others implied – very little would or could be done about it, and that indeed Mr. Lynch was well aware he'd been put, for political reasons, on a pretty weak scent. There was plenty of mad action, perversions and a strange parade of "innocent victims" that, even on paper and in careful police language, was enough to tax the credulity of the dullest police reporter. Any bundle of information off police blotters is bound to reflect a special viewpoint, and parts of the Attorney General's report are actually humorous, if only for the language. Here is an excerpt:

On November 4, 1961, a San Francisco resident driving through Rodeo, possibly under the influence of alcohol, struck

*a motorcycle belonging to a Hell's Angel parked outside a bar.
A group of Angels pursued the vehicle, pulled the driver from
the car and attempted to demolish the rather expensive
vehicle. The bartender claimed he had seen nothing, but a
cocktail waitress in the bar furnished identification to the
officers concerning some of those responsible for the assault.
The next day it was reported to officers that a member of the
Hell's Angels gang had threatened the life of this waitress as
well as another woman waitress. A male witness who definitely identified five participants in the assault including the
president of the Vallejo Hell's Angels and the Vallejo "Road
Rats" advised officers that because of his fear of retaliation
by club members he would refuse to testify to the facts he had
previously furnished.*

That is a representative item in the section of the report titled
"Hoodlum Activities." First, it occurred in a small town –
Rodeo is on San Pablo Bay just north of Oakland – where the
Angels had stopped at a bar without causing any trouble until
some offense was committed against them. In this case, a driver
whom even the police admit was "possibly" drunk hit one of
their motorcycles. The same kind of accident happens every day
all over the nation, but when it involves outlaw motorcyclists it
is something else again. Instead of settling the thing with an
exchange of insurance information or, at the very worst, an
argument with a few blows, the Hell's Angels beat the driver
and "attempted to demolish the vehicle." I asked one of them if
the police exaggerated this aspect, and he said no, they had done
the natural thing: smashed headlights, kicked in doors, broken
windows and torn various components off the engine.

Of all their habits and predilections that society finds alarming, this departure from the time-honored concept of "an eye
for an eye" is the one that most frightens people. The Hell's
Angels try not to do anything halfway, and anyone who deals in
extremes is bound to cause trouble, whether he means to or not.
This, along with a belief in total retaliation for any offense or
insult, is what makes the Hell's Angels unmanageable for the
police and morbidly fascinating to the general public. Their
claim that they "don't start trouble" is probably true more often
than not, but their idea of "provocation" is dangerously broad,

and their, biggest problem is that nobody else seems to understand it. Even dealing with them personally, on the friendliest terms, you can sense their hair-trigger readiness to retaliate.

This is a public thing, and not at all true among themselves. In a meeting, their conversation is totally frank and open. They speak to and about one another with an honesty that more civilized people couldn't bear. At the meeting I attended (and before they realized I was a journalist) one Angel was being publicly evaluated; some members wanted him out of the club and others wanted to keep him in. It sounded like a group-therapy clinic in progress – not exactly what I expected to find when just before midnight I walked into the bar of the De Pau in one of the bleakest neighborhoods in San Francisco, near Hunters Point. By the time I parted company with them – at 6:30 the next morning after an all-night drinking bout in my apartment – I had been impressed by a lot of things, but no one thing about them was as consistently obvious as their group loyalty. This is an admirable quality, but it is also one of the things that gets them in trouble: a fellow Angel is *always right* when dealing with outsiders. And this sort of reasoning makes a group of "offended" Hell's Angels nearly impossible to deal with.

Here is another incident from the Attorney General's report:

> *On September 19, 1964, a large group of Hell's Angels and "Satan's Slaves" converged on a bar in South Gate (Los Angeles County), parking their motorcycles and cars in the street in such a fashion as to block one-half of the roadway. They told officers that three members of the club had recently been asked to stay out of the bar and that they had come to tear it down. Upon their approach the bar owner locked the doors and turned off the lights and no entrance was made, but the group did demolish a cement block fence. On arrival of the police, members of the club were lying on the sidewalk and in the street. They were asked to leave the city, which they did reluctantly. As they left, several were heard to say that they would be back and tear down the bar.*

Here again is the ethic of total retaliation. If you're "asked to stay out" of a bar, you don't just punch the owner – you come back with your army and destroy the whole edifice. Similar incidents – along with a number of vague rape complaints – make up the bulk of the report. Eighteen incidents in four years, and none except the rape charges are more serious than cases of assault on citizens who, for their own reasons, had become involved with the Hell's Angels prior to the violence. I could find no cases of unwarranted attacks on wholly innocent victims. There are a few borderline cases, wherein victims of physical attacks seemed innocent, according to police and press reports, but later refused to testify for fear of "retaliation." The report asserts very strongly that Hell's Angels are difficult to prosecute and convict because they make a habit of threatening and intimidating witnesses. That is probably true to a certain extent, but in many cases victims have refused to testify because they were engaged in some legally dubious activity at the time of the attack.

In two of the most widely publicized incidents the prosecution would have fared better if their witnesses and victims *had* been intimidated into silence. One of these was the Monterey "gang rape," and the other a "rape" in Clovis, near Fresno in the Central Valley. In the latter, a 36-year-old widow and mother of five children claimed she'd been yanked out of a bar where she was having a quiet beer with another woman, then carried to an abandoned shack behind the bar and raped repeatedly for two and a half hours by fifteen or twenty Hell's Angels and finally robbed of $150. That's how the story appeared in the San Francisco newspapers the next day, and it was kept alive for a few more days by the woman's claims that she was getting phone calls threatening her life if she testified against her assailants.

Then, four days after the crime, the victim was arrested on charges of "sexual perversion." The true story emerged, said the Clovis chief of police, when the woman was "confronted by witnesses. Our investigation shows she was not raped," said the chief. "She participated in lewd acts in the tavern with at least three Hell's Angels before the owners ordered them out. She encouraged their advances in the tavern, then led them to an abandoned house in the rear. . . . She was not robbed but, according to a woman who accompanied her, had left her house early in the evening with $5 to go bar-hopping." That incident did not appear in the Attorney General's report.

But it was impossible not to mention the Monterey "gang rape," because it was the reason for the whole subject to become official. Page one of the report – which *Time*'s editors apparently skipped – says that the Monterey case was dropped because ". . . further investigation raised questions as to whether forcible rape had been committed or if the identifications made by victims: were valid." Charges were dismissed on September 25, with the concurrence of a grand jury. The deputy District Attorney said "a doctor examined the girls and found no evidence" to support the charges. "Besides that, one girl refused to testify," he explained, "and the other was given a lie-detector test and found to be wholly unreliable."

This, in effect, was what the Hell's Angels had been saying all along. Here is their version of what happened, as told by several who were there:

> *One girl was white and pregnant, the other was colored, and they were with five colored studs. They hung around our bar – Nick's Place on Del Mante Avenue – for about three hours Saturday night, drinking and talking with our riders, then they came out to the beach with us – them and their five boy friends. Everybody was standing around the fire drinking wine, and some of the guys were talking to them – hustling 'em, naturally – and soon somebody asked the two chicks if they wanted to be turned on – you know, did they want to smoke some pot? They said yeah, and then went with the guys to the dunes. The spade went with a few guys and then she wanted to quit, but the pregnant one was really hot to trot: the first four or five guys she was really dragging, into her arms, but after that she cooled off, too. By this time, though, one of their boy friends had got scared and gone for the cops–and that's all it was.*

But not quite all. After that there were Senator Farr and Tom Lynch and a hundred cops and dozens of newspaper stories and articles in the National News in magazines – and even this article, which is a direct result of the Monterey "gang rape."

When the much-quoted report was released, the local press –

primarily the *San Francisco Chronicle*, which had earlier done a long and fairly objective series on the Hell's Angels – made a point of saying the Monterey charges against the Hell's Angels had been dropped for lack of evidence. *Newsweek* was careful not to mention Monterey at all, but *The New York Times* referred to it as "the alleged gang rape" which, however, left no doubt in a reader's mind that something savage had occurred.

It remained for *Time*, though, to flatly ignore the fact that the Monterey rape charges had been dismissed. Its article leaned heavily on the hairiest and least factual sections of the report, and ignored the rest. It said, for instance, that the Hell's Angels initlation rite "demands that any new member bring a woman or girl [called a 'sheep'] who is willing to submit to sexual intercourse with each member of the club." That is untrue, although, as one Angel explained, "Now and then you get a woman who likes to cover the crowd, and hell, I'm no prude. People don't like to think women go for that stuff, but a lot of them do."

We were talking across a pool table about the rash of publicity and how it had affected the Angels' activities. I was trying to explain to him that the bulk of the press in this country has such a vested interest in the *status quo* that it can't afford to do much honest probing at the roots, for fear of what they might find.

"Oh, I don't know," he said. "Of course I don't like to read all this bullshit because it brings the heat down on us, but since we got famous we've had more rich fags and sex-hungry women come looking for us than we ever had before. Hell, these days we have more action than we can handle."

A MORE COMPLETE HISTORY OF THE OUTLAW CLUBS

William L. Dulaney

William Dulaney's research is the product of five years of participant observation, ten years of experience "in the life", and an intense personal desire to understand what it means to be an outlaw biker.

Here he describes the development of motorcycle club culture since the 1960s.

The American-Vietnam Conflict era (1958–1975) can be seen as the most recent period during which significant and pervading social factors affected group formation of outlaw motorcycle clubs. Just as after the Second World War returning veterans seemed to flock to motorcycle clubs. Returning American-Vietnam Conflict veterans interviewed during my field research feel that all too often they became targets against whom many Americans lashed out. Indeed, for many in this country and others (e.g. Australia) the war and the atrocities being committed in the name of America and against Americans in Southeast Asia was unconscionable. Vietnam veterans reported being labeled "baby killers"; some were spat upon in airports, beaten at demonstrations, and refused gainful employment, all after "doing their duty" for their country.

Among other experiences, returning veterans brought back from the jungles of Southeast Asia journeymen's knowledge of and experience with illegal drugs, which, given a relatively widespread American drug culture in the 1960s, went largely unnoticed or unrecognized by the mainstream citizenry. Whereas WWII servicemen were on average 26 years old, the average age of Vietnam servicemen was only 19. Teenagers barely out of puberty were now experiencing one of the blood-iest armed conflicts in American history. As before, these men would be forever changed by their combat experience, their innocence scorched from their being, their pre-war personal-ities reduced to little more than charred remains to be swept under the carpet, so to speak, by a nation eager to put the experience quickly behind it.

It is during this era that the notorious "one percenters" emerged from the outlaw biker system on a national scale. The dominant motorcycle clubs of the time took the secession a step further and turned the alleged AMA declaration back on itself, claiming the remaining 1% as a badge of honor and forming themselves into a loose association of *truly* outlaw motorcycle clubs known as One Percenters. The original one percenters agreed on a diamond-shaped symbol to denote their marginal-but-exclusive social status, and agreed to establish geographic boundaries – primarily in California – in which each motorcycle club would operate independently. Although this loose association had been around for some time before the American-Vietnam Conflict, the one percenters were not to make the national media scene until the mid-1960s.

A significant point in the evolution of one percenters was evident in California during the summer of 1964. At this time two members of the Oakland Hells Angels Motorcycle Club attending a club rally were arrested and charged with raping two women in Monterey, California. The charges were dropped due to lack of evidence and the two Hells Angels were released, but it seems that the media coverage of the incident caught the attention of certain California state government officials. Cali-fornia State Senator Fred Farr demanded an immediate in-vestigation into "outlaw motorcycle clubs" and two weeks later

California State Attorney General Thomas C. Lynch launched a statewide law enforcement information gathering initiative. The year following the Monterey incident, Attorney General Lynch released to the public the internal report, which was prepared ostensibly for the purpose of outlining activities of California motorcycle clubs such as the Hells Angels. The Lynch Report, as it has come to be known, can be seen as the first large-scale bureaucratic attempt to portray motorcycle clubs as a clear and present danger to local, state and ultimately international constituencies. The report consists of what can be interpreted as little more than law enforcement urban legends: unsubstantiated absurdities such as gang raping of innocent young women and the plundering of small California townships, all of which fall under the heading "Hoodlum Activities". Investigators such as Hunter Thompson debunked the Lynch report as early as 1966. Thompson perhaps describes best the credibility of the Lynch report when he writes, "As a historical document, it read like a plot synopsis of Mickey Spillane's worst dreams". The questionable social validity of the Lynch Report notwithstanding, "facts" from the report continue to find their way into government and law enforcement literature to this day.

News media were quick to pick up on the negative portrayal of the Hells Angels, and many notable periodicals began running stories with alarmingly biased titles. Perhaps Andrew Syder outlines best how the Lynch Report framed the dominant American culture's conceptualization of motorcycle clubs. Syder traces citations of the report in mainstream American news media, noting that most media took the "condemnatory Lynch Report at face value, using it as their primary source of information". Most notable among publications citing the report are:

The New York Times: "California Takes Steps to Curb Terrorism of Ruffian Cyclists," 16 March 1965,
The Los Angeles Time: "Hell's Angels Called Threat on Wheels," 16 March 1965,
Time: "The Wilder Ones," 26 March 1965,
Newsweek: "The Wild Ones," 29 March 1965,
The Nation: "Motorcycle Gangs: Losers and Outsiders," 17 May 1965,

The New York Times: "10,000 in Beach Riot in New Hampshire," 20 June 1965,
Life: "Come to the Riot," 2 July 1965,
Newsweek: "Bikies' Fun," 5 July 1965,
The Saturday Evening Post: "The Hell's Angels," 20 November 1965.

This media coverage had the effect of casting a pall that encompassed not only the charters of the Hells Angels MC, but the outlaw motorcycle club system as a whole. Hollywood moviemakers were quick to cash in on the disturbing image of outlaw motorcycle clubs. *Wild Angels* and *Hells Angels on Wheels* were released as early as 1967, each distorting further the reality of what it meant to be a member of an outlaw motorcycle club. It appears that certain members of the California state government were responsible for casting an unrealistic image of the outlaw motorcycle club system, that certain prominent news media were responsible for "validating" that distorted image, and that Hollywood has perpetuated that image over time.

This is not to suggest that the Hells Angels MC was (or is) an innocent victim of negative government and news media coverage. To be sure, the Hells Angels have played their role well in the crafting of their image. For example, members of the Hells Angels MC seemed to enjoy media attention by allowing Hunter Thompson to associate with them, by gladly participating in the making of certain biker gang exploitation films (e.g., *Hells Angels on Wheels* and *Hell's Angels '69*), by calling in to local California radio broadcast talk shows. Further, the Oakland charter of the Hells Angels MC fanned the flames of media attention through antics such as attacking a group of anti-Vietnam War protestors in Berkeley. Perhaps all this was simply an attempt on the part of the Hells Angels MC to capitalize on hyperbole and set something of a renegade image in the eyes of the dominant culture. However, an incident in late 1969 served to solidify the outrageous image of the outlaw motorcycle club system – no matter how valid or invalid it may have been – in the eyes of American citizens. An HAMC member was charged with the murder of an 18-year-old named Meredith Hunter, who was stabbed to death at the December 6,

1969 Rolling Stones "Gimme Shelter" concert at Altamont Speedway in Livermore, California.

Details of the incident remain unclear: 1) the Hells Angels MC may or may not have been employed as security for the Rolling Stones, and 2) the deceased, Meredith Hunter, may or may not have attacked a member of the Hells Angels MC, and 3) Hunter may or may not have intended to attack Mick Jagger rather than a Hells Angel in order to instigate the melee. According to Sonny Barger, Hells Angels MC Oakland charter president at the time, Hunter shot one HAMC member: "Meredith had shot a Hell's Angel. Since the guy he shot was a fugitive at the time, we couldn't take him to a doctor or an emergency ward. It was just a flesh wound anyway". Of course, Barger's account must be considered in the light of an absolute lack of corroborating information; indeed, even Barger admits that he didn't actually see the alleged shooting. The Hells Angel who was supposedly shot remains nameless due to his "fugitive" status, which also conveniently explains why no medical records are available to verify Barger's claim. One may look to the amount of contextual detail surrounding the Altamont stabbing as evidence for credibility, which Barger seems to provide, but nonetheless his account must be examined critically.

It is still possible today to view some of what happened at Altamont. In a 1970 documentary titled *Gimme Shelter* (directed by David and Albert Maysles and Charlotte Zwerin), viewers are able to see multiple filmed replays of significant aspects of the Hunter stabbing. As Aretakis describes:

And then we see the murder itself: A member of the Hells Angels stabs a man holding a gun in front of the stage. Or, that is, we see it twice. It happens during the performance of "Under My Thumb," but unless you're closely looking, it's hard to spot. Not so in the editing room, where the filmmakers show it to us and to Jagger, rolling it back and forth on their editing machine. Clearly stunned by the images, Jagger walks out of the room toward the camera, a blank look on his face, offering us no guidance, no verdict on what happened, how, or why.

While the film does lack context surrounding the stabbing it is important to view the film footage in addition to reading accounts of the incident in order to make plausible inferences. What can be verified is that the HAMC member charged with the murder was found not guilty. As with the Hells Angels MC members charged in Monterey five years earlier, the Hells Angel charged with murder at Altamont went free; however, the outlaw motorcycle club system was handed down a life sentence of negative public opinion.

During the 1960s and 1970s, newer clubs joined the One Percent ranks. While smaller in membership than older clubs such as the Hells Angels MC, they were considerably more aggressive when it came to carving out geographic areas in which to operate. Outlaw motorcycle clubs joining the elite ranks of the One Percenters during this time include the Bandidos MC from Galveston Texas, the Pagans MC, the Sons of Silence MC, the Mongols MC, the Vagos MC of southern California, and the Warriors MC in Florida. Accelerating to contemporary times, a hierarchy of motorcycle clubs has been firmly established among the One Percenters: "the big three" as they are known to state and federal law enforcement agencies. The big three in order of sociocultural power are the Hells Angels MC, the Outlaws MC, and the Bandidos MC. There are other one-percent motorcycle clubs in the system, including the POBOBs MC, Gypsy Jokers MC, Galloping Gooses MC, and Henchman MC.

Since the beginning of the Transformative period in 1948 the number and types of outlaw motorcycle clubs have swollen the ranks of the system; some clubs meet the criteria to wear the One Percenter emblem but most do not. With due respect to Mark Watson and Daniel Wolf, who have reported that all outlaw clubs are One Percenters, it is important to draw a sharp distinction between outlaw motorcycle clubs and One Percenters. Outlaw motorcycle clubs are simply motorcycling organizations that do not hold American Motorcyclist Association charters, and represent the vast majority of motorcycle clubs in America. The reality is that all one-percent clubs are outlaw motorcycle clubs, but not all outlaw motorcycle clubs are one-percent clubs. The original meaning of the term "outlaw," which denotes a lack of an organizational AMA charter and nothing more, still holds in motorcycle clubs that do not define themselves as One Percenters.

The One-Percenter ethos can be summarized as follows: the demands of the organization are superior to the needs of the individual, which includes the individual's family and occupation. While it is no secret that certain members of one-percent motorcycle clubs have been convicted of illegal acts such as methamphetamine production, distribution and sales; prostitution; contract violence; racketeering; and motorcycle theft, my field research suggests strongly that those members who engage in such behavior represent the minority of the one-percent clubs. Further, of the outlaw motorcycle clubs observed, illegal behavior such as that listed above was non-existent.

The dominant symbol of the One Percenter is the diamond, and a motorcycle club that does not display this symbol on their colors is most definitely not a one percent organization. This diamond-shaped patch, with either the text "One Percenter" or the alpha-numeric symbol "1%er" embroidered in the center, is usually displayed on the wearer's left vest lapel, over the heart; however, at least one club places the one-percent symbol on the back-patch (e.g., the Bandidos MC). The one-percent symbol utilizes the two dominant colors in the club's color scheme (for examples, the Hells Angels MC incorporates a white background with red letters and border, the Outlaws MC places white lettering on a black background, the Bandidos MC uses red lettering and borders on a gold background). As an interesting aside, recently certain American charters of the Hells Angels MC have ceased displaying the One Percenter diamond signifier. According to Sonny Barger, the Hells Angels MC standards for membership are higher than those of any other motorcycle club, One Percent or not. Barger, et al states, ". . . we're not One-Percenters – we're Hell's Angels first and foremost". During my field research this was certainly the case in the Oakland, California; Cave Creek, Arizona; and Charlotte, North Carolina charters; however, the Hells Angels MC website still proclaims "Hells Angels is the oldest, and biggest original 1 % motorcycle club in the world"

Through the selling of particular Hells Angels MC organizational support merchandise, it can be seen that these Hells Angels MC charters are taking steps to deride the status of the diamond signifier. These support items include T-shirts, hats, belt buckles, patches, and key chains that display the diamond signifier, inside of which is displayed the script "81 %er". The number 81 represents the Hells Angels (e.g., the eighth letter of the alphabet is "H" and the first letter is "A," thus 81 = HA). These support items are easily purchased via Hells Angels MC websites and even the online auction house eBay.

During my research compelling evidence emerged that suggests the existence of non-one-percent outlaw clubs that do have factions of members who espouse a one percenter philosophy, individuals I will call "quasi-one percenters". Quasi-one percenters aside, the outlaw motorcycle club organizational ethic, in and of itself, can be a harsh one to live by. This ethic, colloquially referred to as "motorcycle club etiquette," outlines acceptable member behavior given a wide variety of social contexts and dictates the deliverance of swift and severe sanctions to those who violate group and individual roles and responsibilities. Generally speaking, quasi-one percenters hold positions such as Sargeants-at-Arms, special enforcers, or bodyguards. These members display a diamond-shaped patch identical to those described above, usually on the front of their vest, but inside the patch one usually finds the letters of the motorcycle club rather than a "one percenter" or "1%er" signifier. Sargeants-at-Arms are elected positions within a motorcycle club whose primary function is the maintenance of club discipline during official functions, to act as the enforcement arm of the local leadership, and to monitor the behavior of "problem children" (i.e. individuals, both within and outside the club who are known troublemakers or who seem to be displaying signs that point to possible, imminent trouble) during club social events. Special enforcers are not elected positions, but rather are appointed positions based on special training, skills, and abilities that certain members possess. Very often special enforcers have U.S. Special Forces training and are proficient with a number of weapons and hand-to-hand combat techniques. Bodyguards are also appointed positions and those who hold such positions are similar to special enforcers in their military training, but they serve as the personal security detail for state and regional presidents of motorcycle clubs.

The taxonomy offered above is useful in understanding certain social and cultural factors that influenced the origins and evolution of motorcycle clubs in the United States. A common thread runs through each of these eras, that of involvement in American military conflicts and subsequent social organizing around the sport of motorcycling. What seems clear is that neither the American government nor society is attending to the effects of war on such individuals. Indeed, it appears that no process exists by which combat veterans are able to resume their roles as citizens, as people. Because of this lack of structured re-assimilation into American society, certain combat veterans have created over time a culture in which they are accepted as the people they have become. The outlaw motorcycle club system can be seen as a society built along militaristic, hierarchical lines, a highly ordered, controlled, and black-and-white world in which individuals may understand implicitly their role, their identity, their *place* in a society.

What I and other outlaw motorcycle club researchers have failed to examine is the effect that the current American "War on Terror" may have on the continued evolution of the system. Once again a handful of Americans find themselves on foreign fields of battle, waging an increasingly unpopular war for unclear reasons. Given the overwhelming influence armed conflict has had on the formation and evolution of the outlaw motorcycle club system, it seems appropriate to examine if and how the role of women in combat units in Afghanistan, Iraq, and other hostile zones fighting the War on Terror changes the perception of women as full members in outlaw and one-percent motorcycle clubs.

Perhaps an additional period is unfolding in the outlaw motorcycle club system even as one reads this essay, a post-transformative period that begins sometimes in the 1980s and includes the effects of popular culture on the biker system. Future research may reveal that certain members of the system seem to have attained something of an iconic status. American society may well regard members of the Hells Angels MC more as pulp fiction characters than as credible menaces to society. Indeed, the context in which many have come to know members of the system is that of cable television, with the History Channel, Discovery Channel, and The Learning Channel all cashing in on the appeal of outlaw biker documentaries, and with members of the Hells Angels MC appearing on television shows such as the Discovery Channel's popular series *Monster Garage*. While certainly not all members of one percent motorcycle clubs are talented mechanics and artisans, perhaps certain members of one-percent clubs are using these new media as venues to broadcast a more positive image of what it means to be an outlaw biker, or more specifically a One Percenter. The image portrayed in cable television shows like *Monster Garage* is not that of a criminal element; indeed, the image is that of a craftsman. Whereas media coverage of the 1960s can be interpreted as casting an image of outlaw motorcycle clubs as destructive forces in society, certain outlets of modern mass media seem willing to broadcast an image that is very much that of creative individuals. And so the evolution of the outlaw motorcycle club system continues.

PART 2

The Outlaw Biker Lifestyle

"An outlaw biker has turned riding in the wind into something to live for. He has made the motorcycle the cornerstone of his identity, the master symbol of his lifestyle and a metaphor for his personal freedom. He has found ordeals and tests that confirm his manhood. He has found ultimate experiences that transcend the earthbound traps of the ordinary. He has found core values around which to focus a lifestyle."

Daniel Wolf

This section displays the many facets of one-percenter biker lifestyle. As with any subculture, this is constantly evolving in response to internal and external pressures. Regional differences also come into play as outlaw biker clubs spread across the globe.

That said, some generalizations are valid, as they form the core values of one-percenter outlaw biker subculture. For example, outlaw bikers adhere to a rigid code of silence, which cloaks their world in secrecy. And one-percenters still embody the spirit of rebellion, rejecting conformist culture. In fact, the original outlaw lifestyle was deliberately calculated to offend, repulse and deny "conventional morality", with bikers relishing any chance to shock the "straights" or "citizens". In more recent times, one-percenter outlaw bikers live by the following creed:

> A 1%er is the one (1%) of a hundred of us who have given up on society and the politicians' one-way law. This is why we look repulsive. We are saying we don't want to be like you or look like you. So stay out of our face. Look at your Brother standing next to you and ask yourself if you would give him half of what you have in your pocket or half of what you have to eat. If a citizen hits your Brother will you be on him without asking why? There is no why. Your Brother isn't always right, but he is always your Brother! It's one in all and all in one. If you don't think this way, then walk away because you are a citizen and don't belong with us. We are Outlaws and members will follow the Outlaws' ways or get out. All members are your Brothers and your family. You will not steal your Brother's possessions, money, woman, class or his humour. If you do, your Brother will do you. (anon)

Biker brothers are equals, united by a love of bikes and loyalty to the club. "Fuck the World" (F.T.W.) is their collective motto and attitude. Bound by a symbolic dress code (the "colours" that adorn the backs of leather vests), a common jargon (bikes are "hogs" or "choppers"), and an inclination to "show class" (i.e. sexual prowess), outlaws bikers may look like casts from the same mould: but they come from a variety of backgrounds. Some have rich families and live off inheritances. Others have jobs that require them to wear suits and ties during office hours. And others scrape by on various government pensions related to disablement (particularly Post-Traumatic Stress Disorder). Finally – as policemen, politicians, and sensationalist journalists, endlessly dwell upon – some are career criminals.

And yet, it seems that most enter the outlaw biker subculture in search of identity. But entry is closely guarded, an initiation process assuring compatibility between the "nominee" or "prospect" and club. This period of "noming" or "prospecting" can be long and gruelling, pushing would-be members beyond the limits most men are prepared to endure. This minimizes the risk of infiltration by undercover cops, while permitting both club and nominee to do the "hard yards" in order to decide if membership is appropriate.

Having successfully completed this rite of passage, the initiate's former self is dead and his new identity is that of "member of the outlaw club".

The selections in this section express the diversity of outlaw biker lifestyle over time, across the globe, and finally, through the "lenses" of individual writers.

THE TALE OF GRANDPA AND THE BOTTLE OF, UH, MILK

Bill Hayes

It was Bill Hayes and his club the Boozefighters that were the key players at Hollister, the event which transformed outlaw bikers from simple non-affiliated members of the American Motorcycle Association to today's "bad boy" one percenters. Bill and his club disbanded in the 1960s but the Boozefighters reformed as a one-percenter outlaw biker club in the late 1990s.

Long before a spate of chopper-building programs flooded cable television, before one-percenter motorcycle clubs blurred the distinction between fame and infamy, and even before those outlaw clubs became targets for federal undercover agents in search of contraband and lucrative book deals, the Boozefighters Motorcycle Club – the original wild ones – backfired onto the American motorcycle scene like a fat-jetted Harley V-twin engine. These young men, restless World War II veterans eager to exercise the freedom they had risked their lives to preserve, fueled by hooch and pretty girls, unconsciously established the archetype of "biker."

One summer weekend in 1947, the BFMC gunned the

stroked engines of their hopped-up Indians and Harleys and set out in search of a little fun. Instead they made history. A sensation-seeking press exaggerated their boisterous antics at the Fourth of July celebration in the sleepy little town of Hollister, California, and in the process created the biker lifestyle.

A few grizzled old bikers who participated in this seminal event are still alive today. A few of them even continue to ride motorcycles and wear the fabled patch of the Boozefighters MC: the three-starred bottle.

Sometimes they have a little explaining to do. A grizzled old biker usually observes the world in a slightly different light than a five-year-old girl.

Usually.

"Grandpa, why do you have that bottle of milk on the back of your vest?"

Old 'n' grizzled wasn't about to begin a long, morally tinged ramble about the difference between milk and moonshine, which one's good for you, which one's not, and why. Instead he answered with a smile and a kid-like shrug that simply said, "Just because." And to a little girl that was OK, that was reason enough. Her grandpa is a member of the original wild ones: The Boozefighters Motorcycle Club. The "bottle" is the centerpiece of the patch, a sacred green icon that symbolizes a brotherhood and a heritage that few are ever fortunate enough to experience. Is it actually supposed to be a bottle of milk? Probably not. But that really is left up to the imagination. The Peter Pan eye-of-the-beholder that is the fanciful essence of an innocent five-year-old is, in many ways, what also fuels the Boozefighters.

The truth is that the founding fathers of the original wild ones were really just big kids themselves, simply trying to recapture some of the youthful fun they lost out on due to the innocence-destroying interruption of a very adult evil known as World War II.

There were no excuses, no laments, no protests. The country needed young soldiers. They went. War changes everyone. And everything. When young vets like Willie Forkner, Robert Burns, and George Manker returned home, it was difficult to forget the horrors of what they had seen. It was hard to shake off the ingrained military regimentation. It was impossible to shed some of the cold-sweat guilt that comes with surviving while so many others did not. And there was an unnerving restlessness in trying to adapt to the calmness and serenity of "normal" living after drowning in chaos. It was easy, however, to adopt an "I don't fit in" kind of attitude. It was easy for returning vets to feel more comfortable with one another than with those from "the outside."

The recipe had been written. The mix was almost complete. All that was needed was the addition of a potent ingredient to spice up the social soup. Something like, say, racing fast motorcycles. The races and rally organized by the American Motorcyclist Association Gypsy Tour in 1947 boiled the soup into a fiery jalapeno-laced stew.

The green stitched bottle that the five-year-old asked her old gramps about was very different from the real bottles that were gathered from the streets of Hollister by an energized photo-journalist during that infamous weekend. The image on that patch is very different from the horde of broken and empty bottles that were carefully arranged around the seemingly drunk and woozy non-Boozefighter (identified as Eddie Davenport or Don Middleton, depending on the source) by San Francisco *Chronicle* photographer Barney Peterson.

The resulting picture was not exactly a work of art that might have emerged from the all-American portfolios of Ansel Adams, Norman Rockwell, or Grant Wood. No. Instead, we were treated to an urban-ugly portrait of the tipsy "model," astride a "nasty, fire-breathing, Milwaukee-steel dragon," viciously framed by those stale-smelling empties and jagged glass shards.

When that twisted version of American Gothic leaped out at the sophisticated readers of *Life* magazine's July 21, 1947, issue, a frightening chill blew through the calm kingdom air. Some of the common village folk wanted to head for the hills, and some wanted to take up pitchforks, sickles, and torches against the strange new beast.

Some wanted to tell the whole story. Sort of. Filmmaker Stanley Kramer produced *The Wild One* six years later, and the snarling cat was out of the bag. The question is, of course, just how sharp were that cat's claws really?

But more than a half-century has already passed, and the legend has grown. The embroidered green bottles went on in

1946, Hollister swept up all that busted brown glass in 1947, *The Wild One* rolled out on black-and-white celluloid at the end of 1953, and the always colorful stories, tales, and traditions have never stopped.

Today, as in 1946, surviving BFMC members are more concerned with carrying on the most important Boozefighter tradition of all: Having fun. One of the early members, Jack Lilly, has a credo that is woven into the very fabric of that holy green patch when it comes to having a good time: "Do it now!" They did. And they still do.

When that cat flew out of the bag, the popularized fear was that he was bent on shredding and hunting prey. In reality that fast, sleek animal was just living up to his reputation for curiosity and playful prowling. For wanting to sniff out every aspect of life. Eat, drink, fool around, chase an occasional mouse, cough up a hairball or two after a tad too much consumption, and, in general, just enjoy the heck out of living.

"Every original Boozefighter I've met," club historian Jim "JQ" Quattlebaum says, " – Wino, J. D. and Jim Cameron, Red Dog, Jim Hunter, Roccio, Les, Gil, Lilly, and Vern Autrey – all exhibit signs that they are made of common threads: Spirited and daring character, challenging competitiveness, strong bonding friendship, a caring and giving nature, the love of motorcycling, and brotherhood with bikers. They're honest and law-abiding citizens, but not beyond the embellishment of a good story." Even in their old age they've stayed active. No rocking chairs for them! Still riding motorcycles as long as their health and bodies would allow.

"Yeah, they let off a lot of steam, partied hearty, got jailed for getting drunk, got a lot of speeding tickets, and occasionally duked it out with redneck bar patrons that hassled them . . . and sometimes they fought with each other. Then they'd sit down together and laugh about it over a beer.

"But no original ever got put in jail for a serious crime like murder or drugs. They got along with all other MC clubs, sponsored races, baseball games, and different events with other clubs. They never considered themselves outlaws the way that term is used today. This was a term that the AMA applied to riders and clubs who didn't follow the structured AMA racing rules back in the 1940s.

"And the originals didn't discriminate toward any ethnic, religious, or political group. Wino said, 'We fought side by side for all Americans to have freedom of choice.'

"That freedom also extended to the members' choice of bikes to ride, as long as they could keep up! Indians and Harleys were the most available, so they were the most used. However, many old BFers started acquiring the Triumph because of its improved racing speed. Hendersons and other pre-World War II bikes were used, too. When the BSA was introduced in the 1950s, it became the bike of choice for the still-racing BFers, like Jim Hunter, Jim Cameron, Ernie and Johnny Roccio.

"Present day BFMC requires members to ride an American or World War II – allied brand of bike. But some exceptions are made in some chapters for special consideration. 'Brooklyn' is allowed to ride a touring Moto Guzzi in honor of his grandfather, who fought with the Italian underground resistance against the Germans.

"The present-day Boozefighters revere our originals and the club's founders for their intent, purpose, and priorities: Family, job, and club brotherhood. We're family men, engaged in legitimate businesses and careers, enjoying getting together as a social group for parties, rides, and special events. We're into this thing strictly for having harmless, good clean fun. We couldn't care less about 'territory' and things like that.

"We don't push religion on anyone but we do have a national chaplain, 'Irish Ed' Mahan, who, in a nondenominational way, conducts Bible study class every Tuesday night, performs legal marriages and funerals, and visits members that request special counseling or have illness issues. He also conducts Easter sunrise services at our clubhouse every year. It's attended by a lot of friendly clubs.

"And we're involved in giving back to society through fundraising, toy runs, March-of-Dimes, Wish With Wings and such. We have a blood bank for members. We're active in motorcycle rights organizations, and many of us are state delegates to our respective political parties.

"We believe in peaceful coexistence with all clubs, but we don't wear support patches for any other organization. And we don't believe in displaying any antisociety or anti-American items."

Apparently some of the original members' priorities and the

club's eventual evolution based on those principles were ne-
glected just a bit in *The Wild One*. But, with another shrug of
the shoulders, that, too, is OK. The Boozefighters are comfortable with who they are. And who they were. They're very
proud of their founders. And they're happy with the continu-
ance of the all-important "fun" tradition.

They're content with their personalities being somewhere in
between Brando's "Johnny," Marvin's "Chino," and the brilliant 1940s/1950s abandon of, oh maybe, a Red Skelton or a
Jackie Gleason.

In a letter dated September 18, 1946, the San Francisco
Boozefighter prez, Benny "Kokomo" Mckell, wrote to the
L.A. chapter to order four club sweaters for his newest members. They had just passed the rigorous series of seven tests
required of a "prospect":

1. Get drunk at a race meet or cycle dance.
2. Throw lemon pie in each other's faces.
3. Bring out a douche bag where it would embarrass all
   the women (then drink wine from it, etc.).
4. Get down and lay on the dance floor.
5. Wash your socks in a coffee urn.
6. Eat live goldfish.
7. Then, when blind drunk, trust me ("Kokomo") to
   shoot beer bottles off of your heads with my .22.

Would Johnny or Chino do all that?
No.
Would Skelton or Gleason?
Probably.
Would the Boozefighters?
Just ask 'em.

So, are all of the tales and legends surrounding the Boozefighters sworn gospel?

JQ answers that (more or less) in an interesting discussion
about memory and motorcycle lore:

"If you ask me today what I did last night, I'd be hard
pressed to remember all the details precisely right. I know

I started off with 65 or 70 dollars in my pocket and got home with about 7. For the life of me I can't remember what I spent the money on. But to get the story more accurate, that doesn't count that $100 bill I had stashed away for an emergency. Man, I hope I didn't blow that, too. . . .

"Ask the original wild ones what happened fifty years ago and they, too, are hard pressed to remember the precise facts. Once, sitting with three such old-timers, I witnessed a heated – but friendly – debate about what club one of them raced for during the Hollister melee. They finally all agreed on one thing: Whether it was the 13 Rebs, Yellow Jackets, or Boozefighters, they all had one heck of a good time, excluding the jail time for rowdiness, of course.

"I had a good time last night, too. (That is, unless I can't find my $100 bill.)

"But anyway, if Patrick Henry had said, 'If I don't get my rear end outta here, I'm gonna get it shot off,' and some historical writer quoted him as actually saying, 'Give me liberty or give me death,' then what kind of respect would you have for that writer? As historian, I've had to dig deep into the facts about the Boozefighters, and there are times I wished I hadn't found out that some stories just weren't so. But then again, the more I dug, the more I found out that there are great stories that were never told.

"They need to be told, so we'll tell them. Some are fantastic, but I'll let the listener or reader sort out what they want to believe. Most importantly, though, the telling of these stories will be geared to the essence of truth as the old-timers wanted to remember it."

And the heart of that truth – those stories – beats with the same wide-eyed wonder that drives the fertile imagination of that inquisitive five-year-old.

Is there milk in that bottle, some 90-proof hooch, or a genie that will pop out and take us directly into a unique and exotic land, a growling jungle that members of the button-down, mainstream, overly protected, boy-in-the- bubble society fear, envy, and would give their eye teeth to journey into?

Maybe it's all three.

HELL ON WHEELS

Columbus B. Hopper and
Johnny "Big John" Moore

"Big John" was President of a one-percenter outlaw biker club for seventeen years. This article, which appeared in a journal, was the result of his collaboration with the academic, Columbus B. Hopper. It includes a discussion of the role of women in the outlaw biker club scene circa 1967–90 in North America. The work is considered a classic and has historical importance. The scene has changed since this early work, which highlights sexual practices indulged in by outlaw bikers at the time, as well as their overall relations with women.

Outlaw cyclists are generally male and between 21 and 45 years of age. The average age for a club studied was 34. There are black gangs, white gangs, and Mexican and other Spanish-speaking gangs. Although race does not appear to be important as a creed or philosophical orientation to them, virtually all of the clubs are racially unmixed. And it should be mentioned that the bikers who are in prisons, as prisoners have done generally, band together along racial lines.

While most outlaws have little formal education (one group averaged 9 years), a few have attended college, at least for a short period of time. Many are veterans of military service but many others are not. Unlike street gangs whose members are local juveniles, a motorcycle gang's members are from a variety of places. Rarely will a large club (they always call themselves clubs rather than gangs) have more than half of its membership drawn from the city or state in which it is chartered.

The only common factors all outlaws share are a love of motorcycles and a strong sense of being outcasts from society. Although intergang fights are often vicious and deadly, all outlaw groups feel a sense of brotherhood which separates them from "citizens" or non-members. While different clubs hate each other, they still respect all outlaws as people who share their values, the way professional soldiers admire enemies who are brave.

The Impact of the Media

Most people have learned about outlaw motorcycle gangs from the mass media. Since the media cover only sporadic and spectacular biker events, only a few clubs have been thrust into the national spotlight. Consequently, a gang's power and influence may not be related to the attention it has had. In California, the media was focussed on the Hell's Angels. Nevertheless, there are other California clubs that consider themselves equal to if not stronger than the Angels. The Hessions, Misfits, Galloping Gooses, and Vagos are all major clubs in that state. The Mongols are the largest club in California but they have had little press attention nationally.

Due in part to their vast publicity, the Hell's Angels have become the most widespread outlaws. They were founded in 1950 at Fontana, California, but they now have chapters across the United States and in Canada, England, Switzerland, Germany, Austria, and Australia. They are headed by the Oakland chapter which is now considered their mother chapter.

Much of the Angels' notoriety has come about because they have on occasions consorted with popular authors and famous rock groups. Other outlaw groups accuse the Angels of having courted fame rather than having it thrust upon them.

In the Southeast, the Outlaws receive most press attention. There are about 35 chapters of Outlaws that extend from

Florida to Canada and they have at least one chapter in California. Their greatest concentration is in Ohio. The Outlaws became notorious in the Southeast in November of 1967 when three members of a club in Florida were charged with the crucifixion of an 18 year old girl on the limb of an oak tree (*The Atlanta Constitution*, 1967). In recent years, the Outlaws and Hell's Angels have had an ongoing feud in the Southeast which has resulted in several deaths and much newspaper space. Three Outlaws and two of their associates were killed in one night in the summer of 1979 in Charlotte, North Carolina (*Charlotte Observer*, 1979).

Although the Dirty Dozen of Arizona is a very strong club in the Southwest, the Bandidos of Texas have received more press coverage in that area of the country. They were called to the attention of the nation in July of 1979 when ABC's program "Twenty-Twenty" did a feature on them. Since their television debut, the Bandidos have been expanding. They now have at least one chapter chartered in Mississippi.

The Northeast is the stronghold of the Pagan Nation, the club that dominates the biker news in that region. The Pagans began around 1959 in Prince George County, Maryland. Because of increased pressure from law enforcement agencies, their national headquarters was moved to Marcus Hook, Pennsylvania, in 1975. The Pagan Nation is a powerful club numbering more than 1,000 members, stretching from Connecticut to California. Its strongest chapters are in Pennsylvania, New Jersey, Delaware and Maryland.

Relatively Unknown Clubs

It would be almost impossible to list all the clubs we have discovered in our research. There are many strong clubs which keep a low profile, getting little newspaper space or television time because they will not allow photographers or reporters around them. But wherever one might travel in the United States, he could see outlaws defiantly flying the colors of organizations with the names of Warlocks, Savages, Nomads, Invaders, Devil's Henchmen, Grim Reapers, Iron Horsemen, Devil's Disciples, Satan's Slaves, Pharoahs, Stompers, Gypsy Jokers, Iron Cross, Sinners, Chosen Few, Ghost Riders, Satan's Dead, Hell Cats, Family and Barbarians. There is even an outlaw club in Hawaii called Alii (Chiefs) composed of native Hawaiians.

Club Cards

Most outlaws carry club cards (usually the size of business cards) which they give to riders in other clubs they feel deserve the honor. They are called courtesy cards and they are not given out lightly. Members might give them to people they partied with, or to clubs with which they are alinged when intergang conflicts are taking place. The cards show the club name, chapter location and usually the club insignia. Some groups list club officers on the cards and provide a place to write the names of the giver and recipient. Often, cards have popular sayings printed on them such as "Ride to Live, Live to Ride." Members occasionally write the reason the card was given on the back of the card.

Clubs sometimes have a special card they give to motorists they help. It is not often that outlaws stop and help automobile drivers whose cars have broken down, but it does occur. When help is given, the motorist is handed a card which says: "You have been helped by some members of [a particular club]." Thus outlaw cards have two functions: one promotes brotherhood; the other is for public relations.

The Motorcycle

It is impossible to exaggerate the importance of the motorcycle to the outlaw clubs. One would expect riders of motorcycles to be fond of them and to emphasize maintenance and riding skills. The outlaws' focus on motorcycles, however, transcends a simple fondness for the machines. The motorcycle is so dominant as to render other interests not only secondary but trivial. Most of their activities and most of their conversations are devoted to bikes. They discuss new models, old models and compare the merits of each in detail. They debate repair and maintenance techniques as thoroughly as surgeons deliberate surgical procedures.

Since one must be experienced with the mechanics of motorcycles to become a member of a motorcycle gang, a person who is exceptionally adept at diagnosing engine problems is given much prestige; he is looked upon as a guru. To the outlaws, the motorcycle is almost literally a sacred object, having the power to transport them beyond ordinary experiences. Individuals who are especially gifted as repairmen share an edge of the aura of the bike itself. Being a good mechanic alone will not bring high status within a club. Mechanical knowledge must be accompanied by the other values bikers hold dear. In the terminology of the outlaws, one must be "righteous" in all respects.

The favorite motorcycle of outlaws is the Harley Davidson 74. In recent years, foreign models have been preferred by individual outlaws who choose a bike for its power and maneuverability regardless of make. The Harley Davidson, however, has a special place of honor.

An outlaw strips off all the accessories and customizes a bike to his own taste. He changes it so much that it does not resemble the machine he started with. The fenders, handle bars, seat, gas tank, shift lever and other parts are changed, painted and chromed. The motor is hopped up for extra power. Only after long hours of devoted work does a motorcycle become an outlaw's "chopper."

A biker's motorcycle is so revered that nonmembers cannot appreciate its significance to the owner. An outlaw will literally attack anyone who is disrespectful to his vehicle. The rampage at Altamont apparently was triggered by a biker stabbing a person who accidentally knocked the outlaw's motorcycle over. Deadly fights have resulted from such things as spilling beer on a motorcycle or a jesting remark about one. Many outlaws affix a sticker to their motorcycles which says: "If you value your life as much as I value my bike, don't fuck with it."

Colors

Colors is the term applied to the club jacket. Although popularly depicted as wearing black leather, the great majority of outlaws wear a simple denim jacket with the sleeves removed, giving it the appearance of a vest. The club emblem is sewn on the back of the jacket. The insignia for the Hell's Angels is a winged skull with a cracked head wearing a motorcycle helmet. Le Croix, a Mississippi Club, uses an iron cross with a dragon as their insignia. Above the insignia is the upper rocker which is the club name. The lower rocker, beneath the insignia, gives the chapter name or location.

Next to the insignia are the letters "MC" which stand for motorcycle club. On the front of the jackets they wear swastikas, Luftwaffe insignias or iron crosses to shake people up rather than to express political sentiment. On some of the jackets a patch which bears the number "13" is worn. The outlaws say it stands for bad luck, but the police claim it stands for the 13th letter of the alphabet, "M," which in turn stands for marijuana and signifies the wearer is a user.

Almost all outlaws wear the "1%" patch. Some years ago an officer of the American Motorcycle Association, in defense of motorcycling, stated that 99% of all motorcyclists were decent and honorable people and that only 1% of the people who rode motorcycles gave the rest a bad name. Since that proclamation, outlaws have proudly worn the "1%" patch.

Each outlaw's jacket is decorated to his liking. It is impossible to find two that are the same. Many wear a dog chain because they like the way it looks and also because a chain is a good weapon which may be carried legally. Each individual has his own collection of items chosen to shock citizens or to make them angry. We have seen colors with George Wallace buttons on them and others with the Church of God perfect attendance medals. One outlaw's colors indicated that he was a member of the American Medical Association. Each outlaw expresses his individuality in the way he decorates his motorcycle and his colors, and he intends to be irritating to citizens. He would like to look bad enough and disgusting enough to show the world that he is not part of conventional society. Outlaws proudly display the "FTW" patch which means "fuck the world."

Terminology of Outlaws

The outlaw subculture is based on terms which are esoteric. In order to understand the outlaw bikers, one must know a few terms which most outlaws use frequently. The following list is not complete but it does include the basic concepts:

Colors: The club emblem and jacket.

Chopper: A motorcycle customized as described.

Citizen: A citizen is a nonmenber of an outlaw club.

Crash: To pass out drunk; it also means to have an accident. When one has an accident due to going around a curve at excessive speeds, however, this is referred to as "going over the high side."

Garbage Wagon: A stock motorcycle with standard parts and fittings intact, loaded with saddlebags. Most clubs' by-laws forbid members to wear their colors while riding a garbage wagon.

Hog: A Harley Davidson.

Legal: In conformity with club by-laws and customs. Each member has a legal name (club name) such as "Trenchmouth," "Trash," or "Little Jesus." Thus when an outlaw talks about something being legal, he is referring to his club's rules and not the criminal code of his state.

Righteous: This term is similar to the term legal but it is more subtle. It refers to a broader range of things which bikers approve. Roughly, it means that something is to a biker's liking. One might describe a wild party as righteous or a particularly fine chopper as righteous, and if an individual is described as righteous, you know he meets fully the character standards of the outlaws.

Love: When you like something as much as you like your motorcycle. One biker's "Old lady" told us she knew her husband had grown to truly love her because when she crashed on her motorcycle the last time, he looked to see if she was injured before rushing to examine the bike.

Mama: A promiscuous girl who is willing to "pull a train" or have sex with all members of a gang. The term is used only for girls who regularly associate with a club.

Originals: Jeans that have not been washed in three years. A member's originals are "baptized" at his initiation into some clubs when all members urinate on them.

Outlaw: A member of an outlaw club. The term is not applied to a motorcyclist unless he is wearing the colors of some outlaw club.

Participate: To aid a member in a fight by ganging his opponent.

Run: An all day or weekend trip the gang makes as a group. It is an occasion for parties. A run may last several days but ordinarily only two or three. A club has a run about one or two times a month.

Sheep: Clubs sometimes require that a new member bring a woman to his initiation. As part of the ceremony, all members have sex with the "sheep" as the woman is called. She might become a mama if she becomes a regular associate.

Show Class: An individual shows class when he does something malicious or shocking to citizens. If one shows enough class, he might be awarded a *Gross Badge* which indicates that the member has been exceptional in his ability to show class.

Snuff: To kill or be killed.

Turn Out: To be initiated as a member. In the case of a woman, to pull train for the first time.

Wings: Many outlaws wear a set of wings which indicate that one has performed oral sex on a female in front of members of his club. The color of the wings indicates more specifically what a member has done. Green wings indicate that the woman had venereal disease while red wings reveal the woman to have been menstruating. Brown wings mean that the act was performed on the anal aperture; purple means the woman was dead. Gold wings signify that the wearer has done all of the above.

Outlaw Rituals

Although each club varies in its specific ceremonies, the outlaw motorcycle subculture revolves around rituals which help make the clubs viable organizations. When a gang breaks up, it is usually from dissention within; outside forces have not had success in trying to suppress them.

The first ritual an outlaw is exposed to and one he never forgets is his initiation. The initiate in some clubs brings a "sheep" who is willing to submit to intercourse with each member of the club. Frequently a new member's pants are pulled down and he is flogged while everyone looks on. Often he is doused with urine, paint and other substances. As a final touch, each member may urinate on his jeans.

Another important ritual is marriage. After an outlaw goes from mama to mama, he may decide to get married. Many outlaws get married in church or in civil ceremonies, but some marry by their club code. There are two ways of getting married in most clubs. The first is performed by a member of the club who is called "preacher"; he is not ordained but he does usually know a lot of Scripture. He preaches a sermon which is followed by a short ceremony held in the presence of members and guests from other clubs. All members wear their colors. When the preacher has pronounced the couple man and wife, the couple embrace and kiss. After kissing the bride, the groom kisses all of his buddies on the lips; the preacher is kissed last.

The second type of wedding is performed by the president of the club. He reads passages from the Harley Davidson motorcycle manual, and then pronounces them man and wife. After the traditional kissing is over, the newlyweds drive off on a motorcycle with beer cans tied to it. If they want a divorce, they simply rip up the handbook used in the wedding ceremony.

The life of a cyclist is filled with harassment, troubles and death. Even in death, the outlaws have their own rituals. When an outlaw dies, he is buried wearing his colors or his colors are placed on top of the casket. All members attend the funeral wearing their colors to show respect. Usually, there are members from other clubs present. At times there may be as many as 300 outlaws who ride solemnly behind the hearse to the cemetery.

We attended a small outlaw funeral in Mississippi. One of the Le Croix members was killed on a run to Florida. The club held a short ceremony in a gulf coast church. After the sermon, the casket was driven to the cemetery followed by the club members on their motorcycles. The colors of the deceased were laid upon the casket. Parts of the motorcycle were put in the grave with him. That night the club had a party. They were sorry that their brother had died but they felt that he was in a place where the citizens and cops would not bother him.

Outlaw Culture as Religion

Outlaw motorcycle clubs in several ways resemble religious sects. A sect is a small fellowship of converts who seek to realize the good life in a highly stylized and specialized way. A sect does not attempt to win the world; rather, it seeks exclusiveness. It is convinced that it alone has found the answer to the way people should live. At times, sects prescribe specific patterns of dress and set themselves apart from the rest of the world through fervent, ritualistic activities. In essence, a sect rejects the popular or mainstream social environment in which it exists.

Although most people think outlaw clubs anti-religious, many clubs have a preacher who conforms roughly to that role in sects. Outlaw riders talk about God often and they believe that the good life is to be found on a motorcycle. They wish to separate themselves from citizens as much as possible and they wear distinctive clothes to show the world their indifference to its values.

In strong clubs, the members form a brotherhood which is based on love. The motto of the Hell's Angels is "All on one and one on all," The phrase means that an Angel must fight for his club no matter how badly he is outnumbered. Outlaws often are killed fighting for their brothers. In their view, they are laying down their lives for their friends.

Cyclists and Crime

Outlaw cyclists have since their origin had much trouble with the law. They want to ride in a way that society will not allow. A man knows before his initiation that the life of an outlaw will not be easy, that he will be scarred and do some jail time.

There is currently police and governmental investigation of outlaw motorcycle clubs concerning their involvement in organized crime, particularly large-scale dealing in drugs, firearms, welfare fraud, murder for hire and other criminal operations. Some contend that outlaw clubs are not only getting involved in such activities, but that they are rapidly moving into a leading role in them.

Our research has not shed any light on this matter. It seems clear that outlaws, as individuals or as chapters of one or two clubs, are getting into crime for economic reasons. The great majority of outlaws, however, remain in their traditional pattern. They raise hell as clubs and the crime they commit is as individuals or in small units of two or three, usually violent felonies which stem from interpersonal conflicts.

The number of bikers in prisons or in criminal justice

processing shows that they do not pose a threat in the general manner of organized crime for they are easy to arrest and convict. Organized crime has presented a problem because the participants are apt to dress and act like everyone else, following a conventional life style while earning money in illegal ways. Outlaws certainly use drugs frequently and, like all users of modest means, they deal to make money to buy their own drugs. The great majority of bikers live at about the poverty level, a fact which seems inconsistent with large-scale crime for profit.

It is nonetheless true that the outlaw subculture is growing and with growth comes change. The clubs are more complex. Some have moved away from the original types who got drunk together about once a week, drank beer, thundered their bikes on the streets and took over beaches in a display of hedonistic machismo. Bikers now have more frequent meetings, more knowledge of legal procedures, and more company in the world of deviant behavior.

The whole range of deviant behavior in America has become more complex. Interpretations of all deviants and the roles they play are changing. In some instances, they are being viewed as less threatening, as in the case of homosexuals. In the case of the motorcycle outlaws, tolerance is decreasing, and they are being defined as greater threats. The most likely event is that neither homosexuals nor outlaws have changed as much as has the society in which they exist.

We have not devoted much time as yet to the question of why individuals become members of the outlaw motorcycle subculture. It is obvious that one does not become an outlaw overnight, but through a process which covers a long period of time. One could not become an outlaw quickly if he wanted to because he has to prove his commitment in stages.

Logically, there are two forces operating: motorcycling and alienation. Only a few of the individuals who acquire a love for motorcycles become alienated from society and a majority of the alienated do not ride motorcycles. The outlaw has both of these traits and both seem equally reflected in his life. Somehow a man must develop a large amount of both before he is initiated into an outlaw club.

From our study of outlaws, we believe that the love for motorcycles comes first for most outlaws. Many outlaws have loved motorcycles since their earliest memories and began working in motorcycle shops and garages, often without pay. Gradually they moved from a general love for motorcycles to a special love for the chopper, the epitome of a fast motorcycle.

When one becomes a "chopper freak" and starts customizing his motorcycle, his sources of information are those who ride choppers – outlaws. When one has acquired knowledge of bikes and skill and daring in riding them, he has developed the generic trait of the outlaw. And he may become labeled as a motorcycle bum. At this point most stay in the main stream. They finish high school, go to college or start working at a civilian or military occupation. They retain their love for bikes and their commitment to society as well, sometimes with frustration.

The outlaws are drawn from those who love motorcycles and somehow begin a series of experiences which promote disenchantment with society. Some we have studied began their disillusionment as service men in World War II, Korea and Vietnam. Others become alienated in civilian life, but all developed the attitude that leads them to wear the "FTW" patch and feel born to lose. The age of the average biker indicates that most have come into the outlaw culture rather late, after having tried other things. The subculture seems a mixture of retreatist and rebel adaptations. When individuals come into the biker world, they tend to stay until they are killed, die of dissipation or go to prison for a long term where they continue to be bikers without wheels.

THE ONE-PERCENTER SUBCULTURE

Randal Montgomery

Randal Montgomery's selection is now widely regarded as a rather negative view which offends most bikers and is embraced by police. Randal was a "hang around" at various outlaw biker clubs. He claims to have been a member of a one percent club and produced his work after almost twenty years of being "up close and personal" with the one-percenter lifestyle. The piece describes his take on initiation rights, earning one's "wings", "showing class", the biker "code of silence", and also criminality: a topic of major concern since the early 1990s.

It is important to differentiate between the vast majority of "normal" motorcycle riders and the "deviant" minority. In fact it is to emphasize their peculiarity that members of the latter group refer to themselves as "One Percenters". The label "Outlaws" is also commonly used, and very appropriately, given the disproportionate involvement in illegal activities.

Ideally the layman can tell a true "Outlaw" from an ordinary motorcyclist by the fact that, at least when in a group, Outlaws wear their "colours". Colours are dirty blue denim jackets with sleeves ripped off, and with the club crest on the back. On the front left lapel are usually found smaller crests. Common is a diamond-shaped one which reads "1%". Also common are nicknames, rank (if applicable) and bits of jewelry designating sexual exploits (eg. "red wings", "brown wings"). At one time replicas of WW1 German "Iron Crosses" were worn on chains about the neck, and small swastika crests were fairly common. The motorcycle's brand insignia is also commonly worn as a badge or crest. These, then, are "colours", which in warm weather constitute the only clothing above the waist, and in colder weather are worn overtop of black leather jackets.

The Outlaw rider was once also easily distinguished by his "chopper"; usually a stripped-down, customized Harley Davidson motorcycle. The "Chopper Hog", while the stereotyped Outlaw machine, was not quite "de rigueur" insofar as some riders preferred Triumphs and BSA's. However, all this has been recently complicated by several factors. Firstly, colours are rarely worn anymore because they invite harassment by police and resentful citizens. Meanwhile many pseudo-Outlaws (so-called "Cowboys", "Dudes", or "Weekend Posers") have appeared with choppers and cut-off denims (sans crests). Thirdly, the One Percenters have gradually come to accept certain Japanese motorcycles, while many of the "straight" motorcycle riders have dropped their prejudice against a certain model of Harley-Davidson. With the old brand loyalties dying out, the make of the machine (so long as it is a large displacement four stroke which has been chopped) no longer distinguishes the Outlaws from the weekend Posers.

Final definition of the subject-matter again rests on the popular term "motorcycle gangs". As already emphasized, millions of males (and a few females) ride motorcycles for transportation, sport, or hobby. Only a few thousand belong to the Outlaw subculture. But the label "motorcycle gang" is misleading for another reason. Most One Percenters belong to formally-organized clubs rather than informal gangs. Weekend Cowboys sometimes form short-lived gangs, often only for an afternoon, but these are not the fellows who generate most of the bad publicity. Having belonged to both types of social groups, the author is well aware of the differences. Unlike the clubs, the gangs have no name, regular meetings, clubhouse, regulations, officers, dues, elections, etc.

Masculine Adulthood

Firstly, there is the distinct impression an observer gets that members of Outlaw clubs are striving for adult masculine status; even overcompensating for any real or felt deficiencies. The Big Tough Man image is flaunted in many ways. There is the adulation of physical height, muscles, width and obesity. Fellows considered by most people to be ugly and repulsive due to their excessive body hair, barrel chests, tree-trunk arms, and beer bellies are ideal in Outlaw bikers' eyes.

There is much boasting of sexual activity, and an obsession with getting more; often expressed in the form of crude, gross, supposedly funny remarks.

Of course there is always the big motorcycle which swells the rider with feelings of pride and power (especially when pedestrians are intimidated or impressed). Outlaws invariably ride the biggest bikes on the market, and then extend the frames and front forks to make the over-all dimensions even greater. The long front forks (ludicrously and unsafely extended by as much as three feet) are obviously phallic extensions resembling a chromed steel erection. The sole purposes of such modifications are "to look good" (though to non-Outlaws they are ugly) and "to show class" (i.e. to create certain effects on onlookers and to distinguish a chopper from a standard bike).

This despite the fact that such modifications involve considerable time and effort, cost hundreds of dollars, create great stress on the fork tubes and steering head, and make the machine handle so awkwardly that only a big brave man is capable of maintaining some control. The Outlaw chopper is a machine only Outlaws want to ride, and which only Outlaws are stupid and reckless enough to ride. The One Percenter motorcycle is good for only one thing, showing-off.

Other Tough Guy attributes are the ornaments and jewelry (chrome swastikas, etc. . . . .) which Sonny Barger (Hell's Angels' incarcerated President) is quick to point out, have no serious fascist implications other than instilling fear and deference.

Weapons are also part of the One Percenter subculture. Motorcycle chains are often worn as belts. Other than "style", the idea is not so much a spare chain for the bike as a super effective weapon which does not legally classify as one. A 1967 raid on the clubhouse of the Satan's Choice during their first annual national convention) netted a sawed-off shotgun, a .32 calibre revolver, baseball bats, spike-studded belts, chains, knives, grass knuckles and two leather whips. The Vagabonds (Toronto's largest Outlaw club) used to wear steel toed-boots. Again, these could not legally be classified as weapons (steel toes are required in many construction sites and warehouses, and could prevent toe injuries in a motorcycle crash). But these steel tips were on the outside of the boots, one quarter inch thick, and came to a sharp point.

Finally there is the dark clothing (black leather, black cotton shirts, black or blue denims) to effect a sinister image and to give a uniform look. The over-all impression, especially in Canadian clubs who prefer black to blue, is of the Italian fascists or Hitler SS (except for the long hair).

Rites of Adolescence

On the second part of the analysis, it must be said that the Outlaws to practice many of the rites of adolescence.

In regard to decoration (tattoos, jewelery, costumes, fashion accessories) they are the paramount of all North American groups. Common are bandanas, armbands, heavy chrome belt buckles depicting the motorcycle insignia or club initials, chain belts, little chains on boots, single earrings, and big rings.

In regard to the acquisition of new names and language, nickname and argot are conspicuously present. In fact, most members of the Outlaw subculture do not know their peers' real names, nor the proper terms for many sex acts and cycle parts. Ignorance of "biker lingo" marks the outsider. A stranger at an Outlaw gathering or in a chopper shop will be amazed at the bizarre nicknames people go by, and even a straight motorcycle mechanic would be perplexed by such chopper terms as "knucklehead", "panhead", "shovelhead", "mousetrap", "hand banger", "coffin tanks", "Fourfive", "pie wagon", "trumpet", "Hog", "full decker", "sissy bar", "risers", "gooseneck", "jockey shift", "tweek bar", etc.

Break from home and assimilation by the new group is another adolescent rite typical of One Percenters. Those few

Outlaws who still live at their parents' home treat it merely as a crash pad and food source. A Satan's Choice member recently boasted to the author of how he had staggered home drunk and hungry early one morning to be unexpectedly greeted by his father and a hot meal; but as soon as his father attempted a conversation with the son, he cursed, picked up the plate, and threw the meal in his father's face. (This biker could not understand why the author was not suitably impressed, nor why the author asked "Why?")

In regard to sexual ambivalence and homosexuality, the author's first encounter with the Road Gypsies made him walk out of the "meeting" when he saw a few of the members engaged in homosexual "horseplay" activity. There was clumsy grabbing, embracing, and rolling around on the bed. There were jocular "threats" to strip and get more involved, and the levity and girls' giggling was not enough to convince him that some type of orgy would not ensue. The President followed the author outside to ask him why he had suddenly "split". When the author told him he had expected a motorcycle club meeting rather than a homosexual party, he was assured that "Those guys were just fooling around" and that the subsequent meeting would be more serious and organized.

Of course, in a similar vein, the Hell's Angels are notorious for their public displays of French kissing and flying-tackle embraces. Again, they claim this is just "to freak out the squares". The author has a news photo of an arrested Satan's Choice member blowing kisses in a policeman's ear. Despite Outlaw disclaimers that such activities are simply horseplay or showing-off to upset onlookers, one is reminded of the sexual duality in human beings. Innate homosexual tendencies can either be socially repressed or encouraged and just because the Outlaw biker subculture is less repressive is not to say that its members are "more queer" than the rest of us.

Regarding the rites of "hazing" and ordeals to prove fitness to become members, the subculture again jibes with the argument of Bloch and Niederhoffer. For the present, suffice it to say that there is quite a long and serious period of observation, servitude, and insult before an applicant's membership bid is voted on. This period is called "striking", and aspirants are known as "strikers". In some clubs, a striker must also perform a feat or ordeal or test of courage. For example, several years ago in Toronto a female car driver was forced to pull off the expressway by an Outlaw rider. In full view of passing traffic, he ordered the young woman to get out of the car and remove her panties. She complied, expecting to be raped. However, the Outlaw simply stuffed the panties into his pocket and roared off. Doubtless his "prize" proved he had successfully completed his feat, and he was accepted as a member of the club for which he was striking.

Regarding economic profit for older men, the club presidents (usually a few years older than most members) receive all sorts of booty and tribute from their members and from allied clubs. For example, Johnny Sombrero (founder and president of the Black Diamond Riders) in his heyday received both a new Harley and a new Cadillac every year, as well as a portion of the dues and numerous gifts of liquor. The author was told by an ex-Cycle Baron that senior Vagabonds exploit junior members for small amounts of money and labour. One Road Gypsy president had the quaint habit of selling parts and even whole motorcycles which members left in his garage for a period of weeks. When they discovered their possessions had disappeared, and protested, he offered to return the items for exorbitant "storage fees". He was always "borrowing" beer and money. Similarly, an older ex-Californian member of the Road Gypsies still owes several younger members hundreds of dollars for rent, gasoline, dope, food, and clothes which he always promised to pay, but never "managed".

In regard to incorporation into new roles and older groups, the One Percenter club represents an older group and a new role for the new young member. The status of membership in an Outlaw club should not be underestimated by naïve, middle class observers. An Outlaw is akin to a career professional in this respect. The author has heard people cited as That's Big Al – he's a "Vag", or "I don't know his name but he belongs to the Choice".

In regard to the sex fertility theme, there is constant sex banter and crude jokes and anecdotes. A more ritualized aspect is the attainment of red wings, a metal badge (similar to airforce wings) painted red and awarded to members who perform cunnilingus on a menstruating woman. Consensual validation of this feat requires that it be performed before a group of onlooking members. There are other "merit badges" for equally deviant sexual activities. Further in regard to the "fertility theme", one Road Gypsy president was constantly heard boasting of his "four kids floating around Lake Ontario". He acquired the nickname "Pappy Stokes" and, of course, Outlaw motorcyclists are notorious for their "gang bangs" wherein one woman is forced to submit to the entire membership in rapid succession.

While a middle class person may cultivate his or her personality by standing in front of a mirror (checking on demeanour and dress) and by consulting dictionaries (to improve vocabulary), there are lower class and Outlaw equivalents. Some of these "achieved personality traits" are styles of standing, leaning, sitting, and walking (e.g., swaggering, shuffling, clicking heels, slouching), and styles of speech (hip argot, sexual references, "country" accents). There is also a form of non-verbal communication (similar to ideo-motor cues in experimental psychology, and everyday "body language") consisting of glares and sullen frowns (called "heavy eyeshots" in Toronto's corner boy subculture). As Yablonsky noted, gang members tend to caricature or exaggerate minor personality quirks because they receive positive reinforcement from their peers when they act out such roles. A member who casually uses a certain phrase or mannerism and finds it well-received by the group is motivated to keep doing it. He may receive a nickname based on it, which motivates him to live up to his image. In any gang there are such roles as silent cynic, loud mouth, tough guy, clown and crazy. People with personalities slightly in these veins tend to be typecast into them, and soon act them out habitually.

Thompson describes several "characters" or "types" in Hell's Angels whose intrinsic personalities were "developed" so as to receive rewards from peers. An aggressive person became more violent, an erratic person became totally unpredictable, a drug user became an indiscriminate addict, a verbal ponderer became the equivalent of a "resident philosopher", a girl chaser became a "sex pervert", etc. In all such cases, appropriate nicknames were supplied by other club members. Examples were: Charger Charlie the Child Molester, Little Jesus, Freewheelin' Frank, Big Frank, Magoo, Frenchy, Tiny,

Big Al, Mother Miles, Zorro, Terry the Tramp, Skip, Bag-master, Gut, Dirty Ed and Mouldy Marvin.

One could argue that this development is opposite to that found in the middle class wherein people are urged to tone down their peculiarities, and those who don't are psychoana-lyzed in terms of acting out their insecurities. Even so, "role development" of a specific nature does occur via behaviourist (reward or disapproval) techniques in both the middle class, and delinquent and Outlaw biker subcultures. In the One Percenter club I belonged to, one member was known as "Pappy Stokes" because of his penchant for fathering illegitimate children. He often claimed to have "four kids floating around in Lake Ontario". A member who shied away from alcohol, bizarrity, and violence was known as "Clean Cut". One fellow who could do nothing right was called "Bogus". He eventually became a speed freak, was jailed for stealing a 29c key fob, and had his motorcycle confiscated by the police as unsafe after riding it only one block. Another member didn't ride his machine that far, for it was always in pieces supposedly being rebuilt. For the year and a half I was involved, he kept promising to have his bike on the road in two weeks. He soon achieved the nickname "Two Weeks". Another Road Gypsy member, a very eccentric friend of mine with orange-colored hair and beard, who wore W. W. I. style aviator's leather coat and helmet, became known as "The Red Baron". My own nickname, coined by the girls, was "Half Moon", apparently because of my movie star smile and unsullen disposition.

Moving from personality to skills, what are some of the skills peculiar to the Outlaw motorcycle subculture? An advertising agent, a welfare clerk, or a professor would have no use (and hence no familiarity with nor respect for) for such skills as the crude joke, the instant insult, the "fast boot", or the "good rider", but these are highly esteemed amongst One Percenters. The Outlaw biker has no use for much middle class skills as "a mind for figures", "a good editor", "an astute critic", "a meticulous programmer", "a good father", "a fast typist", etc. Of course social skills (a "good organizer", an "ice-break-er", a "con-artist", a "front man", a "joker") are just as in-demand amongst One Percenters as anywhere else, given the appropriate shared background.

There are several colourful skills unknown to the middle class, or even to the average lower class person, which are highly esteemed within the Outlaw bikers' world:

Fighting

It appears that fighting skills are still valued and "cultivated" but that a mellowing trend set in across North American around 1973, insofar as various clubs seem to be realizing the insanity of beating each other up compared to the pleasures of partying together and the political advantage of presenting a united front to the police. Whether this new trend continues will be interesting to see both from the theoretical and spectator perspective. It may be a reaction to the fact that internecine warfare escalated during 1970–1980 from the traditional baseball bats and chains ("that was O.K.", according to an ex-Vagabond) to machine gun showdowns and the dynamiting of clubhouses ("going a little too far", according to the same survivor). This author wonders whether it may not have been only the sheer increase in bloodshed and several deaths which has prompted the present counter-trend, but also the fact that the shootings and explosions resulted in a police crackdown, putting the survivors in jail. With destroyed motorcycles and clubhouses, close police surveillance, and most members either in graves, hospitals or jails, a non-violent era may have been the only choice. At any rate it is too early to say with confidence that fighting skills are less in demand.

Highway Vandalism

A quote from H. Thompson (*Hell's Angels*, London, Penguin, 1996) will suffice here:

> Man we swarmed all over him . . . we whipped on his hood with chains. tore off his aerial and smashed every window we could reach . . . and all this at seventy miles an hour.

Motorcycle Theft and Stripping

Many Outlaws are experts in hot-wiring Harleys and Triumphs, stealing them, and stripping them down into hundreds of pieces in a few hours. I knew several people (in the subculture but not club members) who used to specialize in mixing and matching hot and legal parts, ownerships, obliterating and renumbering engine and frame numbers, and selling the resultant quasi-legal hybrid machine for a tidy profit. Motorcycle theft became almost a business for the Vagabonds and Satan's Choice, necessitating a special Toronto Police squad who are kept busy full time on motorcycle thefts, in co-operation with the Ontario Provincial Police who use a large semi-trailer just for confiscating stolen goods.

Bargain Grocery Binges (a teamwork skill)

While one is gathering hams or steaks another will create a disturbance to draw the clerks. A third will fill a ruck sack full of cans and vegetables on the other side of the store, and then they will all flee through different exits.

Technical-Practical Jokes

Mouldy Marvin is widely admired for his work on crashers. He once wired Terry the Tramp (who was sound asleep) to an electrical outlet, then soaked his Levis with beer and plugged him in.

Reckless Riding (wiping out with class)

Any one of them might take a bike he has worked on for six months and destroy it in seconds with a maniacal top speed run at a curve.

The Hells Angels lose an average of four members a year on the road, but considering the way most of them ride. (it's) a tribute to their skill . . . a hard-running Angel can intimidate traffic as severely as a speeding torpedo. The outlaws are experts with hogs . . . they can outride just about anybody.

Thompson (*Hell's Angels*, 1966)

One occasionally sees Outlaws blasting through city streets on their choppers, riding like suicidal maniacs. York University faculty have been intimidated and forced to stop or swerve by the riding tactics of the Black Diamond Riders, whose clubhouse is close to the main campus. I vividly recall one day in October 1967 at a Vagabond chopper shop where I saw a beautiful chopped Hog (customized Harley) with much money and time obviously invested, but looking as if it had just been rolled or run over. It would have taken hundreds of dollars and hours to restore. I inquired of the owner the cause of this small tragedy, and he blithely replied "got a little carried away at our Field Meet".

Poetry

Lincoln Keiser, in his book *The Vice Lords: Warriors of the Streets* mentions that the delinquents he observed had a penchant for poems dealing with the club name, insignia and related values. This parallels in form and function the Hell's Angels poems printed in Reynolds and Thompson and some Vagabonds' poems I saw scrawled on the walls of the jail cells underneath the Old City Hall courtrooms in Toronto.

Conning

The Vice Lords' "whupping the game" reminds me of my participant-observation in the Road Gypsies M. C. The members were constantly trying to extract money from each other, friends, relatives, and hangers-on. Washington, Vice Lord, was as incompetent at this technique as Bogus, a Road Gypsy, while Blue Goose, a Vice Lord, was as skilled as Jay, the Road Gypsy who managed to "borrow" hundreds of dollars from various members and their relatives before absconding to California. Although he ended up in jail following a barroom brawl, during his stay in Toronto he had accumulated several months' free room and board and a few hundred dollars cash by promising to marry Two Weeks' sister! In the Road Gypsies, the term used to describe the manipulation of parts or money away from another person was "beating", but I have not used it as the title here because it might be confused with "beating up" someone. To clarify, if a Gypsy borrowed something from another, and didn't return the item or a facsimile, the loser would complain that "so-and-so beat me for my such-and-such". I later learned that a similar activity takes place in the larger clubs, wherein senior members use their status to get items or favours from junior members but never repay them

Wholesome recreation

From a middle class perspective, breaking windows, stripping cars, kicking beer cans, shooting bottles, rolling garbage cans and insulting strangers are not "wholesome" compared to skiing, tennis, squash or horseback riding. The problem is that the latter sports are not as available to lower class youths. Such activities are not so much "rejected" as "foreign" to lower class youths and adults. Similarly, one could say from an upper class perspective, that the middle class "reject" wholesome recreation because they find ballet "for sissies" and spending hours in art galleries "boring".

Of course all socioeconomic strata and subcultures have their own forms of recreation. Outlaw bikers really enjoy their runs and parties. Just because such activities shock middle class observers does not render them "unwholesome". As an R.C.M.P. member of E Squad (a B. C. unit formed in 1968 to deal with Outlaw motorcyclists) recently said: "Generally most of them are off work and it's a long weekend. Where we might go golfing with a few friends, their fun thing is to ride." From a One Percenter viewpoint, straight parties are boring, pretentious and restrained. Wrecking the interior of a house in winter or staggering (on foot) or careening (on motorcycle) through the woods in summer, completely stoned on whatever, may deem unwholesome to an observer from outside the subculture. As an ex-participant, however, I can assure the reader that the feeling of total abandon provides a cathartic effect which lasts for days.

SONG OF THE DUMB BIKER

Bob "Bitchin" Lipkin

Bob "Bitchin" Lipkin was editor of several biker magazines and has written about the biker lifestyle for over twenty years. His selection provides the very essence of the art of having fun by being a biker challenging all intelligence. Enjoy the ride with Bob and Jack.

I used to wonder why the words "dumb" and "biker" were almost always used in the same sentence. I mean, I know that some words are independently exclusive, and are never used in the same sentence, like "smart" and "woman" but why is it always "dumb biker?" Just like that. Together.

As I say, I used to wonder. Now I know. It's because all bikers is dumb, I know, because I are one.

The first time I realized just how dumb I really am was when a friend, another dumb biker named Billy Jack, and I decided to take a trip. We were sitting in a semi-stupor, after devouring a few small six packs of Colorado Kool-Aid, when spontaneously, the idea to take a trip came up. Afterward, I remembered what brought the whole idea up in the first place was both of our bikes had managed to make it to the liquor store and back without breaking down. This was a major feat since I live almost three blocks from the store.

"A scoot that trusty is good for lots of miles," I told Billy Jack. We decided it was a great idea, and we should load up our trusty steeds and hook it across the country. There was only one small thing standing in our way. It was December.

But what the hell, we're bikers, and we can stand up to any weather. Besides, all we have to do is take along a few extra things to keep us warm, and we would have no trouble at all.

During the planning, I remember, we decided the bikes we were riding might be the wrong type to take. After all, a rigid frame for 10,000 miles might be kinda hard on the old tail. (Maybe that's why they are called hard tails?)

After checking out a few costs to convert to a soft tail, we decided to take a chance the way we were.

Yes folks, bikers are dumb, there is no doubt about it.

Before the Coors wore off, we made a list of all the things we would need for this big trip. We covered everything we could think of – clothing, food, stoves, tents, sleeping bags, even an extra set of gloves. It was a very complete list.

The second thing we did was take the list and cross out things we couldn't afford.

Left was the following!
    2 sleeping bags
    4 helmets
    2 changes of clothes each
    1 three-man tent
    1 small propane stove
    2 pairs of long johns
    2 pairs of sweat pants
    2 flat face shields
    2 sweat shirts
    2 pairs of snow gloves
    2 pairs snowmobile boots
    4 pairs arctic socks
    2 pairs regular boots
    1 instamatic camera & film
    2 dumb bikers

Keep in mind that we started with a list three times longer, but when we looked at the packing area on our bikes we knew it couldn't all fit. The fact that I am 6'4" and weigh 300 pounds, and Billy Jack is 5'5" and weighs 150, made things a little difficult, also, because we both had to have complete sets of clothing. There wouldn't be too much swapping.

Since this was all before the trip, when we were still under the delusion that bikers were relatively smart, we thought the real smart thing would be to go someplace nice and cold as an official test run. You see, living in Southern California tends to spoil you for estimating the rigors of the outside world.

We decided Yosemite Park was a nice cold place to go in December, so we packed up our bikes and headed northward.

We were right. It was cold.

By the time we got close to the summit at the eastern approach to Yosemite the snow was coming down so hard we couldn't believe it was still California.

We pulled into a place with a "camping" sign in front and asked what the rates were. All the dude did was stare at us. I wondered why?

He finally managed to stutter, "If you really wanted to sleep out in this weather, you can set up for nothing." So we picked out a campsight, which was kind of easy since they were all vacant, and set up camp.

Then we made a big discovery. In winter the sun goes down really early after which it gets boring.

Around 7 o'clock we tired of playing "Hiroshima" with the gasoline which we had been squirting on the fire, and we crashed for the night.

The next morning found two dumb bikers frozen in a couple of sleeping bags. We waited for what seemed like an eternity, and then decided it wasn't getting any warmer, so we got up.

After we limbered up with some more "Hiroshima", we scraped the snow off the tent and rolled it up. We packed our bikes and it was time to try and make it into the Yosemite basin.

As we headed up the pass toward the summit we noticed there were fewer cars. Soon we hit an area where a sprinkling of diehards were pulled over, putting on chains. We kept going.

We got to an elevation with so much snow we had to put our feet down to keep from falling over. We were actually using our feet like skis. And it was working.

We did it. We made the summit at 9941 feet and down into the park. If we could get through that we figured we could get through just about anything.

We headed back to our home base and made a few corrections. First of all, we added a sleeping bag each to the list. This would eliminate any more of those foolish frozen nights. We also added a couple of cans of Sterno to heat the morning tent.

We were set. We were in command of long range wintertime bombing and the North American Continent was our cup of hot soup.

Then the idea hit us. Since we were going across the country in the dead of winter, why not try for a new transcontinental record. It sounded like a great idea. We looked up the record and found out we had to beat 36 hours.

Ya know, bikers are really dumb sometimes.

The big day finally came. The night before Billy Jack and I had made our way down to San Diego as official kickoff point, and got a room where we would be close to Interstate 8, which was the short cut across the country. We had gotten into town early, and decided to get to sleep early so we would get up around 6 a.m. for the start. After dousing a couple of bottles of Tequila, we made it to sleep. We woke up at 3 a.m., all hungover but ready to go.

The sun came up as we headed into Yuma, Arizona, land of nothing. We stopped to dump some 90 weight down our throats, and started the coast-to-coast boogie one more time.

That day we made our way along Interstate 8 to Case Grande, then picked up I-10 through Tuscon, Lordsburg and Las Cruces. As the sun was setting behind us we were headed into El Paso. In one day we had managed to make it through California, Arizona, New Mexico, and into Texas. We knew we would make it now.

Boy, bikers are dumb.

By the time we hit Fort Worth it was early the second morning, and still very dark. I'm not going to say we were tired, but we missed our turnoff and it took almost 45 minutes for us to find our way back onto the track.

Billy Jack fell asleep a couple of times. I had a hell of a time trying to get him to wake up.

About 50 miles out of Dallas, heading toward the Louisiana border on Interstate 20, we decided to stop and have breakfast. It had been a long day and night, and we had covered almost 1,700 miles.

We wolfed down our food and hopped back into the saddle. Surprisingly enough, our butts weren't even too sore, but I think a lot of that was due to the numbness setting in.

We had been very lucky also, the weather was just like summer. It was about 60 degrees at noon. At night it dropped down to about 25. Wonderful, just plain wonderful.

As we hooked it east through Louisiana we started to wake up again. We crossed the mighty Mississippi actually feeling good. We really thought we were going to make it into Savannah under the 36-hour limit.

Bikers are the dumbest people on earth.

As we kissed off Mississippi the sun was setting behind us, and we were working on night number two with no sleep.

Then came our downfall. A road called the George Wallace Highway, also known as Alabama 80, looked like a short cut on the map, so we decided to take it. That was a mistake.

This road is used by all of the big eighteen wheelers to go around the weight scales and they do it at not less then 80 miles an hour, curves and things that no sane man would try at 60 are included.

We dodged the big trucks and tried to stay awake. After 34 nonstop hours we were starting to weaken. Then we hit this foolish drawbridge and almost lost the game. I figure the designing engineers must have hated bikes and know the width of motorcycle tires. They put steel girders just far enough apart to catch bike wheels and hold them. We had to go over almost at a crawl speed, with 18-wheelers disputing our right to be there. I recall this to be the most trick riding required in the entire 10,000 miles.

A large truck crossed the double line a few miles farther up the road and knocked one of the sleeping bags off my bike. Billy Jack tried to turn around to pick it up, but his front wheel lost it in some gravel, and he ended up on his kiester in the middle of the road, with two large 18-wheelers bearing down on him.

When I pulled my hands from my eyes after the longest screach of brakes, I saw Billy Jack sitting in the middle of the road with two large trucks about 5 feet from him, their tires smoking from a kingsize panic stop.

We got his bike out of the way, and loaded my sleeping bag back on the bike. We headed into the next town, Selma.

As we sat filling up our tanks I looked at my watch.

We didn't make it. It was exactly 36 hours to the minute since we left the west coast, and we still had over three hundred miles to go. We thought we could do it, but we couldn't.

To celebrate (?) we got a motel room and had our first good meal in the last two days, thick steak, washed down with mucho Tequila.

That night we slept well. In fact, almost too well since it was almost 11 a.m. the next day when we woke up.

No matter how bad things look at night, you can count on the fact that they will look even worse the next day. Here we were in a place called Selma, and we hadn't seen one bit of the country between Los Angeles and here. We decided that it was time to slow down and start enjoying the trip.

We looked at a map and decided it was a good time to see Atlanta, Georgia, since neither of us had been there before. We headed north-east.

You know something? You can sure see a lot of a town when you ride through on a bike. It was really neat to think that just three days earlier we were at home, and here we were all the way across the country, riding through a strange town on our bikes. We really felt good.

We kept heading north all that day, and by night were heading into Winston-Salem, North Carolina, where my long-lost brother lives. I hadn't seen him since we were kids, so I gave him a call, after searching three phone books for his number, and soon we were in his nice warm house.

After a night of old-time talk and good food and drink, we hopped back on our scooters and headed north again, after promising to return for Christmas dinner in about two weeks.

All that day we wandered up through North Carolina and Virginia.

You know, it is a real trip to ride the back roads of states like that, where so much has happened. I mean, you ride along and see a sign that says "Shilo," and you get a lot closer to the history of the country. It is really a strange feeling.

That night we ran into a dude named Fuzzy Dave, who heads up a biker rights organization called ABATE. They were active in fighting the helmet law.

He invited us to stay for dinner and to crash at his home. We may be dumb bikers, but not dumb enough to pass up an invite like that. After dinner we hopped into his four wheeler (since it was about 18 degrees out) and visited a guy named Gary Zager. We talked about helmet laws and the like until late in the night.

The next day we got up and packed our bikes again, by now a familiar procedure. As we rode out of Fuzzy's driveway we passed a farm house used as a hideout by rebel troops so long ago.

The weather was starting to get cold. Even though the sun was out, it was only about 4 degrees at the warmest. We rode into Washington with Fuzzy, and met Gary there. They gave us the grand tour of D.C., including getting a ticket for not wearing a helmet in front of the White House.

On that parting gesture, we bid ado to our new friends and hit it north again. As the sun disappeared into a west sky cloud we started to think, "good campsight."

Our map showed one at the head of Cheasapeake Bay that looked good, so we headed off I-95. Just as the rain started we found the park. It was totally vacant. The good thing about traveling in the winter is you have your choice of camping. The bad thing about traveling in the winter, as we were discovering, is it's cold. We hurriedly set up the tent and spent the rest of a cold, wet night sitting in it watching the rain fall. What a bummer.

In the morning the rain had stopped, but it was overcast. Still about 40 degrees. Temperature dropped to the low thirties, and still dropping. As we passed New York City it was in the 20's.

We pulled into Bridgeport, Connecticut, about three in the afternoon. Bridgeport temperature was 24. All this cold truckin' was just to get with Rogue, a friend, and International President of the Huns Motorcycle Club. We gave him a call and were soon warming ourselves at the Huns clubhouse.

That night was party time and party we did. The clubs in the east are a lot like the clubs on the west coast except they park their bikes in the wintertime. Westcoasters ride them year around. Other than that there is no real difference between the two areas. It is party + party = party, all night long, in both places.

The next couple of days were spent in warm luxury, just sitting around and checking out the local action. It is weird being 3,000 miles from home and only a short-time gone, seeing strange sights and handling strange flesh. Actually folks they were the same as home folks, but the low mileage woofies were even nicer.

As with all good things, the good times came to an end. In this case the end came when we heard storm warnings on the radio. All we could think of was being stuck here all winter. From the weatherman's tone, we were in for a big one. Billy Jack and I decided to load up our scoots and hook it out of there.

This time we chose west. We passed through New York again (yech) and rode on until we hit the Pennsylvania state line. Temperature was really starting to drop now. We pulled over just before we entered the turnpike and packed every bit of clothing we had onto our bodies. A few hours later the temperature had dropped to zero. We just kept riding.

Damn, bikers are dumb. High in the Pocano Mountains we came upon a sign that said "camping ahead." We followed the signs and pulled into Hickory Run State Park. As had been the case for the whole trip, we were the only people in the whole park, so we had our choice of camping spaces.

After unpacking our tent and setting it up, we started looking around for some firewood. Guess what, there was none.

In the entire park, not one piece of wood was big enough to burn. And the temperature was now down to six-below-zero.

Being smart and resourceful as the average biker, we condemned a picnic bench which had seen better times and reduced it to campfire size pieces. We stashed some and dumped high octane on the rest.

I doused the fire on my leg caused by careless handling of the burn juice, and slid up the evening can of beans. With this weather we should have brought fresh T-bones.

Our dinner guest that evening was a Smokey Bear Ranger. It wasn't until he had stopped his car and walked over to warm himself by the fire that we realized the legs of the bench were sticking out, prima facia evidence a law had been fractured in a very literal sense.

A very long fifteen minutes later the ranger left. He never did say anything about the two legs sticking out of the fire. I know he saw them. I guess he just didn't want to hassle a couple of frozen bikers.

The following day we decided to head for some warmer weather. This cold was OK, but enough is enough. We checked out the map and decided south was definitely a good way to go. We turned left in Ohio, and headed for Kentucky and the blue grass pastures.

That night we stopped in a small town just south of Cincinatti, on the Kentucky side of the street, for a quick cup of coffee. While sitting there Billy Jack informed me his mother lived nearby, and he would like to stay there for Christmas. This meant an unwelcome split of a team of dumb bike bums that had become close and (yes, I'll say it) proficient at bad weather, hard luck wintertime biking.

With me almost 1,000 miles from my brother, where we are supposed to be for Christmas, Billy wants to stay here.

We stopped at his mother's house for the night, and the next day, as the Snow Monster descended on the United States, I left for North Carolina by myself.

As I headed into Tennessee the snow got bad. I hooked it over the mountains and down into Knoxville where the weather was a little better, but that was just to sucker me into trying to make the rest of the trip. Bikers are all pretty dumb, and I am probably the dumbest, because I fell for it.

I made a hard left in Knoxville, and soon I was heading up over the great Smokey Mountains. The snow started to come down again, but this time it was a little thicker. The first hint that I might be in a little bit of trouble was when I noticed there were no more cars out there, just me and the 18-wheelers. It was then I noticed no snow moving equipment was working, and only the big trucks could make it over.

As the snow increased it became a white blanket. My visibility was cut down to about 25 feet. I closed in behind a truck and followed him. All I could see was the left taillight.

For what seemed like an eternity I followed that lone red light. Every once in a while I heard another truck going the otherway, but very few of those. It was just me, my bike and that red light.

After what seemed a long spell of me trailing the red dot against a world of white the snow lightened a little bit and I could see the truck that I had been following. It said "Frozen Food" on the side.

No shit.

The splash guards on the truck were about a foot thick with ice, and that started me thinking. I looked down to find that my feet had become completely encased in frozen slush. It was all the gook the truck had kicked up for the last 60 miles. The ice and snow was about 4 to 6 inches thick, and it was a solid as a rock. The snowmobile boots and the special Calafia riding suit had kept me warm, but the snow and slush froze on the outside.

I knew I was in trouble when I tried to down shift from third gear as I pulled off to get some gas. My foot was frozen solid to the foot peg.

Damn, bikers are the dumbest people on earth.

I made about four figure-eights while scheming what to do. I decided to pull up next to a well in the gas station and stall the bike using my front brake. This I did OK, but I couldn't take my hand off the bars to take off my helmet without falling over, and no matter how hard I called, the gas station attendant couldn't hear me.

I imagined spending the rest of the winter as a frozen sculpture in a abandoned corner of an Exxon station. Just then a Highway Patrol car pulled in and asked the attendant what I was doing over there.

A few minutes later he had taken a hammer and screwdriver and broken my feet loose from the foot pegs.

How embarrassing.

Fifteen minutes of warming up in the station, and explaining how it had happened, got me back on my frosted bike, and started down the hill again. Farther I got, the better the weather got until, as I headed into North Caroline, the weather was almost nice.

All of the snow and ice had melted off the forks and front of my bike, and it just looked like a normal old dirty bike.

As I pulled into Winston-Salem and my brother's pad it was just getting dark. I pulled the bike into the garage and the rest of the night was spent talking about my close call, and getting thoroughly wasted. What a lovely way to spend a day, huh?

The next couple of days were like a dream. Riding around in a car, with the heater on. Eating big steaks and home cooked food. It was really enough to spoil me, even if I hadn't been on the road for awhile. The crowning glory was Christmas dinner. Turkey, ham, and all the fixings.

But all good things must end, and so must the holiday spirit and good times. Before I even knew it, the time had come to pack up the old scoot and head out to meet Billy Jack. We had made plans to meet in Knoxville the day after Christmas. It was hard to do, but I managed it. I made for the mountains again. This time I was lucky. No snow. Just a lot of cold weather.

That night Billy Jack and I tried our damndest to make each other jealous with rundowns of what we had eaten and the warm beds we had lain in. Each claimed the better dinner, and the tenderest care, and neither would believe the other. It turned out a tie.

We decided the best place to go in the winter was the Gulf coast, so we headed south, for Mardi Gras Country. We didn't care if there was no Mardi Gras this time of year, we were going to New Orleans any way, mostly for the warm weather and Creole cooking.

The farther south we got, the more we realized we had made the right choice. Heading out over the long bridge over Lake Ponchartrain the temperature was well into the 70's, and we were riding for the first time without jackets. Life was getting to be almost bearable. In spite of comforting warmth for the first time in what seemed years we stayed only a day then headed out again.

We headed west, out of New Orleans, towards that big Texas state, where we got a big lesson in weather and thermodynamics, which I will pass along to you for future reference:

In the dead of winter, when you putt through a warm front, the next thing you will putt through is a wet front, and in this case it was almost a solid wall of water at the Texas state line.

The folks down there call it rain, but I know better. I've seen rain and this was not rain, it was a solid wall of water. I wondered how they got it to stand up like that.

Well anyway, for the next 300 miles we rode through this mobile ocean, all the way into Houston. There, just as it was getting dark, the rain ended, and once again it was almost nice out. Even though it was dark, the temperature was still in the high 60's and very comfortable.

The next day of riding was uneventful, until we jammed into this little town called Shefield, just as it was getting dark. Shefield stands out so well in my mind because people there are without a doubt the unfriendliest folks in the world.

We were about a quarter of a mile out of town when my chain slipped off the rear sprocket and lodged against the frame, locking the rear wheel up. I borrowed Billy Jack's bike and headed back into town to try and get a hack saw to cut the chain loose so we could tow the bike into the next large town.

No matter how I argued, no one would let me use a saw. I even offered one guy $20 just to rent one, but to no avail. They were real sweet.

Back at my busted scoot, we flagged down a passing pickup truck, and the guy said he would give us a ride into Fort Stockton for just $25 and a tank of gas. Did you know there are pickup trucks with 40-gallon gas tanks? Well, there are. We found out the hard way.

We found a friendly biker in Fort Stockton, Rick, who helped us get a chain from Odessa, Texas, and it only cost us $130. The small town in Texas definitely like to see stuck bikers, and then stick it to them.

After a two-day wait for the chain we found the wrong master link had been sent with it. So, being your normal dumb bikers, we jury-rigged it so we could get on down the road.

And down the road we went. It was December 30th, and we figured on making it back to California in time to celebrate New Years at home with some other dumb bikers we know.

But Texas was not ready to kick us free yet. It seemed like a conspiracy to keep us from making it.

Near Van Horn, still in Texas, the Mickey Mouse master link gave out. It was almost midnight, and the temperature was back around 20 degrees. Just to add to our fun, the wind decided to kick up, gusting to about 60 miles an hour. This made for much fun when the big old 18-wheelers passed at 80. Slipstream and wind almost dumped our scoots.

Then we made one more neat discovery.

The spare masterlink didn't fit. The posts were too big to fit the chain, and we would have to find a way to file or sand them down.

Once again I hopped on Billy Jack's bike, and one more time I headed off on my own to get help. Van Horn was about 25 miles away, but in the clear desert air it looked like it was only about 5 miles off. The longer I rode, the farther away it got. I hooked it up pretty good and finally made an off-ramp. There was now a new problem: red lights flashing in my mirror.

I sat there in numb shock as the Texas Ranger explained that I was going to jail for speeding. It seems they have this neat little law for out-of-state speeders. You go to jail until you pay the fine. Unfortunately, the Justice of the Peace was home sleeping, so this meant I was to spend the night in jail, while Billy Jack sat out in the 20-degree wind storm and froze to death.

It was at about this point that our luck improved, but then again, it had to get better because it couldn't get much worse. The ranger believed my story and called the JP at home and asked him to set a fine so I could pay it and get back out to fix the bike. The JP must have felt sorry for me, because he only fined me $25, which the ranger said was low.

That out of the way, with me 25 skins lighter, I got back to the problem at hand. Soon we would be on the road again, I thought.

I trucked on back to where the bike and frozen Billy Jack were and we proceeded to try and fix my bike.

Do you need more proof that all bikers are dumb? I got it.

We were trying to sand down case hardened steel rollers with sandpaper. That my friends, is dumb.

After about one and a half hours of cold wind and sanding, we realized, dejectedly, that it wasn't working.

Three weeks of freezing my ass off, getting rained on, pushed off the road by trucks, of eating cold beans and constantly suffering the pains of a stiff and sore butt were just too much.

All of a sudden everything went red. I picked up the biggest Harley rock I could find and proceeded to beat the damn pins into the chain. To my amazement, they went! Who said force doesn't work?

We put the master link together and packed up. We still planned to try for New Years at home.

We pulled into Lordsburg, New Mexico, sun-up on December 31st. It was New Years Eve, and we were still 800 miles from home. Not only that, we hadn't slept in the last two days. Tired or not, we still were going to try and make it.

Dumb, dumb, dumb.

As we sat slugging down 90 weight to wake us up, a truck

driver came over and asked us if those were our bikes. After affirmative nods he commenced to tell us how he had ridden for a few years, but had given it up. He then offered us a few hits of this neat little white powder that he swore all truckers used to stay awake while they drove. Being your average dumb bikers, we figured what the hell, and dumped some in our coffee.

Now I didn't know what the stuff was, but in about fifteen minutes not only were we awake, we were ready to tuck our bikes under our arms and run all the way home.

We backed our bikes out of the parking lot and the next thing we knew, the sun was again coming up, and we were heading into California, about 200 miles from home.

Then we found out a neat little thing about crank:

What goes up, must come down. And we did.

In a matter of minutes we had gone from feeling fine, to dead on our butts, and we were not yet home. The next 200 miles took us almost 8 hours to ride. We had to pull over about every 5 miles to try and wake up. We hadn't slept for three days and nights, and we were starting to see things that weren't there, unless pink elephants are back in style.

At 7 p.m. on New Years Eve, we pulled into our driveways. We made it. After 10,000 miles of cold and wet and garbage food, we were back with the comforts of home. There was just one problem. We were so damned tired, all we could do was flop on the bed and deal ourselves out of the world for a time. We both slept though the celebrating and the start of a new year.

Like I said, bikers are the dumbest people on earth, and I am the king of dumb.

THE CLUB RUN

Daniel R. Wolf

Dan beautifully describes the motivations, emotions, and sensations of riding with an outlaw motorcycle club on a club run. It stands as one of the clearest examples of why outlaw clubs do what they do with respect to "riding in the wind".

We all have one thing in common – we live to ride and ride to live.

(Terrible Tom, Rebels MC)

An outlaw biker considers himself a romantic. He carries a strong mental image of himself: leaning back on his motorcycle, feet up on highway pegs, his girl tucked in behind him, bedroll and camping gear strapped to the backrest, mountains in front of him and troubles far behind, flying down a lonesome stretch of grey highway, riding in the wind again. The club run adds a key social dimension to this image. The outlaw patch holder is not a loner; he has his brothers beside him.

A club run is a motorcycle tour where members ride together as a group. A run is the outlaw club's fundamental reason for existing, and it is formally mandated by the club's constitution. On a club run patch holders take risks, engage in exciting and stimulating behaviour, and indulge in the freedom of mobility. Members use a run to express and share a wide range of sentiments and emotions, from the festive atmosphere of an initiation run to the grief of a funeral run. The sight and sound of thirty Harley-Davidson motorcycles roaring down the highway make the club run the group activity that most effectively dramatizes the outlaw-biker identity, that of anti-hero and social rebel.

An outlaw biker constructs his anti-hero image from themes and values that are largely hedonistic in nature, from collective risk taking to the freedom of mobility. For the patch holder, the club run symbolizes these goals and values, which he considers legitimate, and which he pursues in the name of his freedom ethic. Ironically, the response of the police to a run, "harassment," actually strengthens the club's ability to portray the freedom ethic. Harassment heightens the process of group polarization and adds credence and reality to the patch holder's isolation as an outlaw from the mainstream of society. For these outlaw bikers, riding in the wind with their brothers goes beyond being a theatre for episodes of togetherness. It becomes an act of defiance.

The Riding Season

The late spring, summer, and early fall months are the riding season. It is a time of riding hard, partying long, and "good times with the brothers." The patch holder has spent the "friggin" cold winter months repairing, rechroming, and rebuilding his "sled," while "making a dime" to pay for it all. Now he is ready to ride!

The Rebels inaugurate the riding season with a mandatory run in the spring and terminate it with a mandatory run in the fall. Dedicated bikers ride whenever possible; the Rebels expect their patch holders to have their motorcycles on the road by April 1st and to ride until October 30th or the first permanent snowfall. However, it is during the official riding season (from mid-May to September) that most outlaw motorcycle clubs, in accordance with their constitution or by-laws, will apply formal sanctions against those members who fail to keep their machines operational.

If a member's bike is not running for a period of thirty days, unless he is in jail or hospital, his colours will be confiscated. A member's bike must be running for at least one week (e.g., not fifteen minutes), to be exempt from the above rule. This period is subject to change at the discretion of the club. (Rebels MC Constitution)

A member's bike must not be broken down over thirty days at a time, unless the person is in hospital or jail. (Hell's Angels MC by-laws, San Francisco)

The RCMP National Crime Intelligence Branch believes that the purpose of these rules is to make sure that outlaw club members – whom they think have become wealthy and affluent through criminal activities – don't abandon their motorcycles altogether. According to one RCMP bulletin: "Even with the arrival of sophistication, bikers must still own their bikes. With the phenomenal profits made in the drug trade, gang members gravitate to Corvettes and other showy or expensive vehicles. Quite a few members would probably prefer to remain members of these criminal organizations without resorting to bikes at all. The trend away from bikes has been so pronounced that the San Diego Chapter of the Hell's Angels passed a by-law levying a $25 fine to anyone not riding their bike at least once a month" (Intelligence communiqué to Canadian police officers, RCMP, 1980). This interpretation is historically wrong. Riding by-laws pre-date the involvement of any outlaw clubs in organized crime. By-laws ensuring riding participation have been a part of the outlaw club scene since the Canadian Lancers MC of Toronto in the 1950s. Furthermore, one would have to question the logic of viewing a $25 monthly fine as a deterrent to someone who is making "phenomenal profits . . . in the drug trade." During the period of my association with the Rebels a number of the members were indeed told to "get their shit together" as far as their motorcycles were concerned. But none of these patch holders was well off financially, and none was preoccupied with Corvettes.

By the time April brings the promise of clearing skies and dry pavement, the Rebels are eager to be riding together again as a group. For five months the Harley iron has been stored in garages and living-rooms. The club has had to endure the tension of petty disputes and minor aggravations that build up during the winter months of non-riding. During this time a member is also deprived of using his club insignia to symbolize his corporate identity; the Rebels MC Book of Rules stipulates that a member will not wear his colours when he is not currently using his motorcycle. A patch holder will lock away his colours with only his ol' lady and a brother knowing their location. The first club run will mediate the tension of disputes and deprivation; it acts as a spring tonic for the social fabric of the group.

Club patch holders always push the season and their luck. This can turn the enthusiasm of "jamming in the wind" into the dread of "skidding in the sleet." I recall one Warlords' Welcome to Spring party that involved riding through mud and snow at $-1°C$ temperatures to attend an outdoor barbecue that featured a club snowball fight. Rae of the Warlords pointed out that one consolation was that "the snow kept the beer nice and cold." Two weeks later the Rebels paid a price for being overly optimistic about the Great White North. A weekend run to Pine Lake was planned, a 240-mile round trip from Edmonton. That Saturday morning the Rebels gathered at a roadside café for breakfast. Larry told Denise that she had "better enjoy that coffee, it'll probably be the last time you'll be warm for the next couple of days." The Rebels assessed the weather while putting down their bacon and eggs. The sun made a beguiling appearance and, despite the "bitching" of some very sceptical patch holders, the run began at eleven. After the sun had made its token appearance the clouds came, followed by rain, and finally a dramatic drop in temperature that changed the rain to snow.

> *Danny*: It was pretty weird. You'd be coming into a turn and the wind would catch you and your front wheel would just slide across the wet pavement.
> *Snake*: We had guys going both ways. Tiny tried to turn back but he said he ran into snow so thick he couldn't see more than five yards.

The white-out turned the weekend run into a two-day snow-in as the Rebels took refuge in some rented cabins along the highway. "The time passed pretty well though," recalled Raunch. "After a while the management was buying us free beer and we got stinking drunk."

Types of Runs

The Rebels schedule a variety of official club runs. Mandatory runs, stag or holiday runs, and weekend or day runs occur on a regular basis. Other runs mark special events, such as an initiation run, a biker wedding, or a funeral run.

Mandatory runs: Like most outlaws clubs, the Rebels have two mandatory runs. The Victoria Day run in May ushers in the official riding season, while the Labour Day run in September brings it to a close. These two long-weekend runs are of premier importance because of their highly political nature. They become a stage for a club to "showcase its stuff" for the benefit of its own members, other clubs, and the general public. Attendance by outsiders is highly selective: "Each person is brought up for a vote . . . it only takes two negative votes to exclude them" (Wee Albert). Attendance by members is compulsory. If a member is late or absent, the constitution requires him to pay a twenty-dollar fine. In addition to the automatic fine, a Rebel patch holder will be required to appear before the executive board to explain his absence. If the member's lack of participation is becoming the norm rather than the exception, "his colours [membership] will be discussed."

Stag or holiday runs: Once or twice a summer the Rebels hold a stag or holiday run. These runs may last as long as three weeks and cover distances exceeding three thousand miles. The stag run differs from the holiday run in that a member does not bring along his ol' lady. Excluding ol' ladies places a greater emphasis on the comradeship of brotherhood and leads to more adventurous undertakings on the part of the patch holders. "The stag run is designed to be with your brothers," explained Wee Albert. "A lot of the guys tend to be more sedate when their ol' ladies are around." On the stag run the Rebels traditionally travel south to party with the King's Crew in Calgary, head westward and camp along the lakes and beaches in British Columbia's Okanagan Valley, cross the Rocky Mountains and fraternize with the Hell's Angels in Vancouver, take the ferry across the Strait of Georgia to ride and fish on Vancouver Island as the guests of Victoria's Bounty Hunters, head north to share some good times with the Hell's Angels in Nanaimo, and then give some serious thought to returning home.

Weekend or day runs: Every summer weekend, provided that the club has not scheduled a clubhouse party or barbecue, the Rebels organize either an overnight camp-out or a one-day bike excursion.

Specialty runs commemorate occasional events such as an initiation, wedding, or the death of a member. A specialty run enables the club, as a whole, to adapt to a new social circumstance such as the addition (initiation) or loss (death) of a member. Such a run becomes a collective ceremony that involves an active social response on the part of the members. The adjustment value of a specialty run can be demonstrated by briefly looking at what happens when a brother "rides hard" and "dies fast."

If the death is a result of vigilante activities or careless driving by citizens, the actions of law-enforcement agents, or the biker "reaching for the edge" while jamming in the wind, then chances are good that he will become a martyr. The biker magazine *Easyriders* has a monthly memoriam column, "A Tribute to Brothers Lost":

> In memory of Youngblood, 8/3/83, a righteous bro who was killed in a fight. He partied hard and was always on the move. We love you and we'll see you in Harley Heaven. Crazy Ray and the bros, Scorpians MC, Bronx, New York.
>
> In memory of Billy Leary, Hell's Angels MC, Salem, Mass. You are missed and loved by your family and brother Angels. Ride forever with Hogman and Hopper.
>
> In memory of John "Sportster Smitty" Smith, killed by a cage on his favorite south Jersey ocean-view highway. I can still hear your voice singing "Desperado" when the winds blow from the ocean. Boneshaker and all your bros and sisters.
>
> (*Easyriders*, May 1986)

The outlaw fraternity comes together as a whole when a member dies. Feuding clubs will often put aside differences and declare an informal truce as they prepare for the funeral run. The bereavement and the sense of deep personal loss are shared among the brothers. Patch holders will reflect upon the values that they lived and shared with their deceased brother, values that might lead to a grave-side epitaph: "He lived and died like a biker."

The funeral run is laden with outlaw-biker symbolism. The hearse will be escorted by a solemn honour guard of motorcycles in formation, and the casket is draped with the deceased's club colours. Conducting the funeral in this manner prevents the death of a member from demoralizing the group. The funeral run confirms the outlaw lifestyle through joint participation and is an emotive event that is charged with gestures of defiance, such as riding without helmets or the firing of weapons as a final grave-side salute.

> We were supposed to meet Paul [secretary, Satan's Choice MC, Toronto] at 9:30 right by the intersection of highways no. 401 and no. 7. When we got to the turn-off we all pulled over and had a smoke and a few bottles of wine. Paul didn't show: so we split from the T.O. [Toronto] chapter and headed home to Brampton. Next morning we got a call from Bernie [Guidion, president, Satan's Choice MC]. He says: "I've got bad news for you. Paul was killed last night. He was trying to pass a fucking car and he was ripped out of his mind on speed [methamphetamine]. He went front-end into a fucking grader. It was game over. You couldn't recognize him or his bike." You want to see a fucking funeral, man?! There was close to five hundred motorcycles right through the city of Toronto; and not one of them was wearing a fucking helmet. I'd like to see the fuckin' cops try to break that one up! Nothing but a stream of fucking bikes from Richmond to Oshawa. There was a cop escort at the front, and a cop escort at the back. Paul had his bike buried with him. I knew the guy really well; I fucking cried at that. We [Satan's Choice] wore black armbands for the next few days. We took off our colours; we never wore our colours for a week in remembrance of Paul. (Gypsy, road captain, Satan's Choice MC)

For the club, a last run with a fallen brother becomes a show of both respect and strength; it helps the patch holders deal with their individual and collective loss.

Not all jamming in the wind occurs within the scheduled

structure of a club run. Members ride together after regular club activities, such as club meetings or drinking at the bar. One or more of the brothers will often combine personal spontaneity with the mobility of their machines to create some "two-wheeled freedom" on their own. The most accurate personification of the outlaw freedom ethic occurs when a biker mounts his Harley and rides the highway, whenever and wherever the urge takes him. Late one evening after a heavy drinking session at the clubhouse, Caveman and Tiny decided to "putt" six hundred kilometres to visit the Spokesmen MC in Saskatoon, Saskatchewan. Caveman was a little short of funds for gas, but he did remember Raunch saying something about just getting paid. At four in the morning Caveman and Tiny arrived at the house where Raunch, Crash, and Snake were living. Caveman didn't have a key and he didn't want to jeopardize Raunch's public relations with the neighbours by engaging in a lot of door pounding, so he simply broke in. Caveman wasn't sure which bedroom to go to, so he moved through the house quietly calling for Raunch. He walked into the wrong bedroom and the household was awoken by a scream from Snake's ol' lady. Snake got up, looked at the intruder, and said: "It's okay, it's only Caveman. He'll probably go away; maybe he's lost." When Caveman finally located Raunch's bedroom he found himself staring at a twelve-gauge shotgun: "Holy fuck, Raunch! I only wanted to borrow a few bucks, not steal your virginity!" Raunch gave Caveman several bills and said, "Okay, now go crawl back with the rats. I work for a living, and I'm tired." Caveman and Tiny found the Yellowhead Highway, laid back on their hogs, and cranked open the throttle.

Organizing a Club Run: Strategy and Tactics

All runs follow a similar pattern. The description of one Victoria Day run will illustrate the typical problems, logistics, and events that are involved.

The organization of a major run will be set in motion several weeks before the run date. Members will suggest any number of possible run sites or destinations. After members vote on a destination, the road captain and his two assistants draw up an itinerary including highway routes and food and fuel stops.

Their decisions are influenced by factors such as highway road conditions, the presence of service stations, and the past history of relations with various law-enforcement agencies along the route. Other tasks are divided among committees and individual patch holders. Some members have the responsibility of ensuring that the crash truck, a support vehicle, is both operational and adequately stocked with repair tools and supplies, such as motor oil, brake cables, and drive chains. Other patch holders are asked to purchase ample foodstuffs and to procure an inexhaustible supply of beer and wine. The president and treasurer draw the necessary funds from the club bank account to pay for these items, while the treasurer collects a predetermined contribution from each member. The members exchange information and opinions about guests who have been nominated to go on the run, and then they vote on their eligibility. The executive committee advises the members about any improvements that they feel are needed in the club's security measures. Finally, the president informs the RCMP of the club's destination. This information will be passed on to the appropriate provincial detachments in order to minimize the number of unpleasant surprises that might otherwise occur.

On the day of the run, club members congregate either at the clubhouse or at a roadside service station with a restaurant, depending on which is closer to the highway. The Rebels want to avoid riding through the city as a unit. The sight and sound of thirty outlaws rolling down city streets to the deep-throated crescendo of "Harley iron" is as subtle as a military barrage, and "cops come after loud pipes." On this particular Victoria Day run, the Rebels were to meet at the Roslyn Hotel at 9:00 a.m., and to leave at 10:00. That morning, at home, each patch holder "loaded on, strapped down, and moved out." They had spent the last couple of days checking the mechanics of their machines and applying several coats of wax and chrome polish. Now they used bungee cords to strap sleeping-bags, tents, and assorted camping gear to their bikes.

Sandra and I took part in this run, and we set off to rendezvous with the brothers. Five blocks later I noticed flashing red and blue lights in my rear-view mirror. It was a standard "shakedown": "Could I see your licence, registration, and insurance?" "How long have you owned this motorcycle?" "Do you have a criminal record?" "Are you carrying any weapons?" "Are you carrying any dope?" "We're going to [radio in and] check you for any outstanding warrants." The officer very cautiously stepped around the front of my bike while "casing out" the handlebars, and I wondered whether he had seen an RCMP information film that had been circulated to various police departments. The film warns officers that an outlaw biker may have converted the handlebars of his motorcycle into a shotgun-firing mechanism activated by a hand switch on the bars. In the United States, according to Don Parkhurst of the Federal Law Enforcement Training Center in Glynco, Georgia:

> Most officers by now have been warned about the outlaw biker trick of converting a handlebar to a shotgun barrel . . . the outer end of the handlebar was replaced with a threaded tube which held a 12-gauge shotgun shell lightly against a homemade firing pin. A snappy twist of the wrist screwed the tube down on the pin, causing the shell to discharge. Any officer approaching a motorcycle should watch for open ends in the handlebars, and keep an eye out for someone who seems to be aiming a handlebar at the officer, or "lining him up" with the rearview mirror . . . Shotguns have also been built into exhaust pipes, and removable "sissy bars" sharpened into spears have been used in homicidal stabbings.

Knowing that exhaust pipes get hot to the point where steel and chrome discolour, I would get awfully nervous about riding behind a biker who had converted his pipes into a shotgun. You would also have to hope that the guy who had "a 12-gauge shotgun shell [held] lightly against a homemade firing pin" never hit a bump on the road that might cause "a snappy twist of the wrist." I was tempted to tell the cop that that part of the film was more science fiction than fact, but the best – quickest – approach under these circumstances is to keep one's mouth shut and avoid eye contact.

We arrived at the Roslyn at 10:10 a.m., but the club had departed; all that remained on the parking lot was an empty can of Castrol oil. I was walking across the street to buy a road map when Crash pulled into the lot. Crash had also been stopped by the cops. He had been dragged down to "the cop shop" to account for an arrest warrant regarding some unpaid traffic tickets. They let Crash go after he signed an affidavit stating that he would pay his debt to society within two weeks. If he failed to comply, then the next time the police checked Crash out he would be thrown in jail. Apparently these officers were familiar with both Crash and his driving habits: "I would have been all right except that the cops knew me. You know, 'Hi, Crash! Paid any of those traffic tickets we've given you?'" Two police squad cars remained in the parking lot, perhaps anticipating stragglers. When Crash and I left the parking lot to pursue the Rebels, one of the squad cars followed us to the city limits. This sort of "surveillance" is the main reason that the club congregates at least one hour before it is scheduled to leave.

Together, Crash and I "rode hard" until we caught up with the pack as they were leaving a gas station, and we joined in formation. The visual impression that you get when you first see a club on a run is that of military precision. Riding in formation cannot be done in a haphazard manner; it requires the systematic synchronization of the members and their machines. The operation demands that each patch holder show considerable riding skills and a disciplined professional attitude. Every outlaw club has procedural rules that establish efficient communications and effective plans of action. Otherwise the group would be vulnerable when situations arose that demanded a coordinated response; under these conditions any hesitancy or miscue by one member might spell disaster for all. This necessary merging of individual behaviour into a group phenomenon contributes to the members' sense of interdependence.

The patch holders are on parade; their club is on display; they know it; and each rider will ride at his professional best. The motorcycle pack advances as a column of staggered twos travelling in a single lane. It is the responsibility of each rider to ensure that there are fifteen yards between himself and the bike he is following, and three yards between himself and the bike beside him. Adjacent bikes constitute units of two, staggered at approximately 45-degree angles, with the motorcycle on the left positioned about one yard ahead of the bike on his right. If the members are properly synchronized, the formation is technically safe and effective, as well as visually impressive.

At the head of the Rebel column is the road captain, who acts as the chief executive while the club is on the road. He sets the speed at which the club travels. The road captain must have a sound knowledge of how the members' hogs will perform under varying road conditions and be able to coordinate long bike formations that may stretch out for a half-mile. He initiates any necessary group action, and his decisions are communicated to the riders through a series of hand signals. Thus, when the road captain decides to pass a slower-moving vehicle, he will make a right-hand-turn signal followed by a 45-degree point signal to the left. The signal is passed on down the column. Motorcycles riding on the left-hand side of the column will increase the distance between themselves to allow the motorcycles on the right to merge and form a single file. Once in a single file, the bikes will pass the obstacle vehicle and re-form the column upon completing the manoeuvre. In some clubs, such as the Pagans MC and Banditos MC, the road captain will assume the added (presidential) responsibility of being the club spokesman while on the road: "The road captain . . . has been carefully selected for, among other things, a clean record and an ability to diplomatically handle policemen. He often carries the club's bail money, never carries contraband, and makes it a point to be immune to arrest. On a run, he is often the key man to talk to".

The president rides adjacent to, and to the right side of, the road captain. The "prez" and "captain" are followed by the other members of the executive. Next in the column ride the rest of the patch holders, followed by the strikers, friends of the club, and assorted guests. At the rear of the column ride the two assistant road captains. One of the assistants will occasionally pass the formation on the inside shoulder while he conducts a visual mechanical inspection of the members' machines. Both assistants will survey the column watching for "whiplash," large gaps between the bikes caused by members not maintaining tight formation while making turns, and they will pick out which riders are responsible. Should heavy traffic conditions make it necessary to split the column into more manageable units, each of the splinter groups will be led by one of the assistant road captains. If a patch holder "drops out" of formation for mechanical reasons, one of the assistants will fall back to assist the member, while the other assistant road captain will expedite the reformation of the column.

The last unit in the Rebels entourage is the crash truck, a support vehicle. It follows the main column at a distance of one and a half to two miles. A "solid" or established club will have such a transport vehicle that it uses on long trips. For example, the Hell's Angels of Vancouver employ a van; the Bounty Hunters of Victoria use a converted school bus; and the Iron Cross of California have a house-trailer. In the late seventies the Rebels used a "club trailer," a white 1969 Plymouth sedan pulling an open trailer that had the Rebel insignia painted on either side. Today the Rebels use a converted bus that they painted jet black. The crash truck carries essential supplies that would be difficult or impossible to transport by motorcycle: (1) liquor, consisting of wine and cases and/or kegs of beer; (2) foodstuffs, such as wieners, buns, beans, corn on the cob, and watermelon; (3) maintenance equipment, including tools, spare parts, and lubricants that enable the Rebels to make all but the most sophisticated on-the-spot repairs; and (4) personal items, paraphernalia that the members would rather not pack on their bikes, such as tents and sleeping-bags. The crash truck has sufficient room to accommodate any motorcycle that is crippled beyond immediate repair and has to be carried to the run site for "major wrench work."

Communications between the column and crash truck are maintained by the president using a CB radio. If the club is suspicious about entering a certain town or area, they will send a scout ahead with a walkie-talkie radio to check for surprises such as a police roadblock. Another security measure that outlaw clubs often use is to equip their crash truck with a short-wave radio to monitor police radio transmissions. Police forces have countered this tactic by using walkie-talkie systems. Since 1984 police departments have been installing new radios in their squad cars, sending out a scrambled signal that only police radios are able to pick up. The RCMP advises other police forces about additional counteractive tactics that they can adopt to neutralize the bikers' security systems.

> Bikes cannot transport cases of beer, sleeping bags, illicit weapons or drugs, and the bikes themselves must appear to be "clean" if stopped on the highway by police . . . A crash truck . . . will be equipped with a CB radio sometimes in touch with one of the bikers on the run.

When stopping bikes, policemen should be aware that a warning signal may well be sent to the accompanying truck, possibly by CB radio. If possible, both the bikes and truck should be stopped simultaneously. (RCMP *Gazette*, 1980)

As a further precaution against having the crash truck stopped and the police seizing its contents – whether they be legal, such as booze and registered weapons, or contraband, such as illicit drugs – a club may load these items on a separate vehicle. This vehicle, such as a house-trailer, will have no visible club markings; it will be driven by clean-cut, straight-looking males or females, and may travel ahead of the formation, equipped with a CB radio, acting as an additional scout vehicle. To counteract this strategy, Parkhurst of the Federal Law Enforcement Training Center recommends "good intelligence." Specifically, police officers should "be in touch with other agencies along the route, since the night before [the vehicle] will usually have stopped with the rest of the run, and will have been identified by local investigators if they've been alerted".

Another factor on a run is the performance of bike-rider teams. To ride successfully as a club, each member must know not only his own machine and riding skills, but also those of his brothers. Members are aware of the changes in performance that result from customizing their machines. Modifications that will affect performance may include wheel size, tire size, weight of the bike, degree of rake and length of fork extension, the presence ("juice frame") or absence ("hard tail") of a rear shock-absorbing system, and the installation of a "stroker kit." A patch holder must remain aware of how he and his riding partner have combined these facts of design with principles of performance. For example, a longer front-end extension will enhance ease and comfort of handling on a straight stretch of highway. However, there is a commensurate loss of manoeuvrability when negotiating low-speed tight turns. If the biker is following a member who is carrying a passenger, he must take into account that the extra weight will drastically affect the braking capacity of even a large motorcycle. For example, a stock Harley-Davidson Electraglide "dresser" that weighs in at 722 pounds has braking ability that outperforms most cars. However, add 150 pounds of passenger and luggage to that bike at a highway speed of 60 miles per hour, and the required stopping distance increases by 35 per cent. An unwritten rule of thumb is that members will team up with brothers whose riding styles and motorcycles are similar to their own. Similarity of machines facilitates performance synchronization. In addition, familiarity with his brothers' machines allows the patch holder to visually check his riding partner's motorcycle while on the road. Each Rebel eventually gets to know the riding style and idiosyncrasies of ever other member along with the capacities of their machines. It is vital that a patch holder have a good idea of what to expect from his riding partner under any given situation.

> Tiny is a very cautious rider. We always ride near the back of the pack. When in formation, we sometimes leave nearly double the usual space between us and the bikes in front of us. That way, he doesn't have to alter his speed as much when the whiplash of the column comes around when we go into turns. He just lays back when they speed up, and catches up when they slow down as the whiplash takes effect. He's a very good rider. He realizes that with his weight on a bike he can't stop as fast. Like Tiny weighs near 285 pounds. (Wee Albert)

Every patch holder on the run rides a fine balance between fear and fascination. A motorcycle offers no illusion of physical protection; nothing stands between unforgiving asphalt and steel except leather and flesh. A failure in performance can result in a painful death. It is this constant and underlying reality that makes riding a challenge; skilful riding is a defiance of danger. This aspect of collective risk taking further cements the bonds of brotherhood and differentiates the Rebels as an adventurous élite from the citizen, who rides within the controlled and air-conditioned confinement of a "cage."

On this Victoria Day run there was one "gut-wrenching" incident. Dale the Butcher experienced a biker's nightmare, a blow-out of his front tire. Dale would have felt the front end of his bike lift slightly the same moment he heard the loud bang. There is an immediate loss of stability as the wheel rim moves back and forth relative to the tire's tread. After the initial shudder, extreme vibrations shake the bike, causing it to wobble

unpredictably. Steering control vanishes as vibrations are re-
layed from the wheel struts to the steel handlebars. Only the
strongest of riders will be able to maintain his grip. If the biker
is unfortunate enough to be turning at the time, then it all
becomes very simple: "game over." In a turning situation, he
will not have enough control to even afford himself the luxury
of "laying the bike down" and "sliding out" in a gracious
manner. Voodoo, who was riding beside Dale at the time, heard
the explosion and pointed to Dale's tire. The members who
were following the crippled bike moved as a unit to the left;
while the Rebels were powerless to help their brother, they
could at least give him the chance to "ride it out" on the
highway shoulder. Dale was in fact a butcher by occupation;
he handled a meat cleaver eight hours a day and had developed
perhaps the strongest set of forearms in the club. Dale didn't
panic, and with patient determination he managed to slow down
gradually. He eventually wound up in a roadside ditch, but he
didn't "drop his bike." Later that evening Dale's brothers
would toast and praise him for a "class" performance.

In order to minimize the risks, the patch holders conduct
"scooter checks" during the periodic gas stops. Otherwise, any
loose nut or bolt always seems to remove itself at the least
opportune moment. For example, Raunch used one gas stop to
reset his carburettor with Indian's assistance. Meanwhile, the
members and their ol' ladies visit the washrooms, eat snack
foods, smoke cigarettes, drink coffee and sodas, and engage in
good-humoured bull sessions.

The noise of forty hogs coming back to life is overwhelming. I
recall not being able to hear the sound of my own engine or even
sense its vibrations. All was engulfed in a collective thunder. It
was on this Victoria Day run that I concluded that a club run is
the single group event that has the greatest psychological impact
on the members: "The run is really what it's all about. That's
were it all comes together" (Saint). A run is rich with symbolism and charged with excitement and emotion. It provides
meaning within a context of danger, power, and mystique. The
run confirms a patch holder's claim to personal and social
validity as an outlaw biker. Members are able to validate their
identity as outlaw bikers by acting out their freedom ethic:

I dislike to use the word, but we power trip on each other. It's a time when you can let your hair down and be the kind of biker that you want. If you happen to be on the hell-raising side . . . a mandatory run is the time to do it. On a mandatory run we don't take any shit from anybody! (Wee Albert)

They act out their identity as brothers by sharing in mutually enjoyable activities:

There's a social aspect to it. We become one; we're brothers. It's getting closer to your brother. Riding our bikes together makes us more in tune with each other. (Slim)

They act out their identity as social rebels by brandishing their motorcycles as subcultural border markers:

That was beautifully heavy! Like I was riding sixth in line; and you'd look back and there would be nothing but fucking bikes! They were stretched out for about a mile. We must have made a few citizens shit their pants. You can imagine the looks on their faces when we passed them by. (Blues)

There are no welcome mats laid out for bikers at private campgrounds. Their aggressive appearance and raucous style intimidate most campers, especially the proprerietors. When the club reached Long Beach, a provincial camp-ground, the rangers said that the camp-site was full. Two of the Rebels rode past the barricades to see for themselves, and the RCMP were called by the nervous park rangers. The scouting party found the camp-ground to be "packed like sardines, man!" Snake suggested that "One of us should get one site and invite the rest in as guests; we'd have the camp-site all to ourselves in two hours!" When the RCMP arrived they handled the situation very professionally and advised the road captain and president that suitable accommodations were available at Amisk Lake. When we arrived at Amisk Lake the accommodations were indeed found to be suitable, but they were also occupied. The

Rebels decided to take over a field that was adjacent to, but relatively isolated from the main camp-ground. It was the best arrangement for both worlds"; the Rebels would be left alone to enjoy the weekend in their own fashion without bothering any of the citizens.

The tents were set up and the members had begun some serious wine tasting, when I decided to unpack my Spalding J5V football.

Snake: When I was riding beside you and I saw that football, I said: "Jesus, he wants to get us all killed!" A football on a run is a dangerous weapon.

Caveman: He was sent here by the Warlords with a football so that we'd commit suicide with it.

Steve: Naw, he just wants to see what a bunch of fucking primitives will do when you give them a toy.

A wild game of team keep-away began with members taking occasional breaks from the action to guzzle some wine.

Larry: Killerball, that's what it was. Boy, I'll tell you, I picked up some pretty wild bruises. You and that football have gotta go. It's funny, as long as I've been with the club, nobody ever thought of it before . . . we had a lot of fun. It gets everybody off that drinking scene. Sure, everyone had to be drunk to even go out there, but two hours later you've sobered right up . . . but then someone put a bunch of acid in the wine and nobody knew about it.

Coyote: I think that it was Voodoo.

Larry: Yeah, that stupid Voodoo, and all of a sudden everybody was wrecked and I couldn't figure out what I was doing at first. It felt like a kill-or-be-killed situation.

The team that was getting the worst of it grabbed the football, some cans of beer and bottles of wine, along with a hash pipe, and retreated up a tree. Those members on the ground felt that those in the tree were being "elitist assholes" and decided to bring them down. When throwing branches didn't work, they got hold of some axes and started to chop down the tree. The men in the tree defended their position by throwing empties at the axemen. The members on the ground then went to the club trailer, got out the emergency flares, and started shooting them into the tree. While the tree members were able to dodge the flares themselves, the flares started a grass fire under the tree. The treed patch holders surrendered the football, and some strikers were told to put out the fire before it ruined their campsite. And so the weekend went.

Over the three-day period, some Rebels rented row-boats and motor boats and went fishing. Jim, who only brought "a can of beans and my fishing rod," caught nine on one outing and feasted on jackfish for the rest of the weekend. Tiny and Shultz were not so lucky. Shultz was towing Tiny's row-boat, but the weight and drag was too much, and Tiny's boat sank.

> *Shultz*: Tiny went down with the fucking ship. When the water started coming in, he just sat there.
> *Caveman*: Tiny is just too fucking lazy to move.
> *Steve*: They could leave him out there in the lake as a spare boat. Just turn him on his belly, paint two numbers on his side, and get him to hang on to the oars.

A lot of the members caught fish, which they fried and shared with their "bros" over evening fires. There were hopes for roast pig. On previous mandatory runs, the off-the-farm trio of Raunch, Crash, and Caveman had raided a farmyard and brought back a pig. But on this trip, one member of the rustling team, Caveman, had a cast from heel to crotch as the result of an oil-rig mishap. While he still managed to ride his hog, he was unable to run down pigs. Crash did try to steal some chickens from a farm, but "that farmer must have five dogs for every chicken he has."

As with most other Rebel social functions, runs emphasize partying hard, long, and wild. Members expect that "everyone will get wasted." A patch holder has to take his ability to party seriously, or, as Wee Albert advised, "If you leave the party early, someone's liable to piss in your boots or pull out the pegs from your tent, if someone hasn't already fallen on top of it." However, it had been a long day of riding, football, fishing, wrestling, and initiation ceremonies. Furthermore, members had brought ol' ladies along and were eager to enjoy their company. The brothers began to crawl back to their tents and sleeping-bags around 4:00 a.m. However, Terrible Tom was exceptionally keen on partying and was not to be denied. At 5:00 a.m., after the last of his bros has passed out by the fire, Tom started yelling, "Get up! Get up! Let's party!" When he didn't get the response he wanted, Tom began singing his version of Indian war chants while pounding a rock on a garbage can. The next morning Steve jumped Tom and hand-cuffed him to a barbed-wire fence. Steve then proceeded to urinate on him: "Tom, you're going to smell as sweet as you sing!"

These hedonistic practices are very much a part of the freedom ethic. Partying is an expression of the outlaw biker's principle of laidback freedom and pleasure. Such impulses run counter to the Establishment's social tenet of maintaining structure through rigid control, and the middle-class morality of restraint leading to respectable moderation. In contrast to moderation and restraint, many Rebel activities are geared towards spontaneity and the generation of intensity: "it all feels best when we can hang loose and wild." These characteristics of spontaneity and intensity leave members with the feeling that the ties between them are genuine, that nothing between them is contrived or artificially regulated. The interaction and bonding that result have a substantial psychological impact. Specifically, the feeling that their lifestyle is truly genuine forms a corner-stone of the biker's identity and acts as a concrete reference point of meaning when he asks himself, "What makes my world worthwhile?" When a patch holder would talk to me of the difference between his world and that of the straight citizen, the pivotal points of dissimilarity inevitably included the dimen-sions of intensity and emotionality. Bikers often perceive straight society as a theatre of deception, a back-stabbing scenario that is hypocritically disguised by a thin veil of re-spectability; it is polite, but it is also superficial. Straight society is seen as lacking anything in the way of meaningful commit-ment or emotional depth. When the patch holders are on a run, they create a world of risk taking and thrill chasing. Collective indulgence in this kind of adventure leads to the formation of bonds of brotherhood that are "blood true."

BIKER GANG STRUCTURE

RCMP Gazette

Taken from the Royal Canadian Mounted Police Gazette (RCMP Gazette), *this article is important for understanding how the police view the one-percenter clubs, their rules and lifestyles.*

MGs are organized into rigid, hierarchal organizations much like traditional organized crime families or multi-national corporations. The Hells Angels are organized like franchises – albeit paramilitary ones. Each regional chapter enjoys independence in club business, but is required to adhere to the Hells Angels' philosophies and guidelines. In other words, each Hells Angels chapter remains independent as long as it's profitable, low key and avoids undue police attention. And each Hells Angels chapter and member must be successful in promoting the Hells Angels' reputation as the biggest and "baddest" OMG. The Halifax, Nova Scotia Hells Angels chapter violated these rules when, among other things, some members sold drugs to agents. And if gangs violate the rules, they may be placed on probation and another chapter will take over daily business until the gang can regain its independence.

Information seems to indicate that the Hells Angels would have a national president. "Officer" or executive bikers are elected.

The following structure is specific to the Hells Angels and their puppet gangs.

Each Chapter:

- Enforces club rules and punishments for local members;
- Maintains independence over internal discipline and local gang activities/business;
- Conducts local intelligence gathering and keeps tabs on rival gangs/law enforcement;
- Assigns colours, supervises prospects, and organizes voting/seniority rights; and,
- Maintains regular contact with brother/puppet gangs, and associates.

Officers' Ranks and Duties:

Executive members are usually elected once a year by colour-wearing members. The officers are not necessarily the wealthiest bikers. The positions consist of the following by order of importance:

President:

- Leader of the gang with full authority over the members;
- Can overrule any decision voted upon by membership; and,
- Leads all runs.

Vice-President:

- Assumes president's duties in his absence.

Secretary/Treasurer:

- Collects fines, pays bills, expenses, court costs and bail money;
- Keeps all books on club-related business and collects minutes;
- Records names, phone numbers and addresses on all members and associates;

- Issues travel money and keeps track of gang debts; and,
- May act as intelligence officer.

Sgt.-at-Arms:

- Keeps order/enforces discipline during meetings – "church";
- Protects gang's arsenal, acquires new weapons, organizes war strategies;
- Rides at rear of pack on runs; and,
- Carries out President's order during wars.

Road Captain:

- Maps out route, carries money, and deals with police during runs/events;
- Rides at the front of pack with the President during runs; and,
- Plans accommodation, route stops, arrival/departure times.

Soldiers in the Biker Army

Member:
- Is accepted by Hells Angels worldwide;
- May have particular crime speciality or area;
- Attends runs, events and weekly meetings;
- Is either in good or bad standing (no honorary members for the Hells Angels);
- Pays dues and votes in gang business; and,
- Establishes criminal "micro-clubs" or "cells" with other members and associates.

Prospect:
- Has extensive criminal experience and may have criminal expertise;
- Is likely a past member of a puppet club;
- Has no voting power;
- Must be nominated by member then voted in unanimously by gang to become a member;
- Is totally subservient to members;
- Probation period varies according to business (criminal) potential (about one year); and,

- Wears bottom location rocker, MC badge, and prospect badge, not full colours.

Hangaround:

- Has criminal experience and is subservient to all members and prospects;
- Must be sponsored by member and obtain majority vote to become prospect;
- Is excluded from all official business and cannot vote;
- Cannot attend meetings and wears only city patch on front pocket; and,
- Performs menial jobs and acts as minor criminal associate and security guard for members.

Friend

- Is an official status;
- Is sponsored by member and must win majority vote to become hangaround;
- Can be either puppet member or street-level criminal;
- Is subservient to all members, prospects and hangarounds; and,
- Enjoys an increase in status over street criminals as a result of Hells Angels' "friendship."

Associate:

- Has proven useful to the gang;
- Supports or profits from bikers' illicit and/or legitimate businesses;
- May be part of criminal element or legitimate working/professional classes;
- May attend parties, runs, and events; and,
- Cannot vote, wear colours or attend meetings.

Women:

- Wives (common law or legal) are called "old ladies" and are protected;
- Party girls are used by one or all members;
- Cannot wear colours, vote, attend meetings or hold office; and,
- Can gather intelligence for the gang.

Structure for other OMGs

(Outlaws, Bandidos, ParaDice Riders, Satan's Choice, etc.)
Unlike the Hells Angels, other gangs may have regional chapters which abide by national and even international decisions. Each regional chapter maintains a level of independence in day-to-day operations.

National (Mother) Chapter:

- Central or founding chapter of OMG;
- Approves new charters and national/international business decisions;
- Organizes world events;
- Presides over multi-chapter gangs; and,
- Communicates between local and international gangs.

National President:

- Makes final decisions for all regional chapters in key business and financial areas;
- Is often the founder of the gang; and,
- Consults with international president, if one exists.

National Vice-President:

- Is in charge of particular regions or districts; and,
- Handles all problems between regional chapters which affect the gang as a whole.

National Treasure/Secretary:

- Manages all money from the regional chapters;
- Records the national minutes and also collects summaries of regional minutes; and,
- Coordinates regular communication between regional chapters.

National Enforcer:

- Bodyguard to the national president; and,
- Metes out punishments, retrieves colours, and removes tattoos.

Regional (Single) Chapter:

- Maintains regular contact with national chapter; and,
- Follows "by-laws" or "constitutions" laid out by the national chapter.

Criminal Executives (president, vice-president, road captain, etc.)

- Follows the same guidelines as the Hells Angels.

Member, Striker/Probate, Hangaround:

- Similar to the Hells Angels' organization, but probation periods may vary; and,
- There is no "friend" position.

Honorary Member:

- Is retired member in good standing who pays no dues;
- Retains colours and insignia until death; and,
- Is required to attend gang funerals.

Joining an OMG

Prospects (probates and strikers) typically must be white, over 18 or 21 years old, English-speaking males with established criminal histories as drug-dealers or weapons/explosives experts. Each man must own a high-performance motorcycle, typically a Harley Davidson. Applicants used to have to commit murder to enter a major gang like the Hells Angels or Outlaws, but now a keen business sense and ability to make money are just as valued as violence. "MBAs instead of murderers" could be the mantra of major OMGs.

The term "prospect" is reserved for applicants to the Hells Angels and the Bandidos. "Striker" is a common Canadian term for other OMGs, while the Outlaws and Bandidos biker gangs use "probate." While puppet clubs may recruit somewhat inexperienced members from the street, powerful OMGs like the Hells Angels, Bandidos or Outlaws do not. New members are generally recruited from puppet clubs where they displayed the necessary loyalty, violence and initiative.

The prospect must win an unanimous vote by members to become a full member. If successful, the prospect must attend runs and pay a club membership/colours fee. He then adds the club's logo to his bottom rocker. Colours are restricted to members. Friends, hangarounds, and associates wear Big Red Machine clothing or "support your local Hells Angels" t-shirts.

If unsuccessful, the gang may seize the applicant's motorcycle, reclaim his bottom rocker and beat him. Any member, applicant, hangaround or associate in "bad standing" with an OMG also faces this punishment.

If a prospect has a girlfriend or wife, his loyalty to her will also be tested. She must also have an appropriate respectful attitude toward the club and its members.

Very few clubs still soil the initiate with feces and oil. Initiations usually involve parties, with alcohol and sex and the awarding of colours. New members have to provide the gang with the names and addresses of family members, relatives and friends.

There is little evidence that OMGs are relaxing their traditional racist entrance requirements.

"I killed eleven people for these colours," a biker declared, rejecting the popular conception that initiations involve urine and feces, "do you think I would let anyone piss on them?"

SOLIDARITY AMONG THE REBELS

Daniel R. Wolf and David E. Young

This fascinating article describes the changes in identity a young researcher experienced on joining a one-per-center outlaw biker club. Dan Wolf was a student of Anthropology at the time, and his piece serves as one of the best accounts of how one's identity changes as research progresses from an outsider's to an insider's perspective. Dan also reflects on the management of conflict within The Rebels – the club he joined.

The Rebels M.C. arose from a political vacuum that was created in the City of Edmonton when police "surveillance" and subsequent legal action led to the demise of the then Coffin Cheaters M.C. and the Sinners M.C. The Rebels M.C., in conjunction with the Warlords M.C. (origin 1969), have since that time maintained a tight territorial rein – preventing the emergence of other outlaw clubs in the City of Edmonton.

From an organizational perspective the Rebels Motorcycle Club constitutes a formal voluntary association comprised of approximately twenty-five adult males ranging in age from twenty to thirty-six years. The Rebels M.C. operates within the parameters of a well-defined but flexible formal organization. The organizational cornerstones of the club include (i) a

214 DANIEL R. WOLF AND DAVID E. YOUNG

club charter in the form of a written constitution and (ii) a political structure made up of "officers of the club": president, vice-president, treasurer, secretary, sergeant-at-arms, and road captain. In addition to their position-specific duties, these officers constitute a separate decision-making body referred to as an "executive board." Finally, there are (iii) rules and regulations which prescribe the formal structural elements and official mechanisms of control, codified in a book of rules.

The Clubhouse

The Rebels M.C. clubhouse is located on a rented section of farmland along the south-eastern outskirts of the City of Edmonton. This proved to be an ideal location because, as one member expressed: "There's nothing out here but land, our clubhouse, our bikes and us. We can be as loud as we want, get as drunk as we want, get as stoned as we want, have as good a time as we want, doing what we fucking want, and nobody bothers us". Within the isolated setting of the Rebels clubhouse, where displays of inter-member differences do not convey weakness to, and consequently invite threats from, an antagonistic environment, there exist both informal opportunities and institutionalized mechanisms for the expression of differences of opinion on a variety of matters. Variation manifests itself as members verbalize diverse theories of group culture; conflict may furthermore arise as members attempt to operationalize those diverse theories of group culture. Those close to the Rebels come to recognize that the club's operational paradigm (the conducting of affairs and the forming of policy) continually responds to both internal political influences (members acknowledge the presence of conservative, moderate, and extreme factions) and interpersonal pressures which are apparent in the day-to-day life of the club. Of particular interest are the disagreements between the extreme and conservative elements of the club that surfaced during various decision or policy making situations. For example, two members demonstrated variation in operationalizing their theories of group culture when they disagreed on the validity of a member's invitation to two outsiders to attend a party at the clubhouse. Ken, a six-year member and president of the club, had earlier given the ethnographer his version of group identity when asked if there were any rules related to guests coming out to the clubhouse:

> Yeah, we don't allow anyone out at the clubhouse unless he's on a motorcycle, or we definitely know is a biker, with an invitation and an escort by a member. We definitely don't want a hippie coming out and asking what's going on. If anyone came out there without an invitation or escort, they'd be told to take off, or whatever.

The member who issued the invitation, Jack – a member of the conservative faction – felt that the two outsiders were eligible as guests insofar as they both rode bikes, had been friendly enough in the bar, were stopping over in Edmonton as part of a "righteous" 6,000 mile cross-country tour which had originated in St. Catharines, Ontario, and, as the member pointed out: "I'd like to see hospitality to bikers as our (the club's) first name." The member who challenged the invitation, Blues – an extreme one percenter – focused on the fact that one of the guests was riding a Kawasaki 900, a Japanese motorcycle. It is the American made Harley Davidson, with its long and venerated folk tradition, that prevails as the only motorcycle considered worthy of symbolizing the outlaw lifestyle. For Blues the presence of the Kawasaki was an ideological intrusion that was not about to be casually overlooked:

> I'm not going to have that piece of shit here! That's a racer's bike. You drive a Harley (Davidson) because you know where it's at as far as bikes go. I don't want that thing parked by my clubhouse. I drove out here to get away from that sort of crap.

Although Jack and Blues both agreed that riding Harley Davidson was a necessary criterion in order to be a member, or even a friend of the club, Blues had gone one step further and had incorporated "riding a hog" (Harley Davidson) into his interpretation of what the group identity was all about. Blues had in effect drawn the club's social boundaries tighter than Jack.

It is expected that conflict which arises on the inter-individual level – in this case the result of two members differing in their perceptions of the group value system – will be resolved by the member concerned negotiating a compromise. If this process fails to settle the issue and the situation threatens to become volatile, an executive officer will enter the discussion as a third party and, if necessary, effect an arbitrary decision . . . ideally a decision that does not involve the creation of a losing party. In this instance Ken fulfilled his presidential function and regulated the conflict by acting as a mediator between the two opposing parties. In his role as primal leader (president) Ken exercised the judgement of King Solomon: the guest could stay but the bike couldn't. The compromise solution involved the guest parking the Japanese motorcycle in a ditch by the highway entrance, two hundred and fifty yards away from the clubhouse and beyond the view of the members.

If the nature of the issue giving rise to the conflict is such that it holds implications for the club as a whole, a parliamentary strategy will be implemented for its resolution. Within the controlled organizational setting of the group, such as club meetings taking place at the clubhouse, the Rebels Motorcycle Club is relatively isolated from threatening pressures emanating from outside groups. In the absence of external threat, the perception and behavioral expression of diversity does not have negative implications for either group or individual welfare. The parliamentary procedures enacted during weekly club meetings provide for the expression of differences in opinion, the elicitation of conflict through debate, and, finally, the reaching of consensus through a standardized decision making procedure in the form of voting.

During the course of participant-observation of the Rebels M.C., a situation arose which saw members take incompatible positions in regards to a fundamental issue concerning the club's future. The issue was whether or not the Rebels Motorcycle Club should form a chapter in the City of Red Deer. Members promoting expansion wanted to see the Rebels Motorcycle Club become a larger organization. They furthermore argued that a Rebel's chapter located in Red Deer – central Alberta – would deter the northward movement of the Grim Reapers Motorcycle Club, a notorious rival club based in southern Alberta:

> Bloody warfare threatens to explode over an attempt by a
> Calgary motorcycle gang to move into the city . . . Ed-
> monton's Rebels Motorcycle Club has warned the inter-
> lopers their attempt to move into the city will be resisted
> . . . the Grim Reapers have already been involved in
> violence here . . . shots have been fired say police . . .
> The gangs are normally kept under surveillance by the
> R.C.M.P. (Royal Canadian Mounted Police) and mem-
> bers of the city's elite task force. (*Edmonton Sun*, January
> 31, 1979)

The defensive strategy of establishing a chapter of the Rebels
M.C. in Red Deer was opposed by those members who wished
to promote the Rebels Motorcycle Club as a tightly-knit unit
and who felt that expansion would result in the depletion of
both material and personnel resources. When members failed to
reach a consensus through informal discussions the matter was
raised at a meeting, debated, and resolved through a formal
voting procedure; expansion was rejected.

The parliamentary decision-making strategy, as it is enacted in
the context of the Rebels M.C., is characterized by a number of
features that mitigate the possible disruptive consequences of
internal ideological conflict. Preceding the meeting, members will
have inevitably engaged in an informal exchange of information
concerning potential solutions to the problem at hand. These
discussions were observed to take place in informal settings,
under amiable circumstances, e.g., drinking or shooting pool
together. As a result, there is minimal emotional hostility or
aggression. Intermember differences come to be viewed as logical
alternatives, as opposed to aberrations. These brainstorm sessions
promote an undisciplined, sometimes humorous, but always
creative exploration of "raw" ideas. The effects of these pre-
paratory activities carry over to the formal meeting and serve to
reduce the possibility of the members focusing on a we-versus-
they distinction as opposed to a we-versus-the-problem orientation. Members are themselves aware of both the fact of variation
and the inevitability of change:

Blues (Rebels M.C.):   They're (new members) not living up to
my (personal) expectations, but they're living up to my (club)

ideals. We (older members) pretty well built the club; and they live up to the constitution and things like that, that we've laid down. But I'm not saying that they follow us a hundred percent; because then we'd never change, and we're always changing.

Ethnographer: Why do you feel that there would be no change?

Blues (Rebels M.C.): Because the idea of the club would get so monopolized that it wouldn't work. You wouldn't get any change and we would always be staying with the same horses . . . it just wouldn't work without new ideas and change.

Ethnographer: In that case, what, or who, decides what the purpose of the club is?

Blues (Rebels M.C.): It's something that is going on in the mind of each and every member.

During the course of the meeting, orderly communication of opinions is mediated by the president, providing each individual with an opportunity to speak, but avoiding the domination by any one individual or faction. The sergeant-at-arms enacts formalized procedures that ensure the orderly handling of any dispute that threatens to get out of hand. Finally, a formalized voting procedure provides due process for settling conflict. It should be emphasized that a formalized structure and process for decision making does not preclude a group style that is characterized by openness, candor, and general "bullshitting," that produces a relaxed and non-stressful environment. For example, at one meeting, Indian began a pretence that he had gotten drunk during the mid-session beer break. Steve was the sergeant-at-arms at the time.

Steve (Rebels M.C.): Are you drunk?

Indian (Rebels M.C.): (Jokingly responds) Yeah, sure, why not!?

Steve (Rebels M.C.): Good! That's a ten dollar fine. Pay up after the meeting!

Indian (Rebels M.C.): Hey, wait a minute! I'm not drunk!

Steve (Rebels M.C.):Glad to see that you've sobered up. You can stay for the meeting, but you still have a ten dollar fine to pay.

Members accept both the procedures involved in the parliamentary strategy, and the possibility that a *partial* agreement – a compromise solution with which none of the members are in complete accord – may have to serve as the basis for decision making.

> No one can stand there and say, "Well, this is what the club is all about, and that's that." Everything that happens to the club, or that the club does, is put to a vote. Everybody knows what is expected of them, but then everybody also has their say. You don't always get your way, but you always get your say. We work things out. It's put to a vote; majority rules (Raunch, Rebels M.C.).

Members furthermore recognize the fact that while certain club policies may lack total consensus, the club's survival – in an often hostile environment – depends on total commitment in carrying out those plans of action: "In many ways the club is like a safe. There may be a lot of loose change on the inside, but when the door to the safe opens, the Rebels come out as one". Thus, members of the Rebels M.C. participate in moulding the group paradigm through an institutionalized framework (parliamentary strategy) wherein they are able to innovate, evaluate, and control group policies. Individual divergence in effect shapes the ongoing political rhetoric, forms the basis of social change, and is accepted as part of the group process.

The Club Bar

An integral part of outlaw motorcycle club tradition is the establishment of a tavern as a regular drinking spot and rendez-vous point for club members: the "club bar." The club bar complements the "clubhouse," the locus of formal club functions and social activities, by providing an alternative focal point for informal group gatherings. While the clubhouse is the private domain of the Rebels M.C., the club bar is found in a public hotel (tavern). It is this aspect of contact with the public that allows the club bar to serve a number of unique functions in terms of the club and its members. Here potential novitiates can exhibit their prowess, demonstrate commitment to the subculture's ideals, experiment with and perhaps form lasting ties with the club.

The club bar thus functions as a buffer zone or point of cultural interface between the club and the host society. Recruiting new members requires a performance on the part of members which is dramatic enough to attract potential "strikers"; however, club members in the bar must continually negotiate their presence and behavioral style in terms of highly unpredictable and often hostile external variables. Carrying this off taxes the varied abilities of club members and does, in fact, aggravate differences in opinion concerning the desirability of trafficking with "citizens." For example, despite the privileges purveyed by management to the members in particular and club functions served by the bar in general, not all the Rebels evaluate their presence there in a positive sense: "They give us privileges and what not, which is bad in a way because our people start spending too much time in the bar". Some members, such as Blues and Terrible Tom, boycotted the bar. Terrible Tom showed up at the club bar only once over a period of three years. Blues periodically avoided the club bar while actively lobbying against attendance there. On one occasion, this lobbying procedure led to a heated argument when Blues suggested certain members change their colours (club emblems) to read: "Corona Hotel M.C." Finally, the presence of members at the bar had been an issue of formal debate at club meetings:

> There are a few (members) that don't care for bar themselves. They don't like going to bars . . . We don't blame them cause you can't talk to nobody in them. The damn music is so loud . . . It's been brought up at club meetings lots of times, trying to get out of the bar, you know. But you can't do it. Let's face it! You've got (approximately) thirty guys and a lot of guys, including myself, want to go.

Before examining the rationale underlying the disparate attitude towards club bars, it is critical to reiterate that some form of public consensus, however limited, is necessary. The necessity arises from the fact that the Rebels M.C. is neither an economically self-sufficient nor a socially self perpetuating unit.

These reasons alone would preclude total self-containment. Like all urban subcultures, the Rebels M.C. must ultimately rely on the organization and resources of the surrounding society. Thus, the only means by which the Rebels can actualize their ideology as an egalitarian undifferentiated society is to enter into limited interaction with the society whose lack of egalitarian organization is so despised by club members.

Negative sentiments expressed by some members result from two separate aspects of group dynamics that are endemic to urban subcultures. The first of these concerns the preservation of organizational integrity: "It's our own society." The maintenance of this organizational integrity requires the establishment of social structural boundaries between "straight society" and the club on institutional, interpersonal, and personal-value levels of participation. With respect to the preservation of these social structural boundaries, some members reasoned that increased interaction with the public would weaken the club as an integral unit by making it susceptible to outside influence. "I'd just as soon see no contact with them (the public). I don't care what they think of us. The more contact you have with them, the looser you are".

The second concern involves maintaining an operational balance between vested group interests and the psychological needs of individual members. The danger here lies in individuals using the group as a reference in constructing their personal identities, i.e., the psychological payoffs of being a Rebel, yet failing to dedicate oneself and one's resources totally to the group, the brotherhood.

Some of the members . . . mingle with the outside, with the citizens, more than they should. In the sense that they should be with their brothers. They should be learning what their brothers are all about, because they haven't learned that yet.

The paradoxical demands placed on the group by the requirement of organizational integrity (the maintenance of club boundaries), and the necessity of organizational perpetuity (the recruitment of new members), is solved by members who by virtue of disparate attitudes towards outsiders, enact two different types of roles in their presence. One group type might be metaphorically labelled "the wall." The wall is comprised of those Rebels who actively manipulate the harsh stereotype laid upon them by the dominant society in a manner that serves to reinforce the boundaries between the club and outsiders. The demands and dynamics of border maintenance received fairly explicit expression in the ideology of the group:

Ethnographer: Is there a common understanding that you avoid straights and hippies in the bar?
Raunch (Rebels M.C.):   Yeah.
Ethnographer: Is it talked about?
Raunch (Rebels M.C.):   Yeah. It's just generally understood that when you're sitting in the bar, you're not supposed to have any straights sitting around the table. If you've got a friend there, and a member doesn't want him there, all he's got to do is say so, and the guy has got to go, no exceptions.

The dialogue between several members that follows below took place in the Rebels M.C. club bar. The incident revolves around one member, Snake, who for personal reasons and with no particular success, attempted to introduce a degree of variation in the operational group identity concerning outsiders.

Killer (Rebels M.C.):   Hey Snake, what kind of bike does your friend ride?
Snake (Rebels M.C.):   He doesn't. He's a close friend of mine. He just plays the guitar.
Danny (Rebels M.C.):   We don't give a shit! There's no room for him. Tell him to get lost!

An appropriate label for the other subgroup would be "the gate." The gate consists of those Rebels who selectively admit certain outsiders, and who "exoticize" their subcultural image and exploit the popular myth of outlaw biker prowess, adventure and brotherhood in an outgoing fashion: "You have to remember that before a biker strikes for the club, the club strikes for the biker".

The reality or perceptual impact of the wall and the gate are best described by an outsider who encounters them. The outsider in this case was Walter Kowal, a graduate student in archaeology who was working his way through university by singing in a rock band. The band, named Lover, would on occasion play at the Kingsway Motor Inn, a one time Rebel bar.

Ethnographer: How did you originally make contact with the Rebels?

Walter K.:   Well Tony, the drummer, he's a biker. You know, he has a biker mentality and he thinks they're great guys; it was no problem for him to fit right in. Armand (Rebels M.C.) bought dope from the bass player . . . so I got to know these guys but I was kept on a very removed level. I could get along with guys like Clayton, Tiny, and Terrible Tom, but the rest I really didn't care to, because like I said, they tend to be too volatile; like you never knew what they were up to.

Ethnographer: How did you differentiate between the two groups? How would you decide which of the Rebels were approachable and which were not?

Walter K.:   Just by their attitude. Most of these guys weren't too bad, but you could feel that you weren't welcome when you sat down at their table; and this was even after we'd (the band) had them over at several of our parties.

Ethnographer: Were you ever threatened?

Walter K.:   I was never threatened physically by any of them, at any time. But it's just that you could tell. Like a guy, like Tiny, would sit down at the table, break a glass, and eat it. You know, eat the glass! He'd be entertaining and having fun with you all of the time. Whereas the other guys would sit there and remain aloof. They'd stay outside the whole thing. They wouldn't enter into the verbal banter or anything; they'd hang back. You would never know what they were saying, thinking, or anything.

Ethnographer: Aside from stonewalling you with these non-verbal cues (kinesics and proxemics), did you feel intimidated in any other way?

Walter K.:   It was generally what you called the unapproach-able group that got into the scraps. The guys I got along with generally didn't get involved in those things unless it looked like things were getting out of hand. So I didn't feel that they would be sort of explosive and do something weird just because I said something to them. Like Caveman, I saw him drop two guys coming into the doorway of the Kingsway. Those two guys never laid a finger on the sucker. Caveman just decimated them before they even hit the ground. And that intimidated me. Even though it wasn't his fault. They started hurling abuse at him, and he said something like, "You'd better leave for your own good," or something like that. They didn't, and all of a sudden, wham, bam, bam, bam, bam! I never saw anything so fast! I think what stands out most was the force of the blows. I mean I heard those things, and they were bone jarring; bummer! That sucker had arms on him that looked like legs. After that I maintained my social distance as it were. Like I said, that's terrifying. Like I figured, "Wow! Would that ever hurt!" Like "crunch!" There goes the nose . . . another operation.

In response to this ever-present threat of conflict, the mood and demeanor of the Rebels while drinking at the bar is noticeably different from drinking sessions held at the clubhouse. "Putting down brew" at the bar becomes more calculated in nature; that is, while some members may become totally "wasted," others in turn will become more reserved and attentive. They assume the task of constantly surveying the bar for potentially threatening situations into which their inebriated brothers may inadvertently fall. These members personify the image of gunslingers of a bygone era, waiting for some bounty hunter to make a foolish move:

"Once you put on colors [club emblem signifying membership] you draw heat, sometimes fast, sometimes heavy. The cops you can predict; you learn fast where the lines are and where and when you can cross. But with citizens you never know . . . [when] some guy is going to try to waste you by running you off the road . . . in the bar you gotta expect everything from drunks who don't know what they're doing, to guys in kung fu . . . who do know what they're doing and can be tough as nails".

Ken, while discussing the nature and frequency of contact situations the club had with outsiders or "average citizens," stated that: "The average citizen is mostly the person you see in the bar. And as far as any contact goes, that's where it usually is *And I would like to see it end*". However, any extreme policy of isolationism, while protecting intermember ties, would jeopardize the perpetuation of the club itself. Interestingly enough, then, if all members of the Rebels M.C. were one hundred percent committed to the core ideology of the group, i.e., the brotherhood, there would be problems. A comparative analysis of the history of the Warlords M.C. illustrates that the danger of such a situation developing can prove to be more real than hypothetical.

The Warlords emerged in 1968 largely through the organizational efforts of two ex-members of the then defunct Coffin Cheaters M.C. of Edmonton. By the early 1970's, the Warlords had consolidated their position as one of the two established outlaw clubs in the city with approximately fifteen members. However, the brotherhood ties that developed between members were so extreme as to preclude any individual breaking into the club's tight-knit social network. It was during this time that the club had one prospect "striker" (attempt to become a member) for a period of two years before they rejected him. The Warlords subsequently developed a reputation of being largely unapproachable: "The Warlords are more a closed clique of guys who stick pretty much to themselves than they are a club. You don't see them around all that much" (Biker in a bar). The Warlords furthermore isolated themselves from interaction with other clubs in the province:

> Like they (Warlords) want to be a motorcycle club, but they want to be a motorcycle club strictly on their own, with nothing to do with other clubs. We've never once had the two clubs (Rebels and Warlords) come together for a run. Some of their members, like Rae, Dump, and them, come to our parties, drink with us sometimes, but that's about it.

In conjunction with this isolation from the larger biker community, the Warlords did not maintain a club bar. Rather, they restricted their drinking and socializing to their clubhouse (a member's home), or irregular visits to various bars that were often located on the outskirts of the city, e.g., the Airway Motor Inn. While contrasting the style of the two Edmonton clubs, a Warlord commented that: "We're different from the Rebels. We don't go around giving cardiac arrests to little old ladies on the street and we don't put on a show in bars." However, time, alternative commitments, and an internal conflict eventually took their cumulative toll. By 1975, Warlord membership was reduced to five. The Warlords Motorcycle Club was in serious danger of dying from internal atrophy and external threats:

> As far as I'm concerned, the Warlords aren't a club. I've met them three times, once without bikes, once without colors, and another time one of our members received an unsigned card from a supposed Warlord.

The Warlords saw the inevitable fate of their policy of isolation when Onion, a well-known biker who visited and had the respect of many Western Canadian clubs, turned down the overtures of the Warlords, to become a Rebel. The Warlords responded with a change in policy. In order to increase their exposure to the biker community, they began socializing at the Rebels' bar and set about establishing their own club bar by drinking regularly at the Capilano Motor Inn. Invitations to outside bikers to attend Warlord runs as guests were more readily given out. As a result of these initiatives, the Warlords M.C. incorporated two new members and had a third prospect striking for them, all within the space of four summer months of 1975. The Warlords furthermore accepted, for the first time, an invitation to join the Rebels M.C. and the Kings Crew M.C. of Calgary on a joint run on Labour Day weekend, 1975.

In summary, although the Warlords M.C. had always been a solid enough club in terms of their interpersonal commitments, i.e., the ideology of brotherhood, they became overcommitted to that ideology – overcommitted in the sense that they became inflexible with respect to maintaining outside contacts. What the Warlords failed to establish was a club bar which facilitates the formation of supportive bonds with the larger biker community in general, and provides a point of entry for prospective novitiates in particular.

Violent Encounters with Outside Society

Camouflaging cognitive and behavioral diversity within the club is generally sufficient to maintain an image of club solidarity for both bikers and outsiders present at the bar. This image of solidarity allows club members to suppress feelings of unease at being in a buffer zone; it also helps prevent outsiders from initiating rash actions against club members.

There are times, however, when the buffer zone truce is disrupted by active hostility between club members and outsiders. Although club members may not initiate or welcome violence, an occasional violent encounter with outside society is not without its ancillary benefits. It pulls the group together in a way that other group activities cannot.

Just such a social drama was created by the Canadian Airborne Regiment. For nine years the Airborne Regiment was stationed at Canadian Forces Base Edmonton, Griesbach Barracks, located just north of Edmonton. The specially trained paratroop fighting force, which was then part of Mobile Command and numbered more than eight hundred, ". . . was probably the best-known component of the forces stationed in Edmonton with its high profile reputation as Canada's elite fighting force". The Canadian Airborne Regiment achieved international repute as a peace-keeping force as part of the United Nations task force in Cyprus. However, part of their local "high profile" included practicing their combat techniques in local bars.

The Airborne drank regularly at the Roslyn Hotel, located on the northern outskirts of Edmonton, while the Rebels had adopted the Kingsway Inn as their club bar. In the winter of 1975 the Airborne began showing up at the Kingsway after one of their regiment had been hired as a bouncer. On Wednesday, March 5, thirty members of the Airborne's Francophone unit called One Commando (the Anglophone equivalent is called Two Commando), came to "drink." Three barroom fights later, the police were called to help a patron press charges and the Airborne were ushered outside. The Rebels considered the presence of the Airborne a territorial infringement, and were neither happy nor impressed as they watched the proceedings.

Two nights later, the member of the Airborne who was working as a bouncer at the Kingsway wanted to make room for his friends in the crowded confines of the bar. He picked up a chair that had a leather jacket on it, threw the jacket on the floor, and gave the chair to his friend. The jacket held Larry's (Rebels M.C.) colors. Larry, shooting pool at the time, came over and took the chair back. When the Airborne bouncer spit on Larry, Larry returned the courtesy and then proceeded to throw his adversary over a beer laden table. The other bouncers moved in and ushered the Airborne bouncer and Larry to the door. Larry wrestled the bouncer to the ground and then said: "Fuck you! You're a waste of time. I'm going back and finish my beer!" The Airborne bouncer, insulted, perhaps frightened, called the Forces Base for assistance.

The Rebels began to notice the gradual swelling in the number of Airborne present. They began arriving, two by two, groups of six, and finally a group of nine. Jim placed an emergency call to the clubhouse. At 11:45 p.m., Armand was entering the doorway at the same time as three Airborne. One of the Airborne, speaking in French, told the bouncer to "Call those asshole Rebels outside." Armand, a member of the Rebels M.C. who is bilingual, looked down at the Rebel skull patch on his own club tee-shirt, then said: "*Alors! C'est un Rebel*," and then proceeded to deck the startled Airborne. The band stopped as both groups scrambled to get outside into the fracas which moved to the parking lot. Management immediately locked the doors in order to protect the bar and its patrons. Although the Rebels were joined by a number of friends of the club, Rae (president of the Warlords M.C.) and one bouncer, they were still at a numerical disadvantage:

> Police say Saturday night's brawl, outside the Kingsway Avenue, involved about forty paratroopers from the Canadian Airborne Regiment, and twenty-three members of the Rebels Motorcycle Club (*Edmonton Journal*, March 13, 1975).

The Airborne had also brought with them an impressive collection of street fighting hardware, including karate equipment, a steel ball attached to a chain, a makeshift blackjack (a letter ball inside a sock), steel bars, and a baseball bat. But a small group that fights as a single unit has a decided advantage over a larger uncoordinated group. This is precisely what happened.

The Rebels attacked together, with the viciousness of cornered animals. They had shared too much together to think of deserting any of their brothers. It was now a brotherhood of survival, fighting with a vengeance. In the rush to get outside, the Saint, generally a reserved, soft-spoken, certainly not aggressive individual, found himself trapped with two Airborne in the exit way. With him he had a motorcycle battery that he had intended to trade to a friend of the club. Battery in hand, he swung wildly. The Airborne were again caught off guard, and crumpled next to the doorway. Ken, leading the way, fell when struck by a ball and chain. Clayton was slashed on the shoulder while trying to help him. Rae, of the Warlords M.C., had found an old hockey stick in the parking lot and swung at the chain-wielding Airborne, breaking both ribs and resolve.

The Airborne began to disperse as they saw a number of their fellows being beaten. These were not raw recruits but personnel that had completed their training in unarmed combat, weaponry, parachuting, and other special skills ranging from rappelling to riot control. However, they had not yet endured and shared enough as a group to cement the ties of comradeship that result in members presuming, and acting upon, a principle of self-sacrifice. The bonds of brotherhood certainly do not just happen, nor can they be "trained" for; they must be forged over time through open communication and shared experiences. The commitment that results precludes any alternative that hints of compromise by way of desertion: "They just wouldn't stick together" (Jim, Rebels M.C.). "They were out to shut us down and rough us up. For us, it was survival. We were out to maim. We were going after them with our bare hands and doing something about it. They broke and ran" (Wee Albert, Rebels M.C.). The actual fighting lasted approximately fifteen minutes. The results:

Thirteen Soldiers Hurt in Brawl with Gang

A brawl early Sunday morning between members of a motorcycle gang and soldiers from the Canadian Airborne Regiment at Namao sent thirteen of the soldiers to hospi-

tal for treatment of minor injuries. The brawl, on streets
near the Kingsway Inn . . . apparently started as a personal argument, then spread to the streets, said an Armed
Forces spokesman . . . Most of the soldiers were treated
for lacerations at the base hospital at Namao (*Edmonton
Journal*, March 10, 1975).

In order to prevent any further incidents the management of the
Kingsway Motor Inn proceeded to ban from its premises
anybody who even remotely looked like a biker. The process
of establishing a different club bar began anew; but the confrontation was over.

For the Rebels the brotherhood had been reaffirmed. Each
member had taken extreme risk, and made personal sacrifices
for the group:

> I thought, "Well, this is it!" I looked at all the hardware
> those guys were carrying, and I thought, "Well, this is it!
> I'm probably not going to be able to walk for a month!"
> There must have been at least fifty-five of them. I don't
> think they expected us to fight against those odds, but we
> went at them, swinging, kicking, clawing with anything we
> could find. I got a boot in the head and went down with
> sore ribs, but that was about it.

Whether the process is desperate, heroic, or banal doesn't really
matter; the brotherhood emerges as a necessary condition of
life. Loyalty arises out of the midst of danger, out of the tension
and apprehension of possible injury, mutilation, or worse.

As a result of extensive media coverage and articulation by
the members themselves – from mutual praise to joking references – the "Battle of the Kingsway" became part of Rebel
folklore. The Kingsway incident emerged as a historical refer-
ent that serves to vitalize and confirm a collective identity based
upon brotherhood.

INSIDE THE BANDIDOS

Edward Winterhalder

Edward Winterhalder was a long-time member of the Bandidos Motorcycle Club — a genuine one-percenter outlaw biker club. In this selection, Ed describes the fascinating cat and mouse game played between law enforcement officials and one percent clubs. His trials and tribulations follow on from this selection and are detailed in his book Out In Bad Standing. *He is currently producing a reality television show, featuring prominent Harley-Davidson celebrities who ride with one-percenter clubs.*

It was springtime in Washington State; I thought that it always rained there, but this was one of those rare and beautiful days of unexpected sunshine. It was April of 1999, and it was the day I first met Alain. We were both in the Seattle area to attend the funeral for a fallen Bandido who had actually died while having sex with his girlfriend.

Alain could have been anyone in the Red & Gold world, but the first thing I noticed was that his patch was very unusual; for it had red stitching on all the edges. The center patch was an eagle, and the top/bottom rockers and center patch were light silver on black. I maneuvered myself closer in order to read the rockers and then realized that I was looking at a full-patched member of the "Rock Machine" from Canada; actually the first Rock Machine I had ever seen. Later that day, I learned that his full name was Alain Brunette, but when he introduced himself to me in his heavy French accent, he merely called himself "Alain".

Alain and I talked for a little while and then parted ways. I tried unsuccessfully to find him again before I left, because I wanted to spend more time with him. I had no idea why, but found myself intrigued. There was no way I could have known at that time what an important part of my life he would become.

The next Rock Machine member I saw was in New Mexico, at the Red River Biker Rally in late May of 1999. I was quite surprised to see that their patch had now changed: it was red and gold, no longer silver and black. I had just heard a rumor that Bandidos MC Europe had recently designated them a "Hangaround" club, and the Rock Machine had changed their patch colors to red and gold. As the shock wore off, I found myself pleasantly surprised to see that the rumor was indeed true.

A Hangaround club is an existing club that wants to join a larger motorcycle club. Being accepted as a Hangaround club puts everyone in the biker world on notice, both in the clubs as well as the rest of the biker world, that the small club wants to affiliate with the larger club and that the larger club is considering the change. In the Bandido world, after at least a year, the Bandidos vote as to whether all members of the smaller club are worthy to wear the Bandidos patch. If the vote is affirmative, then the smaller club will become Bandidos Probationary members.

In mid-November, 2000, I traveled to Europe for two reasons. First, to attend a world meeting that was to be held in Denmark, and second, to attend the one year anniversary party of the "patching over" ceremony for the new Bandido chapters of Germany, which was to occur later that month. A patch over is a ceremony where the members of the smaller club change their patches, and start wearing the patches of the larger club. In this case, the Ghostriders MC had "patched over" to become Bandidos in December of 1999, and now they were going to receive their "Germany" bottom rockers.

Most of the time that I traveled to Denmark, I flew into Frankfurt, Germany. The Frankfurt airport officials paid much less attention to motorcycle club members than the officials at the Copenhagen airport. A close friend of mine, Dieter Tenter, who lived not far from Frankfurt, usually picked me up at the airport, or I would catch a train to the town where Dieter lived. On this occasion, Dieter picked me up and I spent one night with him and his family, and then met up with a few USA and German Bandidos. To get from Germany to Denmark, we traveled by minivan.

On the way there, before we got out of Germany, a car pulled along side of us. The passenger started making all sorts of motions at us, then pulled ahead and got right in front of us. A lighted screen popped up at the bottom of the rear window, which told us to follow the car to the next exit. At this time I was informed that the car was an unmarked police car, and that we were being pulled over. No one had any idea why we were being pulled over; we all thought it was because we were all Bandidos. In the end, it was only because we had been speeding, about twenty minutes before, in a construction zone on the autobahn interstate highway. Our driver, a German Bandido, got off with a speeding ticket, which included a large fine.

We eventually arrived at our destination in rural Denmark around 7pm, shortly after dark. Although I was still suffering from jet lag and didn't feel well, I was glad to see Bandidos there from all over the world. Many of them had become close friends of mine. There were European Sargento de Armas Helga from Norway; European Sargento de Armas Johnny and European Nomad Clark from Sweden; European Presidente Jim, European Vice Presidente Mike, European El Secretario Gessner and European El Secretario Munk from Denmark; European Vice Presidente Les and European Sargento de Armas Diesel from Germany; Australian Presidente Jason and Australian El Secretario Larry; and El Presidente George Wegers, El Vice Presidente Jeffrey "Jeff" Pike, and me from the USA. Because this was a Bandidos world meeting at which only national officers could attend, I had been appointed an El Secretario (national secretary) just for the meeting.

The meeting was held out in the middle of nowhere, in the country, in a house that was surrounded by trees and armed

Bandidos. Once we arrived, we were not allowed to leave or go outside by ourselves, which was for our own safety. Shortly after we arrived, we were informed that there were three Rock Machine members in the area who would soon be joining us; they were Martin "Blue" Blouin, Alain Brunette and one other who I only knew as "Will". I was quite surprised to hear that Alain was in the area, and I soon found myself anticipating his arrival.

Because I was not feeling well, I knew that I needed to get a good night's sleep. I looked around and found a tiny sauna room where I could try to sleep, but I ended up playing "Ace of Spades" with Johnny all night. "Ace of Spades" was a game that Johnny liked to play, where Johnny would try to sneak up on you while you were sleeping and put an Ace of Spades on you without waking you up. I had told Bandido Johnny that I was a very light sleeper, and that he would be unable to tag me; he tried a few times that night but was ultimately unsuccessful.

The next day we had meetings off and on all morning and afternoon. We would meet for awhile, and then watch TV, then meet again for awhile, then eat then meet some more. All of the cooking was done by the European Bandidos members and supervised by Europe Vice Presidente Mike, who is also known as "Kok" ("Kok" is cook in Danish). Bandido Mike had gone to chef school where he was young, and actually was a very good cook. Over the next few days, we discussed a myriad of items that were of importance worldwide, none of which were illegal. Most of what was discussed that day is reflected in the minutes I took during that time, as follows:

WORLD MEETING NOTES IN DENMARK –
NOVEMBER 15, 2000
Old Business:
1. USA to provide Europe & Australia with disc of correct patch design.
2. Call Tudy regarding German MC club about patch – advise German Bandidos

New Business:
  1. Canada – someday soon is OK – currently there is peace – RM removed SYLB Patch and HA changed

colors on support club – as part of the peace – peace is very important to keep.

2. Relationship with Outlaws in Canada, USA, Australia & England-stabbing of Bandido by Outlaw Probate in Guernsey. George will talk to Frank and set up meetings worldwide between us and the Outlaws.

3. Consider updating Fat Mexican – drawings to be submitted.

4. Check and see if Probationary members in USA are wearing 5 yr. charter patch – if so, remove immediately.

5. Actual color of gold on patches to be determined by patch reps (USA, Europe & Australia) and standardized.

6. The shield is the official 5 yr. patch worldwide.

7. Patch reps (USA, Europe and Australia) to make decisions on officers' patches: President, Vice Pres, Sgt. At Arms, Sec-Treas, Secretary, Treasurer, Road Captain with no periods.

8. Europe – return history books to George via CT Ed.

9. Patch reps (USA, Europe, and Australia) to make decision on Life Member patch.

10. No more mandatory visits to other countries for Europe and Australia members.

11. Whispering Jim and Uncle Mad – giving away ENM patches in Europe.

12. Switzerland HA incident – Munich chapter – Sep'00 – rest area.

13. Relationship with HA in USA, Europe, Germany, Scandinavia, & Australia.

14. Outlaws friendship with Black Ghostriders in Germany; Pagans friendship with Bats in Germany

15. Thailand – support club – Diablo MC

16. USA runs are: Birthday Run (1st week of March) & Memorial Day Run (last weekend in May) & Sturgis (1st full week of August) & Labor Day Run (1st weekend in September) & Thanksgiving (last Thursday in November).

17. Australia's triangle international patch is OK to be given to USA and Europe Brothers that have visited

Australia – all gift patches given to Australia & Europe Brothers are not to be worn on vest without approval from their National officer.

18. If your death is the result of a suicide, you are not deserving of a Bandido funeral.

19. If you borrow a bike, ol' lady, or any other Bandido-owned property while visiting another area, chapter, or country, leave the property in the same or better condition than what you received it in when you leave.

During the afternoon discussions, the subject of the Rock Machine becoming Bandidos was discussed many different times. At that time, the Rock Machine had been a "Hangaround" club for about eighteen months. The European and Australian Bandidos were adamant that the Rock Machine should become Bandidos immediately, while the USA Bandidos there (El Presidente George and El Vice Presidente Jeff) thought that the Rock Machine should never become Bandidos. I had already heard a rumor that El Presidente George had made a deal with the United States and Canadian Hells Angels that the Rock Machine would never become Bandidos. El Presidente George supposedly had agreed with their argument that the Bandidos should never patch (take in) an enemy of the Hells Angels. Whether that rumor was true or not, I did not know, but the subject made for a long and sometimes heated discussion.

A compromise was reached in late afternoon, in which the USA, European and Australian Bandidos settled their differences and finally agreed: that when a peace was firmly established between the Rock Machine and the Hells Angels in Canada, *then the Rock Machine could become Bandidos*. Early in the evening, Alain, Blue and Will from the Rock Machine arrived. All of us got caught up on our personal situations, ate dinner and then sat down at a big table to discuss the Rock Machine becoming Bandidos. At that time, the Rock Machine were told that they would continue to be a hangaround club, but if they could make peace last with the Hells Angels in Canada, then, and only then, would the Rock Machine be allowed to become Bandidos. Everyone sitting at the table agreed to that, but I think El Presidente George agreed to this only because he thought that the peace would never last.

Shortly after the sit-down meeting at the table, Alain and I had time to visit awhile. He was in fairly good health, in spite of all the stress that came from being a member of the Rock Machine. At that time there were more than one hundred dead in Canada, as a result of the ongoing war between the Hells Angels and Rock Machine. Alain did have an awful cold, and I must have caught it from him, because a few days later I became very sick, and it took me more than two weeks to get rid of it. To this day, I still tell him I owe him for that cold . . . or whatever it was I caught from him.

I finally escaped from the house in the woods that evening. I caught a ride into Copenhagen to locate a good friend of mine, a Bandido named Kemo. Bandido Kemo and I had met on an earlier trip to Europe, and had stayed in touch regularly since. I spent the night at his home and tooled around Copenhagen with him the next day. While driving around town, he pointed out a brand new store run by the Denmark Hells Angels, in which they sold clothes and other items with the Hells Angel's support logos. It looked very upscale and since I had never seen anything like that, I convinced Kemo that I wanted to go inside. We agreed that he would go downstairs and visit a friend who had a tattoo shop there, in order to give me a few minutes to browse around the shop.

When I walked in, I was quite surprised, although I don't think I showed it. The shop was beautiful, clean and light, and reminded me of an Eddie Bauer clothing store. All the merchandise therein was related to the Hells Angels. I noticed about a half dozen Hells Angels in there, so I immediately announced myself as an American Bandido. The Hells Angels looked at me first in utter shock, then called upstairs to another Hells Angel who was apparently in charge, whose name was Bent "Blondie" Nielsen.

I had heard his name many times, for Blondie was a well-known leader of the Hells Angels in Denmark. Hells Angel Blondie came downstairs, we introduced ourselves, and then we chatted for a moment about basic world motorcycle club politics and the concept of the store. I told him that I had never seen anything like this store before, and complimented him on the quality of the merchandise. Bandido Kemo returned from the tattoo shop downstairs and we left, leaving them, I hope, with a better understanding of what the American Bandidos were all about.

Not known to us USA Bandidos at the world meeting, on September 26, 2000 the Rock Machine and Hells Angels in Quebec, Canada, had shocked everyone in the biker world when the two mortal enemies sat down in person for the first time ever to discuss peace. The Quebec City Rock Machine President Frederick "Fred" Faucher and the Hells Angel's Nomad President Maurice (Mom) Boucher, met in a room at the Quebec City courthouse to discuss a preliminary plan for peace between the two clubs in Canada.

Two weeks later, in front of the entire world, with TV and newspaper reporters present, Fred and Mom had been seen shaking hands as they announced to the world that the war in Quebec between the Rock Machine and the Hells Angels was now over. But at the time I did not know that, so I was surprised to learn that, in the days since the world meeting had been held, the European and Australian Bandidos had somehow convinced El Presidente George that now was the time to change the Rock Machine into Bandidos.

A week after the world meeting, on November 22, 2000, Bandido George met with the Hells Angels at Peach Arch Park just outside of Vancouver and Bellingham. At this meeting, Bandido George confirmed the rumor that the Hells Angels had heard; he told them then that the Rock Machine would soon be members of the Bandidos. On December 1, 2000, the Rock Machine Motorcycle Club became history and Bandidos Motorcycle Club Canada was born. A party was planned for January 8, 2001 in the clubhouse at Kingston, Ontario, Canada, at which time it would be announced to the world that the Rock Machine were now officially Bandidos.

In December, I was finally notified of the exact date of the patch party, and made my plans to go to Canada. At that time, I contemplated many different access scenarios. I had been allowed into Canada in recent years, but I had also been denied access at times, due to my past criminal record and affiliation with the Bandidos. I truly had no idea if I would be allowed into Canada this time or not. It was very important for me to be there, for I had been assigned the task of organizing the new National chapter of Bandidos MC Canada; in essence I was to teach them how to be organized and function as a club. I was to open lines of communication, compile/verify phone lists/email addresses, and establish all the membership rosters for Bandidos Canada. This was going to be a momentous occasion, and I definitely wanted to participate.

Most of the United States Bandidos members who had decided to go to the patch party had opted to fly into Toronto's Pearson International Airport. I thought that under those circumstances, with lots of Bandidos coming in and all the publicity, it would be much harder to gain entry through the airport. I had heard too many stories of Immigration Canada being well known for turning members of any motorcycle club around at the airport, even if they were not convicted felons. Even El Presidente George had been deported a few years ago from Canada for being a convicted felon. I *was* a convicted felon, and in spite of the fact that it had been almost 20 years since I had last been convicted, I had little doubt I would be caught and turned around if I tried to enter at Pearson Airport.

Eventually, I decided to attempt entry to Canada through the Windsor checkpoint, just outside Detroit, Michigan. (Later, someone from Immigration Canada suggested that I came in through Niagara Falls, and I never bothered to correct them; if you check my Immigration case records, you will see a multitude of notes regarding entry at Ft. Erie, near Niagara Falls.) I figured that if I were not welcome in Canada, the officials would simply turn me around when I presented them with my passport. I also figured that no one from the club would be expected to come in through Windsor, and therefore my chances of getting in would be much better.

On January 4, 2001, late on a dreary, winter afternoon, I successfully accessed Canada disguised as a construction worker, riding in the back seat of a car with my sister and one of her friends, who both lived in Michigan. (I did tell the Canadian Immigration officials that I rode into Canada in a van full of construction workers in an effort to protect my sister who had no idea that I might not be allowed into Canada. This statement was the only lie I ever told them.)

The Canadian Immigration Officer at the gate did not ask any of us for our ID's. I had my passport in hand ready to go, but all he did was talk to the driver for about two seconds and wave us on through. I noticed at the time that most all of the vehicles near us were going through the entry point as fast as we were, but I was told that this was normal procedure. (This was before the events of 9/11 . . . and things were much different then than today.) I traveled with my sister and her friend to downtown Windsor, where I was dropped off at a casino. There, I called the Outlaws MC clubhouse in London, Ontario, and a member of the local Outlaws chapter was eventually sent to pick me up.

The Outlaw's name was Finn; he was a full-patched member of the Windsor chapter of the Outlaws. Finn drove me to London, Ontario the evening of January 4th, and on the trip he told me that he had joint citizenship in both the USA and Canada. As we drove through a light snow storm, Finn offered to get any member of the Bandidos across the border at any time for free, which I found strange. (Several years later, I would find out that he was a law enforcement officer. I have since heard that he was an RCMP officer in Canada and that he was an ATF agent in the USA, but either way, it didn't matter to me. It did matter to most all members of the Outlaws in Canada though, for he would be responsible for the arrest of more than fifty Outlaws in the fall of 2002.)

Outlaw Finn and I arrived at the Outlaws MC clubhouse in London about 8 o'clock in the evening. I wanted to visit with a friend and member of the Outlaws MC London chapter, Thomas "Holmes" Hughes. At the Outlaws clubhouse, I called the Bandidos MC clubhouse in Toronto and two Bandidos (Bandido Gee from Montreal and Bandido Generator from the new Toronto chapter) were sent to pick me up. It was a cold, snowy night, and because of that, Bandido Gee, Bandido Generator and I were forced to spend the night at a local London hotel. We got up early on Friday morning, January 5th, and found our way into Toronto by late morning, in spite of the many inches of snow that had fallen the night before.

Just before noon, Bandido Gee, Bandido Generator and I arrived at the Bandidos MC Toronto clubhouse. After visiting for awhile, I had them drop me off at the train station, and I took a train to Kingston by myself, where I had arranged for some Bandidos to meet me at the train station. From the train station, I was taken to the local Travelodge Inn motel, where I was assigned to share a room with my good friend from Sweden,

Bandido Clark. Clark has a personal interest in Bandidos Canada, since he had dual citizenship, in both Sweden and Canada. After visiting with Clark and some of the other Bandidos in the hotel, I turned in early to get a good night's sleep. I knew that Saturday would be a major milestone in biker history and I did not want to miss a minute of it.

The next morning, I started off the day by catching up on all of the newspaper articles from around the world. I always tried to have my laptop with me to monitor the newspapers, and to keep in touch with friends and family and the club. One of the first newspaper articles I came across from Canada contained a bomb. It was a story about how the police had caught a few Bandidos at Pearson Airport in Toronto trying to get into the country for the patch party. It also mentioned that a few Bandidos had actually gotten in, *including an American Bandido from Oklahoma*. I was obviously quite concerned, for it meant that there was a giant "leak" somewhere I had been in the last two days. (Several years later, I would learn that the "leak" had been Finn the Outlaw from Windsor, who had given me a ride to the London clubhouse. I should have realized then that this was an indication of worse things to come.)

Saturday was an uneventful day; I spent it hanging around the hotel visiting with new Canadian Bandidos that I did not know, as well as some I did know. I was meeting so many new people that I was having trouble remembering a lot of their names. After consulting with numerous Bandidos, I decided not to go to the clubhouse for the actual party, due to the police presence, constant media coverage, and publicity. We heard that there were about seventy-five police around the clubhouse, and eight American Bandidos had already been detained for possible deportation.

The only thing that saved all of those American Bandidos from incarceration and deportation proceedings, was the fact that Immigration Canada officials had legally allowed them into the country, and had stamped their passports as proof of the same. But my passport did not have a stamp. Therefore, I thought it would be safer for me to skip the party and have a quiet dinner with a new Montreal Bandido who called himself "Tout", which meant "beep" in the English language.

Robert "Tout" Leger and I had met earlier in the day and

discovered we had much in common. Bandido Tout had a dynamic personality and like me, enjoyed working on Harleys. Tout had what they call in Canada "stipulations"; what we call in America "non-association"; he was not able to associate with any member of the Rock Machine due to an ongoing court case in which he was alleged to have committed the crime of "possession of a firearm". In spite of the fact that most all Rock Machine were now Bandidos, Tout felt that there was no need to push the issue, so he, too, was not going to the patch party.

After our dinner in the hotel restaurant, Tout invited me to visit his home near Montreal, hang out the next day, and then return to the United States via train through northern Vermont. We planned to leave by 8 pm, in order to drive to his home and get to bed at a reasonable hour. I left the table and went back upstairs to pack and check my email. It turned out to be a decision that I would live to regret. While I never made it to the clubhouse, the patch party was a huge success for more than sixty new Canadian Probationary Bandidos. Everyone had a great time that night except me, as you can see by the following newspaper article from the Kingston Whig-Standard:

Bikers Party In Kingston

By Sarah Crosbie

January 7, 2001

Eight American members of the motorcycle gang, the Bandidos, partied in Kingston Saturday night, after Canadian Immigration officials failed to show up more than two hours after Kingston Police initially detained the men.

One man from Oklahoma was arrested later that night by Canadian Immigration officials for illegally being in the country, Kingston police media spokesman Mike Weaver said.

Kingston Police Staff Sgt. Brian Cookman said Canadian Immigration questions bikers to determine if they are members of a criminal-affiliated group, or if they have a criminal record.

The first bikers started showing up at the Burnett Street location at about 2 p.m. in vans and taxis.

The men who were detained by police arrived shortly after 4 p.m. They were released at 5:40 p.m. to cheers and shouts of "woo-hoo."

Cookman said the police can detain the men to check their identification and photograph them, but beyond that, it isn't within their jurisdiction to hold them.

"This is a federal issue, not a municipal issue," he said.

Cookman said he was surprised it took Immigration officials from Lansdowne more than two hours to get to the Kingston site.

By 10 p.m. on Saturday, 53 men had arrived at 770 Burnett St., for the party called a patchover party, where the motorcycle group the Rock Machine merged with the Bandidos.

The Rock Machine was granted probationary status in the Texas-based Bandidos last year.

"The local eastern chapter are patching over to the southwestern Bandido chapter in the U.S.," said Neil Finn, a Kingston police officer who is a member of a special provincial squad formed to combat biker gangs.

Finn said until the party, Kingston's Rock Machine had seven associates; four members and three probationary members.

He said the merging doesn't mean Kingston will see an increase in bikers.

"What's going on today doesn't mean we're going to have more members," he said.

Throughout the police check system, Bandido members showed their identification and their vests, which are decorated with a cartoon Mexican man holding a gun in one hand and a sword in the other.

Some Bandidos were also wearing bulletproof vests.

The men who were not detained drove or walked to 770 Burnett St. When they reached the property, a man inside would unlock the door, walk outside and greet them and then lock the door behind them.

Throughout the day, men would come out and take photographs of the area, including police and the media, but the *members themselves didn't want their pictures taken. One man covered his face with a bandanna; another pulled his vest up over his head as they walked to the building.*

Although police were braced for possible problems with a heavy presence that included officers from Kingston Emergency Services, a tactical team, the provincial special squad, a joint municipal RCMP-OPP group, as well as Quebec police. Cookman said there were no problems on Saturday at the largest biker gathering Kingston has seen.

"This is the pinnacle of importance. No one's ever seen this, in this magnitude in a long time," he said.

A detective from the Albuquerque (N.M.) Police Department in the U.S. came to Kingston because of the number of bikers coming to the area.

Gary Georgia, who has studied the Bandidos for 10 years, said that while he can't say what effect the Bandidos will have on Kingston, the new relationship shouldn't go unnoticed.

"Anytime you have a criminal organization coming into your town, it does lead me to be concerned," he said.

"The Bandidos have been known to use intimidation and violence," he said, noting that they are involved in selling narcotics, motorcycle thefts and prostitution.

Georgia said it's significant that the Bandidos decided to meet in Kingston.

"It gives the Bandidos a foothold they haven't had in the past," he said.

"I've tracked them all over the world and now we have them in Canada and in Kingston."

Georgia said on Friday night, before he came to Kingston, he was called to Pearson International Airport to confirm the identities of two Bandidos members who were en route to Kingston.

They were both sent back to the United States by Immigration on Friday, he said.

Immigration officials could not be reached for comment yesterday.

PART 3

Old Ladies, Mamas and Broads

By Name
What I am is nothing more than what you see down
on the floor
I'm not a man, I'm not a mutt
I'm just the bitch you call your "slut".
You like to ride me hard at night
That's when the moon looks just right.
"Say, have a seat and open wide," these are the
words you say with pride.
I know the rules; I know the words. But "no" is
something I've never heard.
I know I'm here to keep him sane
That's why he calls me "bitch" by name.
                                        Kimberly Manning

No matter how they are treated, there is no shortage of women
who associate with outlaw bikers. Some one percenters claim that
women are attracted to their "bad boy" macho image "like bees to
honey". But it seems some women are simply drawn to the
exciting lifestyle that goes with the subculture: loud and fast
choppers, drugs, alcohol, parties, and "any way you want it sex".

In the old North American biker world, women were categorized as "old ladies", "mamas", and "sheep", reflecting the outdated attitudes of the 1960s and 1970s. These days the North American outlaw biker subculture appears to be evolving towards a more enlightened view of women. And yet, they still have no official club rights (as there are no "official" women members) and continue to wear "Property of . . ." patches.

One frequently cited ritual involving women is "pulling a train" – biker jargon for vaginal, oral or anal group sex. Most "trains" are described as being either voluntary or punitive in nature. One incredible example I came across during my years of associating with outlaw biker clubs occurred on a run to a small coastal town in New South Wales, Australia, where I'd entered a clubhouse, looking to meet a particular one-percenter club official:

As I entered the building it was curiously quiet. I learned that a "train" was going on out back. The scene was ugly. A woman in her early thirties was being screwed by some outlaw biker and a crowd of about fifteen guys had gathered around the woman, masturbating to maintain an erection. I turned to go back into the front area but the biker to my left accidentally ejaculated onto his neighbour, who was waiting to jump on the woman. This outraged the recipient and a nasty fight broke out. I left immediately the fight started and re-entered the building, totally grossed out.

When I re-entered the building from the back door, the local senior police sergeant was making his way through the front door. Everyone bolted out the back door, through the windows, or straight past the Sergeant. That left him and me in the room. "Where is she?" he asked. I pointed lamely towards the rear door. I could hear the word "Cops!" being coarsely whispered behind me at the scene of the "train". I debated whether to run myself, but decided to stay and see what happened.

The woman was lying on the ground groaning, in a state of total disarray. The Senior Sergeant said: "Marge, is that you?" The woman replied: "Oh, hi Ted." – "Are you okay?" he asked. "Yeah, everything is all right," she replied, with apparently little embarrassment. The Senior Sergeant offered her a ride home and she accepted. I went to a hotel and had a long shower and several beers.

Generally speaking, there appears to be a great deal of interest in women who associate with outlaw bikers. Much has been written on the topic – usually by men. But what about the women themselves? Why are their voices not heard? According to police sources women (as well as men) have been tortured and even executed for violating the biker code of silence.

In the selections below a whole range of views are explored concerning women associates of one-percenter outlaw bikers, including a lengthy piece on "etiquette" for would-be biker babes.

OLD LADIES, MAIN SQUEEZES AND THE MAID OF LIVERMORE

Sonny Barger

Ralph "Sonny" Barger is, without doubt, the best-known one-percenter outlaw biker. The following is a fascinating personal account of his relationships with women associates of one-percenter outlaw clubs. Blunt and forthright, it offers a narrative that readers will readily identify as "a bloke who is telling an honest account of his personal experiences with the women in his life as a one-percenter outlaw club member".

Women. Old ladies. Babes. Chicks. Can't live without them, can't use their bones for soup. Wherever there's Hell's Angels, you can be sure there's girls, old ladies, and good-time broads. The higher-quality the old lady, the better the Hell's Angel. Having an old lady who doesn't mind seeing her man having fun can make the difference between a good Hell's Angel and an excellent one. We go out of our way to make sure the women who either go out on runs with us, visit our clubhouse during parties, or are just associated with us feel one hundred percent safe. Touch a Hell's Angel's old lady and you risk the wrath of not only the member but the entire club.

I've done my share of running around, but I'm generally a one-woman man. Believe me, I'm not an expert on old ladies. Women have baffled me since childhood, starting with my own mother.

After abandoning me as a baby, my mother wrote letters to me and tried to make contact. But I threw her letters away without opening them. Concerned I hadn't answered, she called the sheriff's department to ask them to check up on us. The cops did a lot more social work then and they asked me if I had received her letters. "Yeah, I threw them away. What of it?" The cops told me I'd better write her back or else they'd throw my ass into Juvenile Hall. "Go ahead," I told them, "put me away." I knew my father would stand up for me in return.

When my sister, Shirley, turned sixteen, she eventually met up with our mother, but I wanted no part of her. As a fourteen-year-old boy I felt when your mother leaves you as a baby she becomes none of your business, and I never let it bother me. I had a sister watching over me. Soon enough, I figured, I would have complete run of the streets of Oakland anyway.

That same year I had my first sexual experience. I was lying in bed one morning when a girl who lived down the street sneaked over and knocked on the window. We were both the same age and she wasn't too bad-looking. I let her into my room and then she climbed into bed with me.

During the early days of the Hell's Angels MC, the typical club member was hardly a prime catch for some 1950s foxy lady or sophisticated career girl. Outside of Tommy Thomas being married and me usually having a steady girlfriend, if somebody scored a girl, then chances are she was the town slut and everybody fucked her.

In the 1950s, the most pussy anybody got was lying about it or going to Tijuana. When the 1960s came, the situation exploded. It was mostly a sign of the times when everybody was experimenting with drugs and sex. The Hell's Angels weren't after America's daughters, but we were getting national attention in the media and in the movies, so we were scoring big-time. Many club guys had multiple girlfriends living with them at one time.

A lot of "respected" women are secretly drawn to wilder,

more macho guys while the so-called sensitive guy stands there with his dick in his hand. It's just human nature for a lot of chicks; that's what turns them on.

Gang bangs used to happen all the time. I wish I had a buck for every woman who came up to me at one of our parties and asked to use a spare bedroom with a bunch of horny guys hanging around her ready to get down. For a certain kind of chick, it was an honor to get fucked by a bunch of Hell's Angels. Some women who saw us riding down the road were neither terrified nor repulsed. They wanted to be part of it, even if it meant jumping on the back of some stranger's bike. Bobby Durt used to stand in front of a bar wearing his colors and stick his thumb out for a ride. If a chick drove by and picked him up dressed the way he was, chances were she didn't want to know where he was going, she wanted to know where she could take him. He was an Angel and the road was open.

Earning your Red Wings and Black Wings came from a fifties and sixties HAMC ritual. You got your Red Wings by eating a girl on her period and your Black Wings by eating a black girl. A few members earned both wings at once. When Bobby Durt was drinking with us in the Sinner's Club he took a black girl into the bathroom; we opened a stall door, looked in, and validated him. That's how he got his Black Wings.

Sometimes things between the public and the Angels raged out of control to the point when a situation could boil over into an overblown controversy. The Monterey rape incident, which was one of the big stories that first launched the Hell's Angels MC into a national press phenomenon, was the prime example. I was doin' some county jail time in Santa Rita at the time on that lousy pot bust, otherwise I would have been there myself.

The Hell's Angels rode down to Monterey en masse during Labor Day weekend in 1964 for a run and a party. The locals were plenty freaked out with us being loose in the town, and the Monterey Chamber of Commerce was none too excited because we didn't have much money to spend. The guys ended up getting pushed out toward Seaside and finally found themselves at a place called Marina Beach near the Fort Ord military base. The Hell's Angels stayed out there to crash, party, and do drugs, but there were also local bike riders from Monterey at

Marina Beach, plus about thirty girls who came out to the beach
to hang out with us. Everything and everybody was jumping
and partying. By the end of the day, Oakland Angels like Terry
the Tramp and Mouldy Marvin Gilbert were doing the wild
thing and having big fun. Everybody was swimming in the
ocean and the girls were wearing their skimpy bathing suits if
anything. There were two very young girls there – one black and
one white – walking around the beach. One was wearing just a
shirt and the other one was completely naked.

Mouldy Marvin was taking a piss behind a parked car when
he saw a cop car pull up beside these two girls. The cops rolled
down the window, talked to the girls, put them in the backseat
of their car, and drove off. The next day an entire fleet of police
squad cars swooped down on the party. There were about sixty
people still hanging around Marina Beach, about twice as many
guys as girls. The cops lined up the guys on one side and the
girls on the other, and then another cop car drove between both
lineups with the two girls in the backseat. They identified some
of our guys to the cops.

Another Richmond member was at the end of the guys' line,
and one of the girls identified him. The police motioned for him
to come over, and before he approached the cops, he handed
over his beer to Jim "Mother" Miles, the president of the
Sacramento club. Then they waved over to Miles. "You, too."
Marvin started to laugh, so the cops grabbed him next. Then
Marvin's sidekick, Tramp, who was standing next to him in the
lineup, blurted out some remark to the cops, so they grabbed
him too. The two girls had identified the last four guys standing
at the end of the lineup.

The Monterey cops dragged all four of them downtown,
stuck them inside a holding pen in the county jail, and announced that all four were being held on rape charges. The
newspaper headlines screamed MONTEREY RAPE! HELL'S ANGELS
HELD. The news media from coast to coast covered the so-called
Hell's Angels Monterey rape case. Our reputation had gone
national.

A close relative of Terry the Tramp was a former district
attorney from Monterey (and later went on to become a
Catholic priest). He supervised the defense. Marvin, Tramp,
Mother Miles, and the guy from Richmond were bailed out,

and when they returned for an arraignment, the whole case was dropped. The prosecutors and the cops knew they had a weak case. The Monterey rape fracas never made it to trial, and once again our acquittal made the front page of the newspapers all across the country. We were bad, we were nationwide, and we were innocent.

The next year, California State Attorney General Thomas C. Lynch dropped a major criminal dossier both on the press and the legislature about the Hell's Angels, and the shit came down. This was the first time the state's highest authorities proclaimed us a corroding influence and threat to society. Let the publicity begin! Newspapers and magazines hounded us after the government declared war. Soon everybody wanted to talk to us.

My first wife, Elsie, and I met in 1962. She was a real babe. I dug pretty girls, and I knew her long before she was my girlfriend. Elsie was originally involved with a Hell's Angel named Rick Risner. Rick was in the club for a few years, then left the club – left Elsie – and moved to Kentucky. After Rick left, Elsie and I started going out together. Elsie was a real nice girl who liked to have fun and ride bikes with me. She had long, dark-brown hair and beautiful eyes, and everyone in the club liked her a lot. Elsie also had two kids – a boy and a girl – and for her, everything centered on them. One night Shirley, who was living in SoCal, got a phone call from Elsie. She was giggling. "Hello, this is your new sister-in-law. I just married your brother." We were hitched in Reno in 1965 after riding up to Nevada on my motorcycle with another couple.

Our marriage was touch and go from the beginning. We separated for a while in '66, and then we got back together again with plans to buy a house. I found a small brown single-story pad on Gold Links Road in Oakland, right down the street from the city zoo. Lots of members followed me into the area and found pads – Winston, Fat Freddie, and later on Jim Jim Brandes, Sergey Walton, and Kenney Owen.

In 1967, Elsie became pregnant right after New Year's, and since she already had two kids, we talked about it and decided we didn't need to have any more children. Anyway, children didn't fit into my plans. That February, while I was in Boston checking out a new club charter, Elsie tried to self-abort the child by pumping air into her vagina. It caused an air bubble to enter her bloodstream, and Elsie died an agonizing but quick death.

Although my marriage with Elsie was on-again, off-again, hit and miss, we shared good times together on my bike. Elsie's death devastated me, so much so that I had her headstone – a cross – tattooed on my right arm. Elsie's death came at a really strange time in my life, just as club chapters were beginning to spread nationwide. I had bought the new Golf Links house ready for us to move into. After her death, I plunged deeper into club matters and responsibilities.

When the Hell's Angels began in California, some of the chapters actually had women members, specifically San Francisco and San Bernardino. I've seen a couple of old photographs that show girl members wearing Hell's Angels patches.

Frank Sadilek was the president of the San Francisco chapter during the late fifties. His wife, Leila, was a Frisco member and secretary of the club. When Bobby Zimmerman was president of Berdoo, his old lady, Keata, rode right with him. Keata ended up getting killed – after Bobby died – when the handlebars of her bike came off in her hands while she was speeding on the highway. I'm not sure if she was ever officially voted in as a female Hell's Angel. By then we had already gotten all of the girls out of the club.

When I became president of the Oakland chapter, women were no longer welcome as members of the club. I felt we didn't need girls in our club. The Hell's Angels is an elite men's club. Maybe we're sexist, male chauvinists, whatever, but since we don't take any money from the government, they can't take us to court and force us to change our bylaws and start accepting women. The fact that they aren't members doesn't mean girls don't ride with the club. There are lots of women who ride bikes with the club right now – but none will ever be voted in as members.

When we formed the early charters your patch was something you had to defend. We had a lot of fistfights with other clubs. We beat people up and took their patches. They tried to beat us up and take ours. Women couldn't defend the patch. It's a stamina thing, keeping up as a fighter and as a rider. We have women who ride just as well as the members. Some of them can ride better than me, but when it comes down to riding hundreds and hundreds of miles in one day, they're just not going to do it.

In the late fifties, we had a rule that stated women could wear your patch when they're packing behind you, so people could see the patch riding by. But when she got off the bike, she had to give it back immediately. This exposure was important in helping the club grow. No such rule exists today. Anyone wearing a Hell's Angel patch who isn't a member – man or woman – risks getting beaten half to death.

Sharon, my second wife, was my main squeeze for over two decades. We became – at least in the eyes of the cops – partners in crime. I met Sharon Marie Gruhlke in the summer of 1969 after Elsie died. She was a gorgeous nineteen-year-old who had been crowned the Maid of Livermore. When she was fifteen years old she wanted to be a fashion model, so she arranged to leave high school early and enrolled in a modeling school. The summer she turned sixteen her modeling school-teacher took her aside and told her she needed to weigh 113 pounds. Weighing in at 119, Sharon freaked and went to see a doctor, who once a week would shoot her up with some kind of speed cocktail. That was Sharon's very first introduction to drugs. She didn't even know what she was being injected with, finishing each week with little blue supplemental pills to keep going. At seventeen, Sharon left her mom and stepfather's home in Livermore, moving to San Francisco in 1968. She kept her weight down to a "professional level," ate a lot of cottage cheese, and did her early morning exercises to Jack LaLanne on the television.

Sharon's move to "the City" was busy and successful. She was a fucking knockout. She started out getting paid twenty-five dollars an hour, but after an increased schedule of photo sessions, ramp modeling, and television jobs, the agency forked out a ten-dollar-an-hour pay raise. Although a working model, she still felt out of place with the other girls from the agency. Sharon came from a middle-class East Bay family and was raised by her mom. Most of the other models came from richer families living in nicer places across the Golden Gate Bridge, like Sausalito, Marin County, or the ritzier parts of San Francisco. She was having the same problems I had when I was riding my bicycle in San Francisco when I was eight. It was a them-against-us, Oakland-versus-Frisco type of thing.

After moving to San Francisco, Sharon got used to the sounds of motorcycles driving around her neighborhood. Her roommate began going out with a prospect from the Daly City Hell's Angels, which at first really freaked her out. She warned her roommate, "Gail, you better be careful. You know, you could get in trouble going out with some of those motorcycle guys."

The prospect started bringing a friend of his from the club over to Sharon's flat. Everybody in the club called him Nigger Rick, because he was Portuguese with a dark olive complexion. Sharon went out with Rick on a few dates. They stopped dating, but he still dropped by the house and they stayed friends. Rick would sometimes take Sharon out for rides on his motorcycle.

The Daly City club was ready to split in half and spin off into a new San Jose charter, and Rick figured he stood a good chance of being named president of one of the charters. He needed to come over to Oakland to discuss the new San Jose club with me, so Rick invited Sharon to come along. When Rick pulled up to my house and rang the bell, someone opened the gate and waved them in to make a run for the door: My big Doberman Pinscher jumped out of his doghouse, patrolling the front yard as Sharon and Rick followed me quickly into the house.

As usual, Golf Links was Party Central that day. The house was filled with people. Tiny was there hanging out by the front door. Johnny Angel was lurking around too, and everybody was stoked about chartering a new San Jose Hell's Angels club. Most of the members and their old ladies were kicking back, talking in the bedroom. I was still in bed with a curvy little blond bartender chick who lived down the street. We both drove Corvettes and usually spent Friday nights together. That Saturday morning, she hid under the covers as the room filled up with club members and friends who didn't seem to give a damn whether she was there or not.

When Rick introduced me to Sharon, she seemed all nervous and uncomfortable. I'm sure she felt a little out of place talking with the other old ladies, standing next to Rick at the bedroom door, and trying to avert her eyes from the blonde in my bed. Sharon was younger and much more beautiful than the blond

Corvette girl. I needed to know: Who was this young, blond babe Rick was with?

That night there was going to be a big benefit concert at Longshoreman's Hall in San Francisco, and it cost a dollar to get in. I asked Sharon if she planned on going to the party that night.

When she said no, I turned to Rick. "Well, I have a dollar for her if you don't."

"Thanks anyway," said Sharon, and she left and went home for the night.

I kept in touch with Rick for a couple of weeks, because I was hoping I could score Sharon's phone number from him. I told him to put in a good word for me, since she had seemed uptight at the house. When Rick called Sharon at the exercise gym where she worked, she didn't seem too interested.

"Why doesn't he call me himself?" she asked Rick.

Sharon was scared to go out with me, so Rick planned a party at his house in Daly City, offering himself as a sort of chaperon. I phoned Sharon and arranged a double date with her roommate and another friend of mine from the club, Fat Freddie. That night when I came to pick her up, she was all dolled up in false eyelashes and a fall wig that matched her bleached-blond hair. At the party, Sharon seemed a little uncomfortable, so we smoked some grass together (her first time), and the phone rang all night. Most of the calls at the party were for me and most of them were from other women.

One of the callers said that I needed to get over to Fat Freddie's house, pronto. Another one of Freddie's girls had just gotten out of the California Institution for Women, a women's prison in Fontera, and she had some guns she wanted to sell, stashed from before she was in the joint. As I was planning on leaving the party, I asked Sharon to take the ride with me back to Oakland. I didn't know if it was because she was a little high, but she still seemed scared of me. Rick assured her that it was cool and we left the party together. We smoked another joint on the bike as Sharon held on, desperately trying to keep her fall from blowing off her head. We sped over the Bay Bridge back to Oakland and made a couple of stops. When I finished buying the guns, one of our members walked into Freddie's place wired and worried.

"Hey, Sonny, wh-wh-what do you do if an old lady ODs on Seconal?"

I thought for a second.

"Depends on who she is."

"She's the mother of my children."

"Fix her with speed. That'll wake her up."

I didn't realize at the time that you could also kill a person doing that. Our boy was freaking out. I could see he needed my help.

"Okay," I said, reaching for my jacket. "So much for the party. Let's go wake her up."

We needed to find a drug addict with a needle and kit, not a hard thing to do. We left Freddie's and raced over to the member's house on 82nd Avenue. Sharon felt spaced out. She wasn't used to my pace and didn't know what to expect from one minute to the next. Being so young, Sharon barely knew what the term "OD'd" meant. We walked quietly into the house through the back door, looking for a body.

The situation seemed calm but tense. We looked at the body of a woman. Uh-oh, she looked dead. I asked Sharon to go and get me a washcloth. Sharon tried to find the unconscious woman's pulse while I checked her breathing. She couldn't find a pulse, and we both thought she was finished. We injected her with some speed, and miraculously, she came to. Neither one of us really knew what the hell we were doing. Later that night, Sharon told me how safe she felt being with me, even as people were dying around us.

As Hell's Angels, we lived in our own underground world, barely part of the citizens' world and having as little to do with them as possible. Live or die, we handled our own situations our own way. With drug overdoses, it was *never* an option to run and call a doctor. We were in the sights of law enforcement. We handled our own situations without getting the cops or the paramedics involved. That night the woman didn't die, and I guess I probably saved her life risking it. It was also my first date with Sharon. Par for the course, one gun buy and an overdose of Seconal.

Despite all the excitement, Sharon needed to get home that night so she could go to work the next morning. I tried my best to convince her to stay at my house, but she insisted on leaving.

I arranged for a friend of mine to ride her ride back into Frisco. Sharon thought I was a bit of a jerk about wanting her to stay, but it was my way of saying I didn't want her to leave.

Sharon and I lost touch for a spell in the summer of 1969. I had finished filming *Hell's Angels '69*, and the Hell's Angels were planning a major run. Little did I know Sharon had quit her job at the exercise gym and was waiting for me to call her and take her with me on the big run. She had bought some white plastic Nancy Sinatra go-go boots and a fake fur coat, assuming I was going to call. When I split without her, the next time I heard from her was when she sent me a birthday card special delivery. Inside the card she wrote a long note telling me how angry she was that I had ignored her, writing that she could never really tell what my feelings were toward her, but admitting that she still really liked me. She thought I had other ideas and told me to "have a nice life." A strange thing to say to a Hell's Angel.

That card did it. I picked up the phone and called her. Terry the Tramp had arranged a big birthday party for me that night at his house. It was late, I told her, and the party had already started, but I would wait for her if she would just take a cab straight over to Golf Links. When an old Italian cabby pulled up to Sharon's flat in the Mission district and she gave him the familiar Oakland address most people knew from the newspapers, he tried to talk her out of the fare.

"Why should I drive such a pretty young girl like you to that horrible place?"

Sharon showed up at Golf Links that night and never left.

Johnny Angel's girlfriend was confused about how many girls I had actually brought to Terry the Tramp's party. When I had been back in Buffalo starting a new charter, I had met a girl named Sally, and I rode her all the way back with me to Oakland. I really didn't bring her back for myself. Good club girls were so hard to find in those days, and I thought she would make a good old lady for somebody else in the club. Sally took her things and moved out of my place and in with another club member. When Sharon moved into Golf Links, her brother helped load her stuff in a van to Oakland just as Sally was leaving.

Sharon loved sitting out in the garage, watching me wrench

up my bike. Instead of cleaning house and cooking, she sorted out nuts and bolts on the garage floor. Because Sharon was under twenty-one, I wouldn't let her stick around any of our biker bar hangouts, figuring I'd set an example for the other members.

When the *Hell's Angels '69* movie was released, I took Sharon out on the publicity tour with me. We stopped in several cities across the country from Texas to New York to California. The tour was high-class; limousines met us at each stop. Sometimes they would furnish us with a motorcycle, which I would ride to the premiere to sign autographs. When we were in Dallas, I took Sharon to Neiman Marcus and slipped her five one-hundred-dollar bills and told her she had fifteen minutes to spend it. She had no trouble doing that, buying a cool pair of leather pants for the ride with me.

As my new old lady, Sharon always bugged me to smile more. Elsie had been dead for two years, and I guess I kept my reaction to her death to myself. We never talked much about it. I had a whole bunch of girlfriends between Elsie and Sharon, an endless parade of old ladies. I can't even recall their names or faces. Life at home was chaos as gifts poured in from the other charters – pictures and plaques leaned up against the wall instead of being nailed up. My house was a zoo near the Oakland Zoo with Oakland Orange walls. Rather than mourn my wife's death, I had jumped into a partying frenzy.

On one of my road trips, Sharon and I visited the Buffalo Hell's Angels, which had just started. Denny McKnight was elected president of the chapter, and while we were staying at his house, Sharon and I dropped acid. Sharon went into the bathroom and began washing her face over and over with Noxzema. After what seemed like an eternity, I banged on the door. "Come out, girl, and make us some coffee." She came out with the Noxzema on her face and then spent what seemed like hours in the kitchen. As it turned out, she had never made coffee before, so a bike rider named Thief, who rode in from Philly, taught her how to make coffee, high on acid. Old ladies aren't necessarily known for their kitchen skills anyway.

When we got back from Buffalo, I was parking my bike and I didn't put the kickstand all the way out. The bike fell over right on top of my foot, causing it to swell up badly. Actually, it was already fucked up. I had gotten into a fight with Hi Ho Steve up at Bass Lake and he bit me on the foot. It turned out that the bite had not healed up properly. It's common knowledge that a human bite can be as dangerous as an animal's, but with Hi Ho Steve, it could be even more hazardous.

As a result, I spent the next couple of weeks limping around on crutches. Sharon had a severe chest cold, so I suggested she spend a few days at her mother's to get well. In the meantime, I had gotten a call from the club in Buffalo. Denny McKnight had hit a brick wall on his motorcycle and was dead on arrival. Bad foot or not, I rode cross-country to Denny's funeral. Sharon was upset with me when I insisted she was too sick to make the trip.

After she moved into the Golf Links home, there was a knock at the front door one day. I opened up to find a little lady standing on the porch. It was Sharon's mother, Barbara. We had not yet met.

"Can I help you?"

"I just want to see who my daughter has been living with, and whether or not she's living in a garage."

I told her that no, Sharon wasn't living in a garage. She just turned around and walked away. Later on, we did become good friends.

Sharon had come a long, long way from the nineteen-year-old ex-Maid of Livermore. One time I was fighting a charge of being a felon possessing a firearm, and the gun in question actually belonged to Sharon.

In the courtroom, the U.S. attorney cross-examined me on the stand as he held up a pistol.

"Mr. Barger, is this your gun?"

"No, it belongs to Sharon."

Sharon was in the courtroom, so the prosecutor brought her up on the stand. Holding the gun out to her, the prosecutor asked her, "What do you know about this gun?"

"Well," she said, "one thing, the clip is still in it. Be careful. It might be loaded."

The stupid prosecutor nearly dropped the gun handing it to her, but Sharon caught the piece, jacked it back, pumped the clip out, threw the clip back in, and slid the gun back to him.

"Don't worry," she said, "it's not loaded."

The judge grunted and looked down at the prosecutor. "The gun is obviously hers, now get her off the stand."

The two of us liked to get high a lot around the house, and we used more than our share of blow during the early 1970s. During that time I was getting busted a lot and having huge scrapes with the law. My cocaine mood swings got me into a lot of deep criminal shit and would ultimately land me in Folsom Prison. Sharon was doing a fair amount of speed, but I still wasn't much interested in methamphetamine. My cocaine habit ruled then and was much larger than Sharon's. Sharon's drug use spiraled off in a whole different direction. She was used to taking uppers during her modeling days. To help her cope with me being away in prison, Sharon cut way down on cocaine and increased her reliance on speed. In the short term, it counteracted her depression over me being locked up.

What got Sharon through the rough and lonely times was her being able to ride her motorcycle. It cleared her head. I had taught Sharon how to ride alongside experts in the club like "Flash" Gordon Grow and Fu Griffin. I bought her her first motorcycle, a 650 BSA. I picked that particular bike because it shifted on the same side as a Sportster. Then I built her the special little bike we called *Little Cocaine*. Sharon always loved to ride with the club, so whenever the Oakland guys would get ready to ride off somewhere, Deacon would let her know beforehand so she could meet up and come along with the pack.

One of my craziest battles with the law was when Sharon and I decided to get legally married. I was serving time in Folsom Prison at the time. We never spoke much about marriage until I was sent to prison. While I was waiting for my transfer from the Alameda County jail to Folsom Prison, I phoned Sharon one night and asked her if she wanted to get married. She was totally up for it and went out the next day and got a blood test and a tattoo on her back that read "Sonny" with a small sun. For the longest time I wouldn't allow her to mark up her body, but this time I was inside so I didn't have shit to say about what she did or didn't do.

The doctors in prison gave me my blood test, and after we completed all the preliminary steps to be legally married, we found out not one single judge in Alameda County would volunteer to marry us. They were too nervous to be involved. Every response was "No way."

When they shipped me off from county jail to Vacaville to be processed for Folsom, even though we were still legally single, Sharon signed in as my wife during visiting privileges and received immediate clearance. When I landed in Folsom, Sharon reapplied for visiting privileges. They knew we weren't legally married, and when they ran her rap sheet, they found she had a case pending for possession of methamphetamine. Sharon had gotten into a bike accident on the freeway and the cops had found some speed in her pocket. Once I got to Folsom in the summer of 1973, I couldn't receive visits from a "partner in crime."

Meanwhile, we finally found a legal loophole, which enabled us to marry, thereby granting Sharon visiting privileges. We found a law on the books that stated you didn't necessarily need to be in the "same place/same time" to be legally married. If you lived together for a certain period as common-law man and wife – which we did before prison – we could then get a marriage license regardless of whether either of us had valid blood tests.

My lawyer became the mail-order minister/justice of the peace. Although the prison authorities would not permit a justice of the peace physical access to marry us, they legally couldn't keep my lawyer from visiting and performing the service separately. Sharon started the process; the lawyer married her to me first. Ten days later, he came to Folsom and finalized the arrangement and married me to Sharon. We were officially wedded in the eyes of the State of California on December 16, 1973, but Folsom prison officials *still* wouldn't permit Sharon's visits. They felt we had conned them, which, in a sense, we had.

Being the old lady of a Hell's Angel officer like me was no fucking picnic. Sharon and I faced more adventures together than ten couples, but we spent a lot of time apart. Of our twenty-seven-year relationship together, I was away from her for a total of thirteen years, either tending to club business, sitting in jail, or being on trial for my life. When I got into trouble with the law, Sharon would often bail me out and help plan the details of my defense with my court-appointed attorney. She even sold a line of "Free Sonny" T-shirts when I was locked up in the joint.

Sharon and I were a strong couple, but the cracks began to show through in our relationship. When I was released from Folsom, I had kicked my cocaine habit. On the other hand, Sharon's reliance on speed grew and grew as the years went by. God damn, I know I'm fucking far from perfect and I'm set in my ways. I've been doing things my way all my life, and I can't change that. But it's difficult to explain what it's really like to live with somebody who is constantly loaded on speed. The situation grew worse and worse until suddenly I couldn't take it anymore. I told her she had to leave.

In 1996 we made arrangements for Sharon to check into a detox hospital in SoCal run by the Seventh-Day Adventists. I visited her at the hospital and told her, "If you get straight and want to come back home that's fine."

Personally, I prefer a steady life, a long-term relationship. If our marriage was broken down, I wanted to try and fix it and keep on going. But Sharon ended up staying in SoCal for over a year getting straight. I had a hard time handling such a long break in our relationship.

Just before she left, Sharon made arrangements for an acquaintance of hers to take care of things around the house while she was gone. Noel Black had hung around the club for a while. I have no idea how Sharon and Noel met, although I had seen her at club functions. I never really got to know Noel until she came over to the house a few days after Sharon left. One day she was at the house and did a little bit of cleaning up. That evening she asked me where the blankets were. I said, "What blankets?"

"I'm going to sleep on the couch," Noel said, "because I'm not driving all the way back to Sonoma County tonight."

"You don't have to sleep on the couch," I told her as I pointed toward my bed. "Sleep in here."

Sharon and I still had our understanding that she was free to come home whenever she became straight. When she was ready to be discharged from the detox hospital I asked, "What's up?"

Sharon told me now she was clean and sober, but she couldn't come back. "I can't live with you and not take drugs."

On Christmas of 1996 I wrote Sharon a letter saying in order for both of us to be happy and healthy, we should split up and go our separate ways. We filed for divorce and our long association ended. Even today, we keep in touch. Sharon and

I are still friends, and she's continued to stay off drugs and alcohol and lives happily in SoCal. Noel and I married October 8, 1999, in Las Vegas, and with our young daughter, Sarrah, we live in a house in the desert in sunny Arizona. Noel breeds mares and once owned a world-champion stud. Now she's got me. I've taken on a kid and a beautiful "old lady" as well as three mares on the property. Noel also owns a motorcycle and is a fine rider. What more could I ask for?

THE BIKER BABE'S BIBLE

"Throttle"

The Biker Babe's Bible *is the only published work by a woman life partner of an active member of a one-percenter outlaw biker organization. Holly French — better known by her nickname, "Throttle" — is a rider in her own right, but she has written the book from the perspective of what is considered correct and appropriate behaviour for the partner of an outlaw biker.*

I decided to write this because I see too many women clueless in the biker world. They think that putting leather on and climbing on the back of a bike makes them *Biker Babes*. Well, it's not all fun and games.

It's not a lifestyle, it's a way of life. I grew up around clubs, and I learned my place at a very young age. When my Ole Man says "My Ole Lady knows her place," it's a very nice compliment, and it also means that I get to go out and party with him. I would rather go out and have a good time with the club than sit home alone (which I don't do anyway).

I am a very strong, independent woman and have been riding my own bike since I was eleven years old. By age sixteen I had clubbers picking me up three blocks from my house because I didn't want any trouble. My Dad's rags were different from my friends' rags. I was *Little Sis* back then and I pretty much heard and saw everything. I would never dishonor the trust those Brothers had in me.

I learned quick. I joined the Navy and found out where the scooter tramps hung out. When I wasn't on base, I was out with them. Having traveled the country, I have partied with a lot of different clubs and have had a lot of fun becoming the independent woman I am.

I work and play in a man's world so I know my place. I thank women's liberation because I have a job operating heavy equipment, which I wouldn't have otherwise. One thing I don't agree with is unqualified women trying to take over everything that men have or that men do. Yes, women need their outlets, but telling real men they are wrong makes me angry.

I am Old School, and my daughters are raised Old School. I hope they raise their children the same way – with love, honor, and respect. These qualities are extremely hard to find these days. I am writing this book to let the other women know it is a great thing to be a Good Ole Lady and to give the clueless Ole Ladies a little information backed with a lot of experience. And, I decided that some of the Brothers might appreciate a handbook that explains their actions.

I have had Ole Ladies tell me I just don't get it. To this I reply, "Wake up and smell the coffee." Take your time reading this. Make notes if you have to. Know your place.

Being called a Good Ole Lady is not derogatory. It's a very nice compliment.

Getting Ready to Ride

The name of the game is always *be prepared*. There is no such thing as a quick putt. For instance, we know that if the sun goes down, the temperature will drop. So, always take your leather.

One afternoon, a few of us went for a ride to visit a friend. It was a beautiful summer day, a great day for a putt, and we were only going to be gone a couple of hours. We got to the friend's house after about an hour's ride. His Ole Lady made us lunch and then we talked awhile.

All of a sudden, a wind came up and the sky started clouding up. We decided we better leave to beat the storm home. About twenty miles from home and in the middle of nowhere it hit us. The rain was coming sideways. All we could see were corn fields and a tiny red dot ahead.

We realized the red dot was a stoplight, and we hoped there might be a gas station or a store, so we decided to keep going. The wind, however, picked up even more. It was so strong that I had to lean off the left side of my bike just to keep it straight on the road.

As luck would have it, we were then pelted with hail just as we got close to the light. Then, we found that there was nothing at the light but a brick sign. And by this time the hail was coming down sideways as well.

We decided to park the bikes on the side of the road and look for cover. That was when we heard a sound like a locomotive coming. We knew with the hail and the rain, with the sky turning green and black, there was a possibility of a tornado.

The next sounds we heard were tornado sirens in the distance. We grabbed hold of the brick sign and held tight. It was indeed a tornado, and we had caught the outer edge.

This experience would have *really* sucked if I didn't have my leather, a couple of bandannas, and leather gloves. Fortunately, I was prepared. Even though we got wet, my leather kept the hail from tearing me to shreds.

A prospect's pouch is also good to keep handy. It contains a lot of essential items, and they will be covered in Chapter Ten. For now, though, we are focusing on weather conditions.

Riding in the Rain

Your leather, boots, jeans, glasses, and bandannas are all important. Being pelted by rain at eighty miles per hour is pure hell. It stings and makes your skin feel raw. Tying a bandanna around your face will help minimize this. Being on the back of the bike will lessen the effects as well because your Ole Man will block the brunt of the rain. Hopefully you will have remembered to bring an extra bandanna for his face. I always carry a couple of extras just for an unexpected weather change.

Riding in the Snow

Ideally, you will be in a position to wait out the snow. Even if you do, however, the salt kicked up by other vehicles in the aftermath can hurt worse then the rain we just discussed. So, again, what I am saying is you need to be prepared.

I make neck warmers every winter. You can too. Take a piece of fleece and fold it in half, making sure the stretch is crossways to the fold. Then, sew across the bottom and fold in half the other way making a tube. Slide it over your head, face, and neck. Put a lid on top, then glasses, and you'll be a lot warmer.

Every fall, I buy a case of toasty toes and hand warmers. One in each boot and in each glove lasts eight to ten hours. They are inexpensive and are worth their weight in gold.

A group of us decided one winter to go to Colorama in Tomahawk, Wisconsin. Well, the Friday evening we were to leave, everyone had backed out because the temperature had dropped to thirty degrees. So, I decided to go by myself.

I knew that the temperature had dropped to below zero, but it didn't matter. Heat packs and neck warmers, a couple layers of clothes with chaps, and I was set. I did 850 miles that weekend and could have gone a thousand more. I had a pure blast! My friends who backed out later realized that they had missed out on a really great time.

Make sure that you carry heat packs for your Ole Man and yourself, plus a couple extras for other Brothers. I hate being on a run and having to stop every thirty minutes or so because someone's toes or hands are freezing. And, if you make yourself some leg warmers, you can even put heat packs on your knees. Some of us older bikers have knees that ache in the cold.

Finally, if you're riding on the back of a bike in the snow, sit still. Your Ole Man's got enough to handle with idiots in cages and road spray.

Night Riding

In most states the law requires the wearing of clear glasses at night. I carry yellow tinted ones. They help reduce the glare of on coming headlights. I also always have a thinsulate long sleeved shirt of some kind rolled in ziploc bag on the bike. It will fit in a pocket in your leather, and if you get chilly, it will help keep you warm.

Remember, if you get uncomfortable, it's your own fault, so keep it to yourself. Just because you weren't prepared doesn't give you a license to bitch. It ruins everyone's good time if you are bitching, and it's an embarrassment.

So, grow up. Toughen up. You are a biker's Ole Lady.

Windy Conditions

When riding in strong wind, duck down behind your Ole Man and stay as close as you can. Wind can get between you and him and move you around, making it difficult to control the bike. Hold on and sit still. This will decrease wind resistance. Tuck yourself in and keep your lid in one place. You don't want your lid beating your Ole Man.

As a courtesy, I always carry a pack of non-menthol cigarettes – along with the menthols I smoke – and a good lighter. I duck behind my Ole Man, open my jacket to block the wind, and light cigarettes for him, myself, and other Brothers and Sisters. Just a nice gesture for the smokers on a long trip.

Riding in the Heat

On hot days, when the club stops for gas or bathroom breaks, grab your bandannas, wet them down and wrap ice in them. Then wrap them around your neck and your Ole Man's neck.

Bikers always have to have their rags on, and they are hot. The heat from the engine and the asphalt can be overwhelming. Add a little humidity and a dark lid and it could be a dangerous mix. An iced bandanna around the neck will keep you both cool and comfortable.

Get a couple of bottles of water the night before and freeze them. When it gets warm the next day, you can cool off with the ice. A frozen bottle will last a long time, and as it melts, it makes a good drink on the road. When sharing, though, don't hand the bottle to the right; do it from the left side. Your Ole Man has to keep his hand on the throttle.

One road trick I learned is make sure the water bottle has a top you can pull open with your teeth and drink without spilling while running down the highway at seventy miles per hour.

Back in 1987, my parents went to Sturgis, South Dakota, with some of the club. My mom was on a black sportster and everyone else was on big bikes. It was a really hot summer season, and when they got close to the Dakotas, they pulled in to a rest stop.

My mom had stopped perspiring and was so red in the face she was almost purple. She was fatigued and dizzy. She had to be treated for heat exhaustion. The Brothers put her bike on the trailer, and she had to ride in the chase vehicle.

Of course, she is hard core and didn't say a word. All the Brothers loved my mom they all called her Momma. Talk about Respect!

So, what I am saying is, you need to take this rule seriously: *Be prepared!*

Riding Hard

Being prepared for a ride is one thing. Knowing how to ride is another. You have to know when to keep still, and you have to know when to move. You have to know the procedures for mounting and dismounting and some basic rules for safety. And, it helps to know some biker etiquette and courtesies.

Before leaving anywhere, make it a habit to check the bags and bungee cords to make sure that everything is tied down and tight. This should be the last thing you do before mounting the bike.

I always mount and dismount from the kickstand side of the bike. This way I avoid the hot pipes. The best way to mount is from the ground. Swing your leg over, then put your feet on the pegs. Of course, that can't be done if your Ole Man has a bagger or if you are too short. But if you are able to, it lessens the chances of him dropping the bike.

Communication is the best policy. I always tap my Ole Man's shoulder, and when he nods, I move, but not until then. You don't want to be responsible for the bike getting dumped, all because you didn't communicate. Believe me, that would be embarrassing for both of you. Your Ole Man would be ribbed forever, and you don't want to have to find a place to carry the eightball as a consequence.

Shifting or not shifting your weight is very important. With any shift, the driver has to compensate, especially in curves and turns. In tight curves or turns, I make myself a part of my Ole Man. Because I also ride my own scoot, it's more difficult for me to ride on the back. I want to lean, but I know that would mess us both up, so I stay where I'm supposed to.

Ladies, pick one shoulder from which to watch the road. You may not realize it, but you shift your weight every time you look over a different shoulder. So pick one, and stick to it. Your Ole Man can then compensate for the weight on that side.

You don't have to hold on with your hands all the time. With or without a back rest, you should use your legs and feet. When taking off from a stop, your toes should be pointed down, pegs should be in the arch of your feet. Squeeze your Ole Man's thighs with yours. This will keep you on the bike.

Coming to a stop, keep your toes up, thighs together, and grab the back of the seat. This will keep you from sliding into your Ole Man. Be aware of your lid. You don't want it slamming into his back.

Also, when you are in a group or pack and are leaving somewhere, be aware that a lot of people may be standing around. Your Ole Man may want to show off a little by gunning the throttle. I have seen Ole Ladies fall off because they weren't paying attention. So, always be prepared for a quick take off.

Riding with Others

When riding with others, watch out for them by using hand signals, just like the rules of the road for bicycles you learned as a kid. Left arm out means left turn; bent arm up, right turn. I put both hands down for stopping so the bike next to us – if we are riding on the left – can see we are stopping.

It doesn't matter if your Ole Man has turn signals or not. What if a bulb burns out, or a fuse goes bad? Even when we are riding alone, I still use hand signals for changing lanes or turning. I always know when my Ole Man is going to change lanes because he checks over his shoulder and checks his mirrors. I put the signal out before he does.

Hand signals also give cages a little more warning. And, if a bulb burns out, a police officer can't stop you for not signaling because you have made it a habit to give hand signals. Stay aware of traffic and your surroundings.

If you decide to ride on the back of a bike, hopefully it's in good working order and the seat is comfortable. Remember, it's your choice to get on the bike so make the best of it. Don't get on and then start bitching that your ass and tail bone hurt. You can always ride in a chase vehicle, a subject that will be discussed in another chapter.

I rode on a hard tail with no padding on the fender seat and split leg pegs across the state of Tennessee. I will tell you, I hurt real bad, but I didn't let anyone know. Not a groan, not a single complaint came out of my mouth. It was my choice to go.

Hopefully the bike you ride on is that of someone close to you and is maintained properly. When I was seven months pregnant, I was invited by a Brother to go on a Poker Run. I was still wearing normal clothes. They were tight, but they still fit with a little tugging.

Anyway, when we got to the clubhouse, the Brother who invited me had a problem with his bike. Another Brother told me I could ride with him. I was cool with that until we went out to his bike and I noticed it was a rat bike.

But, I didn't want to miss the run. I was young and dumb and just wanted to catch some wind. We were the very last bike in a double line of forty, maybe more. The Brother was having trouble keeping up with the pack.

All of a sudden, the front of the pack slammed on their brakes to make a right turn. We were all doing at least sixty miles per hour, and those from in the middle of the pack to those in the back were locking their brakes up. The Brother and I started skidding and lost our brakes. We were going up the center of the pack and the horn wasn't working, so I started yelling, "No brakes!"

We got to the place where everyone was turning and he tried to aim the bike between two full dressers toward the outside of the pack in the middle of everyone turning right. My arm, leg, and foot glanced off one dresser, pushing me off the seat. I still had my foot on the right foot peg. I was holding on to the back of the seat with my left arm, and my leg was wrapped around the bottom of the seat.

We made it though the gap and were heading through a gravel

parking lot toward a brick building. He was throwing his weight to the left, but the bike wouldn't turn because all of my weight was off the right side of the bike. I pulled myself back on and leaned with him, and we just missed hitting the building. He got the bike stopped and found that his brake cable had snapped.

I had a bruise on my arm in the shape of a mirror, a bruise from the dresser's handle bar across my inner knee, and my toes were backwards in my cheap boots. I pulled my boot off, worked my toes into place, and put the boot back on to keep the swelling down.

Others who had pulled over were saying they thought we were dead until they saw me raise up and get back on the bike with a floating motion. I didn't jerk the bike or panic, and they said it was amazing to watch. Keeping your head and staying alert can save your life.

This was a lesson I will never forget. I will never get on a rat bike again. Knowing the bike is kept up is very important.

Navigating Road Conditions

If you see a pothole or road debris, point to it so the others behind you can avoid it. If it's a bump, put your weight evenly on the foot pegs and lift your weight off the seat. Your knees and legs will absorb most of the shock instead of your back and it's easier on the bike.

Gravel can be very tricky, as can country roads; Interstates can be oily. If you are in a gravel parking lot or riding on a road that is very slippery, you may have to get off the bike early so your Ole Man can park it. Backing a bike is difficult enough; adding your weight or conditions such as gravel could be treacherous. Bikes don't have reverse. I usually help by pushing on the front of the bike while my Ole Man is backing up. I'm his reverse. The same goes for leaving an area. Let your Ole Man tell you where he wants you. It may easier to mount or dismount someplace where he can get his footing to hold you and the bike up.

Always be aware of conditions at Interstate toll plazas. Tollgates, like the center of lanes on the Interstate, are full of oil, antifreeze and water, making conditions very slippery. Hold on when leaving a tollgate because you need to be ready for a little fishtail. A lot of clubs will plan ahead and have one person pay the tolls for all the bikes. I personally have a change holder on my bike and carry change in my pockets.

I have also learned to carry a few truck lug nuts or ball bearings about the size of marbles in my leather. We were once riding down near Tallahassee, Florida, when a van tried to run us off the road. The driver really started messing with us. He wasn't easing up on us at all. He was trying to ram into us. We thought he was trying to kill us!

When the van got too close, I reached into my pocket, pulled out a few ball bearings, and threw them behind me. They hit the van's radiator, and the driver slowed down and pulled over. We just kept on going. In an extreme emergency, when your life is being threatened by a four-wheeler, a few lug nuts or ball bearings can go a long way in protecting your Ole Man, yourself, and your Brothers.

If you see a collision coming, there are a few actions you can take to minimize injury. A lot of accidents are due to drivers pulling out in front of bikes, which results in the Ole Men slamming on the brakes, trying to avoid impact. If it looks like impact is unavoidable, stand up at the very last second and jump, tucking yourself into a ball, protecting your neck, head, and face, then roll out of it. You will go up and over the car.

This tactic is just in case your Ole Man hasn't thrown you out of harm's way beforehand. Talk to him about this. He may have a different view.

Being a Good Ole Lady is not all fun and games. It can be a very serious business depending on where you live, what you know, and who your Ole Man is – or should I say, what colors he flies.

Riding with the Club

One of the most difficult feats to accomplish is to control a bike with a drunk on the back, hoping the person doesn't pass out and fall off. A lot of Ole Ladies think that when they are invited to go to a party with the club or go out for the evening, it's an excuse to get drunk and act stupid.

First of all, keep in mind your Ole Man belongs to the club. If you don't get invited out much, the reason might be because your Ole Man doesn't think you can keep your shit together. Maybe you have embarrassed him in the past or he thinks you will.

Take my word for it, you'll have much more fun if you keep your shit together. Remember, not just your reputation, but your Ole Man's reputation is on the line. If he can't control you, someone else will, and you sure as hell don't want someone else putting you in check.

On top of that, others might think you wear the pants in the house, and even if you do, you don't do it in public. Do I have to remind you this culture is Old School? Your Ole Man is the man and his Ole Lady is the lady. Act like one, not like some drunk barfly.

Some women can't keep their mouths shut and start trouble with other Ole Ladies or civilians, picking fights and so on. If this is you, behave yourself. You are putting the whole club at risk over your inability to control yourself.

If you mouth off or show disrespect for a Brother, your Ole Man will pay the consequences and be fined by the club. Or, another Ole Lady may be ordered to take your ass outside and straighten you out. Why would you want to put your Sister or Ole Man in that position?

My mom was only five feet, four inches tall, but she was an Old School Biker Momma. I remember once a chick got out of line, and when my mom tried to talk to her, to calm her down, she got mouthy. My mom had more patience than I would have had with this chick. Mom given the order to take care of it with a nod from my dad.

This chick had no clue. She was drunk and belligerent one minute, hysterical the next. When she got hysterical, my mom slapped her. We thought, *cool, maybe she'll calm down*. Not so. She became more belligerent.

My mom talked her to the back of the bar and out into the parking lot and *opened up a can of whoop ass* on the chick. A few minutes later someone ran into the bar and yelled to my dad, "Come quick, it's Momma." My dad continued shooting pool and said, "I'm not worried, Momma can hold her own."

The person said, "No! If you don't come out here and stop her, she's going to kill the other chick!" My dad went out back, and all he said to Momma was, "That's enough." She stopped, backed away from the chick, and the two of them walked back into the bar like nothing happened.

If you think we don't handle our own, you're dead wrong. That chick had to apologize to the whole club at the next function, and she was banned from all functions for a year. If you can't control your drinking and partying, *don't go – stay home!*

If you can't talk or walk straight, how the hell do you think you can ride straight? Your actions on the back of a bike affect the handling of the bike. You could cause a wreck. How would you feel then? Often, by twist of fate, the drunk comes out of the accident fine; it's the responsible parties who get hurt, maimed, or even killed. Do you want that on your conscience?

A bunch of us were in Tennessee partying and having a good time. One of the Ole Ladies got sloppy drunk and we had to bungee cord her to the back of the bike to get her home. A couple of us served as escorts to make sure she and her Ole Man made it home safely. This Sister was more concerned about her good time than safety. Her actions put us all in a situation we didn't want to be in.

This happened in 1981, and I still remember it like it was yesterday. One thing I don't remember is the chick's real nickname because after that we called her and referred to her as "Bungee." I personally refuse to be known or remembered like that.

Jealousy has no place in the club. One Ole Lady (*R.I.P*) was on an overnight camp-out in Illinois and got handcuffed to a bike for starting fights and showing disrespect. When she would drink, she would accuse everyone of wanting her Ole Man, And, when she wouldn't listen to her Ole Man, he handcuffed her to the bike for the rest of the evening. She became known as "Cuff." You wouldn't want to end up like this, would you? Behave and control yourself.

We are family, and everyone hugs and kisses each other. Handshakes are for strangers and civilians; hugs and kisses are for family. And the club members *are* your family, so there is no reason to be jealous. If you have a problem with this, *don't go – stay home!*

If you are with a clubber or one-percenter, you should know that much of the time the guys go to titty bars. If you can't enjoy the show and have a good time, *don't go – stay home!* And don't give your Ole Man a ration of shit or the nth degree about his going.

Every time I go, I have a blast. I talk to the dancers and introduce them to the Brothers. I find out which dancers my Ole Man likes and buy lap dances for him. There's no reason to get jealous or upset. I just watch and find out what he likes, and then I can use it at home.

If you're there, you can see what's going on instead of sitting home imagining what's happening. It's actually a great time. But like I said before, there is no room for jealousy, so don't embarrass yourself by acting like a high school kid.

Biker parties are adult parties unless you are riding with a family club. Get a sitter or stay home with your kids. This stuff is for adults.

I don't have little ones anymore, but when I did, wet tee shirts, weenie rides, knife-throwing, slow rides, dancing, teasing, cussing, and drinking were not activities I subjected my children to. I have done the mother gig. Don't ruin my good time because you don't want to do yours.

I am not going to curtail my behavior because you can't find a babysitter. It's irresponsible when people bring their kids to Sturgis or Daytona. What the hell are they thinking? Don't make us have to take care of your kids after we have raised our own. Have some consideration and good old common sense. If you can't get a sitter, *don't go – stay home!*

The exception, of course, is if you are with a one-piece patch holder, a clean and sober club, or a family club. Even then, there will be questions of whether functions are family-oriented or adult only.

My ex-Ole Man has a problem with clothes when drinking tequila and has been known to walk home from a bar with his pants over his shoulder. We were at a party once where some of the Ole Ladies started sneaking him tequila. A few of them were drinking it too. Between one Ole Lady having weenie checks and him drinking tequila off others' tits, it got pretty wild. So you see, you just never know what's going to happen at an adults-only party.

Hey, it's adult fun!

Remember, don't bring trouble down on your Ole Man, yourself, or your family. I really get serious about this. The club is the only family I have outside of my children, grandchildren, and Ole Man. I would really hate to put a Sister in line. I don't know about you, but I really love my nickname and don't want it changed to the likes of "Bungee" or "Cuff."

Chase Vehicles

If you can't ride a bike or if you choose not to, be prepared to ride chase. If you are in a chase vehicle, you need to carry everything on the Supply List plus a cooler with ice and drinks, a gas can, and motor oil.

Your primary responsibility is to follow behind the club and use your vehicle as a block when the scoots are changing lanes. Your job is to change lanes first, then let everyone in the pack in front of you. The chase vehicle prevents other cars and trucks from running up on the back of the pack.

If a bike breaks down, you need to stop and help. Pull in behind and protect the bike from traffic. If you are riding chase, you'll have a cell phone to call and leave messages with bikers in the pack. They will eventually stop, and when they do they will call you back.

If the bike gets back on the road, stay very close behind and try to catch up with the pack. The chase vehicle may also be pulling a trailer. You may need to help load a disabled bike into the trailer and later get it back on the road.

You should have your Ole Man's cell phone number, but you may also want to carry the road captain's. The road captain is the person who has the maps and directions. He's the one who planned the trip from start to finish. He can better help you get back on course if you get separated from the pack.

One night I was riding chase for a club in Norfolk, Virginia. I noticed a cage in the left lane, weaving like the driver was drunk. The cage passed me and then started weaving towards the pack. As soon as it did, I squeezed my vehicle between the pack and the drunk driver. I was then able to make that driver pull over by laying on my horn and edging him off the road. The pack kept going, and I kept them safe by doing this. On the road, a bike has an unfair advantage against a car or truck.

Riding chase is very important. The safety of the pack is the number one job of the chase vehicle.

Proper Riding Attire

Ever since the yuppies and rubs decided that Harley's and pickups are the latest trend, the riding clothes have become a fashion statement: *Gee, let's match our bikes with our leathers with our boots.* If you look beyond some of this bull, you'll realize that many of the so-called trendy items of clothing are actually not good for riding.

Fringe. Long fringe is okay – provided you want to get whipped to death while riding. Short fringe is best. It's what you want to wick away the rain from your clothes.

Boots. A good pair of boots is a must. You'll recall that my cheap boots didn't keep my toes from being bent backwards inside them. When selecting boots, keep in mind that ankle support and protection are important factors to consider. Your boots may keep you from getting burned by the exhaust pipes or from twisting or even breaking toes, feet, or ankles. Rough soles and small heels are very helpful. In wet conditions, you don't want to slip while mounting or dismounting the bike. A small heel helps keep your feet on the pegs.

Leather. A good leather jacket will shield you from the weather, and if you go down, it will protect your hide and help hold your bones together.

My mom and dad were out for a putt one day – each on their own bike – when they came upon a construction zone where the pavement was uneven. They didn't have any advance warning. My mom ended up in a groove that was four inches deeper than that on my dad's side.

Mom couldn't get the bike to jump the gap, so she decided to ride it out. Not a good idea as it turned out. First, she ran into the curb and gutter. Stubbornly, she continued on. Then she came upon an open grate in the gutter, which caught her front wheel and threw Mom and her bike.

Mom hit the kill switch as she went down. She was doing about fifty miles per hour when she hit the pavement. She slid on her elbows and butt. When she came to a stop, she sat up, looked around and noticed that across the street, people were putting a coffin in a hearse. She had come to a stop right in front of a funeral home.

The leather she was wearing, I had made for her. It dipped down in the back with a kidney belt, and it had double cowhide reinforced elbows. Needless to say, there was nothing left of her jacket in the back and at the elbows. But, while she was bruised, she didn't have a single broken bone, and she had all of her skin.

Can you imagine the scene if she had worn a fancy leather – made for show and not protection – on? Think what her bones and skin would have looked like. I cringe every time I see women on the back of bikes wearing shorts, halter tops, and sandals. Even if you go down at a slow rate of speed, road rash has to be cleaned with a scrub brush.

Not me! I don't want any part of a scrub brush on my raw skin. The scars from tailpipe burns and road rash aren't pretty or sexy. I can always take my protection off when I get to the party or wherever I am going, but the road is no place for a fashion show.

Gloves. A good pair of gauntlet gloves is ideal for riding. They keep the wind from going up the sleeves and stop bugs as well. Beware of June bugs. They can just knock you out. The biggest I've ever seen were at dusk in Illinois. They were about the size of a thumb. The biggest bumble bee I have ever seen came out of a friend's jacket in Minnesota. No joke, it too was the size of a thumb. Scary, huh?

Eye protection. Even though you have a windshield, you never can predict when a rock, a bug or rain might put your eyesight in danger, so *always* wear a good pair of glasses. I also advise wearing a visor that can be attached to your lid. It provides some added protection in bad weather and against bugs. Keep in mind that when the sun starts going down, the bugs get worse, especially in the summer.

My Ole Man told me about a time he was returning from Daytona. He was crossing the Bonne Carre spillway doing about ninety miles per hour when a June bug hit him right between the eyes. Everything went black, and he said it took all he had just to keep the bike on the road. The next day, he looked like a raccoon because his eyes were black all the way into his cheeks. So, a good visor is important.

Chaps. In cold weather and to keep you dry in the rain, chaps are handy to have on. A drawback is that they leave you open in the back, inviting a wet ass. Leather pants are better, but it's your choice.

Helmets. Helmets are a double edge sword. For all the good they do, they can also cause severe injury. What the government doesn't tell you is that in a bad crash, a lid can break your neck, causing paralysis or death. Not to mention that while riding with a helmet on, you have a certain amount of hearing loss, and your peripheral vision is limited.

Most bikers think lid laws suck. I grew up with a rule in our house: under eighteen must wear a lid, after which it's individual choice. But now, the government has taken away our right to choose and has made wearing a lid the law. So, the best advice I can give, I guess, is pick a lid that fits you and try to get one with a removable visor.

Let me tell you a true story about my Ole Man. One night in New Orleans in the 1970s after having imbibed a few brews, he was feeling froggy and decided to *twist the wick* a little. Well, this served to get the attention of the local constabulary. So, my Ole Man decided to play *catch me if you can*.

He was on St. Charles Avenue, which is in the Garden District of New Orleans, one of the oldest neighborhoods. The street has an unusually large median strip to accommodate trolley cars that run both ways on tracks between the vehicle lanes. It also has gentle curves and swells, and at the time of this story, it was in need of repair.

To set the scene, the city was doing construction along the side of the street, and crews had dug a hole three feet deep, four feet wide, and five feet long. They had positioned tar pots to mark the spot. All along St. Charles Avenue were the famous big green metal lamp posts.

With a couple of cages in hot pursuit, my Ole Man was roaring along St. Charles at speeds in excess of 100 miles per hour. He turned his head to see how close the cops were, then turned back and saw the hole, but had no time to swerve. His bike hit the side of the hole and stopped. My Ole Man didn't. He flew thirty feet through the air straight for a lamp post. He put his hands out instinctively to cushion the inevitable crash. He struck the pole, hands first, then head. The impact busted his lid like an eggshell, ripping it off and taking a portion of his face with it.

Catapulting through the air, feet first and with his back to the ground, he landed twenty feet further on the trolley tracks. Even then, his journey was not over. He slid another fifteen feet, finally coming to rest on his back with the track under him at shoulder blade height.

Miraculously, he remained conscious and attempted to survey the damage. He noticed a gritty, sandy substance in his mouth, interspersed with the salty taste of blood. He was able to move only his head.

He became aware of two cops standing over him. One asked his partner, "Is he dead?" The other replied, "Not yet, but I don't think he's going to make it." My Ole Man told them, "F*** you!" But, in doing so, he realized he wasn't talking right.

The helmet saved his life but broke a vertebrae in his neck, and ripped off part of his face, his upper lip on the left side, and bottom lip in the middle. Plus, both sides of his jaw line were lacerated. The impact shifted his frame, and to this day, one side of his body is higher then the other. The index finger on his left hand was ripped from the socket and laying across the top of his hand, which was splintered with thirteen other breaks. He suffered a broken arm, a broken collar bone, broken ribs and broken left leg. The gritty sandy substance in his mouth turned out to be broken pieces of his teeth. He had chipped all but one of them.

His recovery involved extensive dental work, $250,000 worth

of plastic surgery, and a body cast. During his year in the hospital, he went from 215 pounds to 128. He had to relearn to walk after being told he probably never would. He was left with a large scar on his spine, compliments the trolley tracks.

While my Ole Man's behavior is certainly not condoned, the point is, a biker is not defined by his or her trendy attire. Almost immediately upon his release, my Ole Man was ready to get back on his bike again. This urge – too strong to be ignored – defines a biker. No matter how slight or how serious the fall, a biker gets up, brushes himself off, mends his broken body, and gets back to the business of riding.

My Ole Man *is* a born scooter tramp. His blood brother died when a sports car driver ran his bike off the road and into a guard rail. He was thrown over the handle bars and pinned between the rail and bike. The bike double-kissed the rail and crushed the face and chest of my Ole Man's brother. No open casket for him.

For men like my Ole Man and his brother, riding is everything. Ask them to name a feeling or emotion that makes them feel good, and they respond with something associated with riding a scoot. Riding, to true bikers, is as necessary as the air they breathe or the food they eat.

To sum this up, let me say from experience that there are two categories of bikers: those who have been down and those who *will* go down. Remember this thought when you pick out your riding attire.

A Clean Scoot

A good thing to remember is this. Picture yourself in a parade where all the floats are bright and grand. Then you turn and look at your float, and it's covered in mud, looking small, and ugly. Well that's what it's like being on a dirty scoot. It makes the bike look like a rat bike.

When you are on a bike, everywhere you go, people look. If you are in a club and the Brothers decide to buzz the front of the bar, convention hall, or party, *everyone* will be looking. Remember, Harleys are thunderous, and people naturally want to see what kind of bike is going by. Your responsibility is to make sure that yours looks as good as it sounds.

Now this is where the iffy part comes in. I used to wash my Ole Man's scoot before I owned my own. Some men don't want you touching their bikes. Others may think it's a bad omen to wash the bike because something will go wrong or it will rain. Discuss this with your Ole Man. Maybe he'd like you to help him; maybe not.

Cleaning a scoot is a very personal matter. There are a lot of products out there to choose from. Personally, I have a few favorites.

Mother's Chrome Polish. This is a commercial product every *Biker Babe* should know about and keep on hand. It is easily applied with a cloth diaper, a toothbrush, and a dental pick to effectively polish the chrome.

Dishwashing liquid. A household staple, it's convenient and effective in cutting the grease, thus making the bike easier to clean.

Degreaser. This gives an added power boost to help remove oil, road grime, and grease.

Steel wool pads. Another item commonly found on kitchen shelves, they work great on the rims for rust spots and for removing tar and bugs.

Aluminum foil. When wet, it helps remove rust from chrome.

Toothbrushes and Q-tips. Both help clean paste wax out of tight areas.

Cloth diapers. These work really well for wiping down the bike. Receiving blankets are equally effective.

Nu-Finish. I have found this to be a good product to use to polish the bike twice a year.

Black leather dye. Once a year, I use black leather dye on the bags and seat.

Neats Foot Oil. When the black leather dye dries, Neats Foot Oil helps waterproof the bags. It's also good on boots, gloves, chaps, and leathers. It conditions, softens, and waterproofs all your leather.

When cleaning the scoot, always work from the top down. The bottom has road grime and will scratch the paint. Between washings, I use a baby blanket to wipe the dust off the bike, but I have found that a Swiffer Duster works really great as well.

You should also be aware of a few *don'ts* when cleaning a bike. For instance:

Never put leather conditioner, such as Armor All on the seat. You will slide into your Ole Man or, worse, off the bike. In other words, don't make the seat slippery.
Never wear jewelry when washing the bike.
Never lean over the bike with a jacket or a belt buckle as these may scratch the surface. Always walk around the bike.

Above all – and I emphasize – before you attempt anything that has to do with your Ole Man's bike, remember this rule:

Always ask your Ole Man first!

Your Biker Family

Now that you have an Ole Man who's in a club, your family just got bigger. You should make an effort to get to know everyone and buddy up with the Sisters. You now have an open door, which means any Brother or Sister is welcome anytime, day or night.

Your home just may be in the perfect location for everyone to meet before going on a run. If the club is meeting at my house in the morning, I will usually get a box or two of donuts and have coffee ready. It's a good idea to have soda as well.

If you have been on a morning run and everyone is coming back to your house, try to have lunch or a meat platter, chips, veggies with dip, beer, soda, and coffee, and make sure everyone gets something to eat. Try to be a good hostess. Your Ole Man is your responsibility. Get him a plate and take care of the Brothers who don't have Ole Ladies with them.

The other Ole Ladies should pitch in and help in the kitchen. Likewise, if you are visiting another Sister's house, help get the food together, help serve the Brothers, and most importantly, help clean up the mess. You don't want to be stuck with a mess to clean up all by yourself at your house, so pitch in and help at another Sister's house. The gesture is always greatly appreciated.

Make sure you thank your Sisters for their help. Even when a Sister says, "No, that's okay," she's just being a gracious hostess. Help by carrying food to the table to save her a few steps. Ask where the plates are. Everyone knows how to wash dishes and take trash out, so be a good Sister.

There may also be times when a Brother decides he's tired or has had too much to drink to go home, so he may need a place to crash – a couch, a bed, anything is fine. He may show up at weird hours of the night, so that means you get out of bed, make him a bed and offer something to eat and drink.

No attitude needed!

Ladies, it's a part of being a Good Ole Lady to make a Brother feel at home. I always have extra toothbrushes, razors, towels, washcloths, and a pair of sweats he can sleep in. I also have one multi vitamin and two Tylenol in a hang-over kit. This saves a hang-over the next day. And, I always ask him what time he gets up. I set the coffee pot for earlier than usual if I have to.

Sometimes, the guys may decide to hold church at your house. This is club business, not yours. I set food out, get everyone something to drink and either go to my bedroom and watch television or just leave the house all together. My Ole Man will call me when it's time to come back. Unless you have a basement that is private or a heated garage, be prepared not to be seen for at least a couple hours.

Don't be nosy!

This is their club and it's their business, *not yours*. You and the prospects are on a need-to-know basis. *Club business is club business*, and since you don't have rags on your back, you have no right interfering in club business. It's a man's club and it's your choice to be a Good Ole Lady. If by chance your Ole Man tells you something, remember, you "don't know" anything. And, what you "don't know" is not to be repeated to anyone.

Arriving at a get-together, the first thing I do is make sure everything is secure on the bikes, and then I find my Ole Man and the other Brothers something to drink. After that, I run to the bathroom to fix my face and hair. Then I get myself something.

If we are in a place we aren't familiar with, I watch my Ole Man's back and check the scoots. I make sure my Ole Man has everything he needs. If he gets up, I watch his drink. If he's off talking with the guys, I give him about ten to fifteen minutes, then I take him his drink. Often, the guys get into a conversation and can't reach their drinks back at the table, so it's really cool to hand him a drink.

Watch to make sure your Ole Man doesn't go empty, even if he is drinking soda. He may be talking business or meeting a new Brother. Take care that he doesn't want for anything. Don't interrupt their conversation, and whatever you do, don't stand there and listen. It's not your business.

If he says *let's go*, you best be ready to ride *now*, but if he takes awhile saying good-bye, don't be embarrassing by standing there with your arms crossed, tapping your foot, showing your impatience. You are *not* the boss! If you want to go out and have a good time with the club again, *don't act stupid!*

Treat everyone with respect. A lot of Ole Ladies make the mistake of treating a prospect like shit. Because they see their Ole Man ordering him around, they think they can too. *Wrong!* You are an Ole Lady.

The prospect has enough to worry about. Mind you, he may be the next patch holder and then he'll remember how you treated him. I say treat everyone just as you would like to be treated. Everyone who now has a patch was once a prospect.

The phone will ring at the most inopportune times, even in the middle of the night. A Brother may need help. Even in mid-stroke, the phone gets answered if it's a Brother. It could mean life or death. If he's broke down, he's vulnerable to anyone passing by. If he's in a club and someone starts a fight, he may need backup. If a Brother goes down, someone needs to take care of the bike and his rags.

Don't ever hesitate answering the phone, and get ready to run if needed. You may have to come along to help a Sister in need. Throw jeans, tee-shirt, and shoes on. You can brush your hair later; for now just tie it back. *Never* make your Ole Man wait for you to get ready. You should be waiting on him at the door while he is putting on his boots.

If you are not going with him, help him get out of the door by nuking some coffee and getting together his stuff, such as boots, gloves, phone, leather, and colors. And then, send him off with love and a kiss – *not an attitude.*

My Ole Man has lived a rough life, so the club is his life, and the Brothers are his blood. Ole Ladies, listen. Jobs, homes, and kids come and go, but his Brothers will always be there. Don't be a nag; let your Ole Man do his thing. If you're a Good Ole Lady, it will be more difficult for him to ever let you go. Especially if you are Old School.

Know Your Place!

Be Your Own Person

Ladies, please stop annoying everyone with a hundred phone calls a day. That's henpecking, and it's very embarrassing to your Ole Man. You, likewise, should be embarrassed that you're so insecure about yourself.

Have you nothing better to do than call him and hound the shit out of him? Worse, what do you hope to gain by cussing him on his voice mail when you can't get hold of him? If he is in church, phones are not allowed. Having them results in big fines. If he's not in church, he may otherwise be busy or in an area with no signal. If you're a Good Ole Lady, you'll let him call you.

Lose the attitude!

I couldn't believe my ears when I heard an Ole Lady threatening her Ole Man on his voice mail, "You better f****** call me now!" The Brothers were on the road, and the whole time she was having a temper tantrum and leaving these disrespectful messages. If I were her Ole Man, I would have saved the messages and played them for everyone to hear at the next club function. That would teach her to grow up and stop acting like a spoiled brat.

Sometimes, I think the reason Ole Ladies call so much is because they're worried about their Ole Men cheating on them. Well, believe me, a hundred phone calls is not going to stop him. Usually, when the Ole Men are out of town, they are working. If they are cheating on you, they most likely are doing it close to home and not out of town. And, if they are cheating, phone calls are not going to stop them.

Take Care of Your Ole Man

Taking care of your Ole Man's appearance is one way to let other women know that he is not available. When I was single and on the prowl, I wouldn't look at the men who had their hair perfectly braided or banded in hair ties. These were indications that these guys were taken care of. For a Good Ole Lady, it is a pride issue. Her Ole Man's hair, his dress, and the way his bike looks are reflections on her. I would look for those men who were not perfectly put together. That was a sign they did not have Good Ole Ladies taking care of them.

I take care of my Ole Man every day and even more so before he leaves town. I have a lot of trust in him and wait till he calls me. Don't get me wrong, I don't stay home and wait with baited breath. I have a life of my own and a cell phone.

Ole Ladies' Night Out

When my Ole Man goes out of town, I have things I like to do. I can pamper myself and do girl stuff that I don't have time for when he's home. I can spend quality time with my wonderful daughter.

One of my favorite activities is having a sleep-over with other Sisters. We can talk girl talk and get buzzed, and no one has to worry about drinking and driving. We play music and board games and in general just have a blast while the guys are off doing their thing. This is a good way for Sisters to bond.

At someone's house, we can be ourselves, something we can't do when we go out. We sometimes get together and go out dancing, for instance, but we can't let our hair down because at some point, some guy is going to act stupid. It never fails. Some drunk idiot is going to be belligerent, and that ruins the fun.

Just remember: When the Ole Men leave town, it's the Ole Ladies' time to be on vacation.

Be a Good Sister

We are all Sisters, and I respect each one of you and your individual idiosyncrasies. I will bend over backwards and put myself out for my family. But, when I feel a Sister has disrespected me, I will tell her in no uncertain terms how I feel. And, if she does not change? Then, I still consider her family, but I will not do anything to help her in any way.

I never like to see a new Sister sitting by herself; I try to make everyone feel comfortable. I don't shake hands with a new Sister; I hug her and welcome her and introduce her to the other Sisters. And, I make sure she gets up on the dance floor along with the rest of us.

I returned to my hometown after being gone for thirteen years. My parents were going to a party and invited me to go along. A lot of the women there didn't know or didn't remember me. Faces had changed a lot. I noticed one group, members of which were all buddies.

I was trying to have a conversation on philosophy with one of the guys. This group kept getting closer, and then they started elbowing me and bumping into me. I kept my cool as long as I could because I was a visitor and didn't want to start any shit.

After I had taken enough, I walked over to my mom and told her I wasn't going to take any more. She said, "Do what you got to do." So I walked over to the group, elbowed the ring leader, and told them all that their goofy shit wouldn't be tolerated. I made it clear that the next person who bumped or elbowed me was going to get her ass kicked. They didn't bother me anymore, but an atmosphere of whispering, pointing, and gossiping was heavy for a while.

Gossip is one of my pet peeves. It only causes problems

between Sisters. If I have something to say, I will usually say it
to that person face to face. The exception is if I think saying
something will do more harm then good. Then, I keep it to
myself. Gossiping behind one's back doesn't help anyone.

Watch Out for Each Other

If a Sister gets out of line or tipsy and that is not her usual thing,
I don't mind helping her out. I will watch over her to make sure
that she doesn't get in trouble. I'll get her a cup of coffee or a
soda. But, I'll only do this if her behavior is a rare occurrence.
My Ole Man's needs are more important, and I am out to have a
good time, not to babysit. So, please, ladies, know your limits.
You don't want everyone to know you as a drunk, and you don't
want to end up an outcast.

When out in a public bar or other such places, it is very
important to watch each other's backs. If one of your Sisters
goes outside or to the rest room, someone needs to go with her.
You never know when a person with a grudge or a drunk may
decide she is an easy target. I especially try to keep an eye on
officers' Ole Ladies at all times because their role makes them
vulnerable.

You can be sure, there are a few unfriendly clubs, whose
members come into parties and watch for a chance to mess with
others. Their Ole Ladies stake out rest rooms or hallways,
waiting to jump an Ole Lady from a rival club. The longer
you are around, the more adept you will become at spotting the
troublemakers.

Some friends of ours – a foursome – are in a mom and pop
club. (In this club, the Ole Ladies wear a patch too, but it's a
one-piece patch.) The four of them like to ride together on the
weekends. On one such outing, they pulled in for gas in a place
where a troublemaking club was hanging out. These weekend
riders, who were minding their own business, got the hell
knocked out of them. So you see, you really need to watch
your surroundings.

I have also on occasion put myself in front of drunk civilians,
blocking their path so that they couldn't bother patch holders.
Being female helps in this regard. I can usually get past an
unsuspecting drunk and then position myself so he or she can't

get past me. This is a maneuver they tend not to expect from a woman, and it catches them off guard.

Just as in traditional families, where siblings are honor bound by blood, Sisters in the biker family need to recognize our special connection and realize that harmony and loyalty among ourselves are gifts to be cherished and not qualities to be taken lightly.

Prospects and Patch Holders

Ole Ladies need to know what a prospect is and what he does to earn respect and show loyalty to his future Brothers. In some cases it takes a prospect two years to earn his patch.

Many times, prospects have been hang-arounds for a good while before becoming prospects. Once they become prospects, they catch a lot of shit. They make runs for anything and everything. They stand out in the cold and watch the bikes while everyone else is inside having a good time. They fetch for patch holders (but for patch holders *only!*). Some patch holders are cool, but others can run the hell out of a prospect. In fact, prospects spend a year or more running their asses off.

If your Ole Man is prospecting, he will be gone a lot that year. You will be sitting home a lot too. Sometimes, he'll be able to bring you around, but don't expect to go out too often. When you do, whatever you do, *don't mess up!* Your Ole Man is trying to earn his patch. Don't be the one to ruin it for him.

A prospect carries everything you can think of – extra cigarettes, lighters, magnesium sticks, leatherman, electrical tape, fuses, spare bulbs, tire patch kits, flashlights, spark plugs, emery boards, gum, and a few other things mentioned in the supply list. Your job as his Ole Lady is to make sure he has everything he needs. He's running hard, so when he comes home, take care of him. He'll be tired, sore, hungry, and possibly wet if he's been out in the rain. Just remember, behind every good man is a good woman. Be true to that saying.

Wearing the Patch

When your Ole Man puts that patch on, your status is still his Ole Lady. As a patch holder's Ole Lady you'll be able to go out more, because he will be able to party now too. It is a good practice, however, for you or your Ole Man to continue to carry everything in a prospect pouch or in your purse or even in a bag on the bike. It is always good to have backup supplies in case of emergency. (See Supply List for items to carry, the reasons why, and uses of these items.)

Depending on the club, your Ole Man could be a hang-around for a year and then a prospect for another year. Prospects really go through a lot for their patches, as well as for the love, honor, and respect of their Brothers. Once he puts the center patch on, he is married to the club. The best thing you can do is be a Good Ole Lady.

Patches are always worn while riding and at club functions. They are never to touch the floor. If you want to be a Good Ole Lady, hold on to your Man's colors while he puts his jacket on. *Never* lay them down anywhere.

Don't take offense to your Ole Man handing his rags to one of his Brothers. This is the proper thing for him to do. No one is to handle or touch the colors except for a Brother. That is, of course, unless your Ole Man asks you to or hands them to you. If you're asked to handle them for any reason, guard them with your life. If you are holding them, fold the rags so that the patch is inside.

If a clubber is riding in a cage, his rags are folded and put inside the cage. It is disrespectful for colours to be worn while in a cage, just as it is disrespectful for colors to be covered up while worn.

If you get out of line or if your Ole Man does something wrong or against the bylaws, then he has to go to patch holder's court. He can get fined and get his patch pulled. If you – his Ole Lady – are the cause of this, then you may as well kiss your relationship good-bye. This is especially true if he is a one-percenter or is in an outlaw club. Remember, it took a lot for him to earn that patch. For you to do something that could result in him losing it would be unforgivable.

Club Hierarchy

Clubs are at different levels in the hierarchy. This is very important in the biker world. Topping the list are the Big

Four. They sanction other clubs. They are the one-percenters, and if you don't know who they are, you need to ask your Ole Man. These clubs are highly respected, and they are worldwide. The biker world is a way of life, not just a weekend thing.

These are words they live by:

Show respect – Get respect.
Act like an asshole – Get treated like an asshole.
Treat us good – We will treat you better.
Treat us bad – We will treat you worse.

One-Percenters What defines a one-percenter? A good example is this. Imagine you are in a big crowd of people and a person is acting out of line and obnoxious. An average civilian would whisper under his or her breath, "What a jerk, someone should do something!" A one-percenter would just walk up and knock the shit out of the jerk.

Taking care of business. This, I think, is what defines a real man. These guys back each other up and stick together, but more important, they do not back down or wimp out. That's why I wrote earlier about woman's lib having no place in the biker world.

One-percenters are real men, not people who have been beaten down by society. They set examples for our young men. My daughters are raised Old School, and I hope they raise their children the same way – with love, honor, and respect. These qualities are extremely hard to find these days.

How can you recognize a one-percenter? You will know him by his three-piece patch and by the diamond shaped patch on his rags. Years ago, the diamond was worn above the top rocker. Hence the nickname, *diamondback*. Now it is worn on the front left side over the heart.

One-Percenter Outlaw Clubs. Next in line are the one-percenter outlaw clubs. Each of these clubs is affiliated with one of the Big Four and also sanctioned by that club. Clubbers wear one-percenter diamonds and three-piece patches. They also wear support patches for *the* one-percenter clubs they are affiliated with. These clubs are considered outlaw because they are not sanctioned by the American Motorcycle Association (A.M.A.).

Outlaw Clubs. Clubbers wear three-piece patches and may or
may not wear support patches. These clubs are each sanctioned
by a one-percenter club. They do not fly a diamond.

"Other" Three-Piece Patch Wearers. After the outlaw
clubs come those who in the biker world are known as the
"other" three-piece patch wearers. But, because of who they
are, they do not abide by the same rules or code of ethics the rest
of the biker world adheres to. These are law enforcement clubs.
They do what they want, when they want.

One-percenter and outlaw bikers adhere to the law of the
land, and we respect the laws we have so that we can maintain
our freedom. Individual rights are becoming fewer and fewer. I
wear a patch with a saying in which I believe strongly:

Legalize Freedom!!!!

Women's Clubs. You will find a lot of women's clubs out
there. They abide by the same rules the men's clubs go by. They
must be sanctioned, and the outlaw women's clubs have prospects.

I have been riding my own bike since I was eleven years old,
and I still haven't had a patch on my back. My mom rode with
the ladies that started *Harley Woman* Magazine. I remember
the first issue of that magazine, which my mom sent me. It
looked like a newsletter instead of a magazine. I really miss that
magazine. Those women paved the road for all of us.

Mom and Pop Clubs. At the base of the hierarchy are the one-
piece patch wearers. They are mom and pop clubs. Their Ole
Ladies wear patches, ride in the pack, and hold officer positions.
These are considered family clubs and are sanctioned by the
A.M.A.

A related point I want to touch upon about club hierarchy is
this. Sometimes, outlaw clubs decide to become one of the Big
Four. If they do, they may be starting a new charter or chapter.
When they decide to go this route, these full patch holders are
considered hang-arounds for a year. Then they get voted in as
prospects. This is a rough way to go. These full patch holders

trade in their colors for prospect patches and start running again for a whole year or more.

This is not easy on our men, and it's even harder on a relationship. If you aren't an understanding Ole Lady, you probably won't survive as a couple, especially when your man is running to different states, parties, and functions. He needs to earn his patches and meet other charters or chapters. And, while the prospecting may be for only a year, he will still be in a probationary period for another year after that. Only then does everything go back to normal. So let your Ole Man do what he's got to do. You just need to be a Good Ole Lady.

Riding Order

Although rules vary by such factors as region, this is typical riding order for biker clubs:

President and Road Captain
Vice President and Treasurer
Other Officers
Full Patch Holders
Prospects
Enforcer
Hang-Arounds
Ole Ladies
Civilians

The president and road captain lead, followed by the vice president and treasurer. Other officers fall in behind, then other full patch holders, followed by prospects and then the enforcer. Hang-arounds, women who ride, and civilians bring up the rear. This is the way it is and it's not going to change.

I have seen some three-piece patches that allow their Ole Ladies to ride in the pack, but higher up in the hierarchy it is *not* allowed. This is a man's club.

I love riding with my Ole Man, just the two of us. Hell, we run down the road side by side and hold hands at eighty-five miles per hour. But when we are with the club, I ride in the back, and I don't mind at all. I have been in the back of the pack almost my whole life. I am comfortable there.

Be forewarned, if you are going to ride your own scoot, be prepared to ride fast, hard, and close. If you are not comfortable or are new to a bike, *don't even think about* riding pack. There is a whole lot more to riding in a pack than just jumping on a bike and cruising along side by side. You have to know what you're doing. I highly advise that newcomers take a motorcycle safety course.

Showing Respect

Always show respect for patch holders, especially three-piece patch holders. The difference between a one-piece patch and a three-piece patch is that most one-piece patch holders do not earn their patches like a three-piece patch holder does. Many of the one-piece patch Ole Ladies get their patches handed to them just because they are Ole Ladies. Personally, I never felt the need to wear a patch on my back. Everyone knows whose Ole Lady I am.

Years ago, Ole Ladies wore *property of* patches that signified who their Ole Men were. This was so that when the big clubs got together, nobody would mess with another Brother's Ole Lady. If an Ole Lady got out of line – especially if she was disrespectful – the Brothers from other chapters would know who to go to.

Now, the property patches are considered very Old School and are fading out. I believe if you are a Good Ole Lady, everyone can see who you are with. I have my pins and patches from a lifetime of travel. These are a part of my memories, that's all.

When meeting new people, I introduce myself as Throttle, (___'s) Ole Lady with the (___) Motorcycle Club from (state). Then, my acquaintance knows who I'm with. If I am sitting with other Ole Ladies, we introduce ourselves or each other by name and by whose Ole Ladies we are.

One other rule is worth mentioning because I have seen plenty of men and women make this mistake. It is considered a very big show of disrespect if you shake someone's hand with a glove on. Most Ole Ladies give and receive hugs when we meet, but sometimes the handshake situation comes up. For example, you may pull up to a party, and some Brothers and Sisters will come over as you are getting off the bike. If you see this happening, a good practice is to take your gloves off before even getting off the bike. After that, you can remove your helmet. This is a really good rule to make everyone in your club aware of, especially if they are going to party with one of the Big Four.

As noted, Brothers are fiercely loyal, to each other and to their cause. If a Brother or his Ole Lady gets out of line, the other Brothers will defend their own *in public*, no matter what. But, be assured, the matter will be addressed *in private*. Therefore, it bears repeating: If you're a Good Ole Lady, you won't do anything to jeopardize your Ole Man's patch.

SEX AND HEDONISM AMONGST ONE-PERCENTER BIKERS

James Quinn

The following account provides a fascinating picture of the changing role of women in outlaw biker subculture. James "Jim" Quinn – a Professor at the University of North Texas – is an expert on one-percenter biker organizations.

One percent motorcycle clubs restrict their membership to adult Caucasian males. A few clubs, e.g., the Bandidos, accept anglicized Hispanics; the Mongols are largely of Mexican-American heritage. Women cannot formally become members of these groups but must gain acceptance through a union with a male biker. A woman's status in this type of motorcycle club is almost completely contingent upon her affective, economic, and sexual ties to a male club member. The attraction of some women to this subculture in spite of their second class status should not be considered too unusual. These women have been socialized in such a manner that they cannot conceive of a feminine role existing for them that is not subordinate to males and based to some extent on their sexuality. Most female associates of outlaw bikers have been enculturated to saloon society and/or some mode of prostitution prior to their activities as "biker's ladies". These women can best be described as having internalized an expectancy to be socially subordinate to males and thus are able to easily accept the sexual-economic role they hold in the outlaw subculture.

The saloon society milieu from which this subculture emerges is highly conducive to prostitution because women who are both sexually available and attractive are a rather scarce resource. The racist outlook that is characteristic of the lower class white population makes the, invariably white, female associates of bikers more attractive to prospective clients than the more frequently encountered, non-white girls who tend to predominate in that business. The subculture's conventionalization over the last 20 years has ameliorated their racism and sexism to a very limited degree.

The highly mobile lifestyle generated by the male's involvement with his bike and in club affairs restricts the variety of jobs that he may hold as well as their duration. The subculture's definition of "class" also predisposes bikers of both sexes to define prostitution as lucrative, expedient, and easily justifiable. The attractiveness of prostitution as a livelihood is further enhanced by the orientation of saloon society participants to tavern life and hence to afternoon and evening hours of activity. Thus, biker's ladies tend to find their most feasible means of support in topless bars, massage parlors, and similar establishments. It is not unusual for a large chapter to own or control one or more of these businesses to provide employment for its members' ol' ladies.

The Outlaws M.C. is widely reported (circa 1973) to own a forced brothel near Meridian, Mississippi. It is said that the women there were forced into prostitution after becoming associated with members of the Outlaws. Ol' ladies from the Outlaws M.C. consider being sent there a severe punishment. Other clubs are reputed to engage in forcible prostitution as well. These sorts of enterprises make the detection and control of prostitution difficult or impossible, although such employment has been described as stigmatizing in itself. Employment in such a questionable line of work may lead some women to associate with bikers for the excitement inherent in the subculture and/or protection.

In some cases male bikers work at legitimate jobs and require only supplemental income from their female companion(s). More commonly, however, their legal sources of income are sporadic, minimal, or non-existent. A very large portion of a club member's time is devoted to carousing with other members and performing club business. This tends to leave much of the role of providing day-to-day economic support to the ol' ladies and other female associates, who, in the biker's perception, are ideally equipped to provide it for the reasons discussed above.

Reinforcing this perspective is the belief in female inferiority that is common among American lower class males. This constellation of beliefs is found in extreme form among outlaw motorcyclists who value and depend upon the comradeship of their brothers for social support, rather than intimacy with women. "Bro's before bitches" is a common biker slogan. Part of the rationale for this social ranking structure is based on the violence of interclub rivalries that makes one's brothers the only people that can be depended on to guarantee day-to-day survival in saloon society. The "us or them" mentality of warfare with the suspension of basic norms it implies, combine with the threats posed by a criminal lifestyle to create a chronic state of near-paranoia in many bikers. Use of methamphetamine and similar drugs can further aggravate such tendencies. In the homo-social world of the 1%er, women are often seen as little more than expendable sources of pleasure, money, information and convenience.

Female Status Roles

A biker's ol' lady is protected from the unwanted advances of other bikers by the possession of ol' lady's rockers. This protection is especially necessary on runs and at other large gatherings where individual relationships are not universally known and unattached women are considered "fair game" for any male in any manner he may select. An ol' lady's rockers are referred to as a property patch. This infers that she is the property of her ol' man, and, through him, his club. Under no circumstances may a woman wear the full club insignia or designate herself a one percenter. The property patch is provided to the female by her ol' man who must obtain it from the chapter treasurer at a cost ($15 to $50). Many clubs restrict their members to one "patched ol' lady" at a time, though some members may have several women simultaneously available to them as sexual partners and/or income sources. Rockers consist of the club name and chapter location. Bandido women sometimes wear belts with the club name rather than a patch and the Pagans' MC does not permit any club symbols on its women.

A biker's ol' lady is expected to hand over all money she obtains to her ol' man. Deception in this regard, if discovered, is punished severely, usually by a beating or gang rape. In one, somewhat exceptional, case, a woman caught withholding money from her ol' man (the amount is said to have been approximately $20) was nailed to a tree in full view of a major highway as an example to others. This was done by Outlaw nationalists in Palm Beach County, Florida and demonstrates the extremes of behavior manifested by Outlaws Nation members. Many bikers require their ol' ladies to provide them with a given amount of cash each day. This amount usually ranges between $50 and $100. This demand can only be met by the woman resorting to prostitution on a regular basis.

A casual female companion or a discarded ol' lady may be more or less adopted by members of a club chapter and designated a mama. This status infers that the chapter or its members will provide shelter, transportation, and protection for her so long as she makes herself available to any member who desires her services. Such women are considered the property of the chapter. They are generally older than most ol' ladies and cannot compete with them in the more lucrative prostitution trade. Some club chapters may have several mamas residing at their clubhouse(s) or drifting between member's homes. Other chapters may have no mamas at all. Some clubs issue rockers to their mamas labeling them as "Property of (Whatever) M.C. / Any town". In this case ol' ladies will wear property patches naming their ol' man by his club name. If ol' ladies patches name only the club and chapter, then mamas will wear no patches at all. The custom of keeping mamas seems to be declining east of the Mississippi River. The lack of uniformity in the insignia assigned to biker women is indicative of the overt (but not always pervasive) disdain for females that is normative in the subculture. Historically, this status role disappeared from the large US clubs in the 1970s. "Party girls" who are employed at biker controlled sex businesses serve much the same role in many modern clubs but are brought to club-houses or party venues only for special occasions.

A woman who is a biker's regular sex partner and/or income source but is not protected by a property patch is often referred to as a "sweetbutt". Such a woman is generally a groupie-like follower of the biker subculture. She is not considered to be as close to the club as is a patched ol' lady and thus is fair game for the advances of others. It is these types of women who are most often victimized by groups of bikers. A sweetbutt is likely to be more freely shared sexually with other members than is an ol' lady. She cannot, however, be bought and sold (as an ol' lady can be) since she has not been formally claimed (i.e. patched) as the property of a member. In recent years, this role still exists but has become the equivalent of a "mistress" for married bikers. A few club members maintain a "stable" of prostitutes whose loyalty they try to assure thru this sort of role.

Some Boundaries between Group Dictates and Personal Choice

Under normal circumstances a club will not force a woman to stay with one of its members regardless of her status. However, if a patched ol' lady should attempt to desert her ol' man while he is in jail, owes the club money, or for other reasons immobile, club members will often make an effort to track her down. They will take revenge for her ol' man and/or collect the required money. Unless one or more of these three conditions exists the club will not become formally involved since women are per-ceived as an expendable commodity. Action may still be taken by the offended member and his friends but they would be acting as individuals, not as representatives of the club. In modern times, the more entrepreneurial of the clubs make a similar distinction between individuals or cliques of bikers and the club sui generis to avoid organized crime prosecution

The male biker is just as unalterably bound to public ad-herence to the code of absolute masculine domination as is his ol' lady. Should he allow her to express herself in opposition to him – or any male of approximately his status – the consequences for such a breach of subculture norms would fall upon him, and with very little hesitation. Rapidly escalating demands would be made for his behavior to come into conformity with one percent norms by the male's unequivocal assertion of dominance.

A female may not criticize or berate a male when others are present and is expected to be constantly alert to the felt needs of any male present, in any manner approved by her ol' man. Such felt needs may be manifested in forms varying from a man's desire for a fresh can of beer to his wish to use the woman sexually. A properly inculturated biker's lady would automatically keep pace with demands for more beer, liquor, etc., while her sexual activity is supposedly under the exclusive control of her ol' man. A man who got up to get his own beer while a woman (or a male of significantly lower status) was available to get it for him would be in normative error for not demanding such service. At the same time, a male would be correct in asking the woman's ol' man for the temporary use of her body, rather than asking the woman herself. Whether a biker will assent to the latter request is a matter of personal choice and chapter custom, but; it is unusual for a club member to deny a brother's request. Similarly, it is rare for a biker to make a request of a brother if he believes it will be denied. Thus, if tactfully handled, the woman can come to exert some degree of control over this aspect of her role through private discussions with her ol' man. The loaning of ol' ladies (and sweetbutts) is very common in the more nomadic (i.e., purist) chapters, but is reserved for special circumstances (such as the release of a veteran member from incarceration) in the more sedentary (i.e., entrepreneurial) groups.

Many veteran biker women, in reaction to their own objectification, come to see their male companions as more or less interchangeable. Certainly, sincere and loving relationships do exist within the subculture. They are, however, more the exception than the general rule. The longevity of even the best of relationships in this milieu is hampered by the sporadic poverty (and occasional wealth), extreme mobility, and physical excesses that permeate it. While a few biker couples manage to maintain long-standing ties to one another, most break up after less than two years. This is because it is more expedient (and exciting) to find a new partner or do without one than it is to work out the problems of a troubled relationship. Modern US clubs are less nomadic, wealthier and somewhat more conventionalized and this allows a much wider variety of female roles but neglect and/or abuse of women are still common.

Women as the "Property of" Males

Biker's ladies are shared with other club members at the discretion of their male companions. Under some circumstances this liberty is a fairly universal expectation, such as the release of a particularly close brother from incarceration. Such "loans" may range from a brief act of fellatio to a period of days of servitude of any desires. Club members are free to sell or trade their ol' ladies if they are incompatible, need money, or expect to be indisposed (i.e. jailed or hospitalized) for some time. Most biker's ladies can be counted on to cooperate in such transactions since they allow females to remain continuously involved in the subculture. Because most biker women work as prostitutes, the idea of being bought and sold is not nearly as repulsive to them as it would seem to someone socialized to conventional society.

An ol' lady may be sold for anywhere from $0.25 to $500. The lower the price asked by her ol' man, the more abusive the buyer's intentions are likely to be. It is also a serious blow to the woman's self-esteem to be sold for much less than $50. Women sold at impromptu barroom auctions can expect to first be inspected and manhandled by prospective buyers and then bid on by a drunken and hostile audience. Buyers at such auctions expect to keep the woman only briefly and are usually quite abusive after the sale has been finalized. Transactions that take place privately between bikers who are friends do not carry these negative implications and generally maintain or enhance the woman's social standing among her peers.

In earlier years, the ol' ladies of club officers who concluded an interclub pact of some kind were traditionally loaned for a night to seal the agreement. There is an almost honorary connotation attached to women who are useful to the club in this manner. There is also a relative degree of certainty that they will not be abused by the officer to whom they have been loaned by members of his club. Between 1975 and 1985, this practice disappeared as the "big four" clubs consolidated territories and adopted more conventional methods of resolving disputes.

Women and Club Business

Within the subculture, the term "club business" refers to any activity that is supported or sponsored by the club. Generally the term refers to all types of interclub and intraclub affairs. This can include activities related to warfare as well as illegal enterprises (e.g. drug sales, bike thefts, etc.) and legal businesses (e.g. bars, tattoo parlors, bike shops, etc.) that have been entered into by the chapter or club. The term is used frequently as an excuse for a male to participate in activities of which he does not wish to inform his ol' lady.

Club by-laws forbid women to have any knowledge of club business whatsoever. However, most patched ol' ladies are aware of many details of on-going club business, although exact procedures, people, and locations involved often remain hidden from them. A patched ol' lady would probably know which area clubs are feuding and over what issue as well as which member was fined for sleeping at the last meeting or why the brothers felt it necessary to take action against someone. She will probably not know the details of illegal transactions or the precise roles taken by individuals in violent crimes. An unpatched female associate will be directly aware of very little in this regard but can usually ascertain whether or not trouble is expected in the near future and whether its source is expected to be the police or a rival club. Women are probably less acquainted with the details of club business today than ever before as biker enterprises have grown more sophisticated and security issues have become nearly "paranoid" due to police efforts to infiltrate clubs or "turn" members and associates into informants.

Pulling a Train

Sexual gratification is seen as a male right rather than a privilege of intimacy among outlaw bikers. Women are defined as an expendable and rather interchangeable commodity. This attitude toward the sexual use of the female body has been linked by some prominent feminist writers such as Susan Brownmiller, to rape – an act for which bikers have developed quite a reputation.

Media-initiated myths seem to abound as to the wanton gang rapes of virginal victims by one percent motorcycle clubs. Most such rape victims however, are rather worldly "biker groupies". who are quite familiar with the mores of saloon society and have somehow run afoul of one or more bikers who they probably know fairly well. In earlier years, every clubhouse had one room designated as the "train room". This room may have been a large closet with a mattress on the floor to one or more rooms equipped with beds and bondage devices. The "train room" was used by club members for quick sexual encounters as well as for the semi ritualized gang rapes of women who are said to "pull a train". During a train, club members (and other males friendly with them) wait in line, usually at the clubhouse bar, for their turn at the victim who has been physically restrained (or beaten into submission) in the train room. In more modern times, trains still occur among 1%ers, especially in small purist clubs, but specific designation of a "train room" has disappeared.

Most trains are defined by their perpetrators as either voluntary or punitive in nature. Some women, who may or may not be otherwise associated with the club, will periodically offer themselves to a small group of bikers. These offers are based on the woman's own sexual desires and are timed so as to apply to only two to five men. Club (and subculture) protocol demands, however, that all males welcome at the clubhouse be allowed to participate in this sort of purely sexual activity if they wish. The unexpected arrival of a large number of bikers at the clubhouse after a woman has committed herself to have sex with several bikers already there (either simultaneously or successively) often results in the voluntary "train broad" coming to define the situation as rape when her refusal to accommodate the additional men is ignored and their attentions are forced upon her by whatever means necessary.

Some bikers will periodically instruct their ol' ladies or sweetbutts to perform fellatio on all the men present at a small social gathering. In these instances no implication of punishment is intended even though the term "train" may be applied to the act. Such accommodation of one's brothers is not required by group norms and generally occurs with the woman's collusion, or at least her tacit consent, among a group of two to ten of her ol' man's closest or most esteemed brothers. Biker slang of the 1970s denoted such an act as a "face train;" and subcultural slang for fellatio is known as "running face", at least among southeastern American 1%er bikers.

If the ol' lady of a club member is unfaithful with a non-biker, withholds money, publicly embarrasses, or otherwise severely angers her ol' man, he may elect to have her pull a train. The offended male may stipulate that intercourse be oral, anal, or vaginal. An anal train is considered within the subculture to be the most severe punishment, while an oral train is the slightest. Normal intercourse is intermediate in its punitive effect and is the most common form of train. A less severe and punitive form of this dominance strategy is employed to accustom reluctant sweetbutts to prostitution at times. If this is the case, the woman will be found to have offended someone and told she is being punished for this. This practice is most common in chapters whose members are heavily involved in prostitution rackets.

If a train is punitive in its intent and the woman is known to have a particular phobia about sex, that fear will be exploited to a degree commensurate with her violation of group norms. An extremely angered biker may keep a woman (almost always his ol' lady) confined and available in the train room for a period of days while selling use of her body to even the most casual barroom acquaintances.

Except for the few women who regularly tolerate, and even enjoy, small, oral trains, those who are violated in this manner can be expected to leave the man, and probably the area, as soon as possible. In many cases, however, they simply find another man in another club with whom to ride. Women who have been subjected to vaginal or anal trains of over ten men have reported continuing gynecological problems as a result.

A woman acquainted with members of a club, but not formally patched by any, may be lured into the clubhouse and trained if a member feels she has offended him in some way. While she will probably be held only a few hours, all men present at the clubhouse will be encouraged to repeatedly participate in the train. Any woman familiar enough with bikers to have offended one to such a degree is almost invariably aware of the practice of, and motives for, trains.

Occasionally a woman may be unfortunate enough to find herself threatened with pulling a train through mere bad luck or naïveté. However, the chances of such an individual blundering into a club controlled area (e.g. a clubhouse, bar, or campsite) makes the frequency of such occurrences very small indeed.

Many women make the mistake of assuming that knowing one club member protects them from the advances of other members. However, there are both formal and informal hierarchies within clubs and chapters and men rarely use their influence to assist a woman.

A female who teases one or more bikers in a sexual manner but subsequently refuses to satisfy him/them is inviting a train if the situation is private enough to allow it. If this is not the case the woman's offense will be remembered and she will be forced to pull a train at a later point in time if club or chapter members can manipulate her into a situation that will permit them to do so. This is also true of cases where a woman becomes belligerent towards club members while on territory controlled by the club or chapter. Hunter S. Thompson notes that rape was always the mode of revenge most salient to members of the Hell's Angels.

It must be emphasized that this practice of gang rape provides far less sexual gratification for bikers than do the other outlets available to them. Trains stem more from a felt need to assert masculine dominance, reinforced with physical pain and psychological terror, than from any explosion of hedonistic desire. Indeed, after several bikers have subdued and forcibly taken a woman in this manner those following them may find it difficult to perform sexually because of the victim's physical state. The train is, however, a very effective social control measure within the club and the subculture. This is to say that the sex acts are performed as a means to an end, but *not* as an end in themselves. It is extremely rare for a biker to come to the aid of a woman threatened with pulling a train. Taking a female's side against a fellow male's, and especially a brother, is an almost unheard of violation of subculture mores.

The outlaw biker's desire to reaffirm his identity as a social pariah is evidenced in the ritual required to obtain the common club decorations that are variously referred to as "white", "red", "black" and "brown wings". The practice of awarding these wings originated as part of the Hell's Angels initiation ceremony and remained so within that enigmatic club up until the late 1960s. In most other outlaw clubs the ritual is not a prerequisite to membership, but the wings are obtained by most bikers within a few months or years of joining a one percent club. The procedure for earning these wings varies between clubs on a few details but is basically the same as that described by Hunter S. Thompson.

The biker who wishes to earn white or red wings must provide a menstruating woman to pull a train for his entire chapter or clubhouse (i.e. fifteen to twenty-five bikers). Immediately after the train has been completed, the candidate must perform lengthy cunnilingus on the woman with other chapter members remaining present as witnesses. If the woman is white then the member providing her and performing cunnilingus on her will receive from the club or chapter a cloth set of white or red wings to wear on his colors. There is no difference between white and red wings. Black wings refer to performing the same sexual practice as described above for red or white wings with the difference being that the act is performed with a woman of African American descent. Since most bikers are racially prejudiced, black wings carry somewhat higher status than do white/red ones because this sort of contact with a black woman is considered to be even more revolting. The fact that bikers are well known for their racism (much as their proclivity to rape) makes the acquisition of a cooperative black woman more challenging. In most cases where black wings are desired, a black streetwalker is abducted under false pretenses by the candidate-biker to fill the female role in the ritual. Women associated with black motorcycle clubs are also frequently targeted for aggression by white one percenters. It is important to understand that the custom of awarding wings disappeared in the 1970s but the savagery of 1%er sexual practices was instrumental in creating the hardened pariah image that still prevails in the modern subculture.

Female Sexual Aggression

The notion of diminishing hedonic returns also has applicability to biker women. As prostitutes and as associates of one percenters, these women are quite sophisticated in the areas of sexual behavior and drug use. Thus, like their men, bikers' ladies are constantly seeking new forms of sensual gratification by experimenting with various sexual positions, techniques, settings, drugs, partners, and combinations thereof. Biker women have been known to abuse young males that they lure into the clubhouse or their residence for their own pleasure. In these situations the women can be every bit as brutal as were their male companions to female victims. Such abuse of males will be stopped if male bikers are present and come to perceive the activity as an attack on masculinity in general. Otherwise such occurrences, which usually involve prolonged sexual teasing, anal penetration with an object, painful manipulation of the erect penis, threats of castration, and the like, are perceived as entertainment by those present.

This sort of aggression by females is, however, relatively infrequent in comparison to male abuses of women. Trains occur roughly once every six to eight weeks. In contrast, female bikers' abuse of fifteen to twenty year old males occurs only about once every six to twelve months, if it occurs at all within the chapter.

Some biker women will participate in trains pulled by other women at times. This is only permitted by some chapters and then only at the woman's specific request. Substantial minorities of biker women are openly bisexual and regularly enjoy the same or similar pleasures of the train room as the men. More frequently the woman wishing to participate in a train has a sadistic and/or bisexual tendency as well as a grudge against females with whom they feel they are in competition in some area (e.g. prostitution). Changes in female sex roles over the last 25 years have made female sexual aggression even more rare but many bikers' ladies are still quite violent in comparison to the dominant society.

Male bikers are very tolerant of bisexual females and many biker's ladies sporadically indulge in lesbian relations. However, they rarely, if ever, form lasting lesbian relationships with

other women. In chapters where communal living is predomi-
nant and two or more of the women in a household are bisexual,
the household and its guests may be entertained occasionally by
public lesbian lovemaking. There are, of course, some biker
women who are disdainful of all homosexuality, but they are
forced to keep their sentiments to themselves. Women, in this
writer's experience, were never coerced in any way to perform
lesbian acts for the entertainment of male bikers.

"I AM A BIKIE SLUT"

Arthur Veno

The following piece illustrates regional or international differences in the way one-percenter clubs treat women associates. It includes interviews and case studies of Australian women associates that depart from the pictures painted by other writers in this contentious area.

I participated in a weekend "Poker Run" organised by an OMC which was open to family members and the public (biker) community. Poker Runs are club events which travel to five pubs and then the pack of riders come back to a clubhouse or other biker friendly environment for a party. At each stop, a card from a deck is given to each registered rider. The person with the best poker hand at the end of the run earns a prize.

Approximately 100 bikers (as well as media cars, media helicopters and numerous police escorts – motorbikes, marked and unmarked cars) rode from pub to pub through a picturesque historical rural area. At each pub stop, the men congregated at the pub, drinking, eating snacks, and forming primarily male discussion groups. Interested village people tended to collect at a distance, watch the bikers, admire the impressive show of Harley Davidson's, and take photographs.

Police, after tending to their video surveillance machinery, retreated to eat lunch and take breaks in discreet eateries, and wait for the next stage of the bikers' ride.

At each village, the women who were riding with the bikers tended not to congregate with the men around the pub – women had their own business to attend to and male researchers are not privy to it. For example, the women's rest rooms were a hive of activity, as were the local antique shops. The women tended to wander through the village in small groups searching for trinkets and souvenirs for their children and family who were not on the runs. Some women searched for the police contingent so they could take photographs. These events occurred far from the so-called "centre of activity", i.e., at the pubs where the men were. The depth of information about women's participation in the OMC bikers' world gained from these informal conversations is not available to male researchers – this is women's business.

Previous male researchers have reported that women who associate with biker men are largely from dysfunctional working class families whose upbringing prepares them for domination in their relationships with biker men. They are said to be tough in character, mostly unattractive and show signs of premature aging in appearance. Their roles in the clubs are as objects used for club sexual rituals, and they are required to perform work tasks which bring economic rewards to the man or club. The women are portrayed as powerless pawns, submissive and meek, who are bullied into demeaning roles within the male domain of the clubs.

I found a drastically different picture of women who associate with OMCs, when guided by a feminist colleague about women associates of the clubs. Below, I present some short stories of the women who I interviewed. These include indepth and intimate conversations with family members of OMCs, business women who are an integral part of OMC life (e.g., Sam the stripper, and Veronica the manager of a strip business), and a rare report from a self proclaimed "bikie-slut" – Grandma. These stories are simply examples of powerful women in their own cultural setting.

Veronica

Veronica is the manager of Richo's – a strip club located directly across from Parliament House. For several months, I worked out of Richo's back room as an office during the course of the main research. As such, I came to know staff reasonably well. One striking example of women who associate with OMCs was Veronica. Veronica commenced working as a performer (i.e., as stripper and a pole dancer) at Richo's five years previously. When I met her, she was the Manager. Richo has the reputation of being the kindest and most gentle nightclub owner in the city. He tries to get the women who work for him to resolve their personal issues and strongly supports their obtaining training and education to further their career prospects prior to when they age past the point that they are employable as strippers. Veronica had taken advantage of these opportunities, for when I met her; she was in her third year at university studying Psychology and Business. Veronica was stunning in her intellect and her beauty – she was accomplished, urbane and confident. Part of her job was to manage the OMC members when they attended the premises. She said it was easy work, and her prime management technique was to "flatter the male ego". The only real problems in respect to OMCs were times of interclub wars and intoxication from "whizz" (methamphetamines). The solutions were formulized for Veronica – she used the OMC club structure to intervene, if any intervention was necessary. She had the personal telephone numbers of all office bearers of OMCs and would simply telephone the Clubs' President if one of his members was behaving badly. She most definitely felt that OMC members were quite easy to manage.

Sam the stripper

Strippers, stripper enterprise managers, prostitutes and brothel madams all indicate without exception that working "a bikie function" is much more preferable to working a "suits party". The consensus is that the bikies are much better behaved and much more respectful of the women than the intoxicated "suits". I wanted to find out the details of this relationship, and was directed to talk to "Sam the stripper". I interviewed her where she wished to be interviewed – at the nightclub where she worked. I arrived at the specified time with my tape recorder, and was, of course, dressed appropriately for the occasion. I asked the doorman for her and was told she was working behind the bar serving drinks. The interview was a difficult one as she was naked except for a pair of cowboy boots and a fake gun and holster. In spite of the setting, I was able to ascertain that she did not work at a particular OMC club as her brothers both were members of a rival OMC and they would have been "overzealous" in their defence of her should any problem occur. As I eased into the interview environment, I sought her story about her life, her occupation in providing voyeuristic sex to OMCs, and her relationship with OMCs more generally. She was guarded in her responses and I felt the "iron curtain of women's business" drop between me and Samantha. It became patently obvious that she wasn't going to tell this male researcher what I wanted to know about women and the OMCs. Clearly this is a job for a female researcher – preferably a feminist as Samantha defined herself as a feminist.

Grandma

There are also very few women who are "groupies" or as the previous researchers would call them "mamas". They have strong allegiances to the club and for one reason or another are keen to be identified as "belonging" to the club. One particular woman who stood out in my mind was a grandmother – with a difference. She had a club tattoo which she happily showed myself and the President of an OMC by hiking up her skirt and pulling down her panties to reveal a 15 cm tattoo of a dagger and the OMC colours tattooed on her upper thigh and hip. As this was done in a five star city hotel, the incident was striking due to the context! I had a further opportunity to interview this woman. She had recently moved from interstate and had moved to her new residence specifically to be near the OMC. She had left her husband, children and grandchildren based in a small rural town in Victoria and said her family unanimously agreed that "I am a bikie slut." She went on to say that she couldn't explain it, but; she was simply overwhelmingly attracted to the OMC and had literally "given up her life to be with the club". I suspected party drugs may have been part of her motivation to be near the club. When I put this motive to her, she replied "I can get drugs at any club or many, many other places. That's definitely not the reason. It's more like the club gives me a cause and a meaning in life. I feel like I am a part of something now". I came across only two such women in my many years of studying ΘMCs and the behaviour is highly unusual in the OMC context. Nevertheless, such women do exist and they have a fascinating story to tell.

Family members

By far and away, however, women partners, sisters, mothers, aunties and children, particularly female children are the central meaning of an OMC member's life. In the vast majority of cases, the children and partners of the OMC members are the reason for their existence as men. The job of the men is to protect the women and children.

The women are fiercely proud to be partners of OMC members. They are aware of the sexual proclivities and goings on at the clubhouse and are not distressed by the situation. Most believe that their men are no more likely to cheat on them than other men. The women partners seemed to particularly enjoy the scheduled "runs" that the men went on. This was seen as a time when they could have their own space and do their own thing. The same attitude was held by the women about the long hours spent at the clubhouse by the men. The women enjoyed their freedom.

Many women partners and family members held a wide variety of jobs and professions including public service jobs, childcare duties, lawyers, medical technicians, graphic designers and a variety of other middle class and some factory occupations. Many had achieved significant levels of education and training. In some cases, the men were the child minders and the women were the primary source of income. No biker women (Ol' Ladies) I came across worked as a stripper or prostitute. The women generally earned their own money and most generally, the money was family money, where the earnings of both the man and the woman were pooled and used as the total family budget.

The main complaint by the women was the police harassment that they experienced as family members of OMC members. A second was distress experienced during times of war between the differing clubs of the OMCs. In one notable example, the women and children of one club were taken to several "safe houses". The location of one of the safe houses was leaked to the opposite club and the women had to leave urgently. As the women left, laser dots from gun sights were shone on them by persons unknown. The women were livid. Later, as they drove through town to another safe house, the woman who had leaked the information was discovered. The women pulled the car over and gave "the dog" or in North American terminology "the rat" a severe flogging. The women can be very violent and seem to accept violence as a viable means to "payback", or as a means to punish others for their misdemeanours.

Mothers and sisters and daughters

One particular OMC member wanted me to meet with his mother. His club nickname was Terrible ("Why?" I asked another member of the OMC. "Because he is f. . . .n terrible" was the response). At 35 years of age, Terrible had a long history of convictions for assault and possession of narcotics. I was at a bikie function with him on the night we were to meet his "Mum" as he called her. The function was to end at 9:30 pm but; it had dragged on until nearly 11:00 pm. Terrible came over to me in the middle of seven people and said "Hey, Arthur, it's time to go." "Can't we put it off for another night?" I said as I was feeling tired and had some unfinished business to attend to with the crowd gathered around me. Terrible's eyes narrowed and his heavily tattooed arms flexed as he said directly to me "What, you don't want to meet my Mum?" We departed immediately for Terrible's apartment which was located in a notorious brothel. His Mum had already gained entry and was waiting for us.

It became apparent why Terrible had wanted me to meet his Mum. She was a nurse and her former husband (Terrible's father) was a senior school administrator. After exchanging pleasantries, I asked Terrible to go down to the pub and get me some Tasmanian beer. This was done as it was obvious that Terrible's Mum wanted to speak to me alone about Terrible.

Upon Terrible's departure, she said "Arthur, all I really want
to know is what happened to my little guy. He was so sweet and
loving and then something happened to him when he went to
his first school. He was never the same after that." She had
brought along three large notebooks full of memorabilia and
pictures from Terrible's life.

It seems that Mum had recently asked Terrible to write down
what he saw as having "gone wrong" with him. His sister was a
lawyer; his brother was an ambulance driver and an ex-rugby
star. When Terrible got the request from his Mum, he worked
on it for months and finally produced a letter which his Mum
wanted me to read, and to comment upon. The letter indicated
that an incident had occurred in his third grade class in which
Terrible believed he had killed a child. He claimed that he then
split into two characters – one character was benevolent, the
other whom he called "The Punisher" emerged whenever
situations became threatening for the "dominant persona".
The Punisher was mean and vicious.

Terrible re-entered the room as I finished reading the letter
and I had started to address the issues with Terrible's Mum.
After only moments of conversation, both were crying profu-
sely, Terrible made amazing admissions, including a "need" for
sex up to 13 times a day. Later in the evening "Mum" tearfully
admitted she was very proud of him, but; she just wished he
could rid himself of the pain that caused his violence and his
profuse drug use.

Terrible's sister came by at about 1:30 am to pick up her
Mum. After speaking with his sister at some length, it became
clear that they were as two apples from the same tree. One apple
happened to fall on the outlaw side of the fence (Terrible) and
the other on the law side of the fence (his prominent lawyer
sister). There were several other meetings with Mums and
families which could be discussed here, but; hopefully the point
is taken. The families are not, necessarily or even mostly
dysfunctional. Much could be learned by spending time with
Terrible's remarkable mother and his sister, and listening to
their stories.

PART 4

Bikers and Crime

OK, there is no doubt that both criminals and non-criminals belong to one-percenter outlaw biker clubs. But the real question is: are outlaw motorcycle clubs criminal organizations or simply groups whose members include some criminals? The question is central both to the policing of outlaw clubs and their ultimate survival.

While it is clear that, on the whole, outlaw motorcycle clubs do not exist to provide illegal goods and services, it is also clear that many of their members engage in some form of illegal behaviour at some time or other. But in the final analysis, the decision to engage in criminal activity is up to the individual.

While the Lynch Report first identified one-percenter clubs as criminal organizations, it was not until 1969 that the association between outlaw bikers and organized crime was presented to the public, and a club subsequently prosecuted under new legislation. It happened like this . . .

J. Edgar Hoover (then Director of the Federal Bureau of Investigation of the United States) was under pressure from Robert Kennedy (then Federal Attorney-General) to crack down on the US Mafia and other organized crime entities. Legislation was passed by the United States Congress and Senate that enabled law enforcement agencies to utilize special powers in their attempts to curtail organized crime. This legislation was known as the Racketeer Influenced and Criminal Organization Act, or "RICO". But it was later discovered that

Hoover had strong connections with the Lansky faction of the US Mafia: so, presumably because of his connections, Hoover made an executive decision to make the first RICO prosecution against the Hells Angels Motorcycle Club (New York). The prosecution was unsuccessful, but Hoover's action sealed the fate of outlaw bikers with respect to law enforcement agencies and public opinion.

The upshot is that outlaw bikers run a high risk of arrest. But arrests are widely accepted as a poor indicator of criminal activity. At best, they simply reflect the attitude of police command. In the end, it is convictions that count. But law enforcement agencies do not fare so well in this area, with respect to outlaw bikers. How come? Well, if one accepts the information contained in some of the selections below, the reasons are as follows: witness intimidation, juror and judicial bribery, and murder of key witnesses. According to the lawmen, tactics like these are frequently used to foil legitimate attempts to curtail the criminal activities of individual members of outlaw biker organizations.

To date, nothing seems truly effective in eliminating criminality in outlaw biker organizations, and extinction is the probable outcome for the clubs unless they can control criminal elements within the subculture.

Finally, there appears to be a connection between government election campaigns based on the politics of fear and high-profile arrests of outlaw bikers. Outlaw bikers are a wonderfully soft target for law and order campaigns, as their code of silence assures little opposition to official attempts at demonizing them. Thus it may not be in the interests of governments to achieve a peaceful resolution to the problem of outlaw biker clubs and organized crime.

The readings below include some discussion of the politically motivated nature of the problem of criminality and organized crime in outlaw biker organizations.

A JURY DECIDES

Paul Cherry

> *Paul Cherry is a freelance writer who is not a biker, and his material is based on court proceedings against several members of The Rockers (who may have been affiliated to the Hells Angels Motorcycle Club in Canada). A trial jury found the men guilty of the murder of two prison guards.*

Madeleine Giauque appeared calm for someone waiting to see what a jury would think of the evidence she and a team of prosecutors had worked on for more than three years. After the jury was finally sequestered in February 2004, Justice Pierre Beliveau decided he wanted to meet with lawyers from both sides every morning in the courtroom while the jury members deliberated on the fate of Hells Angel Richard (Dick) Mayrand and the eight other bikers underneath him in the gang's hierarchy. The morning meetings in the large courtroom were informal and friendly. The tension between the defense and the prosecution that had built up over the duration of the trial was subsiding.

The Morning News

Beliveau allowed a number of Montreal newspapers to be made available to the jury as long as all references to the trial and the Hells Angels were removed. Someone from the defense team was always present to verify that any potentially influential articles did not make their way into the jury. One morning there was even a debate over whether an article about the jury hearing the trial of Martha Stewart, the home-decorating mogul on trial for stock fraud in New York, should be cut out.

A courthouse clerk was assigned the duty of removing all the potentially influential articles. Her scissors were very busy on one day in particular when Operation South was carried out. A police operation much smaller in scale and of less significance than Operation Springtime 2001, it still resulted in the roundup of several members of the Hells Angels' South chapter and many more underlings.

Among those arrested on February 26, 2004, was Éric Bouffard, one of the Hells Angels who had been caught delivering money to the Nomads chapter's bank. He had quickly pleaded guilty to the charges brought against him in Project Ocean, and was already out on parole when he was arrested again. The investigation centered on the South chapter, based in Saint-Basile-le-Grand. At the time, the police said the South chapter appeared to have been filling the drug trafficking void created by the roundup of the Nomads chapter. But the investigation was also heavily focused on loan-sharking. When it was carried out, it made the front pages of all the Montreal newspapers and several pages inside. Some lawyers joked that the jury members were going to be intrigued by the amount of vetting done to their papers that morning.

While waiting for the verdict, Giauque managed to keep her sense of humor as well. While talking to reporters after one of the morning meetings in front of Beliveau, Giauque said that she and other members of the prosecution team killed time waiting for a verdict by watching DVDs. "But there is no way I'm going to watch *Runaway Jury*," Giauque said in reference to a film that had just been released on DVD starring Gene Hackman and John Cusack, portraying two sides engaged in a heated and very illegal battle to sway a jury.

Ladies and Gentlemen of the Jury

It seemed to have taken forever to get to the point where a jury could actually deliberate on the charges filed in Project Rush. The question on many minds was whether the average person could accept that doing things like contributing to a fund, or performing guard duty, or acting as a personal bodyguard facilitated a criminal act and therefore was also a crime. It had taken a long time to get to that point. Jury selection had begun on January 13, 2003. The jury sat for 118 days over a period of a little more than one year. Much more court time was spent without the jury present, as lawyers argued various motions.

The evidence was broken down into 10 stages. The first involved informing the jury of what had been seized at the bikers' homes during Operation Springtime 2001. Rather than allow much of that evidence in without challenge, the defense decided that it had to be scrutinized before the jury. That meant police officers who had seized the items had to be called in to testify. The process created delays that Beliveau would later criticize as being very unnecessary.

The second stage involved showing the jury hours of video-tape police surveillance teams had taken of gang members doing things like attending meetings or doing guard duty – "the watch" as the gang called it. Things did not get interesting for the jury until stage three, when they were shown the videotapes police had secretly made of meetings the Rockers held in hotel conference rooms. It was Dany Kane who had tipped off the police as to where the meetings were going to be held. Stage five involved the informant testimony, and stage seven involved much of the evidence gathered on the Nomads Bank.

Giauque was able to begin her final arguments on February 3, 2004. The task before her was to attempt to make sense of all the evidence the jury had heard and seen. In a very thorough multimedia presentation which took four days to complete, Giauque explained the reasons why the jury had watched hours of videotape and listened to countless wiretapped conversations. She went over the highlights of the Masses, bringing out the importance of some of the comments recorded as they

applied to a gangsterism case. For example, in one of the
Masses, the gang had discussed where Éric (Pif) Fournier
was going to go when the Rockers divided the gang into two
chapters, one to remain in the east end of Montreal and the
other to give them a presence in the west end.

What became apparent during this Mass was that Fournier
was a heavily prized bodyguard to Louis (Melou) Roy. Michel
Rose and Roy had discussed the issue, and the possibility of
Fournier losing his patch was mentioned. The gang also discussed how difficult it was to protect Roy and that there simply
weren't enough guys to act as his bodyguards. Fournier was
believed to have committed several murders for the Hells
Angels since his introduction to the Hells Angels in 1996.

The police found it interesting that a couple of years after
joining the Rockers, Fournier disappeared for several weeks,
around the same time as his boss Louis (Melou) Roy. The
longtime Hells Angel disappeared off the face of the earth, and
was last seen alive some time in June 2000. The police believe
Roy was purged from the gang. His name stopped showing up
on the gang's membership lists, whereas others like Paul (Fon
Fon) Fontaine and Richard Vallée, who turned out to have been
in hiding, continued to be noted on lists seized by the police.

Fontaine was found in May 2004, after spending more than
six years in hiding. He had been made a full-patch member of
the Nomads chapter on June 24, 1998, while on the lam. When
the police found him, he had changed his appearance slightly by
growing a beard and had gained weight. He was brought back to
Montreal to learn he still faced charges for murdering a prison
guard as well as the new charges brought against him in Project
Rush. Fontaine's arrest made David (Wolf) Caroll the only
member of the Nomads chapter still being sought after Operation Springtime 2001.

Another sign that Roy had been purged was that when police
did an analysis of the Nomads' accounting ledgers, investigators
noticed Roy's account with the gang was closed and his drug
profits split up among the members of his former chapter in
Trois Rivières. After Roy and Fournier disappeared, the police
originally assumed they had both met the same fate.

But Pif popped up again. He was arrested in Jonquiere,
Quebec, much later in 2000, carrying a .357 Magnum and some

cash. The cops suspected the cash came from drug sales he had made in a Jonquiere bar. It appeared that Fournier had been ordered to lay low in the aftermath of Roy's disappearance.

During the same Mass, Fournier's membership was debated, the jury got a hint of just how successful the Rockers were as drug traffickers. In the videotape, Normand (Pluche) Bélanger openly complained about always having to collect the ten percent fund during Mass, and that it caused him to carry around a suitcase with a lot of money.

Another meeting Giauque highlighted for the jury was one in which Dany Kane had worn a body pack and given the police a goldmine of evidence. The meeting was held on July 4, 2000, in a restaurant where Robitaille announced the new going price for a kilo of cocaine would be $50,000.

Couture, one of the accused in the Beliveau trial, was at the meeting where the police were able to confirm their suspicions of the high level at which the Nomads chapter was operating in terms of drug trafficking. Robitaille provided an update to his underlings about the state of the Nomads empire. The Rockers present at the meeting informed Robitaille that they were collecting $30,000 a month in the ten percent fund, a clear sign they were making at least $300,000 in profits per month in drug sales.

Paul Brisebois was recorded asking Robitaille about Montreal North, a suburb of Montreal where drug trafficking is normally controlled by street gangs like the Bo-Gars. Robitaille responded by saying the Hells Angels did not want to leave any territory vacant.

Pierre Laurin was also interested in Montreal North, saying the gang could do some "cleaning up" of the potential business in neighborhoods near those controlled by the Mafia. But Robitaille then mentioned that he would have to talk to Mom about Montreal North, saying the Rockers would have to respect the "Italians'" territory. They had right to what was theirs, but they should not be allowed to expand, Robitaille said, adding the Mafia controlled Little Italy and some other parts of the city, but that Montreal North was "wide open" for anyone who wanted to take it. Robitaille also lectured the Rockers on controlling the quality of their cocaine, because the Nomads chapter didn't want it to be too cut by the time it was retailed.

Giauque told the jury that this meeting in particular was clear evidence of a Hells Angel giving orders to the Rockers. But it also reflected a constant theme in Rockers meetings – everyone had a say but the Nomads chapter's authority was undeniable. A key part of the gangsterism charge was whether the Rockers used the ten percent fund to buy weapons. If that had been the case, it would be easier to convince a jury that the gang was paying into a system that murdered people. Giauque pointed out one mass in particular where Rocker Pierre Provencher explained to another gang member that the ten percent fund was used to pay for the clubhouse and "for this," while he made the sign of a gun while the videotape recorder rolled.

Giauque also told the jury the informants who testified were not there to incriminate anyone in particular, but to facilitate a general understanding of the evidence. They were there to explain the hierarchy of the gang, Giauque said, adding that the case could have been prosecuted without the informants. They were there to support evidence, for example that "business" was the gang's euphemism and code word for drug trafficking. The informants were able to explain why gang members were often seen talking into each other's ears when they were captured on video.

"Only certain people, of confidence probably, knew who really committed [a serious] crime. It is an important measure of security, because if someone became an informant they couldn't say this person did this and that other person did that," Giauque explained while describing the whispering as symptomatic. "They were doing it all the time."

The prosecutor acknowledged that informants were criminals who'd only turned when they were put into a corner. "The defense will tell you that they are witnesses who are degenerates and you should not believe them. They have good reason, on one point, they are degenerate witnesses. But here you should believe them. And why? Because they are corroborated by the evidence presented before you. It's certain these are not people you would invite to have supper at your house. None of them. But everything they said here was uncontestable."

She explained her reasons for using Stéphane (Godasse) Gagné while acknowledging that the murders of two prison guards were "*crapeleux*," a French term for villainous that has a better emphasis than the English equivalent. She noted that Gagné was only made a striker in the Rockers for the first murder and was going to be a full-patch member of the gang after the second. It gave the jury something to consider when deciding what it took to eventually graduate to the Nomads chapter.

Gagné was a valuable witness, Giauque told the jury, because he was able to explain the terms the gang often used. For example, when a Rocker said he was "occupied," it was enough to explain to the other Rockers that he had an important job to do for the Nomads chapter and shouldn't be asked questions. Giauque also felt it necessary to explain why witnesses like Peter Paradis had been called.

"His situation was a bit different. He was the enemy, a duck, a bird, a quack-quack, call him what you want," Giauque said drawing a few giggles from the jury. The reference was to the logo featured in the Rock Machine's patches. It was apparently supposed to depict an eagle's head, but it appeared cartoonish and ducklike. According to Giauque, "you probably understood, when you saw his patches, why the Hells Angels call them ducks or quack-quacks. It is very clear when we see the patches."

Giauque also told the jury that despite being a high-profile drug dealer in Verdun, Paradis was left so down and out in his final days as a member of the Rock Machine, he had stooped to stealing food from grocery stores. This was around the same time that Pierre Provencher had declared, during a Rockers Mass, that the east was theirs but that places in western Montreal like Verdun were still to be conquered.

Giauque described Paradis as a regular witness and not an informant. He had already fulfilled his first contract by testifying against his former gangmates. He was out of prison when he agreed to sign the second contract, and placed his life on the line to come out of hiding and testify. Giauque also fully acknowledged that Stéphane Sirois might have been looking for revenge over his failed marriage when he decided to become an informant. The prospect of making $100,000 when he was broke also didn't hurt. "The Sirois aspect is important because it involves real evidence that directly implicates members of the organization," she said.

That "real evidence" included a conversation with André Chouinard in which Sirois asked what it would take to get back into the good graces of the Nomads chapter. Chouinard told Sirois to call Jean-Guy Bourgoin. Chouinard also told Sirois to just keep working, make his own path and get as much information on their rivals as he could.

On December 23, 1999, Sirois set up a meeting with Chouinard where he said he wanted to officially ask to be made a member of the Rockers. Chouinard said it was up to the Rockers and that they were 25 members at that point who all thought differently. He said he even felt he had lost control of them. Giauque brought up the now-infamous sushi dinner where Bourgoin said the Hells Angels had a price list rating the value of each rival gang member who was killed. But Bourgoin also explained that Sirois could climb up in the gang without killing someone, that it would just take longer. Giauque reminded the jury of the evidence they'd heard from Gagné, who testified, among other things, about the plan the Hells Angels had to level the Rock Machine hangout in Verdun.

"It demonstrates that the identity of a person had no importance when they were part of the enemy. It is a clear evidence of the intentions of the gang to eliminate the competition through murder," she said.

Down to the Nitty Gritty

The following day, on February 4, 2004, Giauque continued her final arguments, now narrowing the evidence down to each of the accused. She asked the jury to consider several things. First, she asked them to remember a gathering on Provencher's maple syrup farm, where several Rockers from prison made collect calls to talk to the rest of the gang. During one conversation, Ronald Paulin told Beauchamp that there were 30 members of the Rockers at that point. Beauchamp had replied, "We're a nice clique."

"Don't forget that our theory is to the effect that the Hells Angels' Nomads [chapter] controlled the trafficking of diverse drugs while generating huge profits. The proof shown [earlier in the trial] clearly shows how it was done," Giauque said. "It is evident from the evidence that these are not autonomous drug dealers but an association of people who dealt in drugs in a way that was highly organized." Giauque added that videos proved things like how Beauchamp had done guard duty on Michel Rose, who was importing a lot of cocaine for the Nomads.

She also reminded the jury that at one of Luc Bordeleau's residences the police found several weapons and an agenda that indicated he was doing a lot of intelligence gathering for the Hells Angels, and was going to set up gang members with courses on wiretapping and courthouse research. He also had notes concerning the Café Cosenza, known to be a favourite hangout of Vito Rizzuto's at the time. In his bathroom, underneath the mirror, Bordeleau had kept a stash of money.

When going over André Couture's involvement, Giauque pointed to video evidence that indicated he was heavily involved with Normand Robitaille's drug business. Couture helped do himself in by talking very openly during some of the Masses videotaped by the police.

"Remember that the simple fact of being at a Mass is important, very important. The full-fledged members have to attend or they would be sanctioned or have to face the Nomads. It is a significant presence for the gang and the pursuit of their activities," Giauque said.

On April 27, 2000, during a gang meeting at a motel, it was Couture who announced that Dubois had quit the gang. Couture was reminded that he owed $3,400 to the ten percent fund. He was videotaped saying he had no problem with paying the money. The money was due from a period when he was in prison, a clear indication that his business was operating even while he was behind bars.

Couture had had his share of run-ins with the law while he was with the Rockers. On November 29, 1997, he was arrested after two officers patrolling the Hochelaga Maisonneuve district noticed Couture driving erratically on Bennett Street, in front of the Nomads chapter's hangout. He had backed up into a pole left over from a former railway crossing. When the officers pulled Couture over, they asked him for his licence and registration. When he opened the glove compartment they couldn't help but notice the chrome-plated revolver inside it.

Couture refused to get out of the car. As the officers prepared to arrest him, they could hear someone inside the Nomads chapter's hangout shout, "If you shoot him, we will shoot you." One of the arresting officers would later say in court that he wanted to get out of there fast because he knew who occupied 2101 Bennett Street.

While Couture was being processed, the police opened a sports bag he had with him. It contained a bunch of papers and a note pad. For some reason, Couture consented to having the pages photocopied by the police. He was able to plead guilty and received a $350 fine with a sentence of just two years probation.

But the papers he allowed to be photocopied would later come back to haunt him. Some of the most damaging evidence against Couture in the megatrial was contained in those papers. His lawyer fought to have the documents excluded, because they were evidence from a previous conviction, but lost. It helped prove that Couture worked for Normand Robitaille, collecting money that dealers owed and keeping an accounts receivable. Among the papers was a to-do list citing things like "debug the vehicle" among Couture's chores.

Stéphane (Godasse) Gagné would later recount how Robitaille was furious with Couture when he learned the police had photocopied the documents. Couture was only supposed to have been in possession of the papers for a short while. Gagné would later explain just how important the documents were to Robitaille and the Nomads chapter, as they contained information on how Robitaille had his cocaine cut and listed some of his major clients, including one of Gagné's brothers. But the documents also contained evidence that Robitaille was in the process of gathering personal information on every member of the Nomads chapter's organization to help prevent people from turning informant. Gagné had testified that Maurice (Mom) Boucher once ordered everyone working with him or under him to hand over all personal information, such as their social insurance numbers. Included among the documents photocopied with Couture's permission were personal details, like the social insurrance numbers of Donald (Pup) Stockford and Walter (Nurget) Stadnick, the two Ontario members of the Nomads chapter.

As she continued to make her final arguments, Giauque broke down the evidence the prosecution team had on each of the accused. She mentioned how when the police searched Bruno

Lefebvre's house in Sainte-Marthe-sur-le-Lac, west of Montreal, they found paperwork in the kitchen indicating he was ready to sell it for $435,000. He also had a mortgage for $150,000. The police also found a document that claimed he worked for a company, earning $317 net per week. Yet Lefebvre could afford to pay $50,000 cash as a down payment on a house and was sometimes videotaped by the police driving around in a brand new Cadillac. Stéphane Sirois had said Lefebvre was introduced into the Rockers while dealing drugs for Pierre Provencher in Verdun between 1996 and 1998. In 1997, Lefebvre took one for the team when he was shot while he and a few other Rockers were breaking up a Rock Machine drug den. But the shot didn't come from a Rock Machine gun.

Informant Aimé Simard testified in a trial a few years earlier that it took Lefebvre a few minutes to realize he had been shot by accident by a fellow Rocker while they were shaking down the rival drug dealers, torturing them for information on who ran the drug den. The gang was left to search for a doctor who would remove the bullet, which had lodged in Lefebvre's upper body, without calling the police.

While going over the evidence against Richard (Dick) Mayrand, Giauque focused on his apparent role in the brief truce between the Rock Machine and the Hells Angels. Mayrand had been present at the dinner at the Bleu Marin restaurant where the two gangs had agreed to a ceasefire. "What you have to understand of this is that the people who were present [at the dinner] and represented the two rival gangs had the authority to stop a war that had lasted for years. These were the heads of each organization," Giauque said.

Giauque also used wiretaps to show that Mayrand had apparently been brought into the Nomads chapter as a leader, in particular over diplomatic issues. On November 28, 2000, at around 9 p.m., the police listened in as Mayrand called George Wegers, the U.S. leader of the Bandidos. Wegers lived in the west coast state of Washington. The conversation was brief but polite, considering it was between the leaders of two rival gangs.

"How are you?" Wegers had asked. Mayrand laughed and said that things "could be better" and repeated that he was willing to take a plane to meet with Wegers somewhere "to fix something."

"So Mr. Mayrand was the person designated by the Hells Angels' organization to meet a [member of the] Bandidos at the other end of the country to settle business," Giauque said, adding it was obvious the conversation was related to the biker war. "Does this not give you an idea of Mr. Mayrand's importance in the gang?"

What Giauque was not able to tell the jury was that the police had tracked Mayrand to the eventual meeting with Wegers. Sûreté du Québec Sgt. Guy Ouellette was informed that the meeting was going to take place in British Columbia. Based on past experience, he figured Mayrand and Wegers would meet at the Peace Arch Park, which sits on the spot where Washington Interstate 5 meets with Highway 99 at the Canada/U.S. border. The park is a sort of no man's land where both Mayrand and Wegers could meet without technically having to cross an international border. Both men had criminal records, and could have been arrested crossing into either country. Wegers had already been arrested years earlier for meeting with the Rock Machine in Quebec City.

The meeting was believed to be related to something that had happened at a motorcycle show in Europe a week earlier. Several members of the Rock Machine had attended the show and were shown what their patches as new members of the Bandidos were going to look like. This was while the Hells Angels and the Rock Machine were supposed to be in a truce. Mayrand was recorded calling his former Hells Angel brother in the Montreal chapter, David (Gyrator) Giles, who had moved to B.C. to join a Hells Angels' chapter there, asking him for bodyguards for the meeting. Giles said he would take care of it.

On November 30, 2000, Mayrand met with Wegers in Peace Arch Park while the police watched from a distance. Mayrand had two bodyguards with him, Rick Ciarnello and John Bryce. Wegers also had bodyguards. The two gang leaders talked for a while, with Mayrand appearing to do most of the talking. Wegers listened with no expression on his face. The meeting ended without incident. Judging by what happened almost immediately afterward, it appears that Mayrand let Wegers know that the Hells Angels were going to respond to the fact the Rock Machine was to be patched over by the Bandidos in Quebec and Ontario.

Within days of the meeting with Wegers, it was apparent Mayrand was helping to lead the push to create new Hells Angels' chapters in Ontario. On December 7, 2000, Mayrand and Mathieu were recorded in a phone conversation discussing an order of some 100 new Hells Angels' patches. By December 12, that number had increased to 160, apparently thanks to Donald (Pup) Stockford. Mayrand was recorded talking to Jacques Emond, a longtime member of the Sherbrooke chapter, informing him of the good news. Emond had once lived in British Columbia and apparently still had ties there.

"So it's going to happen in eight days?" Emond said of the eventual patch-over party to be held in Sorel.

"That's it."

"Okay."

"Is that all right?"

"So, I'll alert the west."

"You're going to alert the west and your chapter," Mayrand told Emond before saying goodbye. Giauque pointed to the calls as proof of Mayrand's importance in the Hells Angels.

"The defense might tell you that Mr. Mayrand only joined the Nomads on January 12, 2000, that his actions before that date prove nothing and that they were meetings between friends and that is all. I believe it is impossible to believe this. Could you really believe that Richard Mayrand had been a member of the Hells Angels' Montreal [chapter] for more than 15 years without having anything more than an amicable relationship with them? It is impossible," she said.

When Giauque talked about Sylvain Moreau, she mentioned how his passport showed he had traveled to Barbados on November 4, 2000, and to Cancun in February 2001. Giauque said it was not bad for a guy who claimed to make $511 net for two weeks and $10,915 net annual income for 1999.

Closing Arguments

"All of the manifest acts committed with the goal of eliminating the competition by the co-accused named in the indictment are opposable to each of the accused," Giauque said as she began to wrap up her arguments. Even the objects seized at their homes, which might have seemed somewhat banal at first, could be considered as important.

"We submit that the different objects found are manifestly proof of an agreement between the co-conspirators and can serve as evidence on all three charges. All of these objects can be considered as manifest acts against the accused because they were used in the pursuit of the common goal. Think of the patches on different clothes, the laminated cards [with each member's phone numbers listed on them], the plaques, the trophies, the greeting cards, the photos of friends and of enemies but also the map, the weapons, the money found and the money found in the Nomads Bank. All of those objects had one utility: to assure the cohesion of the gang, its visibility and its supremacy."

The prosecutor also explained the importance of the boring videos the jury had watched of gang members standing in front of restaurants and hotels obviously doing guard duty.

"They showed the importance of the gang and the hierarchy. Think of the watch. Think of the way the Nomads accepted that the Rockers were doing their watch. It was their due," she said. "If there is one [type of] evidence that should be considered as the pursuit of a common goal it is the Masses. In looking at them, you realize immediately that they were only held to assure the proper function of the gang and its diverse activities. There is no other reason for its existence. Presence was obligatory and they were held in secret. Any absence had to be justified. It is impossible to think that we can take part in a Mass by chance. We pass by and see a closed door, we open it and sit right down. It's impossible to think that happened."

The wiretaps the jury listened to also opened a door to life in the Nomads chapter and the Rockers. The calls gang members made from prisons in particular were revealing.

"Even in prison they were combating their enemies. Even if they were detained, the situation did not change. You know that in the case of André Couture and Sylvain Moreau, they continued to pay their ten percent while they were detained," Giauque said. "Prison changed nothing when it came to business. Just because they were detained, that didn't mean they couldn't continue to take part in their gang activities and were still part of the gang. To the contrary, everyone took care of them."

The prosecutor then explained the gangsterism charge the jury was going to have to decide on. "I would submit to you that the evidence demonstrated that all of the members of the gang regularly committed criminal acts punishable by a sentence of five years or more, and that [they did so] with the knowledge of all of them. So, all of them knew that the other members were trafficking in prohibited substances," she said.

"I will repeat again that being part of the Hells Angels is not a crime in itself. But we have surely proven to you that the organization is a gang in the sense of the Criminal Code, and that it is a criminal organization. A criminal organization does not exist on its own. It is the members who compose it that commit the crimes."

When the defense lawyers took their turn, the main theme that ran through their final arguments was that the Crown had presented very little direct incriminating evidence against their clients. Perhaps the most impressive final arguments from the defense side came from Lucie Joncas, the lawyer who represented Sebastien Beauchamp, who said it would take a "contortionist from the Cirque du Soleil" to perform the "intellectual gymnastics" required to convict her client. In an attempt to destroy the credibility of one of the most damaging witnesses against Beauchamp, Joncas portrayed informant Serge Boutin as a man still fuming over an insult made towards his wife.

"If there was one [informant] who wanted to bury my client, it was [Boutin]," Joncas said. She referred the jury to a wiretapped conversation from October 7, 2000, before Boutin had become an informant and was still facing a possible first-degree murder trial in Claude De Serres' death. Boutin was upset because a not yet full-patch member of the Rockers had insulted his wife at a Rockers' party. At the time, Beauchamp was just days away from becoming a full-patch Rocker. Boutin said two or three friends informed him of what was said while he was behind bars. Provencher tried to keep things cool, apparently aware of how potentially explosive the situation was.

"He didn't know she was my wife?" Boutin asked during the conversation.

"You know him, him there," Provencher replied.

"But even if he didn't know it was my wife. You know, even if he didn't know it was my wife."

"That's it."

"You can't . . . you have to pay attention to what you say."

"Yes. Yes."

"To anybody's wife."

"There are times, you know, when you get unglued."

"Yeah, yeah."

"There are times when you don't know what you're saying."

"Hmmm. Hmmm."

"You know, there are times when you are drunk, when you don't even remember what you did."

"Ah yes."

"So, you know, the next morning he apologized and everything."

Joncas argued that the apology wasn't enough, and that when Boutin testified Beauchamp sold drugs for the Hells Angels on Saint Denis Street, he was doing it to get back for the slight to his wife. The proof of that, Joncas said, was in another wire-tapped conversation, taped a week later in which Boutin talked to another Rocker and called Beauchamp a nut. He also said he would look into what had happened if he ever got out of prison.

Lawyer Jean-Pierre Sharpe pointed to the most damaging direct evidence against his client Bruno Lefebvre and tried to downplay it. Before his arrest, Lefebvre owned a house in Sainte-Marthe-sur-le-Lac that he was preparing to sell for $435,000. He had made a $50,000 cash down payment when buying the house for $200,000, despite claiming to earn only $370 a week. Sharpe suggested this should not be taken as a sign Lefebvre was a drug dealer. "Some people make a living that way," Sharpe said, alluding to the real-estate deal. "Donald Trump does it. Should we charge Donald Trump with conspiracy for that?"

Guy Quirion, the lawyer who represented Éric (Pif) Fournier, tried to convince the jury that the accused were victims of police planting evidence. He pointed to inconsistencies in how evidence seized at one Hells Angels' home was recorded and accused the police of planting one of the incriminating photo albums containing pictures of most of the members of the Alliance.

Ronald (Popo) Paulin's lawyer, Lise Rochefort, tried to get on the jury's good side by suggesting that everyone involved in the lengthy trial should be given a T-shirt with the phrase "I survived Gouin" written on it, a reference to their time spent in the specially built courthouse in northern Montreal. Rochefort likened her client to a kid who badly wanted to be part of a hockey team but couldn't skate.

"That kid is willing to do menial tasks like fill water bottles and carry pucks but is not part of the team," she said. She pointed out that the jury had heard a wiretapped conversation where one Rocker had said Paulin did nothing but arrange for T-shirts and plaques to be made for the gang.

After Judge Beliveau made his instructions to the jury, they were sequestered and left to assess all that they had heard and seen over the past year. It would take them 12 days to come up with verdicts.

The Verdicts

March 1, 2004, was a spectacular day weather-wise in Montreal. Instead of charging in like a lion, a bright sun ushered in March with a reminder that spring was on its way. In a park less than a kilometre away from the courthouse sat a payloader and other equipment being used to break up ice on the Riviére des Prairies which was overflowing as the weather got warmer that winter. As the trial neared its end, people making their way to the courthouse on Gouin Blvd. could see work crews pounding away at huge blocks of ice, hoping to prevent serious flooding in Laval across the river. The announcement that the jury had a verdict came early in the afternoon.

Because of the number of lawyers involved, there was a long delay between the time the jury informed Beliveau that they had verdicts and when they came out to deliver them. As he waited, Éric (Pif) Fournier paced in the enclosed prisoners' dock, looking somewhat like a caged predator. His fellow Rocker André Couture paced as well. Richard (Dick) Mayrand appeared to be keeping his cool. He joked with his lawyer through a phone that connected the prisoners' dock with the courtroom. Mayrand shrugged often during the conversation, as if resigned to whatever fate was about to befall him. After he hung up with his lawyer, Mayrand and Beauchamp shared a joke and laughed.

But as the wait grew longer a sense of tension filled the air.

Beliveau felt it necessary to address the situation. He told everyone assembled in the courtroom that if they couldn't take the pressure they should leave. He did not want any outburst reactions to the verdicts.

As the jury entered the courtroom, their eyes were fixed on anything but the accused. Beliveau thanked them for their work and the sacrifice they had made. He also publicly thanked their relatives for putting up with the incredibly long trial. Then juror number eight, a young man, was asked to read out the verdicts.

Following alphabetical order, Beauchamp's verdicts were read first. Some people gasped as they heard the "not guilty" verdict on the first count against him. But Beauchamp had been behind bars for most of the time Project Rush was carried out, so those who had followed the trial closely were not surprised to hear he had been cleared of conspiring to murder members of the Alliance. But he was found guilty of drug trafficking and participating in the activities of a gang. Despite being convicted on the lesser counts, Beauchamp' reaction was not difficult to read. He had a smile that stretched from ear to ear, and he shot a wink towards his lawyer Lucie Joncas that was plainly visible from the back of the courtroom.

All of the remaining eight gangsters were found guilty on all three counts. Luc (Bordel) Bordeleau appeared genuinely stunned as the foreman repeated *"coupable"* three times in his case. Mayrand raised his eyebrows and shook his head in apparent disgust. He then turned towards the section of the courtroom reserved for the audience and stared toward a friend, his face revealing little emotion. Alain Dubois appeared to be furious with the verdicts. His arms were folded tightly across his chest and his face turned crimson red. But he'd obviously expected to be convicted of something. He was the only accused out on bail in the case and had packed a gym bag full of clothes that day. After he was led into the prisoners' dock to sit with his former gangmates, he fumed. One of the Rockers tried to make a joke out of it, but Dubois wanted nothing to do with it. He appeared to tell the others to shut up, or something to that effect. Paulin sat quietly, sometimes shaking his head in apparent disbelief. Before being arrested in Project Rush, the most serious thing Paulin had ever been convicted of was unemployment fraud and neglecting his dog by not feeding it. Now a jury had concluded he was a gangster.

Sentencing Those Who Went the Distance

All that was left to decide was how the convicted would be punished for their crimes. A few weeks after the verdict, the two sides debated what sentences were merited. Because they hadn't plead guilty, like most of the others arrested in Project Rush, it was argued by Giauque that their sentences should be exemplary. Luc (Bordel) Bordeleau slapped his knee and laughed out loud when he heard Giauque say she was seeking a 29-year sentence for Richard (Dick) Mayrand. Bordeleau also laughed when she mentioned, during sentencing arguments of March 22, 2004, that she was seeking 24 years for him. Alain Dubois would be at the low end of the sentencing recommendations. But even though he had only been with the Rockers for a matter of months, Giauque was still asking for a 14-year term.

The sentence recommendations did not seem out of order considering that just two weeks earlier, two members of the Nomads chapter, André Chouinard (who left the Hells Angels just before Operation Springtime 2001 was carried out) and Michel Rose, had pleaded guilty to similar charges and received 20-year sentences. Unlike Mayrand, they had spared the province the cost of a lengthy trial. Other members, like Mathieu and Robitaille, had agreed to plead guilty in exchange for 20-year sentences.

Before the defense lawyers made their sentencing arguments, François Bordeleau made an odd request by seeking a publication ban on the identities of some of the people who might testify as to the good character of his client, Bruno Lefebvre. He said he had witnesses lined up who would testify only if their names wouldn't be mentioned. For example, Bordeleau said, he had the owner of a golf course ready to come in and vouch for Lefebvre, but who did not want his business associated with the Hells Angels. Beliveau said he could understand why someone wouldn't want to be associated with the Hells Angels, but rejected the request.

In Paulin's case, one witness was willing to testify on his behalf. It was the owner of the Montreal embroidery shop where Paulin had ordered all of the Rockers T-shirts over the years. Paulin was so good for business, the owner had hired him as a part-time salesman in 2000, after Paulin decided to retire from the Rockers.

Witnesses portrayed Dubois as a loyal and loving hockey dad who gave a lot of his free time to the Chateauguay Hockey Association. He sometimes coached games and treated the kids to dinners. After his arrest, Dubois limited his work to being a volunteer for hockey tournaments, doing things like selecting the stars of games and serving as a goal judge.

"I don't know one kid who doesn't like him," said one witness. Another witness said she'd known the Dubois family for years. "They have family values," she said as Dubois' father Jean-Guy, a convicted killer, looked on from the audience section of the courtroom.

By April 8, 2004, Beliveau was ready to deliver his sentences. His 69-page judgement was the first real glimpse into what the Superior Court judge truly thought of the Crown's case. He agreed with the Crown arguments that, at least in the cases of Bordeleau, Couture, Fournier, Lefebvre, Mayrand and Moreau, exemplary sentences were appropriate. He noted that it hadn't been proven that Bordeleau and Fournier sold drugs for the network. But it had been proven that all members of the Rockers paid into the ten percent fund, so the pair had to have been doing something to earn their salaries. It had also been proven that Fournier had done "the watch" on several occasions, and that Bordeleau was an organizer of the guard duty. In doing so they played necessary roles in maintaining the gang's turf.

In Dubois' case, Beliveau took into consideration that he had apparently been a drug dealer for a long time. But he also felt that Dubois' departure from the Rockers after only a few months reflected that he didn't believe "in the values of the organization." It was a value system where Rockers knew that if they became Hells Angels they were joining a lifestyle. In his judgement, Beliveau quoted Sylvain Laplante acknowledging, during one of the Masses the police recorded, that life as a Hells Angel was "24 hours out of 24 hours."

Beliveau rated Paulin's involvement as "medium," because while it was obvious he adhered to the gang's values, there was little proof he participated in their more serious activities. Beliveau didn't see any hope of rehabilitation except in the cases of Dubois and Paulin. He accepted the argument from Paulin's defense lawyer that he was like the kid who didn't have enough talent to make the local hockey team so he was willing to do any minor tasks to fit in and be accepted. But he noted that such an attitude in the context of the Hells Angels presented a real danger for society. He couldn't look the other way on the fact that Paulin had held down regular jobs in his life and chose, well into his adult years, to become a member of the Rockers and remain there for six years, knowing full well what the gang did.

Beliveau also let his opinion be known about how some of the defense lawyers behaved during the trial. When it came to factoring in the time eight of the nine accused had already spent behind bars awaiting the outcome of their case, Belivcau could not look past the irritating delays caused by some of the defense lawyers, calling their refusal to admit certain evidence nothing but a stall tactic. He estimated that without the useless delays, the trial would have lasted about six months, half as long as it actually did. He also pointed out that during the English-language trial of Donald Stockford and Walter Stadnick, which had just begun at that point, the lawyers involved had agreed to submit 213 admissions which took prosecutor Randall Richmond just four days, and several sips of water, to read before Justice Jerry Zigman.

In Sebastien Beauchamp's case, Beliveau sentenced the Rocker to eight years for his conviction on the drug trafficking charge, and another five to be served consecutively for participating in the activities of a gang.

In Luc Bordeleau's case, Beliveau noted his lengthy criminal record and association with the Hells Angels, right up to the point where he became a prospect in the Nomads chapter. The judge sentenced him to 10 years for conspiracy to murder, 10 years to be served concurrently for drug trafficking and another 10 to be served consecutively for participating in the activities of a gang.

Alain Dubois received only a two-year sentence for conspiring to murder rival gang members but also an eight-year sentence to be served concurrently for drug trafficking. He was also sentenced to two years to be served consecutively for participating in gang activities. Beliveau did not require that Dubois serve at least half of his sentence.

In Richard Mayrand's case, Beliveau took note of the fact he had been a member of the Hells Angels for years. He was sentenced to 10 years for conspiracy to murder, another 10 to be served concurrently for drug trafficking and 12 years to be served consecutively for participating in gang activities. With time served factored in, he would be required to serve 16 years and 9 months, and do at least half of it behind bars.

Beliveau felt that if anyone in the bunch had a chance at rehabilitation it was Paulin. He was sentenced to seven years for conspiracy to commit murder, seven to be served concurrently for drug trafficking and five years to be served consecutively for participating in the activities of a gang. With time served factored in, he had to serve six years and nine months, with the obligation of having to serve two and a half years before being eligible for parole.

While Beliveau's tough stance towards the defense was applauded by some, the Quebec Court of Appeal did not agree with him. In June 2005, more than a year after the sentences were rendered, the appeal court reduced Beauchamp's and Dubois' sentences by nine months each.

In the summary of the judgement Justice Francois Doyon wrote that Beliveau "went too far" in lumping together the eight lawyers as a whole. Beauchamp's lawyer Lucie Joncas in particular had not taken part in the aggressive tactics the others employed. Joncas has fought a clean fight and therefore her client did not deserve to be punished.

The appeal court also determined there was no proof that the bikers knew their lawyers were going to act in an unacceptable manner.

Cast of Characters

Sebastien (Bass) Beauchamp – Joined the Rockers as a striker on March 26, 1999, and became a full-patch member on October 16, 2000. He was convicted of drug trafficking and gangsterism but dodged a bullet when a jury also acquitted him of conspiring to murder rival gang members. He was sentenced to serve seven years and nine months beginning from the day he was sentenced, April 8, 2004. The Quebec Court of Appeal later reduced the sentence to seven years.

Normand (Pluch) Bélanger – A close friend of Maurice (Mom) Boucher. He was considered an important player in the Hells Angels' expansion into the ecstasy market. He joined the Rockers on March 26, 1998. He became a prospect in the Nomads chapter on October 5, 2000. He was excused from one of the Hells Angels' megatrials because he suffered from cirrhosis caused by hepatitis B, diabetes, hypertension and the after-effects of two heart attacks and was too ill to assist his lawyer. When he was arrested a second time in a loansharking case brought against him and other Hells Angels in February 2004, he had to appear in court in a wheelchair. He died in May 2004.

Luc (Bordel) Bordeleau – A founding member of the Rockers when the gang was created by Boucher on March 26, 1992. Served a five-year term for the Hells Angels after he was caught scuba diving while looking for a large quantity of cocaine gang members had to toss overboard during the early 1990s. He had close ties to Boucher and lived near his compound. He was made a prospect in the Nomads chapter on its fifth anniversary. When the police searched his house in 2001 they found a grenade launcher among a collection of other weapons. He was convicted in the only Project Rush-related trial to go before a jury. With the time he served awaiting the outcome of his case counting as double, he was sentenced to serve more than 14 years starting from April 8, 2004, his sentencing date. He has to serve at least half that behind bars before he can apply for parole.

Françis (Le Fils) Boucher – The son of Hells Angels' leader Maurice (Mom) Boucher. He was made a member of the Rockers on March 26, 1999. On November 18, 2002, he pleaded guilty to his role in the biker war and was sentenced to serve a 10-year sentence from that date. He is required to serve at least half his sentence before he can apply for parole.

Maurice (Mom) Boucher – Became a Hells Angel on May 1, 1987. Created a gang of thugs and drug dealers called the Rockers in 1992. Split off from the Montreal chapter and formed his own elite Nomads chapter which was charactered on June 24, 1995. Many informants describe him as the leader behind the Nomads during the biker war and the person who started the conflict. Sentenced to life in prison on two first-degree murder convictions and an attempted murder conviction after he ordered the Rockers to kill prison guards in an effort to destabilize the justice system. He has appealed the verdicts.

Jean-Guy Bourgoin – A founding member of the Rockers. He remained with the underling gang throughout the biker war and was still a member when he was arrested in 2001. On September 23, 2003, he and a group of fellow Rockers and Hells Angels ended their megatrial by agreeing to a plea bargain that saw first-degree murder charges dropped. Bourgoin was sentenced to 15 years. With time served factored in, he had only 10 years left on the sentence from the day he pleaded guilty.

Serge (Pacha) Boutin – Started out the biker war as a drug dealer for a group called the Alliance which opposed the Hells Angels. Joined the Rockers on October 12, 1999, and decided to turn informant after being charged with helping to kill an informant and several other criminal accusations. He was sentenced to life for the murder of the informant but he managed to plead guilty to manslaughter which meant he would have quicker access to parole.

Paul Brisebois – Was named a member of the Rockers around the same time he and Laurin killed a Verdun drug dealer. He became a prospect in the Nomads chapter on December 11, 2000. His case was severed from one of the megatrials and he later managed to plead guilty to second-degree murder even though his DNA was found at the scene of the murder of drug dealer Patrick Turcotte. As part of his plea bargain he is serving a life sentence but is eligible for parole in 2011.

Salvatore Brunetti – Served time in prison near the beginning of the biker war as a member of the Dark Circle, one of the rival gangs that took on the Hells Angels. When the war ended he was serving a short sentence as a member of the Hells Angels. He defected to the Nomads chapter on December 19, 2000. On November 18, 2002, he agreed to plead guilty to drug trafficking and was sentenced to three years. By late 2004 he was released on parole after reaching the two-thirds mark of his sentence.

David (Wolf) Carroll – Was a founding member of the Hells Angels' Halifax chapter on December 5, 1984. Transferred to the Montreal chapter in 1990 and then joined the Nomads chapter in 1995. Disappeared when a warrant was issued for his arrest in March 2001 and has never been seen since.

René Charlebois – Joined the Rockers in April 1997. Evidence tied him to at least two murders committed during the biker war as well as the slaying of a police informant. Charlebois was apparently rewarded well for his work as a Rocker and was made a full-patch member of the Nomads chapter on April 14, 2000. Originally sentenced to 20 years when he pleaded guilty in his megatrial case on September 23, 2003. He also later agreed to a plea bargain in a case where he was charged with killing an informant. He was sentenced to life after pleading guilty to second-degree murder.

André Chouinard – Joined the Rockers on July 15, 1994. Quickly became a close confidant to Boucher because his clean-cut image and lack of a police record did not draw police attention to the Hells Angels' leader. Four years later he became a full-patch member of the Nomads chapter. He left the gang "in good standing" on July 20, 2000. Despite leaving the Hells Angels he was charged in Project Rush and was in hiding for several months until the police tracked him down. He had been hiding in a house in the Eastern Townships. On March 8, 2004, he pleaded guilty to conspiring to murder rival gang members, drug trafficking and gangsterism. He agreed to a twenty-two-year sentence, one of the harshest given in connection with Project Rush. It is believed he agreed to the sentence because he was also facing the possibility of being extradited to the U.S. to face a trial for drug smuggling which might have produced an even tougher sentence.

Raynald Desjardins – A key member of Montreal's Mafia who spent all of the biker war behind bars. He was doing time for his role in a major drug bust that netted members of the Mafia and the Hells Angels in the early 1990s. During the investigation, Desjardins was seen meeting with Maurice (Mom) Boucher. He was released in 2004 after serving 10 years of a 15-year sentence he received. While behind bars he hung out with members of the Hells Angels.

Alain Dubois – the son of a notorious gangster who himself was part of an organized crime gang. He was made a member of the Rockers on August 24, 1999, but left the gang on April 26, 2000, but was still charged in connection with Project Rush. He was convicted by a jury and was sentenced, on April 8, 2004, to nine years and nine months. The Quebec Court of Appeal later reduced the sentence to nine years.

Paul (Fon Fon) Fontaine – A member of the Rockers early on in the biker war. He was made a prospect in the Nomads chapter on July 1, 1997, and later promoted to full-patch member in 1998, while he was on the lam attempting to avoid being tried for the murder of a provincial prison guard. He would be found by the police in 2004.

Éric (Pif) Fournier – Joined the Rockers on October 24, 1999. He was the bodyguard of Louis (Melou) Roy until Roy disappeared. Fournier got away with murder early on in the biker war after evidence was mistakenly destroyed before his criminal trial could begin. He was convicted of conspiring to murder rival gang members, drug trafficking and gangsterism. On April 8, 2004, he was sentenced to nine years on top of the time he spent behind bars awaiting the outcome of his case. In June 2004 he also pleaded guilty to murdering one of the innocent victims of the biker war and received a life sentence with no chance at parole until he has served 15 years behind bars.

Stéphane (Godasse) Gagné – The trigger man in the murders of two prison guards. Gagné turned informant after he was arrested in 1997. He would become the key witness in the trial that ultimately sent Maurice (Mom) Boucher behind bars.

Normand (Biff) Hamel – A close friend of Boucher who became a Hells Angel on October 5, 1986, only months before Mom did. He was chosen to be a founding member of the Nomads chapter. Was murdered in Laval in April 2000.

Patrick Henault – An aggressive member of the Alliance who turned informant after he was arrested in a botched hit on a friend of Maurice (Mom) Boucher. He would help give details, in the Hells Angels' megatrials, about how the gang war looked from the other side.

Stéphane (Archie) Hilareguy – Was made a member of the Rockers on March 26, 1999. He disappeared about a year later when his name was tied to two murders he helped carry out for the Hells Angels. His remains were later found in the Eastern Townships.

Denis Houle – Became a Hells Angel on October 5, 1982. Was chosen to be among the elite of the Nomads chapter in 1995 even though he had spent several of the previous years behind bars. Survived at least two attempts on his life during the biker war. Pleaded guilty to conspiracy to commit murder and other charges on September 23, 2003, and was sentenced to 15 years on top of the equivalent of 5 he spent behind bars awaiting the outcome of his case.

Dany Kane – Part of the Hells Angels' massive underling network for years, he secretly worked with the police for most of the biker war. Near the beginning of the war he worked as a tipster for the RCMP, handing the Mounties information about the Hells Angels for cash. The RCMP dropped him after he was charged with murder in Nova Scotia. He got off in the case and was hired by Quebec's anti-biker gang squad to infiltrate the Hells Angels again. His work was crucial to gathering evidence but he committed suicide before ever having to testify in court.

Daniel (Boteau) Lanthier – A member of the Rockers since April 1994, before the biker war started. He remained an important figure in the underling gang and was part of a committee that ran it. He was part of the group that pleaded guilty on September 23, 2003, and was sentenced to serve 10 years from the day his plea bargain was accepted.

Sylvain Laplante – Joined the Rockers in 1995 after apparently following Gilles (Trooper) Mathieu into the Nomads chapter's vast organization. Before that, Laplante was part of another Hells Angels' puppet gang that operated in western Quebec. He pleaded guilty on September 23, 2003, and was sentenced to serve 10 years from the day his plea bargain was accepted.

Jean-Richard (Race) Larivière – Was made a prospect in the Nomads chapter on December 11, 2000, the same day as Guillaume (Mimo) Serra. Police surveillance on Larivière was one of the keys to unlocking the Nomads chapter's system that managed their millions. In June 2004 he pleaded guilty to conspiracy to commit murder, drug trafficking and gangsterism and received an 18-year sentence.

Pierre (Peanut) Laurin – Joined the Rockers on August 24, 1999, as a drug dealer already well established in Montreal's west end at the time. Was involved in the May 2000 murder of a drug trafficker in Verdun and was made a prospect in the Nomads chapter later that same year. He pleaded guilty to second-degree murder and received a life sentence. He is eligible for parole in 2011.

Bruno Lefebvre – Joined the Rockers in December 1998. Became a prospect in the Nomads chapter on December 11, 2000. He was shot once by accident by a fellow member of the Rockers when they raided a drug den that was controlled by their enemies. He was sentenced, on April 8, 2004, to serve 12 years and 9 months from that date. He has to serve at least half that time before being eligible for parole.

Guy Lepage – A former member of the Montreal Urban Community police who had to resign from the force in the 1970s. He later joined the Rockers and was considered a close associate of Maurice (Mom) Boucher. During the Project Rush investigation the police noticed that Lepage chauffeured Boucher to important meeting with Hells Angels and other drug dealers. He also was making lengthy trips to Colombia which the police later learned were to help arrange cocaine shipments for the Nomads chapter. He was extradited to Florida where he pleaded guilty to drug trafficking and was sentenced to 10 years in September 2002. As part of his plea agreement he was allowed to serve most of his sentence in Canada.

Gilles (Trooper) Mathieu – Became a Hells Angel on December 5, 1980. A constant presence around Boucher when the police were monitoring the gang. He was a founding member of the Nomads chapter in 1995. Was apparently one of the Nomads who decided who among their rivals would be targeted for murder. Mathieu, Mayrand, Houle and a few others were caught looking over photos of their enemies in a hotel suite in 2001. He pleaded guilty on September 23, 2003, and was sentenced to serve 15 years on top of the prison time he already did awaiting the outcome of his trial.

Richard (Dick) Mayrand – Became a member of the Hells Angels on March 1, 1984. Stayed with the gang even though its members killed his brother Michel in an internal purge in 1985. He was not a founding member of the Nomads chapter but joined it later, on January 14, 2000. He was involved in much of the chapter's diplomatic issues as 2000 neared its end. Appeared to be heavily involved in having gangs from Ontario join the Hells Angels en masse and flew to Vancouver apparently just to warn an influential member of the Bandidos from the U.S. that they shouldn't move into Canada. He was convicted of conspiracy to commit murder, drug trafficking and gangsterism in a jury trial. He was sentenced to serve 16 years and 9 months beginning on April 8, 2004. He must serve half that time before being eligible for parole.

Sylvain (Vin Vin) Moreau – Joined the Rockers on August 24, 1999. Before that he was a petty criminal who was often caught trying to pass bad cheques. Before being made a member of the Rockers, he collected drug debts from inmates for the Hells Angels. He was convicted by a jury and sentenced, on April 8, 2004, to 14 years and 9 months. He has to serve at least half the sentence before being eligible for parole.

Peter Paradis – A former member of the Rock Machine who turned informant. He would later testify in the megatrials against the Hells Angels who tried to kill him during the biker war.

Pierre Provencher – A member of the Rockers throughout the biker gang war. As part of his plea bargain he was sentenced to 15 years on September 23, 2003. After factoring in the time he served awaiting the outcome of his case, he had 10 years left to serve.

Normand Robitaille – Joined the Rockers on June 23, 1994. An ambitious young gangster who often paired up with Charlebois in drug trafficking when both were Rockers. Survived at least two attempts on his life during the war. He became a member of the Nomads chapter on October 5, 1998. He pleaded guilty to conspiring to murder rival gang members, drug trafficking and gangsterism on September 23, 2003, and received a 20-year sentence. In March 2005, he saw a year added to the sentence after he was found guilty of hiding the profits of his drug trafficking in real estate.

Michel Rose – Reputed to be an important drug trafficker before he became a prospect in the Nomads chapter on October 5, 1998. He was given his full patch on the chapter's four-year anniversary. On March 8, 2004, he pleaded guilty to a variety of charges and received a 22-year sentence. With the time he served behind bars factored into his sentence, he had 16 years left to serve and will be eligible for parole after serving half of that.

Louis (Melou) Roy – Became a Hells Angel on June 24, 1991. Survived an attempt on his life and beat murder charges after leaving the Trois Rivières chapter and joining the Nomads chapter in 1995. Was last seen alive on June 20, 2000, and is believed to have been purged from the gang.

Guillaume (Mimo) Serra – Was made a prospect in the Nomads chapter on December 11, 2000, just a few months before being arrested in Operation Spring-time 2001. Informants would later say Serra brought international savvy to the Nomads chapter and had contacts in foreign countries. He pleaded guilty to conspiracy to commit murder, drug trafficking and gangsterism on September 23, 2003, and was ordered to serve 10 years from that date.

Stéphane Sirois – Joined the Rockers as a drug dealer early on in the biker war. He was forced out of the gang but later returned as an informant. He would secretly record conversations that would be used in the megatrials.

Walter (Nurget) Stadnick – Became a Hells Angel on May 26, 1982. Was once the gang's Canadian national president. He joined Boucher in leaving the Montreal chapter and became a founding member of the Nomads chapter in 1995. An influential figure among the Hells Angels across Canada and described as a key player in helping to spread chapters across Canada. He was convicted by a Quebec Superior Court judge on June 23, 2004. On September 13, 2004, he was sentenced to the equivalent of 20 years – 13 years and 1 month on top of the time he served awaiting the outcome of his trial. Stadnick and his fellow Ontario Hells Angel Donald Stockford were proven to have dealt in more than $11 million worth of cocaine for the gang in a mere matter of months. During that time they were estimated to have made a profit of more than $2 million.

Donald (Pup) Stockford – Became a Hells Angel on May 26, 1993. Like Stadnick, he was a biker from Ontario who was frequently in Montreal during the biker war and joined the Nomads chapter in 1995. He played an important role in convincing Ontario gangs to join the Hells Angels. Worked as a stuntman when he wasn't busy working with the Hells Angels. Like Stadnick, he was convicted by a Quebec Superior Court judge on June 23, 2004. On September 13, 2004, he was sentenced to the equivalent of 20 years – 13 years and 6 months on top of the time he served awaiting the outcome of his trial.

André (Toots) Tousignant – A founding member of the Rockers who was eager to be promoted to the Nomads chapter. He was Maurice (Mom) Boucher's bodyguard and henchman early on in the biker war and took part in the murder of a prison guard in 1997. Tousignant was made a prospect in the Nomads chapter on July 1, 1997. But he disappeared after the Hells Angels learned someone had turned informant in the murder and his body was discovered on February 27, 1998, in the Eastern Townships.

MOTORCYCLE GANGS OR MOTORCYCLE MAFIA?

Steve Tretheway and Terry Katz

The following article was written by (then) Sergeant Steve Tretheway and (then) Lieutenant Terry Katz and appeared in Police Chief *in 1998. It illustrates the police perspective of one-percenter clubs in relation to organized crime, clearly indicating that the law enforcement agencies believe one-percenter outlaw clubs now exist as organized crime entities.*

Once considered nothing more than rowdy toughs on two-wheelers, motorcycle gangs have evolved into crime units that are sufficiently well-oiled and well-organized to rival the Mafia. It's not just police officers who lump these groups together. Documented evidence in state provincial and federal courts throughout the United States, Canada. Europe and Australia suggests that motorcycle gangs have become organized crime entities equal to the Mafia on many fronts. Biker gangs are organized internationally, with chapters in Europe, Australia, South America and Africa. As retired Illinois State Police Sergeant Joe Satercier noted in 1993 at a Chicago-area Outlaw Motorcycle Gang training seminar. "Biker gangs are the only sophisticated organized crime groups that we export from the United States."

The international problem has become clearer through Interpol's "Project Rockers," which demonstrated that American-based motorcycle gangs such as the Bandidos, Hell's Angels and Outlaws (three of the larger gangs) use their networks to spread criminal activity overseas. Indeed, at least six motorcycle gangs in the United States now have chapters outside the country's borders. The Hell's Angels gang alone has chapters in 20 countries and is expanding so rapidly that it's difficult to keep up with prospective new chapters. By moving outside the United States, biker gangs can enhance their international criminal connections through involvement with the Italian Mafia, Columbian cartels and other organized crime enterprises.

Most motorcycle gangs are well-organized. They have written constitutions, bylaws and a hierarchical leadership structure. Members pay dues and attend regular meetings to confirm loyalty to the gang leadership. Enforced gang member contact is achieved by mandated attendance at club-sanctioned functions (runs). If members break rules or bylaws, their misdeeds are punished with penalties ranging from fines to murder. Many motorcycle gangs have incorporated: some have trademarked their gang logos. Some call their meeting nights "church." According to some sources, the Hell's Angels gang maintains its own Church of the Angels. This is significant since a gang that owns its own church gives its "ministers" the right to visit members in jail. It also provides the "church" with local, state, and federal tax exemptions.

A Closer Look

Categorizing this counterculture is complicated because of the interrelationships and networking not only with other motorcycle gangs, but also with prison gangs, street gangs, racist groups, drug groups and traditional organized crime families. Adding layers of insulation to the network are the gang associates who do not wear a gang patch (set of denim or leather colors with the gang's logo or patch on the back). Estimates suggest that for every gang member, there are 10 associates doing work for the gang. They may obtain utility or criminal justice information, provide sophisticated weapons and other equipment through military connections, or offer their services as chemists, thieves, prostitutes and even contract hit men.

Unlike the traditional Mafia, motorcycle gang members flaunt their membership and proudly acknowledge an existence outside of society's norms. Most are overt about their affiliation, advertising their identity by sporting gang colors, gang tattoos or T-shirts with the gang's insignia. To increase the shock value, gang colors, patches, tattoos and nicknames often incorporate Nazi symbols, devils' heads skulls, vulgar phrases and satanic types of symbolism.

Historical Perspective

Motorcycle gangs got a kick-start after World War II, when they were thought to be nothing more than a symbol of youthful rebellion. Thanks to a few high-profile Hollywood movies and other well-publicized events, gangs gained substantial notoriety as the years went by. *The Wild Ones* in 1954 and *Easy Rider* in 1969 both served to glamorize gang activity and the biker lifestyle. The Hell's Angels gained broader exposure when they were hired to handle security for a Rolling Stones concert at the Altamont Speedway in California in 1969. Sometime during the show, some members of the Angels reportedly turned on the audience and killed a fan. These events helped capture the imagination of many, who swelled the ranks of the outlaw motorcycle gangs.

During the 1970s, nearly 900 outlaw biker gangs – some of them with numerous chapters – operated inside the United States. By the '80s, the FBI had recognized motorcycle gangs as a priority in its organized crime program, just behind La Cosa Nostra. Other federal law enforcement agencies, such as ATF and DEA, also initiated successful conspiracy investigations. Federal agencies have joined with state and local police in task force operations to arrest and convict members of the major motorcycle gangs. Racketeer-Influenced and Corrupt Organization (RICO) investigations, which used gang members-turned-witnesses, were devastating to these gangs, which had been convinced that no one – least of all their own members – would testify against them.

While these concentrated law enforcement actions were disruptive, the gangs responded by hiring attorneys who specialize in organized crime cases and have expertise in fighting federal prosecutors and multi-agency task forces. Some biker gangs even discovered that being sentenced to jail had its benefits. Those who spent time behind bars learned new and possibly more efficient criminal techniques from other prisoners. And as those arrested during the '80s began to be released in the '90s, many embarked on the next phase of their criminal careers better educated in the world of crime, having learned from their mistakes and developed new contacts.

Increasing Sophistication

Clearly today's motorcycle gangs are little like those in the early years. Realizing that they need to be more covert about their criminal activities to survive, these gangs have become sophisticated criminal enterprises over the last 50 years, refining their criminal skills by associating with and learning from traditional crime families and other criminal groups and gangs. Motorcycle gangs have learned to manipulate the criminal justice system with courtroom maneuvers, such as filing numerous discovery motions. These motions have nothing to do with the specific case, but are intended to gather information, such as the names of informants and law enforcement investigative techniques. The discovery process gives gangs the information they need in order to intimidate witnesses through "private investigators," who will report the witnesses' addresses to the gang.

Another way today's motorcycle gangs attempt to manipulate the criminal justice system is through bribery. Documented evidence shows that gangs will use money, drugs or sexual favors to develop intelligence files on rival gangs, as well as on the police. This corruption has even been known to include the occasional police officer.

Better dressed and better educated, many of today's biker gang members and associates are earning college-level degrees in computer science, finance, business, criminal justice, and law. These curricula improve the gang's expertise in highly profitable criminal enterprises. Education has allowed gang associates to entrench themselves in government positions (including the military) and other legitimate professions. These legitimate jobs give gang associates access to technology, weapons and other informational banks where security records, motor vehicle files, personal data and police reports are maintained. Furthermore, like traditional organized crime groups, biker gangs have made a concentrated effort to invest their illegal gains into legitimate businesses. The result is that biker gangs in the '90s have more power and wealth than most people realize. Armed with an education, organizational wealth and criminal savvy, gangs can more easily chisel out a larger slice of the criminal pie.

Of course, none of this means that motorcycle gangs have abandoned violence as the most efficient method of furthering their criminal enterprises. Similar to traditional organized crime syndicates, motorcycle gangs continue to protect their drug distribution networks through whatever means necessary – including murders, rapes, arsons, assaults, intimidation and torturous interrogations. Because of their desire to deal with issues swiftly and violently, motorcycle gangs must be considered equal to their counterparts in organized crime families and the South American drug cartels. Indeed, they have proven themselves capable of beating organized crime families at their own game.

A Growing Threat

Biker gangs have re-established themselves during the past decade. And because law enforcement efforts have been channeled in other directions, such as narcotic or street gangs, the biker gang threat is growing. Finding they could not afford the manpower to work both biker and street gangs, police administrators in many departments have been forced to make painful choices. Although there is no comparison between the violence levels of motorcycle and street gangs, street gangs have gained attention because they are involved in well-publicized violent crimes. This publicity has prompted communities to demand political solutions; politicians have responded by making street gangs the target of violent crime task forces.

Since street gang enforcement typically yields high arrest ratios with less effort, the natural inclination is to use scarce resources in this fashion, further eroding the officers' availability to conduct the long-term covert operation investigations needed for organized motorcycle gangs. In the meantime, biker gang sophistication continues to escalate with the use of modern business technologies: computers keep club records, fax machines bring out-of-country chapters closer together, cellular telephones and pagers make communications easier for gang members to conduct business, and even Internet websites are common among motorcycle gangs in the '90s.

Some gang members and associates operate spy shops, and make good use of surveillance equipment, including electronic bugging and countermeasures equipment. Some of the bigger and more powerful gangs have the financial backing to obtain the most sophisticated weapons and equipment, while police department budgets continue to shrink – making it extremely difficult for law enforcement to keep pace. For example, some gangs now use private investigators to polygraph suspected informants, while other gangs have bought and operate voice stress analyzers to test potential members.

Gangs often use "smoke screens" in their attempt to deceive the public. They want people to believe that while they may look bad on the outside, they have hearts of gold. Some of their "philanthropic" gestures have included raising funds for the Statue of Liberty restoration, carrying the Olympic torch, conducting benefits for disabled children, organizing blood drives, and involving themselves in other kinds of charity events. This has been somewhat successful, as some people still consider bikers as fashionable rebels in leather attire. It is an image that is promoted when movies, the fashion industry, TV commercials, actors, athletes and politicians embrace the "bad boy" image and lifestyle.

And gang trends have blended into the "RUBs" – rich, urban bikers. Larger gangs recognize this and use it to their advantage. They insulate their operations not only with puppet clubs (smaller gangs), but also with other associates who believe motorcycle gangs are nothing more than fun-loving bike riders. The gangs' own mottos, however, offer insight as to how they should be viewed:

Hell's Angels: "Three people will keep a secret if two are dead."

Outlaws. "God forgives, Outlaws don't."

Bandidos: "We are the people that our parents warned us about."

Organized Criminals

Motorcycle gangs are recognized as organized crime not only by the FBI, but also by other police agencies and courts throughout the United States. Within the past two years, Australia and Canada have successfully used immigration laws to prohibit organized crime members – such as non-citizen members of Hell's Angels – from entering their countries. Although Canada's laws were initially designed to keep the Mafia out, they have been interpreted to include all organized crime, and these exclusions are based on documentation that outlaw motorcycle gangs are international criminal organizations.

With more than 50 years to hone their criminal "skills," outlaw motorcycle gangs have become a criminal force to be reckoned with. They have organized behind a hierarchical structure with bylaws and meetings. Some gangs are so concerned with their image that they have copyrighted and trademarked their logos and gang names. Members attend functions (runs) together to solidify their unity and brotherhood as a "family." These gangs don't simply work parallel to traditional organized crime, they cooperate on joint ventures and compete in other areas.

Furthermore, their inter-gang connections with prison gangs, the Ku Klux Klan, other white supremacy groups, street gangs and drug groups have enhanced their criminal networking – allowing their tentacles to reach all parts of society.

It is imperative that inter-agency joint law enforcement task force operations re-think their efforts to combat this threat, since no one agency has the means to investigate and prosecute outlaw motorcycle gangs successfully. Recent cases by ATF and DEA have resulted in multiple arrests of Hell's Angels and Hessians. FBI agents have arrested members of the Devil's Disciples and the Outlaws. The more successful cases involved the experience and expertise of local and state police who joined with the federal agents. There is no time like the present to devote the resources and develop effective strategies to combat the growing threat of today's more sophisticated outlaw motorcycle gangs.

RELENTLESS HEAT

Daniel R. Wolf

*Dan Wolf was one of the leading researchers on outlaw
biker culture. In the following piece he writes beautifully and clearly about the level of police surveillance
experienced by outlaw bikers.*

The cops are always going to be there, and we're always
going to be hassled. It comes with the territory, like rain
on a run.

(Terry, Rebels MC)

When they deal with bikers, law-enforcement agencies find
themselves in the very difficult position of having to separate
legitimate attempts at creating cultural alternatives from criminal deviance. For their part, outlaw clubs come to expect and
bitterly accept the fact that they are subject to selective law
enforcement. "Harassment" occurs when bikers are singled out
for differential treatment for extra-legal reasons. Under these
circumstances, the interaction between the police and bikers
goes beyond the parameters of upholding the law; it takes on the
added dimension of enforcing social norms and values. The
direction and vigour of the "arm of the law" becomes prejudiced by social concerns as well as legal ones. In effect, the

policeman uses criminal law to enforce social norms by treating the bikers – who are perceived as social deviants – as criminals, which they may or may not be.

The biker wants to avoid a confrontation with the police officer, an individual whose power and resources far outweigh his own. A patch holder quickly learns what tactics he can employ and under what situations those tactics can be used, when he is "pulled over by a cop."

In the spring, when you first get on the road, for about a month everybody is on your ass, hot and heavy. We need a sensible delegate like you to go down and talk to them. But like you say, it all starts in the [police] locker room. Like I got picked up, and this one cop [in a different squad car] says on the radio to the cop that pulled me over: "What are you trying to do, keep those Rebels broke this summer?" And this cop says, "Yeah, I'm going to do my best." And I just told him straight, I said: "There's no doubt in my mind that you're a prick!" And he couldn't say nothing to me because it was just him and I; and if he wanted to get smart, I could get just as smart as him. He said "Well, why do you say that?" I said: "Because you're hassling me about pick-ass bullshit stuff that you don't really give a fuck about; but you just want to be a prick!" I was riding baffle drag pipes, and my bike was quiet. I got a thirty-dollar ticket for loud mufflers, and I told him: "You're a prick!" But you know, what can he do if it's just you and him? He can't prove sweet fuck-all. When there's two cops, I don't say nothing, I just take my ticket and go straight home. But if there's only one cop and he's a prick, I'll tell him so. But I told that guy: "I hope you have lots of time for holidays!" and he said: "Why?" And I said: "Because I'm going to be an asshole, plead not guilty, and take you to court and delay the proceedings till I'm sure the date comes on your holidays." I talked with the crown prosecutor, and the charge was dropped. Same as I was charged twice for driving while under suspension [loss of licence due to accumulated demerit points]. I got out of it both times . . . inadequate attempts to contact me in regards to my licence being suspended . . . I never sign for or accept a registered letter . . .

Yeah, that's maybe what the club should do, use a fucking club lawyer all the time. But the trouble is most of the guys in the club don't have the phenomenal fees that a lawyer wants to handle cases to fight helmet tickets and muffler tickets and speeding tickets that are all of the bullshit variety. And that's also a heads-you-win, tails-I-lose scene. If I want someone in court with me to fight a fucking charge, it's going to cost me $450 to fight a $50 speeding ticket. You beat it and you're out $400. (Caveman)

The "can't-win/can't-break-even" situation is part of the price that a patch holder has to pay. I had two Edmonton cops follow me for five miles in the city. Eventually, I was pulled over, my bike was searched, and I was given a ticket for doing 35 mph in a 30-mph zone. The police constable said: "You were breaking the law! That's why you were searched!" When the Rebels' Wee Albert and I were travelling through the city of Calgary, we noticed that we were being tailed. We made a conscious effort to stay under the speed limit. But we were pulled over, and I was given a ticket for having an inadequate helmet. The officer apparently did not like the appearance of my old Bell "lid." He tried to force me either to abandon my bike or to walk it, but Wee Albert lent me a spare helmet that he was carrying. After consulting a lawyer, I returned to Calgary to contest the ticket in court. The officer dropped the charge one hour before court proceedings. "That's the way it goes," commented Caveman. "You travel 200 miles for the trial, and they drop the charges. Like, it's no skin off his nose." My old friend Gypsy of the Satan's Choice recalled an interesting variation on the theme of harassment: "I was being tailed by the OPP [Ontario Provincial Police] on Highway 401. No way that my insurance company would stand for another ticket. So I slowed down so much that most of the cars were passing me. I got a ticket for going too slow. The fucker says I was impeding traffic."

A hostile reception from both citizens and police may greet an outlaw club that rides into a community while on a run. The police feel that the annual westward migration of Alberta clubs "poses a security problem in British Columbia":

Motorcycle Gangs from Alta. to Face Surveillance in BC
[Cpl. Don] Brown said in an interview the outside clubs
will combine with local gangs on weekend rides. "Clubs
realize one hundred bikers look more impressive than
twenty," he said. "When they ride into a town which is
hostile to bikers they can put up more resistance." Clubs
which police will observe closely this summer include the
Rebels and Warlords of Edmonton and the King's Crew,
Grim Reapers, and Minority from Calgary . . . Brown
said some bikers with hunting permits will legally carry
shotguns. "We are aware of the potential but there is
nothing we can do. And we don't care as long as they
keep the peace." Members of Brown's team will travel in
cars behind the clubs on weekend rides and step in to
prevent local residents from starting a fight. (Edmonton
Journal, 28 April 1977)

In Vancouver, BC, the citizenry are particularly sensitive to the
presence of outlaw clubs. Public visibility is the key factor here;
the Vancouver city police had told the Satan's Angels not to
wear their colours within the city limits. Public indignation in
1966 over the activities of the Satan's Angels MC prompted
provincial Attorney-General Robert Bonner to demand that
pressure on bikers continue:

Nobody Waved Goodbye
Police don't often bother to welcome tourists to the city,
but made an exception Tuesday with five members of the
Rebels motorcycle club from Edmonton. Since arriving in
BC a week ago, they have been subject to police checks
twelve times. (*The Province,* 12 August 1975)

From the public-relations perspective of the police, either
outlaw clubs should not be seen or the police should be seen
to be controlling them.

When the five Rebels got to Vancouver, they were pulled over
by five police cruisers and one motorcycle unit, a total of eleven
constables. They were checked a second time within a hour.
The Vancouver city police were hard-pressed to find any new
faults, but they did issue three additional tickets for mechanical

problems. The second "check-stop" was a tribute to the creativity of the officers involved: Whimpy got a ticket because his spare helmet had loosened from his pack and was covering part of his licence plate. Gerry gave one of the constables his licence, registration, and insurance cards as requested. The constable took a quick look at Gerry's licence, handed it back to him and said: "I can't read this!" and wrote out a ticket for not having a driver's licence. The same card had been accepted by another constable one hour earlier. Danny received a summons for driving an unsafe vehicle: a balding tire. The total cost in fines for tickets received during the two Vancouver shakedowns was three hundred dollars. The Vancouver police were enforcing a claim they had made earlier to the Rebels: "There's only one club in this town! That's us!"

Underlying this selective law enforcement is a more subtle aspect of police strategy. None of the tickets was for a moving violation that could be cleared by a voluntary payment of fines by mail. These citations all required a court appearance. The police assume that outlaw bikers will not be willing or able to travel 3000 miles to appear in court. If the bikers do choose to contest what they feel are trumped-up charges, the officers can exercise their option of dropping the charges up to a half-hour before the scheduled court proceeding. However, if the bikers do not appear, a warrant will be issued for their arrest. Outstanding warrants are an effective deterrent against a club's return. If club members risk re-entering the province, they will do so as fugitives from the law. In effect, by not responding to a traffic citation, the patch holder turns himself into a bona fide outlaw: "I left this BC town and I held her at 60 [mph], because this squad car was following me. He followed me for about ten miles. It turns out the speed limit is 55, and he gives me a ticket for doing 85 . . . No, I'm not paying it. Fuck 'em! I'll take the [arrest] warrant" (Onion, Rebels MC).

Police try to discourage outlaw clubs from visiting their areas by subjecting them to continuous check-stops. This strategy is most effective when adjacent detachments coordinate their efforts.

Don Stevenson, president of the King's Crew, out of Calgary, says that throughout the 300,000 or so miles the club logs every year, it is subject to increasing hassles from the RCMP's "E-squad" and local police. Riding hours are eaten up while officials check for drugs, stolen bikes, illegal weapons and I.D.'s; the search policy only intensifies ill will between riders and police. He claims that although his club members have made a practice for years of phoning ahead to RCMP units to advise them of their routes, local officials duplicate the check-stops impeding riding even more. That could be avoided if the RCMP would radio ahead to local law enforcement units advising that the group has already been checked over, but Corporal Brown explains he can do nothing if local police want to check for themselves. (*Alberta Report*, 2 May 1979)

However, the RCMP do indeed radio ahead to local law-enforcement units. While I was in RCMP headquarters in Penticton, BC, the following message came over the radio dispatch at 1:00 p.m.: "Car 7760 . . . we have the Tribesmen motorcycle gang . . . approximately 30 bikers . . . now approximately ten miles out of Princeton . . . heading east, Highway 97 . . . Estimated Penticton arrival at 14:00 hours . . . Will advise." The Princeton officer was advising the Penticton detachment, so that they could take appropriate action. The Penticton RCMP decided to set up their own roadblock. The frustrated Tribesmen tried to run the blockade but were pulled over. According to Spider, the Tribesmen's road captain, the opening conversation went something like the following:

Constable (RCMP): Why the hell did you run the blockade?!
Spider: You just finished checking us out two hours ago. What the fuck do you want?
Constable: We're going to give you so much fucking heat, you'll never come back here again!

In the search that followed, thirty-eight cases of beer were confiscated, the charge being suspicion of bootlegging. Four arrests were made; two were for possession of unopened beer and two for obstructing an officer. Apparently one member became very upset at the prospect of the club's beer being confiscated. He hung on to the door of the Volkswagen van (crash truck) until two officers managed to break his grip by using their clubs on his hands.

The RCMP are well aware that applying this kind of repetitive surveillance may result in violence. When they advise police departments on the proper strategy for "Stopping and Checking a 'Run'" (1980), they warn officers of the possible confrontational and legal ramifications.

> Bikers may have been checked several times during the course of their run and this may be only one of several times that they have been checked. Normally they will attempt to maintain a low profile, however, one cannot underestimate the potential for any sudden action on their part. Be ready for any violent explosion but don't over-react.
>
> A bike gang on a 100 mile run may have been stopped 11 times. Confronted by police the eleventh time, language may become abusive on both sides. Bikers have been known to record such conversations, then take them to their lawyers. So watch what you say and how you say it.

Once the bikers have reached their destination and are off the road, the "heat" will not necessarily stop. When the Tribesmen finally arrived in Penticton, police officials told them to stay out of town. The Tribesmen begrudgingly complied and set up camp in a remote area outside of the town-site. However, the RCMP continued to monitor the club's movements; that night the RCMP raided the Tribesmens' camp-site.

The Rebels "Invade" Coronation

For seven years the Rebels ended their riding season with a Labour Day run to the town of Coronation, Alberta. A five-man detachment of RCMP managed to police the rally site with no major incidents or complaints from the local citizens. But in 1981 the annual Labour Day run resulted in what the RCMP called "the largest such police action to have ever occurred in Canada" (Corporal Brant Murdock, public-relations spokesman, RCMP). This exceptional incident provides insight into some of the political considerations that underlie the manoeuvres of both police and bikers on a club run.

North American outlaw clubs have traditionally adopted the Labour Day long weekend as a date for a mandatory run. The Labour Day run not only marks the end of the official riding season, for many clubs it becomes a major political event as well. Existing political ties among clubs are strengthened, and the possibility of establishing new ones is explored as "the booze flows" and the members "let the good times roll." Over the years the Rebels established themselves as power brokers in Alberta and Saskatchewan. The Rebels became active in this role in 1975 when they issued invitations to the King's Crew MC of Calgary and the two Spokesmen MC chapters of Saskatchewan to attend the Labour Day run and celebrate the informal alliance that they had fostered among the three clubs. With the approval of the Rebels, the King's Crew in turn invited the Lucifer's Union MC of Calgary. The King's Crew hoped that an alliance with Lucifer's Union would help them survive a power struggle with the Grim Reapers of Calgary. The highly sensitive Labour Day run is a "colours only" event. Only club members, strikers, and their female companions are allowed to attend.

A provincial camp-ground north of the town of Coronation (pop. 1500) was originally chosen (1973) as the regular Labour Day run site because of its central location. Situated 120 miles east of the city of Red Deer, Coronation was relatively equidistant for the Rebels chapters and their guest clubs. The success of the initial and subsequent runs resulted in the annual event being nicknamed the Coronation Run. Several factors contributed to the success of the run. These included the availability of provincial camp-ground facilities, an adjacent rodeo racetrack where members could race their bikes, and a nearby town-site that allowed the patch holders to buy meals, refuel their motorcycles, and restock their beer supply at the Longhorn Saloon. However, the most critical factors were that the rally site was isolated and the local RCMP were very accommodating. The mandate of the RCMP was to protect the citizens and their property; the main concerns of the Rebels were to strengthen inter-club ties and to have a "righteous good time" while doing it. Both the RCMP and the Rebels realized that their mutual interests could best be served by avoiding citizen/biker contact. There was only one access road into the camp-site, and the RCMP would park a patrol car at the entrance. For their part, the outlaw clubs placed a sentry at the gate whose job it was gently but firmly to send on his way anyone who wasn't dressed in the familiar uniform of dusty jeans, leather jacket, and denim-jacket cut-off with club patch. " 'They're a good bunch,' said one constable, 'They just go up there and have a good time. The thing we worry about is that some of the locals might go in and stir things up.' For the most part, the locals respect the bikers' wish to hoot and holler in privacy" (*Calgary Herald*, 5 Sept. 1977: 1). The joint strategy of controlled isolation on the part of the RCMP and the Rebels proved effective. After the third annual Coronation Run, an article appeared in the *Calgary Herald*, newspaper entitled "Bikers invade Coronation but nobody's worried":

> The first bikers' convention two years ago caught the farmers and 1,200 townspeople offguard. Some feared for their children and property . . . they doubted that the RCMP could do much if things got out of control. Now it seems, folks look forward to the annual Labour Day "run" of the hairy young men on their noisy machines. Coronation mayor Bud Carl said the first time the bikers came to town, "we were quite concerned. There were about one hundred of them and we didn't know what they were going to do. There are some pretty wild characters in that outfit . . . but they have been coming here for three years and to my knowledge, they have caused no trouble whatsoever. I have had no complaints from the police or civilians; in fact, they bring quite a bit of business to town." "We're not looking for any trouble," said one biker from the Rebels Motorcycle Club of Edmonton, "we just want to have a good time." (*Calgary Herald*, 5 Sept. 1977)

The unofficial policy of cooperation between the Rebels MC and the RCMP resulted in a good time for the bikers and an uneventful weekend for the police. According to the Rebels, the formula for success was one of mutual "trust": "We had a trust deal with the RCMP. We [the club president] would phone them up and let them know where we were going, how many guys would be there, along with dates and times. The idea was that there would be no surprises for either them or the club" (Tramp). The Edmonton RCMP would then forewarn those police detachments that could expect the Rebels in their area. It was this "trust deal" that enabled a local five-man RCMP detachment at Coronation to handle an outlaw-club convention that involved more than 120 bikers without incident. However, all this would change in 1981.

Instead of the local five-man detachment, the Rebels ran into a small army of over two hundred police officers who stifled the biker bash with relentless "heat." In addition to over one hundred regular Mounties, the force included a heavily armed and camouflaged RCMP tactical squad from the city of Red Deer, a forty-man contingent from the City of Edmonton police force, the E-squad special biker task force from the city of Vancouver, numerous plain-clothes officers, special police photographers, a videotaping unit, and police-dog units drawn from various central Alberta RCMP detachments. The equipment used in the military-styled operation featured a mobile police command centre, a telecommunications truck, a helicopter, two fixed-wing observation aircraft, two chartered buses, a vehicle for storing evidence, forty police cruisers, and an arsenal of high-powered scoped rifles, shotguns, automatic weapons, flak jackets, bulletproof vests, and tear gas. This small army was quartered in the local school gymnasium, which was converted into a barracks; a hotel banquet room served as a mess hall.

The 1981 Coronation Run was an important political event to the Rebels. They were hosting the Grim Reapers and King's Crew of Calgary, Vancouver's Satan's Angels, Hell's Angels from Quebec and Massachusetts, Les Gitans (Gypsies) from Sherbrooke, Quebec, and a representative of the Vagabonds from Toronto – approximately 155 bikers in total. The Rebels were determined to show their guests a good time and had arranged for unlimited free beer and steaks for all. A successful run would enhance the national prestige of the Rebels and affect their future relations with these powerful clubs.

Chilly winds and ominous grey skys foreshadowed the extraordinary events that began to unfold on Friday evening. The

Rebel entourage included thirty-five bikers from the Edmonton chapter, along with several motor homes and pick-ups that carried the extra supplies. The Rebels had been on the road all day, the weather had been poor, and they were cold, wet, and tired. Bob, the road captain, was a ten-year veteran of the club; but he decided against sending scouts ahead to check out the situation on Highway 12. The Rebels had already informed the RCMP of their route, destination, and intentions. As far as the club was concerned, the "trust deal" was still on. It would prove to be a costly mistake. The Rebels had no idea of the "shit that was about to come down":

There were about thirty bikes riding with us. We were maybe a half-mile from the camp-site when they hit us. Just as we came over a rise in the road we saw the road-block. There were twenty or thirty cruisers lined up on either side of the road, with two cars in the middle of the road. There were buses and vans parked all along the highway. A couple of the guys tried to turn around and scramble out of there; but they were surrounded by cruisers and a helicopter that closed in from the rear. I wasn't counting, but it looked like there were four cops for every bike. When we pulled up six guys surrounded me. Before I even had a chance to shut off my bike, one cop puts a numbered card on my chest while another cop takes my picture. They were armed to the teeth. They had handguns, shotguns, and there were four or five sergeants with automatic weapons, all nice and shiny, primed and drawn. There were a couple of cops patrolling around with German shepherds and Dobermans. Then I noticed that they had this plane circling over us. I was surprised, really stunned by what was going on. While I was getting out my licence and registration, Gerry yells out: "Look over there! They've got a fucking SWAT team in the fields!" Sure enough, there were cops dressed in camouflage, their faces painted in camouflage. These guys were crawling through the fields and hiding behind bushes, drawing a bead on us with their scoped rifles. It was unreal, like an ambush scene out of Vietnam. From then on it was the usual hassle and shakedown. It seemed like a lot of trouble to give me a ticket for running loud pipes [having inadequate baffles in the muffler system]. (Terry, Rebels MC)

The police handlers of the canine corps attempted to have their dogs sniff out any caches of illegal drugs that they thought the Rebels had hidden on their bikes or stashed away on any of the support vehicles. No drugs were discovered, but the RCMP did confiscate all the beer and wine that the club had in the bus on the grounds of liquor violations. The Rebels and their ol' ladies were then computer checked for any outstanding warrants. Corporal Murdoch of the RCMP stated that strip-searches were done only when police had "reasonable and probable grounds to conduct such searches" (*Calgary Herald*, 9 Sept. 1981). One ol' lady, a 30-year old nurse, who was pregnant at the time, was strip-searched by three female officers after a computer indicated that she had failed to pay a ten-dollar parking ticket. The woman spent the evening recovering in a Stettler hospital. She was charged with failing to submit a change of address form to the Department of Transport. The charge was later withdrawn by a provincial court judge, Ken Cush, in December. The police proceeded to inspect the motorcycles and issued twenty tickets for minor traffic violations. One bike was inspected three times for equipment violations. On the third check the police decided that the lowest point of the seat was twenty-five inches above the ground instead of the required twenty-seven. The licence plate was seized and the member had to ship his motorcycle home on a trailer. One particularly zealous officer confiscated Tramp's new Sturgis model Harley-Davidson; apparently it had a crack in the licence plate. The police seized six motorcycles for suspected serial number alteration. The motorcycles were loaded on to a hay trailer that the RCMP had requisitioned from a local farmer and transported to the police mobile command headquarters in Coronation. All the suspect motorcycles were returned by the end of the weekend.

The RCMP planned to apply the same "check-stop" procedures to the other clubs when they approached the campground. However, a scout bike evaded the roadblock and returned, cross-country, to Coronation in time to warn a contingent of eighty King's Crew, Satan's Angels, and Hell's Angels patch holders. The bikers at all costs wanted to avoid having their motorcycles confiscated, and "there was no way we would submit to any skin frisk" (Ron, Satan's Angels MC). They decided to "hole up" in the Coronation Hotel bar. The police task force responded by swooping down and sealing off the town. Time began working against the bikers; they realized that as the hours passed and sunset neared, they faced imminent charges of vagrancy. The bikers outmanoeuvred the RCMP by accepting an invitation from the proprietor of the local drive-in establishment to attend a marathon midnight-to-dusk movie showing. After last call at the Coronation bar, the patch holders bought fifty cases of off-sales beer and retired with their ol' ladies to the drive-in. They paid off the proprietor, spread out their sleeping-bags, and settled in to enjoy *Superman II*, *The Dogs of War*, and *Clash of the Titans*. The RCMP ended the stand-off the next day when they ordered the town's gasoline stations not to sell fuel to bikers. The patch holders were stranded and submitted to the check-stop, but still managed to negotiate for a "pat-search" (outside the clothes) instead of a "skin frisk" (strip-search). They wheeled their motorcycles, rented trucks, and Lincoln Continental into the police lines, where they were checked for identification, photographed, and searched. In the meantime, the camouflaged tactical squad had deployed itself in the bushes of the Rebels' camp-site and continued its round-the-clock surveillance after the outlaw clubs gathered together for steaks and beer. "They were out there all the time. At night you'd go to the trees to take a piss, and you'd hear the branches and twigs breaking. During the day they'd be flying over our camp-site with their planes and helicopter. They forced us to change; the trust deal was over. In the future we'll be a lot more prepared for them" (Raunch). By Sunday afternoon the party spirit had dampened and the bikers began to roll out of town with police cruisers and planes following them.

The joint RCMP and Edmonton city police action resulted in the confiscation of five rifles and a handgun, but as the weapons were registered, no charges were laid. Five motorcycles were seized on suspicion of altered serial numbers, all were returned on the weekend. There were four charges for restricted and offensive weapons (one unregistered handgun and martial-arts implements), one charge for possession of stolen property, fourteen liquor offences, seven charges of possession of marijuana and one of cocaine, ten arrests for outstanding warrants (unpaid traffic tickets), and one hundred and twelve Highway Traffic Act charges, mostly for minor equipment violations.

The Rebels MC of Edmonton decided to take collective legal action to contest the charges. The club organized "boogies" (public dances) to help defray the costs. Both the members and friends of the club contributed to a collective fund. Approximately $5000 was raised and used to hire George Parker to act as a club lawyer. Parker appeared in provincial court on 27 October of that year. His actions resulted in fifty-one of the fifty-five tickets issued to the Rebels being quashed on technicalities. For example, a number of the summonses failed to indicate that the accused had the option of making a voluntary payment instead of appearing in court. Six of the other assorted charges were also dismissed by provincial judge J.A. Murray.

The RCMP and city-police action was sanctioned by the Alberta solicitor-general's department and the Edmonton police commission. The exercise cost the federal and provincial governments more than $150,000. But the police forces claimed that it was worth the money because it showed the bikers that they could not get away with antisocial and criminal behaviour, such as terrorizing people in a small town. Public-relations officer Corporal Brant Murdoch stated that past biker gatherings in Coronation had resulted in a gang rape, assaults, break-ins, and thefts. However, none of these alleged occurrences was ever substantiated by official complaints registered with the RCMP. Coronation mayor Muriel Heidecker said that the bikers had not caused any problems in the past and that the town council had not asked the RCMP to crack down on the bikers. However, she did have reservations about her town being chosen as a convention centre for outlaw motorcycle clubs: " 'They have never done any damage to the town but they fight among themselves and the people don't like them coming' " (*Edmonton Journal*, 3 Sept. 1981).

Colleen Richardson, 19, who lives on her family's farm 300 yards from where the Rebels camped, says there were no problems, nor had there been during the two previous years the bikers had been at the camp-site. In fact, Miss

Richardson said, her family let the bikers use the phone several times and her grandmother, who lives in a nearby trailer, invited several bikers in for hot chocolate. Another lady, who lives about five miles from the camp-site and helps maintain the grounds says, "They never cause any problems; they don't do anything wrong." And she observes that the bikers leave the camp-site cleaner when they leave than many other campers do. (*Alberta Report*, 18 Sept. 1981)

However, the town of Coronation's reaction to the outlaw bikers was not altogether positive. Some of the prairie town's businesses advertised that they would be closed for the long weekend, apparently in apprehension about the biker rally: " 'The last time they were in here [Tasty Mill Restaurant] they took over my restaurant like they owned it and then left without paying' ". In the final analysis, there were no violent confrontations between the bikers and police, no fights between the bikers and the townspeople, no public rowdiness, and no complaints from any citizens about abuse from the bikers. All charges that were laid against the bikers stemmed from the checkstop. " 'We go a thousand miles out of our way to be in the middle of nowhere, where we won't bother anyone, and they're all here waiting for us' " (member, Satan's Angels MC; ibid.). According to the publisher of the Coronation weekly newspaper, the townspeople were not happy with the actions of the police: "I look at it as a form of harassment" (*Edmonton Sun*, 9 Sept. 1981).

There was "no reason at all" for the operation, according to RCMP spokesman Murdoch, "other than the fact that it's about time. They've ridden into town for six or seven years pretty well unchecked." Plans for a large-scale police mobilization had been under way for two years; the purpose was to test police capacity to move large numbers of men and equipment on short notice. The operation was not "specifically targeted" at the bikers; "having the outlaw gangs here just added to the rationale for having this operation now . . . we just seized the opportunity" (Murdoch, RCMP). However, the reason that the Coronation Run became the specific target was probably influenced in part by the clubs that the Rebels had on their guest list, particularly the Hell's Angels. One can speculate that the RCMP were concerned about potential coalitions and mergers. The Rebels themselves were laying the groundwork for another chapter in Calgary. "The club was growing," stated Terry of the Rebels; "the RCMP wanted to show us some power." The RCMP were likely also worried about the possibility of the Hell's Angels extending their influence into western Canada through a process of either incorporating or affiliating with clubs such as the Rebels, Grim Reapers, and Satan's Angels, a club that did indeed become a Hell's Angel chapter two years later in 1983. The RCMP would view an increased Hell's Angels' presence as having the potential of destabilizing the "biker problem" in western Canada. In eastern Canada, these kinds of political developments indeed had led to a direct increase in inter-club territorial warfare, homicides, and illicit drug trafficking.

Edmonton Police Chief Robert Lunney would later tell the Edmonton police commission that police intelligence had established "without a doubt that the gangs are primarily large scale criminal syndicates" (*Edmonton Journal*, 11 Sept. 1981). The check-stop operation provided the police with both identification and photographs of "gang" members. The police viewed the weekend gathering of clubs as a major threat to peace in central Alberta: "Intimidation through appearance and overt threats has been a trademark of the gangs. We have been exceedingly fortunate in Alberta that we have not been subjected to the violence and fear that has overcome some communities resulting from large assemblies of bikers" (ibid.) According to Chief Lunney, the RCMP feared that the gathering would result in more crime in the province.

What is lost in these public-relations statements is any explanation as to why it was deemed necessary to use such an unprecedented and disproportionate show of force. For the past five years, the job had been handled by a local five-man detachment, with an accommodating attitude. There were no registered complaints from the citizens, nor did town officials request increased policing. The whole task-force operation was the brainchild of the RCMP, and it is possible that they may have had a hidden agenda: to demonstrate their usefulness and effectiveness. The future of the RCMP in Alberta was uncertain. Their high costs and lack of accountability to provincial complaint boards had caused eight provincial governments to consider replacing the federal RCMP with provincial police forces.

Contract Hassles Jeopardize Mounties' Future in Alberta
Rumours and talks at strategy sessions in provincial offices have shifted to talk of creating police forces to replace the RCMP . . . Eastern Canadian police administrators (Ontario and Quebec) have urged their western counterparts to take the big step – to unload the expensive and unaccountable RCMP. (*Edmonton Journal*, 8 Sept. 1981)

The concern senior RCMP officers would have over these "contract hassles" would stem from the fact that only half of Canada's twenty thousand mounted-police officers work on federal matters; the other half provide police services for the provinces, which reimburse the federal government for costs. If the provinces chose to replace the RCMP with provincial forces, the RCMP would be dealt a devastating blow to their policing presence and political prestige. The number of RCMP officers would be drastically reduced, their training costs per officer would increase, the opportunity for graduate officers to get grass-roots provincial experience would be lost, and the force's ability to integrate and influence both federal and provincial policing would be severely curtailed.

Despite their high cost and lack of accountability, the provinces felt that there was a national aspect to the RCMP that was worth retaining. In addition, the RCMP back their men with an extensive array of support services, special investigative units, laboratories, and an impressive inventory of armaments, dogs, all-terrain vehicles, snow-mobiles, boats, and aircraft. One can speculate that the RCMP wanted to show themselves to be indispensable by profiling their sophisticated personnel and arsenal. The check-stop operation featured several unique components of the RCMP, including Project Focus – part of their national database and intelligence centre – and E-squad, a special investigative corps; both of these units are equipped to deal with "the biker-gang problem" on a national basis. Outlaw motorcycle clubs have a highly negative public image and easily grab frontpage media attention. Picking the bikers as targets –

traditional symbols of antisocial and criminal behaviour –
would ensure that the RCMP's *tour de force* would not go
unnoticed. Ironically, coverage of both the "crackdown on
biker gangs" and the RCMP contract dispute appeared side by
side in the *Edmonton Journal* (8 Sept. 1981). Shortly thereafter,
the Alberta solicitor-general chose to retain the services of the
RCMP.

RCMP public-relations spokesman Murdoch stated that the
checkstop operation would deter the bikers from returning to
Coronation: "'They're not coming back . . . No matter where
they go in Alberta, we'll be around'" (*Edmonton Sun*, 9 Sept.
1981). But next year the Rebels did indeed return to Coronation. "We were just hoping that we could have our party
without any trouble," said Gerry, the club president. When
the Rebels pulled into town, the sign on the Longhorn Saloon
said; "Welcome Bikers."

RIPPING OFF SOCIETY

RCMP Gazette

Written from a Canadian police perspective – but also reflecting the international stage – this piece highlights the concerns of law enforcement agencies that outlaw clubs are becoming sophisticated criminal networks.

Motorcycle gangs have been glorified over the years – "Easy Rider", the mystique of the leather-clad rider on the Harley, an image the bikers want to continue to propagate, in addition to their charity runs, etc. – and in large part, they have been quite successful in doing so, as authors Antonio Nicaso and Michael Welzenbach agree: "Yet all the while, the Hells Angels have successfully maintained one of the most inventive and enduring public relations campaigns in criminal history. Thanks to their increasingly sophisticated PR efforts . . ."

What you may not realize is that like most other things, the reality is often different from the myth – the soft underbelly of the bikers is not quite so soft. The outlaw faction of the motorcycle gang is a force to be reckoned with and their presence is indeed, formidable. In an interview with Ian MacLeod in the *Ottawa Citizen*, Commissioner Murray agreed.

"While you talk about 1,200 (members) and 12,000 associates, the sheer pervasiveness of their influence is almost unbelievable. We see them a couple of times a year dressed in their colours and out doing their thing as a group, but behind the scenes, these people are very astute businessmen."

The Hells Angels, some 50 years old now, is the largest and most sophisticated motorcycle gang in the world. Their expansion rivals that of the biggest of Fortune 500 corporations. As of August 1997, the Hells Angels are the biggest outlaw motorcycle gang in the world, 123 chapters throughout the United States, Canada, Austria, Belgium, Denmark, Finland, France, Germany, Great Britain, Italy, Liechtenstein, Norway, Sweden, Switzerland, the Netherlands, Australia, New Zealand, South Africa and Brazil. The total membership of the organization is estimated over 1,600 members. In the near future, it is expected that six new Hells Angels chapters should be established in the United States, with an additional two in Canada. By the year 2000, less than two years away, the Hells Angels should be no less than 140 chapters throughout the world.

Less than two years away . . .

Puppet Clubs

A puppet club is an outlaw motorcycle gang that is aligned with a major biker club like the Hells Angels. It is usually required to perform "dirty" business – like murders, acts of violence (arsons, bombings). A puppet club also distributes and sells drugs and makes drug debt collections, etc. When members of the Hells Angels attend funerals or other official ceremonies, puppet club members act as bodyguards.

A puppet club is no more than a subservient group which insulates the Hells Angels from prosecution as they carry out their criminal activities. It also expands the organization without having to "share the wealth".

For example, in Quebec, there are at least nine puppet clubs which are aligned to the Hells Angels. Three of the five Quebec Hells Angels Chapters – the Nomads, the Montreal and Trois-

Rivières Chapters – control and supervise the puppet clubs and their activities.

This is by no means an exhaustive list of the activities outlaw motorcycle gangs are involved in. It does however, highlight the reality of their "work" – and their sophistication which is second to none:

"Make no mistake about it, bikers are now as sophisticated as the old organized crime families. They are far more prone to violence when provoked, and certainly more arrogant. They seldom miss an opportunity to make money or to kill someone in the way of profits. The more illegal the scam, the more it is preferred. If you can rip off society and put one over on the establishment in the process, that's showing class" (*RCMP Gazette*).

Drugs

BC chapters are overseeing the cultivation and distribution of hydroponic marijuana which is subsequently sold in Canada and the United States.

As noted in a CISC report: "Drug trafficking is the most lucrative activity for criminal motorcycle gangs. This is particularly true of the Hells Angels who, thanks to support from their affiliated clubs, are a major distributor and seller of drugs from coast to coast."

One raid in Lower Mainland Vancouver by the Vancouver Police netted approximately $1.5 million to $2 million of marijuana – this was the conservative estimated street value, according to a report in the *Vancouver Sun*, December 5, 1997. In actual fact, the "BC Bud" would have yielded much higher profits for the club as it would have likely been transported to the United States where it is traded pound for pound for cocaine.

In the past year, Vancouver police have raided about 50 associates of the Hells Angels and seized about $10 million worth of the stuff. In the same story, Insp. Peter Ditchfield of the coordinated strike force, reports this would account for nearly half of the $23 million worth of marijuana seized by police in Vancouver in 1997.

Drug dealing and trafficking are also staples of outlaw motorcycle gangs in the United States and Europe.

Prostitution

In 1984–'85, a police investigation in the Halifax area revealed that members of the Nova Scotian Hells Angels were acting in concert with another outlaw motorcycle gang from Newfoundland to take over the prostitution trade in both provinces. Prostitution-related charges were laid against all members of the Nova Scotian Chapter and convictions were regsitered against three of them on a plea bargain agreement. The investigation revealed the following:

- they were procuring women from Newfoundland and Nova Scotia for the purpose of prostitution in Halifax;
- the Hells Angels were using intimidation tactics to force other pimps and their girls out of the area;
- they were using violence to control the prostitutes working for them; and,
- one prostitute who left the area after a severe beating from a HA member stated the Hells Angels received 40% of the gross profit from each girl.

There are examples in kind from around the world – from Hambourg, Germany, to Adelaide, Australia, to almost anywhere in the United States. In 1989, the US Attorney General described the Hells Angels as pursuing a wide array of criminal activities including prostitution, burglary, rape, assault, murder, contract killing, as well as sophisticated crimes such as illegal banking and financing drug deals

Obstruction of Justice

Outlaw motorcycle gangs, in particular the Hells Angels, are notorious for their use of fear and intimidation. In many cases, their reputation has been used to establish an aura of fear, as a means of control and also protecting members of the organization. Club colours, insignia, tattoos and other identifiers are frequently worn by members to intimidate the public and the police. This has been often noted in court proceedings where HA members appeared as defendants or were present as spectators.

Money Laundering

From September 1990 to August 1994, undercover RCMP agents ran a storefront money laundering operation in Montreal. Operation Contrat-Compote was undertaken to identify the money laundering procedures originating from the proceeds of crime. The operation showed that members of the Hells Angels Sherbrooke and Trois-Rivières Chapters were collecting money from other criminal organizations to purchase several hundred kilos of cocaine. It also revealed that HA had laundered $30 million over a period of 30 months.

In June 1996, the Quebec Police Force's Proceeds of Crime Unit executed a warrant for the seizure of property of a Hells Angels member, on the grounds that it was obtained from the proceeds of crime. The total value of the property seized was estimated at $500,000. The individual pleaded guilty.

Biker Wars

The Hells Angels have been at war with the Canadian-based Outlaws since 1978. Several murders and assaults have been recorded as a result of this conflict between 1970 and 1986. During that time, 859 murders occurred in Quebec. Outlaw motorcycle gang members were responsible for 118 (13.7%) of these.

Over the years, the biker war between the Hells Angels and the Rock Machine has raged – all over control of the province's illegal drug trade. You need only pick up any French periodical in Quebec to get the latest update. Over the last year, like Montreal, Quebec City has also been subject to bloody turf wars – the Rock Machine is reported to be negotiating an alliance with the Bandidos motorcycle club to wrestle control of the trade from the Hells Angels.

Since 1994, there have been no less than 85 murders and 92 attempted murders related to Quebec's biker wars, including the much-publicized death of an innocent 11 year-old boy. The wars have also resulted in a reported 129 arsons and 82 bombs that either exploded or were located in time by the police.

By the end of the 70s, the Hells Angels in the United States had become increasingly involved in gang wars or confrontations, primarily to protect or expand their lucrative drug market. In 1978, the Hells Angels' ruling council officially declared war on the Outlaws.

The Hells Angels have been vigorously pursuing worldwide expansion and continue to face some strong and violent opposition in the forms of the Outlaws and the Bandidos, both originating from the US. Both the HA and the Bandidos have increased their chapters and members in Europe since 1995, particularly in Scandinavia. Most outlaw motorcycle gangs, for fear of retaliation, sympathize with the Hells Angels and support them in several ways, namely through donations to the "Hells Angels Defence Fund". Since 1994, 14 murders and 74 attempted murders have been linked to outlaw motorcycle gangs through letter bombs, bombs, drive-by shootings and bazookas. Anywhere is "fair game" – prisons, clubhouses, airports and city streets – and at least two people have been innocent victims in these wars.

CHROME AND HOT LEATHER

Mark L. Bastoni

This beautifully written piece by freelance author Bastoni appeared in the Boston Magazine *in July 1988. It focuses on organized crime and one-percenter clubs in the United States.*

The "Log Cabin" bar squats by a railbed near the crumbling, grafitti splayed bridge that carries Rt. 114 over Rt. 107 in Salem, Mass. And though part of the building actually looks like a log cabin, the rest was knocked together and it's all coated with a greasy chocolate-brown substance that is probably paint.

Inside, the reddening grey glow on the western sky somehow shoves its way through the nicotine glazed windows and makes you wonder if one of the sooty mills nearby is in flames. On cue, Hendrix is on the radio . . . "lord, somebody's house is burnin', down down, down down . . ."

At one end of the bar a bleachy blonde wrapped in the brightest tightest red dress, with matching lips, pushes off her elbows and struts her black patent stilettos past the small empty tables opposite the long bar. New faces stand out in the Log Cabin. She wants to glue a hungry look on the stranger, to be sure the stranger has checked her up and down. She stops to

talk with the only other woman in the place, a mousy "brown-
ette" in Frye boots and faded jeans so tight you could read the
the change in her back pocket. A few working men in dirty jeans
and Ts, breast pockets bulging with decks of Luckys, check out
the show. But only briefly – to them it's an old act.

This is Hell's Angel turf.

At about ten o'clock a faint drone stirs the stale barroom air,
steadily swelling into a bristling roar as a dozen motorcycles roll
to a halt outside the door. Twisting their front forks and
flashing their headlights into the bar, the riders neatly angle
their massive, chrome laden machines into curbside slots.
"Here's the boys," someone intones. A few drinkers glance
casually at the door but turn quickly back to their beers as the
tach'ing engines rattle the faded boxing photos hanging around
the walls.

Suddenly the bar fills with leather. Thumping helmets and
groaning bar stools blend with a fusillade of popping brass
snaps and zippers. The April nights hadn't warmed much since
Breakout day, the 1st, the day the bikes hit the road after winter,
and the frosty air demands extra gear. Hearty handshakes and
greetings fly all around as the Hell's Angels form a ragged circle
on the far corner of the bar.

"This is C.J., Carlos, Big Al, Nasty Nick, 'Z', Tony A,
Bouncin' Bob . . . ." go the introductions. Each Angel nods
warily. The eye is automatically drawn to the studs and insignia
on their leathers, and the colors, their patch, on their backs – the
menacing club trademark: "HELL'S ANGELS" in red letters
arching over the gold-and-white winged and helmeted death's
head, and "SALEM", the chapter location, on a rocker below.
Some scratch where their helmet strap crushed their wind-
scattered beards. Others take their long hair off their faces. Yet
most have short hair and are clean shaven. And none are
wearing dirty clothes.

But make no mistake. This is the genuine item. Individually
they're impressive. As a pack they're imposing.

"Every time a Hell's Angel gets into trouble the media
reports it and the papers print it and everyone just assumes
that it's true," C.J., the current Salem chapter president,
quietly declares. "Then when it's over and we're innocent
the story is never written. There's never a retraction," says

the stocky, short haired man in his mid-thirties. Like their brothers across the country, the Salem members insist that the club is a victim of bad press, tall tales, and police harassment. The club is not, they say, a front for organized crime. And the actions of individual members should not reflect on the club as a whole.

"We make the club. The club don't make us," calmly explains the massive, six-six Big Al in a deep baritone that would be the envy of an opera star. His huge, gold "Big Al" belt buckle makes him look like a professional wrestler.

Bouncin' Bob, the most articulate Angel, and also the most agitated, jumps in. "They're targeting us. If you target any group long enough you're going to find something dirty," shouts the frizzy haired biker in a cut-off denim vest. "If they targeted the *Elks* and watched the *Elks* they're gonna find something dirty!" he exclaims.

But the cops say they've found more than dirt – they point to the recent arrest of Mark "Rebel" McKenna on loansharking charges as proof that the local Angels have graduated from petty crime and intimidation into a dangerous partnership in the local Mob's loansharking and drug enterprises.

"Are you affiliated with any federal agency or local or state police group?" drawls Nasty Nick somewhat dreamily, totally out of context, his thin face hidden behind dark aviator shades and his long hair pulled into a tight ponytail.

"Sure some Hell's Angels are convicts," Bouncin' Bob persists, stabbing a beefy finger downward as if to nail each point to the floor. "But that doesn't mean anything about the club. If one guy in the K. of C. goes sour does that mean the whole K. of C. is bad? No! And why don't the papers and the cops and feds target some of these crooked politicians? Why aren't they calling the Senate a criminal organization, and harassing Senators and politicians?

"The feds are just using us to justify spending money they get to go after bikers," Bouncin' Bob continues. The Angels know that their colors and bikes, their pack habits, make them easy targets.

"Hey Bob, why don't you just shut the fuck up and let someone else say somethin'?" Tony "A" shouts from a few stools down. "You never stop shootin' your mouth off!" scolds the lanky, balding man with a death's head tattoo on one side of his high forehead and the acronym A.F.F.A, "Angels Forever – Forever Angels' tattooed on the other.

"No I won't shut the fuck up because I want to know," Bouncin' Bob retorts, raising the temperature a few more notches. Confusion reigns as the others crowd closer with rapid-fire support until the soft-spoken C.J. cuts it all off with a point of his own.

"Look at how much cocaine and pot has been stolen out of State Police property rooms," he begins, "and how much was probably stolen by the State Police and sold. That doesn't make the State Police a criminal organization. And neither are we," he concludes, restoring a rough sort of decorum to the scene.

But the K. of C., the Elks, and the Senate and State Police aren't *all* convicts. And when confronted with the fact there isn't a single Massachusetts Hell's Angel who isn't a convicted felon, C.J. answers with a mischievous grin. "Yeah," he says, "that's a safe bet. I think we're all felons".

It's this kind of proud, smirking embrace of outlaw status that has defined the Hell's Angels for the last three decades, and shaped America's attitudes toward the club. From Jesse James to D.B. Cooper, Americans have always been fascinated by outlaws, seeing something of themselves in the defiant loner who trashes society's rules, who gives the law a run for its money. Solid citizens envy the outlaw's reckless freedom – and there is nothing freer than a half-dressed Angel roaring his gleaming Harley down the highway on a hot summer day.

Throughout history, every war has produced marauding bands of disenchanted vets unable to re-assimilate the social norm. When the Civil War ended they were on horseback, but the horse was supplanted by a gas-guzzling steed after World War II when some servicemen returning to California rejected the pre-war routine of wives, homes, and children, and decided to chase action and speed on big bikes in the company of like-minded vets. The Angels were formed by men like these in Fontana, California, in 1950, but the public image of the Angels – and, to a degree, the Angel's image of themselves – has been molded by Hollywood and the mass media right from the start.

Take the name. The Angels say it's taken from a Los

Angeles-based WWII fighter squadron, but a more likely source is a 1930 Jean Harlow movie of the same name about a mythical Air Corp fighter group. But far more significant in terms of image was the 1954 Marlon Brando movie "The Wild One" – loosely based on a 1947 incident in Hollister, California – which would indelibly stamp all motorcycle clubs, particularly the Angels, as plundering thugs on wheels, a clear and present danger to tranquility, sobriety, and virginity. Forget that the Hollister riot was much less than what Hollywood made of it; and forget that the Angels didn't even exist at the time. The die was cast.

Of course, the Angels did their best to improve upon the foundation Hollywood had provided. Taking their cue from Brando's response to the question, "What are you rebelling against?" – "Whattaya got?" – the Angels slowly transformed themselves from a gang of hard-drinking, hell-raising ex-servicemen into a savage-looking tribe of outcasts, bristling with hair, tattoos, earrings, and menace. Gone was the World War II service cap made famous by Brando, replaced by the helmet of the German *Wermacht*. The leather flight jacket stayed, but the Angels improved it, festooning it with malicious-looking studs and chains, and – improbably enough, given the club's bellicose patriotism – swastikas, SS lightning bolts, and Iron Crosses, the military regalia of the enemy their founders had defeated. Little or none of the Storm Trooper paraphernalia survives today, but the idea was to shock and frighten the two-kids-a-dog-and-a-mortgage crowd. And it worked. Finally, true to the biker's motto "Live to ride, ride to live," some Angels rejected steady work, finding petty crime more conducive to life on the road.

This, along with their native hostility, brought the Angels into frequent contact with their natural adversaries – if spiritual brethren – the local cops. Which was fine when the charges were assault, drunkenness, and destruction of property. But when a string of gang-rape charges were brought against club members (few ended in convictions) in California beginning in 1964, panting press coverage turned the Angels into a national threat overnight. In uniquely American fashion, this notoriety blossomed into a kind of celebrity for the Angels: Ken Kesey and the Merry Pranksters bestowed a hip benediction on the Angels by inviting their participation in his California acid tests in 1965; a string of B-movies celebrated their new status in the late sixties; and on the advice of the Grateful Dead, who had met the gang while performing as the house band for the acid tests, the Rolling Stones hired the Angels – for $500 worth of beer – as security for their free concert at Altamont Speedway in December 1969. The Angels' repeated beatings of spectators, and their role in the killing of Meridith Hunter, crushed the promise of Woodstock and stomped the decade to a close.

The sixties were a kind of long, ferocious coming-out party for the Angels, but all the noise served only to attract more police attention in California, and, later, in other states. But the law effort was fragmented and more of an annoyance to the club than a deterrent, serving only to heighten the confrontational nature of cop-biker relations. Chapters spread through California and finally, in 1967, to the East Coast when Skeets Piccard went West to convince Ralph "Sonny" Barger, legendary president of the Oakland, California Angels, to grant a charter for a Lowell, Massachusetts chapter. Barger, reluctant at first, feeling that the distances involved would create a control problem, finally relented. A New York chapter followed and in 1969, another charter was issued for a chapter in Salem, Massachusetts. Barger's concerns soon proved unfounded, and over the next decade the club would grow into a worldwide organization boasting chapters throughout the U.S., Canada, Europe and Australia, with sprinklings around the globe – 64 chapters in 13 countries. And though police did their best to keep a hard thumb on the clubs, using many of the tactics they still employ, like motor vehicle violations, unlawful assembly and disturbing the peace, the Hell's Angels were fast becoming an organization over which local authorities had little or no power.

In the early seventies the feds entered the picture. Alarmed by the growing number of bikers involved in federal crimes, like truck hijacking, manufacture of drugs, and interstate transportation of explosives and weapons, and recognizing the threat of a connection between bikers and the traditional Mob, the feds turned their attention primarily toward the big four – Hell's Angels, Outlaws, Pagans and Bandidos. Armed with toughened gun control laws and the RICO Act of 1962, the feds have spent much of the last two decades busting the bikers out of existence, an endeavor which, to a great extent, is succeeding. Since 1972, the Department of the Treasury, Bureau of Alcohol, Tobacco, and Firearms, has investigated over 8,000 suspects who are gang members or associates, as well as about 4,000 fringe members, and another 8,000 female associates. The investigations were part of "Operation One Percenter", (so named because of estimates that only one percent of motorcyclists are outlaws). And in March, 1986, ATF arrested seven New England bikers, five from Massachusetts, including two Hell's Angels and one H.A. associate, on charges ranging from assault and battery to unlawful possession of firearms and explosives. ATF concludes that over 800 outlaw motorcycle gangs [OMG] are operating worldwide.

In May, 1985, a two year national investigation by the FBI called "Operation Roughrider" reached 11 Hell's Angels chapters in seven states. More than 125 arrests were made on charges ranging from assault to drug trafficking, and more than 100 of those arrested were identified as members of the Hell's Angels Motorcycle Club. Four Massachusetts Angels – two from the Salem chapter and two from the Berkshires chapter – were convicted. Then in November, 1987, 16 Hell's Angels from Alaska, California, North and South Carolina, and Kentucky were indicted for interestate transport of explosives and explosive devices with intent to kill and injure. The feds say the charges stem from the Angels' ongoing feud with the Outlaws, a rival OMG operating in the southeast. Sonny Barger was among those arrested.

So the Massachusetts clubs, particularly the Salem and Berkshire Hell's Angels chapters, have been sweating the legal heat shoulder to shoulder with Angels all over the country. The kind of heat that makes a sharp lawyer an even better ally than a brother Angel.

The sun hovers low and looks like a porthole to a blast furnace as it begins to cook the moist morning air, but the coolness left from the night chills the sheets over Michael Natola, a young Boston criminal lawyer, and his wife Jill. It's 6:06 on Tuesday, June 9th, 1987. The phone beside the bed rings. Natola's been expecting this call for a year and a half. He takes a deep breath and rests the receiver on his ear as a Salem Hell's Angel tells him that federal agents looking for Mark "Rebel" McKenna have just beaten down his door with a sledge hammer.

It's a familiar scene. Men dressed in blue nylon windbreakers with FBI stenciled on their backs for a quick make in a fire-fight, burst into a suspect's home in early morning, roust the sleeping occupants and usually take someone out in bracelets. In the bust business it's your basic early morning raid. But this time the hooks come up empty. McKenna, the upstairs tenant in the Lynn duplex, wasn't home.

Natola slides the phone back onto the nightstand. "They're looking for Rebel," he says as he rolls out of bed. His wife Jill, also a lawyer, isn't surprised. Natola pulls on a pair of jeans, heads downstairs and begins making calls – the FBI, Justice Department, and personal contacts who can help him locate his client before the feds.

From the cellular in his white BMW humming along the Mass Pike he gets within one call of his client. By 9 a.m. he's sure he'll find McKenna before the feds do, and walk him in. Later that morning, with Rebel safely beside him in the car, he calls the FBI in Boston and leaves a message and his number. Within minutes his call is returned.

"I told them I had McKenna with me and I'd be bringing him in shortly, but I was going to stop by my office first just to wolf down a sandwich," he says. "The agent said, 'Take your time, enjoy your lunch. If *you've* got him that's good enough for us' ". Natola is well known in the Law Enforcement community and believes that a policy of voluntary surrender is in a client's best interest.

Ten days later, Friday, June 19th, Mark McKenna and 10 other men, including one paroled murderer, are arraigned in Federal court on 82 counts in connection with a $3.5 million loanshark operation. The indictments result from wiretaps of private lines, bugging of Fasad's, a Revere nightclub frequented by Mob figures and some Hell's Angels, and the seizure of an alleged loansharking record book during a January 8th, 1986, FBI and State Police raid on the club.

McKenna – slight, perhaps five-five in boots, the only Hell's Angel indicted – looks pretty harmless despite his long, un-kempt beard, scraggy hair, and leather jacket. Yet the feds say he is a collector, an enforcer. And as any seasoned cop or criminal lawyer can tell you, weapons, not appearances, constitute the threat.

"It's all bullshit," said McKenna. But his arrest is viewed differently by the feds, who believe it's added confirmation of what they have long suspected – that the Angels in Massachusetts have graduated from minor league criminals to a dangerous free agent partnership in the big league of the Mob. The feds hope to bring more indictments related to an alleged drug ring operating out of Fasad's, and they believe more Hell's Angels are involved.

"In some cases the government and local authorities have been overzealous in their pursuit of the Hell's Angels," says Natola, McKenna's lawyer, and at 34, thanks mostly to the Hell's Angels, a seasoned pro in the criminal courts. From his stylish Boston waterfront office the Medford native coolly lists "all of the Hell's Angels in Massachusetts" as his clients. However his reputation with the club crosses state lines and Natola has travelled the country defending Angels on charges ranging "from littering to murder one". He is quick to caution his clients against answering questions from the press and readily admits that it's nearly impossible to mount a defense when evidence against a client includes his own recorded words.

Natola earned his street sense while growing up in Medford and the North End and, later, his Law Degree at Suffolk. He travels with ease between the two personas – the articulate court pro explaining an intricate case and the street wise kid confirming an observation with a hearty "you got that right, bubba!". Natola "hooked up" with the Angels while working for Everett attorney Al Farese. His first case involving a Hell's Angel was Commonwealth vs. Dennis Ring, a former club member accused of murder in a 1980 shooting at Jessel's Grill in Malden. Ring was acquitted. "He [Farese] would send me into court and they [Angels] liked the way I worked and the results. It's as simple as that". His cases come strictly through referrals, and though he's often introduced as the "Hell's Angels' attorney" he only works on a fee per case basis, and not on retainer.

Natola's tastes run more to natty clothes and sports cars than to cut-off denim jackets and bikes. And he is far more likely to devour a Le Carré novel than to thumb the pages of *Easy Rider*

Magazine. His objective attitude toward his clients, toward the Angels in particular, is blunt. "I'd rather associate with some of those guys [Hell's Angels] than with a lot of lawyers I know," he says. He is a family man, with one infant child and another on the way, and a shrewd businessman who has aligned himself with a group constantly in need of a good criminal lawyer. "Many of the Hell's Angels I know come from shattered homes, alcoholic parents, and just about the worst possible childhood experiences imaginable," he says, explaining why some may be incorrigible. "Many end up with their own drinking or drug problems," he adds, describing a world far removed from his own professional grooming and solid family ties. But like any good businessman, he feels his fee must be secure before he can invest his time.

Natola is aware that his defense of the Angels, both in court and on a personal level, is a nettlesome stance. He knows his work puts him in direct opposition to the law guys. Some of them respect him, consider him a square shooter concerned with doing his best for his clients. But others are less than complimentary. "As far as I'm concerned, he's too involved with these people," says State Police Sergeant Mike Phair, 42, who keeps tabs on bikies. "When they call he's there in two minutes. It's like they own him."

But the need for legal representation is foremost in Natola's decision to take a case. "The fact that somebody did a particular act," he says, "like strike somebody else or even stab or shoot somebody, doesn't necessarily mean they are guilty of anything. And guilt or innocence is the ultimate question that either the judge or the jury must answer." But the deck is stacked against him to begin with, Natola insists: "Let's face it," he says. "A Hell's Angel couldn't get a fair trial in this state, not with the kind of publicity that's been engendered over the past few years."

What Natola says may be true – but it's not as if the Angels are merely hapless victims of bad press. Sure, despite their history and well-earned reputation for skull-cracking and unpredictable mayhem, today's Hell's Angels won't surround you some night on Route 128, force you off the road, beat you and rape your wife. Although they are the same hardcore bikies who roared out of California and onto America's front pages in the sixties – trailing a dark exhaust of beatings, rape charges and outrageous public behaviour and hysteria – today's Hell's Angel is more sophisticated, more subtle.

But they aren't Eagle-Scouts-run-amok, either. And the feds say that Hell's Angels and other outlaw bikers are becoming the oddfellows of organized crime here in Massachusetts and in other Mob strongholds around the country. As the Justice Department sifts through the small change in the pockets of the Mob, Hell's Angels and assorted bikers turn up like bad pennies, over and over again.

The feds have long feared the Mob-Bikie connection. In his opening statement before a Senate subcommittee on Investigations in February, 1983, Oliver B. Revell, then Assistant Director of the Criminal Investigative Division of the FBI, said that ". . . in some instances these gangs [Hell's Angels, Bandidos, Outlaws and Pagans] have established relationships with the L.C.N. [La Cosa Nostra] and are acting as enforcers."

In Massachusetts, authorities believe the Hell's Angels have taken over ancillary mob enterprises, such as loanshark enforcement and drug distribution, once tended by the defunct East Boston/Revere-based Trampers, a rival motorcycle gang which disintegrated in 1985 and 1986 in a prolonged burst of bad luck and violence. Numerous street informants link a Hell's Angel called "Buster" with Jason Angiulo, 31, son of jailed Boston Mafia kingpin Gennaro Angiulo. And wiretap applications from the Strike Force investigation centering on Fasad's, the Revere bar, are said to prominently link the two. The loansharking charges which felled Salem Angel Mark "Rebel" McKenna are likely only the first round from the Fasad's surveillance. Another wave of indictments is expected, and more Hell's Angels may be going down hard.

Although the feds and the State Police have been tracking an Angel–Angiulo connection for years, McKenna's arrest is the first to make it explicit. Yet the strength and breadth of the association remains unknown. Current evidence only implicates members of the Salem H.A. chapter, and the Lowell and Berkshire chapters are yet to be connected. (The cops say the Angels comprise 60 of the state's estimated 200 outlaw motorcylists, and about 30 are members of the Salem chapter;

the Angels say their *total* state membership is 25, and about half
are Salem chapter members.)

Naturally, the Angels bitterly deny any connection to the
Mob, chalking it all up to police targeting and prosecutorial
harassment – the desire of the law guys to ice them, at any cost,
on any charge. They are outsiders to the Mob, they say, and the
Mob doesn't trust outsiders. And though their social habits may
overlap those of known Mob associates, they insist that as a club
they aren't involved with *any* other group, whether it be the
Mob, the Masons, or the Red Cross.

"That thing about us being Jason Angiulo's bodyguard just
isn't true," C.J. says. "I know him, personally, and think he's a
nice guy. And some other members know him, and some have
gotten help finding regular jobs. Whether that led to anything
else, though, I don't know," he explains. "And I don't *want* to
know, because it would be harmful to the club," he adds, ever
mindful of the conspiracy aspects of RICO. C.J. says that the
only protection he might afford Jason Angiulo is not letting him
drive drunk.

But not even the Angels' high-octane blend of paranoia and
denial can incinerate the violent record of the Massachusetts
club during the last ten years.

Consider:

November 4, 1979: Children playing in a Lynn dump find the
handless, headless body of Robert Garbino, 22, of Lynn,
wrapped in carpet bound with lamp cord. His head and hands
are later found buried in the yard of his Lynn residence. He had
been shot in the head, back and shoulder, and sections of his
skin were peeled, presumably to remove identifying tattoos. His
blood-soaked clothes were found in a dumpster nearby, along
with a Hell's Angels patch. Police say Garbino, a disapproved
Hell's Angel prospect, was killed by the club as payback for a
drug rip-off. No charges are brought.

January 11, 1980: Lynn police follow Angels Alan Hogan and
Robert Montgomery to a Middleton house trailer being converted into a methamphetamine lab for a million dollar a year
business. Hogan and Montgomery are jailed in the scheme,
along with brother Angel Thomas Apostolos, from New Hampshire, the "cooker"/chemist. Two non-Angels turn state's evidence and enter the witness protection program. State Police

say the Angels attempt to track them down and silence them. Three Canadian murders – a Hell's Angel, his wife, and mother, are directly linked to the case.

August 4, 1981: In the first case linking the Hell's Angels in New England to organized crime, two Bridgeport, Conn., members, Daniel Bifield and his father Richard, are convicted as loanshark collectors for made members of the Genovese crime family. Both get 20 years.

May 1985: The FBI's "Operation Roughrider" nets five Massachusetts Hell's Angels. Steve Sullivan, 32, known as "Fee", from Lynn; Linwood Barrett III, 30, a.k.a. "Lee", from Lynn; and Glenn "Hoppy" Main, 35, also from Lynn, are charged with conspiracy to distribute cocaine. Barrett is released, but Sullivan and Main get three years. Berkshire Angels Frank Briggs, 29, from Pittsfield, and Julio "Jules" Lucido, 34, from Pittsfield, are also snared on drug charges. Briggs gets one year, 90 days served and the rest suspended, and Lucido receives 4 years committed, 3 years parole, 3 years probation, and is fined $10,000.

March 1986: ATF's "Operation One Percenter" fells Hell's Angel George Harvey, 36, of Revere, and Peter Lazarus, Jr., 28, of Lynn, an associate and Hell's Angel prospect who never made membership, on firearms charges. Lazarus gets probation but later, in an unrelated case, pleads to coke charges and gets 7 to 10 years in the state prison at Walpole. Harvey serves a year in Danbury.

Guns, dope, conspiracy, possibly murder and dismemberment. Even the Angels would admit it's hard to roll up a rap sheet this long and lurid without really trying. And despite McKenna's arrest, there is no real evidence to suggest that the club as a whole has thrown in with the Mob – just a long list of individual members caught in pursuit of various scams.

But these are only the highlights in the Angels' running skirmish with the law. Far more indicative of the bruising relations between the Angels and the cops was the September, 1984 State Police arrest of Salem Angel Billy Leary – since killed in a bike crash – and another biker for OUI after following them from Jacob's Ladder, a nightclub in Revere. While the staties were attempting to strip-search Leary at the Peabody barracks, all hell broke loose. Three counts of assault and battery, and three counts of making threats are brought against Leary, who was ultimately acquitted. But it is this kind of fracas that defines police harassment for the Angels, and confirms the Angels' bad-ass reputation with the cops.

Anti-police feelings are so strongly woven into the Angels fabric that C.J., president of the Salem chapter, says it was his prime motivation for joining the club. "When I was young and we'd hang out on Lynn beach, the cops used to harass us," he explains slowly and quietly. "Like some of the people were like hippies who were just sittin' on the beach with a bottle of wine or something, and the cops would come by and push them around or arrest them," he relates. C.J. says he was drawn to the Angels "because then there'd always be someone to stick together with and not have to take any crap".

There's no doubt that many losers, misfits and tough guys seek out the Angels because it's the only fraternity that exalts their station. But camaraderie and mutual defense were the membership benefits that appealed to C.J., the same kind of appeal the police force might hold for a young recruit.

This connection helps explain the unlikely mixture of grudging respect and hatred that characterizes Angel–police relations. The cops represent the authority that the Angels despise; the Angels celebrate the subversion, license and chaos that the cops fear. Yet, in many ways, the Angels and the cops are remarkably similar: both consider themselves elite groups, apart from the rest of society, with their own unwritten codes, a strong suspicion of outsiders, and a familiarity with force and violence. The cop's badge is the Angel's colors. The biggest thing that separates them is the law.

In his 1966 book, *Hell's Angels*, journalist Hunter S. Thompson says this of the link between the Angels and the law guys:

"In most cases, and with a few subtle differences, they operate on the same emotional frequency. Both the cops and the Angels deny this. The very suggestion of a psychic compatibility will be denounced – by both groups – as a form of Communist slander. But the fact of the thing is obvious to anyone who has ever seen a routine confrontation or sat in on a friendly police check at one of the Angel bars. Apart, they curse each other savagely, and the brittle truce is often jangled by high-speed chases and brief, violent clashes that rarely make the papers. Yet behind the sound and the fury, they are both playing the same game, and usually by the same rules."

It's a long, long way from the Angels' seamy Log Cabin den to the pale, shadowless quarters of the federal Bureau of Alcohol, Tobacco and Firearms in the towering JFK federal building in downtown Boston. The walnut, carpeted office of ATF Special Agent-in-Charge Terrence McArdle, a quiet corner oasis amid the stark cubicles, is unusually cluttered with stacks of papers and cartons as the bureau prepares to comply with a GSA "forced move" directive. Atop one box is a framed copy of the U.S. Treasury Prohibition Bureau credentials carried by the legendary Elliot Ness, head of the "Untouchables", the forerunner of the ATF. McArdle, a fit man of 44, moves bruskly about the office, packing and speaking rapid fire. Tom D'Ambrosio, 33, ATF's motorcycle coordinator, is listening calmly on the couch. His quiet, unobtrusive manner and preppy attire is striking contrast to McArdle's agressive street-cop, black-shoe-blue-suit bureaucratic style. But despite their apparant differences, their philosophies merge when talk turns to outlaw bikers, whom both describe in the same relentless terms that the Angels use on the cops. McArdle and D'Ambrosio stand on one side, the Angels on another, separated by Ness's credentials and the respect for the law that they imply.

These are the law guys.

Yet even in the heart of the federal law enforcement apparatus, there is some ambiguity about the Angels and what they represent. "They *do* possess a strange charisma," observes D'Ambrosio. "And if you admire anything about them," he continues, sliding to the edge of the couch, "it's that they are principled, and they live by those principles," referring to their pledged loyalty to the club above all else.

McArdle, on the other hand, is quick with his own view of those principles: "The crimes they are associated with start on the letter A and end on the letter Z," he states without the slightest equivocation, and D'Ambrosio agrees. A 1986 ATF press release called bike gangs the "1986 version of Murder Incorporated," and McArdle insists that "outlaw motorcycle gangs are organized criminals who would use any type of resource to obtain their goals."

"They'll tell you they're just a fun-lovin' group of guys – and that's a bunch of bullshit," he adds. "They are hard-core, career criminals and I personally think they'd do anything for a buck, for anybody," McArdle argues. "They rent out their facilities, their resources, to other organized groups, such as the LCN, the Mafia."

McArdle and D'Ambrosio insist that the proof is in the Angels–Angiulo connection, which they say transcends the cocktail-hour socialities the Angels describe. D'Ambrosio believes that Jason Angiulo bankrolled several companies called American Towing. The business, which is considered a high-activity spot frequented by Hell's Angels, is located at 60 Bennett street in Lynn but was formerly located at Captain Fowler's Mariner in Revere, an Angiulo property. "You can see the trucks all over Lynn," D'Ambrosio says. "There's an awful lot of Hell's Angels driving those trucks."

Sources say Jason's money and contacts are also behind a coke business run by a Hell's Angel called "Buster" who employs other club members. Future indictments are expected that will likely prove these allegations at least partially true. But D'Ambrosio feels that enough evidence already exists to suggest that the club is in fact a criminal organization. "They are trying to say that anyone who is a member operates as an individual. Be it a legitimate citizen or a lawbreaker, he's not acting on behalf of the club. But I just don't buy it," he says.

Ninety-nine percent of ATF arrests are on weapons charges – mostly felons who are prohibited from owning or posessing guns – and the Angels' police record makes them worth watching. Drugs, on the other hand, are the foremost concern of State Police Sergeant Mike Phair, who's been keeping tabs on the Angels since 1971.

"They're the people doing the major part of the selling of drugs on the North Shore, especially in Essex and Middlesex county," Phair says. To back his charge, he describes a surveilance the Staties conducted at a Revere nightclub he refuses to name.

"We saw a Hell's Angel come, in his colors, on his bike, and make a sale to a doorman. We knew who the Angel was," Phair says, lounging in a swivel chair in the office of Don's Tow on route 99 in Malden. A single fluorescent tube casts a shadow over the massive man's face, and everything is caked with a fine grey dust of metal, paint and body putty grindings. "We sat there longer. The doorman made some sales because they [customers] came right out to their cars, did their lines, then went back in for a drink," he continues. "About two hours later, here comes the same guy back again. Another sale."

But Phair says the Angels' involvement with drugs goes well beyond street sales of the kind he describes. The gang is big and sophisticated, he says, working alonside the Mob, and he agrees, as sources suggest, that it is possible they're operating a massive drug smuggling network complete with trucks, planes, and boats. The Angels' fear of electronic surveillance, one source says, has more than once reduced their meetings to a series of orders written on a chalkboard in silence. "Some writers in the past have made them look like a great bunch of guys," Phair says, explaining that the public view of the Angels swings between fear and fantasy. "Most people are intimidated by them and wonder why anyone would want such a lifestyle. But there are people who envy their freewheeling, reckless attitude," he says. "But you've got to remember," he cautions, "these guys hurt people."

The Angels' threat doesn't necessarily fade once the law guys have done their job and charged a member with a crime, they say. The Angels have a knack for giving pause, a talent for intimidation that the law guys say they use handily during a trial. "I had one trial where seven or eight Angels wearing colors spread themselves through the courtroom to intimidate the jury," Phair says as he describes a drunken-driving arrest he made several years ago in Salem. "One juror recognized me several months later at a shopping center and said she thought they were 'scary looking.' The verdict was not guilty. The tactic may have worked," he says.

"I have already been in court with one of the Angels who made threats that he was going to blow up my house and all this bullshit," he says. "And you see one thing prominent in all their records. Crimes against the person."

Yet, despite the ATF's "Murder Incorporated" rhetoric, and the single-minded dedication of Phair, D'Ambrosio and other law guys, some are a little less dramatic in their assessment of the Angels' importance in the world of crime.

Says New England Organized Crime Strike Force chief
Jeremiah O'Sullivan: "If you think about it in terms of its
significance across the whole community, controlling substantial criminal activities and, more importantly, of its having the
ability to corrupt police departments or court systems in order
to protect their criminal activities, then the Mafia is important
and the Hell's Angels pale in significance, because they just
don't have that ability."

Then O'Sullivan quickly adds: "That's not to say that they're
not individually madmen and dangerous. And to the degree that
there's interaction between violent members of the Mafia and
violent Hell's Angels, it's a problem.

"I look at their records from time to time," he says, "and, I
mean, there are some pretty bad dudes . . . . ."

The empty brown bottles are crowding the bar and the noise
level in the Log Cabin has mellowed along with the Angels'
interest in the stranger. "The guys in Toronto gave me this last
summer when I was up there," says "Z", affably showing off a
maple-leaf pin on the collar of his brown leather. "This too," he
says, proudly tugging his sleeve to show an embroidered "Canada" patch on his shoulder. At the end of the bar a couple of
Angels begin to collect their gear. The prospect of a cold ride
home inspires thoughts of warmer weather, and travel. "You
gonna make the Sun Jam this year?" someone asks, referring to
one of the many weekend runs, social mainstay of the clubs, that
happen throughout summer. By now the rippling horsepower is
firing up outside, and most of the Angels are drinking up and
readying to leave.

"If you have the time you should come to our summer cook-
out and meet the families," "Z" says as he offers his handshake
and heads for the door. "You'd see we're not just a bunch of
criminals. We have families, kids. We barbecue chicken and
stuff, and get a couple kegs of beer. It's a real good time," he
says.

Outside, several Angels are astride their warming machines,
polishing a gas cap with a rag, pulling on fleece lined gloves,
admiring each other's iron. Most of the bikes are stock spec –
the days of the street choppers are gone. But they dress their
road bikes with perfect paint jobs, and replace many painted

factory parts with chrome. And even the closest scrutiny wouldn't produce a smudge.

Singly, or in pairs, they begin to pull out. "See you Wednesday." "Ten o'clock." Nod. The compression from the tailpipes kicks up the gutter dust and the big Harleys thunder away. Their woes with the law guys have been shoved aside to make room for a brighter outlook on the upcoming motorcycling season. For now, the Angels have had their say, have spelled out their position, completely, articulately, and angrily. But they know their complaints of harassment will be largely unheeded, and their contention that they're being unfairly persecuted will be largely ignored. And, above all, they know that the constant vigil of the laws guys will continue to be a way of life as long as they wear the Hell's Angels patch.

OUTLAW BIKERS POLISH THEIR THUGGISH IMAGE

*This police-originated article asserts that one-percenter
outlaw bikers are involved in public relations campaigns
designed to influence public opinion in the clubs' favour.
It presents the police take on what are, ostensibly,
charitable acts by outlaw bikers. Make up your own
mind . . .*

Pamela Anderson Lee, Jean-Claude Van Damme and Sylvester
Stallone. Maybe these aren't people you would normally associate with the Hells Angels, but they all use members or their
body guard agencies for personal protection. Members of outlaw biker gangs are owning and controlling more and more
"protection services." It puts them in contact with influential,
powerful and wealthy people. And it's very lucrative.

Hollywood "Hulk" Hogan strides into the ring to begin
another World Championship Wrestling promotion for the
next big fight. Fans are screaming – growing more excited as
the Hulk promises an unforgettable fight. Suddenly the air is
filled with a loud revving, which becomes louder as six Hells
Angels wearing colours roar into the ring on Harleys. Above the

deafening noise of the Harleys and the crowd, Hulk explains that he has the support of the Hells Angels. "The Hells Angels are now behind me," he announces. After such a public display of alliance, the Hells Angels enter the mainstream of the television wrestling world. It's a highly calculated commercial plot designed to portray the bikers as glamourous, slickly vicious role models. It's also largely directed at young members of the audience who would be open to buying Hells Angels' affiliated products – Big Red Machine merchandise.

And the Hells Angels' promotion of their name, image and products has been successful. Students attending some high schools in BC have been seen wearing Big Red Machine T-shirts. The larger OMGs have products through which consumers can display their support of the gangs – telephone cards with "Support your local Hells Angels" logos and bumper stickers with "Support your local Outlaws." This merchandise provides a much-needed source of legitimate revenue, but more importantly, it brings the gangs into the consumer mainstream.

OMGs are growing increasingly adept at using (and abusing) the media to portray outlaw biker gangs as unfairly and wrongly persecuted, legitimate motorcycle clubs. As in most OMG activities, the Hells Angels lead the way in using sophisticated public relations. OMGs' public relations campaigns – or sanitizing campaigns as they are known to law enforcement – are methodically designed to discount the gangs' past criminal history. They all admit they were "wild boys" in the "old days" before they reformed. But they continue to deny that they are organized crime groups. Gangs also deny that an individual member's criminal record is the result of organized criminal activities in the club.

Outlaw biker gangs have a policy to avoid police and public scrutiny as much as possible. They prefer that their criminal activities be shrouded in myths and misinformation. But when outlaw bikers do enter the public spotlight, they emphasize their "charity" work. As many in law enforcement have noted, outlaw bikers only perform good Samaritan acts in front of cameras or to manipulate local communities. Along with the already familiar Teddy Bear runs and Toys for Tots, the Hells Angels have participated in blood donor drives, motorcycle rides for handicapped children in France, tours of club-houses in Australia and have given presents to needy children at Christmas. In San Jose, California, bikers erected a billboard saying, "Hells Angels Against Dope." Definitely not true. The Hells Angels have written books and made videos explaining that their gang is a legitimate motorcycle club.

In Denmark, some Hells Angels wrote Parliament to ask for interviews with various parliamentary committees. Some Hells Angels also volunteered to lecture Danish Parliament on organized crime. Bikers Against Child Abuse (BACA) offer the following solution to abused children. The participating bikers will gather en masse to greet an abused child in front of his/her neighbourhood and the perpetrator/s. After this intimidating show of force, they give the child a patch to demonstrate his/her protected status.

Outlaw biker gangs are also making legal and constitutional challenges supposedly to protect and promote the rights of all bikers. They've joined with groups like BRO (Bikers' Rights Organization) to protest helmet laws, among other issues. The Hells Angels have applied for protection under human rights legislation, claiming members, while wearing their colours, are discriminated against by restaurants and bars. The Confederation of Clubs, formed of outlaw and non-outlaw bikers, has a mandate to inundate the Public Complaint systems in Canada and the US and initiate civil suits against the police and other government agencies. The Confederation is controlled by major OMGs like the Hells Angels who seek to disrupt police activities and paralyse the courts.

BROTHERHOOD OF OUTLAWS

Bob "Bitchin" Lipkin

This selection describes the bonding of both club and non-club riders in their perception of government and police as their main lifestyle problem. In his own colourful and insightful fashion, Bob describes one attempt at organizing bikers to break laws which are driven by economic motives of the Establishment rather than alleged concerns for biker safety. A truly biker story . . .

Leroy Makelray of KABD news felt his body instinctively flinch in fear as 30,000 motorcycles rumbled toward him. He stood on an overpass to do the network feed while the cameras would tape the pack passing below them like an endless, roaring snake.

Traffic on the Golden State freeway sped on mindless. Sometimes being in the news business gave a real insight into the stupidity of man. Leroy wasn't sure that he liked that. He could remember when he thought man was an intelligent animal, endowed as no other with free choice. But that was long ago. He'd lost a little of the pride he used to have in his species. *Homo Sapiens*. Wiseman. He now realized how futile it really was to try and fight the real power: Money.

Like the stupid-ass bikers that would soon pass below. They had worked for almost a year solid trying to put together this protest, trying to get the helmet law repealed nationwide. Leroy knew that they were right, that law was about as unconstitutional as slavery, but there was more money on the side of the helmet manufacturers and the federal government than on the side of the bikers. So their cause was lost from the start.

The mandatory helmet law for motorcyclists was a brainstorm of the safety establishment in the federal government. On the surface the reasoning was simple: Bikers are too dumb to know what is good for them, therefore the police must force them to wear hard hats whether they like it or not. In truth, the safety bureau didn't give a damn about the bikers' heads. They were going to ban motorcycles anyway. What they needed was a legal precedent to force mandatory self-protection on car drivers and passengers. That's where the big money was. Nobody would pay much attention to a biker's rights and the motorcyclists themselves were too dumb and disorganized to do anything about it.

What worried him was what might happen when the bikers learned how futile their fight was. This was the first time that bikers had ever joined together for a political cause and it scared him a little. These people are not your normal citizens. They are just apt to really get mad, and if they do there was no telling what might happen.

Earlier he had asked what they would do if they lost the helmet law battle. Their leader was a large and scary individual by the name of Treb Lincoln. Lincoln stepped off his bike, towering above the newsman and camera, looked hard at Leroy and shrugged.

"Hell man, I'm just a dumb biker. If they don't drop the lid law I don't guess I can control my brothers here. They're likely to get a mean attitude."

Leroy knew that it was all carefully staged. For the first time the bikers had a cause and a real leader. Lincoln may have said he was just a "dumb biker," but there was something different about him that translated on tape. He was smarter than the rest of the bikers and they showed a fanatical loyalty to him. He had settled all the local gang wars and disputes and brought all of them together for the first time.

Cameraman and sound crew checked their equipment for the last time. Leroy wanted this shot to be just right. They would pick it up at the network in New York. It would be seen by the biggies. This could help his career, although it was a mystery why the network was interested in this bizarre biker item. The glint of chrome cut through the song and haze like needles in his eyes.

It was frightening. All that noise and power could be felt as well as seen and heard. It was like a barbarian invasion, loud and menacing. Leroy swallowed.

When the bikes were in range he gave the sign for the sound to start, and then the camera. He wanted this to be very dramatic. He turned his back to the camera and watched Lincoln lead the bikes down the freeway. Just before he turned to speak, his eyes met Lincoln's and Makelray was startled at the energy that shot through him.

Slowly he turned to face the camera and began to speak.

I glanced up from my speedometer and saw the broadcaster eyeballing down on me. Hell, I hope the pack is centered. I would hate to go to all this horsecrap and lose out on any of the exposure.

My fatbob Harley was running as good as it had ever run and the feel of the vibrating power came right through the handlebars. All I could think about was the snake behind me. I looked into my rearview mirror and once again my heart beat a little harder. Jesus H. Christ, there is no better feeling in the world than leading 30,000 bikes down the road. Unless it might be leading 40,000 bikes down the road.

Just before we passed under the bridge I looked back up at the broadcaster. I had seen him before, at the park. He was kind of a little guy, but he seemed to know the score. I liked him. Most of the newsmen that were sent to cover this protest were cocky new, because, after all, it was just a bunch of bikers sniveling about their rights being stepped on. Makelray was different. Like he knew I had plans for this group. I don't know how, but he knew.

Passing under the bridge made us sound even louder. The thunder roared and it was beautiful. I glanced next to me at Rom and he had this big shiteating grin on his face. I guess the sound was getting to him too.

Rom and I had been through a lot in the last two years together, and this was going to be the payoff. I reached into my cutoff jacket and felt for my security. It was a 357 Magnum. The heft alone made me feel good.

We turned off the Golden State and onto the Pasadena freeway, toward the civic center. Hell, I hope those cops got the blockades up and the traffic re-routed. If they don't, I would just as soon take this pack through downtown Los Angeles. I was sick and tired of the bureaucracy bullshit that had been going on for the last few days and right now I really didn't give a rat's ass if they were ready or not. We got a point to make and brother are we going to make it.

We turned off the Pasadena and onto the Hollywood freeway. Just one more mile to go. As we dropped into the hollow under some bridges the echoing sounds of the pack came back to me and I was ready for anything. I could ride like this forever.

Our off ramp loomed ahead and I slowed the pack from 45 to 30 miles an hour. No use dumping some sidewalk commando and listening to the government turkeys harp on unsafe riding or other such horsecock. This day was set aside for bikers and damnit, that's whose day it is. Period.

As we approached the civic center I could see all the police there. A quick glance up showed a couple of helicopters in the silver sky. I could see this was going to be a well-chaperoned event.

I pulled my Hawg out of the pack and motioned Rom to lead them to where the police had set aside parking. I aimed my scoot toward the curb and hit the throttle. The front end came up off the ground about a foot and jumped right over the curb. I saw a couple of cops unlatch their holsters as I headed for the stand where the loudspeakers were set up. I knew that no cop was going to shoot me with all the bikers pulling in. As I hit the grass I turned on the throttle a little harder and felt the back wheel swerve as the brand new Goodyear Eagle cut its initials into the nice green lawn of city hall.

I could almost hear the groundskeeper swearing, but what the hell, he's getting paid.

When I was next to the pulpit I dropped my kickstand and turned off my engine. All I could hear was the sound of thousands of bikes pulling in.

I pulled a stick of gum out of my pocket and stripped it, throwing the wrapper on the ground. I could see the folks standing around were a little un-nerved so I decided to try and take advantage of it.

I found a long time ago that when you stand six-feet-four and weigh close to 300 pounds there aren't a whole lot of folks who will mess with you.

For the next few minutes Rom and I walked through the bikes as they parked, talking with the presidents of the different clubs. We had established a chain of command and we didn't want to violate it. The clubs all retained their own identity and officers, all we did was try to aim them in one direction. I had kinda picked up this idea from the Romans. They didn't conquer, they just sort of absorbed. They would bend. So did I.

When you're dealing with clubs like the Hell's Angels, Mongols, Hessians and Vagos you can't afford to make mistakes. So far we had been pretty lucky. We had settled their fights and differences, re-aligned the territories to where most of them were happy and gotten most of the outlaw bikers to go along with a truce. That in itself is a chore.

The hard part was getting them to work together. Each club has a terrific pride in its own reputation; they hate to share any glory with any other club. It had been pretty damn ticklish.

The hardest part was to get the police to lay off during this protest. Hell, the police have books on each of the clubs, with the members' rap sheets and what they're wanted for. It took a lot of talking to get them to promise to leave all the bikers alone during this protest. I was still a little leery of their promises, but we had to believe in something.

It took over an hour for the bikes to pour into the parking areas. The place was wall-to-wall bikers. As I stood on the steps looking over them I knew we would win. There was no way we could be ignored now.

I could see television cameras all over and the different newsmen were picking out the dumbest looking bikers to interview so they would look stupid on TV. They didn't know it, but that was exactly what I wanted. Nothing will lull an adversary into a state of overconfidence easier than letting him think you are a bunch of dummies.

I tested the microphone a little bit and when I knew it was working I started to quiet them all down. This was what we had been waiting for.

PART 5

Infamous Biker Wars

Turf disputes have been a part of outlaw biker subculture since 1950. At first there was a certain unity among one-percenter clubs, but then the "patch" or "colours" came to symbolize dominance over area and/or activities. This is understandable, considering the military environment that spawned the new breed of club – the one percenters that emerged at Hollister. But some disputes have escalated into all-out biker wars, complete with very real casualty figures for "killed", "wounded" "missing" and "collateral damage", as described in the selections below.

The first turf war to be referred to in any detail was the conflict between the San Francisco and Oakland Chapters of the Hells Angels. The San Francisco Chapter was an "old-fashioned" outlaw biker club, with women – or more correctly, family members – being associates and even office-bearers. Frank Sedelek was President at the time and his wife, Linda, was Secretary. After a brief but nasty encounter, the Oakland Chapter took the "colours" from the San Francisco Chapter.

A second war occurred in Australia. A small, home-grown outlaw club known as the Comanchero MC split into two factions. The President of the Comancheros ran his outfit on military lines, complete with compulsory physical training. But the leader of the rebel faction (which was more party oriented) flew to the States to receive the blessing of the Bandidos Motorcycle Club to establish the first Australian Chapter of the Bandidos MC. The ensuing war culminated in a shoot-out at Milperra, New South Wales, and is known in one-percenter folk-lore as "The Milperra Massacre".

Another infamous biker conflict – the Great Scandinavian War – is described in a selection from Sher and Marsden's "Angels of Death" and a selection from the *Royal Canadian Mounted Police Gazette*. A final selection from the *Royal Canadian Mounted Police Gazette* describes the bloodiest and longest lasting biker war on record: the epic battle between the Canadian-based Hells Angels and the Rock Machine who were later to become the Bandidos MC.

There are seemingly endless wars and turf battles which have been and still are being waged in the outlaw biker world. That's just the way it is. A form of military mindedness which compels one to defend the colours and the right of the colours to control the turf is said to be behind the madness of murder and mayhem. Well, that is the benign interpretation of the wars. The alternate version is that the wars are about control of criminal activity within that turf.

In the years up to the late 1970s, there seemed to be an understanding amongst the clubs that problems were to be handled at set venues well away from the public eye. Certainly, in Australia and the UK, there were designated venues where the warring clubs battled. However, over time, this changed dramatically. More and more, the clubs attacked each other in the public eye. It is still quite remarkable at this point in the history of the clubs that there have been less than 5 innocent people killed in the battles innocent people meaning non-club members or associates.

The now public wars are a festering boil which fuels public outcry against the outlaw biker clubs. Until the clubs find a way to go private with their disputes and wars, they play directly into the hands of police and government law and order agendas and this may, ultimately, see the end of the counter culture as it is known today. As well, the measures taken by government will even further erode the civil liberties of the dominant culture.

These selections also illustrate that regional differences and/ or cultural factors greatly influence the nature of one percent clubs. It is perplexing why the most liberal countries produce the most violent in the counter culture of one percent clubs.

THROUGH THE EYES OF SNAKE: THE 1984 MILPERRA MASSACRE

Geoffrey Campbell and Felicity Zeiher

Geoff was one of six Campbell brothers, five of whome were shot on the day of the infamous Milperra Massacre in Australia. Three of his family brothers died, while Geoff survived to remain haunted by the events of that fateful day. Geoff's tale is a chilling account of "old-style" biker wars at their worst.

For those of you who are old enough to remember that time in history, what are your recollections? What springs to mind when *you* hear the phrase: *"Milperra Massacre"*

More than likely, it's not too favorable. Thoughts of warring, rampaging savages; wilfully and unconscionably inflicting acts of violence upon innocent citizens: Perhaps. Don't be surprised – those words were gathered from media clippings that you as the public, had, as your only source of information at that time.

For those of you too young to remember, the Milperra Massacre was the dramatic yet completely misleading name given to a piece of Australian history which arose from the confrontation between the Comanchero Motorcycle Club and the Bandidos Motorcycle Club, at the Viking Tavern, Milperra on Father's Day, the 2nd of September 1984.

We were once the same Club, the Comanchero. The Comanchero were divided due solely to the arrogance and violence of the then President, Jock Ross (JR). JR's obsession for revenge against those he felt had deserted and disrespected him led to JR splitting the Comanchero first into two Chapters (City and West). He then abolished our Chapter (City) and dismissed our members as Comanchero. Eventually, our faction was to become the Bandidos MC.

The Campbell family had six brothers in the Bandidos – Caesar, Shadow, Bull, Chop, Wack and I. I was known as "Snake-Eyes".

We were all founding members of the Bandidos MC (Australia). We were the core, strength and backbone of the Club. JR specifically blamed us (the Campbell brothers) for the split in Comanchero loyalty and he believed that we were responsible for several other like minded Members departing from loyalty to JR along with us.

Milperra was JR's ultimate act of redemption against the Campbells. We were the first to be targeted and shot on that day and we were the only Bandidos killed in the Massacre.

Not many people saw a human face and terrible family tragedy woven into this tale of terror. Few, if any, people even entertained the thought that there could have been an alternative picture to be painted of the events and people that were involved in the incidents of that fateful day due to the media and police hysteria about the events of the day.

Think back and ask yourself how many assumptions *you* made. What judgments did you pass on those involved? Did you ever consider that these "rampaging savages" were ordinary men that were unintentional victims of the extraordinary circumstances which took place on that fateful day . . . that a single day may have destroyed families and friends' lives for ever?

Was your voice one of the many that screamed for justice? So moralistic and law abiding in your demand that someone be held accountable for this outrage, that you remained oblivious to the conspiracy of lies and fabrications that your politicians, police and legal system wove so cleverly in their politics of fear to get your vote? While police corruption, as we now know, was rife in the 1980's – what do our Government and Courts offer as their excuse for the gross miscarriage of justice that was the 'Milperra Bikie Trial"?

Treated as we were – guilty until proven innocent – we were held in a maximum security prison while the system sorted through the evidence to see if they had enough evidence to take us to trial. During this committal process we were held on remand for the longest period ever recorded in Australian legal history.

In the end, evidence was fabricated in order to secure convictions, regardless of innocence or guilt. The abuse of the legal system was for the sole purpose of creating a scapegoat for the death of an allegedly innocent bystander and nothing to do with judicial process or justice in the true sense of the word. Police and judicial procedures used against all involved in the Milperra Massacre were illegal and breeched the sanctity of basic human rights in which law abiding and moral citizens take so much pride.

What would you have done, if you were confronted by a man aiming a gun at you? What would your reaction be if that weapon was pointed at someone you loved in your family – your child or your parents? – *What would you do if that gun was aimed at your brothers?* For the Campbells, that was the real and true question at the Milperra Massacre.

Do you think that you would desperately grasp at any means available in order to protect them, even if it meant taking the life of another? Could you honestly say that you wouldn't fight and defend your family's survival in any way possible and that you weren't justified in doing so?

I'm sure that most of you have probably never been shot by a shotgun. The experience is a sensation of searing or burning pain as the tightly knit pellets of lead enter your body. This is soon followed by a sense of excruciating pain as the dozens of small pellets go every which way inside your body. Can you imagine the pain? Picture in your mind the rising terror of thinking that you are dying. Fear and panic overtaking you.

Look up from your book as you sit in the comfort of your surroundings and glance around the room you're in. Could you even begin to comprehend the horror of having *four* of your family, in this case, brothers lying in close proximity, all in the same agony as you – bleeding, moaning, gasping for breath as their life slowly ebbs from them. Imagine the desperation of watching all that is familiar in your life, slowly crumbling in front of your eyes – and there's not a damn thing you can do about it.

I was once like you; never in my wildest dreams would I have thought that I'd experience anything close to what I've described above. It did happen to me, though. It was something that I lived through and now live with.

My first exposure to swap meets and bike shows was at Milperra's Viking Tavern. That was the saddest most gut wrenching day for both my blood and Club brothers as well as me. It was a bolt out of the blue – something that should not have happened. It was a lot like an accident for which you are not at fault but it did . . . all because of a fucked up old Scotsman.

This was my first swap meet and I was really looking forward to it. It was to be held at the Viking Tavern, a popular watering hole located in the Western Sydney suburb of Milperra. It was going to be a chance to spend the morning of my first Father's Day with my wife Pam and our little girl. The rest of the day was to be spent doing what any riding bloke would love – hanging with my bro's amongst motorbike parts and machines. The girls had us on a time limit though – we had to be back at Caesar's house for his son's 6th birthday party by 4pm that afternoon.

The beginning of the day started out according to plan with my beautiful six week old daughter Angie cradled in my arms. My wife Pam was fussing after me as usual, fixing coffee and breakfast. I kissed the top of Angie's head as I handed her back to her Mum, I gave Pam a kiss on the cheek and started getting organized to ride over to my brother Shadow's. I pulled on my Colours and waved goodbye to Pam as I roared out the driveway. I thought about that little kiss I gave Angie and Pam many times in the years to come. I would never have thought for a second that it would be the last time our family would have any kind of normality to it.

I had Shadow to thank for giving that memory to me. A few weeks before we'd been leaving for a run and Shadow had come to my place to meet up before we left. As we went to go, he pulled me up. "You're not going anywhere until you give your girls a kiss, bro."

Heeding those wise words from my older brother, I gave Pam and Angie a kiss goodbye. Pam smiled softly at Shadow. "Thank you," she said.

I was unaware of the imminent trouble. All I was looking forward to was seeing my brothers. I didn't have to wait long; Shadow only lived down the road opposite the train station at Wentworthville along with his girl Joanne and their two young children, Adam and Amy.

Both Pig and Snoddy were already at Shadow's with Bull, Wack and Chop arriving soon after in Bull's gold HZ Holden station wagon. With the boys all gathered we started out toward Lance's house at Bankstown, that's where we were going to decide the day's plans and to leave together as a Club.

Pig got on the back of my bike and we rode off next to Snoddy with the other boys following in Bull's wagon. A few of the Brothers were missing that day. Bongo Snake had been beaten up the week before and was still licking his wounds and Bushy had pulled out sick.

Riding over the railway bridge at Wentworthville, I glanced to my right and spotted a Comanchero standing on the verandah of a ramshackle house. It was Glenn Eaves. He was part of JR's crop of new recruits. These new recruits had been patched up within a matter of months; none had to prove their worth as brothers – just an unquestioning and fanatical loyalty to JR.

I was startled. I had no idea he even lived in the area. I wasn't as startled as Eaves though. As the rumble of Harleys passed him, he bolted inside the house slamming the door behind him. I sniggered to myself, "bet he's shittin' himself".

We pulled up at Lance's and told the bro's about Eaves; "there's no doubt he seen us" I said. The general thought was he would be straight on the phone informing JR that the Bandidos were heading towards Milperra, as it was in the same direction as Lance's house. In the back of my mind though, I knew JR was more interested in where the Campbells were headed rather than the Bandidos MC.

We decided to send some Prospects down to the Viking Tavern. If the Comancheros were down there, the Club planned to head over to Brighton le Sands Pub. The pub had a band on and was in the opposite direction to Milperra.

None of us wanted to go anywhere that was going to have any dramas. So, Val and Maverick left for the Viking Tavern and returned about half an hour later to Lance's place.

"Were there any Commos down there" I asked them.

"No, Snake," they both replied.

"Did you check the bars, the cars, toilets . . . . . . everywhere?"

"Yes," they nodded in affirmation.

Still not satisfied, I asked, "Did you check the ladies toilet?" They responded, "No."

"Well you should of!" I said.

"Snake," they answered in exasperation, "there were no Colours there."

With that we decided it would be safe to go to Milperra. If only we knew that five minutes after the Bandidos Prospects left the pub, the Comancheros had pulled in. They had rode in, Colours blazing with baseball bats and machetes held in scabbards tied to their motorbikes.

Along with JR were our former Club brothers: Sparrow, Leroy, Tonka, JJ, Snow, Leroy, Kraut, and Foghorn. There was also a huge amount of new recruits. Some we had met briefly when the Commos were split into two chapters and before we left completely to become Bandidos: some we'd never seen before. We learnt later they included: Sunshine, Terry Parkes, Andy Thomas, Blowave, Bones, Chewy Lorenz, Glen Eaves, Littlejohn, Morts, Pee Wee and Dog McCoys.

They had the boots of their cars loaded with guns and had deployed their members to both entrances of the Viking Tavern car-park and behind all vantage points around the pub. They were ensuring that there was no chance of escape for us.

We had no idea that the Comancheros would be there – think about it – would you go to a place knowing that there are scum waiting there to ambush you . . . to take your life? I had five family brothers in the Bandidos and there is no way we would have gone to the Viking Tavern knowing that these cunts were there. Why would any of the Campbells endanger their family and their own Club brothers? If we had known – why the fuck weren't we fully armed up? You don't go to a gun battle without guns? It just makes no sense!

★   ★   ★

But we didn't know – none of us did. That's why we headed off toward Milperra. The gold HZ Wagon was first to pull out with Bull behind the wheel. Chop had jumped in the passenger seat next to him with Wack and Roach in the back.

Pig got on the back of my bike and we headed off through the streets of Bankstown. It was a short ride from Lance's to the Viking at Milperra and not less than 15 minutes later we were pulling into the car-park. The sun had bore down on us as we rode along and my thoughts were on a nice cold schooner of beer. I could hear the band playing as I pulled up on the bike and put the side stand down.

Dressed in a singlet and my Colours with a chain in my jean belt, I started making my way down toward the pub. Walking no more than a few paces I looked up, and what I saw stopped me dead in my tracks.

The barrel of a shotgun was aimed straight at me.

In disbelief, I glanced backward over my shoulder to see if there was someone behind me at who he was pointing the gun. No one was there; even Pig had seemingly vanished into thin air!

I turned back and looking him in the eye, asked "Is that for me?"

I lifted my Colours and turned slowly around to show him I had no weapons except for the chain through my jeans and a little buck knife about 4 inches long, in its sheath. I pulled the chain from the belt loops and arms still outstretched I dropped it and the buck knife on the ground.

He didn't move and he didn't reply. The scum was as big as me and I weighed around 18 stone at the time. "Use these," I said in disgust as I held my fists up in the air.

He just shook his head.

Suddenly a gunshot rang out. The first fired on that day. I felt my Colours go back past my left side; as I put my hand down to my stomach I felt the hot spray of blood streaming from my gut.

I realized that it was me who had received the bullet.

. . . I am sure that most of you have probably never been shot? Never experienced the hot sears of lead enter your body and the excruciation of pellets exploding inside you . . .

I was so pissed at this scum I just stood there in disgust.

"You gutless cunt" I glared at him venomously.

I thought about making a run for him, but it was a pump action shotgun and there was no doubt in my mind he would have used another round. The injury had dropped me to my knees by this stage anyway and I lay on the ground, blood continuing to pour from my gunshot wound. It was there as I stared skyward trying to cope with the excruciating pain, that my view was suddenly obscured by the barrel of another shotgun.

Holding on to the trigger was a Comanchero by the name of Leroy. Although Leroy had remained with JR, he was a good man and still a close friend to all the Campbell brothers. Many times, we would egg Leroy, "Come on Bro, come join us over at Birchgrove"; he said he would, but then privately he would say "I can't Snake, I owe him, I'm a man of my word and I can't". He'd given Jock his word that he would remain with him, and being a man of honour, he did.

This is probably why, when I looked at him over the shotty stuck in my face and challenged him with the words "do it then", he just winked at me, turned his gun up toward our bikes and started emptying his bullets into them.

"Not today Snake," he said to me, "not today".

"Put the guns down, fight with your fists," challenged Caesar. The imposing figure of my brother, along with Lance and Zorba, had, in the meantime, walked down to confront the heavily armed Comancheros.

"Just you and me," he said to Leroy? "Everyone else stay out of it".

Just as Caesar drew to his opponent's eye level, a gunshot rang out through the car-park. Startled, he turned toward the sound in time to see me drop to the ground.

"Fuck! That's Snake," was all he could think as he automatically ran to help me. He got no more than a few steps when he was blasted through the back with two shotgun blasts. A third bullet struck him in the shoulder, the power of which, at such close range, ripped through his body so forcefully that it spun him around; which is when he copped the fourth, almost fatal, gunshot wound to his chest.

The gun fight had started in earnest.

Chop fired his gun as he risked running the gauntlet of bullets, trying to get to me. He never made it. Chop was a family brother that, while not a Campbell by birthright, was so incredible that he became a Campbell by choice at just 12 years old. Someone so amazing that to have his light snuffed out by a meaningless moment of bullets was incomprehensible.

Chop would have saved a lot of family lives that day. How so? You ask. He acted to protect his brothers. He arrived at Milperra as a Bandido, but took to arms to defend his family. The only men that had been shot so far were Campbells. It was an obvious set-up, and Chop had realized that it was he and his blood brothers that were the targets. You think – why was I the first to be shot that day? Why was Caesar the only one to be shot when he was standing with two other men in the firing line?

. . . . . . What would you do, if you were confronted by a man aiming a gun at you? What would your reaction be if that weapon was pointed at your brothers? Do you think that you would desperately grasp at any means available in order to protect them . . . even if it meant taking the life of another? Could you honestly say that you wouldn't – and that you weren't justified in doing so?

Chop did, and he is the reason why some Campbells survived to tell the tale and he is the reason so many of the rest of the Club were able to walk out unhurt.

My little brother Wack didn't have a chance. He was shot as he got out of the back of Bull's wagon the blast catapulting him back into the car. By that time I had been carried to the footpath. Grasping a leg each, Charlie and Lewy along with Lance holding my upper body, dragged me out of the car-park to where I lay slumped in the gutter near the road. Shadow had arrived in Bear's white Ford along with Podgorski, Lard, Lout and Tiny. Stepping into the fray he was confronted by a Comanchero and his shotgun.

"Put that gun down and fight like a man," Shadow challenged him.

With that, the coward lifted the gun, pointed it at my big brother, and pulled the trigger.

In that split second – time stopped. Shadow fell to the ground as if someone was playing the scene in slow motion. The guns fell silent. The birds stopped singing. The world ceased to turn. The heart and soul of the Campbell brothers momentarily united as together, we crashed with Shadow toward the ground . . . Then time, as if making up for the lost moments before – jarred brutally back into reality.

Chop – already dead, his last breath already spent and Caesar, Wack, Shadow and me – all shot, struggling to stay alive.

> . . . Look up from your book as you sit in the comfort of your surroundings and glance around the room you're in. Could you even begin to comprehend the horror of having five of your brothers lying in that space, all in the same agony you are – bleeding, moaning, gasping for breath as their life slowly ebbs from them. Imagine the desperation of watching all that is familiar in your life, slowly crumbling in front of your eyes – and there's nothing you can do about it. . . .

It had taken less than 5 minutes to nearly wipe out an entire generation of men from our family. To destroy not only our lives, but the lives of our mum, our sisters, our wives and our young kids, some of who would never see their fathers come home, others who would not see their fathers for many years to come except in the confines of a prison visiting room.

MILPERRA MASSACRE

Ron H. Stephenson

Ron H. Stephenson was the Detective Superintendent who led the enquiry into the Milperra Massacre, later receiving a police commendation for his work. According to Stephenson, the massacre was a local "old-style war" between biker factions, with no links to organized crime. Ron died in a car accident in 2004.

In 1968, an enigmatic Scotsman named William George "Jock" Ross organised the formation of a Sydney based Outlaw Motorcycle Gang named the "Comanchero", so named from a John Wayne movie which had sufficiently impressed "Jock". Their Clubhouse was set up in the western suburbs of Sydney, the membership grew and all were committed to the following (described in their terms) Comanchero Law:

"As the Brotherhood of the Comanchero is run on a paramilitary basis and not as a do as you like social club, the following laws must be absolutely obeyed".

Club Rules

1. The President is the Supreme Commander of the Comanchero.

2. Any member found guilty of cowardice, will be thrown out of the Club.

3. Any member found guilty of stealing from a member of the club itself, will be thrown out of the Club.

4. Any member found guilty of screwing another member's real Ol'Lady or taking advantage of a rift between them for future conning up, will be thrown out.

5. Any member found guilty of selling, distributing or using hard drugs, will be thrown out.

6. Any member found guilty of breeding dissention in the Club (i.e. running down the President of the Club or Club policies by discredit in any way, shape or form – or bad shit rumours), will be thrown out of the Club.

7. Any member found guilty of using their superior ability to con another member or (Nom) nominated member out of their bikes, money or valuables, will be severely dealt with.

8. Any member found guilty of not helping another member who is in genuine trouble (not bullshit trouble), will be severely dealt with.

9. Any member found guilty of divulging Club business or Club policies to anyone that is not a member, unless directed by the President, will be severely dealt with.

10. Any member found guilty of wearing his colours on or in anything other than a British or American motor cycle of 500cc or more, will be severely dealt with.

Regulations for Firearms. Failure to abide by these regulations will result in severe disciplinary action by Jock.

1. No woman will handle any firearm for any trivial reason.

2. Firearms will not be handled by anybody except the owner or authorised person by the owner.

3. No owner will be permitted to handle his own weapon if he is drunk.

4. No firearm is to be discharged in the Clubhouse, grounds or surrounding grounds.

5. No firearm is to have a shell in the breech.

Naturally, if the Clubhouse is attacked, the abovementioned regulations will not apply.

The Comanchero Club prospered through to 1983 when Jock's authority began to be challenged and dissention grew among the members. Shortly after Christmas 1983, a number of members left as a breakaway group and called themselves "Comanchero 2".

Bandidos

The President of the breakaway group, Anthony Mark (Snoddy) Spencer and another member Charles Paul (Charlie) Scibberas visited the United States of America where they associated and were accepted by the Bandido Bikie Gang. Permission was granted for a Chapter of the Bandidos to be formed in Australia and adopt the "colours" of the parent group, a Mexican bandit dressed in serape, holding a revolver and machete.

Those who defected from the Comancheros and joined the newly formed Bandidos, burned their former "colours" and began wearing those of the Bandido. It was evident from the start that both groups would be bitter enemies as Spencer, who was elected the Foundation President of the Bandidos was once a life member of his former club. As for the others, unauthorised resignation was classified as desertion. Whatever the reason for the split, great animosity and violent rivalry existed.

The Bandidos adopted the By Laws of the Parent Chapter in Texas and were somewhat similar as to those they had previously accepted as Comancheros.

Tension Builds

The Comancheros set up their clubhouse at 65 Harris Street, Harris Park and the Bandidos at 150 Louisa Street, Birchgrove. Both clubs trained in a para-military fashion and drew up their own rules of unacceptable moral and social behaviour. Tension between the two gangs increased with a number of assaults and property damage taking place.

There were a number of "bashings". During July 1984, a lone Bandido was assaulted by a number of Comancheros while attending a motor cycle swap meet. He received a broken jaw and a stab wound to the neck.

This sparked a reaction by the Bandidos who grouped, then ventured into Comanchero territory at the Bull and Bush Hotel at Baulkham Hills. There three Comancheros were badly beaten. Later shots were fired from a shotgun into the Bandido clubhouse by two Comancheros who were incidentally killed in the Fathers' Day Massacre.

Fights occurred at the Royal Oak Hotel at Parramatta which was described as a Bandido hotel from which Comancheros were barred. Territorial disputes were later given as the reason for the assaults. The incidents became more frequent and violent. Again during August 1984, "Jock" Ross was shunted off his Harley Davidson and pushed sixty five metres along a roadway by a Bandido in a hire vehicle.

On three further occasions shots were exchanged by the opposing gangs and the position became acutely evident that their differences would never be settled peacefully.

War Declared

On Friday, 10 August 1984 the Presidents of both gangs, "Jock" Ross and "Snoddy" Spencer spoke on the telephone and war between the two groups was officially declared. Rules of that war were drawn up which included a prohibition of members being "hit" at their homes or places of employment, but if they met at any other location a full scale armed confrontation would take place.

Shotguns, rifles and an extensive range of weapons were gathered by all members. Both Clubhouses were turned into fortresses with windows being boarded up, gun parapets erected and barbed wire stretched across entrances. Savage dogs were kept and an armed guard was rostered on watch duty.

At that very time, four men presented themselves at the Australian Embassy, Los Angeles, United States of America seeking visas for travel to Australia. Their intended travel arrangements were to enable their arrival in Sydney in time to celebrate Father's Day. Their Bandido identity was revealed as Ronald Hodge the National President, Charles Gillies the President of the Albuquerque Chapter, Keith Miller and Dennis Gnirk office bearers of a Nomad Chapter. The visa applications were refused and hindsight, being easier than foresight might indicate that the purpose of their visit was a war expedition.

The Massacre

On the morning of 2 September 1984, Father's Day a large number of Bandidos, in full colours rode past the home of the Comanchero Sergeant at Arms in a taunting manner, this was a breach of the rules of war. As a result the Comancheros were summoned to their Clubhouse where a decision was made to do battle that day with the Bandidos. The car park of the Viking Tavern, Milperra was named as the battleground. A Bikie Swap meeting had been organised to take place at that hotel and the rules of war declared swap meetings as neutral ground and not protected by the declaration. What an ideal location for each to show their superiority in front of other bikie groups who were expected to be in attendance for the swap meeting.

The midday scene at the Viking Tavern displayed a carnival atmosphere with members of the British Motorcycle Club congratulating themselves on the success of the barbecue and swap meeting that they had organised. Most of the motorcycling fraternity were represented with stalls displaying motorcycle parts for sale or swap. Approximately five hundred people packed the carpark with another two hundred enjoying the facilities offered by the Tavern's trade.

The residents of Beaconsfield Street, Milperra (which led to the Viking Tavern) were fascinated by the traditional "bikie convoy" proceeding along their street Twenty members of the Comanchero, wearing full colours were armed with shotguns, baseball bats, chains, knives and knuckle dusters. In the lead was their President "Jock" displaying a large machete with the words "Bandaid hair parter" painted on it. He was followed by the full membership of his gang, with the "Sergeant at Arms" and the "War Waggon" at the rear for security.

Three scouts were deployed each equipped with walkie talkie radios to plot the location of the Bandidos. The convoy drove into the Viking car park, dismounted from their machines, loaded their firearms and with weapons held at the ready dispersed themselves into the already nervous crowd.

At 1.50pm the throbbing vibration of approaching motor

cycles signalled the arrival of the Bandidos. Thirty in all drove their vehicles in a wedge shaped formation into the car park. It was noticeable to all that many machines had scabbards across the handlebars of the cycles which held rifles and shotguns. Those who had not brought a weapon with them went to their own war waggon and were issued with their arms.

With "colours" displayed both groups advanced upon each other without regard to the safety of other persons in the crowded car park. The battle began. For approximately 20 minutes, bats, bars, guns and knives were used. People screamed, people ran, people hid. Shotgun pellets peppered buildings, fences and motor vehicles. Bandidos, Comancheros and bystanders were struck; limbs were broken, people were stabbed, people were shot. Four Comancheros, two Bandidos and a fourteen year old girl died instantly. Twenty one bikies received serious injuries. This scenario was to be drawn by Justice Roden at later court proceedings.

Police Response

The intial alert to patrolling police vehicles by Police Radio V.K.G. was somewhat uncertain:

> *"For 19 Division cars, any car in the vicinity. We have a few calls on this one. The Viking Hotel. Beaconsfield Street, Milperra. Alleged man gone berserk with a rifle. Shots have been fired".*

That broadcast was enough to increase the pulse rate of police in the immediate vicinity with them responding to an incident that would shock the most experienced on arrival. Father's Day, a balmy Spring afternoon in a southern Sydney suburb – five hundred terror stricken people trapped in the midst of a violent battle in the large open car park of a hotel, which, minutes beforehand had provided an entertainment area – two hundred motor vehicles mostly motor cycles, the Harley Davidson, the symbol, the close relative of the bikie – the dead and wounded lying beside their machines – the warriors, bearded, plaited hair held back by headbands, dressed in jeans, metal studded gloves, Comanchero and Bandido colours vividly displayed and holding smoking firearms and blood stained baseball bats. One seasoned street hardened police sergeant was heard to say to a probationary constable.

"Have a good look around here son. You won't see anything like this again".

At the entrance to the car park, the body of Gregory (Shadow) Campbell the Bandido Vice President was being mourned by his brother/bikie Philip (Bull) Campbell. Shadow had drowned in his own blood after being hit in the throat with a shotgun load. How ironic that his brother would later be charged with his murder. "Shadow" carried the driver's licence of another bikie, James John Posar, of Marion Street, Leichhardt who was well and truly alive.

Mario (Chopper) Cianter lay on his back in the carpark with a load of shotgun pellets shattering his chest through the Bandido emblem proudly worn on his "colours". The "Death Before Dishonour" tattoo on his arm seemed all too incongruous.

Robert (Foghorn) Lane, Vice President of the Comanchero was the victim of a .357 magnum blast and indications were that a "hit list" had been executed due to the officer ranking of the dead bikies. A search of "Foghorn's" wallet revealed a driver's licence, in the fictitious name of John Simon Carlton, of Harris Park which added more confusion to the existing bewilderment.

Foghorn had a premonition as to his death making out his will the previous night and giving it to a friend.

Tony (Dog) McCoy received his load of shot in the face and chest and probably died before he hit the ground. A short distance away his brother Comanchero, Phillip (Leroy) Jeske, the Club's Sergeant at Arms lay sprawled with his "colours" saturated in blood. Leroy may well have been identified as Terrence William Parker, of Forster as the driver's licence in his wallet indicated.

The fourth Comanchero, Ivan (Sparrow) Romcek had been shot at such a close range as to notice the wadding from a spent cartridge embedded in his neck.

The shootings, although well directed at those meant to be killed, showed evidence of indiscrimination as the body of Leanne Walters, a 14 year old girl was found near the entrance to the hotel lounge. She had been hit by a single stray .357 magnum bullet which removed the entire lower half of her face.

"Jock" who had shown a high visibility during the battle and was a natural target for his many enemies, had miraculously escaped death. A spray of shotgun pellets had struck him in the head with a metal fragment penetrating his brain. Surgeons who later operated on the Comanchero President expressed amazement at his survival from injuries which left him more mentally unstable than was his norm.

"Snoddy" also survived and at the time the result seemed a hollow and meaningless finality to a war with the two main dissidents alive and still in control of their forces.

Bikie Funerals

The funerals of the victims posed some apprehension for the Task Force as bikie groups followed unique procedures in farewelling their departed brothers. Still vivid in the minds of the investigators was a recent colourful burial ceremony at Palmdale Memorial Gardens on the Central Coast where the Comanchero club had purchased a number of burial sites. In the midst of an industrial dispute involving funeral directors, the Comancheros suffered the loss of one of their members. The coffin, attached to a Harley Davidson minus its sidecar, was escorted from Sydney in convoy to the cemetery where "Jock" shouted to all present, "No one tells the Comanchero when to bury their dead", and a seven gun salute broke the silence of the surroundings as the body of the late "John Boy" was buried. An unconfirmed intelligence report indicated that the melted down motorcycle of the deceased was buried with him.

Four thousand dollars had been sent by the Bandido parent Chapter in America to purchase floral tributes for their fallen brothers which indicated the "feeling" that concerned the Task Force. One group armed with firearms for the final salute to their fallen might well be expected to celebrate the funeral wake by a further confrontation with their well financed rivals. However, due to a visible police presence and the acceptance of advice given to each group, commonsense prevailed and each victim's funeral passed without major incident.

The Investigation Continued

Copies of all television film footage was obtained and a group of detectives assigned to identify as many persons appearing in those films as possible and have them interviewed. A room was set aside for witnesses to view the videos and identify offenders who had participated on the day of the massacre. A number of motorcycle enthusiasts had their personal cameras with them on the day of the shootings and had taken photographs whilst the affray was in progress. The films were developed and the task of placing a weapon with an individual offender commenced.

To the credit of one bikie (not involved in the incident) who came forward with information of a package of explosives that had been taken to the Viking Tavern on the day of the massacre and the probable location in the carpark where it had been abandoned. This package had never been located by police and the conclusion was reached that it may have been placed in or on a motor vehicle and carried away unsuspectingly by the owner. By use of photographs and the plan that had been produced, the registered number of a Holden utility was identified. The vehicle was located at the owner's place of employment and when searched by police; a newspaper dated 1 September 1984, the day before the massacre, was found wrapped around three sticks of deteriorating gelignite, detonators with fuse wire attached, and an army simulator hand grenade. The package had been placed in the spare wheel compartment of the vehicle and may have proved fatal to the innocent occupants if carried much longer.

The injured bikies who had been admitted to hospitals were interviewed when their condition improved and upon their discharge, they too were charged with "Causing an Affray". Within seven days of the offence, forty offenders had been so charged.

The Raids

Pre dawn, Friday 21 September 1984 and "Operation Hard-walk" was underway. The Command Team assembled at 3.30am in the Operations Room at the Police Technical Support Branch building with the field operational teams gathering at their predetermined locations. The Special Operations police radio channel was opened at 4.30am and the action began:

> *"TANGO ON" came the first call. Then "BLUEBAGS ON", "SHARKS ON" until forty-three teams had registered.*

A clear and simple message to the Commander who then knew the exact location of every officer involved in the operation. Not so clear though for the sleepless media hounds that monitor police radio channels for worthwhile activity.

At 5am further concise messages as each team reported off at their target location:

> *"TIGERS OFF AT TARGET" Then "TIGERS BACK ON WITH TARGET".*
> More communication,
> *"PANTHERS BACK ON WITH TARGET. ALSO HAVE SAINTS TARGET".*

Every officer involved in Operation Hardwalk understood what this jargon meant and where all personnel would be located with their prisoner. The Command Post team although aware of the success or otherwise of the house entries, were nevertheless deprived of the operational stimulus of "being there".

"Target Scarlet off" and the six man team of detectives, uniformed police and T.R.G. officers surrounded the weatherboard house at 993 Old Northern Road, Dural. Two detectives went to the front door, demanded entry after announcing themselves and a female voice shouted, "You'll have to go around the back". This proved to be the logical means of entry as, once inside the house the police found that the front door had been securely locked and secured with a piece of four by two timber nailed across the door jamb and a similar sized length nailed through the carpet into the floor and wedged against the door. "Bob" Watkin was the Bandido occupant and armed with a .22 calibre rifle, he was taking no chances on an invasion from the Comanchero.

Watkin's home was searched and, although he was taken into custody to be charged with seven charges of murder, his main concern seemed to be the future care of his Bandido "colours" that hung on the back of a loungeroom chair. Satisfied that his wife was an acceptable custodian, the police and their target left. "*Scarlet back on with target*" came the radio contact.

"*Target Carlton off*" and premises at Leitch Avenue, Londonderry were searched by the four man police team. A short time later, "*Carlton back on without target*". Each team leader had been instructed to pursue all avenues of inquiry to locate their target, so it was not surprising that this particular Team continued the search for Comanchero Richard "Chewey" Lorenz into the following day. At 5.45pm on Saturday 22 September 1984, the detectives returned to Leitch Avenue, Londonderry after surveillance reports of significant movement. Had the police arrived several minutes earlier they would have witnessed the marriage of "Chewey" to his "Real ol' Lady" Kezra. Lorenz's reply to police questioning was that he would like to spend five minutes with his new bride, but then added "What's the difference, we may as well go". Go they did and the bridegroom left, possibly for the ensuing twenty years.

"*Target Alpha off*" and the search for the giant 194cm Bandido Anthony "Tiny" Cain began. His address at Birchgrove was deserted and as the news media publicised the operation later that day, it was to prove extremely difficult to locate Cain at his usual haunts. Investigators prefer to call it good policemanship rather than luck, but on 20 October 1984, members of the Criminal Investigation Branch Motor Squad attached to the task force were scanning one of Sydney's daily newspaper car sales columns when they observed for sale a Ford sedan, registered number ALQ-164. The owner of this car was "Tiny" Cain.

At 12.30pm that day an undercover police officer knocked on the door of 81 Crawford Road, Brighton Le Sands. The nom de plume given by the person who answered could not disguise the giant frame of "Tiny" . . .

"I've come about the car for sale," said the detective.

"She's right there," came the reply with an indication towards the white Ford parked in the street.

"Can we take her for a test drive?" asked the bogus buyer and Cain entered the passenger side of the car with the detective taking the wheel.

The car was driven slowly along Crawford Road and upon reaching the first intersection was greeted by a convoy of police vehicles.

"Tiny" with what remained of a sense of humor said,

"It's cool. Okay, you've got me – I don't suppose you want to buy the car now?"

The major operation was completed by sunrise on 21 September 1984 with Hardwalk continuing in instances as just mentioned.

The final tally of the operation would be forty-three persons, each charged with seven counts of murder. Three hundred and one charges of murder, the thought of the ensuing legal proceedings was awesome.

Police Informant – "Supergrass"

Bernard Stephen Anthony Podgorski was 33 years of age and resided in the western Sydney suburb of Glossodia. Educated at St Patricks College, Strathfield to the Higher School Certificate standard, Bernie was now married with a four months old son. He was employed as a builder's assistant with the Hawkesbury Shire Council and by way of recreation he participated in competition tennis at an "A Grade" level. One could be forgiven for thinking that Bernie Podgorski typified the average Australian male.

Unfortunately Podgorski had more than one cross to bear. He was better known to his bikie "brothers" by his street name "Sheik", the secretary of the Bandidos. "Sheik" who had been a participant in the Father's Day Massacre, had been arrested following Operation Hardwalk and charged with seven counts of murder. He was to break the bikies' strictest law, "the code of silence" and earn the new street name of "Deadmeat".

On 30 October 1984 Podgorski, with his legal representatives sought immunity from prosecution of his murder charges upon the understanding that he would reveal all that he knew relative to matters leading up to, and including the massacre.

The story that unfolded was as though a script had been written for a Mad Max movie. Podgorski was originally a member of the Loners Motor Cycle Club but that club was disbanded after the members were assaulted by "Jock" Ross and his Comancheros and coerced into that gang. He described the club "merger":

"One of our blokes was at the Milton Hotel and his mate was king hit by one of the Comancheros. The member of the Loners returned to the Milton hotel with a shot gun and threatened several Comancheros. They then hit our club house at 148 Palmer Street, Sydney. They assaulted three of our members (that were living there) with baseball bats and put them in St Vincents hospital for seven or eight days. Later we were contacted by the Comancheros for a friendly meeting at the Milton Hotel, but when we arrived cars surrounded us from side streets, blokes jumped out of the cars and started bashing us with baseball bats and iron bars. A number of shots were fired at us. There were about twenty of them".

"Sheik" went on to become a full member of the Comancheros until joining the breakaway group in 1983, when he became a foundation member of the Sydney Chapter of the Bandidos. He described the rift in the Comancheros being caused after "Jock" Ross had declared himself Supreme Commander with total power overuling the previously accepted voting system. The incidents of violence between the two gangs leading up to Milperra were vividly described by Podgorski who had been present on several occasions.

At a July 1984 meeting of the Bandidos at their clubhouse, the members were addressed by the President "Snoddy" Spencer:

"Something has got to be done about Jock and the Comancheros and anybody in the Club who has got any guts and wants to get rid of the problem, not by just bashing them, meet me in the bar after the meeting. We want to get rid of Jock permanently."

Podgorski detailed the declaration of war between the two gangs and at a club meeting prior to Father's Day personal targets were allocated with the instructions. "They are to be bashed and their colours taken." He then described the events of 2 September 1984:

"I left home about 8 o'clock in the morning from my home at Glossodia – I celebrated Father's Day with my family and had lunch with them at their home – later I went to Lance Wellington's home at Pringle Avenue, Bankstown – the members of the Club were in ones and twos. 'Caesar' said to me, 'You're a rover' I said, 'What do I do'. He said, 'Certain blokes have certain targets and the rovers are to bash anyone that are getting on top of our blokes' – we left for the Viking Tavern. 'Bull' was driving his Holden and 'Chopper' was in the passenger's seat. 'Wack' and 'Roach' were in the back. I went in the Falcon station waggon with 'Shadow', 'Lard', 'Lout', 'Tiny' and 'Bear'. Then the bikes came out. 'Davo' was on his trike, 'Lance' on his sidecar with one on the back. Then there was 'Tony' and 'Rua', 'Hookey', 'Zorba' and 'Luey'. 'Caesar' was on his own bike, 'Charlie' on his bike then 'Kid Rotten' and 'Opey'. We travelled towards the Viking in formation.

"The bikes pulled up and the members got off – we walked briskly towards the Comancheros – I was standing to the left of 'Zorba', there were five or six Comancheros facing us with guns. There was 'Leroy' with a shotgun, Eaves and also 'Sparrow'. 'Zorba' went to grab the shotgun that Eaves was carrying and it discharged. Then I saw 'Sparrow' hit 'Zorba' over the head with a club. 'Zorba' wrestled 'Sparrow' down and a girl came and hit 'Zorba' over the head with a baseball bat. Guns went off and I hit the ground – I could see 'Jock', he had a machete in his hand and was waving it above his head and shouting 'Kill em all'."

Podgorski's confession was by way of a twenty three page Record of Interview and indemnity was subsequently granted to him by the New South Wales Attorney General. He would give evidence at future court proceedings, but one could only speculate that the indemnity was from lawful prosecution and not given from the Outlaw Motorcycle Gangs.

The Trial

To the average person, the appearance of 43 defendants daily in a Court was an immense task. What an understatement. The daily routine for Police on the Comanchero escort was the 6.30am transfer of 17 prisoners from Long Bay Gaol into the Police vans. Then with a convoy of 4 support vehicles containing T.R.G. personnel, the vans would be escorted uninterrupted through traffic control signals to the Penrith Police Station.

The receiving procedures, precourt interviews with lawyers and the presentation of the prisoners in Court prior to the commencement of the 10.00am proceedings became meticulous. Morning tea and lunch adjournments added to the workload with the removal of the defendants from the Courtroom. The conclusion of the day's proceedings saw the same functions in reverse. At 8.00pm the vehicular convoy was completed for that day.

The Bandido group of 26 from Parklea Gaol undertook an identical procedure. Only the distance of transport varied.

Bernie Podgorski and his family were given personal protection on a 24 hour basis by members of the Special Weapons Operations Squad. Escorted to and from Court, he was flanked by 4 officers observing a close personal protection pattern, but once in the witness box he was very much alone.

As a member of both the Comanchero and Bandido gangs, Bernie could identify each defendant as being involved in the massacre, what part they had played and their prior knowledge of the war declaration and "hit list", vital and damaging evidence which had some defence lawyers uneasy in their chairs. Podgorski was limited in his knowledge of many of the defendants' correct names and relied upon their "street" names for identification. The bikies were seated in the enclosures at the rear of the Court, 17 Comanchero on one side and 26 Bandido on the other.

"Would you identify each defendant from your left to right," asked the Coroner.

Bernie commenced,

"Tiny, Bear, Lance, Chewey, Jock, Sunshine, Snoddy".

The defence counsel interrupted which observers thought might terrify Podgorski to the state of being incapable of continuing.

"The witness is being asked to identify these men from quite a distance away and he is keeping his head down. Could he be brought to the rear of the Court to face the defendants in order that there can be no mistake and we might hear him better".

"Sheik" visibly shaking was led by a Court attendant to the enclosures holding the accused where face to face he began his identification. The defence action almost succeeded as Bernie stammered and stopped. The glares and motions that passed between accused and witness were the pinnacle of body language.

"Tony", continued Podgorski as he identified his friend to whose son he was godfather. The moment of truth having passed, "Sheik" proceeded with his evidence with increasing confidence. 3 months would elapse before this witness could complete his evidence and survive an avalanche of intense cross examination.

Nervous Reflections

Bernie Podgorski was not the only witness who suffered from nerves as a series of perhaps coincidental incidents did nothing to instill a sense of security in those to follow.

One bikie comment directed to me from the rear of the courtroom at the conclusion of the day's proceedings near the Christmas vacation;

"Your Christmas present is running late, but don't worry, it will be a surprise. You won't know when to expect it".

A civilian eye witness associated with bikie groups received several anonymous threatening telephone calls at his home and place of employment. One afternoon, as he left a Berala Hotel in the western suburbs of Sydney, he was shot in the leg by an unknown gunman. No evidence existed to suggest or prove the incidents were bikie promoted, but his reluctance to attend Court and give his evidence could be well understood.

Comanchero Anthony John "The Rat" Brennan had not been involved at Milperra as he was completing a 10 year gaol sentence received for the shotgun death of a bikie who allegedly had not conformed to Club regulations. However, on his release from gaol, he became a familiar figure in the public gallery of the Court. Witnesses who knew "The Rat" became nervous of his presence, but this subsided when Brennan's Parole Officer advised him that he was in breach of his parole conditions to associate with his "brothers" at the Court.

Three female witnesses complained to the Task Force of the

receipt of telephone calls threatening murder and pack rape, but the anonymity of the threats made the task of identifying the offenders responsible an impossibility.

More anonymous telephone calls, this time to the home of Mr Allan Viney Q.C. leading the Prosecution team, simply having the effect of him knowing that his family home had been identified.

Michael and Deidre Langley, the licensees of the Viking Tavern found the pressure too great and following their evidence and on reflection, they vacated their employment and moved on.

The parents of Bernic Podgorski were listed in the Sydney Telephone Directory and it came as no surprise when they reported the receipt of nuisance telephone calls and unwelcome motor cycle traffic outside their home.

The obligatory bomb threats to the Courthouse diminished in regularity when they no longer remained disruptive. A night fire was set amongst the records of the Office of Public Prosecutions within the Penrith Courthouse complex, but papers destroyed fortunately were not associated with the bikie trial.

An emotional scenario had developed in the minds of many associated with the court case. It would be unjust to believe the men standing in the prisoners' dock were directly responsible for this sensitive feeling, but perhaps the increasing knowledge gained by those involved, of the intense physical force associated with the outlaw bikie movement, created a concerned reaction that might otherwise be disregarded.

The Death of a President

Anthony Mark Spencer "Snoddy", President of the Bandidos was losing control of both his bikie gang and his mind. Cell 3233 in Wing 3 of Parklea Prison had been home to "Snoddy" since his arrest in September 1984. He kept a private diary in which he recorded his feelings, frustrations, depressions and the future of the Bandido group. The writings began with the hope of bail and acquittal of all charges, slowly degenerating to extreme despair. In his own words, here are extracts from his diary.

"We are people that have not been in jail before and they put us in the most max jail in N.S.W. All it will do to us, well 'me' anyway is make me bitter towards the people that put me hear."

My mind is starting to crack. I just don't understand what is happening to us. I don't know how much longer I can hang on to my sanity. I wish we could get bail soon, it is sending me round the twist".

Finally:

"I Tony Spencer

Do not want my wife to have any past in my life or death. Lee Denholm is my lady and Joel is my son & they get all my belongings. Lee I am sorry for this but remember I will always love you & my son.

Plus I want my bros to not think of me as week, but as for fighting for the well beeing of the club have tall made I dont no. But I do no some one will do the right thing for the club".

Sunday, 28 April 1985 at 6.00am, "Snoddy" was found hanging from the shower railing in his cell, a strip of white cloth knotted around his neck. A short time later, after Spencer had been placed on his cell bed, the Bandido inmates gathered around the body and paid their last respects to their deceased President.

The Verdicts

Friday, 12 June, 1987, saw the verdicts delivered. A total of 560 days had been devoted to the legal system to achieve this result. The Courtroom was filled to capacity with reserved seats only in the public gallery containing Police, media representatives and selected relatives of the accused who had maintained a daily vigil for the endurance of the trial. The foyer of the Court complex was partitioned to form an enclosed area for members of the public adjacent to the Courtroom with a sound system provided for the overflow. Security had been increased for this day as it was impossible to predict the reaction from accused and friends if convictions were recorded.

The formalities commenced. "Members of the jury. Have you reached your verdicts?" "We have," replied the foreman, a young man with a ponytail similar to those whose future rested with his decision.

Then individually each accused heard his fate.

"Guilty of 7 charges of murder and guilty of affray" or "Not guilty of murder, but guilty of 7 charges of manslaughter and affray", as each bikie faced the requital of his deeds at the Milperra Massacre.

Relatives and friends wept, sighed or sat stunned as each verdict was announced. The final reckoning.

9 each guilty of 7 counts of murder and 1 count affray. 21 each guilty of 7 counts of manslaughter and 1 count affray. 1 guilty of 1 count of affray. A total of 63 convictions of murder, 147 convictions of manslaughter and 31 convictions of affray.

Three hundred and thirty-two days of evidence had been converted into a determination by the jury as their foreman affirmed the unanimous agreement of each verdict.

All prisoners were remanded until Friday 26 June, 1987 for sentence with the exception of Bandido, Phillip (Knuckles) McElwaine a former Commonwealth Games boxing gold medallist.

Selected passages of His Honour's judgement sketched the futility of the bikies' Father's Day war and probably the unanswered question, "why did it have to happen?"

(Drawn from the Judge's decision)

"Throughout the sentence hearing, I sought a greater understanding that I was able to obtain of the nature of the clubs and the relationship between their respective members.

"There was, I thought, very good reason for that. Some are in their thirties and forties have no significant prior convictions and have good family and work backgrounds. I felt that there had to be some explanation for the marked and perplexing difference between their behaviour as club members and their behaviour in other contexts. I also wanted to know more about the clubs themselves and what it is about the way of life that they offer that led these people, many of whom would in all other respects be regarded as law abiding and responsible citizens of commendable character, to indulge in what on the face of it is irresponsible, anti-social behaviour of extreme violence, bringing with it obvious danger to human life, and in the facts of this case the tragic consequences of 7 deaths.

"It is not possible to sit looking at these men for more than one year, as I have done, without feeling that there is more to them than the popular image of bikie gang members. It is unfortunate that so many of them have chosen to play no part in the sentence hearing, although years of their lives are at stake.

"A fierce loyalty and a propensity for violence, which rightly or wrongly typify the popular image of such clubs are clearly indicated by the evidence in this case. That image seems to be fostered by such clubs by the almost intimidatory appearance adopted and the emphasis on strength and power to be found in man and machine alike.

"A need to belong and to enjoy a close relationship and bond with others can be readily understood. So too can a pride in physical strength and courage. But like most admirable qualities, these can be carried to excess. The ugly side of loyalty seems to demand enemies against whom the loyal can be united and the ugly side of physical strength and courage is seen when violence is unleashed against those enemies. When you have two groups like these in conflict with one another a 'Viking' is always likely.

"As patriotism can lead to jingoism and mateship can lead to cronyism so bikie club loyalty. it seems, can lead to bikie club war."

KAMIKAZE RIDERS

William Osgerby

In this piece William Osgerby offers an interesting overview of the Japanese one-percenter outlaw clubs and their own interclub rivalries. As the subculture spreads through Asia, one-percenter outlaw clubs again change in appearance, values, and regard by law enforcement authorities.

Japan's first motorcycle gangs roared into life during the early 1950s. As in Europe, Japan's postwar affluence delivered a new spending power into the hands of the nation's youth. As a consequence, Japanese cities saw the emergence of new youth styles and subcultures, dubbed zoku or "tribes" by the media. Many of the young zoku borrowed styles from their counterparts in the West, especially the US. Leather jackets and jeans, for example, were typically favored by Japanese bikers who became known as the kaminari-zoku – or "thunder tribe" – on account of their bikes' raucous exhausts.

Although the Japanese press complained about noisy motorcycles and the occasional traffic accident, throughout the 1950s and 1960s the kaminari-zoku weren't considered much of a problem. But the image of motorcycle gangs changed during the late 1960s and early 1970s following several widely reported episodes of violence. One of the most serious was 1972's Toyama Jiken (Toyoma Incident), when a motorcycle gang led 3,000 rioters in a fierce battle with the police. In 1974 and 1975 a series of clashes between rival motorcycle gangs in Kanagawa (a state close to Tokyo) attracted more media attention. But, above all, it was the disturbances that took place in Kobe in 1976 that guaranteed the media's vilification of Japanese bikers. The confrontation began when police tried to stamp out an illicit race meeting held by an assembly of local motorcyclists. Events took an ugly turn, and a crowd of several thousand went on the rampage, wrecking patrol cars and stoning a police station. The Kobe incident became notorious and gave currency to a new term – bosozoku. The name was used to describe the new tribe (or zoku) of sharply dressed young bikers whose lives were dedicated to the excitement of boso – high-speed, high-risk riding through Japan's hectic city streets.

The mid-1970s through to the early 1980s were the heyday of the intrepid bosozoku or "speed tribe." Mostly in their teens or early twenties, bosozoku gangs such as Black Emperor, Hell Tribe, and the Fierce Tigers transformed the city streets into their playground. On summer weekend nights Japan's congested cities exploded with the din of souped-up motorcycles as tens, often hundreds, of bosozoku assembled to show off their machines and stage impromptu races through the crowded metropolis.

Like the American outlaws, the bosozoku had a taste for the outrageous. Their motorcycles were modified virtually beyond recognition, with bland factory models transformed into breathtaking kaizosha (modified vehicles) that reflected the owner's personal style. While US outlaws favored hulking 1200cc Harleys, the bosozoku generally opted for more-readily available Suzukis and Yamahas; and the strict Japanese traffic laws meant they were generally limited to bikes of around 250–400cc. But the diehard bosozoku always stamped his personality on his machine. Frames were resprayed in bright, primary colors, gas tanks were painted with enigmatic Chinese characters (chosen for their visual appeal), while an array of custom mirrors, fenders, sissy bars, and headlights added style and attitude. For some, the original purchase price of the motorcycle was nothing compared with the total costs of modification.

In appearance, the well-groomed and carefully dressed bosozoku were a far cry from America's greasy chopper crew. In place of leathers and denims, the bosozoku of the 1980s favored tokkofuku. Literally, tokkofuku means the uniform of the kamikaze, but in contrast to the dull, utilitarian overalls of the original suicide pilots, the bosozoku's elegant outfits were finely tailored in shades of yellow, pink, and white as well as black and gray, and were painstakingly embroidered with group names, Chinese symbols, and phrases suggesting strident nationalism – for example, "Patriot" or "Protection of the Nation and Respect for His Majesty." Similar slogans also decorated headbands embroidered with the Imperial rising sun crest, which was also resplendent on the flags held aloft by young hatamochl (flag holders) who rode pillion.

The nationalist symbolism, however, didn't point to a close relationship between the bosozoku and Japan's political right wing. On the contrary, the bosozoku had little respect for nationalist movements, and used the symbols for their shock value. Just like the US outlaws, the bosozoku loved to "show some class," with displays calculated to infuriate the ippanjin (ordinary citizens).

THE GREAT NORDIC WAR

William Marsden and Julian Sher

Turning from old-style wars to alleged crime syndicate wars, this piece was written by two journalists who relied heavily on police data. Their account details the war in Scandinavia between the Hells Angels Motorcycle Club and the Bandidos Motorcycle Club during the late 1990s.

Amsterdam's red light district is a lonely ghetto that's left largely to its own vices. It's located just beyond the city's oldest and most sacred church, the gothic Oude Kerk, and hugs two secluded dead-end canals. Sex and porno shops, window prostitutes, brothels, cannabis cafés, strip clubs and cheap hotels line the still waters in teetering buildings huddled shoulder-to-shoulder like shivering old men with tin cups. The district sits in stark contrast to the rest of the inner city with its broader streets, elegant townhouses and carefully planned waterways. You don't stumble across it. It's not on the way to anything. It's an end in itself.

It was here in 1983 that Joanne Wilson and her boyfriend, Stephen Hampton, came to work and play. They couldn't have known it, but they were moving into Hells Angels territory. Joanne was a flirtatious Irish girl with an eternal smile, bright brown eyes, a cute nose and a mass of dark curly hair. She came from one of the most violent and intolerant regions of Europe. Portadown in Northern Ireland is a small rural town whose history is soaked in sectarian conflict. When she was eighteen, she and her Ulster boyfriend hoped to leave all that behind by travelling the world – India, Asia – before settling in seemingly peaceful Amsterdam.

Joanne had trained as a dental nurse, but the only job she could land was as a chambermaid at a downtown hotel. It didn't bother her. She was young, and the money was enough to live on.

Stephen worked in a bar in the red-light district. Among his customers was Louis Hagamann, nicknamed Long Louis, who came in for a drink a couple of times a week. He was a tall, lean, muscular guy of thirty who wore his hair in a ponytail and tied a red bandanna around his head. Most of all, what separated Long Louis from the rest of the red-light patrons was the fact that he was a full-patch member of the Amsterdam Hells Angels. Long Louis made his money dealing drugs and pimping in Holland's eager sex trade. He was also involved in armed robbery and extortion, but neither Stephen nor Joanne knew about that. Stephen said he found him "very friendly." Joanne also liked him. In fact, she liked him so much that she dated him in secret several times.

September 20, 1985, had been an all-nighter for Stephen. He had worked at the bar into the early morning and come home exhausted. Joanne was up early. She made him a breakfast and, before he drifted off to sleep, told him she'd be out most of the day but expected to be back for dinner. That was the last time he saw her alive.

Joanne later left their apartment and walked to Amsterdam's Central Station. Along the way she met up with a girlfriend. The two chatted briefly, and Joanne told her she was going to meet somebody. When they got to the station, the two girls parted, and Joanne vanished into the bustling crowds.

When she didn't arrive home that evening, Stephen thought that maybe she was staying with friends. When she didn't return the next day, he began asking around. He called friends – including the biker Hagamann. Nobody had seen her. Finally, he went to the police station. The police suspected it was a lovers' tiff and assumed she would show up sooner or later, so they did nothing other than file a missing persons report. After three days and still no word, a frantic Stephen launched his own investigation. With the help of Hagamann, he searched the streets and canals of Amsterdam.

Six weeks later, a sluice-gate operator in Amsterdam spotted a curious-looking plastic bag floating in his lock along the Amsterdam-Rijn canal. He grabbed a barge pole, hooked the end around the bag and hoisted it onto the concrete bank. Inside, he found human remains.

The problem for police was that the body had been dismembered, much like Steve Chocalaad's would be almost twenty years later. There were no arms, no legs, no head. There was a knife wound in the chest, but that didn't necessarily mean it was the cause of death. All they knew was that the torso was a woman's.

One week later, the gate operator found another plastic bag floating in his lock. He fished that out too and discovered a left leg. A pathologist concluded it belonged to the torso. Police began combing through missing persons records and found Joanne Wilson. A sandal in her apartment fitted the foot, and a hair found in her bathroom was similar to pubic hair on the torso. Still, they couldn't be certain; there was no DNA analysis at that time. They questioned Stephen and his biker friend, Hagamann, about their whereabouts the day she disappeared.

Louis Hagamann should have stayed at the top of the cops' list of suspects – not least because they were well aware he was a Hells Angel with a violent criminal record. Hagamann's apartment was only about three hundred yards from where the body was found. Joanne's girlfriend told police she had mentioned that she was meeting a man named Louis. Hagamann even admitted meeting her at the station for a drink, but after that, he claimed, he didn't know where she went. Police did not pursue him further, other than to mark him down as a suspect.

Police decided that they couldn't be sure the body was indeed hers, so they closed the file, which they callously labelled "Operation Annoyance." Because the identification was uncertain, they refused to release the body to her mother, Ann Donaghy, in Armagh. Instead, they had the body interred in a small corner of Amsterdam's largest cemetery reserved for unknown cadavers. And that's where the remains of Joanne Wilson lay buried for the next fifteen years.

Joanne had been Ann Donaghy's only child. Joanne's reassuring letters home had not assuaged a mother's fear for her daughter's safety. Now, her daughter's murder together with the remarkable indifference of the Dutch police would make Ann Donaghy's life what she later described as "a complete hell" for many years to come. Had the police been more astute or just a little more persistent, they likely would have discovered that Joanne Wilson was one of several victims of a lawless subculture of terror and intimidation proudly invented in America and now ready to sweep through Europe.

One of the leaders of this outlaw biker invasion was Willem van Boxtel, a muscular street-gang leader determined to become Europe's Sonny Barger.

Willem grew up in east-end Amsterdam, a lover of motorcycles, speed and gang violence. He gorged on American biker movies and tales of the Hells Angels. In 1973, at the age of seventeen, he started his own biker gang, calling it the Kreidler Ploeg East. The club quickly staked out its territory. On his eighteenth birthday, his gang beat up the manager of a late-night convenience store. When the manager complained to police, Willem and his boys came back and beat him up again. A few weeks later he raided a school, beating up two teachers, several schoolboys and some girls, throwing them to the ground and kicking them. His gang then tossed the husband of a teacher into a stairwell and bashed the owner of a nearby snackbar. Police arrested Willem and eleven other gang members. He got six weeks in prison and six weeks' probation, but that didn't stop him. He was determined to become the most feared outlaw biker in east-end Amsterdam.

Even though he didn't have an official charter, van Boxtel decided to call his gang the Hells Angels. Under that American banner, he was ready to take on all comers. When a British gang called the Mad Dogs came to Holland to party, his gang went to war, beating them badly in a sandlot fight before police broke it up. Alarmed Amsterdam youth commissioners decided that the way to tame Willem was to give his gang a place to hang out, so in 1974 they voted his gang 172,500 guilders (US$103,386 today) to build a clubhouse in east-end Amsterdam. The council then approved an annual grant of 21,300 guilders (US$12,772 today) to the biker gang to organize charity events and activities for young people and to promote motorcycle riding.

In 1977 Willem's Amsterdam club became a prospect chapter for the Hells Angels, with a clubhouse – called Angel Place – fully financed by Dutch taxpayers. It would prove a costly mistake. Far from being an oasis of goodwill, Angel Place would soon gain a reputation for murder, drug dealing, torture and gang rape.

It would take fourteen years before the council stopped paying the annual grant after they realized most of the Angels were well over thirty years old and had no interest in helping young people. Commissioners also discovered that Willem believed charity began at home and had used the money to expand his clubhouse while the youth department continued to pay the lease on the land.

Willem had command of his own fortress and the neighbourhood around it. He figured that what he needed now was a new name for himself – one that people wouldn't forget. He chose something straightforward and easy to remember: Big Willem. The name would stick. In fact, Big Willem would fast become a legend. He had caught the Hells Angels wave rolling in from California early: when he applied for a Hells Angels charter, there were just seven other HA clubs in Europe. England had five and Germany and Switzerland had one each. In other words, mainland Western Europe was a vast untamed territory ripe for the Hells Angels' picking.

Delegations of Hells Angels from the United States arrived to assess the Amsterdam club. German, English, Austrian and Australian Angels followed. The international attention was no accident. Amsterdam was becoming the drug centre of Europe, and the country's increasingly lenient laws meant it could serve as a safe haven for outlaws. The ports of Amsterdam and Rotterdam were already major drug transportation hubs. As the Angels planned an aggressive expansion throughout Europe, Amsterdam would play a pivotal role, quickly becoming the mother club. This was why the international Angels wanted to assure that the members who controlled it were up to scratch. Big Willem had to prove his mettle.

In May 1978 police raided Angel Place after the father of a nineteen-year-old girl claimed she had been gang-raped in the clubhouse. Some visiting Danish bikers had come to Amsterdam to party with the Hells Angels, who were hoping to expand into Denmark. They brought the girl to Angel Place for a drink, where they sexually assaulted her. The bikers were so drunk that she managed to escape when they passed out. She ran through the steel gates, up the small commercial road, under a railway bridge and into Amstel subway station, where she called her father. Police raided the clubhouse and arrested six bikers, who were convicted the following year. They never did serve their two-year sentences: the Dutch court allowed them to return to Denmark.

It was harder for Big Willem to calm his angry neighbours, who demanded that the city close down Angel Place. Willem defiantly declared, "We live by our own laws; one of them being that apart from our own girlfriends, girls are only permitted in Angel Place for sex." When opposition intensified, Big Willem took a more conciliatory tack out of the Toys for Tots gimmick book used by the North American Angels. He donated money and delivered free toys to children's hospitals. The chequebook diplomacy worked, and the incident was largely forgotten.

Big Willem's club finally gained full-patch status on October 28, 1978. At three o'clock in the morning, two members of Sonny Barger's Oakland club called with the good news. The German Hells Angels president from Hamburg was on hand to present them with their colours. Their wives and mistresses spent the night sewing the new Death Head patches onto their jackets. As Big Willem stood by proudly, his fellow Angels raised the Hells Angels banner above the clubhouse.

Big Willem's dream had come true. But his work was far from finished. He was determined to make his chapter the most powerful in Europe. For the time being, though, those plans could wait. For the next three days, the Amsterdam Hells Angels drank themselves into oblivion.

Nobody saw what was coming. Not the politicians. Not the police and certainly not people like Joanne Wilson, who found the outlaw bikers an intriguing, even exciting, subculture.

Big Willem wasted no time in expanding the Hells Angels

throughout Holland. By 1980 they had opened a second chapter in Haarlem, about twelve miles east of Amsterdam. Then in 1986 the Nomads opened a clubhouse in Limburg, in southern Holland. Four years later the Angels added another club in the north. By the mid-1990s the HA had the four compass points of Holland covered. They owned the country and now could concentrate on the rest of Europe. Over the next twelve years, they would spread north through Denmark, Sweden, Norway, Finland and then into Eastern Europe and Russia. The expansion would spark one of the most vicious and daring internecine wars in the history of outlaw biker gangs.

Willem and his Hells Angels prospered in Amsterdam. They moved into the red-light district and established cafés and nightclubs with names like the Excalibur and the Other Place. Here they could build their forces and make alliances with existing crime figures while they fortified their drug business and began to build one of the most powerful underworld organizations in Europe.

They had little reason to fear arrest or conviction. Penalties were so lenient in the Netherlands that drug dealers rarely served much jail time. Holland became a country where, as one British journalist wrote, it seemed the legal system was drawn up "by a bunch of people out of their gourds on dope." In its more lunatic moments, the system allows criminals to deduct the expenses of their crimes. A Dutch court, for example, in 2002 ordered an armed robber to reimburse the 6,600 euros he stole from a bank – minus the 2,000 euros he had paid for his gun.

Dutch drug laws represent a tradition of tolerance and a will by the vast majority of its fifteen million people to decriminalize the use of soft drugs while at the same time perhaps stopping people from migrating to harder drugs such as cocaine and heroin. The Dutch regard drugs as a health issue. Licensed cannabis cafés – there are about 860, including 290 in Amsterdam alone – can legally sell up to 5 grams of cannabis to patrons and can keep up to 500 grams (about a pound) on the premises. Dutch citizens can grow up to five marijuana plants for personal use, so it's not unusual to see marijuana plants popping out of the roofs of houseboats tethered to canal walls or among the lovingly tended flower gardens and windowboxes of Holland.

Dutch authorities also tolerate the possession of up to 0.5 grams of cocaine or heroin.

What is illegal in Holland is trafficking in large quantities of any illicit drugs, including cannabis. Yet the Dutch have in the past largely closed their eyes even to that. Holland's politicians have made it clear that they would probably legalize all drugs, if not for opposition from the rest of Europe and the United States.

The Dutch ambiguity toward drugs has scored some successes as a social policy: a far lower proportion of the population in Holland uses cannabis than in the United States, with all its draconian drug laws. But it has been a disaster as a criminal policy, in effect allowing organized crime to thrive in Europe's open market.

For the outlaw bikers in Holland, the drug trade has been a gold mine: they have become the continent's gatekeepers. Cocaine flows in from Colombia, heroin from Turkey and Afghanistan, cannabis from Morocco. Laboratories in Holland pump out enough chemical drugs such as amphetamines and ecstasy to supply not only Europe but also parts of Asia, Australia and North America. Holland is the Colombia of synthetic drugs.

From his ever-expanding base in Holland, Big Willem launched his invasion of Scandinavia. Eager to bring the hundreds of ragtag Nordic biker gangs under the banner of the Big Red, he allied himself with a Danish biker as bold and ambitious as he was. His name was Bent Svang "Blondie" Nielsen, and he was eager to light up the land of Hans Christian Andersen.

Nielsen led a union of five local clubs operating under the surprisingly tame title Galloping Goose. In 1979 they were given prospect status under the Hells Angels. A year later the Geese acquired Angels' wings. Just two years after the Hells Angels had moved into Amsterdam, they had succeeded in creating their first Scandinavian club in Copenhagen, celebrating the new charter on New Year's Eve 1980.

Then the war began.

One club refused to join. They called themselves the Bullshit and they controlled a good chunk of the drug market in Copenhagen – especially the lucrative trade at an abandoned military base in central Copenhagen called Christiania. After squatters and hippies took it over in the 1970s, they declared it a self-governing state, and it remained as such until late 2005. They refused to pay taxes and utility bills. Tree-lined canals and brick walls brightly painted with graffiti art encircled and separated the community from the rest of Copenhagen. Christiania had its own sports clubs and social services. Thousands of visitors poured through its colourful gates each week to enjoy its cafés, restaurants, jazz clubs, theatres and art shows.

Christiania did a brisk business selling hash and pot out of numerous smoke shops. Police estimate they grossed anywhere from 500,000 to 1 million DK (US$78,600 to $157,200) worth of hashish and pot a day.

A lot of that money went into the hands of the Bullshit. They refused to ally themselves with the Angels, so the HA set out to destroy them. The Angels struck hard and fast, as if they were sending a message to all of Scandinavia.

Blondie Nielsen seemed to have his spies everywhere. In 1983, after he'd received a telephone tip from a barman, he walked into a Copenhagen restaurant where he found four Bullshit. He instantly killed two with his knife, stabbing them and cutting their throats, and wounded a third.

Still the Bullshit refused to surrender. So the Angels struck at the head.

Hells Angel Jørn Jønke Nielsen drove a stolen van to the home of the Bullshit president, nicknamed the Mackerel, and shot him with a machine gun as he walked to his car. With the Mackerel's wife looking on, Nielsen calmly walked over to his prone body, rolled him onto his back and emptied his magazine into his chest. Nielsen fled to Canada, where he hid out with the Vancouver Hells Angels. When he came out of hiding a year later and returned to Denmark he got a sixteen-year murder sentence. Prison turned him into a man of letters. He wrote an autobiography – *My Life* – and quickly became a popular author/murderer/biker guest on radio and TV. Nielsen bragged about his early days as a rebel biker: "Dirty, ragged clothes, and preferably with as many offensive symbols as possible. White Power T-shirts, swastikas and other Nazi badges could really get the bourgeois animals out of the armchair."

By 1988 thirteen people were dead, and the Bullshit no longer existed as a motorcycle club. Most of their members had been assassinated.

"They eliminated the Bullshit totally," Troels Ørting Jørgensen, commander of the Serious Organized Crime Agency (SOCA) in Copenhagen recalled. "They killed everybody. After that the HA were alone in the Danish criminal scene and in the Nordic as well."

For the next five years, the Angels enjoyed unrivalled supremacy in Europe. Sonny Barger's boys were firmly established in Holland, Copenhagen, France, the United Kingdom, Germany, Austria and Switzerland. Europe was their turf. But it wouldn't last. Their next adversary would prove far deadlier.

The Bandidos

The Texas-based group rivalled the Hells Angels in numbers in the States and had moved into Australia in a big way; now they were eager for a European beachhead. Signs of an approaching war first appeared in France in August 1989, when the Bandidos patched over a club in Marseilles. Like the first Bandidos in Australia, the Marseilles gang was selling used Harley-Davidson motorcycles shipped duty-free from the brotherhood in the U.S. Harleys were rare in Europe and commanded a premium price – at least double their American worth. The Hells Angels took immediate action to discourage the Bandidos' expansion. Four Angels from Geneva drove their bikes to Marseilles and shot the Bandidos vice-president dead and wounded two other club members. The murders sparked fears of a continent-wide battle for territory as both the Angels and the Bandidos planned massive recruitment campaigns, primarily among the hundreds of small biker gangs, many of them eager to wear American colours. Some included white supremacist groups such as Combat 18 (18 being the numerical initials of Adolf Hitler), soccer hoodlums and skin-heads with a reputation for unbridled aggression. Some were culled from the ranks of Europe's prison populations. Others were just disaffected bourgeois youth. It was a recipe for extreme violence.

American executives from both clubs met in Paris in the late summer of 1993 to prevent all-out war and make a peaceful division of the continent. Both clubs wanted to avoid police and government countermeasures that could slow their expansion.

In Germany, Hamburg officials had already outlawed the wearing of the Hells Angels patch, grounding the club and rendering it practically invisible. An Angel without his patch was clipped. The bikers wanted to forestall more of that kind of legislation, so they signed a non-aggression pact similar to the one they had in the United States. Basically, the Bandidos would inform the Angels where they would open a new club and give them the names of its members. If the Angels objected, some kind of compromise would be reached.

The Paris pact was the outlaw motorcycle gang version of Munich. As far as the European bikers were concerned, this was pure America hubris. While Europeans were impatient to embrace the American biker culture and adopt its most powerful symbols, they would do it on their own terms. As Churchill said in 1938, Europe had peace now; it would get war later.

It's not certain what exactly triggered the Great Nordic Biker War or even who fired the first shot. Both sides were primed for action. They were full of eager young disciples steeped in the lore of Sonny Barger and outlaw biker gospel. "Fuck the World." "Expect no mercy." "Real power can't be given – it must be taken." They were human tinderboxes dying to explode. Anything could set them off. So whatever the trigger, when the biker wars in Scandinavia began, they were bloody.

The Bandidos' expansion into Scandinavia began in Denmark in December 1993: they patched over a small gang called the Undertakers and set up chapters in Stenlose and Sandbjerg near Copenhagen. The Hells Angels sanctioned the takeover under the condition that the Bandidos confine themselves to just these two chapters in Scandinavia. "As far as we know the Bandidos promised not to expand further, but they did," Det. Insp. Christian Möller of the Danish police said.

The Bandidos leader was Jim Tinndahn, who was every inch as much an outlaw biker as Blondie Nielsen, the ferocious Danish leader of the HA. Determined to expand, he welcomed remaining supporters of the Bullshit plus several Hells Angels who had been tossed out in bad standing. "He filled his club . . . with this dirt," a Hells Angel said. "Tinndahn recruited all that garbage, and such a sick mixture produces more sick things."

The Angels, of course, had their own "sick things." Blondie's Copenhagen Hells Angels had already expanded into Sweden in

1990, awarding hangaround status to a club called the Dirty Draggles (Swedish for "scum") in Malmö, a port city on the southern tip of the country and just across the water from Copenhagen. The Draggles had won a violent struggle with two other clubs vying to become the first Hells Angels chapter in Sweden. It was typical of the way the Hells Angels selected new clubs. They sat back and watched as local clubs killed each other for the privilege of wearing the HA Death Head. The last club standing won. The Draggles become a full-patch HA club in 1993.

Tinndahn and his Bandidos had no intention of sticking to what they considered Hells Angels-imposed protocol. They too intended to expand. The Bandidos opened talks with the Morbids in Helsingborg, a port just north of Malmö. Once HA supporters, the Morbids were so angry with the Angels' recruitment of the Draggles that they opened talks with the Bandidos. That prompted the furious Malmö Angels to declare war on the Morbids. When Tinndahn patched them over as a Bandidos probationary club in late January 1994, the Hells Angels responded by sending a support club called the Rebels to spray the Morbids' clubhouse with bullets. The Angels launched a second attack a week later. The president of the Malmö chapter, Tomas Möller, a biker who, according to a Swedish police detective, used a giant Nazi flag as his bed cover and kept an elaborate museum of Nazi paraphernalia in his home, climbed onto the roof of a van with a high-calibre submachine gun and opened fire, riddling the club-house with bullets. Aside from one biker getting a finger shot off, nobody was hurt. The Angels then patched over the Rebels, making them their Helsingborg hangaround chapter. And the war began in earnest.

The first death occurred just after midnight on February 13, 1994. Fifteen Bandidos from Denmark held a party at the Roof Top Club in Helsingborg. The Hells Angels crashed the party. Thirteen shots were fired. When it was all over, one biker lay dead and three others were wounded, including HA hangaround Johnny Larsen. Nicknamed "Seven Bullets, No Problem," Larsen gained notoriety when he was shot seven times in a previous fight over either a woman or a motorcycle. Nobody ever really knew.

After that, the bikers brought in the heavy artillery. Literally.

Throughout Sweden and Denmark, the military had built small-weapons' depots for their civilian militias. Most males undergo obligatory military training and therefore know how to use these weapons. They also know where the depots are located. But most of all they know that they are unguarded. On the night of February 20, 1994, the Bandidos raided a Swedish armoury, stealing sixteen shoulder-fired light anti-tank weapons. They also stole hundreds of hand grenades and crates of small arms, including pistols and military rifles, plus ammunition. The bikers would raid these depots many more times before the government finally took steps to secure them. "It was probably dozens of times that they broke in," one intelligence officer with the Swedish police said. "Only the defence department really knows." Bikers also broke into the homes of militia members and stole their army rifles. How many weapons in total were stolen from homes and military installations during the four-year war has not been made public. Swedish and Danish military authorities have kept these numbers a secret even from the police. But an analysis of official police reports from Denmark and Sweden show that between 1994 and 1997 there were at least 36 thefts, including at least 16 Bofors anti-tank rockets; 10 high-powered machine guns, about 300 handguns, 67 fully automatic military rifles, 205 rifles of various calibres, hundreds of hand grenades, land mines and 17 kilos of explosives, plus detonators. Police believe the Bandidos or their support clubs were responsible for most of the break-ins. For their part the Hells Angels obtained Russian- and Yugoslavian-made rocket launchers, as well as surplus machine guns from former East Bloc countries.

The bikers were well armed to fight the kind of protracted gang war that Scandinavians had never experienced.

Back in California, the Hells Angels worried about the Bandidos' expansion. They also wanted to avoid a drawn-out war and the legal repercussions it could entail. Sonny Barger's Oakland club summoned Swedish Hells Angels leader Tomas Möller of the Malmö chapter to California to remind him that the Paris pact was, after all, a non-aggression deal. At the same time, they emphasized that the agreement did give the Angels control of Sweden, and they were determined to hold the Bandidos to that.

The Oakland chapter then met again with the Bandidos in Houston, where they reaffirmed that Sweden was indeed HA country. But the Bandidos central command in Texas could not seem to control the Morbids, who wanted to avenge the HA attacks. And European Bandidos leader Tinndahn reaffirmed his support of his newly chartered, violence-prone probationary club.

More futile diplomacy followed when a delegation of Bandidos from Houston visited Denmark and Sweden to meet with the Hells Angels clubs in Copenhagen and Malmö. Neither side would give in, and the talks ended in failure. That spring Helsingborg turned into Dodge City. "There were shootings almost every day," one police officer said.

The war found plenty of willing soldiers, even though at the time there was only one Hells Angels chapter in Sweden and one probationary Bandidos chapter in Denmark. But there were about fifteen homegrown biker gangs in both countries, most of them favouring the Hells Angels. That created several thousand bikers in Scandinavia itching to go into battle.

The war quickly revealed the differences in strategies of the two sides. While the Bandidos just blasted away in apparent indiscriminate attacks designed to terrorize the Angels into submission, the Hells Angels, if anything, showed themselves to be more strategically aware. They appeared to plot their attacks with the aim of decapitating the Bandidos. But neither side surrendered.

The first important attack on the Bandidos came on July 17, 1995: a carefully planned assassination of Swedish Bandidos president Michael "Joe" Ljunggren. As he drove his Harley along a largely deserted highway at more than seventy miles per hour, a sniper hiding in a roadside forest picked him off with five shots from a 9 mm automatic rifle. That same day saw two more assassinations of a couple of Bandidos outside their clubhouse in Helsinki.

The Bandidos responded over the next two weeks with two robust rocket attacks, one at the Hells Angels clubhouse in Helsinki and the second at the Helsingborg stronghold, where the rocket destroyed the roof, penetrated a wall and finally blew up a swimming pool. By sheer luck, nobody in either attack was injured.

As the war spread throughout Scandinavia, machine-gun

battles broke out in Oslo and Copenhagen. Both sides lived in constant fear of attack from car bombs, drive-by shootings and rocket attacks. They heavily armed themselves, fortified their clubhouses and checked their automobiles for telltale signs of explosive devices. It wasn't unusual for a biker to find a hand grenade rigged to his ignition. Ample weaponry was within reach. Swedish police raided the apartment of the girlfriend of one Bandido and found machine guns, hand grenades, land mines and explosives.

Then, eight months after their first sniper attack, the Angels struck again at the Bandidos' leadership. This time the attacks occurred in broad daylight amid thousands of people.

March 10, 1996, began like any other day at the Kastrup Airport in Copenhagen, with the busy cycle of arrivals and departures as cars and buses pulled up. Hundreds of travellers milled outside the glass-and-concrete terminal, expecting the safe and efficient processing of people. Except not on this day.

One of them was Jan Anderson. At 4:23 in the afternoon he was idly gazing out the window of a double-decker bus that was to take him to a ferry and then back to his native Sweden. "About eight or ten men emerged from a parking place," he later told a local newspaper. "Two of them walked over to a parked vehicle and began shooting directly through the windshield." The men jumped into a getaway car, which raced past his bus and disappeared down the highway. "I could see a guy dragging somebody away who was bleeding all over. The car was shot to pieces. Two of the tires were flat, but the driver had escaped."

Bandidos Danish leader Uffe Larsen was killed instantly. Three of his comrades were wounded. They had flown in from Helsinki, where they had attended a Bandidos party.

About 280 miles away at Fornebue Airport in Oslo an identical ambush was in process. Again the victim was a Bandido who had attended the Helsinki party. Four Hells Angels involved in the airport shootings got their Filthy Few patches.

"It was a very good professional job, like a military operation," said Commander Jorgensen of SOCA. "The Hells Angels are not like the Bandidos, who are kamikaze pilots. The Hells Angels always try to measure out the pros and cons, what is good, what is bad. The Bandidos have recruited the worst of the worst. The scum. But that made them extremely strong. So there was retaliation after retaliation."

After the airport ambushes, rockets rained down on the Angels.

On April 11, the Bandidos attacked the HA headquarters in Snoldelev, near Copenhagen, a prospect club in Jutland, and the HA club outside Helsingborg. A week later two anti-tank rockets were fired at two HA strongholds in Copenhagen, killing a woman and burning one of the clubhouses to the ground.

The Angels struck back a week later. On April 26 they somehow managed to cut through a perimeter fence at a prison in Copenhagen, smash a window and lob a grenade into the cell of a sleeping Bandidos VP named Morten "Traeben" (wooden leg) Christiansen. The grenade rolled under his bunk and exploded. They then sprayed the room with machine-gun fire. Although badly injured, Christiansen miraculously survived, saved primarily by his wooden leg, which absorbed most of the grenade blast. The Hells Angels sent another imprisoned Bandido a shaver with a small bomb inside. In a third jailhouse attack, the Angels simply walked into a low-security prison and threw a hand grenade into a cell.

The violence continued throughout 1996. Another rocket was fired at the Angels' Helsingborg clubhouse in September. Four days later they tied the launcher to the second-storey window of an abandoned factory. They then rigged a string around the trigger, strung it to their getaway car and pulled the cord. It was exactly as diagrammed in the army manual for remote firing of the anti-tank weapon. The rocket cut through electric wires over railway tracks before hitting the HA fortress. Nobody was hurt, despite the fact that the Bandidos had also tossed two hand grenades and a smoke grenade into the building before making their getaway.

When the Bandidos struck again soon afterwards, the results were quite different.

Denmark is a flat country, so if you want a clear shot from a secure perch in a city crowded with apartments, you have to climb up onto on one of the steeply slanted tiled roofs. This was exactly what a prospect Bandido did one evening two weeks later, taking two anti-tank rocket launchers along with him.

Below, he had a clear view of the Hells Angels Copenhagen clubhouse compound, with its steel gate and chain-link fence. He could see guests arriving to help celebrate the Angels' anniversary party with a "Viking fest." About three hundred people showed up, plus about a hundred cops taking pictures and copying down licence numbers. One of them was Det. John Verlander. "I was talking to the people going in, and one of the Hells Angels told me to fuck off and lifted his beer to me as sort of a mock toast and closed the steel gate. He was lucky. If the steel door had been open, he would have caught the full force of the blast to come."

Seconds later the Bandidos prospect fired his first rocket. The projectile tore right through the clubhouse. Nobody saw it coming. All they saw was a huge explosion that rocked the compound. Verlander was the first one in.

"People were screaming and walking around, wounded. I called for two ambulances, but when I walked farther inside I told them to send everything they got," he said.

He started working on one victim, a twenty-nine-year-old woman named Janne Krohn who had been badly hit by fragments of stone from the wall, desperately trying to massage her heart, but she died in his arms. So did a man badly hit nearby, a Hells Angels prospect named Louis Niesen. Eighteen people were injured, many of them badly burned.

"If the rocket had hit about one foot to the right, it would have hit a steel plate and exploded with three-thousand-degree heat," Verlander said. "A lot of people would have been killed."

Police later found the abandoned launching tube on the roof of the apartment. Next to it was the second rocket. The prospect was too eager to escape to fire it.

The attack was a wake-up call for politicians and police, who, until then, had taken the stoic attitude that there was nothing they could do if two gangs wanted to kill each other. Now, however, another innocent woman lay dead, killed by a high-powered military rocket fired in the middle of Copenhagen. Within ten days the Danish parliament passed what became known as the "Rocker fortresses law," evicting bikers from their clubhouses. Police moved in quickly to execute the new law. In Copenhagen angry neighbours took sledgehammers to the Hells Angels Nomad clubhouse, levelling it to the ground. The irony was that many of the outlaw biker clubs had originally received state subsidies to set up their clubhouses, under the mistaken impression that the bikers wanted simply to pursue their passion for motorcycles. Some bikers sued for loss of property, while others went to welfare offices seeking state relocation subsidies. They were rarely successful. One mayor, however, decided to pay each biker an undisclosed sum to get them out of town. They took the money and ran.

In the end, the sudden flurry of evictions was too late. The bikers were so well entrenched and organized that they quickly re-established themselves in new and often improved accommodations, and the war continued unabated. Over the next ten months, well into 1997, police logged more than two hundred acts of violence, including three murders and twenty two attempted murders. It seemed no one could stop the bloodletting.

Then Drammen happened.

Torkjel "The Rat" Alsaker had been carefully planning the attack for months. President of the Hells Angels chapter in Oslo, Norway, Alsaker, thirty-six, was eager to make his mark in the ongoing war with the Bandidos. On the evening of June 4, 1997, six members of a Hells Angels support gang packed a stolen minivan with explosives. Bikers wearing longhaired wigs drove the van to the front of the Bandidos' headquarters in Drammen, a small city just east of Oslo. The car bomb exploded at 11:45 P.M. collapsing the building, sending debris two hundred yards away and blowing out the windows of surrounding buildings. Three Bandidos were sleeping inside when the bomb exploded. The floor gave way beneath them, and the impact blew off their clothes. They walked out of the debris dazed and naked but uninjured.

The same wasn't true for Astrid Bekkevold. The fifty-one-year-old woman and her husband were driving home after an evening out. As they passed the minivan, the bomb exploded, and Bekkevold took the full impact. She died instantly. Her husband was badly injured but survived.

Fallout from the Drammen explosion shocked Scandinavia. Politicians from all four countries met to discuss banning the motorcycle clubs and pooling police resources for an intense clampdown. The sudden, universal condemnation spooked the biker gangs. According to a document later discovered in a raid on a Hells Angels clubhouse in England, the Angels began making plans to win public support and considered legal action if governments passed laws that they felt violated their freedom of association.

The bikers themselves, exhausted, bloodied and losing public support, seemed eager for an end to hostilities. Tensions had been at hair-trigger level for years. Bikers in Oslo had even shot a woman in the head when she drove by their clubhouse once too often. Most of all, though, "it was very expensive," Det. Insp. Christian Möller of the Danish police said. Wiretaps picked up bikers complaining about lack of money: the war was ruining their business. "We could see it in our investigations that they had no money and they had to use it all on this war," he said. "A lot of the bikers were older and had children and were not interested in having this war going on."

The incentive to find a solution was strong on all sides. American and European leaders of the Hells Angels and Bandidos met again in the United States, first in Colorado and then in Seattle in June 1997, to discuss yet another peace agreement. In the end, however, it had to be reached among the Nordic clubs. Police helped smooth the way by supplying security for peace conferences. "We picked up the people from the HA and the leaders of the Bandidos and brought them to the meetings," Möller said.

Finally, on September 25, 1997, on live television, Danish Hells Angel president Bent "Blondie" Nielsen, and Bandidos European president Jim Tinndahn shook hands. Dressed in their full-patch biker gear like two war-weary heads of state, they gave a press conference during which they declared an end to what police had dubbed the Great Nordic Biker War. The announcement headlined the news throughout Scandinavia. It seemed that the only thing missing was the declaration of a national holiday.

There were well over four hundred violent incidents during the three-year war, which killed eleven people and injured more than a hundred, many seriously. Given the ferocity of the war and the weapons used, it was miraculous that the mortality rate was not higher. Police say some people simply disappeared, their fates unknown. Authorities counted seventy-four murder attempts, but there were probably many attempts they knew nothing about.

The peace agreement held. The violence stopped. And the two clubs got down to the business of making money. What police didn't realize at the time was that this was more than a peace accord. This was a precursor to a Versailles Treaty, where the two gangs carved up Scandinavia and eventually all of Europe.

It began with the four Nordic countries. As police later discovered in raids on their Danish clubhouses, the bikers signed treaties designating exactly which areas they controlled, right down to individual bars, cafés, nightclubs and restaurants. "It was because they wanted to avoid a confrontation," Möller said. Police regard these documents as the strongest evidence of how far the enormous power of the two outlaw bikers clubs extends over Scandinavia's underworld economy.

The bikers quickly expanded into their allotted territories: By 2005 the Angels had added two more chapters in Denmark, going from six to eight, for a total of about 168 full-patch members. In Sweden they had eighty members in six chapters, in Norway five chapters and in Finland four.

Not to be outdone, the Bandidos formed thirteen clubs in Denmark with 171 members. They also have four in Sweden, plus two probationary, two clubs in Finland and five in Norway. Both clubs also beefed up their support gangs. In Denmark, for example, the HA formed twenty-five Red and White support chapters with 250 members and the Bandidos had about thirty support groups – called X-Team chapters – with 350 members.

For reasons that mystify the police, Denmark has the highest concentration of outlaw bikers in Europe and perhaps the world. "No one has ever done a sociological investigation as to why in this small, extremely peaceful country of Denmark we have so many chapters of outlaw motorcycle gangs," Commander Jorgensen said. "They are very much hardliners, they are fierce, they are violent. We are the country of Hans Christian Andersen. We should not create crooks like that."

From their Scandinavian base, the bikers were poised to conquer Europe – and with a peace treaty under their belts they were ready to take advantage of the newly emerging markets of the European Union. When the borders fell in 1992 between EU countries, it gave the bikers unrestricted access to one of the world's richest markets – 376 million people with purchasing power of US$11 trillion. "Some of the greatest beneficiaries of a single market have been organized crime," said Europol, the police intelligence agency created to monitor organized crime in the EU. "Perhaps the most potent threat to the European Union, its economy and social fabric is organized crime groups that can now operate in a bigger, virtually unregulated, market. Sophisticated organized criminals are now operating closely together."

Indeed, since 1998 both clubs have doubled in size on the continent. Fifteen years after the Bandidos opened their first European chapter in Marseilles in 1989, they have expanded to seventy. The Hells Angels have moved into Spain, where the south is the central transit area for cannabis from Morocco and also a major money-laundering centre. Police investigations show that drug money has fuelled the enormous real estate boom along the Costa del Sol, helped somewhat by the transfer of some Scandinavian Angels to the Spanish clubs. In Italy the HA now have eight chapters, and the Bandidos have three. Europol officials are worried that police in both Spain and Italy are making the same errors that the Scandinavians made by ignoring the early-warning signs of the expansion of outlaw biker gangs in their countries. Already Italy has seen several high-profile biker murders in 2004 and 2005. "They are too preoccupied by their homegrown Mafias to care about what they think is just biker subculture," Mogens Lundh, a Europol intelligence officer from Denmark, said. "They are more or less developing this type of criminal society without really knowing it and understanding the danger."

That danger has been quite deliberately planned: documents found in 1988 by Danish police in a Hells Angels bunker in Roskilde reveal the Angels' intention to divide Europe into three power blocs. The first was Scandinavia, including the Baltics and Russia. The second was Great Britain and the third Western Europe, which would be in charge of expansion into Eastern Europe.

True to plan, both clubs have begun expanding aggressively into Eastern Europe and Russia. The Hells Angels opened a chapter in Prague in 2000 and a prospect chapter in Moscow in 2004, where they patched over part of the Night Wolves gang. The Bandidos moved into St. Petersburg that same year and established a prospect chapter in Turkey run by Muslims from Denmark.

The American-based clubs – the Hells Angels, the Bandidos and, to a lesser degree, the Outlaws – have in typical corporate fashion "rationalized" the outlaw biker gangs of Europe. During the past fifteen years, they have merged and amalgamated hundreds of largely white neighbourhood street punks, soccer thugs and racists into disciplined organizations that now rival traditional ethnically based organized crime groups such as the Italian Mafia and the Asian Triads. That has been the greatest success of the Hells Angels and Bandidos. They have empowered Europe's criminal underclass. They have given it structure and common purpose. They have turned the marauding punks of Europe into a finely tuned, intimidating machine without depriving them of their freewheeling independence. In so doing they have given them stature, power and wealth – or at least the expectation of wealth. It has been a typical American corporate invasion that has rewarded the Hells Angels and Bandidos with a truly global reach.

Indeed, many Hells Angels from North America are in awe of the stature their brethren have across the ocean. "There are European countries where we are literally looked on as gods," says Donny Peterson, a leader of the Ontario Angels in Canada. "In Scandinavia we're revered, feared."

It didn't take long for Europe's newly invigorated bikers to cast their eyes abroad – to Asia and Africa.

The Bandidos are expanding into Asia, where they have opened four chapters in Thailand led by Danish members. They have invested in bars and nightclubs. Commander Jorgensen thinks they are looking for a nice country to retire in. "It's all that they want. There's power, corruption, females, nice climate, no police to hamper them."

If Thailand is the retirement home for Bandidos, South Africa is where aging Angels want to settle. Danish leader Blondie Nielsen has bought a large estate in the northeast, close to the Elephant River game reserves. Malmö HA president Tomas Möller has an estate outside Cape Town on the cliffs overlooking the ocean. Möller lives in Cape Town half the year, where he collects 14,000 Kroners (US$1,707) a month in tax-free workman's compensation. He claims he has a bad back. "How did he hurt his back?" one Swedish detective scoffs. "He has a good doctor." Indeed, for a man who supposedly scrapes by on disability payments, Möller lives well. Swedish police records show he drives a Ferrari, a Hummer and two Harley-Davidsons. When not in South Africa, he has a number of apartments in Malmö, plus a small private museum for his collection of Nazi paraphernalia, including uniforms, flags and banners, weapons and even Nazi cars and motorcycles.

The police reaction to this renewed biker onslaught on Europe had been slow and uneven. Only in 1999 did one of Europol's priorities become outlaw motorcycle gangs. Headquartered in a large fortified former convent in The Hague, Europol set up a separate intelligence unit to monitor OMGs throughout the union. "Biker gangs are now entrenched in Europe," said chief analyst Mogens Lundh. "In the European Union there are outlaw motorcycle gangs present in every country except Cyprus, and the Hells Angels are present in almost all of them."

The brightest spot on the law enforcement map in Europe is Lundh's home country of Denmark, where police have applied tremendous pressure on the outlaw bikers since the peace treaty, designating them a "national security" issue. "We have had more or less a zero-tolerance policy," Lundh said.

As of the end of 2004 the 1,086 Hells Angels, Bandidos and supporters in Denmark had a total of 7,937 convictions, according to a survey by Danish police. In fact, only one biker in the two largest outlaw motorcycle gangs in Denmark did not have a criminal record.

"The whole philosophy here has been that after the biker war ended we would not allow ourselves to relax and let them share in their criminal activity," Jorgensen said.

Since the crackdown, many Danish bikers have sought safer harbours elsewhere. Norway was not much of a refuge. Police there have taken a similarly aggressive stance and convicted all six Hells Angels involved in the Drammen bombing that killed the fifty-one-year-old woman driving home. Torkjel "The

Rat" Alsaker, the president of the Hells Angels chapter in Oslo, was sentenced in 2004 to life in prison.

Sweden proved to be more hospitable to the bikers. Almost none of the crimes have been solved there, primarily because police are too afraid to get involved: threats from the bikers are constant, and the government has done little to protect its police.

Swedish police got a taste of biker intimidation back in 1990 when they arrested every member of an Angels support gang called the Belkers, only to find themselves under siege. Bikers threw hand grenades into the homes of a detective and prosecutor. In the summer of 1999, when a patrolman approached a suspicious car in the harbour and opened the front door, he ignited a bomb that blinded him. A year later a bomb blew up a SWAT team member's car outside his house. Then in 2002 another bomb was placed just outside the door of a police officer's home, where he and his son were asleep; one of the clock hands on the timer snagged on a wire and stopped the explosion one minute before the scheduled ignition.

"Because of all the threats against police officers, I think policemen close their eyes," said one police intelligence officer who was reluctant to have his name published. "They don't want to see. They're afraid."

At least in Sweden the cops knew the power of the bikers. But in Holland, the police remained blithely unaware of the storm gathering around them.

For almost two decades, Dutch police had ignored the 1985 murder of the twenty-two-year-old Irishwoman, Joanne Wilson, whose body had been chopped up and the torso and left leg found in an Amsterdam canal. Despite the constant pleading from her mother no further action had been taken. Even after DNA analysis became a proven forensic aide in identifying victims and perpetrators, the Dutch police made no effort to use the science on the body parts they believed were Joanne Wilson's.

But one person didn't forget.

Peter de Vries is a journalist who specializes in digging up cold cases and solving them on TV. More than a million Dutch viewers watch each week as he unearths new witnesses and clues to the many unsolved mysteries that for one reason or another have stymied Dutch police. De Vries is particularly interested in murder where time is about to run out. Holland is one of only a few countries with a statute of limitations on murder. It's eighteen years; it's not good law, but as the clock ticks it can make great TV.

In 2001 de Vries decided to take one last look at a March 1984 murder in an Amsterdam apartment: someone had stabbed Corina Bolhaar and her two young children and then slit their throats while a third child, who was only one year old and too young to talk, looked on. The statute of limitations on the case would end in a year. De Vries didn't have much time. He learned from his police contacts that the main suspect was the Hells Angels' Long Louis Hagamann. He also learned that Hagamann had been a suspect in another long-forgotten murder: that of Joanne Wilson.

Now he had four murders to solve and one prime suspect. Because Dutch law had turned murder into a stopwatch game, de Vries found himself racing against time.

Since Joanne's death, Hagamann, known as the Hells Angels' assassin, had been a busy criminal. He had more than a hundred convictions for aggravated rape, drugs, armed robbery, assault, torture and tossing a hand grenade at a police officer. He had become one of the most feared men in Amsterdam's underworld. De Vries and his staff began questioning anybody who had anything to do with Hagamann and his case: old witnesses, pensioned police officers. At one point the Hells Angels Nomads attacked de Vries's crew with rocks, kicking in their car doors and forcing them to flee. Intimidation of journalists wasn't an entirely unusual occurrence in Holland. The Hells Angels had once walked into a studio and beaten up two TV journalists for daring to suggest on air that the HA were a criminal organization. But de Vries and his team were not easily frightened. Eventually they came across one of Hagamann's old girlfriends, with whom he had had a baby in the late 1990s. Renetta van der Meer's interview was the crucial break they hoped could blow both the Bolhaar and Wilson murders wide open.

She admitted that Louis Hagamann had bragged to her about killing a woman and "her brats." He also bragged about strangling a former girlfriend, cutting her to pieces and feeding some of her body parts to pigs and throwing the rest in the canal. "He laughed about how he walked around with one of her arms after cutting the body into pieces in a bath. It was horrible. He told me he would do the same with me if I ever crossed him." In fact, he once tried to strangle Renetta. He gripped her throat so hard that the veins in her eyes popped and she needed an operation to save her sight. She said that Hagamann had also shot her former boyfriend in the legs.

De Vries then discovered that after the Wilson murder, Hagamann had been forced to move out of his apartment because he didn't pay his rent. The next tenant made a chance discovery. He found Joanne Wilson's passport behind the wallpaper.

With only one week left before the statute of limitations expired, de Vries broadcasted his findings, and police were forced to reopen both the Wilson and the Bolhaar cases. (They had initially lost the Wilson file.) They still faced one major hurdle: they didn't know with 100 percent certainty that the body buried in the unmarked grave was Joanne Wilson's. Without a body, they had no case. Worse still, when they went to the cemetery, they found that the grave had been dug up and the remains dumped somewhere in a giant landfill. Joanne Wilson had vanished, again.

The police, while incompetent, were at least lucky. In their forensic laboratory they discovered a technician had preserved a vial of Joanne's blood. DNA tests proved the butchered cadaver pulled out of a canal eighteen years earlier was indeed Joanne's. Now police, if only in spirit, had a body. They also had plenty of reason to go after Hagamann.

Long Louis wasn't going anywhere: he was in prison serving time for rape. But the police had only a few days left to charge him with the murders. Two inmates came forward and signed statements that Hagamann had bragged about the killings of Wilson and Bolhaar. What body parts he didn't throw into the canal, he smashed with a sledgehammer and fed to pigs on a farm, one inmate said of the Wilson murder. "He told me that he slept in the same bed and snored away beside the corpse for a couple of nights."

In the end, however, the police were too late: they had no

corroborating evidence about how or why Wilson had been murdered. Without proof of premeditation, the clock had run out on justice for Joanne Wilson. Ann Donaghy, her mother, was devastated: "Now he will not be punished for murdering my beautiful daughter. He will live the rest of his life as an innocent man as far as Joanne's death is concerned. The Amsterdam police have a lot to answer for."

But the police were more successful with the Bolhaar case. Hagamann, forty-seven, was convicted and given a life sentence, which means he could be out in fifteen years.

"He told me he'd kill me if he got a chance," de Vries said.

Too violent even for the Hells Angels, Hagamann was kicked out well before the trial, despite testimonials in court from Big Willem.

If the Dutch police thought they could go back to sleep, they were wrong. Another equally gruesome murder remained unsolved. Steve Chocolaad's Hells Angels killers still walked free. That would soon change, as even more bodies were about to come bubbling to the surface of yet another Dutch canal.

BLOOD SPILLED

RCMP *Gazette*

Another take on "The Great Nordic Biker War", offering a slightly different perspective. It takes the view that the war was over control of drug and other criminal activities in Scandinavia.

The war between the Hells Angels and Rock Machine in Quebec was not the only biker war to erupt in 1994. In March of 1994, another biker war broke out in Denmark and Norway with violence quickly spreading to Sweden. As in Quebec, the two gangs were violently competing for territory and control over criminal enterprises – markets for drugs, weapons, sex, and smuggled and stolen goods.

Outlaw biker gangs are not new to Scandinavia. OMGs have prospered in Nordic countries partly because of the relatively lax gun laws, the "open borders" policies between most European countries and a long standing cultural tolerance of unconventional behaviour. The Hells Angels took advantage of this tolerance when they began moving into Denmark. "The first thing the Hells Angels did before coming to Denmark was to send their lawyers," says Danish journalist Ambro Kragh, an expert on the Hells Angels. "They looked at every law and regulation here to see what they could use to their advantage."

The Hells Angels found a regulation that made any group exhibiting a particular interest eligible for government funding. Under Danish law the Hells Angels were a legitimate motorcycle club. "The government gave them taxpayers' money to set up their clubhouses," Kragh says. "They treated the Hells Angels as if they were providing adult education." The bikers were supposed to be teaching young people to drive motorcycles. Organized crime figures encouraged to teach young people obviously sets a dangerous precedent.

The Hells Angels opened their Copenhagen, Denmark chapter on January 1, 1980. In 1984, a Hells Angel murdered the President of Bull Shit, a rival gang. This led to retaliatory violence between Bull Shit members and the Hells Angels, supported by its affiliate the Morticians.

Between 1985 and 1987, the Danish Hells Angels wiped out Bull Shit. "There were 13 killings," says Per Larsen, head of CID for the Copenhagen district of the national police force. "But they were using normal methods – guns and knives. It was down to earth."

After this skirmish, members of the Danish Hells Angels embarked on a massive public relations campaign to rehabilitate their image. They held local television specials, handed out toys to sick kids and, at one point, sent a delegation of bikers to address the Danish parliament on the issue of organized crime. But all this soon changed as violence broke out again. In 1988, a breach developed between the Hells Angels and the Morticians, now the Undertakers Northland and the Undertakers East Coast. In 1992, against the Hells Angels' express wishes, the Undertakers applied for admittance to the Bandidos. The Hells Angels had recently declared they would not tolerate any more Bandidos chapters in Europe.

The war over territory began when the Bandidos moved into a region already occupied by the Hells Angels and set up a clubhouse close to them. In early February 1994, there had been clashes between Hells Angels and Bandidos in Finland and Sweden. At this time, a violent gunfight broke out between the two gangs in the Swedish port of Helsingborg. One Hells Angel was killed in the fight. The Hells Angels retaliated by killing two members of the Bandidos – one in Sweden and one in Finland.

Another phase of biker attacks began in May of 1995, when a Bull Shit member was severely wounded in a Hells Angels' attack which was launched to settle a score from the war in the 1980s. Between that rivalry and the newly erupted violence in 1995, most surviving Bull Shit members became Bandidos. Members of the Hells Angels were seen walking around Scandinavia wearing bulletproof vests – a sobering indication of the escalating violence.

The Hells Angels and Bandidos began gathering support – front-line soldiers – from existing or new biker gangs. When these gangs joined either the Hells Angels or Bandidos, cities became divided and unwittingly entered the war. "These are fellows from the same villages; some went to school together," says Pers Jaldung of Sweden's national police. "But one club went to the Hells Angels and the other to the Bandidos."

Military hardware stolen from an army depot in 1992 suddenly appeared in the biker war. The stolen anti-tank rockets were first used in Finland. In the summer of 1995, on the day a funeral was being held in Sweden for a high-ranking Bandido, the Helsinki clubhouse of a gang allied with the Hells Angels was attacked. Between 1995 and late 1996, the Hells Angels' bunker in Helsingborg, Sweden has been hit six times with anti-tank rockets. "After a bombing attack in Malmo, homes of 30 families had to be evacuated," says Jaldung.

The war climaxed on March 10, 1996. At this time, Danish members of both the Bandidos and the Hells Angels had been in Helsinki, Finland to take care of separate business. The Bandidos were opening a new clubhouse and the Hells Angels were attending a tattoo convention. In a horrible, ultimately deadly coincidence, the two gangs were booked on the same flight back to Copenhagen.

As they met at the Helsinki Airport before their flight left, the atmosphere was extremely hostile. According to police surveillance tapes, the four Hells Angels called their clubhouse in Copenhagen and requested a support team to pick them up upon arrival in Denmark. One of the Hells Angel travellers called to his brother bikers in Copenhagen: "Can't you send a couple of guys. We'll be arriving four men. But the whole plane is filled up [with Bandidos members]."

The flight was extremely tense, but uneventful. At the Copenhagen International Airport, four Hells Angels and two prospects waited in three cars. The Bandidos had also called for, or expected a support team upon arrival. Their members waited in seven cars.

Before the arriving Hells Angels and Bandidos left the Airport, the members of the support teams starting shooting at one another. Thirty-three shots were fired. The Danish Bandido leader was killed by Hells Angels' gunmen. Three other Bandidos were wounded. Both gangs then fled.

At about the same time as the Copenhagen attack, another violent incident occurred in Oslo, Norway. A Bandidos' probate was shot and wounded as he left the Fornebo Airport where he had just arrived from Helsinki. He was shot by a member of a Hells Angels-allied gang. The two simultaneous attacks indicated they were likely planned in advance.

A contributory cause to the tension was likely an attack in a restaurant by seven to ten Bandidos on three Hells Angels. The restaurant was a Hells Angels' hangout.

Two days after the attack, on March 12, police in Copenhagen arrested three Hells Angels. They were charged with murder. A Hells Angels' prospect was later charged. The court case began on November 11, 1996 and ended on December 20. Two Hells Angels were acquitted. One was sentenced to 16 years in prison. The prospect, now a full Hells Angels' member, was sentenced to six years for driving one of the cars. Shortly after the trial ended, the three originally charged Hells Angels and two other members were given the Filthy Few patch. The patch is a mark of honour for Hells Angels who have killed for the club.

But this was not the end of police action in this murder – particularly in light of the acquittals. In early 1997, the Hells Angels smuggled a cell phone into the prison for the convicted member. Police learned about the phone and secretly monitored and recorded his calls to his brother bikers.

Based on evidence gathered from the recorded conversations, Danish police arrested three Hells Angels. On October 16, 1997, one received 15 years and seven months, the second received nine years and six months, and the third received nine years and ten months. All were found guilty of murder and five attempted murders.

After the shoot-out at the Copenhagen Airport, police across Scandinavia increased patrols at airports and ferry ports. Officers with submachine guns and bulletproof vests also checked documents and searched vehicles going in and out of airports.

Justice Ministers from Finland, Norway, Sweden and Denmark met in Copenhagen in 1996 to seek a joint strategy to curb the growing biker war. The ministers adopted broader legislation and agreed to adopt stricter border controls and immigration restrictions. Judicial institutions agreed to strengthen their ties with neighbouring jurisdictions. Police began cooperating with their international counterparts by providing intelligence on the cross-border movements and transnational activities of biker gang members.

Anti-biker gang legislation was introduced throughout Scandinavia. In Denmark, police gained the power to stop and search bikers for weapons. On October 6, 1996, Danish police handed out eviction notices to the more than 200 bikers in the country's twelve clubhouses. Danish parliament had ordered all clubhouses closed immediately on the evidence that they attracted attacks which could injure or kill innocent bystanders. Anyone wearing a gang's insignia can be searched and jailed for thirty days if a weapon is discovered on his person. Norway outlawed clubhouses where civilians can get caught in the "cross-fire." By forcing clubhouses out of urban areas, legislators hope bikers will go elsewhere. Sweden introduced the country's first comprehensive anti-gang law.

Since May 1996, police have carried out hundreds of searches of bikers for weapons. In 166 criminal investigations opened because of the gang war, 132 offenders have been jailed.

On June 4, 1997, the war claimed an innocent victim and outraged citizens across Norway. The Hells Angels bombed the Bandidos' clubhouse in Drammen, a city close to Oslo. A woman and her husband were driving home – she was killed and he was severely injured. The car-bomb completely destroyed the clubhouse and severely damaged the surrounding buildings and shops. "They heard the blast 30 kilometres away and it shook windows 15 kilometres from here," said a neighbour. The woman's death was the eleventh death attributed to the Bandidos.

The morning after the bombing, Norway's prime minister

visited the site. He promised laws would quickly be in place to curb the violence. Within a month, legislation was in place which outlawed biker clubhouses in any area where gang rivalries could threaten civilians.

In Norway, as in Quebec, tough antibiker gang measures were introduced with the death of an innocent bystander. In Quebec, the death of an eleven-year-old boy brought the formation of the Carcajou squad. The woman's death resulted in strict anti-gang legislation and enabled tough police action.

From 1994 to 1997, the biker war resulted in eleven killings, 73 attempted killings and 96 wounded persons, of which 21 were innocent bystanders or police officers on duty. Several of these attacks were carried out with heavy military weapons such as anti-tank weapons, grenades and explosives.

In Sweden it was noted that Hells Angels' members and supporters most frequently use small arms, while the Bandidos more frequently use antitank missiles. Bombs were used by both gangs. The size of the bombs used during this war, one to five kilograms, are smaller than the ones used in Quebec, occasionally 50–90 kilograms.

An anti-tank missile, Type AT 4 – Swedish model, was used eight times and a Type RPG 22 – Russian model was used three times. Hand grenades were used in four attacks and a booby trap in one case. Car bombs were used in three cases and "other bombs" used in three cases.

On September 25, 1997, the Hells Angels and Bandidos in Denmark released a much-publicized press release in which they proclaimed an armistice for all of Scandinavia. Bandidos and Hells Angels were shown arm-in-arm on television. The armistice, negotiated on more neutral ground in the US, was not a simple peace agreement between the gangs. It was deliberately and publicly designed to ease public pressure on law enforcement for arrests and parliaments for even greater antibiker gang legislation. Police believe both gangs also experienced resource problems, including an acute shortage of funds to continue procuring weapons and pay for expensive bail and legal bills. Also, the psychological pressure of "war fatigue" was likely experienced by some members of both gangs, as well as their families. There was also the possibility that the Danish Public Prosecutor would ban both biker gangs.

The threat that biker gangs may have been outlawed in Denmark would certainly have concerned both clubs. However, as this would have infringed upon human rights and the Danish constitution, the Danish Ministry of Justice concurred with the recommendation by the Public Prosecutor not to ban the gangs.

In their peace settlement, each gang agreed not to establish any more chapters other than those existing on the date of settlement. This condition has not been respected. Both chapters have been actively expanding and creating support chapters.

The Hells Angels and Bandidos have now apparently turned to bureaucracy to settle their differences. According to police sources, committees comprising members of each gang have been appointed to settle any disputes. Members from both gangs have generally obeyed a directive to observe the peace settlement and neither carry weapons nor wear bulletproof vests. But some members, especially those heavily involved in the past violence, have found it difficult to adjust to peace.

There are many who watched the war, and its subsequent peace deal unfold, and they question whether the violence has ended. "There may be members of each group who are tired of the killing, tired of wearing bulletproof vests," says Jalung. "But I don't know whether [the peace] will last. A lot has happened. Too many people have been shot."

As always with outlaw bikers, the bottom line is profit. According to CISC, the war and the growing public outrage and political action against the bikers was cutting deeply into profits. The peace deal was the quickest, simplest way to appease everyone and return to making money. And the peace deal as it stands may be profitable – at least for a time. But territory and control over criminal enterprises will likely still be in dispute. And when profits are threatened again, violence will return.

There was, and is, an international context to this war and peace deal. As both the Hells Angels and the Bandidos are gangs with chapters around the world, it was crucial to ensure the war did not spread. Other chapters from each gang obviously had influence in encouraging the Hells Angels and Bandidos to choose peace, or at least a facade of peace. But although other chapters may exert some influence, every region is self-sufficient and may persist in ill-advised wars. For example, the Quebec Hells Angels refuse to listen to any chapter and insist on handling their conflict with the Rock Machine their own way.

The Nordic war and its peace deal are also complicated by the Hells Angels' bloody war with the Rock Machine in Quebec. The Bandidos in Denmark have been the principal players in attempts to patch over the Rock Machine as Bandidos. The Bandidos and Rock Machine were apparently strengthening their ties during negotiations of the peace deal, threatening its implementation.

Law enforcement will continue to watch closely any developments in Scandinavia, particularly any indications that violence may again erupt. And police will also monitor any effects the interactions the Hells Angels and Rock Machine have on Hells Angels–Bandidos relations.

HELL'S ANGELS VS. THE ROCK MACHINE

RCMP *Gazette*

This 1999 excerpt from the Royal Canadian Mounted
Police Gazette *illustrates the enormous costs of interclub wars, allegedly fought over control of criminal
activity in Canada.*

Canada is home to some of the world's most violent outlaw
bikers. The war between the Rock Machine and the Hells
Angels in Quebec is the longest and most violent war – sur-
passing the biker war in Scandinavia. No other biker war has
been fought so overtly and with such brutal intensity. And the
violence continues.

The province has a history of biker violence. The battle between
the Hells Angels and the Rock Machine is the province's third such
brutal dispute. In 1970, a bitter rivalry broke out between the
Devils Disciples and the Popeyes. In 1978, war erupted between
the Outlaws and the Hells Angels, who had taken over the Popeyes
in 1977. Animosity still lingers between the Outlaws and the Hells
Angels, though members of those two gangs in the US have been
photographed arm-in-arm recently. The violence which characterizes the current war in Quebec is also not unprecedented.
Between 1970 and 1986, there were 890 murders linked to organized crime in Quebec; 118 of them biker-related.

Although the war between the Hells Angels and the Rock Machine has been fought throughout Quebec, Quebec City is the brutal epicentre, characterized by murders, attempted murders, arson, and bombings.

Prior to 1994, the Hells Angels allowed the Rock Machine to control the sale and distribution of a large portion of the Hells Angels' drug market in downtown Montreal and the East-End. The Rock Machine was officially described as an OMG in 1991, though as a non-traditional gang. However, the gang was observed by law enforcement exhibiting characteristic biker gang behaviour as early as 1989.

There are old ties between the Hells Angels and Rock Machine. The Rock Machine is composed of some former Devils Disciples and SS biker gang members.

The gang was already weakened by the arrest of a member in May 1994 for conspiracy to import 11 tonnes of cocaine from the US into Canada. According to the Hells Angels, the Rock Machine was too disorganized and weak to continue independently managing a lucrative drug network. Around this time, the Nomads offered to absorb the Rock Machine, but the gang refused. The Rock Machine wanted to keep its independence and members were willing to fight for it.

The Hells Angels found a new business partner – the Rockers MC which is a puppet club to the Nomads. The Rockers was formed in 1989. The gang had two waves – the original Rockers died or retired in 1991 and 1992. The second wave came when the Rockers replaced the Rock Machine in 1994. Since 1994, the Rockers has managed the Rock Machine's former drug network.

The Rock Machine, preparing to preserve its independence from the Hells Angels, sought support in other organized crime groups. They gained the support of the Dark Circle, made up of some former Devils Disciples, a few of whom used to fight the Popeyes. The Devils Disciples were involved in and approved murders of the Hells Angels and their affiliates during the war. The Dark Circle also contained members of other organized crime groups – the Pelletier, Bertrand, and Cossette clans. The Bertrand clan is better known as the Palmers. Members were in a street gang and the palm tree became their symbol and name. The Palmers had a close relationship with the Rock Machine because the gangs shared some common territory. There were also some independents in the Dark Circle who wanted territory for themselves or who were enemies of the Hells Angels. The union of these forces and the Rock Machine became known as the Alliance. Members wore a ring with a large "A," similar to the Rock Machine's ring.

The Rock Machine again had strong criminal backers. They were ready for war. So were the Hells Angels.

On July 14, 1994, an individual involved with the Hells Angels was murdered. Two days later the Surete du Quebec thwarted a Rock Machine conspiracy to eliminate three members of the Evil Ones MC, a Hells Angels affiliate. Five Rock Machine members were arrested with explosives in territory controlled by the Evil Ones.

"After the war began, some members of the Alliance – a few of the Pelletier clan and some of the Palmers and Cossettes – defected to the Hells Angels," says Cpl. Pierre Verdon formerly of the Carcajou squad. "Some defections were the result of territory shifts. Many of the independent low- and mid-level drug traffickers are controlled by whoever runs their territory. Some had no choice but to work for the Hells Angels." These defections may occur on both sides as territory changes hands, but the Rock Machine, as they lost almost all territory, lost many more supporters.

Throughout the war, frontline "soldiers" on both sides carried on a vicious battle, attacking each other's associates, hangarounds, strikers and prospects, and even members if they were unwisely unprotected. Soldiers were often expendable, controlled by members who wished to command but survive the violence.

During the war, both gangs used a large number of powerful explosives to attack clubhouses, places of business, residences, vehicles, hangouts, and members and their supporters. Both the number and the size of the bombs used were unprecedented in Canada. From January 1992 to May 1997, 241 bombs exploded in Quebec. Another 110 bombs were dismantled, including 44 in Montreal, by bomb technicians in Quebec. This was the worst wave of bomb activity since the 1963 to 1970 *Front de Libération du Quebec's* terrorist campaign in which 200 bombs exploded.

Although the Hells Angels and Bandidos in Scandinavia occasionally used larger arms – even rocket launchers – against one another during their war, the bombs used in those countries were much smaller.

Many of the bombs in Quebec were made by incompetant in experienced guys says Cpl Jacques Morisset of the Intelligence Section, Surete de Quebec "The bombs were way too large; they'd destroy everything, not just the intended target. A few of them which luckily didn't explode could have destroyed more than one building in residential areas. In these cases, they weren't made properly," he explains. "A lot of the guys who made the bombs were hangarounds or prospects. Luckily they didn't always know what they were doing. These guys were trying to prove themselves."

Between 1994 and 1995, 1.3 tonnes of dynamite was stolen in Quebec in four major thefts. Part of this dynamite soon began to show up in Montreal and Quebec City's war zones. This marked an escalation in the size of bombs used. In August 1996, a 90 kg dynamite bomb was found in a residential area near a warehouse used by the Rock Machine as a meeting place. In November of the same year, police dismantled a 23 kg bomb left near a Hells Angels' clubhouse in St. Nicholas, Quebec City. On January 27, 1997, a 35 kg bomb was found outside a Hells Angels' bar in a Quebec City suburb. On May 19, 1997, in Montreal, police found two 20-litre gasoline containers wired to a powerful explosive charge. Four Hells Angels' associates were arrested and 250 kg of dynamite was seized on September 13, 1997, following raids in Sept-Iles, Quebec, northeast of Quebec City.

And these are only a few of the bombs characteristic in the war. From 1994 to 1997, bombs and arson attacks occurred with terrifying regularity in Montreal and, particularly, in Quebec City. Although both the Rock Machine and Hells Angels used bombs and arson attacks, the Rock Machine was responsible for a larger number of attacks, particularly on Hells Angels' owned or controlled businesses and hangouts. One reason is that the Rock Machine has more of an incentive to destroy property. The Hells Angels controlled the majority of the territory and have no reason to destroy their own strip clubs and bars.

*   *   *

The destructive potential of the large bombs and the frequency of the attacks occurring in public or residential areas concerned police and the public. It was only a matter of time before an innocent person was killed.

This occurred on August 9, 1995. On this date, an eleven-year-old boy became the war's youngest victim. The youngster was wounded by debris while riding his bicycle past a Jeep as it was blown apart by a powerful remote-controlled bomb. He died a week later. The man who owned the Jeep, not the intended target, also died in the explosion.

On the two year anniversary of her son's death, his mother spoke about the biker gangs and their attempts to silence her. "The year it happened, I received a letter from the Hells Angels asking that I meet with the president," she said. Five offers were made by members of both gangs in signed letters and telephone calls. "They wanted to give me an exorbitant amount of money. I won't say how much, but I refused. I told them they could never buy my silence or compensate me for the sadness."

Both gangs obviously regretted the intense media publicity that the death of the boy focussed on the war and the problem of outlaw biker gangs in Quebec and Canada. The mother said members of the gangs offered to pay for funeral costs and gifts for her family. Before the boy's funeral, a member of the Hells Angels even offered 16 bikers to accompany the funeral procession.

After her son's death, his mother made frequent public appeals for tougher anti-gang legislation. Her appeals guided public outrage into a persistent call for politicians to take action to end the war and combat OMGs.

Public outcry surrounding the young boy's death resulted in the provincial government setting up the Carcajou (Wolverine) anti-gang squad in October 1995. Before Carcajou, police shared intelligence and carried out informal joint operations. Carcajou formalized cooperation between the Montreal Urban Community Police (MUC); Sûreté du Quebec (SQ) (provincial police); and the RCMP. Its mandate was to stop the biker war and achieve public security. And the squad succeeded – Carcajou has been responsible for numerous raids against the Hells Angels and Rock Machine, large seizures of drugs and weapons, and the closure of clubhouses. The squad also arrested nearly all the Dark Circle's Devils Disciples after they attempted to murder a prominent member of another gang. The successes of Carcajou were published almost daily in the media, making the investigative unit very well known to the public.

In October 1998, one of Carcajou's priorities was to include Laval, which has been a site of war violence. Municipal police officers were paired with officers from the SQ. Partnerships between regional, provincial, and federal police created mini-squads – each dedicated to combatting local organized crime while effectively sharing information and resources. These joint forces projects are operational in 1999 – in Montreal, Trois-Rivières, Chicoutimi, Quebec City, Hull, Sherbrooke, Laval, and a division from the South Shore.

Unlike Carcajou, *Project HARM*, formed in 1997, concentrated upon the street level activities of the two gangs – both their daily criminal activities and acts of war. This project, named after the initials of the Hells Angels and Rock Machine, was staffed by officers from the MUC police force's biker squad. It was closed on May 31, 1999 with the reformation of Carcajou.

As much of the war-related violence has calmed, Carcajou has adapted to meet different investigational needs. The second Carcajou will investigate the OMG's criminal activities within Quebec in a cooperative, integrated manner. Officers will be drawn from a number of municipalities to staff the unit. The management structure of the squad has also changed. The former Carcajou was managed primarily by the SQ, but this version will be run by the MUC and SQ.

As bombs exploded regularly in Quebec, members of the Rock Machine and Hells Angels both knew that the war was bad for business and attracted intense and unwelcome police interest. Some Hells Angels were particularly concerned about adverse publicity – especially the kind which leads to tougher laws or more police investigations. In 1996, after a bomb destroyed a house in which children lived – the children were away at the time – the Hells Angels' war cabinet decreed there would be no more bombings without the express approval of senior bikers. The Hells Angels claimed they didn't want to involve children in the war. But the Hells Angels' public relations campaign only exists to sanitize the gang's image and preserve its criminal activities from police investigations, political interference, and public scrutiny. There is no room for children.

Bombs are no longer a key component in the Hells Angels' arsenal, but the Rock Machine made no such decree.

In April of 1997, Canada introduced new legislation intended to combat OMGs. It was designed to give law enforcement greater powers to investigate and deter criminal organizations and their members. "This is only a first step," said Alan Rock, former Federal Justice Minister, when he presented Bill C-95.

In November 1998, Quebec's Justice Minister Serge Menard promised to start using the seized proceeds of organized crime to reinvest in police forces. The use of seized proceeds to fund police work has been a standard practice in the US for years. More than $20 million in assets has been seized since 1996. With more than $11 million worth of property, vehicles and other costly items already auctioned off, half the proceeds will go back to the police forces that participated in investigations, raids, and seizures. The other half of the funds will be split evenly between organizations that help victims of crime and crime prevention community groups.

Although the violence has calmed considerably, there has been no peace treaty announced or cease-fire in the biker war. The record of war-related incidents is staggering. From July 1994 to June 1999, there were 69 deaths, 143 attempted murders, 82 bombings, 9 missing persons, and 140 cases of arson against biker affiliated businesses and hangouts. Larger death tolls (115 murders) include acts of violence not directly related to the war but to the OMG's "regular" criminal activities, including internal purges.

The Rock Machine has been severely weakened by the extended conflict. All of their original leaders are dead, jailed, or retired. The Hells Angels control nearly all of Quebec, but the Rock Machine are recruiting heavily. Members have been spotted across the country, attempting to establish enclaves receptive to the gang. And many younger bikers are joining the gang.

For several years the Rock Machine has been trying to negotiate a much-needed alliance with the Bandidos. Talks seemed to be failing recently as, according to intelligence sources, the Bandidos ordered the Rock Machine to establish better relations with Bandidos in the US. But in the first week of June 1999 at a ceremony in Lac la Tortue, Quebec, the Rock Machine successfully convinced the Bandidos to give them the right to wear Rock Machine colours. Prior to the gang receiving colours, Rock Machine members wore a $30,000 ring – diamond and gold with an eagle's head emblem. The Bandidos' colours are red on gold, while its affiliates receive gold on red colours. The gang's name is on the top rocker, with the gang's eagle's head symbol in the centre, and "Canada" on the bottom rocker. On the front of the colours, along with the characteristic OMG patches, there is a front left patch – "Support Bandidos World."

There have also been new developments with the Rockers. The Rockers now have a new gang working for them – the Scorpions. The gang, primarily formed from a group of local drug dealers, each wear a gold ring with their name above the emblem of a scorpion and "DBD" below – "death before dishonour." On the side of the ring are two letters, "SR," – "support Rockers." The Rockers must replace their war dead and have enough members to expand the gang.

The Hells Angels remain in control throughout the province and continue to expand. Tensions remain high between the gang and the Rock Machine. Law enforcement will be watching closely to determine what effect the formal support of the Bandidos for the Rock Machine will have on Quebec's OMG situation.

Extensive news coverage on OMGs documents their use of violence to expand or protect their territory or criminal activities, to punish, and to intimidate, but it also serves to further the gangs' brutal images. And, according to law enforcement sources, outlaw bikers are capitalizing upon this image. They use their much-publicized brutal images to intimidate by reputation. And the war in Quebec must not be used to further their already well-known reputations. It's a fine, often difficult line between providing accurate information on OMGs and unintentionally promoting their image.

MURDER OF PRISON GUARDS IN QUEBEC

RCMP Gazette

Perhaps the biggest – and lengthiest – of biker wars has been that between the Hells Angels Motorcycle Club (Canada) and the Bandidos Motorcycle Club (Canada). The following selection suggests that in Canada, like Scandinavia, law enforcement agencies believe that the clubs have basically declard "war" on the agencies.

On June 26, 1997, a prison guard was shot as she drove home from the Bordeaux Institution North of Montreal. On September 8, of the same year, another guard was driving the prison bus to the Rivière des Prairies, Quebec jail to pick up prisoners. The bus was sprayed with bullets and the guard was shot dead through the windshield. He was unarmed. Both guards were killed by semi-automatic gunfire. Both were married and had children. Another prison guard, a partner of the bus driver, was also in the prison bus and was wounded by the gunfire.

Two days after the June 26th killing, a person was shot and wounded as he left a public meeting at Saint Vincent de Paul Penitentiary in Laval. Police have said they believe this person was targeted in the mistaken belief that he was a prison guard. Both murdered prison guards were wearing their uniforms when they were killed.

After the second murder, corrections officers staged a daylong wildcat strike. They were replaced by provincial police officers. The guards returned to work after the province answered their demands for weapons and bulletproof vests. Prison guards also received police protection for the transfer of any prisoners.

Michel Lacoste, Quebec's regional director of correctional services for Montreal, accused organized criminal groups of trying to bring down the judicial system. The murders did slow down the justice system for a while. All court appearances involving prisoners in the Montreal area were temporarily cancelled after the second murder.

In December 1997, Montreal police arrested a striker for the Rockers and, a short time later, a biker sympathizer. The two agreed to become informants after their arrests. The sympathizer implicated a prominent biker figure who was charged with two counts of first degree murder and one count of attempted murder. Prosecutor Jacques Dagenais said the person charged is a leader in the Hells Angels' Quebec organization and a principal player in the gang's turf war against the Rock Machine. His arrest was seen as a strong blow to the Hells Angels and a victory for the Carcajou (Wolverine) squad.

In March 1998, the sympathizer was sentenced to life in prison on a charge of first-degree murder for the death of a prison guard. He was also sentenced to ten years in prison for attempted murder. He will serve both sentences concurrently which means he will not be eligible for release until he serves 25 years. In exchange for his testimony against the prominent gang member, the Crown dropped another charge of first-degree murder. Because the sympathizer was sentenced for one charge of first-degree murder, he will have the right to use the "faint-hope clause" to ask for release after he serves 15 years. This clause isn't available for multiple murderers. This person is in the witness protection plan in prison.

The sympathizer agreed to become a police informant – the Crown's principal witness against the prominent gang member. He testified about his participation in prison guards' murders and gave information about the general structure of outlaw motorcycle gangs. The sympathizer admitted he killed the guards and claimed the prominent gang member ordered the murders to intimidate Quebec's justice system. The sympathizer further testified that two other Hells Angels prospect members were his accomplices in the murders.

These two gang members were both prospects for the Hells Angels' Nomads at the time of the murders. The two men disappeared in December of 1997, shortly after warrants were issued for their arrests and just before the prominent member appeared in court. Nationwide warrants were issued for their arrests. The two bikers were last seen at the 20th anniversary celebration for the Quebec Hells Angels, held in Sorel, Quebec on December 5, 1997. In early 1998, the men were rumoured to be in Edmonton, Alberta. Although there were numerous sightings, none were confirmed by police. "They are considered armed and dangerous; they're in hiding and they don't want to be found by police," said a RCMP spokesperson. Rumours of Quebec bikers in Alberta renewed concerns about bikers evading police by hiding in different provinces and countries.

The rumours didn't last long. On February 27, 1998, a shot, burned and mutilated body was found by a farmer in his orchard south of Montreal. "The body was burned, probably to delay the identification of the body," said a Quebec spokesperson. The body was identified by dental records nearly a month later. The gang member was probably lured into a trap by fellow bikers who killed him to make sure he didn't talk to police.

The other gang member is still missing. There have been rumours that he's hiding or being hidden by bikers in western Canada.

Extraordinary security precautions were taken during the prominent gang member's two-week trial. He was surrounded by three court constables in the dock. Two constables sat at the front of the courtroom and two stood at the back. Provincial police used seven vehicles to accompany the patrol wagon to and from Sherbrooke, Quebec where the accused was held at the beginning of the procedures.

After he was moved from Sherbrooke, the prominent gang member was isolated in an empty wing of the prison to ensure he did not receive special treatment from the other prisoners. "We don't want 200 guys cheering and applauding when he shows up, like he's some kind of hero," said Rejean Leguard, president of the provincial jail guards' union. No men were cheering – he was held in the Tanguay women's detention centre. There was a special surveillance team of about ten officers to watch him at the detention centre. Guards must enter his cell in pairs.

The jail guards' anger and fear is understandable. "It's like you're a father and someone has raped your daughter and then you're being asked to drive him to court," Leguard said angrily. "We have a problem with anyone who participates in the murder of a peace officer." Leguard stated guards received assurances from the Public Security Department that their security concerns would be met.

Guards have been threatened by outlaw bikers in the past. Some guards have been photographed outside their homes by bikers who then use the photographs to intimidate them.

The security precautions also extended to the jury. Jurors were sequestered from the moment they were sworn in until they reached a verdict. This was the first time since 1983 that jurors were sequestered for the entire trial. The names and addresses of each candidate were revealed only to the parties in each case. Superior Court Justice Jean-Guy Boilard said, "sequestering the jury will prevent a mistrial caused by an event over which I have no control because it occurs outside the courtroom." Boilard cited a Leger & Leger poll of 1000 respondents commissioned by the Crown which found the public's fear of reprisals and threats while serving in a murder trial was heightened if the accused was a member of either the Mafia or the Hells Angels. While making his decision, Boilard referred to previous cases of jury tampering. He specifically mentioned a 1986 murder case in which four Hells Angels were charged with killing five of their brother bikers. In that case, after fourteen days of deliberation, Boilard received a confirmation of jury tampering – a note from a juror: "I was bought – Hells Angels. Juror No. 8."

Before their deliberations, Boilard instructed the jury to focus solely on whether or not the accused had ordered the murders. He said the jury should not take into account the prominent biker's activities as a Nomad or his position as Nomad leader. The judge also said the accused was linked to the murder only by indirect evidence – the testimony of an informant without corroboration. The accused must be convicted on all counts, he said, or acquitted completely. Boilard also instructed the jury to determine if the informant, who has a lengthy criminal record beginning in his adolescence, could be believed beyond a reasonable doubt. Boilard said he regarded the informant's testimony as unreliable and cautioned the jury to examine all of his testimony carefully.

On November 27, 1998, after a two-week trial and ten and a half hours of jury deliberation, the prominent gang member was acquitted on all three counts. He was now released after having been in custody since December 1997. He gave no comment to reporters as he left the courtroom. Outside the courtroom, his supporters exclaimed, "We got them!"

The Crown filed a notice of appeal of the not-guilty verdict in December, 1998. By coincidence, the notice of appeal was filed on the anniversary of his arrest by the Wolverine squad. This date will likely be one he remembers.

The Crown claims that Judge Boilard was at fault in his instructions to the jury before their deliberation. France Charbonneau, a Crown attorney who assisted prosecutor Jacques Dagenais, is heading the appeal of this acquittal. According to Charbonneau, Boilard "obliged the Crown to prove beyond a reasonable doubt all charges and then instructed the jury that if this condition was not met to acquit on all charges. The judge didn't have to make this condition," she says. "There was no opportunity for the jury to vote guilty on the first murder and not the second, or vice versa. The jury didn't have a choice to rule on one count and not another."

According to Charbonneau, Boilard also did not allow the jury to consider certain evidence. "He first said the jury should not take into account that the accused is a Hells Angels' leader," she says. "The prosecution provided a tremendous amount of evidence proving his leadership. As a leader, he must have given authorization for the murders. The sympathizer could not undertake the murders without this authority," Charbonneau states. The man and his leadership role in the Nomad cannot be separated. Boilard later said the jury may take the accused's leadership into account. But Boilard's initial statement had already been entered as part of the jury's instructions.

"Judge Boilard also misled the jury on certain evidence of reasonable doubt," Charbonneau states. "He required the Crown to prove all of the informant's statements beyond a reasonable doubt," she says. Boilard also misled the jury on the issue of corraboration.

A decision in the appeal is expected next winter or in the spring of 2000.

The aquittal highlights some serious underlying problems in Quebec's fight against OMGs. In particular, the use of informants to provide key, and sometimes principal, information against outlaw bikers is problematic. In OMGs, much of the criminal activities are carried out by junior criminal underlings – members of puppet gangs, prospective members, hang-arounds or associates.

And because underlings carry out much of the dirty work, they make ideal informants for police to connect more senior members with organized criminal activities. Since 1995, the use of informants by police has gone up steadily, and this is dangerous for biker leaders.

For the Quebec Hells Angels and its leadership, the murders served a dual purpose. They indicated that the Hells Angels wielded a significant influence in the province's prisons, and that the gang could and would intimidate (and murder) law enforcement officers. Equally important, the killings demonstrated the leader's need to establish complete control over his members. Absolute loyalty is imperative for the protection of the gang, its criminal activities and members. Any biker or associate who entertained the possibility of becoming an informant to lessen or avoid criminal charges would find prison a particularly harsh environment after the deaths of two prison guards. Similarly, the murders show there are few, if any, places safe from outlaw bikers.

It's difficult to infiltrate biker gangs or to locate and utilize an informant with valuable, first-hand contact with senior bikers. The more valuable an informant's information, the greater (generally) his involvement with the gang, and, likely, the greater his criminal record. And whether the informant is street-level or more established, the jury is likely to be concerned about his past criminal activities. And his present honesty. For someone who has a graphic knowledge of murders, arson, bombings and other crimes may not necessarily be believable to a jury. Particularly if the informant receives money and reduced sentences in exchange for information.

A great part of the problem is intimidation by the bikers. During the prominent biker's trial, courtroom spectators were offered $100 or $200 for their seats by his supporters. Although none of the bikers wore colours, both the jury and spectators were obviously aware who they were. All the spectators gave up their seats. During lunch, underlings reserved seats for more senior members. This attitude toward the public is common.

According to sources, the bikers spent most of their time glaring at members of the jury. One could think that the glares were meant to intimidate the jury. Was the jury scared? How did they feel when faced with a Hells Angels' leader and a courtroom packed with his loyal supporters? Unfortunately we cannot answer these questions as the jury's deliberations are secret.

Given these problems with juries at trials of OMG members, other alternatives to the current jury model seem to offer greater security to jurors. Trials of outlaw bikers could be restricted from the public to prevent large groups of biker supporters from gathering in the courtroom. Jurors could participate in court proceedings from behind a screen or via video. Or outlaw bikers could be tried by three to five judges instead of a jury.

Unfortunately, murders and an attempted murder of Quebec prison guards may only encourage OMGs to intimidate corrections officers. Every court case which results in an acquittal or is dropped for lack of evidence or intimidated witnesses fuels further biker aggression toward law enforcement. And it makes outlaw bikers believe they are untouchable.

The murders of these prison guards are being used by other Hells Angels chapters to intimidate corrections officers. During his incarceration at the Halifax County Correctional Centre in May or June of 1998, one Hells Angel showed a guard a newspaper article which described the murder of two Quebec prison guards. The Hells Angel's comment was "this is how we handle prison guards."

PART 6

Rats, Snitches, Dogs and Undercover Cops

"In an organization like the Hells Angels, which is based on brotherhood, freedom and your word, a rat is the true enemy."

Ralph (Sonny) Barger

Supposedly, no outlaw biker rats on another biker. That is the "golden rule". This section includes stories of former outlaw bikers who have rolled over and informed on their clubs, plus accounts of undercover cops who have managed to infiltrate the one-percenter outlaw motorcycle subculture.

Contrary to their stated hatred for snitches, some outlaw bikers have turned against their brothers. Bikers probably do not inform on their brothers from a desire to redeem their souls: they usually have ulterior, self-serving motives, such as saving their own hides and securing their futures.

But whatever the reason, the consequences for snitches, if caught, are dire. As noted, one-percenter outlaw bikers have a rigid code of silence:

"If you break the code, you will be hunted down and killed."

It is alleged that the bikers honour informants with an un-marked grave.

In October 1972 a long-time member of the Oakland Hells Angels was arrested for narcotics possession. His name was George "Baby Huey" Wethern. The Hells Angels MC had used George's ranch as a burial ground (possibly as one of those locales where wars were conducted out of the public eye) and he was granted immunity from prosecution for informing on the Hells Angels MC. Coming off massive addictions to heroin and methamphetamines, George was partially blinded when he sat down to write his deposition against the Hells Angels MC. He took the pencils provided him and stuck them in his eyes, piercing both sockets. Nevertheless, he continued to provide authorities with information that temporarily devastated the Oakland Chapter of the Hells Angels MC.

Danny Kane was a trusted confidante of the Quebec Nomads MC. He worked as a hit man but was also employed by the RCMP as an informant. Kane wanted revenge on the Hells Angels MC for "taking advantage" of his years of service without rewarding his efforts. His proximity to the Hells Angels MC gave police forces across Canada access to the inner work-ings of the members of the club. Kane was paid over a million dollars for his services. A few weeks before Kane was to "disappear" into witness protection he died a mysterious death.

But rats and snitches aren't the only threat to the closed world of outlaw motorbike clubs: undercover cops also pose a danger. But that said, outlaw motorcycle clubs have an internal dis-cipline that makes infiltration a long, arduous, risky process. And yet, it has been done.

For most cops, the line between enforcing the law and break-ing the law is clear. But for undercover agents that line some-times blurs. When you work undercover, you walk an invisible line between doing your job and breaking the law. Basically, the undercover cop must "live in a sewer without getting dirty". But this is no easy task. There is a constant struggle to keep anchored in the "straight" world, while living in that of the outlaw biker. Some undercover officers have paid for their years of covert work by losing their personal identities, their families, and their friends.

From 2001 to 2003, in an effort to bring down the Hells

Angels MC, ATF Federal Agent Jay Dobyns went deep under-cover and became a member of the club. Allegedly, there is now a contract on his head.

Meanwhile, ATF Federal Agent William Queen infiltrated the Mongols MC – reputedly the most vicious outlaw motor-cycle club in the United States – for a period of twenty-eight months, leading to the arrest of fifty-one club members. Like Dobyns, he had to abandon his old life, family and his friends, in order to wear the "colours". At one point Queen became so close to his biker brothers he felt he would lose his cop soul . . .

MEETING A HIT MAN

Mark G. Murphy

*This is a compelling story of an undercover Royal
Canadian Mounted Police member who died under
suspicious circumstances just before he was scheduled
to "disappear" under the Witness Protection Act. It
provides an insight into the traumas of deep cover work
by police among biker gangs.*

Sitting in my surveillance vehicle, a loaded shotgun across my
lap and a bullet-proof vest hugging my chest, I watched as a
blue sedan circled the parking lot and slowly approached our
undercover agent. There were four men in the car – three more
than expected.

It began to look as though the Mafia was doing a take-down of
their own. I had told our agent to drop to the deck if anything
went wrong. Reaching for the door handle, ready to hit the
pavement, I couldn't believe how a simple phone-call had led to
these increasingly dangerous encounters between the biker, the
Mafia, and the Mountie.

The 10th of November, 1980, began as a regular day. The
shrill sound of the phone at 12:55 PM was to change all that. The
NCIS (National Crime Intelligence Section) of the RCMP
(Royal Canadian Mounted Police), located on the 8th floor

of the RCMP Headquarters at 225 Jarvis Street in Toronto, routinely receives calls and visits from citizens feeling that organized crime somehow plays an important part in their lives. Most of the callers and walk-in visitors are referred to the RCMP by their professional counterparts, either Metro (Metro Toronto Police; recently changed to Toronto Police) or the OPP (Ontario Provincial Police). To be charitable, let's just say the NCIS has a wide variety of calls and visitors of questionable nature, whom they, by reciprocal agreement, refer back to Metro or the OPP. This call was different.

Over the lunch hour the phone rang. There were only a couple of people in the office and I answered the phone. The conversation went as follows:

(M.M.: Cpl. Mark Murphy; U.M.: unknown male, later identified as Cecil Kirby)

M.M.: NCIS, Murphy.

U.M.: Yeah, is the Staff Sergeant in charge there, please?

M.M.: No, I'm sorry, not at the moment. Can I help you?

U.M.: Well, I want to speak to the man in charge.

M.M.: He's out of the office at the moment. (Recognizing a tone of urgency, I suspected this guy had something to offer.) If there is something you wish to discuss, I'd be happy to help you. In all probability, the boss would ask me to speak to you anyway.

U.M.: Yeah, O.K. Well, I'm not going to tell you my name, but I'd like to meet you.

M.M.: Well, I'd like to have some idea of what you want to talk about.

U.M.: Yeah, O.K. Well, myself, my girlfriend and a friend of mine are charged with a break, entry and theft into my friend's neighbour's house. Now, we were caught cold turkey because York Regional had us under surveillance at the time. I'm looking to work a deal and I was wondering if you could help me.

M.M.: If there were exceptional circumstances and you had something really worthwhile to offer, maybe I could speak to the coppers involved and to the Crown and go from there. What are we talking about here?

U.M.:   Well, I'm charged with robbery, extortion, mischief and assault causing bodily harm, but they're all bullshit charges. What happened on that was, me and my girlfriend were living common-law and we got into a fight and decided to split up. So, I took some of the furniture, which I bought to begin with, and she called the police and the bastards charged me on a bullshit charge. My girlfriend and I are back together again so she'll be dropping the charges. It's the break, entry and theft that I'm worried about. They want to get me really bad and they are looking for two years.

M.M.:   O.K., what kind of information are we looking at? Do you have any ties or connection to organized crime, because that's our main interest?

U.M.:   Well, to be honest with you, I'm an ex-Satan's Choice biker. I was a biker for seven years, but I got out. I can get you some guns.

M.M.:   Well, to be up front with you, I can get all the guns I want. In fact, I can have a Sherman Tank on your front lawn tomorrow morning if you want it. Guns aren't of too much interest to me.

U.M.:   I have some information on some old murders. In fact, do you know Terry Hall from OPP and Ron Tavenor, Metro Police, that work on the bike gangs?

M.M.:   Yes, I do.

U.M.:   Well, I went to them to try and work a deal and they really tried to jerk me around. I gave them some information on a murder. I told them who did it and that the guy who did it was shot and still had a bullet inside him. They picked the guy up and got him for the murder. I gave them that information because I was in court for an assault charge. They said they would help me, but they went and told the Crown I was a biker, and that they were asking for heavy time. They even testified against me. When I saw I'd been double-crossed I changed my plea to not guilty, beat the charge, and walked away. I can't trust them, and that's why I'm coming to you.

M.M.:   O.K. Well, listen, I'm very interested in talking to you, but you understand we have to be a little bit careful. You don't want to tell me your name?

U.M.: No, I won't tell you my name, but you got nothing to worry about. I want you to come alone and don't be wired (no hidden tape recorder).
M.M.: I'll take the chance. Where do you want to meet?
U.M.: How about the Casa Loma? (An old castle and well-known Toronto landmark)
M.M.: O.K., I'll meet you there at 1:30 PM.
U.M.: O.K., come alone and no wires.
M.M.: What are you driving?
U.M.: A green Chev. I'll watch for you.
M.M.: O.K., 1:30 PM at the Casa Loma.

By the time the conversation was finished, my remaining fellow officers had left the office. I tried in vain to raise another member for back-up. The only other person in the office was the secretary, Marlene Jones, whom I held in very high esteem. I gave her the details of the planned meeting and asked that she stand by the radio. I said I would call back a licence plate number of the unknown male's vehicle before we conversed.

It was exactly 1:30 PM when I pulled into the parking lot at the Casa Loma. The unknown male was circling the lot looking for the person he had arranged to meet. When we saw each other, there was only a slight nod of acknowledgement. We went to a remote area of the parking lot to find a place to talk. In the meantime, I held the police microphone on the seat of the police car, to prevent being seen, and called in Ontario licence plate number PKK-109 to Marlene Jones, my only conceivable back-up.

When the unknown male stepped out of the 1973 green Chevrolet, he didn't give the appearance of being a biker. What's more, he didn't even look like the stereotypical criminal. He stood 5'–10" tall, had light blond hair and a moustache, and was clean-cut, dressed in a dress shirt, brown corduroy jacket and blue jeans. Extremely well-built, with arms like tree stumps, he presented an extraordinarily clean appearance, like an applicant for a new job. Little did I realize at that point in time that he was to be an applicant for a very dangerous and special job, that of an undercover agent for the RCMP.

Dealing with people over the course of many years in situations such as this, one develops a sort of a sixth sense, an ability to read personalities and intentions quickly. Body language speaks volumes if one knows what to look for. Despite the casual appearance of a law-abiding citizen, I noticed he was always glancing around, surveying his surroundings. This is a classic trait of a criminal, particularly one involved in organized crime. But I also detected an element of sincerity and good faith, and began to feel a little more comfortable about the lack of back-up support.

When this unknown male sat in the police car, he looked at me with piercing blue eyes and stated that his name was Cecil Kirby. He grinned, and we carried on with small talk for a few moments. Let me say that no matter what you read in the pages that follow, Cecil Kirby is a very personable and likeable man. I later learned the details of his youth that led him into crime – a broken home, the lack of education and opportunity, the usual conditions that cause young people like Cecil Kirby to fall through the tears in our social fabric. Cecil left school at an early age to work with his father. Although not formally educated, he was intelligent, street-wise, and had a phenomenal memory which was later demonstrated by his ability to recall in detail something that had taken place years before. He was also generous, the kind of person who would literally give you the shirt off his back if he liked you. I would later see his other side: the fierce and intense violence of a temper that was, although never directed at me, uncontrollable at times; the egotism and love of attention that drove him to finish first, no matter what the challenge.

At our initial meeting I discovered that Kirby might be an experienced criminal with a great potential as an informant, although I had no idea at the time how valuable he would become. Yet during his time as an informer, he would also prove to be quite unpredictable, and at times very difficult to control. In spite of Kirby's volatile personality, he would end up providing the police with phenomenal amounts of information on organized crime, and investigators have yet to find errors in the details he has supplied. It was not Kirby's nature to be a trusting soul, yet from the moment we shook hands on that fateful day a trust and friendship were initiated that would stand the tests of time and play an integral part in the events that followed.

During our first conversation in person, Kirby explained the circumstances of the break, entry and theft charges. He stated that he did not expect to walk on the charge, and was willing to plead guilty. The only problem was that Hall and Tavenor had earlier approached the Crown and were insisting on a two-year sentence; Kirby was looking for a two-year suspended sentence for himself and his two associates. Kirby pointed out that the Crown Attorney handling the case was Steven Leggett, and that Sergeant Robert Silverton, 31 Metro Police Division, was the police officer in charge. Kirby reiterated that if we could help him he would be willing to hand over some stolen guns, maybe a few machine guns, and provide information regarding old, unsolved murders. I again told him I had little interest in stolen guns (this being a common bargaining tool among criminals and police when the criminals are looking for help), since I could easily obtain stolen guns, machine guns, AR-15's, and any other type of weapon. I told Kirby I was interested in the information on old murders, but my main focus and that of the NCIS was organized crime. I mentioned that if Metro Police were handling the charges, they would be interested in crimes such as armed robberies, murders, major break-and-entries, and other criminal code offenses. I told Kirby I would find out the circumstances of his charges. We arranged to meet again on November 13, 1980.

There was something about Kirby that made me eager to pursue his case. When I arrived back at my office on Jarvis Street, I spoke with Constables Mike Atkinson and Paul Lennerton, two members of NCIS assigned to liaison with Metro and the OPP. Metro and the OPP had formed a JFO (Joint Forces Organization) to gather intelligence on biker gangs operating in Ontario. Atkinson quickly produced a large binder containing a dossier on known bikers. Listed under the caption "Satan's Choice", along with a photograph, was the individual that I had just met, one Cecil Murray Kirby.

A quick check also revealed that Kirby was well known to the police in a wide variety of circumstances. Kirby was known as Cecil Murray Archie Kirby, fingerprint section #35B777A, born on August 17, 1951. The following is a rundown of his criminal record from 1969 to 1980. It also includes charges that were eventually withdrawn:

DATE	PLACE	CHARGE	DISPOSITION
09 Dec. 69	Toronto	Unlawfully in dwelling house	30 days
		Assault causing bodily harm	$50/10 days
10 Oct.70	Toronto	Illegal poss. of narcotics	$250/30 days
31 May 70	Toronto	Break, entry & theft	All withdrawn
		Possn. stolen property	
		Possession of weapon	
		Dangerous to public peace	
		Indecent assault on female	
04 Jun. 71	Toronto	Possession of weapon	No disposition
23 Sept. 71	Toronto	Wounding	Withdrawn
17 Nov. 71	Mississauga	Dangerous driving	Withdrawn
21 Dec. 71	Collingw'd	Break, entry, & theft	Withdrawn
		Mischief	Sentence suspended
30 Dec. 71	Toronto	Possession of stolen property	Dismissed
		Break, entry & theft	6 months on theft charge
23 Nov. 72	Richm'dhill	Break, entry & theft	Withdrawn
15 Dec. 73	Toronto	Assault causing bodily harm	50 days
22 Jun. 76	Toronto	Wounding	Withdrawn
15 May 78	Toronto	Assault causing bodily harm	Withdrawn
03 Jan. 79	Toronto	Threatening (3 charges)	Withdrawn
		Assault (4 charges)	
22 May 80	Toronto	Attempt to obstruct justice	Acquitted
23 Sep. 79	Toronto	Break, entry & theft	Withdrawn
29 Oct. 80	Newmarket	Robbery, extortion, mischief,	Withdrawn
		Assault causing bodily harm	

Given this history, it wasn't difficult to imagine the kind of individual Cecil Kirby was; nor was it difficult to comprehend his potential as an informant. I could appreciate why Hall and Tavenor wanted him so badly. Now I was interested.

At our next meeting just 3 days later, I was far better prepared to deal with Kirby. Now that we were able to establish that he was not just a kook, but was heavily involved in crime and tied in with the notorious Satan's Choice Motorcycle Gang. Our second meeting took place at Casa Loma, under much the same conditions as the first. Kirby was driving a different vehicle, a new Chevrolet Caprice Classic.

During this meeting Kirby supplied information about a murder in Newmarket; the news that a prominent Toronto lawyer (who had recently been appointed a judge) and his wife were cocaine freaks; and information on a bombing involving an individual who owned a prominent disco on Bloor Street and wanted it bombed for insurance purposes (Kirby told me this individual stated he could do the bombing himself, because he had experience with the Palestine Liberation Army as a mercenary and knew how to make bombs).

Kirby's next statement was of particular interest. He said that his information was that Chuck Yanover, known enforcer for Toronto Mob Boss Paul Volpe, had someone come from Europe to kill Ian Rosenberg. Rosenberg, also an enforcer for the Volpe Mob, was killed on April 22, 1977.

The execution of Ian Rosenberg and his common-law wife, Joan Lipson, was of utmost significance in affecting the direction of the investigation that was to follow. The moment Kirby mentioned the name Rosenberg, I reinforced his belief that Rosenberg probably knew too much, was in jail and the Mob was afraid he would talk. I told Kirby that I felt it was the Volpe organization that bailed Rosenberg out of jail for $50,000 one day and arranged his execution the next. The death of Rosenberg, and more significantly that of Joan Lipson, had a tremendous effect on Kirby's way of thinking. Rosenberg and Lipson were both shot in the head by an unknown assassin while sleeping in their newly acquired apartment in Toronto. Their five-year-old child had the horrifying task of finding the bodies and calling for help. Kirby, facing a term in jail while living in commonlaw with a woman, Linda Caldwell, and her young daughter, drew an uneasy parallel between his own situation and that of Rosenberg.

During our conversation Kirby mentioned that his main occupation was armed robbery. In fact two years earlier he had travelled to Vancouver to rob a guy involved in the fish industry who reportedly would be carrying $300,000 in cash on his person. Fortunately for this individual, Kirby had arrived one day too late. He intended to return in the fall and try again.

Kirby mentioned another name of particular interest. He stated that while in Vancouver he was met by Carlo Gallo, well known underling of the late mobster Joseph Gentile. Gallo took Kirby to his restaurant in Vancouver and told Kirby if he was successful in grabbing the $300,000, he would have to give Gallo two-thirds of the grab; Kirby could keep only one-third for himself.

Carlo Gallo was of extreme interest to me. I explained to Kirby that I knew Gallo. In fact about five years earlier, Gallo and Joe Gentile had arrived in Toronto to visit some heavy people connected with the Mob. While in Toronto, they stayed at the Holiday Inn on Dufferin Street, where Toronto RCMP Intelligence Squad kept them under surveillance. As it turned out, it was fortunate that I mentioned to Kirby that while in Toronto, Gallo and Gentile had visited the Commisso brothers at the Casa Commisso, 1275 Lawrence Avenue West, Toronto. Kirby looked at me with his unique kind of grin.

"Yeah, I know the Commisso brothers," he said. "In fact, I've done some work for them. It was Cosimo Commisso who had asked me to go to Vancouver."

I asked Kirby if it was the same Cosimo Commisso who owned the Casa Commisso on Lawrence Avenue.

"Yeah," Kirby replied, "I have his phone numbers for the Casa and his home."

Kirby supplied the phone numbers, and I told him I would check them out. If what he said was true, we were really in business.

This meeting had taken place in Kirby's Chevrolet. After some small talk I got out of the vehicle and prepared to leave. We had already arranged to meet at the Holiday Inn next to the City Hall in downtown Toronto on Monday, the 17th of November, for a proper debriefing. It was going to be difficult to meet and talk freely, with Kirby's fear of police surveillance and both of our fears of being seen by other criminals. I was standing outside the vehicle on the passenger side when I mentioned to Kirby that I would call him and make some final arrangements for the meeting on the 17th.

I was about to close the door when, as an afterthought, I leaned in the door and said to Kirby, "By the way, if you call me at the office and I'm not there, don't leave your own name. You never know who might be around the office. How about leaving another name . . . how about Jack Ryan?"

Kirby looked at me like a man who had just seen a ghost. His eyes were popping and his face went completely white. I knew I had touched a sensitive nerve, but I had no idea why. Talk about body language – in a few seconds he had told a whole story. He was visibly upset, so I got back in the vehicle and tried as delicately as I could to have Kirby explain his extraordinary reaction to the name of Jack Ryan. He was reluctant to elaborate. The only thing he did say was, "You people know quite a bit about me, don't you?" Not wanting him to think any differently at this point in time, I bluffed and said, "Yeah, I guess so." We shook hands and parted company.

Policeman are trained to be composed, but when I arrived back at RCMP Headquarters in Toronto and confirmed that the phone numbers Kirby had in his possession were indeed those of Cosimo Commisso and the Casa Commisso, a huge banquet hall operated by the Commisso Family, I must be honest, I was excited. Since my arrival in Toronto in 1973, most of my efforts dealing with organized crime were concentrated on the Paul Volpe Group. As of then I had had little to do with the Commisso Family, nor did I know much about them.

SMOKESCREEN

Paul William Roberts and Norman Snider

This is the true story of an undercover cop and his battle to infiltrate one-percenter outlaw bikers. Unusually, it describes a relatively smooth undercover operation. Nevertheless, the cop in question still received threats – including the ominous presence of an "enforcer" from a biker gang outside the condominium complex where he lived.

Cal had exhausted Montreal – although he still had dormant LOAs going there – and his list of enemies was hitting critical mass. He still worried about that troll, Little John, popping out of a doorway and coming at him with a hammer. It was time for a change. So he and Simone moved to Toronto, taking an apartment in North York. It would make her career much harder to pursue. The French and the English in Canada aren't called two solitudes for nothing. The possibility of a French singer finding work in Toronto is about the same as a transvestite being asked to address the Empire Club. But she loved her man more than she loved her job. Without him, what reason would there be to sing anyway?

Before long, Cal had devised an extremely cunning idea for

relieving both Richards of the $100 million. When Bob Osler heard it, he liked it too. In fact, he liked it a lot. But he had to get approval from upstairs before they could proceed with the scheme. It isn't prudent to say precisely what the plan was, since it's still in operation, reeling in millions of another gang's dollars at this very moment, but suffice it to say that it enabled those with too much unbankable cash to make investments that, theoretically, they could later recoup, with profits, through a legitimate bank account. If deployed in a more imaginative fashion across North America, such a scheme would have organized crime unwittingly funding everything from public housing to new schools – something that undoubtedly would count in their favour when those responsible stood before a judge.

With a new city to sniff out, Cal, while he waited yet again for the go-ahead from on high, made the most of it. In no time at all, he'd located the main biker hangouts and selected a bar on Front Street for his cold approach.

While we think of the biker bar as somewhere between a strip club and a pool hall, wreathed in smoke, awash in beer, the Front Street bar was actually a quite pleasant family restaurant that gradually became a biker spot as the night wore on. It's probably safe to say that this experiment in clientele contributed to the bar's eventual demise: although a lot of people enjoy slumming it, they don't want to feel unsafe. When you look up from your steak au poivre and your conversation with Granny to find the bar now thronged by scarred, tattooed, leather-jacketed Cro-Magnons waggling their tongues at your wife, you know it's time to get the bill.

As he usually did, Cal targeted the barman, Tommy, a personable young Jamaican. He would go in three or four nights running, dropping three or four hundred a pop, plus a hefty tip. Then he'd stay away for a while – absence sometimes being the highest form of presence. When Cal returned, Tommy – whose income probably doubled when Cal was in – would be overjoyed. Cal dropped all the usual hints too – Bulgaria, import-export, big show-roll, bigger bank balance – and soon he was being introduced to the late-night customers: Benny the Pig, Meathook, Shark, Billy Goat, Big John Bat – it was *Animal Farm* in there after nine o'clock.

The owner wanted to meet him as well, but Cal played hard to get. He came there for pleasure, not business. The more he insisted on this, the more interested everyone became in doing business with him. When Richard Aran flew down from Montreal to discuss progress on the $100-million laundering job, it was good for Cal to be able to take him to the bar, where he now appeared to have tight friends – some of whom Richard, naturally enough, knew himself. Because no one wants to introduce an undercover agent into their criminal circle, there's a great emphasis on the longevity of acquaintanceships. People Cal had known for only a few months introduced him as if they known him for years – and some even came to believe they *had* known him for years. When you've been drinking a bottle of Jack Daniels and snorting a gram or two of blow every day for a decade straight, a month and a year aren't so different anyway.

The main Ontario biker gang Cal worked with has since merged with the Hell's Angels – although you can take it for granted that they originally applied for an Angels charter but were rejected (conditions for charter membership are fairly rigorous; many are called, though still not a few chosen). Shark and John the Bat were their main enforcers. If you were among the bike gang's network of pushers and had failed to pay for your weekly ounce or pound, Shark or John – and sometimes, if the debt merited it, both of them – would show up unannounced and remind you of it. They were very polite. The first time. If they had to come back and remind you again, however, they probably wouldn't speak at all. But just the sight of them was enough to make most people find the money, even if it meant selling their children for medical experiments.

Shark looked as if he'd been beamed down from 100,000 B.C., where he'd lived in a damp cave on a diet of raw hedgehog and toadstools. His teeth alone were terrifying, and he rattled as he walked, as if laden with metal implements to use on your debt. John the Bat was far more contemporary in appearance, a good 98,000 years ahead of Shark. He had actually been one of the Visigoths in the film *Gladiator* and was flown over to England with other bikers from North America (since Europe no longer breeds a convincing barbarian). He wasn't named after the flying rodent, however, but rather after – originally, at least – the baseball bat he kept clamped to his bike winter and summer. Although the only pitcher he'd ever faced held a gallon of beer. The nickname had evolved into Batty, the way these things do, and there was now speculation that its origins lay in insanity rather than mere violence.

The story was that Batty had found his girl with another man, and before dealing with her, he'd tied the man's testicles to a radiator with a length of piano wire. Then he threw the man clean through a second-storey window. The girl merely had her nose cut off. It was joked that Batty still had the testicles – which was why some people called him Four Ball. No one ever called him John – not to his face, at least. He'd mutilate you – that was how bitterly he resented being named after a penis, a can, a mark. He stood around six-foot-six and weighed a good 400 pounds; a great deal of this flesh was covered in jailhouse tattoos (achieved by making ink from burnt matches, cigarette ash, and saliva, then using a red-hot pin to work the ink into the skin – the result invariably becomes a blurred mess after a few years, so don't try it at home). On the Macedonian-sausage fingers of his left hand was L-O-V-E, and on the right H-A-. Cal wondered whether he'd meant to add T-E but had run out of ink or been interrupted. Or had the intention been to write H-A-H-A, but the joke wore off? Now, of course, it would be presumed to stand for "Hell's Angels" and viewed as evidence of supernatural prescience. But as with anyone whose legend is writ large, Batty kept the details of his life vague. He was touchy about these things, so you didn't ask. You didn't ask about his beard either. It was falling out in great clumps, and he was always smearing strands over the gaps and trying to glue them down with saliva. Maybe he was on chemo? Or maybe the toxins in his body were having the same effect? It was hard to imagine tumours daring to grow in there.

Cal became tight with Shark and Batty, mainly because he bought them thousands of drinks, but partly because his own legend was writ far larger than theirs. He'd mastered the art of the smokescreen, which, not unlike the silver screen, is about myth, not reality. And here big *is* better. The same story, when dipped in the wax of the myth-making sub-conscious of successive listeners, becomes at once grander and more basic. By making his yarns suitably short on detail and long on innuendo,

Cal knew that human nature would elevate them to mythological epics before a week was out. This engendered in the two bikers a thirst for Cal's companionship that could not be slaked, as well as a ravenous hunger for his thoughts on business, his take on life.

Shark, who'd never left Ontario in forty years, yearned for information about other countries – especially Bulgaria, which Cal painted as bandit heaven. Shark couldn't hear enough about hunting wild pigs and ambushing trucks in the mountains. He wanted to go there so bad. You could tell he imagined himself arriving at the airport in Sofia, where he'd be greeted by customs officials and immigration inspectors who looked just like him: "Velcome 'ome, brother!" they'd say, waving him through the formalities and indignity that lesser mortals could not avoid.

Shark was very proud of his enforcing skills, and the members of the bike gang were clearly grateful for his services. In fact, to show their appreciation, they had purchased for him a monstrous $25,000 diamond ring, which Shark always wore. Owing to the state of the rest of him, however, strangers must have assumed he'd found the ring in a Christmas cracker. It looked incongruous, like a bison with a wistwatch or a crocodile with shoes.

Much pomp and ceremony had, it seems, accompanied the presentation of the ring, and Shark would often fondly recall this, his finest hour. It had taken place in a strip club on Gerrard Street and was by invite only. Everyone had worn tuxedoes – not your boring black tuxedos, but ones in powder blue and chocolate brown, with velvet trim. The most stellar dancer in all the bike gang's vast stable had emerged from a huge cake and given Shark his own personal lap dance, followed by a blow job. Everyone was drunk and stoned; the cocaine flowed like champagne and the champagne flowed like water. They all went for breakfast at Fran's on College Street at dawn. It was magical.

"I never paid for a single fucking drink," Shark would say in awe.

This was just as well, Cal mused, because Shark never seemed to have two cents to rub together. One night, after an exceptionally punishing attack on Cal's show-roll, Shark suggested that Cal might like to do a little business with the bikers.

"I keep my business separate from my pleasure," replied Cal, ever coy.

He did agree, however, to go back to Shark's place for further discussions. It was 3 a.m. Shark lived way out in the east end of Toronto, in an area that time had forgotten. It looked like the set from *Our Mutual Friend:* blacking factories, smokestacks, choking tenements, ancient hand-painted signs for Pear's Soap. You wondered if this part of town had a member to represent it in Parliament. Even the hookers were old and shrivelled.

Shark lived off a brick-surfaced alley in what appeared from the outside to be a garage. It appeared that way from the inside too. In fact, it was a garage. Dark, cold, lit by a single hanging bare bulb, it housed a good deal of garbage, many tools, and a spectacular, gleaming, customized 1996 black-and-platinum Harley Dyna Wide Glide 80ciEvo.

"CV carb with Dynojet thunderslide and Screamin' Eagle hi-flow air cleaner. . . . Here," Shark said, handing Cal a beer he'd taken from a ledge outside the window. "They chill on the sill." He laughed. Well, he made a guttural sound in the back of his throat, kicking an up-turned oil drum across the floor to Cal and adding, "Have a seat."

They sat on oil drums.

Some people, thought Cal, apologize for living in filth and squalor when they actually live in surgically sanitized, spotless environments; others live in filth and squalor and feel like kings. He kept thinking Shark would soon show him into a house via the rear door, but as he found when he went for a piss, the rear door opened onto another alley. It was a free-standing garage.

"So this is where you live?" Cal ventured.

"Yeah," said Shark, looking around himself expansively. "Got all me stuff here."

"Where'd you sleep?"

"In me bed," Shark replied, pointing to a small rectangle of what appeared to be oily rags just behind them. "I don't need much."

"I can see."

It was embarrassing. Shark offered Cal cornflakes. Cal politely declined. Shark poured himself some in a dirty mug, then tipped his beer over them, commenting that they tasted far better with beer than with milk. As there were no spoons – there were a good many wrenches – Shark slurped his cereal from the mug, and then began talking business. He mentioned millions of dollars, tons of dope, and the desire to get into real estate in a big way.

"We need to clean up some cash," he said.

Cal wondered if Shark ever felt like cleaning up himself or the garage. A lot of folks less attuned to the criminal milieu might have found it hard to believe that a man who lived in a garage and slept on a pile of rags ever knew what money laundering was, but Cal had seen worse. It's not called the underworld for nothing. Besides, it was kind of peaceful in Shark's garage; there was even an odd charm about the place when you viewed through its occupant's eyes. No doubt Shark had the mandatory nightmare of a childhood – the dozen siblings, the succession of brutal stepfathers, Children's Aid, the foster homes, the diddling vicars, young offenders, then older offenders – and all he'd ever wanted was a room of his own, a (sliding) door with which to shut out the cruel world. What was it, though, that made the brutalized want to be brutal? You'd think they'd know better than anyone the horrors of brutality, and want to spare others from them. But they don't. They want to inflict others with their own pain. They want to perpetuate the cycle, not end it. Cal had experienced his own share of brutality as a child, yet harsh as it was, that brutality still had love behind it. It instilled a belief in the sanctity of life and in a man's infinite ability to rise out of the ashes, no matter how often he goes down in flames. To be men, not destroyers.

You couldn't have this kind of discussion with Shark, though. He'd think you were fucking with him. There was no still, small voice in there telling him what was right and what was wrong – and if you tried to insert one, you'd be fucking with him. "Don't fuck with me" – it was the most common thing some of these buddies said, and it meant "Don't make me look at myself." Shark had no introspection. He just reacted instinctively. Like an animal.

Cal played coy during this first meeting, saying he didn't do this and he wasn't into that. But he knew Shark was hooked.

Once the others saw Shark hanging with Cal, they too got interested. No one wanted to be left out – of what, they weren't sure, but they wanted in on it anyway. It was always suspected that people were doing private deals, and since Cal was good at feeding the rumour mill about himself, the late-night crew at the bar soon saw him as Big Money, Russians, Big Time. They saw Réal Dupont's Caribbean fantasy, because they all wanted out in their own way, wanted to be far from the rips and the beatings and the detention cells, in some feudal fiefdom of their own. Where no one would fuck with them. Failing this, however, they'd stay in the gang. There was safety in numbers, and these boys were hopeless on their own. They never looked for trouble by themselves, Cal found, and they were unusually easy to intimidate.

"I'm not gonna introduce you to my people dressed like that!" Cal once told Batty, whom he'd promised to fix up with some Russian mob contacts.

"Like what?" Batty asked, theatrically opening up his denim vest and leather jacket to peer down at his stained, filthy jeans and beat-up cowboy boots, as if he was the acme of sartorial splendour. "What's wrong with what I'm wearing?"

"For a start," Cal told him, "you look like shit. You smell like shit too. *And* you're a fucking heat score, man! Jeeeezus! You look like a fucking biker! I don't wanna be seen dead with you on the street. A cop looks and thinks, Oh, fuck. There's a biker . . . and who's that with him? You gotta show some respect, man. You bring heat around my people, you won't even have time to kiss your ass goodbye. You understand what I'm saying? And get a fucking shave – you look like a fat spider!"

Batty had beaten people into blood pudding for less. Much less. But he just stood there and took it. Next day, he appeared in a suit and tie, clean-shaven, face *and* head.

"How d'I look?" he asked.

He looked like an over-inflated Mussolini, but he did get an A for effort. He felt good about himself too, you could tell. He wasn't even fazed when the cream of Russian thuggery failed to show. Trouble was, the next time Cal saw him, Batty had reverted to fat spiderhood. Obviously, feeling good about himself didn't make him feel good. He needed to feel bad about himself. "Don't fuck with me" means low self-esteem too. But when all you've done in life is steal, peddle dope and beat people into blood pudding, you have no reason to experience anything but low self-esteem. Bad is good.

Good is bad sometimes, also. When bad things start happening to good people, they get pissed off. They feel the times are out of joint. Around now, this is what Cal was starting to feel.

You know that old cinematic device where dates start peeling off a calendar, faster and faster, to get blown in the wind, whirled into a tangle? Well, imagine it here.

January 11, 2001

Réal Dupont was released from prison during the first week of January. High up on his list of old friends to reacquaint himself with was C. Calvin Broeker. Cal still had his cellphone then, and it would ring as we worked on this book. People he knew to be associates of Dupont's urgently wanted to see him about a deal. It was never Dupont who called – perhaps he didn't trust himself not to tell Cal about all the crunchy, meaty things he was going to do to him at their reunion.

Tragically, however, this reunion was not to be. On the night of January 11, Réal Dupont was driving on the south shore of Montreal when – model citizen that he was – he stopped at a red light. He didn't notice someone slip out of the van behind him; all he heard was a tap on his side window. He turned to see a man he recognized, and he could just about make out what the man was saying: "*Au revoir*, motherfucker!"

When the lights turned green again, Dupont didn't move. He just sat there. He'd been shot five times in the head and died instantly.

Cal was told by his old handlers that the Banditos, a rival biker gang, had done the deed. But it could have been almost anyone. You didn't come across many people *là-bas* who wanted Réal Dupont alive. You probably couldn't find many who want Cal Broeker alive either. But he's nowhere to be found.

He calls from time to time, usually from the road, heading to another joint, but we don't know where he is. It always sounds peaceful, though, wherever it is. And so does he. He sounds like a man who, after his season in hell, has finally found himself.

A WAYWARD ANGEL

George Wethern and Vincent Colnett

Confronted with his property in Ukiah, California being discovered as a burial ground for Hells Angels Motorcycle Club enemies, George "Baby Huey" Wethern turned snitch in exchange for immunity for himself and his wife. He told his story to a journalist and the result is a first-hand view of the forces that motivate snitches.

UKIAH, California, October 30, 1972. By 6 A.M., about three dozen law enforcement officers had taken up positions around a single story redwood house nestled at the base of a wooded hillside. Crouched behind cars and flattened against tree trunks, they drew beads with pistols, rifles and shotguns. But there was no movement from the house other than the wisps of smoke curling from the chimney. They waited and listened.

Then, at the sound of scrambling feet inside, one officer raised his bullhorn:

"COME OUT WITH YOUR HANDS HIGH!"

The first response was a paper bag sailing out the door. Then a 280-pound bearded man lumbered onto the porch with his hands up. "Don't shoot," he yelled. "This is my family in there."

George Wethern walked forward with a ponderous sway. In a moment, his wife, Helen, a tiny woman with an elfin face and close-cropped blond hair, was standing in his shadow along with their chubby nine-year-old son and thirteen-year-old daughter. Raiders from state, federal and local jurisdictions swarmed around them with guns drawn.

They handcuffed the parents, then state narcotics agent Jack Nehr read from a search warrant that referred to narcotics, firearms, explosives and "human skeletal remains."

With his family under guard and a dozen investigators fanning over his 153-acre ranch, Wethern took bomb squad experts and some other officers on a tour of the house and a children's dormitory. A pair of stolen .30–06 rifles and seven legal guns were seized along with the paper bag's contents – an ounce or two of methamphetamines, a pound of marijuana, some Seconal and other pills.

Later, Wethern was driven a few miles to the Mendocino County jail and interrogated by Nehr, Bruce True and other agents. He admitted being a former Hell's Angels motorcycle club member, but he remained faithful to the club code of silence and dodged questions with word games and roundabout answers.

The questions, however, indicated someone in the club had betrayed him, and possibly was trying to set him up. He gaped when Nehr said matter-of-factly, "Ya know, Tiny's dead . . . He took his last boat ride. Was cut to pieces by nine-millimeter slugs. He squealed like a pig."

"Tiny" was Michael Walter, a close friend and the Oakland Angels No. 2 man. He had vanished the previous month, leaving behind his motorcycle and all personal belongings. The agent was stating hearsay as fact, but Wethern didn't know that. He was certain authorities were putting a murder on his doorstep, although his only crime had been providing two empty pits to Angels leader Ralph "Sonny" Barger as a favor. He didn't even know the names of the dead buried on his own ranch.

"I don't know anything about it," he said.

When the agent asked him whether there were any well holes

on his ranch, it became obvious that authorities had been told about the burials. Wethern's family and his own life were at stake. So he put aside the possible consequences of breaking silence, then let out fragments of information. Finally, he took a long breath and said, "I'll show you the wells."

When they returned to the ranch, backhoes and other machinery were already scooping dirt at the front of the property where an informant had directed them. Wethern pointed out a spot twenty-five feet from that excavation, then, after some hemming and hawing, guided authorities to a flower garden less than fifty feet from the house.

Later that day, the stench of decayed flesh rose from two yawning excavations at those spots. The skeletons of two men were lifted from a twenty-two-foot-deep, dirt-filled well shaft. The partially mummified body of a red-haired woman was exhumed from the second hole. An informant had reported that Tom Shull and Charlie Baker – a pair of Georgia cyclists missing for more than a year – were buried on the ranch, and the two male corpses matched their descriptions. Yet the unidentified female corpse was a total surprise to the raiders.

The news rolled across the country. "Hell's Angels' burying ground" was the phrase thrown out by the state Attorney General's office and fielded by news media. Helicopters flew over the ranch for aerial photos. And a herd of journalists soon was at the bootheels of Sheriff Reno Bartolomie, a paunchy, silver-haired lawman who looked like a cattle rancher.

In the same twenty-four-hour period, two other widely reported events also gave the Hell's Angels winged skull emblem a new, more sinister meaning:

– In Sacramento, the California Attorney General's 1972 Crime Report branded the Angels a major narcotics distributor. It credited the hitherto loosely organized clan with trafficking $31 million in illegal drugs from the West Coast to the East in one three-year period alone. Club members, it said, were hitting the big time, getting credentials as large-scale organized crime operators who actively purchase land, invest in legitimate businesses and deal with major crime figures in the state. The report said the Angels availed themselves of sophisticated electronic devices to intercept police communications, thus enhancing their extreme mobility. And it said the Angels,

Chinese youth gangs and other organized groups accounted for more than 100 California gang slayings in the previous few years.

– In Oakland, home of the club's controlling chapter, Angels President Ralph "Sonny" Barger and three other members were going on trial, charged with executing a Texas drug dealer over an estimated $80,000 in cocaine. They were accused (and later acquitted) of shooting the man as he slept, throwing the body in a bathtub, then setting the home afire. Authorities said the murder weapon was the same silencer-equipped pistol used to kill one of three men found murdered in a nearby house the same day.

The Wetherns were held on bail of $100,000 each while their children remained in protective custody at the home of a deputy sheriff. From past experience, Wethern knew the Angels drew no lines at retaliation – torture, kidnaping and murder were possible. His violation of the club code made it a good bet they would try to silence him temporarily by getting to his family or permanently by getting him. He realized it was only a matter of time before Barger would be connected to the burials – and implicating the club chieftain almost certainly would be a capital offense.

Still, he and club leaders maintained a semblance of loyalty that first day. He tried to warn those drug dealers whom he might incriminate, and Angels acting president "Big Don" Hollingsworth offered him legal aid and any other club assistance, presumably hoping to keep a lid on things. The club's offers were transmitted through J.B., Wethern's closest friend and a retired Angel, during a jail visit.

Later, Wethern was reunited with his wife in a special cell on the women's side of the jail – a compact room within a room, like a gas chamber with bars, four bunks, a metal table, toilet and stall shower. Agents with mud-caked boots had come to her cell earlier and told her about the grisly find. And the television news had said the same thing. Once they were alone, Wethern told her what he had done. And she wept, knowing he was a dead man whether he went to prison or not.

The next day, after an Angels attorney excused himself from the case because of potential conflict of interest, the Wetherns met with a Mendocino County public defender named Richard Petersen. The attorney convinced the family that an immunity deal was the best long-term answer, if they could be provided with protection against the club. Immunity also was attractive because Wethern felt an acute psychological need to flush all the dark secrets from his mind.

Two days after the raid – with several Angels in custody and several more fugitives in the case – a formal immunity deal was proposed by county District Attorney Duncan James. During the Superior Court session, the Wetherns were chained together in their jail blues. The couple were puzzled by the legal jargon and alarmed by the seemingly rushed procedural matters, a commotion in the bulging press section and the last-minute substitution of another public defender. And all too suddenly Judge Timothy O'Brien was asking them whether they were willing to reveal everything about the Hell's Angels.

"Your honor," Wethern declared, "I don't fully understand this and won't agree to anything unless I do." He also thought the proposed deal was too narrow. He wanted immunity binding on both federal and state courts, plus protection for his entire family. He demanded all or nothing.

By day's end, the Wethern children had been placed in a foster home. And the parents found themselves back in their cell, without their children, immunity or means of making bail. The vise of Angels' law and society's law clearly was tightening on Wethern.

But his patience and bravado paid off by that weekend. Under the deal, he and his wife agreed to plead guilty to misdemeanor charges stemming from the confiscated guns and drugs, but they were granted immunity for all other crimes except any capital offenses in which they may have been principals. Authorities knew of no such offenses.

The government agreed to relocate the family in the U.S. locale of their choice, with new names, government-issued identification, all necessary appearance changes, guarantees of housing and subsistence payments until they could reestablish.

In return, federal and state investigators would draw upon their memories of a fourteen-year association with the Angels, including Wethern's two stints of active membership:

After joining the club in 1958, he became a vice-president around 1960, just as the club began to actively recruit the roughneck kids who hardened into the world's most elite corps of outlaw motorcycle riders, the Oakland Hell's Angels. In the mid-1960s, he turned his close leadership ties into big money as the Angels slid into drugs, guns and explosives. He became the club's top psychedelics distributor and kept several other Angels in his stable of peddlers. As a drug businessman, he dealt with the royalty of that realm, particularly the infamous underground chemist and "LSD King" Augustus Owsley Stanley III, and he was there when the Angels played acid games with author Ken Kesey and his Merry Pranksters. He joined other Angels in exploiting San Francisco's Haight-Ashbury flower children and their petal-thin revolution. In the late 1960s, he made between $100,000 and $200,000 a year, adopted a free-spending life-style and witnessed the first known Angels execution of a club member. And in 1969, after shooting his partner during a drug-triggered violence fit, Wethern turned from narcotics and retired from the club. Still, his friendship with club leaders endured, and he continued to traffic guns and drugs with the club right up to his arrest.

As word of immunity leaked to the press, District Attorney Duncan James proclaimed triumphantly on November 4: "This may not shut the Angels down right away, but most law enforcement officials think it would be the beginning of the end.

"A Hell's Angel doesn't tell on a Hell's Angel," he explained to reporters. "At least that's the way it's been. If they get arrested, they do their time in county jail and don't talk.

"But now there's a person who has had a friendship with Sonny Barger, the Angels maximum leader, and he's turning state's evidence. Now that their code has been broken, other Angels can be expected to come out and do the same thing just to save themselves . . . After all investigations have been concluded, and arrests made, the Angels will probably be no more than a fragmented group of motorcyclists."

This heralded a parade of law officials. From all regions of the state and every level of government, they descended upon the former Angels leader day and night, with questions about the club and its people, hundreds of questions. Even when the long debriefing sessions were over for the moment, the questions hounded Wethern. Normal memory lapses frustrated him. It became increasingly difficult for him to distinguish between things forgotten and things never known. Tranquilizers temporarily released tensions, but drug dependency further irritated him, so he quit them.

On the morning of November 8, after a night of pacing, Wethern ventured a few thoughtful steps each way across the cell. He had been trying to figure out possible identities for the dead woman. He awakened his wife to pick her brain.

"Go to sleep," she urged. "You need some rest."

He apologized for waking her, resumed pacing for a minute, then told her, "I gotta get you outa here."

"Whatta ya mean?" She cleared her eyes and her head.

Stolidly, he sat and pondered, as though listening to someone.

"Whatta ya mean?" she pressed, rolling from under the sheets.

"Shush. God's talking to me." He shut his eyes.

"What's he say?" She held his face in her hands, but he remained mute. His eyes popped open and glazed over. "George," she whispered urgently, "you gotta talk to somebody."

When Deputy Jim Tuso arrived, Wethern was hanging on the cell bars, reaching desperately for the deputy's gun. "Kill me, Jim," he screamed. "Do it. Do it."

Embracing the big man and stroking his forehead, his wife explained to the deputy, "He's feeling bad. He's upset. He won't take his tranks."

After a few minutes of more reasoned talking, Wethern canceled his death wish. "Never mind, Jim," he said. "Forget it. I'm okay now." When he rose from his knees, dropped into a chair and seemed to calm himself, the deputy departed.

Suddenly, Wethern was up again. "Lemme talk to Petersen. Dammit, lemme talk to him."

"Okay. Okay," she said. "He's already on his way."

"Can you handle it?" he added. "Can you get yourself out of here?"

"Whatta ya mean?" It was unclear to her whether he meant out of jail or out of the entire mire.

"Can you do it?" he replied with great emphasis.

"We can talk to Mr. Petersen," she said, terrified that she had lost his thoughts.

"Well, if you can't do it, I've got to," he said.

The attorney showed up, but, try as he might, he couldn't communicate with the former Angel.

"Don't give up," Helen entreated her husband. "Talk to Mr. Petersen. He's here to help you."

Wethern remained tense, frighteningly intense, obstinate yet incoherent. "No. It ain't workin'. No good."

After the attorney left, Wethern pounded and pounded the metal bed frame with his fist, telegraphing a crude message to himself.

"Come on, George," a jail matron called from the corridor doorway. "Calm down. Come on."

He smiled sheepishly and asked her to close the door so he could use the toilet in privacy. She hesitated until Helen assured her it was all right. Once the door latched and the matron's footsteps pattered off, he sprang to his feet, then fiercely pulled his wife to her knees. "Let's pray," he murmured. Then another thought struck him. He picked up a pencil, wanting to write a letter, so Helen joined him at the metal table.

With deliberation, he formed the letters of his first name. GEORGE. He stopped. Almost involuntarily, his head bobbed, rhythmic yet ponderous, a tousle of hair and whiskers. Images filled his mind: feelings intensified the images. Guilt for the life his wife and children would inherit. Fear for their future hells. Regret for abandoning old and loved comrades.

"Gimme another pencil," he said.

He seemed to be writing two-handed, right to left and left to right; then he turned the pencils point-up in his fists. He flicked away one lead with his thumb. His muscles bunched. His wide forearms wrenched upward. The pencils sank deep into his eyes, past the whites and toward the target. The brain, the source of his pain, had to be pierced, killed. His thick hands strained, but Helen threw herself across the table, with all her might prying them away, screaming for his life. To get the lances deeper, he tried to ram them on the table. Yet, as his head plunged forward, the woman gripped the bloody pencils and swiftly yanked them out.

Blinded by blood and pain, he clutched her throat, tearing her rosary and driving her back to the shower floor. "He's going to kill himself and take me with him," she told herself. She held her breath at first. Then, when she desperately needed air, she found her throat passages closed. Panicking, she mustered all her strength to try to push him away. But her legs were hopelessly pinned under his huge body and her arms were too weak.

As she started to lose consciousness, deputies dragged George away and pinned him to the bed. After they held him for a while, he went placidly to a holding area.

A few minutes later, Helen watched from the corridor as he was led toward an ambulance. Her throat was bruised and her knees were quaking. "George," she called.

"Honey. I'm sorry. I'm sorry," he cried back.

"It's all right. I'm okay," she assured him. "Don't worry."

"Gimme a kiss, Sugar," he said – and they were allowed a brief embrace.

Speeding toward the hospital, he enjoyed a queer, peaceful joy in his blindness. The darkness relieved him of his real world concerns, but they rushed back on the hospital operating table, when one eye picked up the outline of the overhead light. "Oh, no," he told himself. "You didn't do it good enough."

Back at the jail, he was manacled so he couldn't touch his eyes. He cursed the chains, he cursed the deputies, he cursed the world, he cursed himself. He growled and snarled and shook the bars of his cell. When the doctor came, he demanded, "Gimme a shot. Gimme a shot." The first shot made him cry for more, reverting into a complete Hell's Angel.

He created such a disturbance that deputies finally wrestled him to an old storage room. His feet shackled and his hands chained to a belt, he stretched across the floor. He yawned, pretending to be sedated. He bummed a cigarette from one guard. As he smoked, he worked slack in his chains. Then, rolling over as though to snuff his smoke, he jammed the entire butt into his eye. Cursing their own stupidity, the deputies were immediately upon him, but the damage had been done.

With his chains cinched tighter, he was returned to his cell. Alone in the darkness and the eery, echoing jailhouse, he wanted in a desperate way to talk to his wife to make sure she was unharmed. He clamored until several deputies were standing in the doorway of his cell.

"I'm comin' out," he roared. "I wanna see my wife."

"No, you're not," one of the deputies said, but George exploded through the human barrier. Like a runaway elephant, he charged down the hallway with deputies clinging to his dangling chains. He reached the guardroom before a gang tackle brought him down just short of the women's side of the jail. "I'm goin' to her, and that's it! God help me!" He screamed it until a guard literally choked off the words.

The commotion carried to Helen's cell. Hunched at the edge of her bunk, she fingered her broken rosary. She ached to go to him but was helpless. She reconstructed the rosary, bead by bead. The matron left for a couple of minutes. "He had another sedative," she returned to say. "He's sleeping, finally."

At that, Helen surrendered to her own sedatives and slept too.

UNDERCOVER MOUNTIE

Robert Sheppard

Marital strife, nervous breakdowns, deep shit – the moving story of a cop working under cover in an outlaw biker organization.

Bob Stenhouse was one of the RCMP's shiniest stars. He joined the force in 1982, barely out of his teens, and fairly shot through the ranks. Staff sergeant while still in his 30s, a significant achievement, he garnered performance reviews that characterized him as "outstanding" or "exceptional," of leadership calibre. What's more, he earned his spurs the hard way, on the streets. Stenhouse was one of the Mounties' top undercover specialists in Western Canada. He had the personality to befriend suspected murderers and get them to cough up their secrets. Once, playing a mobbed-up tough guy, he tricked a small-time killer into showing where he had stashed a body, deep in the bush in central British Columbia.

Stenhouse also had the guts to wade into a bar full of bikers – his special target – and put them on notice. A cop's cop? He certainly looked the part. Big, raw-boned, soft-spoken. After receiving special assault training early on, he was part of the team that would be called out at all hours, anywhere in north-central Alberta, whenever someone was barricaded in a house with a rifle: given the order, he was one of the guys who would storm the house.

But it was not just his brawn or his courage that moved him through the ranks. A colleague called him one of the Mounties' foremost experts on undercover police work. He also organized, on his own initiative, seminars for officers in outlying regions on how to deal with bikers. He had a knack for challenging his subordinates – and his superiors. In the year and a half leading up to his suspension, he had confrontations with three different senior officers about how to handle bikers. Though that didn't stop two of them from writing laudatory memos as Stenhouse went through the processes for promotion.

His future looked bright. In 1997, he quarterbacked one of the RCMP's very few successful investigations of a biker gang. Called Project Kiss, it was an elaborate sting that went on for nearly a year and resulted in the conviction of 13 Edmonton bikers and the confiscation of $1 million in drug money. Then he did, by his own admission, a very stupid thing.

In the spring of 1999, with his marriage crumbling and his job frustrations mounting, Stenhouse sent a package of RCMP policy documents to Toronto journalist Yves Lavigne. The package included letters from fellow officers criticizing the force's way of handling investigations into motorcycle gangs, then considered the RCMP's No. 1 law-enforcement priority. One was a memo Stenhouse himself had written, arguing for more coherent, targeted investigations into suspected gangs – instead of the turf-based system that divided the force into intelligence gatherers and criminal investigators. (And further divided the drug squad into units based on commodities such as marijuana and heroin, with the result that cops were chasing after small-timers with drugs in their possession rather than focusing on the kingpins.)

Another, more contentious part of the package, marked "confidential" and "for police eyes only," included memos and minutes of meetings of the national strategy committee to combat outlaw motorcycle gangs, a policy-making group of the Canadian Association of Chiefs of Police.

Stenhouse and Lavigne had never met, but they had talked on the phone several times. Stenhouse saw Lavigne as a friend of the police: he had written three books on the Hells Angels and spoken at police functions. And he felt Lavigne would use the documents as background, as an aid to understanding the frustrations of frontline officers. "It never crossed my mind he would publish them the way he did," says Stenhouse. When the memos hit the fan, Mountie honour forced him to 'fess up.

Within hours of Lavigne's book *Hells Angels at War* hitting the stands in October, 1999, Stenhouse sent e-mails to superiors and fellow officers outlining what he had done. "I didn't want someone else taking the blame for this," he says. The internal rumour mill was already pinning the rap on someone else. Close colleagues were shocked. So were his superiors. There may be consequences, they told him, but for the meantime continue on. In this instance, oddly enough, that meant going forward as a candidate for management ranks.

Then, three months later, everything suddenly changed. Stenhouse was suspended from duty. That is still his status two years later. The RCMP has tried (and failed) twice to suspend him without pay – an extremely rare initiative. It also tried to charge him with a criminal offence, only to be told by the Alberta justice department there were no grounds. And earlier this spring, the force held a disciplinary hearing in Edmonton, one that went on for 10 days over a seven-week period, heard from almost 25 witnesses, and in the end – in very harsh and uncompromising terms – ordered Bob Stenhouse dismissed, an order he is appealing more for reasons of honour than anything else.

There are two stories here, and sometimes they intertwine. One is the personal tale of the burned-out Mountie, the over-committed officer whose life was the force – he had married a Mountie, all his close friends are police officers – and who lost sight, perhaps, of how to go about changing an institution he loved. There is also the story of the RCMP's failed attempt to get a handle on organized crime – particularly outlaw motor-cycle gangs, the scourge of the '90s. That's a policy that is even now spinning around 180 degrees, towards a vision of policing that Stenhouse, among others, has been advocating, ironically as the RCMP tries to drum him out of the force.

Part of that is due to changed circumstances: the new fight against international terrorism has forced the Mounties to combine their intelligence gatherers and criminal investigators into single targeted units aimed at specific groups. But even before, the wheels were turning in that direction. "This was something that was being talked about at a lot of different levels," says Don McDermid, the recently retired assistant commissioner who headed the RCMP's Alberta operation. "Were we on the right track with that in Alberta? Maybe not to the point that everybody was doing it. But you don't make a shift of that magnitude overnight."

From outside law enforcement, it's tempting to see the police as looking after their own, either to close ranks in support or to root out with a vengeance those who are considered bad apples. The Stenhouse case is not nearly so clear-cut. If anything, it shows the class divisions that bedevil the national force, divisions between what one officer calls, half-jokingly, "the cowboys" on the front lines and the "admin wienies." One after another, officers who worked directly with Stenhouse, including long-serving investigators from his earlier posting in B.C., appeared before his disciplinary hearing to sing his praises.

Did the documents he passed along compromise police operations? Not at all, they said. Has the leak affected their ability to share information with other forces? No again. "I found Bob to be a character person with the RCMP, a person with guts," said his former boss on the biker intelligence team, retired Staff Sgt. Del Huget. "If he ever made an error in judgment, he would certainly get my forgiveness in a second. And I believe he should get that kind of forgiveness from the force."

On the opposite side were a handful of senior officers in the Edmonton detachment, some of whom were directly or obliquely criticized in the Lavigne book. But their points were still valid: Stenhouse betrayed his colleagues; some of these documents were clearly marked for police eyes only – some were from sister organizations, a measure of inter-force co-operation that was delicate at the best of times; how can we trust him again?

Oddly enough, the main antagonist in this drama was a non-Mountie: Toronto police Chief Julian Fantino. A big, bluff man who has headed three southern Ontario forces, Fantino was also chairman of the police chief's strategy committee against outlaw bikers, the group that came together in 1996 shortly after an 11-

year-old bystander was killed during the long-raging biker wars in Quebec.

When an RCMP investigator faxed him sections from the Lavigne book in January, 2000, and told him an internal inquiry was under way, Fantino blew his stack. It was, apparently, the first time he had been made aware of the leak; he fired off a hard-hitting letter that same day to Philip Murray, then commissioner of the RCMP. Under a bold headline – "Deeds speak" – Fantino called the leak one of the most corrupt acts he'd witnessed in 30 years of policing. Within days, Stenhouse was suspended and, for months after, in almost every internal report, the RCMP incorporated Fantino's views.

Bikers, of course, have bedevilled police for years. Indeed, since the national strategy group was formed, the largest of these gangs, the Hells Angels, has moved into every major province where it didn't already have a foothold – Alberta in 1997, and subsequently Saskatchewan, Manitoba and Ontario – taking over rival gangs and their livelihood in what police call a "patchover," a sharing of insignias. And as Stenhouse was arguing with his superiors, drugs were the mainstay of motorcycle gangs. (Quebec's recent crackdown has proved this in spades.) But because drug squads and biker intelligence units were two different groups with two different agendas, coordinated attacks on motorcycle gangs foundered. "It's always been like this within the RCMP," Stenhouse says. " 'We're drug enforcement. We're customs and excise.' And within drugs, 'we're heroin. We're marijuana.' It's all about turf and that's why the Hells Angels have fallen through the cracks for 20 years."

The conclusion of Project Kiss in the fall of 1997 should have been a time of sweet victory for Bob Stenhouse. It was anything but. His marriage was disintegrating, he was despondent from job stress, and his frustration that front-line officers did not have greater input into biker strategy was so great, he handed in his resignation. Close friends talked him out of it. Then, a few months later, the RCMP sent him as its representative to a provincial policy committee on organized crime – which only started his cycle of frustration all over.

The committee, headed by a consultant and composed of

representatives from the RCMP and the Edmonton and Calgary police, was struck because the Alberta government was withholding nearly $2 million in organized crime funding because it didn't trust the feds to contribute their fair share. Stenhouse was on the committee to add an operational perspective, but what he saw only crystallized his view that there were deep-seated problems with funding and strategy. The RCMP was then saying it had budgeted $16.5 million and 183 people to combat organized crime in Alberta. But with only five full-time biker investigators in the province, the numbers looked like a shell game. More worrisome, to Stenhouse at least, was that the biker policy emanating from the police chiefs seemed more concerned with telling the media about the gangs than with frontline policing. "I just felt this was unethical," he says now. "It seemed all about trying to get money from government."

He started to write memos on how biker investigations ought to be organized. At least four of them went up the lines and were swatted back. They were his personal "wish list," the disciplinary board called them later. From his point of view, they were a way of saying the force could do more with less, by combining priorities. (He was not alone in his concerns – at Stenhouse's disciplinary hearing, senior RCMP officers from B.C. and Alberta, men with 15 to 20 years' experience as criminal investigators, came forward to tell the same story, almost as a lament. Mountie pride was at stake. They were the national police after all. Yet because of their own internal battles and trying to do too much with too little, they were losing ground against bikers.)

In late December, 1998, Stenhouse went to see McDermid. They spoke for 90 minutes. The assistant commissioner seemed sympathetic. He acknowledged the force seemed too content to pick low-hanging fruit, and asked for more documentation. He said he'd see what he could do. A few months later, they met again in a corridor. Recollections differ. McDermid recalls saying change was coming but it would take time. Stenhouse says the message was more like business as usual. A week or so later, Yves Lavigne called, asking what was new.

"UNDER AND ALONE"

William Queen

William Queen was an undercover agent working in the United States who infiltrated the Mongols Motorcycle Club. He worked his way up through the club hierarchy, but in the process almost lost his mind. This story is about trying to keep sane in insane situations, shifting between identities, and somehow coping with two diametrically opposed lifestyles. Queen's work eventually led to the conviction of virtually all Mongols Motorcycle Club members in the United States.

"All right, Billy, how long was your fuckin' academy?"

Red Dog pressed his ruddy, windburned face three inches from mine. I smelled that thick mix of Budweiser and crank-fueled sleeplessness on his breath. The words he spat felt hotter than the midday Southern California sun. He cocked his head to one side and pushed closer. "I'm askin' you a fuckin' question, Billy!"

Red Dog, the national sergeant at arms of the Mongols Motorcycle Club, stood six feet tall, with long, stringy hair and a rust-colored handlebar mustache that drooped below his chin. From his pierced forehead, a silver chain swept down ominously past his left eye. His powerfully muscled arms were sleeved out with a web of prison tattoos, and his right hand clutched a loaded 9-mm Glock semiautomatic. Behind him, six other Mongols – Evel, C.J., Domingo, Diablo, Bobby Loco, and Lucifer – all in various states of drunkenness and methamphetamine highs, were slapping magazines into their Glocks and Berettas. More than one had his Mongol colors decorated with the skull-and-crossbones patch, boldly announcing to the world that he had killed for the club.

Here at the end of a long dirt road, in an abandoned orange grove about 80 miles north of Los Angeles, what had begun as a typical Southern California day – that perfect golden sun beating down on a ribbon of black highway – had quickly turned into my worst nightmare.

For several months now, working deep undercover on assignment for the Department of the Treasury's Bureau of Alcohol, Tobacco and Firearms (ATF), I'd been posing as a Mongols "prospect" – a probationary member of the club, a position that allowed me to wear my black leather vest with the lower rocker reading CALIFORNIA but not yet the official black-and-white center patch and top rocker that distinguished a full-fledged member.

As a prospect, you're a slave, the property of the club. You have to do everything a member tells you to do, from hauling drugs and guns to wiping a member's ass if he orders you to. Some members were good for simple orders like "Prospect, go get me a beer," or "Light my cigarette," or "Clean my bike." But other members, guys like Red Dog, took inordinate pleasure in making a prospect's life a living hell.

Prospecting inside the Mongols was a dangerous game. According to intel developed by ATF, the Mongols Motorcycle Club had assumed the mantle of the most violent motorcycle gang in America, a tight-knit collective of crazies, unpredictable and unrepentant badasses. With 350 full-patch members, the gang was a small fraction of the size of the Hells Angels, their hated rivals, but the Mongols had wreaked more than their fair share of havoc since they were founded in the early seventies.

Their most significant violent acts in the 1970s and '80s were committed against the Angels, with whom they fought (and ultimately won) a seventeen-year war. But by the mid-nineties, infused by the ruthless Latino gang mentality of East Los

Angeles, the Mongols' indiscriminate violence spread outside the biker underworld and began to terrorize the general populace of Southern California. When the Mongols frequented mainstream bars and clubs, where people were not as familiar with the gang's fearsome reputation, the result was a series of vicious assaults, stabbings, and gunfights. In late 1997 the Mongols got into a confrontation in a club in the San Gabriel Valley, just outside of L.A., which resulted in a shoot-out, leaving one man dead. Also in 1997, the Mongols went to two nightclubs in the Los Angeles area and stabbed patrons in plain view of dozens of witnesses, but no one would come forward to testify against them.

Nor was the Mongols' violence limited to the outside world; even within the ranks of the club, the gang had such a reputation for assaulting its prospects that by the late nineties, the membership was dwindling. No one wanted to join a club if it meant that every day and night he had to worry about taking a savage beat-down. In 1998 they adopted a new national policy: No beating on the prospects. And almost everyone stuck by it, except for Red Dog.

Despite the fact that as national sergeant at arms he was supposed to be enforcing the club's rules and constitution – yes, the club had a seventy-page constitution – Red Dog was a loose cannon, riding his Harley through life with a "fuck everyone" attitude. For months he was in my face, smashing his heavy fist into my chest, at times uppercutting me as hard as he could. More than once he'd sucker-punched me in the gut, leaving me doubled over, gasping for air, and ready to puke. But I was a prospect, so I gritted my teeth and sucked it up.

That morning we had all hooked up at C.J.'s house, where the dudes drank hard and I did my prospect thing, fetching beer for the patches (as fully inducted members of the club are called), lighting their cigarettes, watching them do line after line of crank and coke. Then when Red Dog figured everyone was drunk and high enough, he gave an abrupt order: "Let's go shoot."

This was a Mongols membership requirement: Before any prospect could attain full-patch status in the club, he had to prove that he owned a firearm and was a decent shot. When I got behind the wheel of my bullet-pocked red Mustang, I thought we were heading out to an actual firing range – and so did my ATF backup. We formed a ragged convoy behind Red Dog's burgundy Monte Carlo as we left the Visalia city limits. I kept glancing in my rearview mirror, checking to see that my backup was still there. But as we got farther and farther into the countryside of vineyards and orange groves, eventually turning down a remote dirt driveway, I realized we had completely lost my backup. I also realized this wasn't going to be a standard firearms-qualification exercise. There was nothing ATF could do to help me now. If shit went bad, it just went bad. I was alone.

Now, with a collection of new semiautomatic pistols on the hoods of our cars and the loaded magazines clicking into place, the mood in the orange grove suddenly turned dark and twisted. One Mongol brother stood loading rounds into a street-sweeper, a high-capacity, drum-fed semiautomatic 12-gauge shotgun that looks similar to the old Thompson submachine gun from the Prohibition era. An awesome assault weapon, beloved by drug dealers and hard-core gangsters, the street-sweeper has since been banned by the feds. I knew that a gun like that was useless for target shooting; like the tommy gun, a street-sweeper is a pure killing machine.

Without warning, Red Dog was up in my face again, head cocked to one side, hollering crazily – accusing me of being an undercover cop. "How long was your fuckin' academy, Billy?"

"What are you talkin' about, Red Dog?"

"You know what I'm talking about, Billy! Who the fuck did you tell you was comin' up here? Who the fuck did you tell you was gonna be with the Mongols today? Who, Billy?"

"I didn't tell nobody. Come on, Red, why you acting like this? I didn't tell nobody I was coming up to Visalia."

He locked his slate blue eyes on mine and, in torturous silence, stared at me for fifteen seconds. "So you're saying if I put a bullet in the back of your fuckin' head right now, ain't *nobody* gonna know where to start looking for you? Is that right, Billy?"

"Yeah, I guess that's right, Red Dog."

He gestured across the dusty, desolate, trash-strewn field, told me to go set up some cans to shoot at. My first thought was of the infamous 1963 Onion Field case, chronicled in Joseph

Wambaugh's bestseller and subsequent movie, in which two young LAPD officers, after stopping a vehicle in Hollywood they suspected had been involved in a series of armed robberies, were kidnapped by a pair of ex-convicts and taken to a remote onion field outside Bakersfield. Officer Ian Campbell was shot dead while Officer Karl Hettinger watched in horror before escaping with his life.

When I turned my back to Red Dog and the other armed Mongols, the icy realization hit me: After the firefights in Vietnam, after twenty-five years in law enforcement, this was the way it ended – I was going to die on a gorgeous Southern California day, by a Mongol bullet, in the middle of a god-forsaken, abandoned orange grove somewhere outside Visalia.

I closed my eyes and began to walk, waiting for the bullets to start tearing through my back. I couldn't even turn to shoot it out: Red Dog and Domingo had made certain that I was the only one without a gun. It was a simple equation: If they'd made me, I was going to die today. I stumbled across the field in my motorcycle boots and suddenly saw an image of my two sons standing tearfully over my open casket. I'd felt similar eerie premonitions during my tour of duty in Vietnam, but here, without question, there was nothing worth dying for.

Suddenly, I heard a loud pop and felt my boot crunching an empty beer can. My knees buckled, but I bent down and picked up the can. I glanced back toward the Mongols and saw them talking in a tight circle instead of pointing their guns and training their sights on me. No, they weren't going to shoot me, at least not right now . . .

"Queen, line one!"

It was a bright morning in late February 1998, and I was sitting in my office on Van Nuys Boulevard, typing up reports, when I got the call that changed my life. Picking up the receiver, I heard the voice of Special Agent John Ciccone, calling from ATF Group II in downtown Los Angeles. "Billy Boy," he said, "how'd you like a shot at riding with the Mongols?"

I stared down at the stream of muscle cars and motorcycles speeding down Van Nuys. Ciccone was known for his bad practical jokes as well as his choice of bad nicknames, but I could tell he was dead serious on this one. "What's going on, Johnny?"

Ciccone knew I'd been hanging out with the Hells Angels for a few weeks, gathering intel for another case agent. At the time, ATF was working an investigation in conjunction with the Internal Revenue Service and the Ventura County Sheriff's Department, trying to make a prosecution against the Angels. Ciccone also knew that the Mongols were the gang responsible for much of the biker-related murder and mayhem in the L.A. area.

"Billy, why don't you forget that Red and White crap and take a look at the Mongols?" The Hells Angels are often called the Red and White because of the colors of their patch. The Mongols are known as the Black and White.

Ciccone, an eleven-year veteran of ATF, wasn't your stereotypical agent: "One-man, one-gun" cases really didn't excite him much. Five feet seven, wiry, clean-cut, Ciccone was the kind of guy you might easily pass on a sidewalk or in a shopping mall and take no notice of. Despite his small stature, he had the fierce determination of a long-distance runner – he ran marathons and pumped weights with fanaticism – and, within ATF, carried himself with tremendous command presence.

Ciccone and I had worked together from 1992 to 1998 in the ATF's Special Response Team, the federal version of SWAT. Over the years I'd developed a deep admiration for John's skills; he could manage complex investigative cases like no one else I had seen at ATF. It's not a talent they can teach at the ATF academy in Glynco, Georgia. John was gifted with the ability to juggle the fragile egos and self-promoting attitudes of ATF management, often a good-ol'-boy network with an ingrained us-versus-them mentality. I had also come to recognize Ciccone as a barracuda who could swim in the shadow of great white sharks and still manage to come away with dinner.

"Talk to me, Johnny," I said. "What you got on the Mongols?"

Over the previous few months Ciccone had been receiving increasingly disturbing reports on the surge in the Mongols' criminal activity across the United States. Those of us who worked the biker underworld for ATF had become alarmed as the Mongols' penchant for assaults, gunfights, and cold-blooded murder spread from the biker scene into the general population.

While this "Mongol Nation," as they refer to themselves, spans the southern and western United States and Mexico, with growing chapters in Oklahoma, Arizona, Colorado, and Georgia, its stronghold is Southern California, in particular the Hispanic communities in and around Los Angeles.

Ciccone told me that he had a confidential informant – or CI – who looked promising. The young woman was willing to make an introduction to the gang. And if I was interested, Ciccone said, he'd deal with the administrative types, handle the paperwork, and we'd be good to go.

I watched the candy-painted Chevy Impalas blasting bass-heavy Latino rap and the roaring Harley-Davidson bikes chewing up the asphalt. "Well, then . . . line it up."

Neither Ciccone nor I realized the extent of the perils we'd be facing or the personal sacrifices we'd be making over the next twenty-eight months; neither one of us dreamed that this routine phone call was about to become the most extensive undercover operation inside an outlaw motorcycle gang in the history of American law enforcement.

In March 1998 I'd gone up to Oakland to trade motorcycles with Special Agent Steve Martin, the group supervisor, also known as the resident agent in charge (RAC), of the Oakland office. I held Martin, a graduate of the U.S. Military Academy at West Point, in high esteem; we'd had a friendly but intense rivalry during our time at the ATF's Special Response Team school. He and I were the two oldest candidates in our class. He'd finished number one and I'd finished a tight number two.

Earlier in his ATF career, Martin had ridden undercover with another outlaw motorcycle gang (or OMG), the Warlocks, out of Florida, and managed to send a well-deserving group of them to prison on federal drug, guns, and explosives charges. He had a soft spot for the bike he'd ridden in that case. When he relocated to Oakland, he'd brought the bike with him as a trophy of his accomplishments. Now I hoped it would bring me a little luck.

It was definitely a biker's bike. A stripped-down version of a Harley-Davidson FLHTC, it was black with leather bags and a badass, hot-rod engine that would rival the fastest bike in any gang. With straight drag pipes and a compression ratio well above a stock Harley, this hog could be heard from a mile away. If you were a cop, from two miles. The fact that I would enjoy riding it was simply icing on the cake.

After lining up all the required paperwork, Ciccone called me to say that he'd just talked to his CI and she was going to meet us at the Rose Bowl parking lot in Pasadena at about nine P.M. It was a Thursday night, and we knew that various Mongols would be at The Place.

It had always struck me as appropriate that the Mongols, not the sharpest knives in the drawer, would pick a place called The Place as their watering hole. Reminded me of a little kid's sneakers with *L* and *R* written in Magic Marker on each rubber-tipped toe.

"Okay," I told Ciccone. "I'll be there."

Strangely enough, I didn't really think too much about the plan at the time. It was going to be just another undercover caper. Merely an introduction. No buys, no recordings, no big deal. A basic intelligence-gathering mission.

At this early stage, Ciccone and I, as ATF special agents working out of different offices, answered to different group supervisors. The chain of command in the field looks like this: The special agent (sometimes called a field agent) answers directly to his group supervisor (or resident agent in charge), who oversees six to ten field agents. Directly above the RAC is the assistant special agent in charge (ASAC, pronounced "ay-sack"); for Los Angeles there are two ASACs, each responsible for overseeing half of the groups of special agents. Next in line comes the SAC, or special agent in charge; in L.A. the SAC is responsible for all of Southern California, from the Mexican border to as far north as Paso Robles. Administrators above the rank of special agent seldom leave ATF offices to see action in the field.

I left Van Nuys after informing my RAC that I would be working that night. He ran his standard admin-babble by me. "Be in the office in the morning, and don't forget your duty-agent assignment." "Duty agent" was yet another genius boondoggle dreamed up by ATF administrators wherein they assigned senior investigators to do secretarial work – answering telephones and sorting messages. I doubt this was what Uncle Sam had in mind for his tax dollars when he trained me to be a federal law-enforcement officer.

At about 8:30 P.M. I jumped on my new hot-rod Harley and headed for the Rose Bowl, where I found Ciccone sitting in his black Pontiac Grand Am. John loved that car but drove it like he was going to turn it over to the junkyard tomorrow. I'm not a deeply religious person, but every time I rode anywhere with Ciccone, no matter how short a distance, I said a prayer for myself and any innocent bystanders in his path.

The Rose Bowl, focus of the sports-loving nation every January 1, is a huge venue that holds more than ninety thousand people during college football games. It's located in a narrow pass that separates the San Fernando and San Gabriel valleys. The area is mostly residential, with an affluent, old-money feel. Even during periods with no special events, people come from all over to walk around the area. But on this night the Rose Bowl was dead calm and the parking lot dark. A thousand stars spread out across the clear California sky.

In his Pontiac, Ciccone and I mulled over the upcoming operation while waiting for our CI to show up. Ciccone hadn't said too much to me about the CI. I knew that she'd contacted an LAPD detective and was willing to introduce someone into the Mongols. She claimed, according to this detective, that she was pissed off at the Mongols because of what she'd seen them do to a friend of hers. Not that the bikers had stolen everything he owned, or beaten him within an inch of his life, or some other god-awful thing. Nope, she was angry because she'd watched as the Mongols scooped up one of her friends and turned him from a good family man into a flaming Mongol asshole. The fact that he was an eager participant in the transformation (or that she herself continued to be a willing Mongol hanger-on) didn't play into her twisted logic. Personally, I didn't care why she was doing what she was doing; I was using her, albeit with her permission, to further our noble cause.

Within the law-enforcement community there is a saying about confidential informants: "You never know when they're gonna piss backward on you." I knew that an introduction into any undercover operation by way of a CI was risky, but I really had no clue how risky until I met Sue (not her real name) face-to-face.

Within a few minutes a pickup truck rolled into the parking lot. It was old, dirty, banged up, reflecting no pride of ownership. It pulled up under the sole streetlight where Ciccone and I were sitting in his Pontiac. Although I'd never really given it much thought, I suppose in my own wishful mind I'd envisioned the CI to be a cute little biker chick who'd been turned around by an attack of conscience.

But what rolled out of the truck was two hundred pounds of bleached-blond tweaker that could neither stand still nor shut up. "Tweaker" is cop vernacular for a methamphetamine addict; anyone who knows anything about meth can tell you that its physiological effects are brutal. It can take an attractive young woman and make her look like Medusa in no time. In Sue's case, she had probably started from a disadvantaged position, and it had all gone downhill from there.

As Sue rambled on, I glanced over and gave Ciccone a little nod of gratitude for his expert selection. The three of us agreed to split up and meet at a joint called In-N-Out Burger on Foothill Boulevard in Tujunga. Sue would get on my bike, and we would ride over to The Place from there. So that was that. With a loose game plan, we headed out.

Tujunga is a bedroom community within the boundaries of Los Angeles proper, on the northeasternmost edge of the San Fernando Valley. It borders Glendale and Pasadena, nestled quietly into the surrounding mountain range. The residential terrain runs the gamut from beaten-down shacks to palatial custom-built homes on substantial horse property.

Tujunga, per capita, has more than its share of white trash and rednecks as well as an ever-present biker element. In police circles, Tujunga is referred to as The Rock, after Alcatraz's beloved nickname. In my tenure as a criminal investigator, I'd participated in many cases on The Rock, and in this community I began my odyssey.

I rolled into the parking lot of the In-N-Out Burger followed by Sue and Ciccone. Sue parked her truck and got herself ready while Ciccone waited in his car and I sat on my idling bike. Ciccone and I looked at each other across the parking lot and gave a thumbs-up.

Sue walked over to my bike and then, like something out of an old western, hopped onto one of the back passenger foot pegs as if it was Trigger's stirrup. For the uninitiated, any Harley-Davidson could rightfully be called heavy metal, and an

FLHTC is heavier still. There was no way I was going to be able to hold up that bike with her big glow-in-the-dark white ass hanging off one side. Though I held on for dear life, down we went with a horrific crash in the parking lot – me, my CI, and Steve Martin's revered Harley. It was a less than auspicious start.

From the ground where I lay, I looked up at Ciccone. It's impossible to describe the look on his face. I think he wanted to laugh, wanted to apologize, and was praying to the ATF gods that this was not a harbinger of things to come. I picked up the bike and my ego and prepared for round two. As if I were talking to a six-year-old, I explained to Sue that there was no way I was going to be able to hold up a thousand pounds of motorcycle and her at the same time. She was going to have to use a different technique to get on the bike. She looked at me with a wounded expression but then took a deep breath and carefully got on.

With its reputation for casual violence, The Place was the worst of the many biker bars that dot the Tujunga landscape. There had been frequent assaults and melees involving a variety of weapons both inside and outside the bar, and there was no way in hell I would have set foot in there under normal circumstances, at least not without a warrant, a gun, and maybe a backup unit. As we approached, I felt something in the pit of my stomach. Something I'd felt before on other undercover assignments. The edge, I guess. Keeping me sharp, appropriately nervous, greasing the skids for bravado to move front and center, if necessary.

There were six or seven bikes parked at the curb out front. As I got closer I could hear the hard-rock tunes blaring through the front door. A disheveled patron, who had obviously consumed more than his fill of alcohol, stood by a pay phone mounted on the front of the building. I rolled past the bar and turned around in the street to get in a position to park my bike. No one paid us any attention, which was fine by me. Although I carried my gun, I still felt uneasy. I was about to meet some of the infamous Mongols for the first time.

I stopped the bike just short of the front door so Sue could get off. With the In-N-Out incident fresh in my mind, I held on to the bike for dear life. Dropping it in front of The Place would have made one hell of a first impression. Sue managed to dismount without pulling the bike and me down to the ground. I backed the bike against the curb and killed the engine. As I got off I saw Ciccone roll by in his black Pontiac. I took off my helmet and put it on one of the rearview mirrors. *Game time*.

Surprisingly, considering that it's such a dump, The Place is located in a historic building that was a Pony Express stop in the 1860s. Above the bar were five or six one-room apartments sharing a common bathroom. The inside was cramped. Carrena, the owner of The Place, had managed to squeeze two pool tables in and maintain an area for throwing darts. The two bathrooms were filthy. The wood floor looked like it was original construction from the Pony Express era, warped and aged by the constant soaking of Budweiser, piss, and puke. And of course there was the requisite jukebox full of Marilyn Manson, Metallica, and Santana.

The walls were painted black and white, the Mongol colors, and adorned with biker paraphernalia in honor of the Mongols. Carrena was a hard-core biker chick, the "ol' lady" of a Mongol called The Kid, who was away doing a prison sentence. She had the words PROPERTY OF THE KID tattooed on her back. Ironically, Carrena's father was a retired cop.

I strolled in behind Sue. The joint was dimly lit, filled with stagnant cigarette smoke and unsavory patrons, including two full-patch Mongols huddled together towards the back of the bar, beers in hand. Sue could have dropped me right in my tracks when she openly pointed at them in her death-defying effort to identify them for me.

"Jesus Christ!" I hissed. "What the hell's the matter with you? Settle down, before you get both our asses killed."

She was not only a hard-core tweaker but felony stupid on top of it. Luckily, no one saw her blatant move. I moved toward the bar, dragging her in my wake. Of course, I'd known that I was going to have to watch my back, but now I realized that if I wanted to stay alive, I was going to have to keep an eye on Sue also.

The bartender, an older, hard-looking soldier from The Rock, looked my way. I yelled, "Two Buds!" over the guitar-crunching music and passed one of the beers to Sue. I'd planned to stay on top of things and nurse my beer for the entire evening. Apparently Sue had no such intention. In less than thirty seconds, her bottle was empty and she was hollering, "Let's have another!" Jesus, I could see trouble coming. I gave her ten dollars to cover her beer tab for the next few minutes and watched as her beer, and my federal money, quickly vanished.

Sue moved around the bar on her own, hugging and talking with one patron after another until she finally reached the two Mongols. My moment of truth. I watched as she reached out and hugged the first biker, then the other. Neither hugged her back. But they didn't shrug her off either. She turned and motioned for me to come over. "Billy," she said when I got there, "this is Rocky."

He frowned menacingly and tipped his beer bottle my way. I returned the gesture. "Good to meetcha, Rock."

Rocky looked more American Indian than Mexican, with long – almost to his butt – black hair that he wore braided like an Indian warrior. Dressed in all black, he carried a thick length of chain on his belt, along with a large hunting knife. He was on the young side, maybe mid-thirties, and had only been in the gang for about a year and change. He didn't have that real hard-core, badass look yet, but he was working on it.

Sue nodded toward the second Mongol. "This is Rancid," she said.

I tipped my Bud and said, "Good to meetcha, Rancid."

The moniker fit. Rancid had long, black matted hair that hung well past his shoulders. The amount of grease and dirt under his nails was surpassed only by the grease and dirt in his hair, which had turned the top rocker on his patch almost black. He had an array of tattoos that started with an Uzi on his neck. There was a big black MONGOL tattoo across his enormous beer belly, which was displayed for everybody when his T-shirt rode up. He was "sleeved out," meaning that there was no more unmarked skin on his arms for inking. His gruff voice was loud enough to be heard over the Santana guitar riffs blaring from the jukebox he was leaning against. He was wearing black jeans and sported a huge chain and a hunting knife on his belt. I would later learn that the chain and knife were standard equipment for Mongol patches. His black steel-toed boots had chromed metal spikes on the tips – designed for nothing less than ripping open the flesh of whomever he kicked. He was equipped for battle, and made an ominous impression on me.

Sue was talking faster than her brain could function. I knew she was only trying to help, but in her reckless, intoxicated efforts she was digging a hole both of us could fall into. She went on and on about how well she knew me and all that we'd supposedly been through together. This caused me anxiety for more than one reason. First, she was no prize to be seen with. Second, I knew how easy it would be to get caught in the tangled web of bullshit she was weaving. I had to get her out of there, fast. She'd served her purpose for the night. I turned to her and said, "Look, Sue, we need to go – I got some things to take care of."

She threw back her head and laughed. No way. She was in an alcohol-and-crank-induced party frenzy. She was *home*. This was her niche. She'd dug in for the night with her Mongol buds, and there was no way she was leaving.

After a few more tense minutes, *I* made my way toward the exit. It was tough, but like dragging an unruly dog on a chain, I managed to pull Sue out to the street with me. I felt like I had walked out of the twilight zone back to reality. No runs, no hits, no errors, and nobody left on. Just like that, our first night of the Mongol undercover investigation was over.

APPENDIX: WHAT ARE A BUNCH OF MOTORCYCLES DOING IN AN ART MUSEUM?

Bernard E. Rollin

Rollin is a long-time rider whose current "scoot" is a 1986 Harley-Davidson Low Rider. He is also a distinguished academic based at Colorado State University. Bernard's contribution to this anthology examines the motorcycle as "Art", offering a mature understanding of the motorcycle as part of popular American culture.

In June of 1988, the Solomon R. Guggenheim museum in New York, one of the world's most prestigious art museums, opened an exhibition entitled "The Art of the Motorcycle," wherein the history of the evolution of the motorcycle was chronicled through more than 130 examples. The exhibition was the best-attended installation in the history of the museum, and also broke attendance records at the Guggenheim museum in Bilbao, Spain.

An obvious question arises concerning both the exhibition and its unparalleled success. In what sense can motorcycles be viewed as works of art? The introduction to the exhibit begins as follows:

> Perhaps more than any other single object of industrial design, the motorcycle can be considered a metaphor for the 20th century. Predating the automobile by 25 years and the airplane by 36, the motorcycle was the first form of personal mechanized transport to emerge from the beginning of the industrial age; its subsequent evolution follows the main currents of modernity.

This statement certainly justifies an historical exhibition on the motorcycle. But it fails to explain why the motorcycle is to be viewed as art.

If the Guggenheim were to have devoted an exhibit to potato peelers, people would simply not have lined up in droves. In any event, we know from ordinary experience that ordinary people see motorcycles – particularly Harleys – as aesthetic objects. One popular picture book of Harleys is subtitled *Rolling Sculpture*, and any Harley owner can tell stories of groups of people admiringly surrounding the motorcycle and extolling its beauty. My own mother, who saw motorcycles as death traps, and professed no interest in them, would actually address bikers with phrases like "What a beautiful machine!" In other words, many motorcycles evoke an aesthetic response from people, and are considered "beautiful." And since they are man-made artifacts, we can surmise that most people would have no problems seeing them as "works of art" in both the descriptive and evaluative sense of that phrase. The question before us, then, is what is it about at least some motorcycles that evoke such a positive aesthetic response?

Some initial light on our task is shed by the final paragraph of the introduction to the exhibition stated earlier:

> The motorcycle is an immortal cultural icon that changes with the times. More than speed, it embodies the abstract themes of rebellion, progress, freedom, sex, and danger. The limits imposed by its possible forms and functions, and the breadth of variation that has been expressed within these limitations, provide a framework in which

to examine the motorcycle both as object and as emblem of our century.

One can argue, as does an essay in the catalogue to the exhibition, that the essence of modern culture is speed. Thomas Krens affirms in the essay serving as a preface to the Guggenheim catalogue, "The pursuit of speed can be seen as a primary factor in the advance of singularly twentieth-century technologies from the measures of light, sound, and particles to the development of military weapons and the nature of warfare to the transformation of our concept of distance." The rate at which humans could travel was relatively fixed from antiquity until the advent of engines; the speed of a fast horse, or roughly forty miles per hour. The motorcycle was going considerably faster – over sixty m.p.h. – by the first decade of the twentieth century and, in 1907, Glenn Curtiss, riding an experimental V-8 motorcycle, set the world land speed record at an astounding 136 miles per hour. By the 1920s, commercially produced bikes were guaranteed to exceed one hundred miles per hour. Today, the motorcycle speed record is owned by Harley-Davidson, over 320 miles per hour.

Vehicles that could achieve high speeds gave people a sense of possibilities never imagined; the ability to travel far in brief periods, and the ability to do so totally on one's own (unlike the speed achieved by a locomotive), and with one's own life more or less in one's own hands. And though there are indeed vehicles that go faster than motorcycles absolutely, from an experiential, phenomenological living of speed, nothing feels faster. A jet plane traveling at 500 miles per hour does not at all give us a sense of speed, we rarely even spill our drinks, and often fall asleep. No one falls asleep on a motorcycle. Twenty miles an hour on a moto-cross trail is enough to take the breath away from a novice rider. Despite my now having logged a quarter of a million miles on a motorcycle, I vividly recall my own first ride on the back of a Triumph Bonneville, rocketing from 0 to 60 in a few seconds, feeling like I was sliding off and flying, out of control, an odd amalgam of exhilaration and fear.

Then too, on a motorcycle you are part of the world through which you speed, the wind in your face and hair, the bugs in your mouth and beard remind you constantly that *you* are speeding through the world, rather than, as in an equally fast auto, a machine with you in it. No wonder then, in my experience, that American Indians, whose civilization flourished on fast horseback, revere Harley-Davidsons as "iron horses" and wear T-shirts (as do many bikers) showing a motorcyclist in tandem with a ghostly Indian warrior with the logo "brothers in the wind." Though few reservation Indians can afford a Harley, the shirts are actually ubiquitous on the vast Navajo reservation.

I recall being approached in Albuquerque by two plainly alcoholic Indians. This is common in the Southwest, as they are usually hustling a few bucks from strangers, particularly from bikers, who they see as "bros." These two however, were after something else. They told me that they had just been released from prison after a number of years. "Would you just start the Harley up so we can hear it, please?" they asked. "It helps us realize that we are free." Motorcycles, unlike much faster cars (what bikers call "cages") are archetypal symbols of freedom, and of the danger the freedom brings, and make one savor life.

In the early 1900s, a school of Italian artists known as Futurists captured the essence of modernism as speed obtained through the machine. Embracing violence, speed, and machines as symbols of the future, and condemning traditional art and museums as passé and "cemeteries," the Futurists were drawn to war and Fascism and above all to motion as destroying middle-class comfortable torpor. The most successful Futurist art freezes motion with astounding success – Umberto Boccherini's bronze sculpture *Unique Forms of Continuity in Space* or Gino Severini's painting *Armored Train in Action* could not be more suggestive of movement if they moved; Futurist music froze the sounds of industry and motion. Though often deploying trains and racing cars as symbols, their ideology applies equally well to the motorcycle, for its looks, function, and sound (= music).

The first *Futurist Manifesto*, written in 1909 by Marinetti, could well have been written for the Guggenheim exhibit, and as an aesthetic guide to the motorcycle experience. Indeed the *Manifesto* begins with the following declaration:

We suddenly heard the famished roar of automobiles [= engines]. Friends, away! Let's go! Mythology and the Mystic ideal are defeated at last [i.e. the historically sanctified Platonic reality]! We're about to see the centaur's birth!

(The centaur is a recurrent symbol for the motorcycle.)
And the eleven elements of the Manifesto read as follows:

We intend to sing the love of danger, the habit of energy and fearlessness.

1. Courage, audacity, and revolt will be essential elements of our poetry.
2. Up to now literature has exalted a pensive immobility, ecstasy, and sleep. We intend to exalt aggressive action, a feverish insomnia, the racer's stride, the mortal leap, the punch and the slap.
3. We affirm that the word's magnificence has been enriched by a new beauty: the beauty of speed. A racing car whose hood is adorned with great pipes, like serpents of explosive breath – a roaring car that seems to ride on grapeshot is more beautiful than the *Victory of Samothrace*.
4. We want to hymn the man at the wheel, who hurls the lance of his spirit across the Earth, along the circle of its orbit.
5. The poet must spend himself with ardor, splendor, and generosity, to swell the enthusiastic fervor of the primordial elements.
6. Except in struggle, there is no more beauty. No work without an aggressive character can be a masterpiece. Poetry must be conceived as a violent attack on unknown forces, to reduce and prostrate them before man.
7. We stand on the last promontory of the centuries! . . . Why should we look back, when what we want is to break down the mysterious doors of the Impossible? Time and Space died yesterday. We already live in the absolute, because we have created eternal, omnipresent speed.
8. We will glorify war – the world's only hygiene – militarism, patriotism, the destructive gesture of free-

dom-bringers, beautiful ideas worth dying for, and scorn for woman. [Recall that the Hell's Angels offered their services in Vietnam.]

9. We will destroy the museums, libraries, academies of every kind, will fight moralism, feminism, every opportunistic or utilitarian cowardice. [Bikers are known for contempt of feminism. Compare the famous T-shirt, "If you can read this, the bitch fell off."]

10. We will sing of great crowds excited by work, by pleasure, and by riot; we will sing the multicolored, polyphonic tides of revolution in the modern capitals; we will sing the vibrant nightly fervor of arsenals and shipyards blazing with violent electric moons; greedy railway stations that devour smoke-plumed serpents; factories hung on clouds by the crooked lines of their smoke; bridges that stride the rivers like giant gymnasts, flashing in the sun with a glitter of knives; adventurous steamers that sniff the horizon; deep-chested locomotives whose wheels paw the tracks like the hooves of enormous steel horses bridled by tubing; and the sleek flight of planes whose propellers chatter in the wind like banners and seem to cheer like an enthusiastic crowd.

Though decidedly not politically correct and even somewhat ugly, what the Futurists extol does capture some elements of the biker experience – the dimension of the outlaw that Americans are decidedly warm towards (such as Jesse James, Billy the Kid, gangsters in popular culture), the anarchist and rebel, the fighter and warrior. The symbols worn on shirts and skin by outlaw bikers or outlaw wannabe Harley riders – skulls, Vikings, SS runes, iron crosses, werewolves, pirates, even swastikas – extol rebellious outsiders (though, in my experience, these are largely not pro-Nazi political symbols, but rather symbols of rebellion aimed at shocking and engendering unease and even fear). In a world ever increasingly erosive of personal freedom and even of free speech, these symbols stir a sympathetic chord even in people who do not wear them. Unquestionably, then, the Futurist aesthetic captures a number of elements of the biker phenomenon, and helps explain the exhibition.

But there is more to the motorcycle experience than this, and many motorcycles are not symbols of rebellion and non-conformity.

For another perspective on the aesthetic of motorcycles not related to the rebel, but equally explanatory as to the aesthetics of motorcycles, we can turn to the aesthetic theory of John Dewey, as developed in his *Art as Experience* early in the twentieth century. For Dewey, art replicates and attempts to create in people a special feature of ordinary life; having *an experience*, a consummatory passage of time having a beginning, a middle, and an end that can clearly be identified. Such experiences occur all the time as little jewels in one's life, in the most mundane of contexts. Imagine, for example, waking up at dawn after a heavy snowfall in the country, seeing the snow glistening on your driveway, putting on a coat, finding the snow shovel, getting into a rhythm shoveling as you warm up, and finally ending up with a clean driveway, a satisfying glow in your muscles, and a sense of accomplishment. This would exemplify an experience in Dewey's honorific sense, and can occur at any time pretty much in all aspects of life. Artworks are codifications of such experiences, capable of evoking in those who appreciate them an experience. Matter and form combine to produce an object capable of creating such an experience, and requires both the artist and audience, though at different moments in time. Thus art is continuous with life, and Dewey condemns repetitive jobs where workers gain no aesthetic satisfaction from what they do.

A motorcycle is an endless source of experiences in Dewey's sense. Consider a very mundane task such as driving to work. You enter the garage, pull out the car, and are barely conscious of the drive, thinking instead about trivial or major problems. Not so on a cycle – as one rider said to me, "It makes magic out of going to work." With a 360-degree view of the sunrise, the sound of the engine, the never-ending thrill of initial acceleration, the waves and thumbs-up from other bikers and cars, and the need to be totally aware, to avoid the semi-zombie state of a car driver, to watch for gravel and oil and other vehicles, the thrill of morning cold piercing your clothing, the changes in temperature as you move from green fields to city streets, each ride is a potential experience in Dewey's sense.

Since my son was eight, for eighteen years he and I have taken a two-week motorcycle summer trip through the American West, Montana to New Mexico, Nebraska to Nevada. Unlike other vacations and trips we have taken, which are vague in our minds, every bike trip remains as a Deweyan experience made up of smaller Deweyan experiences – the time we drove into the Jemez reservation and watched construction workers build a Kiva, and sprinkle us with their hose to mitigate the 100-degree heat, and giggle as we spun around, angry, and then laughed together. The time my engine blew when my son was nine in the middle of nowhere at twilight and his unspoken fear: "What will we do, Daddy?" And we were picked up by the driver of a ranch truck who tied the bike down and found us a motel, in a little town where all the restaurants were closed, but we bought canned spaghetti and bologna and chocolate chip cookies and white bread and milk to create a splendid feast. And our joy the next day when my friend brought his truck to rescue us. And the Navajo police chief on a Harley, who stopped us to tell us that a helmet was required on the reservation and as our faces fell, he added, "You'll note I'm not wearing one! Have a good day." And the envious looks of children trapped in station wagons cast at my son, who swelled up with pride. And the time the starter went out 300 miles from a shop and my eleven-year-old had to push his 250-pound father on the 700-pound bike with a hundred pounds of luggage to a start each time we stopped, with people yelling, "That's child abuse, Mister."

To look at a bike in a museum is to live these experiences again for those who ride. And for those who do not, the beauty of the machine foreshadows such experiences, and the experience of freedom and speed and infinite possibilities offered to the rider. "Some day I'll have one of those" is the aesthetic reaction of nonriders to all motorcycles, but particularly to Harleys. People feel, briefly at least, how their lives could be transmuted, how they could soar above the mundane into a mode of being replete with Deweyan experiences.

I wish I had a dollar for every time, riding alone, burned brown by the sun, clad in the black, weary yet quintessentially alive, I have been approached by women of all ages, who say, "I've always wanted to ride one of those, could you give me a ride?" And when I say "sure," they back away, afraid that a fantasy realized is a disappointment, content to appreciate from outside, yearning for the speed, sound, wind and risk from a safe distance. My wife has talked of buying me a little flag to wave, which says, "I'm not your fantasy object, I'm just a philosophy teacher."

A final aesthetic-theoretical approach to understanding the lure of the motorcycle grows out of the Bauhaus revolution against the ornate and ultimately degenerate excesses of *fin-de-siècle* art – the froufrou art that prevailed at the end of the 1800s. For the Bauhaus, form should follow function; hence elephant feet umbrella stands and lamps fashioned of nymphs and satyrs cavorting on bronze rocks with landscape-looking shades were monstrosities. The founder of the Bauhaus school, Walter Gropius, aimed at obliterating established distinctions between fine art, crafts, and industry. Under the influence of Bauhaus principles, the Museum of Modern Art would exhibit polished ball bearings or airplane propellers as objects of art whose beauty consists in their perfect adaptation to their function.

Motorcycles and their components are paradigmatic examples of design where form follows function. A motorcycle at rest suggests the possibility of fast movement, and of power, and of new Deweyan experiences. There are few extraneous decorative fillips on any motorcycles, and they are, aesthetically, what they do. And in the only purely aesthetic aspect of a motorcycle, the paint jobs, we experience the free play of fine art, from the inherent beauty of primary colors like fire-engine red gleaming from paint jobs that look permanently wet, to airbrushed renditions of abstract designs, to meticulously rendered skeleton figures of the four Horsemen of the Apocalypse or surrealist landscapes. In the end, motorcycles are Bauhausian sculptures that do what they look like with room for infinite modification expressing the rider's individual aesthetic.

Any motorcycle – but particularly Harleys – which are, in a sense, the Platonic form of a motorcycle emulated and plagiarized by others, is a piece of industrialized sculpture, as elegantly at home in a gallery or store window as it is burning up the roads. And in addition to its functional nature, a motorcycle is an investment in a work of art. What other object can be used for years as it is meant to function, and yet not only keep its financial value but actually grow in value? My own Harley has ninety thousand miles; I purchased it for six thousand dollars and could now sell it for twelve thousand. Although mass-produced vehicles, Harleys are almost never left as they came from the assembly line, but are customized by individual riders to reflect their own aesthetic. A bike bought for $25,000 from a dealer may immediately be majorly rebuilt for an additional $10,000 or $20,000 more, with the aim of turning it into one's unique aesthetic creation. This is truly an example of how high technology and mass production can make each individual an artist, creating a work that, like fine art, will usually appreciate in value.

Finally, motorcycles have ever-increasingly diverged from cars. Cars have become increasingly automated, replete with cruise control, navigator computers that talk to the driver, and electronic parts that take the "I" out of driving. There are those who project a future automobile that does not require a driver, where the machine is centrally controlled and the would-be driver becomes a passenger. Such changes are not seriously projected for motorcycles, for motorcyclists largely do not ride for practical reasons, despite those who extol their mileage per gallon; many cars get better mileage than some bikes. Motorcyclists ride largely for the aesthetic experiences riding provides, from being nearly out of control or extending total concentration not to get killed, from getting soaked in warm summer rain to being totally dry an hour later. In a deepest sense, riding takes skill that driving a car does not, skill that one can take pride in, much as we once took pride in horsemanship.

Finally, whereas death and danger were constant companions for our ancestors, be it from infection, highwaymen, wild animals, or enemies, Western society has sanitized our lives. On a motorcycle, in Heidegger's immortal phrase, we come face to face on a regular basis with "the possibility of the impossibility of one's being," the prospect of death. Whether this serves, as in Heidegger's philosophy, as a call to authenticity in one's life choices and decisions, or merely, like hot sauce, enhances the experience of ordinary life, it unquestionably creates a profound aesthetic experience which in and of itself licenses a motorcycle to be considered a fountain of aesthetic experience and thence a work of art.

As philosopher Gilles Deleuze remarks in *Proust and Signs*, "The modern work of art is a machine and functions as such. . . . Why a machine? Because the work of art, so understood, is essentially productive – productive of certain truths."

ACKNOWLEDGEMENTS AND SOURCES

The editor would like to thank the following for their kind permission to reprint the extracts indicated:

Anthropologica for Daniel R. Wolf and David E. Young, 'Solidarity Among the Rebels' in *Culture II* (1983), pp 59–71; *Australian Police Journal* for R.H. Stephenson, 'The Milperra Massacre', Parts 1 and 2, *Australian Police Journal*, vol. 41 (No. 4) and Vol. 42 (No. 3); Mark L. Bastoni for 'Chrome and Leather', *Boston Magazine* (July 1988), text © Mark L. Bastoni; Blackwell Publishing for Columbus B. Hopper and Johnny 'Big John' Moore, 'Hell on Wheels' in *Journal of American Culture*, Blackwell Publishing 1991; Edward Winterhalder for 'Inside the Bandidos' in *Out in Bad Standings: Inside the Bandidos Motorcycle Club*, Blockhead City Press 2005, © text Edward Winterhalder; Canadian Criminal Justice Association for Randall Montgomery, 'One-Percenter Subculture', Parts 1 and 2, *Canadian Journal of Criminology and Corrections*, published by the Canadian Criminal Justice Association and the University of Toronto Press Inc. 1976; William L. Dulaney for 'Enter the Outlaw Motorcycle Club', *International Journal of Motorcycle Studies*, text © William L. Dulaney; ECW Press for Paul Cherry, 'A Jury Decides' *The Biker Trials: Bringing down the Hell's Angels*, ECW Press 2005, text © Paul Cherry; Ross Fuglsang for '800 Pounds of Steel' in 'Motorcycle Menace: Media Genres and the Construction of a Deviant Subculture', PhD Dissertation, University of Iowa 1997; International Association of Chiefs of Police (IACP) for Steve Tretheway and Lieutenant Terry Katz, 'Motorcycle Gangs

or Motorcycle Mafia?' in *Police Chief vol. 56 (No. 4), text* ©
International Association of Chiefs of Police, 515 North Washington
Street, Alexandria, VA 22314 USA (further reproduction without
express written permission from IACP is strictly prohibited); Knopf
Canada and Hodder Headline for William Marsden and Julian Sher,
*'The Great Nordic War' Angels of Death: Inside the Bikers' Empire of
Crime,* text © William Marsden and Journalism Enterprises Inc.
2006; Little, Brown and Company for Brock Yates, 'Birth of the
Terror' and 'First Contact' in *Outlaw Machine,* Little, Brown and
Company 1999, text © Brock Yates; Robert Lipkin for extracts from
Song of the Dumb Biker, 'Brotherhood of Outlaws', FTW Publishing
1982, text © Robert Lipkin; *Macleans for Robert Sheppard, 'Under-
cover Mountie', first published 26 November 2001, text* © Robert
Sheppard; MBI Publishing Company, for Michael Dregni, 'The
Wild Ones: The Photograph, The Marie, UC, The Anti-Hero, The
Real Boozefighter Speaks, Meet the Hell's Angels, The Enduring
Myth of the Outlaw Biker Mystique by Michael Dregni from *The
Spirit of the Motorcycle: The Legends, The Riders and the Beauty of
the Beast.* Michael Dregni 2000, reprinted by permission of publish-
er MBI Publishing Company LLC, MN, USA www.mbipu-
blishing.com; MBI Publishing Company LLC for Bill Hayes,
'The Riverside Riots: "Typical Speed Demons", "The Riverside
Riots", "An Honest Sheriff", "Wild Red Hair", and "The Electric
Seat"' in *The Original Wild Ones: Tales of the Boozefighters Motor-
cycle Club* and Bill Hayes, 'The Tale of Grandpa and the Bottle of,
uh, Milk' in *The Harley-Davidson Reader,* text © Bill Hayes 2006,
reprinted by permission of Publisher MBI Publishing Company
LLC, St Paul, MN, USA. www.mbipublishing.com; Minister of
Public Works and Government Services for 'Biker Gang Structure',
'Building a Criminal Army', 'Hells Angels v. The Rock Machine:
The War in Quebec', 'Ripping off Society', 'Murder of Prison
guards in Quebec', 'Sanitizing Campaigns: Outlaw Bikers Polish
Their Thuggish Image' and 'The Great Nordic War' in *The Royal
Canadian Mounted Police Gazette,* vols 60 (No. 9) and 61 (Nos 712),
JulyAugust 1999, text © Minister of Public Works and Government
Services 2007; Mountain State Publishing for 'Throttle', *The Biker
Babe's Bible: A Guide to Being a Good Ole Lady* (selected pages),
Mountain State Publishing, Martinsburg, West Virginia, text ©
Mountain State Publishing 2005; Open Court Publishing Company
for Bernard E. Rollin, 'What Are a Bunch of Motorcycles Doing in
an Art Museum?' in B.E. Rollin, C.M. Gray, K. Mommer and C.
Pinco (Eds), *Harley-Davidson and Philosophy: Full-Throttle Aris-
totle,* text © Open Court Publishing Company, a division of Carus
Publishing Company, Peru, IL; Penguin Books Ltd for Paul Lunde,
Organized Crime: An Inside Guide to the World's Most Successful

Industry, Dorling Kindersley 2004, text © Dorling Kindersley; James Quinn for 'Sex and Hedonism Amongst One-Percenter Bikers', text © J.F. Quinn and S. Koch; Raincoast Books for Paul William Roberts and Norman Snider, 'Smokescreen', *Smokescreen: One Man Against the Underworld*, Stoddart Publishing Co. Ltd 2001, text © Paul William Roberts, Destrier Inc., Norman Snider; Random House Pty for Sonny Barger, 'Old Ladies, Main Squeezes and the Maid of Livermore' in *Hell's Angel: The Life and Times of Ralph 'Sonny' Barger* (2000), text © 2000 by Sonny Barger Productions. Reprinted by permission of Harper Collins Publishers, Random House Inc., and Mainstream Publishing for William Queen, 'Under and Alone', *Under and Alone*, text © 2005 William Queen used by permission of Random House Inc.; Richard Marek Publishers for George Wethern and Vincent Colnett, 'A Wayward Angel', *A Wayward Angel*, Richard Marek Publishers 1978, text © George Wethern and Vincent Colnett; University of Toronto Press Inc. for Daniel R. Wolf, 'The Club Run' in *The Rebels: A Brotherhood of Outlaw Bikers*, text © University of Toronto Press Inc.; Julie van den Eynde for 'I Am a Bikie Slut', text © Arthur Veno and Julie van den Eynde 2007; Geoffrey Campbell and Felicity Zeiher for 'Through the Eyes of Snake: The 1984 Milperra Massacre' in *Milperra Massacre: The True Story*, text © Campbell and Zeiher 2007, reproduced by permission of the authors; Lyons Press, and The Ivy Press, for William Osgerby, 'Kamikaze Riders', text © William Osgerby.

Every effort has been made to trace the original copyright holders of the following, without success: the editor and publishers would be pleased to hear from any claimants to legal copyright of:

John Dorrance, 'Forty Hours in Hollister', *Life* Magazine 1967; C.I. Dourghty Havok in Hollister: 'Motorcyclists Take Over Town, Many Injured', *San Francisco Chronicle* 1947; Mark G. Murphy, 'Meeting A Hit Man' in *Police Undercover: The True Story of the Biker, the Mafia and the Mountie*, Avalon House Publishing Ltd 1999, Toronto, Ontario; William Murray, 'Hell's Angels', *Saturday Evening Post*, 20 November 1965; Frank Rooney, 'Cyclists' Raid', *Harpers* Magazine, date unknown; Hunter S. Thompson, 'Losers and Outsiders', the *Nation*, 17 May 1965.